# A HISTORY OF THE
UNITED STATES MARINE CORPS

Colonel Archibald Henderson in the Uniform of 1845

# A HISTORY OF THE UNITED STATES MARINE CORPS

CLYDE H. METCALF
*Lieutenant Colonel, U. S. Marine Corps*

ILLUSTRATED

*New York*
G. P. PUTNAM'S SONS

COPYRIGHT, 1939, BY CLYDE H. METCALF

All rights reserved. This book, or parts thereof, must not be reproduced in any form without permission

Fourth Impression

MANUFACTURED IN THE UNITED STATES OF AMERICA
Van Rees Press, New York

TO
**THE MARINES**
WHO HAVE FOUGHT THEIR
". . . COUNTRY'S BATTLES
ON THE LAND AS ON THE SEA"

# THE MARINES' HYMN

From the Halls of Montezuma
To the shores of Tripoli;
We fight our country's battles
On the land as on the sea;
First to fight for right and freedom,
And to keep our honor clean;
We are proud to claim the title
Of United States Marine.

Our flag's unfurl'd to every breeze
From dawn to setting sun;
We have fought in every clime and place
Where we could take a gun;
In the snow of far-off Northern lands
And in sunny tropic scenes;
You will find us always on the job—
The United States Marines.

Here's health to you and to our Corps
Which we are proud to serve;
In many a strife we've fought for life
And never lost our nerve;
If the Army and the Navy
Ever gaze on Heaven's scenes;
They will find the streets are guarded
By United States Marines.

# PREFACE

For a number of years the Marine Corps has felt the need of a comprehensive history of that organization for the purpose of presenting to the nation an account of its many services and one serving as a background for its present and future personnel. In attempting to present the services of the Marine Corps, the writer has endeavored to examine the more important activities of the organization from the broader point of view. When marines were used, for example, as an instrument to help carry out the foreign policy—that has been their more common use for several decades—the writer has attempted to indicate the national policy which occasioned their use and as each situation developed, particularly in the case of interventions, to set forth the local conditions which led to the specific operations undertaken by contingents of marines. Many facts pertaining to our foreign relations have herein, it is believed, been published for the first time. It is therefore hoped that this work will prove to be a contribution to the knowledge of our foreign policy as well as to that pertaining to our naval history. The activities of the Marine Corps during recent years, when engaged in interventions in more or less backward countries, have often been presented as though they were participating in free-lance expeditions of their own choice. As a matter of fact, they have never acted in any foreign countries except under the closest supervision of the President, the State Department, or the Navy Department.

This history of the Marine Corps was prepared almost entirely from original source material contained in the headquarters of the organization and in the Navy Department. While neither footnotes nor bibliography are contained herein—omitted for the lack of time to tabulate and arrange them and to save space—all of the conclusions as to what were the salient facts were arrived at after careful consideration of all available documentary and other evidence. The conclusions and opinions are of course those of the writer; criticisms are not made unless the occasion was one where mistakes were obviously made, or when the contemporaries of the parties concerned were practically unanimous in condemnation. The failures of the organization and its members as well as the successes have been frankly stated. Where success followed failure, every attempt has been made to ascertain the reasons for both and submit them to the reader.

Effort has not only been made to trace the physical and material growth of the organization but also its spiritual and mental development and the rise of its position and reputation in the minds of the people of the nation. When definite advances were made or reverses suffered, the writer has attempted to ascertain and set forth the reasons therefor. The Corps grew larger and more useful as time went on, as a result of the forces which brought about the growth of the nation. While many of its leaders had much to do with directing its destiny, its outstanding *esprit de corps* has grown up and been maintained largely through the efforts of its rank and file. While the noncommissioned officers of the organization are not as frequently mentioned as the commissioned officers, large credit must be given them for helping to maintain its efficiency and fighting spirit, especially in times of great stress.

In writing the work the author has found that certain traditional accounts of episodes in the history of the Corps were not (in his opinion) founded on facts; but, on the other hand, he has been able to bring to light a number of heroic deeds which have long been lost sight of or never heretofore presented. After examining the vast amount of material, only the outstanding episodes and trends of events which were considered most significant could be presented in the limited space allowed in a single volume. The importance of the event determined whether or not it would be selected, and characters were brought into the work as merely incidental to the happening narrated. The reader will perhaps be struck with how frequently some characters reappear, and they at times all but "steal the show." In order to evaluate the acts of individuals in connection with the accomplishments of the organization, their later rewards were disregarded, but every attempt was made to judge them on the merits of each case as found in the records. The reader may suspect the author of feeling that several of the Corps's outstanding individuals were never properly rewarded for their accomplishments. Several outstanding characters of well-recognized ability failed for various reasons to receive advancement commensurate with their accomplishments.

In selecting the material for inclusion in this work, the author has been guided by a desire to present as complete a record of the organization as could be contained in a single medium-sized volume.

He was perhaps more anxious to include all incidents which he considered important than to present in great detail human interest material. But outstanding records of courage, self-sacrifice, and heroism have not been entirely neglected.

The writer acknowledges his particular indebtedness to Dr. Dana G. Munro's *The United States and the Caribbean Area* for many essential facts about the diplomatic background and local conditions which governed many steps taken by the Marines in several of the Latin-American countries. Indebtedness to Lieut. Colonel E. N. McClellan, U.S.M.C., retired, for many of the pertinent facts contained in the early chapters is acknowledged. That officer spent several years researching all available sources pertaining particularly to the early history of the Marine Corps, and the studies left by him were freely used. Indebtedness to the work of Captain Harry A. Ellsworth, U.S.M.C., entitled *One Hundred Eighty Landings of United States Marines*, is also acknowledged. The writer is especially indebted to Mr. James C. Jenkins, Senior Clerk of the Historical Section, Headquarters, U. S. Marine Corps, for the valuable assistance he has rendered in locating material, as principal research assistant, and for valuable help in revising the manuscript and in copying the greater part of it. Valuable assistance was also rendered by Mr. Jesse Mello during part of its preparation. Mr. Rupert H. Guertner and Miss Irene L. Scott assisted in copying parts of the manuscript. The writer acknowledges the valuable assistance given by Mr. Joel D. Thacker in the preparation of the chapter, "On the Western Front." The series of full-page illustrations, showing the uniforms worn by the Marines from the year 1810 to the present, are the work of Second Lieutenant Donald Dixon, U.S.M.C.R., who painted them under the direction of the author of this work. Without the confidence and encouragement shown by my fellow officers, it is doubtful whether or not the work could have have been accomplished. The writer feels especially grateful for the encouragement shown by Thomas Holcomb, Major General Commandant, Clayton B. Vogel, Brigadier General and Adjutant and Inspector, and Colonel Henry L. Larsen of the Marine Corps, and to several other officers with whom the writer has been associated during the preparation of this work.

## CONTENTS

| | | |
|---|---|---|
| I. | The Continental Marines | 3 |
| II. | The Early Years of the Marine Corps | 28 |
| III. | The War of 1812 | 53 |
| IV. | Indian Wars and Larger Usefulness | 81 |
| V. | The Mexican War—Operations in Eastern Mexico | 106 |
| VI. | The Mexican War—Operations in the West | 138 |
| VII. | The Marines See the World | 167 |
| VIII. | The Civil War | 192 |
| IX. | Marking Time in the Gilded Age | 223 |
| X. | The War with Spain and Operations in the Far East | 253 |
| XI. | Supporting the Foreign Policy | 286 |
| XII. | Interventions in Cuba under the Platt Amendment | 312 |
| XIII. | Occupation of the Dominican Republic | 339 |
| XIV. | Twenty Years in Haiti | 371 |
| XV. | Interventions in Nicaragua | 408 |
| XVI. | The World War | 449 |
| XVII. | On the Western Front | 473 |
| XVIII. | Twenty Years After | 524 |
| | Index | 557 |

# ILLUSTRATIONS

|  |  |
|---|---|
| Colonel Archibald Henderson in the Uniform of 1845 | *frontispiece* |
|  | FACING PAGE |
| Tun Tavern—Birthplace of the Marine Corps | 8 |
| Pay Roll of the *Enterprize* | 9 |
| Marine Corps Uniforms of 1775 | 40 |
| Commandant Burrows with President Jefferson | 41 |
| Typical Marine Corps Uniforms, 1810 | 41 |
| Early Commandants (1776-1864) | 60 |
| Lieutenant O'Bannon Raising the Flag over Derne, Tripoli | 61 |
| The Harbor of Nukahiva, 1814 | 68 |
| Marine Corps Uniforms of the Mexican War | 69 |
| Marine Corps Uniforms of 1834 | 69 |
| Landing of Commodore Perry at Yokohama, Japan, March 8, 1854 | 170 |
| The *Hartford* and *Tennessee* at Close Quarters | 171 |
| Commandants of the Marine Corps (1864–1910) | 226 |
| Captain McLane Tilton, Corporal Brown, and Private Purvis with the Flag They Captured from a Korean Fort, 1871 | 227 |
| Marine Guard on the U.S.S. *Galena*, 1885 | 248 |
| Uniforms of the Civil War Period | 249 |
| Marine Corps Uniforms of the Gilded Age | 249 |
| Officers of the Guantanamo Battalion, 1898 | 256 |
| Marine Detachment under Lieutenant Dion Williams, Cavite, P.I., 1898 | 257 |
| Waller with Officers of the Second Regiment Marines, Panama | 292 |
| Hiram I. ("Hiking Hiram") Bearss | 293 |
| Major General John Twiggs Myers (Retired) | 293 |

## ILLUSTRATIONS

FACING PAGE

| | |
|---|---|
| Colonel Lincoln Karmany (Retired) | 326 |
| Major General Littleton Waller Tazewell Waller | 326 |
| Marine Corps Uniforms, 1900 | 327 |
| Marine Corps Uniforms, 1912 | 327 |
| Marine Patrol at San Pedro de Macoris, D. R. | 354 |
| Marines with Pack Train, Seibo, D. R. | 354 |
| Joseph H. (Uncle Joe) Pendleton (Retired) | 355 |
| The Marine Corps Regimental Flag | 384 |
| Fort Riviere, Haiti, after its Capture by the Marines, 1915 | 385 |
| Fort Riviere, Haiti. Marines on the Walls after the Capture | 385 |
| Major General Smedley D. Butler (Retired) | 400 |
| Commandants of the Marine Corps (1911–1930) | 401 |
| Typical Marine Mounted Patrol, Nicaragua | 424 |
| Bull Cart Meeting Marine Transport Plane | 424 |
| Marine Patrol on the Coco River | 425 |
| Major Victor F. Bleasdale with Typical Field Equipment in Nicaragua | 425 |
| Field Uniforms and Equipment, Nicaragua | 444 |
| Major General Logan Feland | 445 |
| Leaders of the Sixth Marines | 460 |
| Major General Ben H. Fuller | 461 |
| Major General John H. Russell | 461 |
| Major General Thomas Holcomb | 461 |
| Major General John A. Lejeune (Retired) | 476 |
| Typical Uniforms and Equipment of Marines on the Western Front | 477 |
| Belleau Wood, 1918 | 477 |
| Major General James G. Harbord, U.S.A. (Retired) | 488 |
| Belleau Wood | 489 |
| The Transport of the Marines—U.S.S. *Henderson* | 528 |
| General Officers of the Marine Corps | 529 |
| Miscellaneous Views, Fleet Marine Force | 550 |

ILLUSTRATIONS

FACING PAGE

Miscellaneous Views, Marine Corps Aviation . . . . . 551

### Maps and Sketches

Map of Mexico . . . . . . . . . . . . 108
Fort Polk, 1846 . . . . . . . . . . . . 112
Second Tabasco Expedition . . . . . . . . . 124
Mazatlan Harbor . . . . . . . . . . . . 163
Map of Panama . . . . . . . . . . . . 289
Map of Cuba . . . . . . . . . . . . . 314
Map of the Dominican Republic . . . . . . . 341
Map of Haiti . . . . . . . . . . . . . 373
Map of Nicaragua . . . . . . . . . . . 410
Belleau Wood . . . . . . . . . . . . . 483
The Soissons Attack . . . . . . . . . . . 493
The Attack of Blanc Mont . . . . . . . . . 505
The Meuse-Argonne Sector . . . . . . . . . 511

# A HISTORY OF THE
UNITED STATES MARINE CORPS

## Chapter I
## THE CONTINENTAL MARINES

### COLONIAL BACKGROUND

The basic idea of a Marine Corps as a part of the armed forces of the United States came down from early colonial times and was in imitation of the British Royal Marines, which organization has existed since 1664. The American colonists had many contacts with the Royal Marines as well as with the Royal Navy. While it cannot positively be claimed that marines were maintained by any of the colonies prior to the Revolutionary War, colonial troops had had many experiences with expeditions against the non-English settlements along the coast of North America in which they performed the duties of marines. The colonists were from the very beginning forced by nature to be a maritime people. For many generations practically the only intercolonial communication was that carried on by sea.

Not many years after the first successful colony was planted by the English on American soil, active hostilities broke out between the English settlements, supported by the British Navy, and the settlements of the Dutch, Spanish, and French. As early as 1613 an expedition set out from Virginia and raided the French settlement in Nova Scotia, and some years later a similar expedition laid waste the French settlement in Acadia. A few years later the English colonists began fighting with the Dutch settlers, who had established a colony in the present state of New York. Expeditions against the Dutch continued until 1664, when they conquered the Dutch colony and renamed it New York. A large expedition from Massachusetts reduced the French colony at Port Royal, Nova Scotia, and destroyed a fort at the mouth of the St. Johns River. During the same year a combined land and sea operation from Boston made an unsuccessful attempt to capture Quebec. In 1710 a large expedition, sent out from Boston, again took the French settlement at Port

Royal, which had been returned to the French after its previous capture. In the following year another attempt, which ended in disaster, was made to reduce the French settlement of Quebec. The English colonists were themselves subjected to raids by the French and Spanish settlers, who claimed that part of North America in which English settlements were made.

During the War of the Spanish Succession, Admiral Vernon, British Navy, organized a strong expeditionary force consisting of a number of British naval vessels supported by a force of Royal Marines and some marine regiments raised in the American colonies. This expedition, by combined operations of the landing forces supported by the Navy, attacked a number of Spanish positions in the Caribbean area. Several other expeditions which included colonial troops acting as marines went out during the following two or three decades against Spanish settlements in that area.

The failure against the French in Quebec checked attacks of the English against that colony for a period of about thirty years; but in 1745 a stronger expedition, composed partly of colonial troops, on about eighty or ninety transports, supported by fourteen war vessels, set out to reduce a strongly fortified position at Louisburg on Cape Breton Island. The task proved very difficult; it necessitated the employment of several different operations and continued for nearly three months before the position was finally taken.

During the French and Indian War (Seven Years' War) the British carried out other operations in which colonial troops acted in the capacity of marines. During all these colonial experiences the idea of soldiers of the sea was being maintained and enlarged upon. It stuck fast in the minds of the leading men in the colonies and no doubt caused them to think of forming an organization of marines almost as soon as it occurred to them to develop a navy or raise an army.

### Washington's Fleet

Shortly after the exploits of Ethan Allen and Benedict Arnold on Lake Champlain and the early encounters between the colonists and the British around Boston, George Washington was selected as Commander in Chief of the Continental Army. He was directed to take command of the sixteen thousand New England Volunteers surrounding Boston. In addition to making a tremendous effort to organize an army, during the fall of 1775, Washington ordered the fitting out of six war vessels. This was a forerunner of the Continental Navy. These vessels were prepared for the purpose of intercepting the flow of supplies to the British Army at Boston and capturing those supplies for Washington's army. The officers and crews for these ships were taken from the army and retained their status as part of the Continental Army while acting as naval personnel.

The first ship commissioned in "Washington's Fleet" was the schooner *Hannah,* about September 2, 1775. Other ships were added early in October, and the remainder of those authorized joined the squadron during November. Washington retained direct control of this fleet and kept it in the general vicinity of Massachusetts Bay. The first engagement of importance by one of its ships took place in November; the cruiser *Lee* captured the British brig *Nancy,* which was loaded with arms and ammunition for the British Army. Two vessels of the fleet went to the St. Lawrence to intercept British transports but accomplished nothing, except making some raids upon the inhabitants—much to the displeasure of Washington.

The British evacuated Boston in March, 1776, and Washington moved his army to New York, where he fitted out a second fleet. He then had a dozen vessels in the two fleets. The vessels at New York carried the usual complement of sailors, or soldiers acting as naval personnel. Special detachments of soldiers on the vessels performed the functions of marines. Washington's Fleet led to the establishment of the Continental Navy; its acting marines were the forerunners of the Continental Marines. Both of Washington's fleets were abandoned in 1777.

## The Lake Fleet

In the meantime another more important fleet came into existence by action of two separate colonies and the Continental Army prior to the establishment of a navy by the Continental Congress. Benedict Arnold developed a fleet on Lake Champlain. A large supply of cannon and other munitions of war was located at Ticonderoga near the head of Lake Champlain at the outbreak of the war. Arnold strongly recommended to the Massachusetts authorities that immediate steps be taken for a secret expedition to go and capture the much-needed war supplies and drive the British from the lake, which formed an important link in the line of communications between Canada and New York. Within two days a Massachusetts committee worked out the details for the expedition, appointed Arnold colonel and commander in chief and supplied him with funds to defray the expenses of the expedition. His authority, seemingly, not only authorized him to recruit the necessary troops but to appoint all subordinate officers as well.

Meanwhile the Connecticut authorities, acting under a similar suggestion, authorized the raising of a force in the Green Mountains to carry out practically the same mission. This expedition was formed, and Ethan Allen assumed command of it without any specific authority and started on the mission ahead of Arnold. Arnold, who had not yet raised his volunteer troops, overtook Allen. A dispute soon arose over who should command, but the Green Mountain boys won the argument, as they would follow nobody but Allen. Arnold joined the expedition as a volunteer rather than be left out of the affair. He raised a small force of his own soon afterwards. Arnold and Allen with only eighty-five men crossed the lake in a few available boats, completely surprised the British garrison, and made a spectacular capture of Fort Ticonderoga with all of its cannon and ammunition.

A party was sent out by Arnold to procure boats from Skenesborough, at the extreme southern end of the lake. They were held off for a time by the inhabitants, but the timely arrival of some additional men enabled them to capture the town and also a schooner. They manned the schooner and promptly sailed it to Ticonderoga, where they renamed it the *Liberty*. Arnold's original plans, to capture guns and ammunition, were considerably expanded after this bit of luck. He decided to capture an armed British sloop known to be somewhere in the lake. Arnold armed the *Liberty* and placed on it a crew of fifty acting sailors and marines recruited from his men. He made John P. Sloan, a sailor of experience, captain of the vessel, while he acted as commander of the expedition. They sailed up the lake on May 14 in search of the British sloop which was reported at St. Johns on the river beyond the northern end of the lake. When they arrived within thirty miles of St. Johns, they were becalmed but took to their boats and after rowing all night reached St. Johns. They captured the sloop, renamed it the *Enterprize,* placed it under Sloan's command, and manned it with men of the expedition. They also captured some valuable stores and retired with them and all boats found in the vicinity.

These humble beginnings by Arnold were the first efforts made by any of the colonies to develop armed forces afloat. One of the oldest remaining documents of this period is a pay roll of the *Enterprize* of July 1, 1775. It bears the names of certain naval officers, Lieutenant James Watson of marines, a number of sailors, and seventeen marines. Some of the enlisted men whose names appear on this roll were given credit for pay from as early as May 3, 1775—the date on which Arnold set out from his home at Cambridge. The roll shows that other men were taken up for pay at various times during the period covered by the pay roll. It seems to be a reasonable assumption that Arnold had naval intentions at the time he left Cambridge:

the principal officers on the *Enterprise* were paid from that date and probably accompanied him. Arnold was, at the time he set out, acting solely under the authority of the state of Massachusetts, and his naval force was not, properly speaking, a part of the Continental Navy. On June 10, 1775, however, all of the American forces operating at Crown Point, Ticonderoga, and on the lake were, by resolution of the Continental Congress, brought under its control. The resolution provided for the men to be paid from May 3. That pay roll is the earliest existing record of United States marines.

No sooner had the control of the lake been obtained, than rumors were frequent that the British in Canada were preparing to retake what they had lost. Arnold was determined to make every possible effort to hold his gains. He requested more seamen for his ships and fitted out additional small vessels. He requisitioned the necessary stores and additional men from New York State.

The little fleet on Lake Champlain together with all armed forces in the vicinity was placed by Congress under the control of Washington on June 15, 1775. On June 27, however, Congress placed all the forces in New York under Major General Philip Schuyler and ordered him to take St. Johns and, in every way possible, induce the people to join the colonists. Congress had yet taken no steps for the creation of a navy: the vessels on the lake operated as part of the Continental Army. The situation then was not unlike that which existed prior to 1798 when the United States had no Navy Department and the Navy, what little existed, functioned under the War Department.

During the fall of 1775 both the British and Americans set about to build fleets to control Lake Champlain. The British with the aid of a detachment of the Royal Navy not only were able to build a superior fleet but manned it more effectively than did the inexperienced colonials. The British developed a flotilla of twenty-five vessels armed with eighty-nine guns and manned by about one thousand men. Despite the urgent requests and recommendations of the officers on the lake, the Continental Congress did not supply sufficient men or material to develop a squadron that could hope to compete with the rapidly growing British force. By early October, Arnold was able to put in commission only fifteen small vessels carrying eighty-eight guns and manned by about seven hundred men, whom he described as a "miserable set" and a "wretched motley crew." Arnold reported that the "marines are the refuse of every regiment and the seamen few of them were ever wet with salt water." The officers of the flotilla were army officers, and the vessels were not suited for serious naval engagements.

But on October 11, 1776, the two opposing forces met in a desperate battle in which Arnold attempted to hold off the superior British forces by anchoring his flotilla in line between an island and the shore. The engagement was not entirely decisive, but by nightfall Arnold's vessels were so seriously damaged that he was forced to retire during the night. He retreated south; the British discovered his movements early the following morning. They pursued but did not overtake him until noon of the 13th. Two of Arnold's vessels then attempted to protect the others—one of these was captured in the engagement; the other escaped for the time being. Five of the American vessels put in at Panton Bay where their crews beached and destroyed them. Arnold's other vessels, except two which fell into the hands of the British, came to a similar end. The British gained control of the lake and made a demonstration against Ticonderoga, but abandoned all their valuable gains on November 3 and returned to Canada for winter quarters.

## STATE NAVIES AND MARINES

The first armies during the Revolutionary War were raised by the different states. They functioned for some time more or less in cooperation with each other before the Continental Congress made any attempt to create an army. Navies of several colonies also came into existence before Congress attempted to form a navy. The first of the state navies was formed as early as June, 1775; others came into existence during the following months. During the course of the war all of the states, except Delaware, developed naval forces of their own. The combined strength of these navies is not definitely known, but it was probably greater than that of the entire Continental Navy. Most of the state vessels were small craft suitable only for the defense of inland waters and harbors. Probably not more than sixty in all could have been rated as deep-sea vessels. The primary function of the state navies was to defend seaports and the coast and protect commerce. Most of the states organized their navies after the British fashion; each had its own marines as well as sailors for duty on naval vessels. The marines of several states antedate the Continental Marines; their existence, no doubt, helped to cause the establishment of an organization of marines serving all the colonies.

Early in June, 1775, the Third Provisional Congress of Massachusetts took the initial step for providing that colony with a naval force for the purpose of protecting its coast and attacking enemy vessels. The citizens of Machias, Maine, fitted out a sloop and a schooner; the revolutionary government gave them authority to

Tun Tavern—Birthplace of the Marine Corps

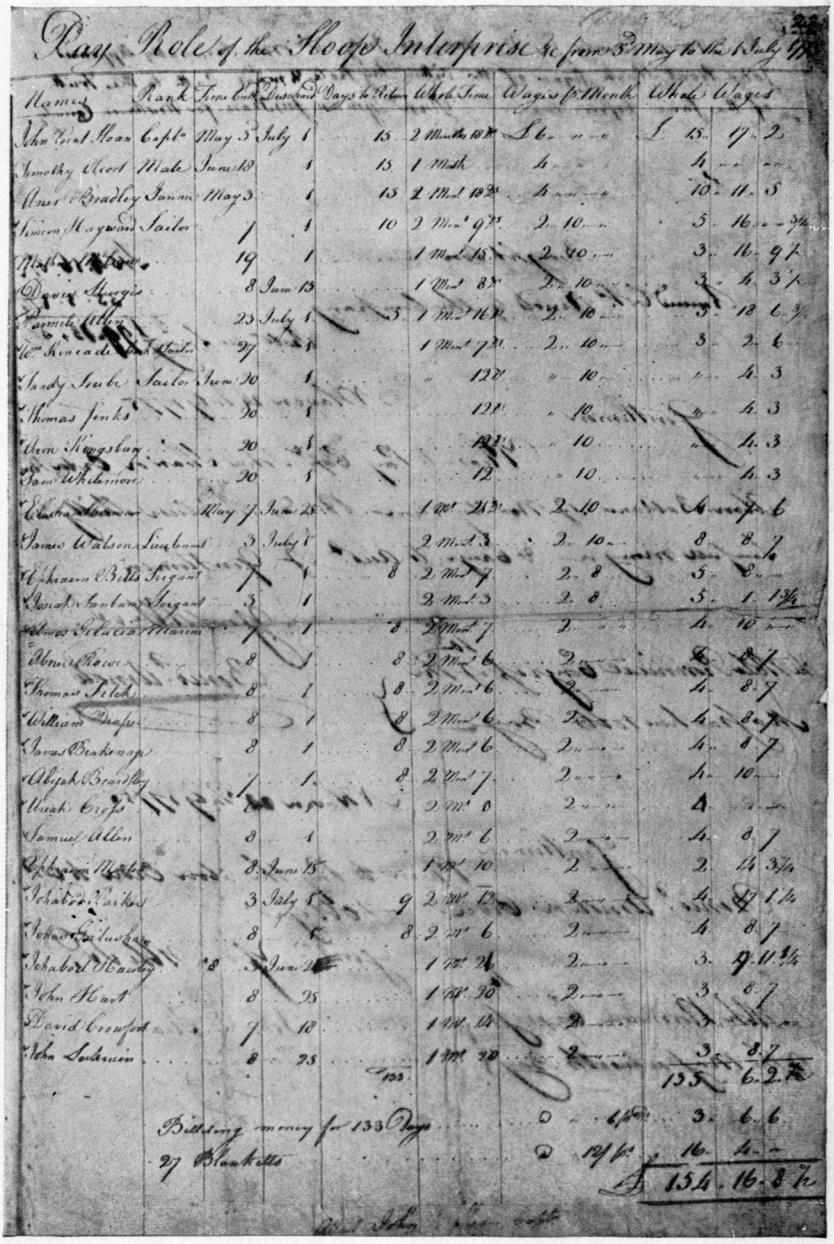

PAY ROLL OF THE *Enterprize*—OLDEST KNOWN RECORD OF AMERICAN MARINES

operate the vessels as the Massachusetts Navy. Within the following year that navy grew to six ships of seagoing size, in addition to some small craft. Massachusetts made provisions for a regular naval organization including officers, sailors, and marines for the several vessels. Before being taken into that service as a marine, the applicant was required to have "a good effective Fire Arm, Cartouch Box, Cutlass and Blanket." During the succeeding years several large ships were added to the Massachusetts Navy. During the war it had sixteen different vessels carrying from ten to twenty guns each. These vessels rendered signal service by capturing a number of enemy merchant ships, transports, and supply ships. The most important operation that they participated in was the Penobscot Expedition—an account of which is given hereafter.

Connecticut established a navy, principally of small craft for defense of its harbors, at about the same time. Its principal ship was the *Minerva* (108 tons), which had an authorized complement of about forty marines, a like number of seamen, and the necessary officers. The total number of vessels in the Connecticut Navy during the war was about twelve. The frequent mention of marines in the Connecticut records indicates that they were provided as part of the crews for most of those vessels.

The first step for providing a navy for Pennsylvania was taken early in July, 1775, when the Committee of Safety directed the building of a galley and, within the following three months, caused twelve others to be added to its naval forces. These small craft, armed with 18-pounders and carrying a crew of thirty-five, were largely used on the Delaware River. By August, 1776, one fairly large vessel, the *Montgomery,* carrying 128 men, a floating battery, and twelve smaller craft had been added to the Pennsylvania Navy. The returns show that it then had a total strength of 768 officers, seamen, and marines. According to the custom of the times probably at least one-third of the naval personnel were marines. These marines wore a distinctive uniform which consisted partly of "a brown coat faced with green, letters 1 P.B. on the buttons, and a cocked hat." The Pennsylvania Navy reached its maximum strength (fifty-one vessels) in 1777. It played an important part in the operations along the Delaware River until it was practically destroyed by the British when they occupied Philadelphia in 1777. It maintained a few small craft, however, throughout the remaining years of the war.

Virginia also established a navy in 1775. In number of ships it was the largest of any of the state navies—comprising from first to last seventy-two vessels of all classes, mostly small craft for the protection of inland waters. The Virginia Navy carried on until

April 1, 1781, when it was practically destroyed during the British invasion of the state. The men from the ships joined Washington's army during the Yorktown campaign. The records of the Virginia Navy show that a considerable portion of its personnel were marines.

The next in importance of the southern state navies was that of South Carolina, which had its beginning in the successful operation of two armed barges which, with the aid of some Georgians, captured a cargo of gunpowder and other munitions at Savannah. This success led to extensive preparations for the capture of other British munitions ships. The first real ship to become a part of the South Carolina Navy was the schooner *Defense,* commissioned in October, 1775. It had, as part of its crew, a detachment of thirty-five marines. Shortly after being commissioned, it engaged two British ships in an indecisive battle. The affair, however, stimulated interest in the navy of that state, which soon added two other seagoing vessels. Sailors were scarce in South Carolina, and arrangements were made for a part of the crews of these vessels to be recruited in Massachusetts. The South Carolina Navy, although smaller than that of Virginia, was more active than any of the state navies except that of Massachusetts. During the first three years of its existence it captured thirty-five prizes off the coasts of the southern colonies and in the West Indies. Several of its vessels, in conjunction with the Continental Navy, participated in an operation in the West Indies which is described hereafter. The South Carolina Navy practically came to an end with the siege and capture of Charleston (discussed below) in 1780. State marines of South Carolina played the usual part of soldiers of the sea in those operations.

Of the remaining state navies, that of Georgia was probably the first created. Although it consisted mostly of galleys, it played an important part, especially in the early stages of the war. The Maryland Navy did not antedate the Continental Navy but was developed to a considerable strength and rendered valuable services, especially on Chesapeake Bay. It performed its most notable service during the closing years of the war by assisting Washington during the Yorktown operations. Its marines wore a distinctive uniform of blue hunting shirts. The remaining colonies made less important naval efforts, principally in defense of their coasts.

### The Origin of the Continental Navy

The first official step taken by the Continental Congress for the development of a navy was made on October 13, 1775, when it authorized the acquisition of two vessels of war. On the 30th of that month it authorized the acquisition of two additional vessels and two more on December 2. The first vessels procured under that authority were probably delivered early in November at Philadelphia. Some of these ships, together with their crews, were acquired in New York and Baltimore. On November 5 the naval committee of Congress selected Esek Hopkins as commander in chief of the Continental Fleet. Hopkins assumed his duties early in December, but Congress did not officially confirm his appointment until December 22. Meanwhile it made provisions for the more complete organization of the naval service.

The first move by Congress for acquiring personnel for the Navy was by the resolution of October 13 mentioned above; it provided for eighty men to man one of the ships. Further authorization for naval personnel was contained in the resolution of October 30, which provided for the acquisition of two ships. On November 2 Congress provided for "such officers and seamen as are proper to man and command" the vessels already procured.

## THE CONTINENTAL MARINES

The first official step taken by the Continental Congress to provide marines was taken on November 10, when it authorized the raising of two battalions consisting of one colonel, two lieutenant colonels, two majors, other officers as usual in regiments, and enlisted men as in other battalions. The resolution further specified that the personnel selected for the battalions be "good seamen or so acquainted with maritime affairs as to be able to serve to advantage at sea." November 10, for that reason, has been officially designated the birthday of the United States Marine Corps and has been observed as such since 1921. It is not apparent, however, that any marines were actually recruited or officers commissioned for the two battalions as such, but the authority contained in the resolution appears to have been used to form more or less isolated detachments of marines who served throughout the remainder of the American Revolution. Personnel for the Navy had, in the meantime, been inducted into service under the resolution of November 2.

Provisions for administering the Navy were effected by a resolution adopted by Congress, November 28, 1775. The rules contained therein marked the beginning of the regulations for the United States Navy. They were concerned largely with the feeding, care, rank, usages, and punishment of the enlisted men of the navy. The resolution also provided for the commissioning of captains and lieutenants of the Navy and five marine officers—captain was the highest rank allowed for marine officers. The disciplinary rules, which also governed the marines, were derived mostly from the naval discipline act of Parliament of 1749 and conformed more or less to the laws that regulated the discipline of the British Navy.

The procurement of ships, the enlistment of marines and sailors, and the commissioning of naval and marine officers proceeded slowly under the several acts of the Continental Congress mentioned above. While Hopkins and probably other naval officers carried on their official duties under the authority of the Naval Committee, the first commission actually granted was not confirmed by Congress until December 22, 1775. The first marine officer appointed, according to known existing records, was First Lieutenant John Trevett, who reported for duty on board the *Columbus* in November, 1775. The oldest existing commission of a marine officer is that of Captain Samuel Nicholas, dated November 28, 1775. At about the same time several other marine officers were appointed for duty on board ships of the navy, then being placed in commission.

The first recruiting of the Continental Marines under the authority stated above appears to have been at Tun Tavern in Philadelphia —at the time a hostelry on the east side of King (Water) Street. The proprietor of the Tavern, Robert Mullan, was made captain of a company of marines and acted as one of the principal recruiting officers for the Marines throughout the Revolution. Similar recruiting rendezvous were probably established in New York and Baltimore for enlisting marines for the vessels of the navy procured at those cities. The method of recruiting was largely by "drumming up" in the technique now used by the Salvation Army. Offers of prize money were early resorted to. The recruit was also lured by a prospective bounty, a pension, and promises of ample grog and other rations.

Congress had called upon Washington to transfer suitable soldiers to the marines, but he objected to such action on the ground that it would seriously deplete his army, already too small, and disrupt the organization of its units. The objection was agreed to; the former method of procuring marines was, thereupon, used, and the necessary marines for Hopkins' squadron were gradually provided.

As to the first Continental Marine unit formed, a regular marine detachment was on board the *Cabot* during December, 1775; another detachment was on the *Alfred*—the first ship procured for Hopkins' squadron—early in the following month. The problem of obtaining suitable arms and equipment for marines appears to have been more difficult than the procurement of men. The difficulty was overcome, to some extent, by the Committee of Public Safety of Pennsylvania making substantial donations and loans of muskets, other munitions, and materials to the several marine detachments formed in Philadelphia.

## THE EXPEDITION TO NEW PROVIDENCE

The naval squadron under Commodore Esek Hopkins was gradually assembled and outfitted for any particular part it might be called upon to play. In the meantime Congress was gradually evolving plans for its use. Several conditions existed which called for the use of a naval squadron. Some British ships were cruising in Chesapeake Bay and around the Virginia capes, interrupting commerce and making raids on shore. Hopkins' squadron had been formed largely for the purpose of combating those enemy ships. Other British vessels were carrying on similar depredations along the Carolina coast. An enemy naval force was at Savannah attempting to prevent the inhabitants of Georgia from taking part in the rebellion. Both the Marine Committee and Hopkins hoped that his little squadron would not only be able to put a stop to the activities of the British along the coast but also capture some of the ships to add to the Continental Navy.

Information to the effect that large quantities of powder and other ammunitions of war had been stored by the British on the island of New Providence in the Bahamas, where it was guarded by only a small detachment of British troops, caused a further extension of the naval plans. The colonies were at the time in serious need of any and all military supplies—especially powder. The prospect of capturing six hundred barrels of powder strongly appealed to Hopkins, and he determined to make that the first mission of the newly organized squadron.

Early in 1776 the squadron consisted of: the *Alfred* and *Columbus*, each manned by a crew of 220, including 60 marines; 2 brigs, the *Andrea Doria* and *Cabot*, having a crew of 130 and 120 respectively, including 30 marines each; 2 sloops, the *Providence* and *Hornet*, with a crew of 90 men each, including 28 marines on the former and 20 on the latter; and 2 schooners, the *Fly* and *Wasp*, each carrying 20 marines as part of their crews. All of these vessels, except the schooners, carried from one to four marine officers. The vessels were frozen in for several weeks and were therefore unable to leave the vicinity of Philadelphia, but Hopkins continued to improve his organization and add military equipment furnished by the State of Pennsylvania. The squadron moved down the bay for a short distance to Liberty Island on January 17. It continued fitting out and, at the end of that month, moved farther down to Reedy Island preparatory for a dash to sea as soon as the weather would permit. Hopkins finally sailed on February 11 for Cape Henlopen, where he was joined by two ships from Baltimore.

Shortly after Hopkins arrived at Cape Henlopen, a cold northeast wind sprang up and made his anchorage unsafe. On February 14 he ordered his squadron to carry out the mission more suitable for the time of year, the weather, and his own taste—cruise south and, if separated by bad weather, to rendezvous at Abaco, one of the Bahama Islands. The squadron sailed three days later and arrived at the rendezvous March 1. The *Fly* and *Hornet* got separated from the squadron in bad weather and did not rejoin until about ten days later. Hopkins made plans for an immediate attack on New Providence. He procured two small sloops to use as transports for a landing force. The marines from the *Andrea Doria* were temporarily transferred to the *Providence;* the remainder of the marines of the squadron (about 220), under Captain Samuel Nicholas, together with about 50 sailors under Lieutenant Weaver of the *Cabot*, were placed on board the sloops during the evening of March 2. In order to surprise the enemy, the sloops carrying Nicholas' landing force were ordered to sail ahead of the squadron, keeping their armed forces concealed to avoid arousing the suspicion of the British.

The squadron followed the sloops too closely, however, and was seen by the enemy, who fired an alarm shot from the fort on New Providence before Nicholas could effect a landing. Nevertheless, supported by the *Providence* and *Wasp*, Nicholas' force moved to a position off the eastern end of the island. Under the cover of the gunfire of those two vessels, Nicholas, with his landing force then headed for the shore, succeeded in landing without resistance or mishap and immediately advanced toward the town of New Providence—greatly surprising the inhabitants by his warlike acts.

Being a good diplomat Nicholas set about to accomplish his mission with the least bloodshed. He received a message from the governor of New Providence desiring to know his intentions. Nicholas replied by messenger that only the military stores on the island were wanted; and, if they were surrendered, no harm would be done to the inhabitants. As Nicholas approached Fort Montague, located about one mile east of the town of New Providence, the enemy fired three 12-pounder shots. Nicholas halted to make further plans, sent a message to the fort advising the garrison of his mission, and received a reply that the shots were fired by order of the governor. The garrison offered no further resistance, however, but spiked their guns, abandoned the fort, and retired to the town.

Nicholas then advanced and took possession of the fort, removed the spikes from part of the guns, and spent the night there.

Hopkins issued a declaration to the inhabitants of the principal town, Fort Nassau, expressing his desire to carry out his mission without doing any harm to them or their personal property. This had the desired effect and enabled him to proceed without further resistance. On the following morning Nicholas marched into Fort Nassau with his detachment of marines and sailors and took possession of the governor's house, which commanded not only the town but also the fort. Nicholas demanded and received the keys to the fort and took possession of it without firing a shot, in spite of the fact that its forty guns had all been loaded for his reception.

Hopkins then moved his squadron into the harbor and came ashore. He found a vast quantity of various military stores including seventy-one cannon and fifteen mortars, but only twenty-four casks of powder. The governor had succeeded in doing away with 150 casks during the night. Hopkins' squadron remained in the harbor until March 17 and loaded the captured stores on its ships and on an impressed vessel. Hopkins then took the governor and several other officials of New Providence on board. After giving orders to his captains, in case the squadron got separated, to make the best of their way to Block Island Channel in Rhode Island and there await the arrival of the rest of the ships, Hopkins sailed away. He had carried out, with practically no resistance, what was perhaps the most successful American naval operation during the Revolutionary War. The Continental Marines had performed their first landing operation. Hopkins' squadron next operated along the New England coast against isolated ships of the British Navy, transports, and supply ships.

### With Washington's Army

After his campaign with Howe's army around New York late in 1776, Washington gradually withdrew westward across New Jersey and in December retreated into Pennsylvania. Howe was not at all vigorous in his pursuit: his army had little taste for a winter campaign under the primitive conditions that existed in the colonies. Washington's army became somewhat demoralized and dwindled to about five thousand men. The British, in their pursuit, extended their army most of the way across New Jersey. Some Hessian troops went into winter quarters at Trenton and Bordentown. In spite of repeated orders they made little effort to provide protection against surprise. Howe thought that Washington had been completely defeated and appears to have taken little further notice of him. Washington, however, was keeping a close watch on all the British forces and was well aware of their having cast aside all caution, even the usual measures for providing security.

Since the fitting out of Hopkins' squadron and the raising of marines in Philadelphia, that city had continued to be the center of naval and marine activity, few details of which are now known. The brief records show that Samuel Nicholas was appointed major of marines and six captains of marines were provided for by the Continental Congress on June 25, 1776. Nicholas soon afterwards raised three companies of marines for three frigates which were then fitting out. In September, Congress directed two companies of marines that were stationed at Philadelphia to report to Washington at Fort Montgomery, but there is no evidence to show whether or not these orders were carried out. By November, however, Nicholas had a battalion of marines in the vicinity of Philadelphia. Continental and Pennsylvania marines were at the time serving on board vessels of the Navy in the Delaware River and helped prevent Howe's army from taking Philadelphia. On December 12 the marines on the *Hancock*, then operating in the Delaware River, landed at Burlington, which they suspected was held by the Hessians. The Hessians had withdrawn, however, and the *Hancock*'s marines returned to their ship on the 17th.

In December, 1776, Nicholas with his battalion of marines was ordered to report to Washington in New Jersey and "continue in the field until the men's time and enlistments expire." Marines and sailors from a number of vessels were also sent to Washington's army at about the same time. Upon reporting to Washington, these naval forces, including Nicholas' battalion, passed to the command of General Cadwalader, who made them a part of his division. The naval forces on the Delaware and Washington's army along its western bank foiled the attempts of the British to invade Pennsylvania. Washington had been careful, when he retreated across the river, to remove all available boats and vessels to the Pennsylvania side. When Washington made his famous crossing of the Delaware, Cadwalader's division attempted to cross near Burlington but was unable to land the artillery and returned to the Pennsylvania side. Washington's army, without that division, advanced rapidly on Trenton, where they surprised and captured the entire Hessian garrison on Christmas night, 1776. In the meantime Cadwalader, with his attached naval forces, succeeded in crossing the river and hurried on to join Washington.

When Cornwallis at New York heard of Washington's attack on Trenton, he hurried to the vicinity, collected seven or eight thousand troops, and on January 2, 1777, advanced on Trenton. Washington withdrew and successfully evaded the British advance. He had a skirmish with some of Cornwallis' forces in the so-called Second Battle of Trenton, or Assanpink, then quickly moved towards Princeton in rear of the British forces, where he routed three regiments moving to reinforce Cornwallis at Trenton. Nicholas' battalion of marines and the marine detachments from several ships were with Washington's army during these operations; but the few existing records do not disclose the particular part they played in them.

Cornwallis had hoped to drive Washington back against the Delaware, but Washington outwitted him and passed well around his rear. Washington then marched to Morristown, New Jersey. Nicholas' marines remained with Washington's army until February 20 and took part in several other skirmishes. That battalion as well as the detachments from the ships returned to Philadelphia in March, 1777, and resumed their duties in that city and on board their vessels. Prior to the detachment of the marines from Washington's army, a number of them were transferred to the artillery as they had had considerable experience in handling guns on board ship.

### In European Waters

The first Continental vessel to operate in European waters during the Revolution was the *Reprisal,* which conveyed Benjamin Franklin to France in the autumn of 1776. It cruised in European waters for several months and captured a number of British prizes. In April of the following year it was joined by the *Lexington.* Soon afterwards the American agents purchased the 10-gun cutter *Dolphin* and added it to the little squadron, which was then under the command of Captain Lambert Wickes. Wickes' squadron made two daring cruises around Ireland and returned to France, after having captured fifteen prizes. The *Lexington* later engaged the British ship *Alert,* off the coast of France, and fought a disastrous battle during which Lieutenant James Connelly of the marines was killed. The *Lexington* was finally forced to surrender, and its crew were thrown into Mill Prison at Plymouth, England. The *Reprisal* sailed for the United States soon afterwards. It foundered on the Banks of Newfoundland, and all hands except one perished. Both the *Reprisal* and the *Lexington* carried the usual complement of marines.

## With John Paul Jones

The next Continental Marines to serve in European waters were those with John Paul Jones during the first of his famous cruises along the coast of the British Isles. Jones had been placed in command of the *Ranger*, which had been poorly fitted out and had practically no provisions. With the usual marine detachment as part of a nondescript crew, Jones sailed from Portsmouth, New Hampshire, for Nantes, France, in November, 1777. There Jones received a salute of recognition from the French admiral and, after being thoroughly refitted, sailed in April of the following year for a cruise in the Irish Sea. In a series of daring exploits he captured British ships, boldly attacked a fleet of British war vessels, and in the face of the entire population burned shipping at Whitehaven, England. While making a raid ashore, his men spiked the guns of a fort, plundered the castle of the Earl of Selkirk, and caused consternation in general throughout that part of the English coast.

Jones ended his cruise in a desperate engagement with the superior British ship *Drake*, off the Irish coast. After a fight of seventy-four minutes the *Drake* surrendered, and Jones with his prize returned around Ireland to France. During the battle with the *Drake*, Lieutenant Samuel Wallingford, in command of the marine detachment of the *Ranger*, was killed. The French were so impressed with Jones's victories that they were willing to place their fleet under his command. But the American commissioners relieved Jones from command of the *Ranger* and turned that ship over to Lieutenant Thomas Simpson, leaving Jones for some time without a ship.

## Other New Providence Expeditions

Early in 1778 the sloop *Providence*, which had been with Hopkins in the first cruise to New Providence, undertook another expedition to that place. It narrowly escaped a British squadron but reached Abaco and, two days later, arrived off New Providence. The character of the ship was disguised as much as possible. It sailed into the harbor at midnight, and Captain John Trevett, Continental Marines, with twenty-eight marines and sailors made a landing at about 2 A.M. and captured Fort Nassau. He then took another fort, four miles away, and spiked its guns. Trevett captured a considerable supply of ammunition and stores which he placed on board the *Providence*. That sloop also captured four small vessels. Having completely finished its job, the *Providence* sailed away four days later with its loot and two of the prizes, having burned the others.

A third expedition, consisting of South Carolina naval forces and

Spanish forces under the Governor General of Cuba, went against New Providence in April, 1782. The skillful handling of the American naval vessels together with the threat of a Spanish landing force induced the governor to capitulate on May 8. The Spanish then occupied the island.

## IN AMERICAN WATERS—1777-1779

During 1777 several Continental naval vessels continued to operate along the coast of North America. The *Randolph*, Captain Nicholas Biddle, was sent on a general mission of co-operating with the South Carolina Navy in clearing the Carolina coast of enemy vessels. It captured six prizes and brought them into Charleston but was blockaded in that port the remainder of the year. Early in 1778 the *Randolph* with four small vessels of the South Carolina Navy put to sea to drive off the British blockading squadron. In addition to the regular Continental Marines on the *Randolph* under Captain Samuel Shaw, the vessels carried 150 South Carolina troops serving as marines. The little squadron soon freed the coast of enemy vessels and early in March sailed for the West Indies in search of prizes. While cruising to the eastward of Barbados, the squadron encountered the British ship *Yarmouth*. Without hesitating, the *Randolph* closed on the greatly superior British ship. The two vessels engaged in a running fight for about fifteen minutes, when the *Randolph* blew up, and all on board except four were lost. Only one of the South Carolina vessels took part in the engagement. The sacrificing of the *Randolph* enabled the remainder of the squadron to escape.

By this time the Continental Navy had been considerably diminished; but a few ships continued to give a good account of themselves along the American coast.

## POLLOCK'S FLEET AND MARINES

The Continental Congress placed naval affairs on the Mississippi River and in the general vicinity of New Orleans under its commercial agent, Oliver Pollock, whom it authorized to commission vessels and officers in the Continental service and to issue letters of marque. Pollock worked in close co-operation with the Spanish governor of Louisiana, Bernardo de Galvez, who was particularly friendly to the American cause and opened the port of New Orleans to all United States vessels. In March, 1778, Pollock procured a small vessel and, after a delay of more than a year, succeeded in fitting it out with twenty-four guns. He provided a crew with Captain William Pickles in command and renamed the vessel the *Morris*.

Pollock commissioned Daniel Longstreet as a first lieutenant of marines to serve on the *Morris* and command its marine detachment. The *Morris* was originally designed to become part of the Continental Navy, but, while waiting for orders from Philadelphia, it was wrecked at New Orleans by a severe hurricane.

In the meantime Congress had made other arrangements for a show of force on the western frontier. It directed Captain James Willing to proceed with an armed force from Fort Pitt (Pittsburgh) down the Ohio and Mississippi Rivers to New Orleans with important dispatches for Pollock and the Spanish governor. With permission of Congress, Willing enlisted a company of marines to accompany him. Congress placed Willing under the general direction of Pollock. General Hand, in command at Fort Pitt, furnished the necessary supplies for the expedition. With his escort of marines Willing started down the river on January 10, 1778, on an old boat, which he had armed and renamed the *Rattletrap*.

Willing engaged in a number of activities on his way down designed to advance the claim of the United States over the western territory. The western settlers who would not declare themselves in favor of the United States were required to give an oath of neutrality. On the way down the rivers Willing recruited more men for his expedition and captured a number of boats, including a small vessel called the *Rebecca* which Pollock renamed the *Morris*. Willing arrived at New Orleans on March 6, 1778, delivered the dispatches, and sold his prizes. Willing and his men took part in some other expeditions along the lower Mississippi. Later in 1778, while attempting to return to Philadelphia by sea with dispatches for Congress, he was captured by the British. His "company of marines" went back up the Mississippi and joined George Rogers Clark in his operations in the Northwest Territory.

## With the Penobscot Expedition

As the war dragged on, a great many American privateers operated from the present coast of Maine against British supply ships and merchantmen. In 1779 the British decided to establish a strong naval base in that part of New England in order to suppress the privateers. A force of about seven hundred soldiers from Halifax together with some naval vessels established a base on Penobscot Bay. They began to fortify it and within a month had erected substantial earthworks and other defenses. In the meantime Massachusetts learned of their operations and began to organize an expedition to drive them out. Three vessels of the Massachusetts Navy and three of the few remaining vessels of the Continental

Navy were assembled for the naval part of the expedition. About one thousand militia embarked on thirteen private vessels which they hired as transports. They took along a few pieces of artillery under Lieutenant Colonel Paul Revere. Approximately three hundred marines, about half Continental and the remainder Massachusetts Marines, accompanied the expedition which finally sailed from Boston, July 19.

The landing force of the expedition, under General Solomon Lovell of the Massachusetts Militia, was organized into three general divisions. The combined marine detachments under Captain John Welsh formed one division, and the militia, two divisions. The expedition arrived at Penobscot Bay on July 25. The naval vessels engaged the British ships in an indecisive engagement which lasted about two hours. The next day the marines landed under the support of fire from the ships and took possession of Nautilus Island, which commanded the anchorage of the British ships and afforded a position for artillery to fire against the enemy's main fortification at Bagaduce on the mainland. The British ships then retired up the river.

A lack of co-operation between Lovell and the naval commander soon developed; it proved the complete undoing of the expedition. They lost valuable time while the enemy on Bagaduce Peninsula strongly fortified their positions. The orders to the expedition for the proper co-operation between the two arms of the service had been most specific, but the naval commander failed in practically every instance properly to support the forces on shore, despite the fact that he knew a superior British naval force was expected to arrive. Lovell apparently thought that the marine battalion was the best shock troops for his next offensive move. He withdrew the marines from Nautilus Island, leaving it to a detachment of sailors who had landed.

In the early morning of July 28, under the protection of the fire of a battery on Nautilus Island, the marines landed on the peninsula west of Bagaduce and advanced through thick woods to the crest of a ridge. There they encountered the British outguards. The marines held the ridge and covered the landing of the militia. On the following day Lovell succeeded in advancing about one-third of the way across the peninsula, through thick woods and up a steep slope, but without the support of naval gunfire, as agreed by the naval commander. Welsh was killed in the attack. Two days later the marines, reinforced by a few seamen, moved in boats and made an unsuccessful attempt to land in a position which would outflank the British. The American naval commander for some reason failed to engage the inferior British squadron and left it free to support the British defenses. By this time Lovell was convinced that he could not successfully attack the British position without proper support from the squadron. Several valuable days had been lost.

Meanwhile, a British squadron of seven ships under Commodore Collier at New York, having learned of the expedition, sailed on August 3 for the Penobscot. On the 13th, while Lovell's forces were still besieging the British and making arrangements for another vigorous attack, Collier's ships appeared in the offing. The American naval commander, with his hopelessly inferior force, refused to give battle. Lovell's troops on shore withdrew to the vessels and attempted to escape by retreating up the Penobscot River. The British ships followed until night came on and then anchored. The Americans landed safely during the night, destroyed their vessels and, after considerable hardships, made their way back overland to Boston.

## On Jones's Second Cruise

After considerable delay the French Government gave Jones an antiquated Indian merchant ship, which he fitted out as best he could and renamed the *Bonhomme Richard*. In spite of numerous difficulties Jones succeeded in assembling a crew of 380 officers, sailors, and marines. With few exceptions, the officers were Americans holding commissions from the Continental Congress, but the crew was of many nationalities—only about fifty-five were native born Americans. The marine detachment consisted of 3 officers—Lieutenants Edward Stack, Eugene MacCarthy, and James J. O'Kelly—and 137 marines, many of whom were French citizens. The *Alliance*, which had been sent over from Boston early in 1779, upon arriving in France became part of Jones's squadron. Jones procured and armed the *Pallas* and the *Vengeance* and added them, together with the armed cutter *Cerf*, to his squadron. The *Alliance*, *Pallas*, and *Vengeance* had detachments of marines as parts of their crews. The squadron made its first cruise in June, 1779, escorting a convoy from L'Orient to Bordeaux. This led to no important engagements but disclosed the fact that mutiny had been planned by British sailors on the *Bonhomme Richard*. Jones replaced them with former American prisoners of war who had in various ways got out of prison.

Jones, accompanied by two French privateers, sailed on his second famous cruise around the British Isles August 14, 1779. He had a quarrel with the Frenchmen, and they deserted the squadron. Jones cruised to the west of Ireland and around the north of Scotland. He then headed for the vicinity of Edinburgh, which was reported to be completely undefended. His ships became separated by bad weather, but Captain Landais of the *Alliance* caused still greater embarrassment by his repeated insubordination and claims of being actually in command of the squadron. Jones attempted to raid Leith, near Edinburgh, but failed because a gale blew his ships back to sea. By this time his presence had spread alarm throughout the British Isles; the captains of his accompanying ships were very insistent on leaving before a superior force could attack. Jones refused: the *Pallas* and *Vengeance* sailed away to safety. Meanwhile, the *Bonhomme Richard* got separated from the remaining vessels of the squadron.

The *Alliance* and *Pallas* fortunately rejoined Jones on September 23. He then discovered the British frigates *Serapis* and *Countess of Scarborough* convoying some merchantmen. Upon signal from the British commander the merchantmen fled. The *Pallas* attacked the *Countess of Scarborough;* Jones's ship closed on the *Serapis;* but the *Alliance* took practically no part in the battle. The engagement between the *Bonhomme Richard* and the *Serapis* was one of the most remarkable and desperate fights in the annals of our navy. The *Bonhomme Richard*'s guns proved to be very unreliable—two of them burst on the first broadside—and the crews refused to man the others on the same deck. This left only the guns on the upper deck to carry on the fight. The reduced gunfire from the *Bonhomme Richard* was more than compensated for by the deadly fire delivered by the marines from the tops and other elevated positions against the personnel on the decks of the *Serapis*. Stack, with a group of marines in the maintop, was able to keep the open decks of the enemy ship practically cleared of all men. The two ships soon became fastened together. While the small arms fire, together with the fire of a gun which raked the *Serapis,* completely dominated her weather decks, she poured an incessant fire from her lower guns into the *Bonhomme Richard* and riddled her with holes—some of which were below the water line and caused imminent danger of sinking. The climax came when Jones's men succeeded in dropping hand grenades from the mainyard down the hatches of the *Serapis:* one of these ignited a powder chest. The explosion demoralized the entire British crew, and the *Serapis* surrendered. Sixty-seven of the marine detachment of the *Bonhomme Richard* were killed or wounded during the fight. In the meantime the *Pallas* had captured the *Scarborough*.

Jones reached Holland with his prizes, but the *Bonhomme Richard* sank the day after the famous fight. Jones and his officers and crew were hailed as great naval heroes. Jones put the *Serapis* in commission and refitted it and his other ships at Texel, Holland, but he was blockaded there for some time by a British squadron. He later took the *Alliance* as his ship and transferred to it all the Americans who had been with him on the *Bonhomme Richard*. Because of neutrality difficulties the Dutch forced Jones to leave Holland on the *Alliance* in the face of a British blockading squadron, which, however, he succeeded in evading. The *Alliance* reached a Spanish port, where it was cordially received, and a few months later returned to the United States.

## PRIVATEER MARINES

In addition to vessels of the Continental Navy and of the state navies, a large number of privateers were commissioned by the Continental Congress and by several of the states during the Revolutionary War. Many of these vessels, operating under letters of marque and reprisal, carried as part of their crews a contingent of men armed in the same manner and commonly called marines. The number of privateers under American letters varied from about 136 during 1776 to about half that number in the following year. Thereafter the number rose rapidly to nearly five hundred in 1781 and then gradually declined to the end of the war. It will be noted that, as the Continental Navy decreased in strength, the number of privateers went up rapidly. Privateers operated not only in American waters but carried on extensive operations under letters issued by the American commissioners in Europe.

The opportunity for prize money and high adventure attracted many "gentlemen sailors" who were not really a part of the regular crews of privateers but formed a sort of special marine guard in support of the officers of the vessels. The total number of such adventurers, who might be termed in a general way marines, cannot be estimated even approximately, but it appears probable that it was even greater than the number of marines serving with the Continental Navy and all the state navies combined.

These privateers engaged in a number of spectacular combats with enemy vessels of all types. In many fights they came off the victors, but in a number they were defeated. Usually, when captured, the vessels were sold as prizes and their crews sent to British military prisons. Privateers often cruised with vessels of the Continental and state navies and, on several occasions, while thus employed, engaged enemy ships. The British privateer *Nanny* was taken in May, 1779, by the American privateer *General Arnold*. The captain of the *Nanny* reported: "We received sixty dozen musket shot from their Marines, according to their own account, besides from their tops."

### THE FINAL CAMPAIGN IN THE SOUTH

Throughout the last three years of the war, operations in the North were practically at a stalemate. The British held New York and, a great deal of the time, Newport. A French fleet, accompanied by a French army expeditionary force, made some futile attempts to co-operate with Washington's army but accomplished little. The British determined to conquer the colonies by starting in Georgia, which was largely loyal to the mother country, and gradually overcome the colonies by working north. While attempting to carry out that plan, they continued to raid the coasts of the other colonies.

The British captured Savannah. General Lincoln, assisted by a French fleet under d'Estaing, attempted to retake it but was repulsed with heavy losses. The British, greatly reinforced by troops from New York, then advanced on Charleston. Lincoln's army and five vessels and a number of small craft, under Commodore Abraham Whipple, attempted to defend the city. Whipple's squadron carried a force of marines of unknown strength commanded by Colonel John Laurens. Whipple's ships were hard pressed by the British squadron. He retreated close into Charleston, transferred his crews, including the marines, ashore with all available guns, and destroyed some of his ships. Whipple's forces ashore then assisted in the defense of the city, but they, together with Lincoln's army, were trapped and captured by the British in May, 1780. This was the last important engagement in which marines took part during the war.

The marines came in for their share of hard luck in that a great many of them were captured at various times and were subjected to unspeakable conditions on British prison ships at New York and Charleston and in prisons in England and in the West Indies. Several spectacular escapes from these terrible prisons were effected by a few marines. Others obtained their freedom by recapture. A considerable number were exchanged or paroled. Some, while prisoners of war, were forced to serve as part of the crews of enemy vessels.

### UNIFORMS AND EQUIPMENT

The uniforms worn by the Revolutionary marines were very similar in style and cut to the army uniforms of the period, which in turn followed the fashions of the times. The distinctive uniform color of the Continental Marines was green. The green coat was made with turnback skirts, faced with white, and was well supplied with decorative buttons. The officers wore silver buttons with foul anchors on them; the enlisted men wore pewter buttons. A waistcoat of white material and white breeches edged in green were worn by officers. Knee-length, black gaiters and cocked hats completed the officers' uniform. The enlisted men wore green shirts, green coats with red facings, breeches of light colored cloth, woolen stockings, and a round hat with white binding. Jones dressed his marines in the uniform of the British Royal Marines—red coats, with the other parts of the uniform, white. The state marines wore their own distinctive uniforms or, in many cases, no uniform at all. There are no existing descriptions of the rank devices and insignia worn during the period. It may be logically presumed that they were the same as prescribed for the Continental Army.

The weapons and military equipment which the marine of revolutionary times was expected to be able to use were of a wide range of kinds and makes. The muskets in use had been collected from practically all parts of Europe. Blunderbusses and even more antiquated types of firearms were at times issued to marines. Pistols were in common use. Powder for the muskets was commonly carried in cowhorns. Muskets were usually fired with flints. A crude type of cartridge was used to some extent. Cutting and thrusting weapons such as the bayonet, cutlass, lance, pike, spear, and even tomahawk were at times placed in the hands of marines. Hand grenades were provided, especially on board ship.

## Duties of Marines

The marines performed a great variety of ordinary duties on board ships during the American Revolution. Cooper says they were expected to impart a high military character to the crews of the vessels. As is still the custom, they furnished guards and sentinels aboard ship, and, "at all times they sustain and protect the stern and necessary discipline of a ship by their organization, distinctive character, training, and, we might add, nature." Mutinies were not infrequent among the unreliable crews of the period, and the marines were expected to be the force behind the captain in dealing with these serious breaches of discipline. Marines were not required to go aloft; distinct provision was made that duties in connection with the sailing of the ship were entirely voluntary on their part. As is still the custom, the captain's orderly was usually a marine. A particular duty of the marine sentries on the quarterdeck was to guard the arms chest. When the crew was called to quarters, the marines habitually mustered on the quarterdeck where, in case of emergency, they were armed from the near-by chest. When a prize was captured, it was the usual custom for some of the marines to go as part of the prize crew. Men having special qualifications were at times used for practically any administrative duty on board ships.

## The End of the Continental Navy and Marines

By the spring of 1783 only three ships of the Continental Navy remained in commission, and during that year only twenty-one letters of marque were issued. After the war the few remaining ships in the Navy were gradually disposed of, and their crews were discharged. The Continental Navy passed into history. In spite of a considerable effort to retain it for sentimental reasons and to keep the American flag on the seas, the *Alliance,* the last vessel, was disposed of in 1785. There is practically no record of the Continental Marines serving on shore during the last two years of the war. The number at sea declined as the number of ships grew less, and finally, with the passing away of the Continental Navy, the organization which we have called the Continental Marines was also discontinued.

The last remaining Continental Marine officer of whom we have any record was Lieutenant William Waterman serving on the *Alliance* in June, 1783. The last mention of a Continental Marine in any of the known records is that of Private Robert Stout, who was serving on the same vessel on April 26, 1784. It is probable that some time after this, but prior to the disposal of the *Alliance,* the Continental Marines passed out of existence. But they were no more forgotten than was the Navy with its glorious record. As soon as the struggling nation again saw the necessity of having a navy, an organization of marines was again created which has existed since then as the United States Marine Corps.

## Chapter II
## THE EARLY YEARS OF THE MARINE CORPS

THE Continental Marines as well as the Navy passed out of existence shortly after the Revolutionary War. The War Department was established in 1789 and placed in charge of the military and naval forces; the Navy, however, did not actually come into existence until some years later. There were a few vessels in the Revenue Cutter Service which attempted to perform some of the functions of a navy. They carried as part of their crews a group of men armed similar to and performing the functions of marines and, as a rule, called marines. There is record of at least one marine officer serving in the Revenue Cutter Service prior to 1798, when the Navy Department and the Marine Corps were formally established. The practice of having a few marines on board revenue cutters continued for some time thereafter. Having soon discovered that the rights of the struggling new republic were seriously being infringed upon, many of its leading statesmen came to the conclusion that the best interests of the United States demanded a naval force of at least sufficient strength to protect its own shores and to offer some resistance against pirates.

The need of a navy was further brought home to Congress by the capture of two American ships off the coast of Portugal by Algerine cruisers that took them back to Algiers and imprisoned their crews. Congress did nothing, however, until matters became more serious in 1793, when eleven American vessels were similarly captured, and their crews imprisoned. Congress then decided to build a navy. It authorized the construction of six frigates and provided for a crude naval establishment. Six navy captains who had served in the Revolution were appointed; each was assigned to supervise the construction of a ship. An act of Congress, March 27, 1794, authorizing the establishment of the Navy, further provided that each of the ships carry a detachment of marines consisting of one lieutenant and from forty-five to fifty-four enlisted men.

There had been considerable resistance in Congress to the building of these ships. In order to overcome the opposition, the navy advocates agreed that if a satisfactory treaty were made with Algiers the work of construction would be stopped. Such a treaty was made in September, 1795, at the cost of nearly a million dollars for ransoms, bribes to officials, etc. The estimated cost of all the frigates was only slightly more. The treaty provided further for a substantial annual payment to Algiers. As previously agreed, the work on the frigates stopped. During the following year, however, in spite of violent opposition, Congress authorized work resumed on three of the frigates—the *United States, Constitution,* and *Constellation*—and reauthorized marine detachments for the three vessels.

## Difficulties with France

Some long-standing difficulties with Great Britain were partially adjusted by the Jay Treaty in 1794, but revolutionary France began to insist that we become her ally in wars against various European powers. A war broke out between Great Britain and France which soon involved the United States in serious questions of neutrality. Both of those countries practically refused to recognize any of our neutral rights, and both began to retaliate for our refusal to comply with their demands. Both captured American ships and in many other ways interfered with American commerce. Our Government made repeated efforts by diplomatic means to adjust the difficulties, especially with France, but to little avail. By 1798 it was apparent that peaceful settlement with France was impossible. French privateers were even then capturing American vessels in our own harbors.

Meanwhile Congress had taken measures for defense by appropriating funds for fortifications, revenue cutters, and the completion of the three frigates. Congress also authorized the reorganization of the Army and recalled the aged Washington from retirement as its commander in chief. President John Adams showed little concern over raising an army at the time; he rightly judged that an adequate navy was the only means to check the depredations of the French naval forces upon our commerce. Resistance in Congress against real measures for defense was not overcome until the publication of the famous X Y Z dispatches, which showed clearly that the attitude of the French Government towards the United States was little better than that shown by Algiers. Congress then took substantial and far-reaching steps for defense. It appropriated funds

(April 27, 1798) for the construction, fitting out, arming, and manning of twelve vessels of twenty-two guns each, and three days later authorized the forming of the Navy Department. Other appropriations for national defense followed rapidly. On May 28 Congress authorized the seizure of French armed vessels which were carrying on belligerent operations in American waters and the recapture of any American vessels. This was the beginning of the Naval War with France.

No declaration of war was ever made by either country, and the affair was not officially classified as a war, despite the fact that, during its more than two years of existence, approximately ninety French vessels were captured, and several engagements took place between the armed vessels of the two countries. On July 7 Congress abrogated all our treaties with France; two days later the President instructed the naval forces to seize any and all armed French vessels and began to issue letters of marque to privateers with authority to carry out the same mission.

### Marines for the New Navy

The procuring of marines for the newly created navy kept pace with its development otherwise. The first appointment of an officer of marines of which there is any remaining record was that of Lieutenant Philip Edwards, who was appointed March 16, 1798, to serve on board the *Constellation*. Lieutenants were appointed for both the *Ganges* and the *Constitution* on May 5, and orders were issued to recruit detachments for those vessels. The date when enlistment of marines began is unknown. The earliest enlistment of which there is any record was that of Stephen Bowden on May 7, 1798. The few existing records bear the names of twenty other marines who enlisted prior to the establishment of the Marine Corps, but there were probably many times that number. A lieutenant was appointed for the *Constellation* on May 22 and ordered to recruit marines for that vessel. By June 15 orders had been issued to recruit two other detachments of marines for ships that were purchased. No information is available as to how many officers were appointed prior to the establishment of the Marine Corps. The appointing of officers and the enlisting of marines appear to have been carried on much the same as during the Revolutionary War. Detachments were formed for duty on board particular ships without regard to any central organization.

## Establishment of the Marine Corps

A Corps of Marines was authorized by the Act of July 11, 1798, which provided for an organization of: "one major, four captains, sixteen first lieutenants, twelve second lieutenants, forty-eight sergeants, forty-eight corporals, thirty-two drums and fifes, and seven hundred and twenty privates, including marines who had been enlisted." The law allowed the President considerable latitude as to the use, organization, and disposition of the Corps. He was authorized to provide a staff for the organization in the event that part of it was ordered to duty ashore. Under this authority President John Adams, on the day following his approval of the act, appointed William Ward Burrows as Major Commandant of the Marine Corps. Burrows, an officer in the Revolutionary War and, at the time of his appointment, a resident of Philadelphia with strong Federalist convictions, was, said Washington Irving, "a gentleman of accomplished mind and polished manner." Burrows immediately set about organizing the Corps by selecting a small staff of officers and enlisted men for his headquarters from the few existing subalterns of the line, the sergeants, and the "musics" (musicians). By August 23, 1798, he was able to open a headquarters in Philadelphia and a few days later established a marine camp near that city.

The first concern of the new Commandant was to provide marine detachments for the naval vessels that were being rapidly put in commission. A few ships had already been provided with marines. Lieutenant Daniel Carmick with a detachment of twenty-four marines had been sent aboard the *Ganges* early in May, 1798. That vessel was the first ship of the new navy to go to sea. The *Delaware*, a packet of twenty guns, was purchased in May, 1798; its detachment of marines went aboard during the following month. Marines had also been provided for the *Constellation*.

Burrows encountered some difficulty at first in recruiting marines, as the Army at that time was attempting to add a considerable number of men to its ranks and was offering a substantial bonus for enlistments, which was not allowed marines. The dates of commissioning of the ships of the new navy and the strength of their marine detachments, as far as can be determined from the remaining records, are indicated on the following table:

| NAME OF SHIP | WHEN BUILT OR PURCHASED | NO. OF MARINES | MARINE OFFICER |
|---|---|---|---|
| United States | Launched July 10, 1797 | Authorized 58 | Capt. Franklin Wharton<br>1st Lt. P. Edwards |
| Constellation, 36 | Launched Sept. 7, 1797 | Authorized 46<br>Nov. 17—41 | Lt. Philip Edwards<br>Lt. B. Clinch<br>Lt. J. Triplett<br>Lt. R. Harwood |
| Constitution, 44 | Launched Oct. 21, 1797 | Authorized 58 | Lt. Lemuel Clark |
| L'Insurgente | Captured from French, Feb. 9, 1798 | 36 | Lt. D. S. Wynkoop<br>Lt. Robert Rankin |
| Baltimore, 20 | Purchased May 3, 1798 | 24 | Lt. R. Harwood |
| Ganges, 24 | Purchased May 3, 1798 | 25 | Lt. D. Carmick<br>Lt. S. W. Geddes<br>Lt. J. James |
| Delaware, 20 | Purchased May 5, 1798 | 25 | Lt. James McKnight |
| Herald, 18 | Purchased June 15, 1798 | 18-25 | |
| Montezuma, 20 | Purchased June 26, 1798 | 25 | Lt. Robert Rankin |
| Retaliation | Purchased July 31, 1798 | 25 | Lt. S. W. Geddes |
| Diligence, 12 | Built about Aug. 30, 1798 | 9 | |
| George Washington, 24 | Purchased about Sept. 25, 1798 | 30 | Lt. Diamond Colton<br>Lt. Henry Caldwell |
| Merrimack, 24 | Built about Oct. 1798 | 21-24 | Lt. David Stickney |
| General Greene, 10 | Built, 1798 | 10 | |
| Eagle, 14 | Built, 1798 | 14 | |
| Norfolk, 18 | Built, 1798 | 12-25 | |
| Pickering, 14 | Built, 1798 | | |
| General Pinckney, 18 | Built, 1798 | 15-25 | Lt. John Hall<br>Lt. John Maine |
| Portsmouth, 24 | Built about Oct. 1798 | | |
| Richmond | Purchased, 1798 | 20 | Lt. Wm. Cammack |
| South Carolina | Built, 1798 | 15-25 | Lt. John Hall |
| General Greene, 24 | Built, 1799 | 34 | |
| Boston | Built, 1799 | 30 | Lt. Jonathan Church |
| Enterprise | Built, 1799 | 16 | Sergeant —— Heyler |
| Experiment | Built, 1799 | 14 | Lt. Nathan Sheredine |
| John Adams | Built, 1799 | | Lt. John Hall |

After the establishment of the Navy Department such matters as the complement of marines for ships became a naval administrative affair, and the responsibility of providing the required Marine Corps personnel for the ships was placed upon the Commandant of the Corps. As a result of the Marine Corps having to furnish detachments to the many ships of the Navy which were hurried into commission and supply personnel for other activities, a serious shortage of men was encountered within the first year of its existence. The situation was somewhat relieved by an act of Congress on March 2, 1799, which authorized an increase of 4 officers and 196 enlisted men. But the little increase of men was soon absorbed into the rapidly expanding naval forces.

## IN THE NAVAL WAR WITH FRANCE

The Marine Corps as well as the Navy was created for immediate use in a national emergency. As vessels could be placed in commission and provided with hastily organized crews, they hurried away to the task of clearing the American coast of French cruisers and privateers, which were committing numerous depredations on commerce. In spite of its having few ships and little experience, the Navy drove the French from our shores during the summer and fall of 1798.

The more spectacular incidents in the war with France, however, were a series of naval duels which occurred between several of our naval vessels and French naval vessels and privateers. These sea-fights conclusively showed that the dash and fighting spirit which had so often manifested itself during the Revolution had been carried over into the newly-created navy. The naval and commercial center of the French in the western hemisphere was at the time in the West Indies. From different ports of these islands French vessels could easily prey upon American commerce which also centered to a large extent on the same area. As soon as the depredations by French vessels along our coasts had been stopped, our Government determined to carry the war into the Caribbean area. The Navy established a convoy system for American merchantmen, and practically all of its remaining vessels were assigned to stations in the West Indies. One cruising station was designated along the Windward Islands, another along the Leeward Islands as far west as Porto Rico, a third in the Windward Passage, and a fourth near Havana.

Our first ship to engage in a fight with a French war vessel was the *Delaware*, which, after a brief encounter, captured the *Croyable* on July 7, 1798. The *Constellation* engaged the 40-gun ship *In-*

*surgente* off Basse Terre, West Indies, February 9, 1799, and, after a spirited fight, captured it. About one year later the *Constellation* also engaged the 52-gun frigate *Vengeance* off Guadeloupe in a five-hour night battle at pistol range; both ships suffered severe losses. The *Vengeance* struck her colors three times, but because of darkness the signals were not seen, and the fight continued. The vessels finally separated, both being barely able to reach near-by ports. Lieutenant Bartholomew Clinch commanded the marine guard during both of the *Constellation*'s battles; his marines contributed materially to the success of the operation and suffered more than their share of the casualties.

The *Vengeance* managed to reach the port of Curaçao, but the Dutch governor refused to assist in its repair. The French thereupon sent an expedition from Guadeloupe and attempted to take the entire island. The Dutch retreated to their forts, leaving the French in control of the remainder of the island. After having been reinforced, the French began operations to capture the forts. The Dutch called upon three American naval vessels lying at St. Christopher to come to their assistance. Two of the vessels, the *Merrimack* and *Patapsco*, came on September 22. The French by that time had captured two of the Dutch forts and were using them to protect fifteen of their vessels lying near by. The American commander decided to send only one of his vessels into the harbor to help save the town and protect American interests. Twenty marines were transferred from the *Merrimack* to the *Patapsco*, which entered the harbor on September 23. Lieutenant James Middleton, U.S.M.C., went ashore with a landing party from the *Patapsco* to assist in the defense of the town. The French kept up a continuous fire against the *Patapsco* throughout most of the following night; they then suddenly withdrew to their ships and sailed back to Guadeloupe. The intervention of the Americans saved Curaçao, but the British took possession of it and promised to protect American interests.

The *Constitution*, which later came in for lasting fame as one of the great fighting ships of the American navy, took a less important part during the French Naval War. It captured three small prizes and engaged in a cutting-out expedition at Puerto Plata, Santo Domingo, which is of special interest because of the part played by its marine detachment. The captured English ship *Sandwich*, held as a prize by the French in Puerto Plata Harbor early in May, 1800, was the objective of the expedition. The *Sandwich* was known to be lightly manned but was protected by the fort of Puerto Plata. About ninety marines and sailors were transferred from the *Constitution* to the sloop *Sally* and boldly sailed into the harbor, well knowing that they could not retreat until the wind shifted to a land breeze the following morning. The *Sally*'s warlike character was completely disguised by having the fighting force hidden below with only five or six men working about the deck—putting him in mind, as Captain Daniel Carmick of the Marine Corps reported, "of the wooden horse of Troy."

The *Sally* ran alongside the *Sandwich;* the marines and sailors quickly boarded and captured that vessel without the loss of a single man. Captain Carmick and Lieutenant Amory with the marines then promptly made a landing, captured the fort before its commanding officer was able to alert his command, spiked all of its cannon, and, before support could be sent from Puerto Plata to the fort, returned to the captured vessel. They then rerigged the *Sandwich* and put it in order for defense against the enemy forces in the vicinity—estimated at about five hundred men. After completely rerigging the *Sandwich,* they sailed out of the harbor when the land breeze sprang up, accompanied by the *Sally.*

During the closing years of the war, the brig *Enterprise,* which carried a detachment of sixteen marines, was the most active ship of the Navy. It was assigned for a time to the Guadeloupe or Windward Station. During the year 1800 it captured nine French privateers, captured eleven American vessels, and engaged and defeated a Spanish brig of war which had sought an encounter. Its most spectacular encounters with French vessels occurred during December of that year. It engaged in a spirited fight and captured the 10-gun privateer *L'Aigle*—a vessel fully its equal in strength. Shortly afterwards it engaged the *Flambeau* in a two-hour fight and also defeated and captured that superior vessel. The small-arms fire delivered by the marines from the *Enterprise* and the damage to the topmasts of the *Flambeau,* which caused them to go overboard, were the deciding factors that gave success to the Americans. The plucky little *Enterprise* was withdrawn from the West Indian operations at the close of the French war and went to the Mediterranean, where it again distinguished itself, fighting the Tripolitan pirates.

The above naval engagements were only the more important ones. Many others, by practically every ship of the American Navy, resulted in the capture of French vessels. The Navy was also active in convoying merchant vessels, protecting channels of maritime commerce, and performing duties on the several West Indian stations. All of these experiences helped to build up in the Navy a fighting tradition which it carried over into the war with Tripoli and into the war with England in 1812, when the fighting spirit of the Navy probably reached its zenith. In addition to the activities of naval vessels a large number of merchantmen were armed for defense and given commissions which permitted them to capture French armed vessels and privateers. A number of these engaged in spirited encounters with French privateers and ships in various parts of the world.

### Supporting Toussaint L'Ouverture

Wars in Europe had left the control of the French island of Santo Domingo to whoever could maintain himself in authority. Toussaint L'Ouverture, a negro who had received considerable training in the Spanish army, led a rebellion against the French authorities and gained control of most of the island. His only opponent for power was the mulatto chieftain, Rigaud, who held the southwestern portion of the island and carried on piratical operations in the adjacent waters. Toussaint negotiated with the United States and, in exchange for trade privileges, was given the support of several American naval vessels. Early in the spring of 1800 Toussaint forced Rigaud to evacuate Grand and Petit Goave and cease piratical operations in their vicinity. In the meantime, the U.S.S. *General Greene*, with a marine detachment under Lieutenant James Weaver, had blockaded Jacmel while Toussaint attacked from the land side and captured the town.

Some picaroons under Rigaud retreated farther to the southwest and continued to prey upon vessels which were becalmed in the vicinity. In March, 1800, the *Boston*, carrying a detachment of thirty-six marines commanded by Lieutenant Jonathan Church, engaged in convoying some merchant vessels, was becalmed in the Bight of Leogane. The *Boston* had its guns housed to conceal its identity. Nine barges of picaroons attacked the *Boston*, but it succeeded in driving off the robbers after a fight that lasted five hours, during which it disabled five barges. The marines took an active part in the fight. The *Boston* remained on that station for some time and had other engagements with the picaroons as well as with some French vessels. Toussaint finally forced Rigaud to flee to France. He received aid from the Americans in getting rid of the French and Rigaud and in turn assisted the Americans in putting down piracy.

### Guarding Prisoners of War

During the belligerent outbreak with France the Marine Corps rendered its principal service ashore guarding prisoners taken from the many captured vessels. The marines, at different times, were called upon to guard such prisoners on board ships and at jails at the principal ports of the country. The marines escorted the prisoners to, and, assisted by soldiers, also guarded them at concentration camps established at interior towns. The principal prison camp was at Frederick, Maryland, to which place the marines at one time marched a miscellaneous collection of French buccaneers, natives of various color from Haiti and Santo Domingo, and a number of French naval prisoners. The marines maintained and guarded another concentration camp at Lancaster, Pennsylvania. Arrangements were eventually made to exchange these prisoners for Americans. It then became the duty of the marines to escort the French prisoners back aboard ships for transfer to West Indian ports. At the close of the war the remaining French prisoners were liberated and taken back to France on board vessels which had been returned to that country in accordance with the peace convention.

A few months after the end of the warlike affair with France, Congress passed the Peace Establishment Act, which provided for a sweeping reduction in the armed forces of the United States. It authorized the sale of all naval vessels, except the thirteen larger ones, and provided that only six of these be kept in commission with only two-thirds of their full strength crews. The vessels that were laid up were assigned a marine guard of one sergeant, one corporal, and eight privates each, as part of a skeletonized crew. The reserve vessels were kept in the Eastern Branch of the Potomac at Washington. While the Act did not specifically reduce the Marine Corps, President Jefferson directed a reduction to four hundred less than authorized by the act which established the Marine Corps.

In further keeping with his policy of retrenchment, Jefferson ordered (May 21, 1802) all marines discharged except guards of one sergeant, one corporal, and fifteen privates at each of the navy yards at Boston, New York, Philadelphia, Washington, and Norfolk, competent guards for the vessels in ordinary, and for the vessels arriving in the country. Such artisans and mechanics as were absolutely necessary to the Corps, he also allowed to be retained. As a result of these reductions, there were only 483 enlisted men remaining by February, 1803; in November of that year the officer personnel numbered only 23. The Corps remained at approximately that strength until increased by Congress in 1809.

## Removal of Headquarters to Washington

The headquarters of the Corps remained at Philadelphia slightly less than two years. The construction of the new Capitol at Washington had progressed sufficiently to require the presence of marines—first at the Navy Yard in March, 1800, for the purpose of guarding the construction at that place, and later to establish the headquarters of the Corps near the office of the Secretary of the Navy, which moved to Washington in June, 1800. Burrows with his staff and headquarters troops arrived at Georgetown and went into camp (July 31) on a hill southeast of the town—the present site of the Naval Hospital, Washington. Barracks for these marines were later rented from the War Department. The detachment moved into them on November 11 but returned to its camp in the following spring.

William Ward Burrows, commandant since July 12, 1798, tendered his resignation because of ill health, and it was accepted as of March 6, 1804. On the following day he was succeeded by Captain Franklin Wharton, senior officer of the Corps, who assumed his duties as Lieutenant Colonel Commandant. During the Naval War with France, Wharton had served on the frigate *United States* until August 31, 1800, and then went to duty as commanding officer of marines at Philadelphia, where he was stationed at the time of his appointment as head of the Corps.

## Customs of the Early Corps

The severe and rather brutal methods of enforcing discipline, practiced in all navies of that time, were adopted by the Marine Corps shortly after its establishment. Commanding officers had broad powers in administering punishment while general courts-martial and courts-martial were authorized by law to award all other punishments that were considered necessary. The former were convened only by the President, but commanding officers could convene a court-martial of three officers, who performed all its necessary legal functions. Flogging was the most usual form of punishment awarded both by courts and commanding officers. The law of 1799 limited a commanding officer's punishment to twelve lashes by the cat-o'-nine tails. An act of Congress in 1800 permitted the liberal allowance of one hundred lashes if awarded by a general court-martial. The lashes were laid on at the tap of a drum, and floggings were made occasions of ceremony. Other punishments, now considered humiliating, such as shaving the head or half the head, drumming a man out of garrison, sentence to hard labor with ball and chain and, if the culprit were addicted to too much drinking, to wear drunkard's dress, were commonly awarded. Taking away the rum ration, then allowed in all branches of the service, was a common form of punishment for cases of drunkenness. Commandant Wharton, who did not look with great favor on the rum ration, on one occasion ordered it so highly diluted that it was impossible for the marines to drink it in sufficient quantity to get a kick out of it.

## Rations, Quarters, and Uniforms

The rations allowed marines in the early days of the Corps consisted of only a very few items and were valued at from 15 to 17 cents. Rented barracks were provided for the marines in Washington during the winter months, but, to economize, they went into camp during the summer. Washington was at that time in its early stages of development. Marines were called upon to guard public buildings as well as distinguished personages in need of special protection.

The Marine Band was established not long after the Corps was authorized and soon earned a reputation for being the best band in the vicinity of Washington. During the first three years of its existence it was the only public band in the city. As early as New Year's, 1803, it played at a White House reception and later in the same year at official parties given at hotels in Washington. It also played on other official and semi-official public occasions. In brief, it then assumed the role which it has carried on throughout its history.

In addition to duty at the national capital, regular stations for marines were established at Portsmouth, New Hampshire, Boston, New York, Philadelphia, and Norfolk within a few years after the Corps was formed. One first lieutenant and twenty-one marines seems to have been approximately the standard garrison for marine barracks at navy yards during the early years of the Corps. It was difficult to maintain even this small number of men during times when the greater proportion of the marines were on sea duty.

Regulation uniforms for both officers and enlisted men of the Corps were gradually developed during the first few years of its history. The period was one in which extremes of design in service uniforms were still in vogue. The spectacular uniforms of Europe, many of which had of course been seen on various European troops in America during the Revolution, had their influence on the design of uniforms for the early marines. The uniforms worn by the Army prior to the organization of the Corps were copied in some detail in its early uniforms. For a few years the uniforms which had been worn prior to the establishment of the Corps by the marines and officers, while serving under the jurisdiction of the War Department, were continued in use.

The officers wore long blue coats with red lining, long red lapels, standing collars, slash sleeves with red cuffs, skirts and pocket flaps, red vests and blue breeches. The coats were lavishly trimmed with buttons of yellow metal bearing a foul anchor and an American eagle. Buttons were freely used for ornamentation on the lapels, collars, and sleeves of the coats. The officers wore one or two gold epaulets according to their rank, which was indicated, in the case of junior officers, by the shoulder the epaulet was worn on (first lieutenant on the right and second lieutenant on the left). Captains and above wore two epaulets; their rank was indicated by other devices. The uniform of enlisted men was not so elaborate but still showed considerable display of color and ornamentation. Their coats and pantaloons were blue trimmed in red. They wore red belts and vests. Cocked hats continued to be worn as during the Revolutionary period. Black leather stocks were early adopted as part of the uniform, hence the term "Leathernecks." The hair was worn queued and powdered according to the custom of the times.

As the period up to the War of 1812 progressed, the uniform underwent a considerable number of changes and refinements. Prior to 1804, uniformity of design was attempted by merely writing letters to all concerned. In that year the first formal uniform order was issued by the Secretary of the Navy, which practice continued thereafter. The wearing of a scarlet sash by officers came into vogue then and continued for nearly one hundred years. Black boots were prescribed for officers in lieu of the former black stockings and low shoes. Elaborate high caps with plumes were worn on certain occasions. The red on all uniforms was considerably reduced; the double-breasted coat came into use for both officers and enlisted men. Trousers were prescribed for enlisted men. A plumed cap superseded the former cocked hat. The short coat of the enlisted men was replaced by a cutaway coat similar to that worn by officers. The white crossbelt for carrying articles of equipment continued in use throughout the period. Black cloth gaiters were prescribed as part of the enlisted men's uniform, and provision was made for the use of linen uniforms for summer.

The early Commandants showed a great deal of concern about the design and manner of wearing the uniform. Officers on parade and on courts-martial were expected always to appear in their most formal attire. Uniforms were ordinarily made for both the officers and enlisted men by local tailors. Considerable difficulty was en-

MARINE CORPS UNIFORMS OF 1775

Typical Marine Corps Uniforms, 1810

Commandant Burrows with President Jefferson

countered in maintaining uniformity of design. The procurement of suitable cloth and other materials for making uniforms was always difficult. As provision was made for more field officers in the Corps, two epaulets were worn only by those grades; a captain wore a gold epaulet on the right shoulder and a gold counter strap on the left.

## THE WAR WITH THE BARBARY CORSAIRS

While the Government was making every effort to reduce the cost of the naval establishment by selling ships, placing others out of commission, and reducing the personnel of both the Navy and the Marine Corps, serious difficulties began to arise with the different Barbary States located along the northern coast of Africa. Peace with France had scarcely been concluded before a squadron of four vessels under Commodore Richard Dale was dispatched to the Mediterranean to protect American commerce from depredations committed by the Barbary corsairs. The squadron arrived at Gibraltar on July 1, 1801, and began a series of blockade and convoy operations. It also carried out diplomatic missions, supported by demonstrations of force. Thus began a period of warfare which continued until the strength of the Barbary States was crushed. The principal duty of the Navy as well as the Marine Corps for the next few years was to carry on these operations in the Mediterranean. Naval officers in charge of the Mediterranean Squadron usually acted as diplomatic agents to negotiate treaties with the Barbary States. The officers were at times assisted by special representatives sent out by the State Department.

The principal trouble maker for American commerce was Tripoli, but other Barbary States were always sympathetic to that country and openly or secretly aided it. The Pasha of Tripoli had become dissatisfied with the treaty that he had made with the United States; he believed some of the other Barbary countries procured more favorable terms. After some heated discussions with the American consul, Cathcart, on May 10, 1801, the Pasha declared war on the United States, and a few days later cut down the flagstaff from the American consulate.

The combined naval strength of the several Barbary States was considerably in excess of that which the United States could place in the Mediterranean. Dale's squadron was able, by making a show of force off Algiers and Tunis as well as off Tripoli, to restrict greatly the activities of the corsairs. His squadron was too weak, however, to deal effectively with the situation. Our Government finally comprehended that fact, and Congress authorized the manning of additional vessels for duty in the Mediterranean. Commodore R. V. Morris proceeded late in 1802 to the Mediterranean on the *Chesapeake*. The number of ships on his station was increased to ten. Morris accomplished little during the early months of 1803, but on May 22 the *New York, Enterprise,* and *John Adams,* while cruising off Tripoli, discovered several Tripolitan merchantmen. They chased them toward the harbor, and a number of gunboats came out to rescue the merchantmen. A brisk fight ensued, but the Tripolitan vessels escaped into port. Their gunboats then returned to the harbor. During the night the Tripolitans hauled the merchant ships on shore and built breastworks of stones and bags of wheat to protect them. The boats of the American squadron went in with a landing force of marines and sailors under Lieutenant David Porter to destroy the vessels. Porter attacked and drove the enemy from the breastworks, set fire to the vessels, and then safely withdrew. He was wounded and lost a number of men in the operation.

Morris withdrew to Malta, leaving Captain John Rodgers in command of the blockading ships off Tripoli. Rodgers soon gave up the blockade for lack of light-draft gunboats for attacking the shore defenses. The Mediterranean Squadron was reorganized and placed under Commodore Preble in the fall of 1803 but was not yet sufficiently strengthened for effective operations. Preble resumed the blockade of Tripoli, however, with the *Philadelphia* and *Vixen*. On October 31 the *Philadelphia,* while pursuing enemy cruisers, ran upon some hidden rocks a few miles to the eastward of Tripoli. After four hours of futile effort to refloat the ship, during which no determined attack was made by the enemy, Captain William Bainbridge hauled down his colors and surrendered his vessel. The entire crew, including the marine detachment of First Lieutenant William S. Osborne and forty-three marines, were made prisoners. They were held under trying conditions which at times amounted to the most cruel form of oriental slavery. Much to the surprise and chagrin of its officers and crew, the *Philadelphia* was refloated by the Tripolitans and brought into port. In spite of the disaster Preble continued the blockade.

On February 16, 1804, a select detachment of seventy officers, sailors, and marines under Lieutenant Stephen Decatur transferred to the captured ketch *Intrepid,* and on the following night they executed one of the most daring feats in the history of our navy. Decatur sailed boldly into the inner harbor, where the *Philadelphia* was lying under the protection of the coast defenses, boarded her, and surprised the Tripolitan crew. He soon had complete control of the vessel, then set her on fire in a number of places, calmly waited until the fires had begun to leap from the ports, and finally withdrew in the face of a heavy enemy fire without the loss of a single life. The *Philadelphia* burned to the water line. The wrath of the Pasha was unbounded. The crew of the *Philadelphia* continued in prison until a treaty of peace was concluded with Tripoli, nineteen months after their capture. In the meantime their lives were spared only by the hope of the Pasha that substantial ransom would be paid for them.

The squadron found that it was greatly handicapped by the lack of light-draft gunboats, which could follow the enemy craft into shallow water and approach near enough to the shore to deliver an effective fire against enemy works and forts. Preble managed to procure a number of lighter-draft vessels. By July, 1804, he had two bomb ketches, six gunboats, three schooners, and three brigs in addition to the *Constitution* and felt prepared for a more determined action against Tripoli. As weather conditions permitted, he made five different attacks against Tripoli, in which he captured or destroyed a number of Tripolitan vessels and bombarded the city and its forts. The gunboats during these operations were divided into two groups under Stephen Decatur and Captain Somers. Part, if not all, of these gunboats carried small marine detachments who played their part, particularly in the close fighting between the gunboats and the smaller Tripolitan vessels.

The news of the loss of the *Philadelphia* had a very pronounced effect in Washington. The Government ordered all ships that were held in ordinary placed in commission and sent to the Mediterranean. These vessels, with those already in the Mediterranean, carried approximately nine marine officers and four hundred marines—four-fifths of the enlisted strength of the Corps. With these increased forces the Mediterranean Squadron carried on the war against Tripoli with renewed vigor and forced the other Barbary States to recognize the increasing power of the United States. Rodgers, in active command of the ships, kept up an effective blockade of Tripoli and cruised to various parts of the Mediterranean but had very few contacts with enemy vessels. Three small vessels were assigned to support another undertaking which proved interesting from the standpoint of Marine Corps history.

## THE EXPEDITION AGAINST DERNE

The ruling Pasha of Tripoli, Yusuf Karamali, who had succeeded to that position prior to the outbreak of the war, was a usurper who had made himself ruler despite the fact that he was the youngest of three sons. He had murdered his older brother and taken control in the absence of Hamet, the next in line. Yusuf held Hamet's wife and children as hostages. Hamet took refuge first in Tunis and then in Egypt. The United States hoped that, if it befriended Hamet and assisted him in regaining his throne, he would then be willing to make a favorable treaty.

William Eaton, a former captain in the United States Army, who had had considerable diplomatic experience in the Barbary States, was chosen as the agent to attempt to place Hamet in power. Eaton arrived in the Mediterranean in the summer of 1804. He was reasonably sure that, if restored to his rightful heritage, Hamet would be friendly towards the United States, but Eaton's first and one of the most difficult problems was to locate the banished Pasha.

Hamet had taken refuge several hundred miles up the Nile with the Mamelukes. Eaton was taken to Egypt in November, 1804, on the *Argus* and after considerable difficulty found Hamet. They then began collecting an expeditionary force for an advance against Tripoli. Eaton, acting as commander in chief of the force, was accompanied by Lieutenant Presley N. O'Bannon, one sergeant and six privates of the Marine Corps, and Midshipman Peck. The expedition further consisted of thirty-eight Greeks—two of whom were officers—Hamet and his immediate following of ninety men, a party of Arabian cavalry, and a number of footmen and camel drivers.

Eaton made arrangements for the *Argus,* with reinforcements and supplies, to meet him near Derne. He planned to march west across the Libyan Desert, along the shore of the Mediterranean. Eaton's motley army finally set out about March 8, 1805, on what proved to be perhaps the most trying and difficult march in which Americans have participated. Disaffection in his ranks broke out almost immediately; a revolt occurred which repeated itself in various degrees of seriousness during the six-hundred-mile march to Derne. Time after time the owners and drivers of the camels threatened to turn back. They demanded pay in advance for the entire march and got it at the cost of emptying the pockets of all Christians in the expedition. They repeatedly received rumors that Derne had been reinforced, which greatly discouraged the African troops and even at times caused Hamet himself to want to turn back. The advance was only about half as fast as had been expected with a resultant shortage of supplies—especially food. On April 8 a serious mutiny occurred. The disaffected faction, drawn up in battle line, faced the Christian contingent, who were also prepared to give battle. With great difficulty Eaton avoided bloodshed and persuaded the African troops to resume the march, in fear of starvation if they did otherwise.

Finally, on April 15, with its food supplies exhausted and no naval vessel in sight, the column reached Bomba. On the following day, however, the *Argus* arrived, and on the succeeding day, the *Hornet* with much-needed provisions for the expedition. Eaton had asked for and expected one hundred marines for the remainder of the march and for the attack on Derne. Commodore Barron, in command of the squadron, agreed to no such arrangements, however, and the only assistance Eaton received was the service of two midshipmen, who had been with him in Egypt.

The column, which had been augmented by a contingent of several hundred tribesmen who had joined some time previous to arriving at Bomba, resumed the march April 24. Conditions during the remainder of the march were less difficult, but reports (greatly exaggerated) continued to come in that enemy reinforcements were approaching Derne from the west and would probably arrive there in time to prevent its capture. Yusuf had learned of the approaching expedition and knew that American naval vessels were operating with it. This knowledge doubtless made him more receptive to proposals for peace which were at the time being made by other American representatives. Eaton, somewhat broken by the trying conditions of the long march and disheartened by the discouraging situation, courageously pushed on even when Hamet and his followers and the Arab contingent of his force showed little desire for a determined assault on Derne.

As the motley army approached the walls of the city, the Arabs again mutinied, and the camel train started to the rear. Eaton promised them handsome bribes; again they joined in the advance. The column camped for the night of April 25-26 on a hill southeast of Derne overlooking the town. The garrison of Derne, estimated at about eight hundred, were disposed for its defense and resolved to fight it out. The governor haughtily rejected Eaton's demands for surrender and made loopholes in buildings throughout the town for a determined defense.

The few marines, twenty-four cannoneers with a gun, and thirty-six Greeks, all under O'Bannon, attacked Derne from the southeast, while Hamet and some Arabs attempted to attack from the southwest. The *Nautilus*, *Hornet*, and *Argus* bombarded the harbor fort as well as the part of the town in O'Bannon's front. They silenced the fort, but both attacks on the town definitely failed. The situation was desperate, as enemy reinforcements were known to be approaching. Eaton knew that his only chance of capturing the town was before they arrived. He gathered up the few remaining Americans and Arabs and went to O'Bannon's assistance.

Upon Eaton's orders O'Bannon's troops withdrew slightly and together with Eaton's small force formed to charge. With a boldness that has seldom been equaled in history, they assaulted the town and drove the enemy out of that part of it they were attacking. O'Bannon and his marines seized the harbor fort and raised the Stars and Stripes for the first and only time (prior to the World War) in that part of the world. The marines then turned the guns of the fort on the governor's castle. This completely demoralized the defenders of the town; they promptly began to retreat. Hamet then advanced and captured the castle. In spite of the several reverses Derne was completely in the hands of Eaton's forces within two hours after the beginning of the attack, and the Arab cavalry were pursuing the retreating enemy. Most of the inhabitants promptly declared their allegiance to Hamet. The attacking Christians had lost thirteen, including two marines: Private John Whitten was killed, and Private Edward Steward died of wounds shortly afterwards.

Eaton immediately set about organizing Derne for defense. He shifted the guns of the harbor fort to cover the town and constructed a fort on a bluff to the southwest which dominated the town and its approaches from the west. The ruins of the fort are still known as the "American Fort." By May 8 a considerable force of Tripolitan troops had arrived in the vicinity. They surrounded Derne and made repeated attempts to recapture it. With the aid of the forts, the guns of which the Tripolitans did not care to face, Eaton succeeded in retaining control of Derne in spite of the attacks until early in June, when Commodore Rodgers ordered him to evacuate it.

Withdrawing proved somewhat difficult since it was necessary to embark Hamet and his troops as well as the Christian forces, with the enemy besieging the town. The *Constellation* arrived and placed some additional marines ashore to help cover the embarkation. The Greeks and Hamet with his suite embarked under the protection of the marines, who, with Eaton, were the last to withdraw. In the meantime peace had been negotiated with Tripoli by Tobias Lear, consul general to Algiers and special agent of the United States. Barron took Hamet to Syracuse and temporarily made him a pensioner of the United States. He is said to have presented O'Bannon with a sword which Hamet had carried while with the Mamelukes in Egypt. That sword was said to have been of a pattern later called the "Mameluke sword," which, with a slight interruption (1859-1875), has been the sword carried by Marine officers since a few years after the Tripolitan War.

Eaton was bitterly disappointed over the failure of his scheme. He later received, as a reward for his services, a year's pay as captain in the Army and a grant of land. O'Bannon was commended for his bravery and presented a handsome sword by the State of Virginia but, feeling neglected in receiving no promotion—not even a brevet—resigned from the Marine Corps in 1807. It appears that, in spite of the outstanding services which he rendered, he was the least rewarded of any of the American officers with the expedition. His distinguished service received belated but substantial recognition in 1917 by the naming of a destroyer of the Navy in his honor.

## The Expedition Against Tunis

A few months after making peace with Tripoli, the Mediterranean Squadron was reinforced by eight gunboats from the United States, giving the squadron a total of seventeen vessels—the largest American fleet that had ever been assembled. In July, 1805, Rodgers, then the commodore of the squadron, concentrated most of his forces in the Bay of Tunis and began negotiations with the Bey of Tunis for a satisfactory adjustment in our relations with that country. The Bey was extremely incensed over Rodgers' having captured some of his vessels and was much given to bluffing during the succeeding negotiations but later grew more conciliatory and sent an ambassador to Washington. The squadron spent the remainder of 1805 affording general protection to American commerce in the western Mediterranean. When Jefferson learned of the treaty with Tripoli, he ordered most of the vessels in the Mediterranean to return to the United States. In June, 1806, all of them except the *Constitution, Enterprise,* and *Hornet,* which remained until August, 1807, came home. This ended the series of wars with the Barbary corsairs, which had occupied practically the entire strength of our navy for about five years.

## Distribution of Personnel

The actual strength of the Marine Corps at the close of the year 1807 was 26 officers and 720 enlisted men. The Act of March 3, 1809, increased the officers in the Corps and brought the authorized strength of the enlisted personnel up to 1,823. The enlarged Corps (considerably under its authorized strength) was distributed to various stations and ships; as follows:

## STRENGTH AND DISTRIBUTION, 1809

| Station | Officers | Enlisted Men |
|---|---|---|
| Washington | 14 | 155 |
| New York | 1 | 33 |
| Boston | 1 | 33 |
| Philadelphia | 1 | 44 |
| New Orleans | 3 | 160 |
| Baltimore | — | 8 |
| *Ship* | | |
| Constitution | 2 | 57 |
| President | 2 | 57 |
| United States | 1 | 57 |
| Chesapeake | 2 | 49 |
| Essex | 1 | 36 |
| John Adams | 1 | 30 |
| Wasp | 1 | 21 |
| Hornet | 1 | 25 |
| Argus | — | 18 |
| Siren | 1 | 24 |
| Vixen | — | 14 |
| Ferret | — | 14 |
| Nautilus | — | 17 |
| Enterprise | — | 15 |
| Revenge | — | 5 |
| Gunboats at Charleston, S. C. | 1 | 32 |
| Total | 33 | 904 |

### AT NEW ORLEANS

Scarcely had the treaty which transferred Louisiana to the United States in 1803 been ratified, when many difficulties began to arise which threatened to sever the newly acquired possessions from the United States. The inhabitants of New Orleans in particular were handled in a way that made them dislike their new allegiance. Not long afterwards the conspiracies of Burr and Wilkinson added to the difficulties. President Jefferson constantly pursued a policy hostile to Spain. Disputes over the possession of West Florida and the boundary between Louisiana and the Spanish possessions farther west complicated our relations with that country. At times our difficulties with France and England indicated that we might at any time become involved in war with either of those countries.

In order to help secure our hold on Louisiana, a detachment of about one hundred marines, under Captain Daniel Carmick, was sent to New Orleans early in 1804. Upon arriving at its new station, Carmick's marine detachment was divided between small posts at Pointe Coupee and Fort Adams. Based on the assumption that small gunboats had proved to be very efficient instruments of naval warfare, Jefferson started a vast program of building these small vessels, particularly with a view to defending our shores. A number of gunboats were sent to New Orleans in 1806, and the marine detachment at that place helped to provide crews for them as well as for the bomb ketches, *Aetna* and *Vesuvius*. New Orleans proved to be very unhealthful for Carmick's marines; late in 1806 the entire detachment was removed and replaced by another detachment under Lieutenant Samuel Baldwin. It was enlarged early the following year, and, in addition to furnishing garrisons for two or three small stations ashore, including one at the navy yard and another at Fort St. John, on Lake Pontchartrain, it supplied marine detachments for six naval vessels.

During the closing months of 1808 our difficulties with Spain became more menacing; at one time approximately 1,500 Spanish troops were mobilized in eastern Texas, and some of them entered what was undoubtedly a part of Louisiana. Our Army assembled several regiments of regulars in the vicinity of New Orleans, and the Navy increased its gunboats in the vicinity to twenty-four. The marines were again increased and had detachments of approximately a dozen men on a number of gunboats. In addition to guarding the lower Mississippi River, some of the small vessels operated as far up the Mississippi as Natchez. Part of them were present when the United States extended its control over West Florida by occupying Baton Rouge after the independence of that territory had been declared by the inhabitants. Carmick returned to New Orleans early in 1807 and remained in command of the marines at that station until his death from wounds received in the Battle of New Orleans, described in the next chapter.

## East Florida

Perhaps the most important experience of the Marines, near the close of the period preceding the War of 1812 and overlapping slightly into the time of that war, was that of a detachment commanded by Captain John Williams operating with the Navy, Army, and Georgia volunteers in East Florida. Florida was still a Spanish possession, but Spain was just beginning to recover from the Napoleonic conquest and her control over the American colonies was practically non-existent. This was particularly true in Florida. The United States Government greatly feared that Great Britain was about to take possession of East Florida. Further to complicate the situation, our non-importation laws had resulted in a considerable smuggling trade of British goods over the frontier into Georgia from East Florida. Amelia Island, lying off the coast of Florida, just beyond the mouth of the St. Marys River, which then formed the southern boundary of the United States, was a veritable nest of smugglers.

In January, 1811, Congress authorized secret steps to be taken looking to the taking over of East Florida—permanently if possible, otherwise temporarily—to prevent it from falling into the hands of the British. American commissioners began to operate in the area soon afterwards, and United States troops went into positions just north of the St. Marys River. The Navy sent a number of gunboats to the vicinity—ostensibly to break up the smuggling trade. A detachment of two officers and forty-seven marines went on the brig *Enterprise* to aid in the operations. The marines established a regular garrison on Cumberland Island, just off the coast of southeastern Georgia, on May 4, 1811. They were instructed to co-operate with both the Army and the Navy. In order to accomplish their mission without an open break with Spain, the commissioners resorted to the use of so-called "patriots" whom they induced to join the plot by promises of five hundred acres of Florida land. The patriots were organized and armed in Georgia, preparatory to an advance into East Florida.

After much delay the patriots advanced on March 17, 1812, to capture Fernandina on Amelia Island, then held by a garrison of ten Spanish soldiers. Nine American gunboats, under Commodore Hugh Campbell, took up position just off the town with their guns pointing at Fernandina, while the patriots advanced and demanded that the Spanish surrender. The Spanish commander, seeing the hopelessness of his situation, complied. That the action of the American gunboats was purely a bluff is evident from the fact that they had strict orders not to fire under any condition. Both the soldiers and the marines appear to have simply looked on during the operation, but as soon as the patriots had gained possession, the army commander, taking Williams' marines with his forces, occupied Amelia Island. The patriots, followed by the army troops, then advanced by marching and in boats furnished by the Navy on St. Augustine, leaving the marines to hold Amelia.

In the meantime Governor Mitchell of Georgia had been made an American commissioner and placed in command of all forces in the vicinity. The Secretary of the Navy tried to extricate the marines from the unauthorized foreign war, but Mitchell countermanded the marines' orders to withdraw and insisted that they continue to take part in the operations. The Army and the patriots soon found themselves involved with maintaining a difficult line of communications through hostile Indian country and called upon Williams' marines to escort wagon trains and other convoys, en route to their advanced positions near St. Augustine. The marine detachment made several trips on convoy duty and was for a short time with the army near St. Augustine. On September 12, 1812, while convoying a train and some volunteer troops, Williams was ambushed by a large band of Indians whose hostility towards the Americans was long-standing; a desperate fight ensued. The marines finally succeeded in driving off the Indians, but only after the Indians had killed and scalped one of their detachment and wounded seven others. Williams was wounded eight times and died a few weeks later.

The command of the marine detachment then fell to Lieutenant Alexander Sevier, who carried on several more operations against the Indians. In conjunction with a detachment of the Army and some volunteers, in November, 1812, the marines carried the war into the Indian country and destroyed the villages of those who had ambushed Williams. In the meantime the War of 1812 had begun, but Sevier and his marines continued in East Florida until May, 1813, when they withdrew by sea and returned to Washington in time to participate in the futile effort to save the capital.

## Résumé

The Anglo-Saxon tradition—that marines are a necessary part of a naval service—had again asserted itself when the government of the United States set about organizing a navy. The services rendered by the Continental Marines were no doubt recalled by Congress when it made the initial step in 1794 to build a navy. Their first thought was for the marines to be in the same status as during the Revolution. The idea soon developed, however, that marines could be made more efficient by having an organization of their own. From this idea grew the Act of Congress, July 11, 1798, which established the Marine Corps.

The consolidation of the scattered marine detachments on the several naval vessels of the United States into an organization, having its own *esprit de corps* and feeling of unity, developed very rapidly during the first few years of the Marine Corps's existence. During its formative years it was perhaps more closely associated with the Navy than it has been in more recent years. It performed few duties other than those closely integrated with the naval service. The Corps was born during the trying times when the struggling

Republic was making a desperate effort to organize a military-naval service in order to defend itself and maintain its national honor. When only a few weeks old, the Corps was thrown into war and scarcely had a breathing spell between different belligerent outbreaks in which it was called upon to participate, until after the close of the War of 1812. Its fighting spirit as well as that of the Navy soon developed to a degree that has caused the American people to look to this early period of our naval history for its most brilliant achievements. The naval war with France, with the attendant experiences in the West Indies, was almost immediately followed by the long war with the Barbary corsairs. In each of these the Marine Corps did its bit by furnishing parts of the crews for naval vessels. Towards the close of the period covered by this chapter, the Marine Corps had its first duty with the Army. The Corps gradually extended its shore activities by furnishing marine detachments to the navy yards and naval stations as they grew up in different parts of the country. In brief, the Marine Corps during the first few years of its history found practically all of its future missions.

## Chapter III
### THE WAR OF 1812

JUST prior to the declaration of war against Great Britain, June 18, 1812, it was practically certain that war was in the offing, but the country did very little towards preparing its military establishments. The approach of war found the Marine Corps as poorly prepared as the other branches of the service. The party in power was suspicious of the naval service and did not give it the needed support until experience during the early stages of the war clearly demonstrated the necessity for increased naval strength. The outbreak of war found the Marine Corps with an approximate strength of only one thousand officers and enlisted men—slightly more than one-half of the peacetime authorized strength. Congress showed no inclination to provide for more marines until April, 1814. In the meantime it did not provide sufficient funds to enable the Corps to enlist even its authorized peace strength. The few marines available for shore duty were scattered among the regular shore stations along the seaboard from Boston to New Orleans and with a small expeditionary force in the field in East Florida. The remainder of the Corps was on board the active ships of the Navy and assigned to the gunboat flotillas. Preparations for war greatly increased the calls for marines, which of course could not be supplied.

The Marine Corps had not yet established a reputation as an outstanding arm of the regular service. The war itself was very unpopular with a substantial percentage of the population of the country. In an effort to raise a number of regular army regiments, Congress made conditions more difficult for the Corps by providing substantial inducements for recruits to join the Army which were not allowed for joining the Marines. The Corps went through the entire war so hopelessly undermanned that it was unable to supply even needed marine detachments for the vessels of the Navy and had no marines for independent service or service with the Army, except when taken from other duties in times of great stress. The shortage of marines for duty was at times so acute that soldiers of the regular army had to be substituted for them on board vessels of the Navy.

Commandant Wharton set about, to the best of his ability, to put the Corps on a wartime basis. He made a considerable effort to recruit enlisted men but procured very few because of the much more favorable inducements offered by the other branches of the service. At the outbreak of the war the only marines on the Great Lakes were a little detachment on board the *Oneida* on Lake Ontario. Wharton took steps to provide more marines for duty on the Lakes as well as for the ships which had been kept in reserve.

## On the Great Lakes

The first year of the war, fought mostly along the Canadian frontier, resulted in a series of disasters to the American forces. Governor Hull of Michigan, in command of a force of regular army troops and militia, attempted to invade Canada in the vicinity of Detroit. He was defeated at every turn and finally surrendered to the British. The United States soon lost control of all the western lakes. The operations farther to the east were no more successful. Both the regular army troops and the New York militia failed hopelessly in every operation they undertook. A new army was organized in the West under General William Henry Harrison but failed to accomplish anything of importance during the remainder of 1812.

It eventually became evident to the administration that the disasters in the West were due largely to the British having control of the Great Lakes. President Madison finally saw that control would have to be gained over Lakes Erie and Ontario or the situation would be hopeless. The enemy forces would virtually be cut in two by controlling Ontario. At the outbreak of the war the Navy had two or three small armed schooners on the Lakes—all but one of which were soon captured by the British. During the summer and early fall of 1812 the Navy took the necessary steps to begin accumulating material for the construction of vessels on both Lake Erie and Lake Ontario. Commodore Isaac Chauncey was placed in command of the naval forces on the Lakes and established a base at Sacketts Harbor on the eastern end of Lake Ontario. He collected all available lake vessels and armed them in spite of many difficulties. By the fall of 1812 he had a force of sufficient size seriously to dispute the control of the lake with the small British naval force that had for some months dominated Ontario. In spite of the fact that there were very few marines and calls for them were many times in excess of their numbers, a few were provided for Chauncey's lake squadron. A detachment of three officers and fifty-seven marines under Captain Richard Smith was assembled at New York and marched to Sacketts Harbor, where it arrived on November 2, 1812. By various other means about one hundred marines were provided for lake duty by the end of the year.

The naval forces on the Great Lakes were gradually reinforced during the following winter and early spring. By April, 1813, Chauncey was able to muster a flotilla of fourteen more or less effective vessels. The Marine Corps gathered up every available marine from stations in the United States and sent them to Chauncey. The marine barracks near Charleston, South Carolina, was abandoned, and its officers and men, under Captain Robert D. Wainwright, marched to Washington and then via Baltimore and New York to Sacketts Harbor. The detachment was gradually increased by adding marines from the barracks along the line of march until it finally numbered what was then a sizable contingent of 3 officers and 121 marines.

Niagara Falls made it impossible to move vessels from Lake Ontario to Lake Erie. It was therefore necessary to have a separate naval force on the latter lake if successful operations were to be carried on, and the disasters suffered by Hull atoned for. The Navy established a base at Erie and began building vessels. Despite the severe weather and lack of skilled labor and material, they made some progress during the winter of 1812-1813. The Marine Corps made an effort, but with unsatisfactory results, to provide the necessary marine detachments for the Erie squadron. Lieutenant John Brooks set out from Washington in April, 1813, with a small detachment of marines to march via Pittsburgh to Erie to report for duty to Commodore O. H. Perry, who had been placed in command of the naval forces on Lake Erie. Brooks had authority to recruit all available men en route to his new station, but he arrived there with only twelve marines. Marines could not be provided for Perry's rapidly expanding squadron, and volunteers from the Army were substituted for marines in the detachments on part of the vessels. Two army officers were in charge of acting marine detachments. Brooks commanded the detachment on the *Lawrence,* and noncommissioned officers of the Corps were in charge of the marine guards on some of the smaller vessels.

General Dearborn, in command of the army in the East, had a considerable force in western New York. In April, 1813, he placed about 1,700 soldiers on Chauncey's vessels and sailed for York (Toronto). Part of his troops landed a short distance west of the town, advanced under the support of the gunfire of Chauncey's squadron and captured York on April 27. Chauncey's squadron carried about one hundred marines who, together with some of the sailors, had been organized as a landing force to support the army in the event they encountered difficulties. Their use was not necessary, however. On May 1 Dearborn withdrew to Fort Niagara, and Chauncey returned to Sacketts Harbor.

Dearborn's forces then began to make preparations for the capture of Fort George, on the Canadian side of the Niagara River about one mile from its mouth. Perry was called down from Erie to take part in the operation. The attack on Fort George was set for the morning of May 27. A large number of boats had been assembled for transporting the troops. The artillery moved into position for firing across the river. The troops embarked in boats and on vessels of Chauncey's squadron and moved to their landing position on the lake shore west of the mouth of the river at 4 A.M. A heavy fog delayed the landing. The schooners took their positions, nevertheless, and silenced the enemy artillery in front of the landing force. The leading troops succeeded in reaching the beach without great difficulty, but shortly afterwards the enemy concentrated most of his forces in front of them. With the aid of effective grape and canister fire from Chauncey's schooners, the troops continued to land and successfully drove the enemy south past Fort George, which the Americans captured without further resistance. The marines of the squadron had been grouped into a special unit and attached to a regiment of artillery, which was held in reserve during the first stages of the landing operation. They landed later, however, and took part in the pursuit of the enemy, who retired to the vicinity of Queenstown.

### The British Raid Sacketts Harbor

While Chauncey was aiding the Army to carry out operations against York and Fort George, he had left his base at Sacketts Harbor almost wholly unprotected. The British promptly took advantage of the situation and tried to raid it. On May 27 the British squadron made an unsuccessful attempt to attack the base. They came back again two days later, accompanied by a landing force, for a more determined attack. The little American garrison, composed partly of marines, seeing themselves greatly outnumbered and thinking that all was lost, began burning their barracks and stores as well as the ships in the harbor and prepared to retreat. They later mustered up courage enough to fight and drove the British back to their vessels. In the meantime, however, the fires that they had started had consumed a greater part of their stores. The marines lost all of their clothing and military equipment and for a time found themselves in a rather trying situation.

## In the Battle of Lake Erie

Perry had made tremendous progress in the construction and fitting out of his squadron at Erie but was able for some time to get sufficient personnel to man properly only one of his schooners. The President gave him orders repeatedly to co-operate with Harrison, who was sorely beset by the enemy on the western end of Lake Erie, but made no provision to furnish the necessary men. All naval personnel coming from the East passed through Sacketts Harbor where they were promptly absorbed into Chauncey's squadron. Perry repeatedly called upon Chauncey for men but received only the castoffs from Chauncey's vessels. In addition to the ships he had constructed, Perry was able to add five captured vessels to his squadron. He finally managed to man his fleet partially and on August 12 sailed out upon the lake with ten more or less effective vessels. He would have none of the long periods of maneuvering for advantage which characterized Chauncey's operations.

A British squadron was at the opposite end of the lake, but its commander did not venture from his base until September 9. On the following day the two little squadrons met. The British had only six vessels but in number of guns were superior to Perry. To their great advantage, they opened fire at long range, but Perry's vessels immediately closed to their effective range. The details of the battle which followed are too many to narrate in this brief account; its decisive results are too well known to repeat. Perry's victory immediately gave him the complete possession of Lake Erie and restored Detroit and vicinity to American control. The political and moral results on the nation were far-reaching. It was the first fleet engagement of the war. Records of the parts played by marines and the soldiers acting as marines in this great naval victory are notably lacking. Lieutenant Brooks and four of his contingent of marines were killed in the battle, and a dozen other marines were wounded. No information is available as to even the approximate number of marines who took part in the battle. Most of the marines on the Great Lakes at the time were probably at Sacketts Harbor or with Chauncey's squadron at Lake Ontario.

With the support of Perry's squadron, Harrison's army crossed over into Canada near Detroit and defeated the British in the Battle of the Thames and soon afterwards regained control over Michigan Territory. Harrison then moved east with his regular army units and left the militia to hold the west. The Navy gradually extended its control over the western lakes.

Chauncey was almost completely lacking in the dash that Perry possessed and was never able to have a decisive engagement with the British squadron under Commodore Sir James Yeo on Lake Ontario. In fact, Chauncey and Yeo seemed to be pretty much two of a kind; both avoided decisive engagements, and each did a great deal of maneuvering in the hope of catching the other at a decided disadvantage. On the day following Perry's victory the two squadrons came together, exchanged a few shots, and both retired. They contacted each other several times during the year, but no decisive engagement ensued. In the autumn of 1813, Chauncey was given the task of keeping the British squadron shut up in Kingston and preventing it from interfering with General Wilkinson's expedition down the St. Lawrence. Chauncey failed in accomplishing his task; some British gunboats with eight hundred troops got by his vessels, followed Wilkinson's army down the river, and harassed them until Wilkinson changed his plans and retreated overland back into the United States.

During the winter of 1813-1814 both naval forces on Lake Ontario spent all their energies building ships in preparation for an attempt to gain control over the lake as soon as conditions permitted in the spring. But maneuvering against each other and avoiding decisive combat continued during the remainder of the war. Whichever squadron was temporarily inferior in strength waited in its harbor for additional ships to be finished, then forced the other to return to its base. As the war progressed, the building contest became more energetic with both sides building larger and larger vessels.

## Sea Duels

At the outbreak of the war there was considerable discussion in Washington as to the best possible use of the frigates and other deep-sea vessels of the Navy. The Navy Department and the Administration were strongly of the opinion that such vessels should be used for the defense of the principal ports of the country, but all of the more experienced naval officers believed that such a policy would lead only to their destruction or being blockaded in port by the superior British forces. These officers held that all of the better vessels should put to sea, either singly or in pairs, avoid the British squadrons by distant cruises, raid British commerce, and whenever possible engage single British war vessels. They finally won the dispute, and a series of glorious and spectacular naval victories on the high seas resulted. These interesting sea fights continued throughout the war in spite of the British efforts to drive the American Navy from the sea. All of the vessels that engaged in these sea duels had the usual marine guards, who did their part of the fighting. In several of the fights marines played a part which contributed very materially to the success of the engagements. About half of the personnel of the Marine Corps was assigned to our deep-sea naval vessels during the War of 1812. To describe all of these interesting duels would involve too much space for this work; therefore only brief mention of the more important ones is made.

During the first year of the war the Navy won four sea duels which did more than anything else to offset the moral effects of the disasters in the northwest and still cause the hearts of the American people to swell with pride. The frigate *Constitution* alone won two famous victories. After some maneuvering to avoid a British squadron, the *Constitution* encountered the *Guerrière* (August 19) off the Gulf of St. Lawrence. Both ships closed and soon became engaged in one of the most desperate sea-fights in the annals of our Navy. During the first hour of the battle the ships maneuvered and bombarded each other at a reasonable range. They then closed to less than pistol-shot distance; the fight became unusually furious, with the *Guerrière* taking most of the punishment inflicted by the superior American gunnery. The vessels then contacted each other, and both called away boarders. The British hesitated about their boarding operation, as the boarders on the *Constitution,* supported by the marines, assembled aft in preparation for boarding the *Guerrière*. In the meantime both sides inflicted heavy casualties on each other with musketry. Lieutenant William Bush of the marines sprang upon the rail to lead the boarders on to the *Guerrière* but was shot dead by Royal Marines. The destructive musketry continued from the decks and tops of both vessels. Other American officers attempted to lead the boarders on to the *Guerrière* only to be shot down by musketry. The musket fire from the decks and tops of the *Constitution* picked off most of the men on the enemy's open decks. With the *Guerrière* in a helpless condition the ships finally separated. The *Guerrière* offered no further resistance and soon surrendered. It was too nearly a complete wreck to be brought into port and was burned. The enemy crew were taken prisoners and brought into Boston on the *Constitution*. The losses on the British vessel were many times those on the *Constitution*.

The next duel, which resulted in another victory for the United States, occurred between the American sloop of war *Wasp* and the British sloop *Frolic*. The latter vessel, while engaged in convoying fourteen merchantmen from Honduras to England, October 17,

1812, was intercepted by the *Wasp* southwest of Bermuda during a severe gale. On the following day, when the storm had somewhat abated, the *Frolic* began to maneuver against the *Wasp* in the hopes of permitting the convoy to escape. The two vessels soon became engaged, and American gunnery again proved greatly superior. In less than an hour after the fight had begun, the *Frolic* was a hopeless wreck and surrendered. Again the losses to the American vessel were insignificant as compared to those of the enemy. Lieutenant John Brooks and sixteen marines made up the marine guard of the *Wasp* during this memorable fight. The fruits of victory were not long enjoyed, however, as the *Wasp* and its prize were captured a few hours later by the *Poictiers,* a British 74.

Not long afterwards the frigate *United States* encountered the British ship *Macedonian* in mid-Atlantic. After a desperate fight which lasted several hours, American gunnery and seamanship again demonstrated their superiority. The *Macedonian* was forced to strike and was brought into port and added to the American navy. The fight took place beyond the range of grape and musketry; for that reason the marines were unable to play as important a part in the victory as in some of the other duels. The marines suffered their share of the casualties, however—two killed and one wounded, out of the total of six killed and six wounded.

The *Constitution* again successfully engaged a solitary enemy frigate, the *Java,* off the coast of Brazil, December 29, 1812. After some preliminary maneuvering for advantageous position, both vessels deliberately shortened sail and closed for decisive combat. A cannonade developed which from the beginning proved very destructive to both vessels. The range was sufficiently close to permit a deadly fire of musketry and grape. With her superior speed the *Java* repeatedly attempted to gain a position for raking the *Constitution,* which vessel, however, successfully maintained a broadside to the enemy and poured into her a destructive fire with superior gunnery. The *Constitution* succeeded in raking the *Java* from the stern and then at close range and parallel to the enemy delivered an effective fire with both guns and muskets. The latter, fired mostly by the marines, inflicted heavy losses on the open decks of the British vessel. The British as a last hope tried to lay the *Java* aboard the *Constitution* and prepared boarders for an assault. During the maneuver, however, the *Constitution* again raked the *Java* and inflicted sufficient losses to make boarding fail. The vessels separated, and the *Constitution* again succeeded in raking the enemy with a starboard broadside. The British vessel was by then in a hopeless condition. Her flag had been shot down causing the Amer-

MAJOR SAMUEL NICHOLAS
1776-1781

LIEUT. COLONEL WILLIAM WARD
BURROWS, 1800-1804

LIEUT. COLONEL FRANKLIN
WHARTON, 1804-1818

COLONEL JOHN HARRIS
1859-1864

EARLY COMMANDANTS

LIEUTENANT O'BANNON RAISING THE FLAG OVER DERNE, TRIPOLI

icans to think she had surrendered. The *Constitution* lay off for making repairs. In spite of the fact that the *Java* was a mere hulk, she again raised her colors, only to surrender, however, when the *Constitution* again bore down on her. The marines had again played an important part with their musketry. They suffered one killed and two wounded while eight seamen were killed and twenty-two wounded. The loss to the enemy was again terrific—forty-eight killed, including the captain, and 102 wounded.

During the next year of the war the Navy was not so successful on the high seas. The British became more aggressive while the number of our ships available for distant cruises was somewhat reduced. On February 24 the *Hornet* engaged the British brig *Peacock* and, after a spirited fight lasting only fourteen minutes, forced the British vessel to surrender—unfortunately the prize soon afterwards sank.

In response to a challenge for a duel, the *Chesapeake* engaged the *Shannon* off Boston, June 1, 1813, with disastrous results to the former. The *Chesapeake* had been newly put in service and had a comparatively inexperienced crew, including many foreign mercenaries. Captain Lawrence, who had been successful in several previous engagements against British vessels, was nevertheless quite sure of victory. During the first few minutes of the engagement the *Chesapeake* put up a spirited fight and with her broadsides inflicted considerable damage to the enemy. She also took considerable punishment, especially on her open deck, but a number of the crew became panicky and left their stations. During this part of the battle Lawrence was mortally wounded and while being carried below gave utterance to the immortal expression, "Don't Give Up the Ship." In only ten minutes after the engagement began, however, the British led by Captain Broke boarded the *Chesapeake*. The mercenaries and many of the inexperienced members of the *Chesapeake's* crew fled below leaving the enemy virtually in control. The officers made several efforts to lead parties from below back to the deck but failed because all but a few refused to follow.

The marines of the upper decks, however, behaved themselves with more spirit; a number of them stayed at their stations in spite of the desperate situation until all were either killed or wounded. From the tops they offered considerable resistance to the British boarders but one of the *Shannon*'s small nines made a direct hit which cleared them out of one top, and the fire from the *Shannon*'s foretop was too much for them in another station aloft. A small group of seamen and marines, at bay on the forecastle, put up a desperate fight against the enemy, who eventually closed in and slew them to the last man. Within five minutes after the British came on board, the *Chesapeake* surrendered. Fourteen marines were killed, including Lieutenant James Broom in charge of the detachment, and twenty were wounded—leaving only one corporal and nine marines. In this fight lack of proper training and discipline proved fatal to the American vessel.

The loss of the *Chesapeake,* however, was somewhat redeemed on September 5 off the coast of Maine by the successful engagement of the famous old brig *Enterprise* with the *Boxer.* The *Enterprise* was then commanded by Lieutenant William Burrows, son of the first commandant of the Marine Corps. The duel opened with destructive broadsides from each of the ships. Captain Blythe of the *Boxer* was killed at the beginning of the action; soon afterwards Burrows, while assisting the crew of one of his carronades, was struck by a canister and mortally wounded. In spite of this he remained on deck until the enemy had surrendered, when he exclaimed: "I am satisfied; I die contented." The records do not disclose the details of the services rendered by the sergeant's guard of fifteen marines during this memorable action. The victory of the *Enterprise* can be attributed principally to skillful maneuvering and excellent gunnery by means of which she repeatedly raked her adversary with terrible results.

In spite of the ever-increasing efforts of the British to blockade the American coast and drive our Navy from the seas, a few vessels were still able to avoid the watchful enemy, continue commerce raiding, and occasionally encounter British ships of war. During 1814 our Navy accounted for four British war vessels but, in the meantime, lost eight. Several of our more powerful frigates were kept blockaded during most of the year. The *Constitution* made some more cruises and captured several prizes but had no decisive combats.

In June, 1814, the American sloop of war *Wasp* successfully engaged the *Reindeer* in a fight which is most interesting for marines, in that the decisive fighting took place on the decks of the vessels. The vessels came together; the British first attempted to board the *Wasp* but were successfully repelled. The Americans immediately boarded, slaying or driving below all the British on the decks of the *Reindeer,* and forced the ship to surrender. The little detachment of sixteen marines played a conspicuous part in the action. They carried out two of their main battle functions aboard ship—repelling boarders and covering a boarding party as it assaulted an enemy vessel. The enemy acknowledged that the musket fire from the marines in the foretop caused great losses during the final stages of the combat. As a result of the hand-to-hand combat, the losses were very severe to the crews of both vessels.

The *Wasp* again distinguished itself on September 1, when it engaged and sank the British sloop *Avon*. At the moment of victory the *Wasp* was forced to flee, however, by the arrival of some additional British vessels. The *Wasp* continued on a cruise in the Atlantic and captured several prizes but disappeared sometime after October 9, when last seen by a Swedish vessel.

Even the signing of the treaty of peace in December, 1814, did not put an end to the naval warfare. The *Constitution* once more put to sea during that month and had one more glorious cruise during which she accounted for two British war vessels and again narrowly escaped capture by several large British ships. On February 20, 1815, the *Constitution* encountered two enemy vessels, the *Cyane* and *Levant,* and engaged and defeated both in an unusual battle which lasted into the night. During part of the battle the *Constitution* was fighting both enemy vessels. She successfully raked the *Cyane* several times, and that vessel surrendered forty minutes after the action began. A prize crew took possession, and the *Constitution* resumed the action against the *Levant,* which it captured about two hours later. The victory over the two vessels was made possible by the skill with which the *Constitution* raked the enemy. The marines did not perform all of their prescribed functions during the battle but were able to deliver effective musketry when the contending vessels got sufficiently close together.

The *Constitution* took her prizes to the Cape Verde Islands. While lying at anchor (March 10), she sighted a British squadron of three heavy frigates approaching. Captain Stewart did not trust the neutrality of the port to protect him and immediately cut loose and stood out to sea with his prize vessels following. The enemy pursued and captured the *Levant,* but the *Cyane* and the *Constitution* escaped.

### WITH PORTER AND GAMBLE IN THE PACIFIC

By far the most conspicuous part played by any marine officer during the War of 1812 was that of First Lieutenant John Marshall Gamble while in charge of the naval base of Nukuhiva, Marquesas Islands, and while attempting to escape on a captured British vessel from that island. Gamble with thirty-one marines sailed with Captain David Porter October 22, 1812, on the *Essex* for what proved to be one of the most exciting cruises in the annals of the American Navy. Porter had orders to rendezvous with the other vessels of

Commodore William Bainbridge's squadron, but, failing to meet them at the appointed place and after capturing a British vessel, he proceeded around South America into the Pacific to operate against any enemy vessels found in that part of the world. Porter arrived in the Pacific with his supplies practically exhausted and without even a friendly port within several thousand miles.

He made his way up the west coast of South America to a base of a British whaling fleet, the Galapagos Islands, in April, 1813. There he found and captured three British whalers. Porter had brought with him an additional complement of officers and enlisted men and was therefore able not only to man these vessels but several others which he captured soon afterwards. One of these, the *Atlantic,* he refitted with twenty guns and renamed it the *Essex Junior.* Another captured vessel, the *Greenwich,* was similarly refitted, and, with a crew of fourteen men under Gamble, was made a man-of-war.

While cruising near the Galapagos group during July with his three armed vessels, Porter sighted three strange vessels. Each of the American vessels chased one of the strangers, which all proved to be British whalers. Gamble soon forced one of them into action with the *Greenwich.* In spite of the fact that he was a marine officer, Gamble maneuvered his ship according to the best principles of naval tactics, frustrated all of the enemy's efforts to escape, and, after delivering a few effective broadsides, forced his adversary to strike. His prize proved to be the *Seringapatam*—the terror of all American whalers in the Pacific. Porter had watched every move of the *Greenwich* during the fight and later highly commended Gamble for the masterful way he handled his ship during the entire engagement. During the following month Porter left Gamble in charge of the *Greenwich* and several other prizes and sailed on the *Essex* in search of enemy vessels.

Early in October, Porter, fearing the arrival of British cruisers, sailed west with his squadron to the Marquesas Islands. He established a base on the island of Nukuhiva, where he planned to refit his ships, rest his men, and then attempt a return to the United States. He found the Marquesans warring with each other and took an active part in their struggle. He soon restored peace among them and on November 18, 1813, took possession of Nukuhiva in the name of the United States and renamed it Madison Island. He concerned himself extensively with local affairs on the island but kept his men busy refitting and provisioning the ships. On one occasion he was forced to interrupt the overhaul of his vessels to assist the natives in the vicinity in a war against other Taipi.

The first day of the war went against Porter and his several thousand native allies, but on the second day Porter, with his motley army, was completely victorious and laid waste the entire enemy country.

Porter gave his men as much liberty as he dared among such treacherous and practically savage people. His situation was made more delicate by the more important islanders' presenting many of his men with concubines as tokens of their hospitality. Many strong attachments soon developed, and Porter had every reason to fear that he might be unable to detach his men from their paramours. While making final arrangements to sail with the *Essex* and *Essex Junior,* he restricted the men of those ships for a few days, only to find that the native girls lined the beach from morning till night, "dipping their fingers into the sea and touching their eyes and allowing the salt water to run down their cheeks," while others threatened to do away with themselves if their sweethearts were not allowed to come ashore. As a result of these demonstrations of love, Porter's men behaved rather badly. Some of them agreed to a resolution to refuse to weigh anchor and if forced to do so to mutiny when out to sea. Porter boldly assembled his crews, however, and after talking kindly to them, directed all who were willing to obey his orders to come to the starboard side of the ship. His appeal was sufficient, and both crews responded. Having discovered the ringleaders of the mutineers, Porter left them behind. In the meantime Porter had erected an improvised fort on a hill dominating the harbor as well as the surrounding country. He placed Gamble in command of the work and named it Fort Madison.

## Porter's Defeat

The *Essex* and *Essex Junior* were finally ready for sea, and Porter sailed December 12 for Valparaiso. He left Gamble with Midshipman Feltus, twenty-one sailors and marines, and a few prisoners of war with three of the prize vessels to hold Nukuhiva until he returned or for a period of five and a half months. In the face of numerous difficulties Gamble was expected not only to maintain the integrity of his own little command but also to keep peace on the island and defend himself against the barbarous islanders. The latter task proved by far the most difficult. Gamble knew that if the natives discovered his relatively insignificant strength they might at any time turn on him. Most of the men whom Porter left with him were not even Americans. Those who had already proved themselves disloyal and the prisoners of war were of course always a potential danger.

Porter reached Valparaiso February 3, 1814, and remained there for some time, keeping the *Essex Junior* cruising off the port on the lookout for the enemy. Two English men-of-war finally appeared, cleared for action, and sailed into the harbor. They tried to induce Porter to violate the neutrality of the port; failing in this, they did not immediately attack him. A few weeks later, however, the British left the harbor for a cruise and Porter attempted to escape. The enemy was not far off and attacked the *Essex* while it was still in neutral waters. The *Essex* put up a desperate fight in spite of the overwhelming odds against her; the *Essex Junior* was not able to render any assistance. After losing more than half of his crew in killed and wounded, Porter finally surrendered both of his vessels to the British. Most of the marines who had left the United States on the *Essex* participated in this gallant action but only nine remained to be paroled and sent back to the United States with Porter and the remainder of his crew.

### Revolt and Mutiny

Scarcely had Porter cleared Madison Island before the natives began to show hostility towards Gamble's little command. Warlike preparations against the Americans were soon very evident. Gamble decided to take forceful action while the *New Zealander*, which Porter had ordered to the United States, was still there to help him. Immediate action was also made necessary by the natives' seriously interfering with his supply of local provisions—particularly the hogs. In spite of Gamble's effort to prevent them, the natives were stealing by the wholesale supplies and provisions.

On December 24, after having placed the disabled and sick on board the different ships with orders to fire the loaded cannon upon receiving a signal, Gamble landed with every available man. With a little army of only thirty-five armed men, Gamble advanced against the hostile native village. Upon his signal the guns on the ships and in the fort fired according to schedule. The show of force was sufficient. In place of encountering two or three thousand natives as they expected, one old chief under a flag of truce came out to meet them and promised to respect their rights and supply them with necessary provisions. The demonstration served to keep the natives under control until the following May when other complications added to Gamble's difficulties.

Food supplies gradually became more and more difficult to secure at Nukuhiva, and Gamble was forced to obtain part of them elsewhere. He put the *Sir Andrew Hammond* in sailing condition, left the base as well defended as possible, and sailed away with an abundant supply of old iron—then the best medium of exchange in the South Sea Islands. On February 10 he reached the Island of Dominica (Hivaoa), where he was able to procure just a few provisions as most of the men on the island were engaged in civil war. He visited several ports and succeeded in obtaining a few hogs and some coconuts and bananas. With the meager supply of provisions he returned to his base on February 16.

Love affairs added to Gamble's troubles. He discovered that his men were permitting the native girls to come aboard his vessels and that the girls were carrying away his much needed supply of bread as they swam ashore. Gamble felt obligated to punish the guilty men, most of whom were thoroughly unreliable for other reasons. But punishment only tended to make them disaffected. Doubting the loyalty of some of his men, Gamble had all of the muskets, other weapons, and powder stored aboard the ship on which he lived and kept them carefully guarded. The situation became more difficult when four men, composing an entire watch, deserted in the middle of the night and took with them a supply of muskets and powder as well as other valuable stores. Furthermore they wrecked all the boats so that they could not be followed. One of Gamble's most trusted marines was drowned, thus further reducing the all too few trustworthy men.

The time was approaching for Gamble to abandon his base in accordance with his orders. On April 12 he set about to rig two of his ships for that purpose. He noted that several of his men were becoming more and more sullen towards him. On May 7, while aboard the *Seringapatam* preparing that ship for sea, Gamble was violently attacked by members of his crew, tied hand and foot, and imprisoned. A few moments later the mutineers threw Feltus and Acting Midshipman Clapp into the brig with Gamble. The mutineers collected the arms on board the *Seringapatam* and spiked the guns on the other vessel as well as in the fort. While a prisoner of the mutineers Gamble was shot in the heel with a pistol; he did not recover from the wound for many months. The mutineers put to sea on the *Seringapatam,* taking Gamble and his loyal men with them. When about four miles out they put Gamble and the few loyal men over the side in a leaky boat, giving them three old muskets and some powder for defense against the natives. With great difficulty and after several doubtful hours they managed to reach the *Greenwich,* where a few other faithful men were anxiously awaiting them.

The news of the mutiny had, in the meantime, reached the Marquesans, who immediately turned upon the few Americans and began to plunder the vessels and the stores on shore. Gamble then saw that his only chance was to put to sea on one of the remaining ships. With his few remaining men he set about shifting the more necessary supplies to the *Sir Andrew Hammond*. While thus engaged, the natives attacked the working party and massacred four of Gamble's most valuable men including Feltus. Only three of the party escaped, one of whom was seriously wounded. While the survivors were attempting to make their way back to the ship in a boat, the natives tried to intercept them, but Gamble, in spite of his severe wound, drove back the savages with a few shots from the ship's guns which he kept loaded. Disregarding all danger, Gamble rescued a sick man from the *Greenwich* and had that vessel set on fire.

Unable to hold the natives off any longer, Gamble spread a couple of sails and partly raised the anchor. A land breeze carried them out to sea. The prospects of reaching safety were none too promising. Gamble had only seven men; only Clapp and one other were in good health. The naval enlisted personnel of the little crew consisted of three sailors and three marines. They had neither compass nor spy glass and were without charts or accurate maps. Having insufficient sails or men to work the ship, Gamble decided to run before the trade winds and steer for the Sandwich (Hawaiian) Islands. While attempting to raise the only available boat, it broke in two. The physical strength of the crew was not sufficient to haul up the only anchor and they were forced to cut it away.

### Captured by the British

After fifteen days of running before the wind, they reached one of the Hawaiian Islands—probably Oahu. They were kindly received by a number of foreign traders as well as by the natives. Gamble heard a report that a mysterious vessel had appeared off the island a few days before. The description of it led him to believe that it could be none other than the *Seringapatam* with its crew of mutineers. With the assistance of the traders and natives he managed to provision, to some extent, refit his ship, and sign up several additional men for his crew. At the request of the native chiefs and in the hope of obtaining more provisions, Gamble agreed to take a number of the leading natives with their tribute to a neighboring island where the king resided. While en route to carry out this friendly mission, they encountered the *Cherub,* one of the British vessels that had defeated Porter at Valparaiso. Escape was impossible, and, having no means of resistance, Gamble surrendered. The *Cherub* kept Gamble and his men around the Hawaiian Islands for some weeks and then sailed for South America, taking him and his

THE HARBOR OF NUKAHIVA, 1814

MARINE CORPS UNIFORMS OF 1834
PREDOMINANT COLOR GRASS GREEN

MARINE CORPS UNIFORMS OF THE MEXICAN WAR

crew as prisoners of war. They remained for a time at Valparaiso and on November 28, 1814, reached Rio de Janeiro. The British allowed them to live on shore with considerable latitude until news of the treaty of peace was received, then set them at liberty but left them completely destitute. Gamble, badly broken in health, finally made his way back to the United States and reached New York in August, 1815. He was promoted to major and later to lieutenant colonel for his heroic services. He continued to be an officer in the Corps until he retired in 1834. What happened later to the three sailors and three marines who survived the experiences at Nukuhiva is unknown.

## Raids in the Chesapeake

Two methods of the British in carrying on the war were: to blockade the ports of the United States; and to raid our more or less undefended towns. Early in 1813 Admiral George Cockburn with four large vessels and several smaller ones, carrying in addition to their regular naval crews a force of about 1,800 soldiers, arrived in the Chesapeake and raided several towns on the lower bay. They destroyed considerable shipping in the vicinity of Gosport (Portsmouth). The *Constellation,* which happened to be in the vicinity at the time, was trapped in the Elizabeth River by the British forces and was unable to escape during the remainder of the war. Early in April, Cockburn moved up the bay and threatened Annapolis and Baltimore. The Secretary of the Navy ordered a battalion of marines to be formed and directed Lieutenant Colonel Commandant Wharton to detach Lieutenant Miller with all the marines that could be spared from headquarters for that duty. Miller with one hundred marines proceeded at once to Annapolis. The British only threatened Annapolis, however, and Miller's marines returned to their regular station. Cockburn raided Havre de Grace and destroyed about half of the town. He raided several other towns near the head of the bay and returned to the vicinity of Gosport, where he was reinforced by several additional vessels carrying a considerable force of soldiers and marines.

## Defending Norfolk

The British then began an operation to capture the Gosport Navy Yard and the frigate *Constellation*. The Governor of Virginia, in anticipation of the British attack, called out a considerable force of militia to help man the defenses of Gosport, which consisted of forts on each side of the Elizabeth River just below the city and fortifications on Craney Island at the mouth of the river. Our naval forces in the vicinity consisted of the *Constellation,* Captain Tarbell, and a flotilla of twenty gunboats, all closely blockaded in the Elizabeth River by British vessels in Hampton Roads. On June 19 Tarbell with fifteen of the gunboats made a surprise night attack on the *Junon,* one of the British frigates lying closest to Gosport and at the time becalmed. Tarbell completely surprised and surrounded the *Junon* and was about to capture that vessel when a breeze sprang up and other British vessels sailed in and forced the Americans to retire. This operation only served to demonstrate to the British the desirability of capturing the navy yard as well as all naval vessels in the Elizabeth River.

Since Craney Island was the key to the outer defenses of Gosport, the British started an extensive operation to capture it. The attack was anticipated by the Americans, however. They sent a number of soldiers, in addition to 150 sailors and fifty marines under Lieutenant Henry B. Breckinridge from the *Constellation,* to reinforce its garrison, raising the strength to 737 officers and men. The naval contingent was assigned the task of working the heavy guns. In the early morning of June 22 the British started their expected attack by landing a force of about 2,500 infantry and marines on the mainland about two miles northwest of the island in an attempt to flank its defenses. Our sailors and marines shifted their artillery to protect the exposed flank of the island's defenses and successfully held off the attack of the British landing force. In the meantime Tarbell had anchored all his available small vessels in a crescent shaped formation across the mouth of the river, extending the battle line which defended Craney Island to the east. The British, from a covered approach, then started another landing force of about 1,500 sailors and marines for a direct attack on Craney Island. Embarked in fifty barges, led by the British Admiral's own barge, the second landing force bore down upon the island from the north. Our naval artillery opened a deadly fire as soon as the leading barges came within easy range and soon forced the enemy to retire. By 10 o'clock the British, having been stopped on every hand, withdrew and made no further attempt to capture Norfolk or the near-by naval establishment.

Three days after the attack on Norfolk, the British attacked and captured Hampton, which was defended by only a few hundred militia and a few marines. They then divided their naval forces and sent one part to threaten and raid the Atlantic Coast as far south as Florida and with the remainder menaced various places along the Potomac. They caused considerable consternation in Washington and other cities, after which they again sailed up the Chesapeake threatening Annapolis and Baltimore. They continued their blockading operations until the summer of 1814.

## With Barney's Flotilla

In order to relieve the pressure against their forces along the Canadian frontier, early in 1814 the British planned to create a strong diversion somewhere on the Atlantic Coast. They sent an expeditionary force under Major General Robert Ross to operate in conjunction with a British squadron under Vice Admiral Sir Alexander Cochrane, who with a number of ships had reinforced Cockburn's squadron. The enemy expedition arrived in the Chesapeake in August, 1814.

The only American force in the bay at the time was Captain Joshua Barney's flotilla of twenty-six gunboats, barges, and other small craft manned by about nine hundred sailors and marines. Barney could not, of course, operate with his small gunboats against regular British warships; he was soon compelled to take refuge in the Patuxent River where the larger British vessels could not follow him. The enemy determined to destroy Barney's flotilla before carrying out any other operations. Barney soon found himself trapped by a blockade at the mouth of the Patuxent. The British then set about finding means for destroying him in his refuge. They sent an expedition of twenty-one barges and two small schooners, carrying about eight hundred men, up the Patuxent against Barney's flotilla. Barney was then at the mouth of St. Leonard's Creek and moved down with five hundred men mostly in barges to meet the enemy. When the two forces met, a desperate, miniature sea fight occurred in which all of the boats became engaged. After both sides had suffered heavy loss of both boats and men, the British retreated to their ships in the Chesapeake.

One hundred marines with three pieces of artillery under Captain Samuel Miller from the Marine Barracks, Washington, and some mixed army troops, including a few more pieces of artillery, then reinforced Barney. With the aid of the artillery Barney tried to break the British blockade and escape from the Patuxent. The officer in charge of the artillery used it improperly, and it had little effect. Miller kept his artillery in operation until his supply of shot was exhausted. He then began to move it to a position for firing grape and canister against the enemy, who were then threatening to make a landing. While making the move, however, the army units with whom he had been co-operating withdrew, forcing him also to retire. The flotilla failed to escape.

The British then organized a combined force of small vessels and soldiers under Ross to destroy Barney's flotilla and then to move either against Baltimore or Washington. Barney saw that there was no hope for him to save his gunboats. He retired up the river as far as possible with the determination of destroying his vessels as a last resort and then fighting the enemy ashore. The army troops and Miller's marines retired in the direction of Washington. On August 18 Ross's expeditionary force, with a flotilla of small craft from Cockburn's squadron, started up the Patuxent. Ross landed his soldiers at Benedict on the following day, and the two British forces began a leisurely advance up the Patuxent without meeting the slightest interference by the American forces.

### Ross Raids Washington

Despite the fact that British raids had threatened the cities along the Atlantic Coast for several months, practically no preparation had been made for the defense of Washington. Most of the regular army units were hundreds of miles away on the Canadian frontier. It was not until July, 1814, that an officer was even designated in charge of the defenses of Washington and even then only at the insistence of the Governor of Maryland. Brigadier General Winder, who was given the task, did practically nothing until the enemy was within striking distance.

When the British were reported at Benedict, Winder hastily assembled some 300 regulars and about 1,700 militia and marched out to a place called the Woodyard, a few miles west of Upper Marlboro. Even then he made no provision for the erection of defenses around Washington. Consternation reigned supreme in government circles; the President and all of his Cabinet attempted to participate in the defense of the city. Winder remained with his little army at the Woodyard, while Ross's redcoats, with their flank dangerously exposed, marched north through the then dense forests, but the Americans made not the slightest effort even to delay their advance. The width of the Eastern Branch of the Potomac at Washington and the ease with which its bridges could be destroyed caused the British to approach Washington through Bladensburg. Winder hurriedly assembled additional militia troops in that vicinity but still took no steps to erect defenses.

Barney abandoned his flotilla and left it in charge of a small group of selected men with orders to destroy it on the approach of the enemy and then rejoin him. He withdrew to Old Fields, a point about halfway between Upper Marlboro and Washington, where he was again joined by Miller and his marines. Miller had been ordered to report to Barney, but no orders were ever issued for Barney's naval contingent to be under Winder's orders. When the British reached Upper Marlboro, Winder withdrew his force to Old Fields, still apparently having no definite plan of action. On August 23 the British force at Marlboro, reinforced by Cockburn with a contingent of sailors and marines, took up the march towards Washington. Winder made no effort to delay their advance but turned his entire attention to the organization of resistance at Bladensburg. He, together with Barney, retired into Washington and prepared the bridges over the Eastern Branch for destruction. Barney's detachment and Miller's marines spent the night at the marine barracks in Washington. In the forenoon of the following day, when the British were known to be advancing via Bladensburg, they marched to the support of the army at Bladensburg.

Winder had hastily disposed about seven thousand troops in positions at Bladensburg in a faint-hearted attempt to stop the British advance. They turned back the attack of the British leading elements, but when a succeeding enemy regiment threatened to turn the left flank, Winder's hastily improvised army began what soon developed into a panic-stricken retreat.

Barney with his sailors and marines arrived upon the battlefield just as Winder's army began to break. They took up a position at the top of a hill, one mile west of Bladensburg, on the road to Washington. A detachment of regulars was then on their right and some Maryland militia on their left. The British, after their first successes at Bladensburg, advanced down the road expecting no resistance; then suddenly they encountered Barney's detachment supported by several pieces of artillery. Three times they were driven back by the deadly musket and artillery fire of the sailors and marines; then they began an envelopment of both flanks. The troops on Barney's flanks fled, leaving his force in a hopelessly exposed position. Barney and Miller, both severely wounded in the battle, ordered their troops to retire and remained in the battlefield, where they were captured by the British. The British army and navy commanders interviewed Barney soon afterwards. They expressed their highest commendations for his and his men's conduct during the battle and immediately paroled Barney.

With the retirement of Barney's detachment from the field, the last resistance to the entrance of the British into Washington was gone. What was left of Winder's army, government officials, and even the Commandant of the Marine Corps fled to the west and north in utter confusion. The remnants of Barney's command made good their escape and later joined a naval detachment under Commodore John Rodgers, who had been attempting to reach Washington in time to participate in the defense of the capital. The marines suffered 8 killed and 14 wounded out of a total strength of 103 during their efforts to defend the capital.

After the British had completely crushed all resistance along the Bladensburg road, they gradually took possession of the national capital, burned a number of public buildings, and then retired leisurely to their vessels in Chesapeake Bay by the route over which they had approached Washington. After the Battle of Bladensburg they were not molested at any time by American military forces.

## The Defense of Baltimore

While only ineffectual steps were being taken to turn back the British from the national capital, tremendous efforts were made for the defense of Baltimore and vicinity. They were rewarded by complete success when the British advanced on that city a few weeks later. Rodgers was in command of the new frigate *Guerrière,* nearing completion at Newcastle, and had part of the necessary contingent of sailors and marines for his crew. With all his available men he was ordered to Baltimore, where a detachment of marines from Cecil Furnace reported to him. Commodore Porter, in command at New York, left for Washington with all available sailors and marines when he heard that the capital was in danger. Neither of these forces arrived in time to help defend Washington. They joined in Baltimore on August 25 and organized a brigade of two regiments having together approximately one thousand sailors and marines. Perry, who had been transferred from Lake Erie to supervise the construction of the *Java* at Baltimore, was given command of one of the regiments. The surviving marines from the Battle of Bladensburg under Captain Samuel Bacon, a small draft of marines from Baltimore, and detachments from Philadelphia and from the *Guerrière* helped make up the brigade.

Soon after Ross's return the British squadron sailed up the Potomac and without resistance captured Fort Washington. Alexandria submitted to the British admiral's demands without opposition and paid a heavy tribute. The Navy Department feared another attack on Washington and ordered the naval brigade from Baltimore to Bladensburg, where it arrived on August 31. It soon became evident that the British had no further designs on the capital. The Secretary of the Navy determined to harass the British fleet and, if possible, with all available forces ashore in the vicinity of Washington, prevent its escape. Porter, with a detachment of sailors and marines and a few pieces of artillery, established an improvised fort on the west bank of the Potomac a few miles below Mt. Vernon. Perry, with a similar detachment, established himself at Indian Head, Maryland, a little farther down the river. Rodgers, with a third naval detachment, was assigned the mission of harassing the British fleet with fire ships. In spite of all its efforts, Porter's detachment, reinforced with a few companies of militia, was unable to prevent the British fleet from passing down the Potomac early in September.

The next probable move of the British was another advance up the Chesapeake. Secretary of the Navy Jones ordered Rodgers with his naval detachment back to Baltimore, and the remainder of the naval brigade soon followed. Rodgers took command of the brigade and immediately went to work helping to prepare defenses for Baltimore. The sailors and marines were given a sector to the northeast of the city where they constructed a number of redoubts connected by trenches and breastworks. What remained of Winder's army and volunteers from Pennsylvania and Maryland were busily engaged preparing defenses in other sectors.

Ross's army and supporting ships reached a point fourteen miles below Baltimore on September 11 and began landing. Ross marched on Baltimore the following day but met determined resistance about five miles from the city. He was killed early in the encounter and his successor, finding that his troops were making little progress, abandoned further efforts and returned to the ships. The marines who served with the Army during the engagement were later highly commended by the army commander in his report to the Secretary of War. The British bombarded Baltimore during the early morning of September 13 and on that evening attempted to land but were repulsed. Meeting with a warmer reception than they had anticipated, the enemy ceased raiding operations in the Chesapeake area.

## Lake Champlain

At no time during the war was the shortage of marines more manifest than when urgent calls were made for them to help man a little naval squadron on Lake Champlain. During the first two years of the war little of importance happened on that lake, but during 1814 it became the most important theater of operations: the British began an advance from Canada with an army of Wellington's veterans in an attempt to cut the United States in two. The Navy Department had anticipated the danger, and Thomas Macdonough had been given the means to construct a squadron of small vessels so that he might be able to cope with the increasing British naval strength on the lake. Macdonough called upon the Department for marine detachments for his vessels, but, no marines being available, none were furnished. When the threatened British invasion began,

# 76  A HISTORY OF THE U. S. MARINE CORPS

General Izard, in command of the army at Plattsburg, despite his own shortage of troops, supplied detachments of officers and soldiers from the 6th, 15th, and 33rd Infantry to serve on Macdonough's squadron and perform the usual functions of marines. With their aid Macdonough defeated the attacking British squadron in Plattsburg Bay and helped to turn back the enemy forces.

### ATTACK ON THE PIRATES OF BARATARIA

During the long struggle between France and England at the beginning of the nineteenth century, it had been the practice of the former country to sell letters of marque and reprisal to all adventurers who cared to buy them. As the result of this policy and unsettled conditions, the Caribbean Sea and the Gulf of Mexico swarmed with pirates and other lawless adventurers. England crushed the strength of the pirates in the West Indies in 1810, but many of them took refuge along the borders of the United States. The activities of a group based on Amelia Island are discussed in the preceding chapter. Another more formidable group developed a base of operations on Barataria Bay, on the southwest side of the Mississippi Delta. With a number of armed vessels a large group of lawless adventurers, under the leadership of the two Lafitte brothers of New Orleans, carried on an illegal slave trade as well as wholesale smuggling and piracy. New Orleans was the principal place for disposing of their plunder.

Since many of the leading citizens of New Orleans profited by the illegal operations, no action was taken against the pirates until it was learned that the British Navy was attempting to entice them into its service by promises of handsome rewards and threats of dire punishment if they refused. At this juncture, however, one of the Lafittes showed unusual patriotism and laid the whole British plan before the officials of Louisiana. In the meantime the British naval activities along the Gulf coast had greatly increased; it was suspected that their next attack would be either at Mobile or New Orleans. The situation demanded prompt action. Still distrusting the Lafittes, Master Commandant Daniel T. Patterson, in charge of the New Orleans naval station, supported by the army commander, made plans for a determined attack on the pirates.

On September 11, 1814, Patterson, with seventy soldiers from the 44th Infantry and a detachment of marines from the naval station, formed an expeditionary force and placed it aboard the *Carolina*. Seven gunboats and their tender, the *Sea Horse*, joined him the following day. The expedition sailed out Southwest Pass on the evening of September 15 and next morning was off the pirate fort on the island of Grand Terre. Under the flag of Cartagena the pirates lined up ten vessels for battle near the entrance to the harbor. They were reported as having at least twenty cannon and between eight hundred and one thousand men. Patterson promptly attacked them with his gunboat; the pirates soon abandoned their vessels and fled in all directions. He captured their vessels, landed his troops, and systematically destroyed the bandit stronghold. The expedition returned to New Orleans about a week later with all of the pirate vessels except one which had escaped. A second small expedition returned to Barataria two weeks later, upon report that the pirates had reassembled, but found no pirates.

## The Battle of New Orleans

By that time the British had established a naval base at Pensacola and had attacked Mobile. Patterson had been at New Orleans for a number of years and had very definite ideas of how the British would attack the city as well as how it should be defended. It is claimed by some authorities that he actually made the plan of defense which General Jackson used. In anticipation of the British advance to the mouth of the Mississippi, Patterson dispatched a flotilla of gunboats to scout in the direction of Pensacola and report the approach of the enemy. Lieutenant Thomas ap Catesby Jones, in charge of the flotilla, sighted the main British fleet off Mobile Bay on December 10. Patterson put into effect a plan which delayed the enemy for about a month. It was apparent that the British would approach New Orleans through Lake Borgne. Jones was ordered to hold that lake as long as possible and prevent the enemy from using it to transport troops in barges and small boats. After successfully delaying the British fleet for a time in Pass Christian, Jones withdrew his gunboats into Lake Borgne, where the British warships could not follow.

The enemy was forced to improvise a flotilla of barges to drive the American gunboats from the lake in order to clear it for a further advance. They prepared sixty barges, manned by approximately twelve hundred men and armed with cannon in the bow, for the attack. When Jones first observed the approaching barges, he retired to the channel between the mainland and Malheureux Island, where he anchored his gunboats in a line across the passage and awaited the enemy. Jones had five gunboats with a total of 23 guns and 182 men, including about 35 marines. The tender *Alligator*, which was unable to join in the battle, was soon captured by the British. Jones held his fire until the British were in effective range and then opened up. The enemy pressed home a determined attack with as many as fifteen barges against one gunboat and completely overwhelmed Jones's greatly inferior force. The British won, however, only with the loss of a number of barges and more than three hundred killed and wounded. Jones's maneuvers and his gallant stand had not only delayed the British for several days while New Orleans was being prepared for defense but also served greatly to arouse the fighting spirit of its defenders.

The British, having gained control of Lake Borgne, pushed forward their lighter transports and, after considerable delay (between December 16 and 20), landed part of their army on the north shore. From that position they hoped to advance in barges by way of the lake and a bayou which extended in the general direction of New Orleans. When Jackson learned of the enemy movements, he ordered all troops which could be made available in the general vicinity into the city and turned it into an armed camp. About 1,700 of the enemy moved in barges across the lake and as far as possible up the bayou. They then disembarked and marched towards New Orleans. The American forces discovered them when they were only six miles away. Jackson immediately advanced to meet them with a miscellaneous force of some 2,200 men, including a detachment of marines under Lieutenant Francis B. de Bellevue. The British went into camp for the night on the bank of the river.

At Jackson's request the *Carolina* took a position on the river covering the Britsh camp and opened a deadly fire at 7 P.M. This was the signal for Jackson's force to attack. Darkness and fog soon threw the action into hopeless confusion, and Jackson's troops were firing on friend and foe alike. The British withdrew a few hundred yards to a less exposed position; the Americans soon afterwards also withdrew, having accomplished but little aside from greatly improving their morale.

The affair also gained time for Jackson: the British not only delayed to bring up more troops but spent two days in dragging up artillery to drive off the annoying *Carolina*. In the meantime Jackson went back about two miles and took up a strong defensive position behind the Rodriguez Canal, with one flank resting on the river and the other extending into a cypress swamp. Jackson's army not only strongly fortified that line but two other positions between it and the city. His order of battle was made up of almost every conceivable kind of hastily thrown together military units. Even Lafitte's pirates held a sector. Another was held by a battalion of volunteers commanded by the creole Major Plauché, to which organization Major Daniel Carmick, U.S.M.C., and his few available marines attached themselves. The remainder of the marines from New Orleans (about sixty-five), under Bellevue, held a sector near the center of the Rodriguez Canal line.

The *Carolina* was forced by a gale and river currents to anchor within range of the British artillery. After a gallant fight it was finally destroyed (December 27), but most of the crew escaped in small boats. The surviving sailors and marines joined Jackson's battle line and manned a battery of artillery. Sir Edward Pakenham, who had taken personal command of the enemy forces, ordered an attack on December 28. When he observed the strong breastworks which Jackson had built, he halted and made still more elaborate preparations. By this time the British had, in Jackson's immediate front, nearly eight thousand troops supported by considerable artillery. Patterson had constructed a substantial fort, armed with navy guns, on the right bank of the river opposite Jackson's line. On January 1, 1815, the British started a bombardment that developed into an artillery duel, but after some hours Jackson silenced their batteries. Once more the Americans gained a moral victory and valuable time.

The British then started to transfer part of their forces to the west bank of the Mississippi to outflank Jackson's position. With tremendous efforts and days of delay they dug a canal up to the levee, over which they dragged their boats to the river. The Americans discovered the maneuver in time to ferry additional troops across the river to support Patterson's naval battery. Pakenham sent 1,200 troops across the river during the night to make an early morning attack; then upon signal the main British army would attack Jackson's position. They were greatly delayed in landing, but Pakenham, having received no signal from them by sunrise, gave the order for his army to attack. The results of the British attack against Jackson's motley army are too well known to repeat. The attack of the British in a heavy column, with their soldiers wearing their full equipment and carrying scaling ladders and fascines of sugar cane with which to cross the canal, resulted in a slaughter almost indescribable. While attempting to rally his troops and lead them in a second assault with lighter columns, Pakenham was killed, and his troops fell back in utter confusion.

The British on the west bank were entirely successful. The volunteers supporting Patterson's naval battery fled when the British attacked; Patterson spiked his guns and retired. But the local defeat had no effect on the general outcome of the battle. An armistice was concluded the following day, and the British, after burying their approximately seven hundred dead, began a gradual withdrawal to their ships. Jackson made no effort to molest them during their retirement or embarkation, which required almost two weeks. While the total number of marines in the scattered detachments that took part in the several operations in the defense of New Orleans was not large, compared to the total American forces engaged, they gave a good account of themselves each time they were under fire. They were highly commended for their services by Jackson, Patterson, and by Congress.

### Marines on the Privateers

The activity of privateers during the War of 1812 was by no means as extensive and successful as during the American Revolution. The British Navy more effectively controlled the seas. American privateers did, however, cause considerable damage to British shipping and engaged in several fights with British armed vessels. The more important of the privateers carried detachments of marines who, strictly speaking, had no official status as such but functioned in the same capacity and rendered valuable service to the country.

### Résumé

The story of the Marine Corps during the War of 1812 might be epitomized by saying that it was a constant struggle with the personnel problem—trying to do many difficult jobs with a hopelessly inadequate number of men. The Corps failed to render its full usefulness to the country through no fault of its own. It had not yet gained a national reputation, such as it has enjoyed in recent years and which evokes the unqualified support of the nation during times of national emergency. The lack of public support was partly a product of the times. The spirit of nationalism was still lacking and most of the people felt that their first allegiance was to their own state rather than to the nation. There were few difficulties in raising state troops—volunteers or militia—but all of the national services were unable to fill their authorized quotas. While at times the Marine Corps could only supply part of the absolutely necessary personnel for certain duties and at other times could supply none because of its hopelessly inadequate personnel, the struggling little organization rendered substantial services to the nation and had no reason to be other than proud of its accomplishments during that war, filled with so many serious reverses and humiliations to the American people. The Marine Corps was doomed to wait a few more years for an outstanding leader and the opportune time to establish a national reputation and then to enter upon a period of larger usefulness to the nation.

## Chapter IV
## INDIAN WARS AND LARGER USEFULNESS

#### Postwar Reactions

Despite the disastrous consequences which the nation had suffered as the result of its total unpreparedness for the War of 1812, and over the protest of both naval and military authorities, shortly after the war was over it determined again to fling aside its military forces. The unpopularity of that war and the outcome of the general wars in Europe, which relieved the country of the constant danger of being drawn into European wars, made the people more determined than ever to mind their own affairs and to have no more wars such as they had just passed through.

The Marine Corps, as well as the Army and the Navy, came in for its share of reduction. It was cut to one thousand, including officers. The Corps was even further reduced in 1817 to an authorized strength of 49 officers and 865 enlisted men. The reduction in officers was effected by a considerable number of resignations during and immediately after the war and by discharge of others as being supernumeraries. The enlisted personnel was discharged in the usual way. The Corps remained at the 1817 approximate strength until 1834. At that time the authorized enlisted strength was increased to 1,224, and the actual officer strength to 58. The increase was made just in time for the Marine Corps to play a considerable part in the Florida Indian War, which began two years later. There were no further changes in the authorized strength of the Corps until the Mexican War.

The personnel of the Marine Corps during the period between the War of 1812 and the Mexican War, covered by this chapter, was largely drawn from the states along the Atlantic Coast and was practically all of English descent. Officers were commissioned direct from civil life, and no specialized preliminary experience or education was required. The records show that recommendations and political influence were strong determining factors in procuring a commission. Influence also had much to do with obtaining desirable assignments. Newly appointed officers were attached to headquarters for instruction prior to going to sea or to other stations. Promotion was by seniority and was, as a rule, very slow. There were no retirements for disability or old age.

The Marine Corps functioned as an integral part of the Navy and had practically no duties except those closely related to that branch of the service. The Secretary of the Navy exercised more supervision over the administrative details of the Corps than was the custom after the Navy had grown to a more complicated organization in later years. In the early 1830's a reaction set in against the national policy of complete isolation, and the country once more began to look beyond its boundaries for possibilities of increased greatness and commercial advantages. This policy was reflected in the Act of June 30, 1834, which gave a substantial increase to the personnel of the Marine Corps, settled the question of its control by definitely placing it in the hands of the Secretary of the Navy, and provided for its larger usefulness to the nation by authorizing the President to order its personnel to duty with the Army. Various reports of the Secretary of the Navy, as well as reports of naval officers, strongly indicate that the marines rated ace-high during the period following the War of 1812.

Herman Melville—the great writer of sea stories of the period—found by his experiences on an American man-of-war that the marines were the elite division of the ship's company. They greatly impressed him by the dignified manner in which they carried on their duties.

## Commandants

Franklin Wharton, despite efforts to persuade the President to make him resign, continued as Commandant of the Marine Corps until his death on September 1, 1818. The records of his official acts throughout his tenure of office indicate that, despite the criticisms of his many enemies, he was an officer of considerable ability as well as one who commanded wide respect. The problem of selecting his successor caused considerable embarrassment to the Corps. Anthony Gale was the next senior officer, but he was not a man of outstanding ability, and he had been, on several occasions, reported for misconduct. A court of inquiry had looked into some of the episodes of his life, but no disciplinary action was taken. His questionable character and reputation were officially reported to the

# INDIAN WARS AND LARGER USEFULNESS

Secretary of the Navy prior to his selection; nevertheless, he was appointed to that important position. His administration was incompetent but was soon terminated by his dismissal from the service for disgraceful conduct in the city of Washington.

Gale was succeeded by the next senior officer of the Corps, Archibald Henderson, who had formerly acted as adjutant and inspector and temporary commandant in the interval between the death of Wharton and the unfortunate appointment of Gale. Henderson had been in the Marine Corps since 1806 and had had a great variety of service, including duty at sea during the War of 1812, for which he had been cited for gallantry in action and given the rank of brevet major. His tenure of office was the longest and perhaps the most eventful of any of the Commandants. Assisted by trusty heads of the staff departments, some of whom stayed in office almost as long, he directed the affairs of the Marine Corps, to what now appears to be almost microscopic detail, until 1859. He was a remarkable man in many respects and appears always to have had in mind the proper function of the Marine Corps and to have conducted its affairs in such a way as to assure its most effective service to the Navy and to the nation.

## DUTIES ON SHORE AND AT SEA

During all of this period the Marine Corps with its limited personnel was called upon to operate its headquarters, furnish marine guards for ships of the Navy, and provide regular detachments for navy yards and stations at Portsmouth, New Hampshire, New York, Boston, Philadelphia, Washington, and Norfolk. During the early part of the period marines were also stationed at Erie, Pennsylvania, and Sacketts Harbor, New York, and, during most of the period, at Pensacola, Florida. The duties of marines at the shore stations had to do largely with guard and police duties; the routine was not unlike that of the present.

The duties performed and the life aboard ships of the Navy were quite different in many ways from those of the present. The number of marine detachments assigned to ships varied from about eighteen at the beginning of the period to twenty-six just prior to the Mexican War. The routine duty of marines aboard ship had to do largely with maintaining order and discipline. Besides performing regular guard duty, they acted as orderlies for high ranking naval officers. They were called upon, at times, to perform many of the duties aboard ship which were ordinarily done by landsmen and ordinary seamen. Many navy captains of the period were of the opinion that marines could perform all of the duties of those two classes and were constantly advocating an increase in the allowance of marines aboard ship with a corresponding extension of their assigned duties.

The wartime duties of marines, as evidenced by the wars immediately before and after this period, differed greatly from the present battle assignment of marines aboard ships of the Navy. Their primary battle stations were the fighting tops, from which positions they acted as sharpshooters against the exposed personnel on the decks of the enemy ships. Part of the detachment was generally stationed on the ship's waist, which was most exposed and dangerous in time of battle. Their duties there were largely to enforce battle discipline over the gun crews stationed in that part of the ship. The marines on this duty were armed with muskets and bayonets, and were expected to use them if necessary. Muskets were also valuable weapons when the enemy ship got within close range. The assignment of marines to regular duties as members of gun crews did not take place until later. They often replaced sailors at the guns, however, when the necessity arose as the result of battle casualties.

When ships closed in battle and boarding parties went on the enemy ships, the marines, as a rule, covered the operation with musketry. They were the primary defense of a ship against enemy boarding parties. The marines were usually called upon to guard the crews of captured vessels, and at times they furnished guards which became part of the prize crew of captured ships. Such duties were then important since it was not unusual for navy ships to capture a considerable number of merchantmen during a war. Naval commanders were of the opinion that marines should be furnished at the rate of about one marine for each gun of the ship. This rule was followed as far as marines were available even if it was necessary to strip the shore stations of practically all marines.

## Pay and Allowances

The marine of those days would not now be envied for the compensation which he received nor the trying duties which he was called upon to perform. The pay of privates varied from $6 per month to $10 per month, with a corresponding rate of pay for other enlisted grades up to $17 per month for sergeants major. The pay of officers was not much more flattering, as second lieutenants were paid only $25 per month and the other officers at a gradually rising pay scale up to $75 per month for the Lieutenant Colonel Commandant. In order to discourage desertions, the practice of withholding part of a man's pay during the early months of his enlistment and paying it to him upon discharge was commonly resorted to.

The rations allowed in those days may well be imagined from their computed value, which varied from fifteen to twenty cents per day. The redeeming feature of the meager ration was, perhaps, that it contained a daily allowance of a gill of grog. Officers were allowed from four to twelve commuted rations in addition to their meager pay. The clothing allowance for enlisted men was $30 per year. Since most articles of clothing were handmade in those days, their prices were, as a rule, very little under present-day prices. The uniform kit of a marine contained such articles as pompoons, stocks, uniform woolen overalls, gaiters, and fatigue jackets, in addition to other articles that are commonly issued today.

## Discipline

In those days of wooden ships and iron men, discipline was enforced more expeditiously and by means which today would be regarded as unnecessarily cruel. Commanding officers had wide latitude for giving punishments, while court-martial procedure was a relatively simple affair. Near the beginning of the period Private John Graham was tried and convicted for being asleep on post and sentenced "to walk post with iron collar and balls for two months." For the same offense another marine was sentenced to a period of hard labor with ball and chain. In 1820 Private Robert Sloan was tried and convicted for desertion and sentenced "to wear an iron collar round his neck for four months and with a 6 lb ball and forfeit all the pay—then to be drummed out of the garrison." For desertion from a ship in 1830, the sentence was three dozen lashes and discharge. It was considered a proper sentence of a court-martial to take away the daily allowance of liquor. In 1820 Private David Wiley was sentenced to "one month to garrison and liquor stopped" for being drunk at parade. A common punishment awarded by a commanding officer, especially at sea, was to "be triced up on the grating" and given a prescribed number of lashes with the "cat" (cat-o'-nine-tails) by the master-at-arms while the entire crew of the ship was paraded to watch the grim affair. Suitable punishments were considered to be "12 lashes with the cat for desertion"; "8 lashes for drunkenness"; and "abuse to sentry, 12 lashes."

It should not be taken for granted, however, that our hardy marines and seamen of those days considered these methods of discipline as unnecessarily cruel. It is evident from the way they expressed themselves near the end of this period, when the abolition of corporal punishment by act of Congress was being considered, that a great many of them did not approve of this reform any more than they had approved of having their grog rations reduced by one-half a few years previously. Nearly everyone then thought that discipline could be maintained only by such methods. After all, it was a way to get the punishment over quickly and to restore the man to his regular station where he was always seriously needed.

## Larger Usefulness

During this eventful period of its history the Marine Corps was called upon to perform many and far-flung emergency duties. Precedents grew up which served to establish definite missions which it has since carried out. The Corps rendered invaluable aid to the civil authorities during several serious domestic disturbances; fought pirates in the Mediterranean, in Florida, and in the East and West Indies; intervened to protect Americans in Haiti and China; furnished a military force in support of the famous Wilkes Exploring Expedition; came to the timely assistance of the Army in wars against the Indians of Georgia and Florida; and took part in the first raising of the United States flag in California.

## Domestic Disturbances

Means for maintaining law and order in the United States were then poorly organized. The marines found themselves called upon from time to time to assist in local emergencies near their regular stations. During a great fire in Boston in 1824 a detachment of marines from the navy yard at that place rendered considerable assistance. A few years later they were called upon to assist in quelling a riot at Charlestown, Massachusetts. The marines and sailors from the *Grampus* assisted in stopping a serious fire at St. Thomas in 1825 after five hundred houses had already been destroyed and more serious damage was threatened. During the same year the marine detachments from three ships of the Mediterranean Squadron assisted in fighting a conflagration at Smyrna, which threatened the complete destruction of that city.

In March, 1833, the Treasury Department in Washington was set on fire for the supposed purpose of destroying certain documentary evidence, and the marines of the headquarters detachment were called out and protected the building. One of the most outstanding examples of courage in our history was exhibited by Major Robert D. Wainwright with thirty marines from the Boston detachment in stopping a very serious riot of 283 inmates of the state prison at Boston. At one end of a court Wainwright lined up his marines with loaded muskets facing the rebellious prisoners, and he told the prisoners that if they did not disperse within three minutes he would fire upon them. The situation was extremely tense as not a prisoner moved until near the end of the third minute. Then they began to retire a few at a time and later rapidly in large numbers. Not a word was uttered. The story of Wainwright's heroic conduct during this episode was made a classic by being included in *McGuffey's Readers,* which were used by nearly all American schools for nearly seventy-five years. But the more interesting duties of the marines were outside of the United States.

## BARBARY CORSAIRS, 1815

After the withdrawal of the American squadrons from the Mediterranean in 1807, American shipping again suffered various indignities at the hands of the Barbary pirates. The Barbary States had flagrantly violated all the treaties of peace which they had agreed to. The corsairs had been especially active against our commerce during the War of 1812. Congress declared war on Algiers, March 3, 1815. Our Navy had learned much about fighting during the War of 1812 and was stronger and better prepared in every way to take a firmer hand in the Mediterranean situation. A squadron of twelve ships under Commodore Stephen Decatur was ordered to the Mediterranean to put an end to the depredations on American commerce. For the purpose of making treaties with the rulers of the pirate states, a peace commission accompanied the squadron. All of the ships of the squadron carried marine detachments, and a battery of army artillery helped to reinforce the squadron. The squadron sailed from New York in May and arrived at Algiers late in June, 1815. While approaching Algiers it engaged and captured two Algerine vessels and five hundred prisoners. During an encounter with one of the vessels the marines on two vessels of the squadron helped defeat the enemy by delivering an effective musketry fire from the fighting tops. The news of the capture of his ships and the show of force by Decatur's squadron served to show the Bey of Algiers that further resistance was useless. He agreed without modification to the treaty presented by our commissioners. The treaty was epoch-making in that it ended tribute-paying by American vessels in the Mediterranean. Shortly afterwards several European countries demanded and received the same exemption.

Decatur then proceeded to Tunis and Tripoli, where the commission settled some diplomatic problems growing out of the War of 1812. Another American squadron of eleven vessels commanded by Commodore William Bainbridge arrived in the Mediterranean in August to support Decatur. Each vessel of this squadron carried the usual complement of marines, who were organized for landing force operations. Such action was not necessary, however, as the show of force alone was sufficient to make all the rulers of the Barbary States concede to the terms demanded.

## Florida Pirates

Shortly after the War of 1812 the marines played a part in eliminating pirate-infested forts along the coast of Florida, which was then still a possession of the decadent Spanish Empire. The United States was at the time carrying on seemingly endless negotiations for the purchase of Florida. The local Spanish authorities were totally unable or unwilling to control the disorderly elements. One of the main places of annoyance was a negro pirate stronghold, located fifteen miles up the Appalachicola River. Marines on two gunboats helped in the destruction of this nest of outlaws on July 27, 1816. Another pirate stronghold had grown up on Amelia Island off the northeastern coast of Florida. On December 23, 1817, the marine detachments of six navy vessels participated in joint army and navy operations which forced the surrender of the island and put an end to its use as a base for illegal operations.

## Suppressing Piracy in the West Indies

As a result of the Napoleonic Wars and internal disintegration, the Spanish Empire was practically falling to pieces in the early nineteenth century. After further disorganizing influences, practically all the Spanish colonies in the Western Hemisphere revolted from the mother country. In support of these rebellious operations many privateers were fitted out, some with more or less spurious commissions, others with no commissions at all, while many were outright piratical adventurers. Many who formerly had been legitimate privateers drifted into piracy. With the strong arm of the law completely broken throughout the Caribbean area, piracy assumed very serious proportions during the early part of the nineteenth century, especially during the period from 1815 to 1825. A great many American ships were captured, and many American sailors were murdered or forced to join the pirates.

During that decade the suppression of pirates in the Caribbean area became practically the major function of the United States Navy. Previously, only a few minor efforts had been made towards their suppression. In 1821 a number of naval vessels went to the area to operate against the pirates. They destroyed a considerable number of pirate boats and ships along the northern coast of Cuba during the succeeding years. An expeditionary force of two hundred marines on board the *Macedonian* and several other ships joined the naval forces operating against the pirates in the spring of 1822.

They had several engagements with pirate ships, boats, and strongholds on shore during the remainder of that year. In one of these encounters Lieutenant William H. Allen, U.S.N., and three sailors were killed.

This incident caused President Monroe to press more vigorously the war against the pirates. With the approval of Congress he assigned additional naval forces to the task. Three officers and ninety-four marines as well as additional ships were added to the West India Squadron, and Commodore David Porter was placed in command. A base for the squadron was established at the present location of Key West. The Navy developed that base, and marines guarded it until it was abandoned about two years later because the locality was extremely unhealthful. The Navy then established another base at Pensacola. During 1823 the center of pirate activity gradually shifted towards the eastern islands, where our naval force had several encounters with them. The situation grew somewhat complicated on March 3, 1823, when one of Porter's schooners, the *Fox*, while attempting to enter the harbor of St. John, Porto Rico, was fired upon by a Spanish fort, and Lieutenant William H. Cocke, U.S.N., was killed. The *Peacock* had previously been fired upon by the same fort.

In October, 1824, Foxardo, Porto Rico, was reported to be a center of piratical activities. The U.S.S. *Beagle* went into that port to investigate conditions. Lieutenant Platt of that vessel, while on shore, was insulted by local officials and detained for some time practically as a prisoner. Commodore Porter considered the acts as an insult to our flag and went there with several ships to demand an apology. Porter landed with a substantial force. Lieutenant Thomas B. Barton, U.S.M.C., with a detachment of marines advanced upon a fort and without firing a shot captured it and spiked the guns. The remainder of Porter's force, including another detachment of marines, under Lieutenant Horatio N. Crabb, then marched upon the town. Upon approaching Foxardo, Porter sent for the alcalde and demanded an immediate apology. The Spanish official made a full apology in the presence of the offended Platt, and the episode was apparently terminated to the full satisfaction of the American naval forces. The Navy Department, however, did not approve of the action taken by Porter and shortly thereafter relieved him of his command and ordered him to Washington for investigation. He was court-martialed, given a mild sentence, but resigned from the Navy.

The operations against the pirates continued intermittently for several years. The British Navy and the Royal Marines were also carrying on operations against these pirates. The pirate forces were gradually broken up, and they ceased to be a menace to commerce.

## FIGHTING PIRATES IN SUMATRA

The experiences of the marines on the famous cruise of the *Essex* during the War of 1812 was only the beginning of their experiences in the South Seas. No part of the world at that time was too remote for our Yankee skippers to venture in quest of trade. Whaling in the Pacific was developing rapidly, even in the early part of this period. The crews of whalers were often subjected to barbarous treatment when shipwrecked or forced ashore by other disaster. Wherever the whalers or merchantmen ventured, our navy vessels soon followed to give all possible protection and to help promote trade by diplomatic means. In addition to committing some lesser interferences with our commerce, the natives of Sumatra seized and robbed an American trader and murdered part of the crew in the harbor of Quallah Battoo in 1831. Our Government decided to send a punitive expedition. The frigate *Potomac*, especially organized and equipped for operations against the Sumatran pirates, went out from New York. The expedition arrived at Quallah Battoo in February, 1832. A combined landing force of 250 marines and sailors went ashore, and, in spite of fierce resistance of the natives, captured several pirate forts and burned the town. The *Potomac* remained in the South Seas as its regular station to protect American interests.

The natives of Sumatra apparently did not learn their lesson from the first retaliatory action and continued to harass American ships. A second expedition of two ships was sent against them in 1838. On this occasion the show of force alone was sufficient to bring the native chiefs to terms for the time being, but their continued hostility necessitated the return of a naval vessel to Quallah Battoo the following year. After its demands had been rejected, it bombarded the place and sent a landing force ashore. The landing party destroyed the forts and burned the town.

On the other side of the Southern Hemisphere marines performed similar duties. On the Falkland Islands in 1831-1832 the marines on board the sloop *Lexington* participated in landing operations to rescue three American schooners which had been detained by Argentine officials who were attempting to establish a claim over the islands.

## ACTIVITIES DURING REVOLT OF SPANISH COLONIES

At various places in Latin America the Marine Corps came in for a share of our naval activities during the years of revolts of the

Spanish colonies. A detachment of marines was on board the *Ontario* during an extended cruise along the western coast of North and South America for the purpose of visiting various unsettled localities and observing conditions during 1817-1818. That vessel went as far north as the Columbia River and attempted to strengthen our claims in the Oregon Territory on August 29, 1818, by landing and raising the American flag at Cape Disappointment at the mouth of the Columbia River. The marine guard of the *Ontario*, commanded by Sergeant McFadian, participated in the flag ceremony.

## HAITI, 1817-1821

The American consul at Port au Prince, Haiti, was reported to have been seriously mistreated by Petion, the mulatto ruler of the southern part of that country, and in consequence had left his post. In July, 1817, the State Department sent a special agent, Mr. Tyler, to investigate conditions and re-establish relations. Tyler, escorted by a detachment of forty-seven marines under First Lieutenant William Nicoll, was taken to the Haitian capital on the frigate *Congress*. He successfully carried out his mission and in addition investigated some reported executions of American seamen by the Haitians. The *Congress* then proceeded to Cap Haitien where Tyler attempted to carry on negotiations with Christophe, the negro dictator of northern Haiti. Christophe declined to enter into diplomatic relations on the ground that Tyler's written instructions were not in due form. The marines on the *Hornet* furnished moral support for a special mission to the same places again the following year. Chaotic conditions which followed the end of Christophe's reign in northern Haiti again necessitated the sending of the *Ontario* to protect Americans at Cap Haitien in 1821.

## WITH CUSHING AT CANTON

American traders had begun to venture to the China coast during the closing years of the eighteenth century. Our commercial interests in that part of the world had grown to sufficient importance for ships of our Navy to begin visiting eastern China in 1820. In 1835 the East India Squadron was organized with its base at Hong Kong. In 1842 the United States decided to send a minister to China. Caleb Cushing was selected, and a squadron of three ships of the Navy (the frigate *Brandywine*, the sloop of war *St. Louis*, and the brig *Perry*) escorted him to his post of duty. He arrived at Macao, February 24, 1844. With a large official party he established a legation at Macao and by making considerable display attempted to impress the Chinese officials with the importance of his position.

A squad of marines from the *Brandywine* remained ashore with the legation for about two months and did its part to help impress the Chinese with the importance of the United States.

Canton was then the only Chinese port open to regular foreign trade. Arrangements had been made in the early part of the eighteenth century for foreign traders to establish factories (trading posts) on Whampoa Island in the river below Canton. Each of the foreign nations had areas assigned for their factories. By 1844 American commerce with China through this port had reached considerable proportions. Difficulties arose between the Americans and the Chinese. A Chinese merchant was killed by an American during a riot on June 16. Two days later a mob gathered in front of the American factory and demanded the delivery of the American who had killed the merchant.

Fortunately our little East India Squadron was near at hand. The American consul immediately notified Commodore Parker on the *Brandywine* and Captain Tilton on the *St. Louis* of the situation and asked for immediate protection of Americans and their property. Without waiting for orders from the Commodore, Tilton sailed the *St. Louis* up the river as far as possible and personally took ashore a landing party consisting of the marine detachment and forty-four sailors armed with muskets and cutlasses. They arrived at the factory on Whampoa just in time to prevent the mob from attacking the Americans. The landing force then became an armed guard in the American compound. Cushing adjusted the difficulties with the Chinese officials and the situation quieted down. The sailors of the landing force returned aboard the *St. Louis* on June 21, but the marines remained at the American factory until July 20. They were highly commended by the consul and other American officials for the manner in which they performed their duties.

## Wilkes Exploring Expedition

The marines had some very interesting experiences in connection with the Wilkes Exploring Expedition during 1838-1842. Lieutenant John Wilkes, in command of six naval vessels, sailed from New York in March, 1838, for the South Seas to make extensive explorations. The experiences of his explorers were not altogether peaceful. The natives of the Fiji Islands were found to be especially hostile to any encroachment upon their domain. They attacked a small party in a boat making scientific observations: the Americans narrowly escaped. Wilkes immediately set out to avenge the outrage. The marines from two of his vessels and a detachment of sailors landed, marched to the principal village, and burned it to the ground. The natives grew still more hostile and shortly afterwards murdered two American naval officers on another island. A second punitive landing force burned the two principal towns on that island. The expedition left the Fiji Islands a few months later, without having had further serious encounters.

In the summer of 1841 they had some difficulties with the natives on Drummond's Island. According to a story which they heard upon arriving there, an American vessel had been wrecked, and all on board, excepting the wife and child of the captain, had been murdered by the natives. While Wilkes was attempting to verify the story and to rescue the woman and child, if still alive, a sailor of a landing party mysteriously disappeared. All efforts to locate him or the woman only made the natives more hostile. Again Wilkes resorted to punitive measures and destroyed the principal village on the island.

As early as 1820 American traders had established regular commercial relations with the Samoan Islands. Wilkes made some trade regulations with the native chieftains during his exploration of those islands in 1839. Shortly afterwards an American seaman was murdered on one of the group. Two of Wilkes's vessels, which were in the vicinity, attempted in vain to obtain redress from the native rulers. Again they resorted to a landing operation of the marines and sailors. The ships supported the landing by a preliminary bombardment. The natives fled during the firing, and the landing party went ashore unopposed and burned three of the principal villages.

The expedition visited many other islands in the South Seas, including the Hawaiian Islands and the Philippines, but had no serious difficulties with the natives. They made extensive explorations along the present west coast of the United States and finally returned to New York around the world in 1842.

## Landing in California

In September, 1842, a small squadron of American ships under Commodore Thomas ap Catesby Jones was temporarily based at Callao, Peru. For some time there had been considerable intrigue by Russia, France, Great Britain, and the United States, each trying to gain advantages which would help establish claims to California and Oregon. The United States was, at the time, especially suspicious of Great Britain. Jones, thinking that California was about to be detached from Mexico in some manner and that war between the United States and Mexico was imminent—if it had not already broken out—decided to sail for California and take possession of Monterey before the British or one of the other interested powers could do so. He arrived at Monterey on October 20, with his flagship the *United States* accompanied by the *Cyane*. On the following day he demanded and received the surrender of the town from the Mexican commander. A landing force of 150 sailors and marines went ashore from the two ships to take possession of the town and garrison the fort which controlled the harbor. They hauled down the Mexican flag over the fort and with due ceremony hoisted the American. The three cheers of the landing force were answered by the ships. The landing force prepared for a long stay on shore and began to make themselves comfortable. But Jones had acted on insufficient information and soon found that he had made a serious mistake.

On the day after the landing Thomas O. Larkin, the American consul at Monterey and later confidential agent of President Polk, showed Jones newspapers which clearly indicated that war did not exist between the United States and Mexico and that Jones's idea that the British were about to seize California was also in error. Jones, finding himself in an awkward position, backed out of it with as much grace and in the most expeditious manner possible. He hauled down the American flag from the fort and, with proper ceremony, ran up the Mexican flag in its place. Jones then fired a salute of thirteen guns to the Mexican commander, which was returned by the Mexican guns in the fort. The landing force withdrew to the ships. On the following day Jones sent ninety-five pounds of powder to the Mexican authorities to replace the powder expended by his landing force while in possession of the fort.

## Indian Wars, 1836-1842

Andrew Jackson's spectacular and apparently thoroughgoing expedition against the Seminole Indians and his encroachment on the territory of Spain in Florida during the so-called First Seminole War only temporarily solved the difficulties with the Indians of that tribe. Shortly after the transfer of Florida to the United States, land-hungry emigrants from the near-by states began to flock into that newly acquired territory and encroach upon the domains claimed by the Seminole Indians, who soon began to retaliate by attacks on the settlers. Arrangements had previously been made to remove all of the Indian tribes from the southeastern states to new reservations west of the Mississippi River. The Seminoles in Florida had agreed in 1832 to move. Attempts to carry out this emigration scheme further embittered the Indians. After two years' delay General Wiley Thompson went to Florida with a force of troops to carry out the removal of the Seminoles who, under Osceola, had refused to go peacefully. While carrying on negotiations with

## INDIAN WARS AND LARGER USEFULNESS 95

Thompson, Osceola was somewhat insolent; the impetuous general imprisoned and put him in irons for a day. Osceola, burning with revenge, incited the Seminoles to such an extent that they went on the warpath and, by various desperate operations, resisted their removal for nearly seven years. They were subdued only after repeated combined operations by the regular Army, Marine Corps, Navy, and volunteer troops from the near-by states.

Actual fighting between the military forces and the Seminoles broke out in December, 1835. The army operating against them was then based on Tampa Bay; the rebellious Indians were located in central Florida. General Clinch, with a small force, while attempting to protect the settlers, had occupied Fort Drane near the present town of Gainesville. The garrison was in a very exposed position and in great danger of being overwhelmed by the hostile Indians. Major Dade, with about one hundred soldiers from Fort Brooke at the head of Tampa Bay, attempted to march to its rescue, but was ambushed on December 28, 1835. Dade and all of his soldiers, except four who later died of wounds, were massacred. On the same day Osceola, with a small band, crept upon Fort King, located a short distance east of Fort Drane, surprised General Thompson dining with five of his friends, and murdered all of them. Osceola got his revenge for being put in irons by personally scalping Thompson. A short time afterwards forces under both General Clinch and General Gaines fought indecisive battles with the Seminoles.

At the outbreak of the Seminole war the West India Squadron, under Commodore A. J. Dallas, was ordered to co-operate with all available men and ships and help suppress the Seminoles. The marines from the ships of the squadron soon became actively engaged in many phases of the war. Shortly after the Dade massacre, a detachment of several officers, fifty-seven marines, and seven sailors, under First Lieutenant N. S. Waldron, was sent from the *Constellation* and the *St. Louis* to garrison Fort Brooke until additional army forces arrived. Waldron arrived (January 22, 1836) just in time to help ward off a serious Indian attack against the fort.

General Gaines, with a force of eleven hundred regular and volunteer troops, arrived on February 10 from New Orleans. Gaines immediately took the field wth his troops, leaving Waldron with his detachment and a few soldiers to hold the base on Tampa Bay. Gaines's expedition into the interior was a failure. He was attacked at Fort King, February 27, and besieged until March 6. After having suffered heavy losses, he was reinforced by General Clinch. Gaines soon left his troops to hold some forts and returned to New Orleans.

Shortly afterwards General Winfield Scott arrived in Florida and assumed command. During one of Scott's operations along the Withlacoochie River in March, 1836, the marines under Waldron took part and engaged in several fights against the Indians. Waldron's detachment continued on shore duty at Fort Brooke and vicinity until August, 1836. In the meantime the vessels of the West India Squadron were called upon many times to support the army and to protect settlements along the coast of Florida.

Early in January, 1836, at the request of the Governor of Florida, a landing force of sailors and marines from the *Vandalia* protected the settlers in the vicinity of Pensacola. Several expeditions went from the ships of the squadron to protect settlements on the keys off southern and eastern Florida. One or more of its vessels remained in Tampa Bay during the greater part of 1836, in close support of Fort Brooke. To make sure that it had a full-time job, the squadron had the additional tasks of preventing the illegal landing of slaves in Florida and of protecting American commerce in that vicinity. On March 31 Lieutenant L. M. Powell, U. S. N., with a detachment of marines and sailors from the *Vandalia*, went on a boat expedition up the Charlotte (Carlosahatchee) River in response to requests for protection by the settlers. While on that duty they also co-operated with the army in a campaign up the Macacca River.

The situation for the army in central Florida gradually grew more difficult throughout the early part of 1836. A force of not more than one thousand was attempting to conquer and deport from the country more than three times that many Indians. The state troops called into the vicinity soon had enough of the trying conditions, and practically all of them left early in the year. The campaign was in many ways most arduous. In addition to the large number of killed, many more died of disease and exhaustion because of the very unhealthful and trying conditions of the campaign. The army, in addition to fighting the Indians, had, with the occasional assistance of state troops, built 90 forts and stockades and opened up 480 miles of road. But still greater difficulties were in store.

## Henderson Takes the Field

The Creek Indians, with whom arrangements had also been made for transfer to the West, went on the warpath in southern Georgia and Alabama in an effort to avoid moving and to help the Seminoles in Florida. The Creeks committed depredations and murderous attacks against settlers, mail carriers, stage coaches, and even against steamboats on the rivers. They burned Roanoke, Georgia, and threatened to attack Columbus and Tallahassee. Thousands of white settlers fled from the area to escape their murderous operations. General Scott was then ordered from Florida to conduct the war against the Creeks. Their outbreak necessitated the Army shifting its main effort from the Seminole to the Creek country around Columbus, Georgia, and neglecting the former area. In the midst of all of these difficulties, the Marine Corps, true to its traditions, threw its sword into the scales.

A law had shortly before been enacted which empowered the President to order the Marines to duty with the Army. All of the regular stations and receiving ships occupied by marines in the United States were hopelessly undermanned, but the situation was one calling for great sacrifice, and Colonel Commandant Archibald Henderson volunteered the services of a regiment of marines for duty with the Army in the operations against the Creeks. The offer was promptly accepted, and on May 23, 1836, President Andrew Jackson issued orders for all available marines to report to the Army. Despite his being Commandant of the Corps, Henderson did not hesitate to offer to lead in person the marines in their operations against the Indians. By taking practically all officers, reducing navy yard detachments to a sergeant's guard, and limiting receiving ships' detachments to one corporal and ten privates—all of whom were unfit for duty in the field—Henderson was able to mobilize more than half the total strength of the Corps for field duty. The mobilization proceeded, and the expedition went to the theater of operations very much like the many other expeditions that have been sent out in the hundred years of Marine Corps history since then.

The marine regiment was mobilized in two contingents which proceeded separately to the scene of the conflict. The First Battalion was assembled at Fortress Monroe under the command of Henderson. Its components came from Washington, Philadelphia, Baltimore, and Gosport (Norfolk) by steamboats. The battalion then proceeded (June 2) on the chartered steamer *Columbus* to Charleston and from there went by rail over the then longest railroad in the United States to Augusta, Georgia. After a few days to get organized, it started on a fourteen-day march of 224 miles from Augusta to Columbus, Georgia. The other battalion, under Lieutenant Colonel William H. Freeman, was assembled in New York from detachments on receiving ships and from the navy yards at Portsmouth, New Hampshire, Charlestown, Massachusetts, and New York. Additional small groups from the stations farther south also joined it. It sailed from New York by steamer to Charleston and proceeded to Columbus in the same manner a few days after the First Battalion.

In equipping and outfitting this expeditionary force of marines, the heavy and burdensome high caps and frock coats of the day were left behind, and only the white fatigue uniforms were taken. Most of the marines were armed with muskets, but a few were supplied with the newfangled Colt rifles, which they later found were prone to explode if carried loaded for a few days before firing. As the result of such experiences, they stuck by their trusted and tried muskets.

## IN THE CREEK CAMPAIGN

Henderson's regiment went into the Creek country fifteen miles below Columbus and established a camp. The camp, located at the head waters of summer navigation on the Alabama side of the Chatahoochie River, was named Camp Henderson and later renamed Fort Henderson. The Creek Indians in that area were very much on the warpath; the marines lived in constant expectation of the Creeks creeping upon them in the middle of the night for their scalps. The Indians twice attacked their camp at night, but on each occasion the marines soon had "the situation well in hand."

By June 3 the regiment was sufficiently organized in its new position to begin active field operations. The First Battalion, under Lieutenant Colonel Samuel Miller, searched the country between the Euchee and the Hatcheechubby rivers for a distance of about twelve miles looking for a hostile Indian concentration which had been reported. The warriors fled, however, leaving only the squaws and papooses to be captured by the marines. A few weeks later Companies A and B, under Captain Levi Twiggs, who later lost his life in the Mexican War, made an extensive search for Indians in the swamps near Camp Henderson. Shortly afterwards Company E went on an extensive patrol looking for hostile Indians. Similar patrols continued to go out during the summer of 1836. One company went to Upton Mills, Georgia, for the purpose of intercepting Indians who tried to escape into Florida. For more than two months the marines were searching for "Jim Henry," the local chief of the Creeks. Supplies from New Orleans for the army in the Creek country were constantly being forwarded by steamboat up the river. In addition to their field operations the marines erected a strong picket work and two storehouses for army supplies.

Scott, who was recalled (June 28) for an investigation of his conduct of the war against the Creek and Seminole Indians, turned over the command of the army to Major General T. H. Jesup. After the usual long-drawn-out investigation, Scott was exonerated and restored to his command— apparently he had done everything possible with the means at his disposal. With the assistance of the marines and some volunteer forces, the army was able to bring the Creek In-

INDIAN WARS AND LARGER USEFULNESS    99

dian War to a successful termination during the summer of 1836. The Creeks gave up completely and were concentrated at various points. Henderson, with three companies of marines, guarded a concentration camp at Talessee, Alabama. Under an escort of the army assisted by part of Henderson's marines, the Creeks went to their new reservation in what is now Oklahoma.

Shortly after the close of the Creek War, Henderson's regiment made its way into Florida. By August 30 Henderson with most of the unit was in Tallahassee. The marines who had taken part in moving the Creeks did not arrive until early in October. The regiment then reassembled at Appalachicola, moved into the Seminole country, and based for some time at Fort Brooke.

### Fighting the Seminoles

During the war against the Creek Indians the West India Squadron continued to co-operate with the land forces in various ways. Waldron with his marines helped to hold Fort Brooke throughout the period. Small expeditions of marines and sailors from the squadron went ashore at various places along the coast in response to reports from the settlers that Indian attacks were imminent. Such alarms were so common at Tallahassee that Commodore Dallas was kept busy sending landing forces back and forth between St. Mark and Tallahassee when in his opinion there was no real need for protection. Dallas manned three steamers with special guards of seamen and marines and kept communications open on the Chattahoochie River between the Gulf and Columbus.

Upon the arrival of the marine regiment at Fort Brooke, the detachments of marines under Waldron withdrew and returned to their ships. They later took an active part in expeditions along the keys, off the southern and eastern coasts of Florida. A typical one, and the largest of these expeditions, consisting of several naval officers, two marine officers, ninety-five marines, and fifty sailors, started out from Key West October 13, 1836. It reached Cape Florida, near Miami, October 21 and after extensive river patrolling returned to the *Vandalia* at Key West, December 9.

For some time after the arrival of the marine regiment at Fort Brooke, the forces in that area were not sufficient to take the field in a determined operation to crush the Seminole rebellion. The operations during the remainder of 1836 consisted only of sending out large patrols and holding forts, located at important places in the interior. Here marines had their first experience in officering "native troops." A number of Creek Indian volunteers had been brought down from Alabama. During some of the operations against the Seminoles these Creeks were largely commanded by marine officers. On November 21 a force of Creeks under marine officers successfully attacked the Seminoles in Wahoo Swamp near Dade's battlefield. First Lieutenant Andrew Ross was killed in the battle. Shortly after this incident a detachment of marines and some Alabama volunteers went into the interior against the Seminoles but accomplished little. The marines, at times, escorted supplies from the base on Tampa Bay through the Indian country to the forts in the interior.

During the closing months of 1836 while the Army was assembling troops for a major offensive against the Seminoles, the naval forces in the vicinity continued to carry out supporting and protecting missions. Boat expeditions of marines and sailors operated among the keys and up the rivers around the southern end of Florida. The Navy developed special barges and shallow draft boats for this class of operations. One or two revenue cutters were on duty with the Navy in Florida waters throughout the period of the Seminole War. When the Army had concentrated sufficient forces to take the field, the naval landing forces took over some of its bases and forts near the coast in order to make all possible army troops available for the campaign. A detachment of sailors and marines from the *Constellation* took over Fort Clinch, located about fifteen miles up the Withlacoochee River from the Gulf. Similar naval forces helped to hold Fort Brooke and Fort Foster. In January, 1837, the squadron sent sixty marines on a special river boat to operate against a reported force of Indians up the Clear River.

After the arrival of additional regular army units, twelve hundred Tennessee troops, a regiment of Georgia infantry, and a regiment of Creeks, General Jesup had sufficient force for a determined operation against the Seminoles. He completed all necessary arrangements and preparations for the campaign early in January. Jesup divided his army into two brigades. The Second Brigade, consisting of an artillery regiment, the Fourth Infantry, the Georgia volunteers, a battalion of friendly Indians, and the marine regiment, was placed under Henderson. It was apparent that the greatest difficulties would be to locate the enemy and supply the troops while operating in a jungle devoid of roads and local food supplies.

### The Battle of the Hatchee-Lustee

After several unsuccessful efforts to gain contact with the enemy, Henderson moved his brigade eastward towards the headwaters of the Ocklawaha, where a strong force of Seminoles was reported. A recently abandoned Indian camp with horses, baggage, and a number of squaws, found on the morning of January 27, indicated that a considerable force was near by. The warriors had fled into the swamps. Henderson left one company behind to guard the Indian camp and pushed on with the remainder of his troops. They soon encountered the enemy, who had taken up a position behind the Hatchee-Lustee River—a stream too deep to ford. The marines and other troops forced the stream by swimming and crossing on foot logs, attacked the enemy position, and drove the Indians farther into the swamps. They pursued the Indians, had several contacts, but lost them in the dense and deep jungle at nightfall. Henderson then gave up the pursuit and withdrew his forces. A number of marines were killed or wounded in the operation. Henderson and several of his officers were recommended for brevet rank for their heroic conduct; a number of marines were promoted for their gallantry in action.

Jesup's army continued to harass the Indians throughout their country. Jesup did not permit them to plant their crops, when the time arrived, nor to make a living otherwise. When his troops found the Seminoles encamped, they promptly attacked and drove them from home. Facing starvation they soon began to give themselves up to our armed forces. After some preliminary misunderstandings Jesup entered into an agreement with the chiefs for a general capitulation. They agreed to assemble their people near Tampa Bay for transportation to the West. The Indians were collected in camps near Tampa Bay; twenty-six vessels were standing by in the bay to take them to New Orleans for further transfer to their new reservation. The sailing was delayed several times by the pleas of the chiefs that still more were to come in. Apparently the war was over. The volunteers and militia were sent home, and the marines were ordered north. Henderson departed on May 22 with all of the marines except two companies (189 men), left in command of Lieutenant Colonel Miller at Fort Brooke. The naval landing forces that had been holding forts returned to their ships and the squadron withdrew its support. Too much trust, however, had been placed in the word of the Indian chiefs.

### The War Renewed

Early in June the Seminoles began to run away from the concentration camps. Osceola was among the first to go and again stirred his people to go on the warpath. Warriors came into the emigration camp and carried away those who were unwilling to leave. Jesup reported that his whole campaign had proved a failure and asked to be relieved. The war was renewed and lasted for five more years. With reduced forces the Army again took up the thankless task. Jesup stayed on in command for several months. Colonel Zachary Taylor took command of part of the troops and made a campaign against the Seminoles, who had retreated farther into the interior—this time towards the Everglades. Taylor came upon them along the south shore of Lake Okeechobee on Christmas day, 1837, and fought a desperate battle in which he lost heavily. The Indians retreated farther south into the Everglades and Big Cypress Swamp. They had lost their chief, Osceola. Jesup captured him under a flag of truce and sent him to prison in Charleston where he died. Despite the efforts of nine thousand troops to run them down, the Seminoles held out in the fastnesses of the Everglades. As the troops could penetrate there only with the greatest difficulty, the Seminoles defied the entire forces of the country.

## With the Mosquito Fleet

The war assumed a different phase for the Navy and the Marine Corps. The command of the small marine battalion at Fort Brooke was taken over by Captain William Dulany in July, 1837. Some of Dulany's marines helped to escort Indians to the West. Several marine officers acted as Indian agents and conducted their troublesome charges by steamboats up the rivers as far as Fort Gibson in what is now Oklahoma. Early in 1838 the Navy again attempted to come to the rescue of the Army in dealing with the seemingly impossible task of rounding up the Seminoles in the Everglades. It organized a special detachment of small schooners, a small steamer, a few barges, and a large number of canoes manned by 160 sailors and marines under Lieutenant John T. McLaughlin, U.S.N. McLaughlin's mission was considered so important that he was removed from the authority of the West India Squadron and ordered to co-operate directly with General Zachary Taylor, then in command of the army in Florida. The strength of the naval detachment was increased shortly afterwards by giving it two regular companies of marines and raising its total strength to 541 men. Ships and additional men were gradually added and by June, 1841, the so-called "Mosquito Fleet" had 7 small vessels, 2 barges, 140 canoes, 68 officers, 130 marines, and an aggregate strength of 622. This little flotilla proceeded to carry out some of the most unusual tasks ever undertaken by a naval force. It was given the additional duty in June, 1839, of intercepting all communication between the Indians and boats operating from islands off the coast of Florida. Many former Spanish subjects were at that time trying to aid the Seminoles in every way possible.

No attempt will be made in this brief account to recite all of the operations carried on by McLaughlin's flotilla throughout the more than three years of its existence. Only a brief mention of its activities as a whole and a short description of the more important operations can be given. The remaining records are as a matter of fact too incomplete for detailed accounts. In March, 1838, a detachment of this force had a successful encounter with the hostile Indians near the headwaters of the Juniper River. They carried out many other missions. During the following year detachments of the Mosquito Fleet, prompted by reports of Indian activities and requests for protection by the settlers, took part in a number of operations along the eastern coast of Florida and into the Everglades. In July, 1839, Lieutenant Sloan, U.S.M.C., with a small detachment of marines, while on a boat expedition in the western edge of the Everglades, ran down and captured a group of Indians. In December the Mosquito Fleet was divided for a time into two detachments; each operated independently but co-operated with units of the Army.

Throughout the following year the task assigned to the Army was becoming more and more difficult. The Indians had dispersed in small groups and hidden themselves in the most inaccessible places of Southern Florida. Every known means was used to locate them, including the use of bloodhounds. The Army as well as the Mosquito Fleet underwent untold hardships in the then vast and almost impenetrable jungle. Their losses from disease were always many times greater than those from occasional encounters with the Indians. They were not deterred, however, by the many difficulties but vigorously pursued the Indians wherever they could be located.

In December, 1840, McLaughlin, with sixty marines under Sloan and ninety seamen, started out on one of his most extended expeditions into the Everglades. In co-operation with an army detachment McLaughlin made many trips by different routes into the Everglades, using various types of boats. Finally in March, 1841, he shifted to canoes in order to penetrate still farther into the less accessible parts of the swampy region. His expedition, which kept going until May, attracted considerable attention, and came to be called the "Florida Expedition." McLaughlin sent similar expeditions into the Everglades and Big Cypress Swamp during July and October. He established a base for these operations near the present location of Miami and called it Fort Dallas. In conjunction with the army he had another base at Fort Lauderdale. Both of these forts were at various times garrisoned by marines attached to McLaughlin's command.

Another extensive combined operation started out in November, 1841, with two companies of the Third Field Artillery and 150 marines and sailors from Fort Dallas. They went around Florida and up the Carlosahatchee River from the west to Lake Thompson, near Lake Okeechobee. They encountered the Indians near Lake Thompson. The enemy fled to the east; the expedition pushed on into Lake

Okeechobee. They then made their way east across the lake and the Everglades back to Fort Dallas. Commander John Rodgers undertook another extensive expedition; he went inland on February 15, 1842, and lived in canoes for fifty-eight days in various parts of the Everglades.

The West India Squadron continued to support the Army throughout the closing phase of the Second Seminole War. Occasionally its landing parties protected settlers who lived outside of the area occupied by the Army. Waldron with his marines from the *Constellation* continued to perform such missions. They protected the white settlers in the vicinity of Tallahassee for some time during the early months of 1838. Dulany's marines at Fort Brooke stayed there until April, when they were transferred by sea to Baton Rouge and to the Cherokee country for further duty with the Army. The Cherokees had agreed two years before to remove to their western reservation but had avoided, in every possible way, actually making the move. In order to effect their transfer, the Army concentrated a considerable force in the Cherokee territory, and General Scott, who was in command, issued what amounted to an ultimatum to proceed peacefully or they would be compelled to do so by all the available military forces. They gave in, and more than fifteen thousand went peacefully and unaccompanied to their new reservation in what is now Oklahoma, where a part of their tribe had settled a few years previously. Dulany's marines, Companies D and E of Henderson's former regiment, were then relieved from duty with the Army and, late in July, 1838, returned via Fort Cass, Tennessee to Washington.

Finally after long years of dreary effort, attempting in every possible way to run down the Seminoles, the task was practically given up, and those who could not be persuaded to remove to the West were given a small reservation in the Everglades where some of their descendants still live. The Florida naval expedition was gradually disbanded between May and August, 1842; the marines, attached to it, returned north in July.

During these operations against the Indians the Marine Corps as well as the Army gained valuable experience which was soon to prove useful in the more important and far-flung operations of the Mexican War. Nearly half of the marines who saw duty at various times in the Florida war were called a few years later to fight the Mexicans. Several army generals who were later successful leaders in the Mexican War got their first field experiences in fighting the Seminoles. The losses to the regular forces were perfectly staggering, when considered in proportion to the number of troops involved. The regular army alone lost 1,466 killed or dead from disease. The total dead of the Marine Corps was 61. A proportionate number of naval personnel died or were killed in various expeditions along the coast and into the interior of Florida. It should be remembered that these arduous and trying duties performed by the marines and the West India Squadron followed shortly after more than twelve years of intermittent fighting of pirates in the West Indies. Notwithstanding the many criticisms that were made from time to time, the country, as a whole, Congress, and the President of the United States showed due appreciation for the duties performed by the regular services in their many expressions of gratitude for the manner in which the duty was performed and by awarding commendations, brevet ranks, and added promotion to the personnel who served during the trying Indian campaigns.

### DISTRIBUTION OF THE U. S. MARINE CORPS, FEBRUARY, 1833

| STATION | COMMANDING OFFICER | OFFICERS | ENLISTED MEN |
|---|---|---|---|
| Headquarters | Lt. Col. Arch. Henderson | 4 | 64 |
| Navy Yard, D. C. | Capt. Levi Twiggs | 2 | 41 |
| Philadelphia, Pa. | Bt. Lt. Col. Samuel Miller | 5 | 60 |
| Gosport, Va. | Bt. Lt. Col. R. D. Wainwright | 6 | 74 |
| New York, N. Y. | Lt. Col. John M. Gamble | 6 | 83 |
| Boston, Mass. | Bt. Lt. Col. W. H. Freeman | 6 | 79 |
| Portsmouth, N. H. | Lt. Col. Samuel E. Watson | 3 | 60 |
| Pensacola, Fla. | Capt. Thomas A. Linton | 2 | 18 |
| *Receiving-Ships* | | | |
| *Franklin* | Capt. Joseph C. Hall | 1 | 30 |
| *Java* | Sgt. H. Theal | | 15 |
| *Sea Gull* | Cpl. Lewis Henry | | 8 |
| *Mediterranean Station* | | | |
| *United States* | Capt. John Harris | 3 | 52 |
| *Constellation* | Lt. L. N. Carter | 4 | 33 |
| *Brandywine* | Capt. Thomas S. English | 3 | 42 |
| *John Adams* | Sgt. Francis Wood | | 22 |
| *Brazil Station* | | | |
| *Lexington* | Sgt. Thomas Bradlee | | 24 |
| *Peacock* | Lt. H. W. Fowler | 1 | 20 |
| *Natchez* | Sgt. John Moore | | 21 |
| *West India Station* | | | |
| *Vandalia* | 1st Lt. Andrew Ross | 1 | 23 |
| *St. Louis* | Sgt. John Montgomery | | 21 |
| *Pacific Station* | | | |
| *Potomac* | Lt. Alvin Edson | 1 | 37 |
| *Falmouth* | Lt. J. L. C. Hardy | 1 | 23 |

## Chapter V

## THE MEXICAN WAR—OPERATIONS IN EASTERN MEXICO

THE approach of the Mexican War found the Marine Corps with only sixty-three officers and about 1,200 enlisted men available for all duties. A number of ships had recently been added to the Navy and, as usual, more calls were made for marines at sea. At the outbreak of the war about 75 per cent of the marines and most of the junior officers were on sea duty. The Navy had for some time considered it sound policy not to have more than 50 per cent of the marines at sea, as that same proportion was needed for the shore establishments of the naval service. To provide the necessary men for sea duty, the detachments in the United States had been reduced in size to the point of seriously handicapping every station. Repeated attempts had been made by Colonel Henderson to obtain an increase in personnel, but the Secretary of the Navy, George Bancroft, was not at all sympathetic and even insisted that the Marine Corps had more officers than it needed.

The Navy had fared somewhat better during the years preceding the Mexican War; several ships had been added to it. It was evident that a war with Mexico would be a decidedly one-sided affair with regard to naval operations because Mexico had practically no navy. If war came the Navy and Marine Corps would be called upon to co-operate in every possible way with the Army, establish an effective blockade of the Mexican coast, and carry on landing operations against places that could not be reached readily by the Army. Except for its almost total lack of bases, the Navy was fairly well equipped for blockade duty, but all except two of its ships were sailing vessels, and most of them drew too much water to enter many of the Mexican ports or rivers. For some time previous to the war the Home Squadron and the Pacific Squadron had been keeping a close watch along both coasts of Mexico by keeping a number of vessels in the waters of that country.

The war was preceded by a period of diplomatic negotiations for the peaceful settlement of the Texas problem and for the purchase of California from Mexico. In addition to the desire for annexing these two large areas to the United States, there was a strong sentiment in favor of procuring, by some means, the territory between the two which was then called New Mexico. When the war finally broke out, the general plan of campaign—so far as there was any definite plan—was to secure all three of these areas as soon as possible, and then to carry on such operations against Mexico as would be necessary to force the government of that country to conclude a peace transferring the desired territories to the United States.

Geographical conditions created two widely separated theaters of operations for the Navy and the Marine Corps: one composing the entire eastern coast of Mexico; the other, California, Lower California, and the western coast of Mexico. The operations in these two theaters of war were carried on practically independently of each other. Since there was almost no connection between the operations in the two areas, the history of the operations along the eastern coast of Mexico and with Scott's army is treated in this chapter and the operations in the western theater in the succeeding chapter.

The general situation outlined above and the desire of the United States for more territory suggest the actual course which the military and naval operations followed during the Mexican War. The Marine Corps functioned throughout the war in its usual capacity as a naval auxiliary and furnished troops for operations with the Army. Since the marines served in close co-operation with either the Army or the Navy in practically all of their participation in that war, it is necessary to narrate a number of the events which constitute part of the general military and naval history of the war in order to show in proper perspective the services rendered by the Marine Corps.

When Texas was annexed to the United States during the summer of 1845, a small army under Zachary Taylor, which for some time had been held in Louisiana in readiness for the purpose, promptly went into Texas to protect it from invasion by Mexico and from Indian outbreaks. The army first moved only as far as Corpus Christi and thus avoided for the time being the region between the Nueces and Rio Grande Rivers—the ownership of which was very much in dispute. Texas claimed the latter river as her southern boundary while Mexico insisted that the Nueces was the extreme limit of Texas. In February, 1846, Taylor was ordered to advance to the Rio Grande; after considerable delay he took up the march for his new position.

MAP OF MEXICO

## Landing at Point Isabel

When Taylor drew near to his new position he established a base of operations and a depot at Point Isabel, located a few miles north of the mouth of the Rio Grande. He then reorganized his forces and advanced to the Rio Grande and began building a fort just opposite Matamoros. War had not yet been declared, and Taylor had orders to avoid hostilities, if possible, but to protect Texas against an invasion by the Mexicans. The Mexicans considered the whole of Texas a part of their territory and were especially insistent on their ownership of the disputed area. Arista, the Mexican commander, had approximately six thousand troops—more than double Taylor's strength —in the general vicinity of Matamoros. The Mexicans attempted to cut Taylor's line of communication, by crossing the Rio Grande about ten miles below Matamoros and starting northward. Taylor had carelessly left his base at Point Isabel practically undefended and had made no efforts to protect his line of communication. Shortly after the Mexicans crossed the river, Taylor learned of the movement and immediately started back with most of his troops to Point Isabel in order to protect his base and to counter the enemy's move. As he approached Point Isabel he found out that the Mexicans were between him and the part of his force which he had left on the Rio Grande constructing a fort. Taylor turned on the enemy and on May 8 defeated them in the Battle of Palo Alto and again, on the following day, in the Battle of Resaca de la Palma.

The Home Squadron, which had been supporting Taylor's army in its advance to the Rio Grande, was lying off Point Isabel while Taylor was thus engaged with the enemy. The naval forces knew that Taylor's army was greatly outnumbered by the Mexicans; therefore they feared the worst when they had no other information than the distant reports of artillery in the Battle of Palo Alto. The ships made ready a landing force to assist in holding Point Isabel in the event that the Mexicans advanced on it. The excitement which prevailed during the tense situation on board the ships of the squadron and the disembarking of the landing force was vividly described by an eye-witness, the chaplain of the *Cumberland*.

The firing continued—at times, louder and quicker—and now, the smoke rose in clouds, distinctly on the view. The land spreading from Point Isabel to Matamoros over which the march lies, is an extensive plain; and the prevailing conviction on board the ships, was that this point, from which rose up the pillars of smoke, *was the field of battle,* some twelve miles distant; and that General Taylor had there been met by all the Mexican forces. The fate of the day, which could not yet be told, was now to be awaited, with anxiety and the greatest solicitude. Indeed, as the hours advanced, the reports of cannon seemed to be yet more distinct, and yet more near, and the volumes of smoke yet more dense, and receding nearer towards ourselves and Point Isabel; and if General Taylor's army was indeed retreating, we could fancy we heard the repeated and rapid discharges of artillery, and the successive volleys of musketry, as the rear guard covered the retreat. I have seldom seen greater sympathy and ingenuous solicitude lined on the faces of a collection of officers, than were now traced in the features of numbers, gathered on the poop-deck of the *Cumberland*. Every one seemed to feel that they would hasten to the rescue, and add their force to the army, in its critical circumstances. '*I can land 250 men* in fifteen minutes,' said one of the captains of one of the smaller ships of the squadron. Other ships could send their complement; and had the order come, every heart would have leaped for the shore, and volunteers have amounted to more than the ships could spare. The order, before the sun went down, did come to land a number of the ships' crews, with all the marine guard of the squadron, to give defence at the encampment at Point Isabel, should it be needed. A steamer came off, and the ships' boats took the men to the steamer—all being enthusiastic for the expedition. And when the number selected for the shore had all been safely embarked from the ships to the steamer, the boat put her wheels in motion and rounded by the stern of the *Cumberland*. The remainder of the crew, still aboard the ship, as the steamer approached us, were ordered to lay aloft, 'to cheer ship.' Nor had the order fallen from the lips of the officer of the deck, before the shrouds of the frigate were literally covered by our men, with their faces outward.

'Stand by,' cried the Lieutenant—'Cheer away!' and a volume of voices was sent over the waves, as the men swung their hats above their heads, and gave the three times hurrah to their leaving shipmates and comrades. The frigate *Raritan,* at our windward, watching our motions, had also sent her men to the rattlings, and their voices joined in with the loud echo of a thousand hurrahs, which sent a thrill home to the heart, such as hardly aught else of earth may equal, as back came the three cheers of the mass of men now crowding the decks, above and below, of the steamer, and told the enthusiasm, and the excitement, and the sublimity of the moment! Onward the steamer went, bearing these heroes, in imagination at least and in reality if the opportunity should present for displaying their deeds, even to a recklessness before any opposing enemy. Without accident, they were soon disembarked, at the encampment on Point Isabel.

The landing force, commanded by Captain F. H. Gregory, U.S.N., consisted of five hundred marines and sailors taken principally from the *Cumberland, Raritan, Potomac,* and *John Adams.* As initially organized, it retained the marines with each of the ship's companies in violation of the approved squadron plan for forming the marines into a separate battalion under the senior marine officer of the landing force. When the irregularity was called to the attention of Captain Gregory, he promptly rectified it and formed the marines, totaling 145 officers and enlisted men, into a battalion under First Lieutenant William Lang. The marine detachments from the *Cumberland* and *Raritan* each acted as companies, while those from the *John Adams* and *Potomac* were combined to form a single company of about the same size. Lang's little battalion was assigned to defend the center sector on the side of the fort facing the enemy as shown on the sketch on page 112. The sketch (submitted at the time and now in the archives of the Marine Corps) also indicates the disposition of the remainder of the landing force while assigned to the defense of Fort Polk, as the enclosure about the depot was called. In addition to defending their sector the marines did the guard duty for the garrison and carried out extensive training which proved invaluable to them during later operations. All danger of Mexican attack had passed by the 13th, and the landing force began to withdraw to the squadron.

The battles of Palo Alto and Resaca de la Palma violently disclosed to the President, to Congress, and to the country in general that war actually existed with Mexico. Congress soon admitted this fact by declaring war. Congress authorized the President to call for fifty thousand volunteers and increase the number of soldiers in each company from sixty-four to one hundred. Despite recommendations by the regular services, Congress allowed no other additions of personnel to the regular army and made no additional allowances for the Marine Corps.

### Expedition up the Rio Grande

The operations of the Mexican army obviously constituted an act of war. Our Navy therefore began operations in open prosecution of war. Part of the Home Squadron was immediately dispatched to blockade Vera Cruz and other important ports; some of the ships remained in the vicinity of Point Isabel to protect the Army's communications and otherwise assist it. Taylor followed the Mexicans to the Rio Grande. On the morning of May 18 a detachment of two hundred seamen and marines from the *Cumberland* and *Potomac*, commanded by Captain John H. Aulick, U.S.N., went up the Rio Grande in boats for a distance of about fifteen miles to cooperate with a few companies of soldiers under Lieutenant Colonel Wilson in establishing a post at Burrita on the south side of the river. These troops proved to be the first to invade Mexico; Taylor's army at Matamoros did not begin crossing the river until an hour or two after they landed. Aulick's naval detachment remained at Burrita for two days. By that time the Mexican army was in full

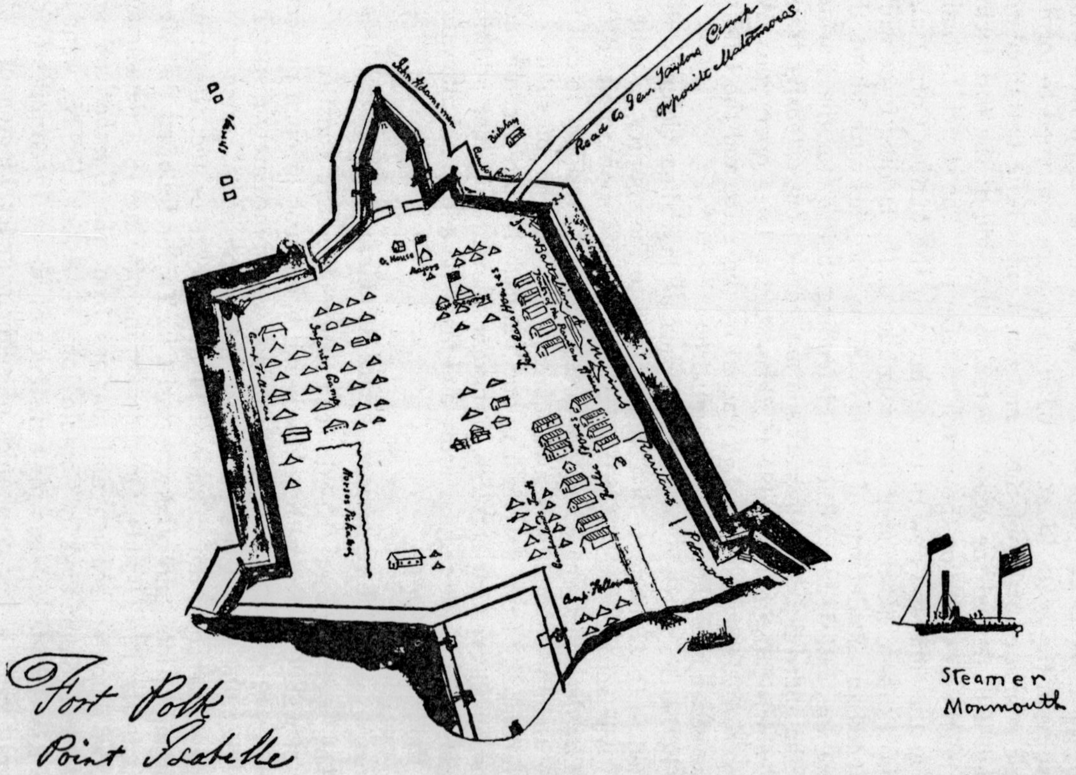

FORT POLK, 1846

retreat towards San Luis Potosi, and there being no further need for the navy force ashore, it returned to its ships on May 20. Both ships sailed for Pensacola to reprovision and fit out for extensive tours of duty along the Mexican coast.

## Attacks on Alvarado

The port of Alvarado, located a few miles southeast of the fleet anchorage which had been established at Anton Lizardo, near Vera Cruz, was second only in importance to Vera Cruz as a place of entry for war supplies for the Mexican Army. Alvarado proved very difficult to blockade effectively with large ships because of the broad bar covering the approaches to it. Commodore David Conner, commanding the Home Squadron, was bent on an early capture of Alvarado, which proved very difficult as the town was strongly defended. Besides, Conner had insufficient shallow draft vessels which could pass over the bar and attack its defenses. Nevertheless, he attempted to attack the strongly fortified place on August 7, 1846.

The steamers *Mississippi* and *Princeton* bombarded the defenses of Alvarado with more or less effect for about six hours. At the same time small schooner gunboats and pulling boats, containing a landing force of marines and sailors, attempted to cross the bar and go up the river to attack the fort under the protection of the fire from the large ships. The current in the river was so strong that the attacking force made little headway, and, at nightfall, finding themselves under heavy musket fire from the shore, with no prospect of success, they withdrew to their ships. They were especially chagrined by this failure because British naval ships witnessed the unfortunate affair, and because they failed to produce material for newspaper noise at home. The Administration was most anxious to popularize the war; they seriously needed a victory at this particular time. The sting of failure was not long to be endured, however; Conner made plans for another attack to capture Alvarado as soon as the necessary men and suitable vessels were available.

The squadron was particularly embarrassed by its lack of small steamers. These were necessary for operations against ports which were usually near the mouths of rivers with their entrances invariably obstructed with bars covered by only a few feet of water. Early in October the new small steamer *Vixen*, which had been built for that kind of an operation, the steam revenue cutter *McLane*, which had been ordered to duty with the Navy, and some small schooner gunboats joined the squadron. With the aid of these vessels Conner made a second attack against Alvarado on October 15. A storming party of marines and sailors from the *Cumberland*

and *Raritan* had been assembled on the *Mississippi,* under Captain French Forrest of that ship, for the purpose of landing whenever support was needed for the close-in smaller attacking vessels. The *Vixen,* with Conner on board, took two of the schooner gunboats in tow, while the *McLane* towed three others. Conner waited outside the bar until 2 P.M. for the usual afternoon breeze in order to maneuver successfully the steamers with the cumbersome tows. The hoped-for breeze did not spring up, but Conner started the attack as planned, notwithstanding.

Alvarado was defended at the mouth of the river by a fort which covered the bar with its fire; three or four smaller forts farther up the river, in addition to two armed brigs, an armed schooner, and two gunboats, were in positions to defend the channel against invaders.

The *Mississippi,* with her long guns, opened fire on the fort at the mouth of the river, while Conner on the *Vixen* led the attacking force over the bar. The *Vixen* with the gunboats in tow next opened fire on the fort; but the *McLane,* which was following, grounded on the bar in the midst of breakers and cast off its tows, which were unable to make their way in against the strong current. The firing upon the fort appeared to have little effect. When Forrest on the *Mississippi* saw the *McLane* aground, he disembarked his storming party and started to the assistance of the Commodore. Before Forrest could get into action, however, the *Vixen* with its tow gave up the attack and stood back out to sea. By this time the *McLane* had got clear, but Conner, much to the chagrin of his forces, called off the attack and returned to the fleet anchorage at Anton Lizardo. The second failure to take Alvarado tended greatly to improve the enemy's morale. The Mexicans were always ready to claim our slightest reverse as a great victory; they hailed the second repulse of our forces as a great triumph. Conner's plan for taking Alvarado did not include a strong landing force, which could have been put ashore a few miles to the west of the town to advance overland against it while he was attempting to attack from the sea. Such tactics were later resorted to by Perry with great success. Conner, however, does not appear to have had much confidence in his men fighting on shore. No further attempts were made to take Alvarado until after the army had landed at Vera Cruz. These attempts are described later.

### First Expedition up the Tabasco River

Immediately after the second attempt to take Alvarado, Commodore M. C. Perry was given a detachment of the squadron and ordered to capture the town of Frontera, at the mouth of the Tabasco River, and then operate up that river against San Juan Bautista—the capital of the state of Tabasco and an important trading center, held by a considerable force of Mexicans. Conner needed control of a river near the fleet anchorage for supplying fresh water; Frontera also offered a supply of cattle. Then, too, considerable trade was getting past the blockade through that port.

Preparatory to operations against Frontera, a detachment of two hundred marines and sailors was assembled on the steamer *Mississippi* and armed and equipped for an extensive landing force and boat expedition. The marine detachments of the *Raritan* and forty-two marines from the *Cumberland* formed a part of the special detachment; Captain Alvin Edson had by that means a squadron marine battalion assembled under his command for the anticipated operations ashore. Perry took his flagship, the *Mississippi*, and the small steamers which had been used in the Alvarado affair. Bad weather delayed the operation for a few days. The landing force aboard the *Mississippi* was transferred to the small vessels and to boats which were formed in tows behind the steamers.

Finally the weather was favorable on October 23, and the attacking force stood in over the bar for an attack on Frontera. When it reached a suitable position to start an attack, Perry made a demand for the town to surrender; the Mexicans yielded without resistance. Perry captured several small vessels, including a river steamer which his expeditionary force immediately put into use.

Perry anticipated that the enemy's main force at San Juan Bautista, about seventy miles up the river, would begin extensive operations for defending themselves; he hurriedly reorganized his forces for a dash to that place. He used the captured Mexican steamer for towing two schooners and a number of barges filled with men of the expeditionary force, while the *Vixen,* his flagship, took in tow another schooner gunboat. The expedition started up the river the next morning and steamed all day and night without serious incident. At 9 A.M. the second day it encountered the first enemy resistance at Fort Accachappa, a few miles below San Juan Bautista. Perry had expected resistance at that place; he disembarked the landing force a mile below the fort and marched overland to attack it, while his gunboats prepared for a bombardment to support the troops ashore. Again the show of force was sufficent; the Mexicans fled. Perry's men spiked the guns of the fort; the landing force re-embarked, and the expedition resumed its advance.

Perry's force reached San Juan Bautista at noon. His armed vessels anchored in line of battle within close range of the city;

Perry summoned it to surrender. The Mexican commander refused to capitulate and told Perry in a spirit of bravado to open fire as soon as he pleased. Three shots from the *Vixen* brought down the flag over the city; Perry then inquired as to whether or not the place had surrendered. The reply being in the negative, the landing force, under the cover of the armed vessels, went ashore and with little resistance captured the city. Scattered musketry fire only was directed against the landing force and the vessels.

The enemy forces apparently had only scattered, and Perry, not wishing to expose his men to a night attack in the town, re-embarked them. The expedition remained in position throughout the night, covering the city with its guns. On the following morning the Mexican forces resumed firing on the vessels, and Perry bombarded the city. The Mexicans soon ran up a white flag and the firing ceased. Perry did not wish to do serious damage to the city, even though the Mexican commander appeared entirely indifferent about the matter. As Perry did not have sufficient men to hold San Juan Bautista, he rounded up the vessels and boats which he had captured and started to retire. The Mexicans vigorously attacked one of the prize boats which was being operated by a naval crew. Perry again bombarded the town, and the firing ceased, but the navy lieutenant, in command of the captured vessel, was mortally wounded in the affair. The expedition with its prizes then proceeded down the river and arrived at Frontera on the evening of October 26. It remained there two days and then returned the marines and sailors of the expeditionary force to the *Mississippi*. Perry went back to Anton Lizardo, leaving only a steamer and schooner to maintain a blockade at Frontera.

### THE TAMPICO EXPEDITION

When Perry and his detachment of the squadron returned from the Tabasco expedition, they found an expedition to Tampico had been ordered by the Navy Department in order that that important place might be in our possession when needed as a new base for Taylor's army, which was advancing rapidly into Mexico from the north. Conner was most anxious to make another attempt at Alvarado to offset the previous failures there, but his orders placed the Tampico task as number one on his calendar. Perry again supplied his small vessels with ammunition and other stores for a river expedition and apparently left nothing undone which would insure the success of the venture. It was anticipated that the city of Tampico would surrender upon an extensive show of force, but Conner made every preparation to take the place, if necessary, by a regular landing force operation. On November 10 two frigates sailed away on the new task while the *Mississippi* and *Princeton* and the small steamers *Vixen* and *Spitfire*, with a number of schooners in tow, left the fleet anchorage the following day. The *Cumberland*, which stayed behind, sent her men aloft to cheer away the prospective heroes and rendered honors similar to those now rendered to departing men-of-war.

The expedition arrived off Tampico November 14 and immediately began to organize for the attack. A landing force of three hundred marines and sailors embarked on the small steamers, schooners, and a number of barges and prepared to cross the bar under the personal command of Commodore Conner. The *Spitfire*, flying Conner's broad pennant, towed the schooners *Petrel* and *Reefer* and a number of boats loaded with seamen and marines from the *Cumberland, Mississippi,* and *Princeton*. The *Vixen* flying Perry's pennant, towed the schooners *Bonita* and *Monata* and five boats loaded with men of the landing force. In addition to the two broad pennants, a number of other flags were flying. All this gave the expedition a pageant-like appearance. The marines in this expedition were again formed into a battalion under the squadron marine officer, Captain Alvin Edson.

The formation lined up just off the bar, and at 11 A.M. when a gun was fired from the *Raritan* as a signal to attack, the expedition headed for the mouth of the Panuco River. Upon entering the mouth of the river they passed, on the north bank, a fort which showed no signs of being occupied. A little farther along a boat carrying a flag of truce met the expedition; a deputation of citizens on it reported that the Mexican armed forces had left the vicinity; the citizens then surrendered the town to Conner. He took possession of five small Mexican vessels that had been abandoned by the enemy. His troops landed, took control of the city of Tampico, and established a temporary garrison composed principally of marines. Edson was placed in charge of the city. Most of the navy personnel then returned on board the ships lying off Tampico.

Shortly after taking possession of the city, Conner received information that the retreating Mexican forces had left a considerable store of munitions, some other supplies, and some boats at Panuco, about eighty miles up the river. A small expeditionary force of twenty marines and twelve sailors, under Edson, embarked upon the steamers *Spitfire* and *Petrel* and started up the river (November 17). It reached Panuco in the early morning of November 19; Edson's marines and sailors landed, took possession of the town, destroyed a large quantity of Mexican stores—including several guns and some ammunition—and captured some other stores which they later took back to Tampico for the use of their forces. Edson's force remained at Panuco until the afternoon of the following day, when it re-embarked and returned to Tampico with the captured boats and stores.

The War Department had anticipated the capture of Tampico and already had ordered its occupation by the Army. The steamer *Neptune* arrived off Tampico from Texas, with five hundred troops on board under Colonel Gates. Gates's forces were landed and ready to assume full charge of the situation by November 23. At 10:30 A.M. that day Gates's troops and Edson's marines were formed on the city square and Edson with proper ceremonies turned over Tampico to Gates. Edson's marine battalion remained on shore, assisting in the occupation, until early in December. Meanwhile, additional army troops arrived to assist in holding Tampico.

The successful operation on the Panuco River gave our government and newspapers good material for publicity and appears to have spurred the Home Squadron on to greater efforts. The Army having assured the complete denial of Tampico to the enemy, Conner was free to proceed with the closing of other important ports. He withdrew the larger vessels of the squadron from Tampico for other duty. The *Spitfire* remained for a time in the vicinity in support of the Army.

## Vera Cruz

The operations of Taylor's army in northern Mexico had proceeded without any very definite plan. As fast as new troops were raised they were sent by sea and concentrated in southern Texas near the Rio Grande. Taylor moved his army up the Rio Grande to Camargo and established a line of communication with steamboats up that river. In August, 1846, after considerable delay in collecting stores, troops, and trains, Taylor's army advanced on Monterey where the Mexican army had taken up a strong defensive position. His little army attacked the enemy of nearly double its strength, defeated them at every turn, and finally made them agree to evacuate Monterey and retire farther south. Taylor then continued his advance into Mexico as far as Saltillo and pushed his detachments still farther south.

Towards the end of 1846 the President and the War Department began to formulate more aggressive plans to force Mexico to sign the desired treaty of peace. They decided first to take Vera Cruz, then, if Mexico did not come to terms, to advance on and capture the Mexican capital. General Winfield Scott, who thus far had been kept from field duty on account of political jealousy, was selected to command a force to take Vera Cruz and was given full power to requisition practically all troops he needed from Taylor's army in northern Mexico and from army units in southern Texas. Taylor was directed to assume a defensive role while Scott gathered his troops near the mouth of the Rio Grande preparatory to transporting them to Vera Cruz. Tremendous preparations were made for the expedition; a large fleet of transports was assembled; and all necessary equipment for landing operations, including siege guns, was provided. The expedition moved first to Lobos Island for final training, equipping, and formulating joint plans with the Navy.

In the meantime Santa Anna, the Mexican President and commander in chief, had assembled at San Luis Potosi an army which numbered at least three times Taylor's force. Santa Anna determined to crush Taylor's small force before Scott had time to attack Vera Cruz. He advanced and attacked Taylor's army at Buena Vista, but, after what was doubtless the most desperate battle of the war, the Mexicans were held off and so roughly handled that Santa Anna began a retreat which soon developed into a rout.

The joint operation of Scott's army and Conner's squadron for the taking of Vera Cruz was carefully planned and was executed with a high degree of co-ordination and precision. Conner convoyed the transports to the fleet anchorage at Anton Lizardo where they made final preparations and last minute plans. Shortly before the landing, the troops were transferred to naval vessels, taking with them only their light equipment. Each army division was placed aboard two or more of the vessels of the squadron. The First Division (about 4,500 men under Brigadier General Worth), embarked on the *Raritan, Princeton,* and the army transport *Edith.* The surf boats, especially provided for the landing, were towed by the steamers. The expeditionary force thus disposed proceeded (March 9, 1847) from its anchorage to a position off the beach two or three miles southeast of Vera Cruz.

The ships carrying the troops anchored; the boats came first to the ships carrying the First Division. Five gunboats and the two small steamers formed in line parallel to the beach to cover the approach of Worth's division to the shore and later to cover by supporting fire its advance from the beach. The First Division, with the squadron marine battalion (between two and three hundred marines under Edson) attached to the Third Artillery, disembarked into the boats, rendezvoused in the lee of the *Princeton,* and then lined up in rear of the covering small vessels. The ships of the squadron shelled the beach; the division headed for the shore as fast as the navy crews could row the boats. Worth's division landed at sunset without a single mishap and without meeting any resistance.

Worth immediately took up the advance and occupied a line on some hills about a mile and a half inland to cover the landing of the succeeding waves of troops. The boats returned to the squadron and by repeated trips transported the remaining three divisions ashore by 10 P.M. Scott's troops then formed a line of investment extending in the rear of the city from the landing beach to Vergara on the opposite side of Vera Cruz, thus completely cutting off its land communications. After landing artillery, horses, and heavy stores next day, the army took up a systematic siege of the city, which was defended by an army of approximately six thousand Mexicans occupying the strong fortress of San Juan de Ulloa and forts along the walls surrounding the city. The Mexicans offered a stubborn resistance and kept up a continual shellfire on the American positions. Scott's heavy artillery being insufficient, Conner landed a number of navy guns. A combined army and navy bombardment breached the wall and materially assisted in breaking the morale of the inhabitants, who eventually persuaded the Mexican commander to surrender the city on March 29.

The squadron marine battalion under Edson had served with Worth's division throughout the siege and advanced with his troops as the investment of the city progressed, moving closer into entrenched positions near the city walls. After the city surrendered, the marines returned to their ships, while Scott hurriedly moved his army into the mountains west of the city in order to avoid the danger of yellow fever—the season for which was rapidly approaching. In spite of the fact that Edson's marine battalion was under fire from the Mexican artillery for about twenty days, only one marine was killed during the operation. Scott expressed a high appreciation for the services of this "handsome detachment of marines" during the siege of Vera Cruz.

## Capture of Alvarado

With the city of Vera Cruz in possession of the American forces and the Army available to support his squadron, Conner decided to make a third attempt to take Alvarado. Major General John A. Quitman with three regiments of volunteers, a squadron of dragoons, and a section of artillery marched overland on March 30 to cut off the retreat of the enemy occupying the place, and, if necessary, attack the town from the rear. Conner sent the *Scourge* to blockade Alvarado until he arrived to co-operate with Quitman's force, which could not get there for several days. Lieutenant Hunter, in command of the *Scourge,* anxious for his vessel to make good its name, immediately upon arriving vigorously attacked the forts at Alvarado. His first assault was unsuccessful, but he repeated the attack the following day, and the enemy evacuated the forts. With his little vessel he proceeded up the river, captured several enemy vessels, but learned that the enemy had fled up the river. Hunter left a small garrison in Alvarado and continued on up the river to Tlacotalpam, which also surrendered to him. The Mexican forces whom Quitman had not been able to intercept escaped with most of their supplies and many horses.

When Quitman's force and Conner with part of the squadron arrived at Alvarado, they found Hunter in full possession. Useless to say, the wrath of these two higher-ranking officers fell upon the impetuous Hunter. He was court-martialed and dismissed from the Navy for disobedience of orders. Quitman's thwarted opportunity to obtain horses and gain glory afforded a great deal of amusement to the American public. The New York *Sun,* May 7, 1848, published the following poem:

> On came each gay and gallant ship,
> On came the troops like mad, oh!
> But not a soul was there to whip,
> Unless they fought a shadow.
>
> Five sailors sat within a fort,
> In leading of a lad, oh!
> And thus was spoiled the pretty sport
> Of taking Alvarado.

By that time forces were available for the permanent occupation of Alvarado. Captain Isaac Mayo, U.S.N., was made naval governor of Alvarado and vicinity and was given a detachment of marines and sailors to garrison the city. Mayo had no further trouble at Alvarado, but during May, 1847, he found it necessary to go up a near-by rapid river in small boats with an expedition of eighty marines and sailors to drive an enemy force from the village of Holescogan. The expedition was attacked in the boats on the return trip down the river after accomplishing its mission, and six of the men were wounded. At various times during the remainder of 1847 the marine detachment at Alvarado was increased by small contingents from the squadron. The garrison was further increased to a battalion of marines in 1848; its further activities are mentioned below.

## Capture of Tuxpan

With the fall of Vera Cruz and the capture of Alvarado, the only remaining important port on the eastern coast of Mexico not in the possession of the American forces was Tuxpan. That port was defended by two forts on the right bank of the river and one on the left. These forts, which contained among other guns some taken from the *Truxton,* which had been wrecked there several months before, were defended by General Cos with 650 Mexican troops. After the several naval landing operations, Commodore Perry conceived the idea of forming a landing force brigade, organized from parts of the crews of the ships of the squadron, and giving it special drills and training in landing force operations. The fleet marines under Edson were assigned as one of the battalions of this brigade. The brigade then at the fleet anchorage prepared for extensive operations against Tuxpan. The ships which were not to take part in the operation transferred their contingents of the brigade aboard the ships assigned to take part. Perry with some small schooners and schooner gunboats in tow of the *Mississippi* sailed for Lobos Island, where his force was joined by the *Raritan,* a number of additional vessels, and additional contingents for the brigade. The brigade, as finally organized for the operation, consisted of an aggregate force of 1,489 officers, marines, and seamen, supported by four pieces of land artillery, with Captain Samuel N. Breese, U.S.N., in command.

On April 15 the attacking force moved into position off Tuxpan Reef, but a norther blew up and delayed operations for three days when final arrangements were made to attack Tuxpan. The brigade was transferred to the small vessels and into thirty barges, preparatory to crossing the bar. With small steamers towing the gunboats and barges, the expedition, led by the *Spitfire* with Perry on board, headed for the mouth of the river in the early morning of April 18. The attacking force entered the river and, as soon as they reached the first enemy positions, they encountered a vigorous fire. The steamers cast off their tows and steamed rapidly up the river, shelling the enemy's position while passing. The gunboats followed under sail, doing likewise. The landing force in barges landed and assaulted the enemy positions from the flanks and rear, while the small vessels covered the enemy with fire from the front. The enemy were, by that method, easily driven from their positions. The *Truxton* guns were recaptured; the forts with their remaining guns were destroyed. Perry's entire expedition lost only fourteen killed and wounded. He left a small detachment of marines, supported by the *Albany* and *Reefer,* to garrison Tuxpan. The remainder of the expedition withdrew to its ships and returned to the fleet anchorage. Perry immediately began preparations for other operations farther to the east.

## THE SECOND TABASCO EXPEDITION

The control of the Tabasco River and of Frontera, at the mouth of that river, had been left to blockading vessels since Perry's first dash up the river. Continuing his thoroughgoing policy as soon as men and ships were available, Perry stopped at Frontera on May 15, 1847, with a part of his squadron, took possession of the town, opened the port under American control, invested a naval officer as governor of the district, and left the *Bonita* as a guard ship. The marine guard of the *Mississippi* under Lieutenant Shuttleworth had assisted in taking the town and remained to garrison it for several days.

Since Perry's first visit to San Juan Bautista, the Mexicans had reoccupied it with a considerable force and had not only fortified the town but a number of places along the river below it. These Mexican positions protected a considerable flow of supplies into Mexico from Central America. Perry determined to take the place as soon as possible because it was the last important point through which foreign commerce was being carried on with Mexico. Perry assembled his naval brigade (then having a strength of 1,173 including Edson's battalion of marines) on fifteen ships of his squadron and sailed for the mouth of the Tabasco River on June 13, 1847. When he arrived off the bar, before entering the river, Perry, as usual, transferred the naval brigade to the small steamers, schooners, and boats. The expedition started up the river on the 14th; it proceeded in the usual manner and encountered no resistance until it reached a point twelve miles below San Juan Bautista, when it was fired upon one evening just before dark. At about the same time, the vessels began to encounter obstructions which the enemy had placed in the river. Firing from the vessels soon stopped the enemy fire and the obstructions were removed, but the flotilla lay in that position for the night.

Perry resumed his advance the following morning and encountered a second more strongly fortified position which he thought inadvisable to pass with his brigade on the flotilla. He had the small boats manned, disembarked with his brigade into them, and "with three hearty cheers pushed for the shore, landed, and formed in separate columns on the bank." Despite difficult landing conditions the brigade was ashore with its seven pieces of artillery in the short space of ten minutes. Within fifteen minutes it had brought off more artillery from one of the small vessels and was ready to advance on the city. The vessels then steamed ahead up the river and supported the marching troops.

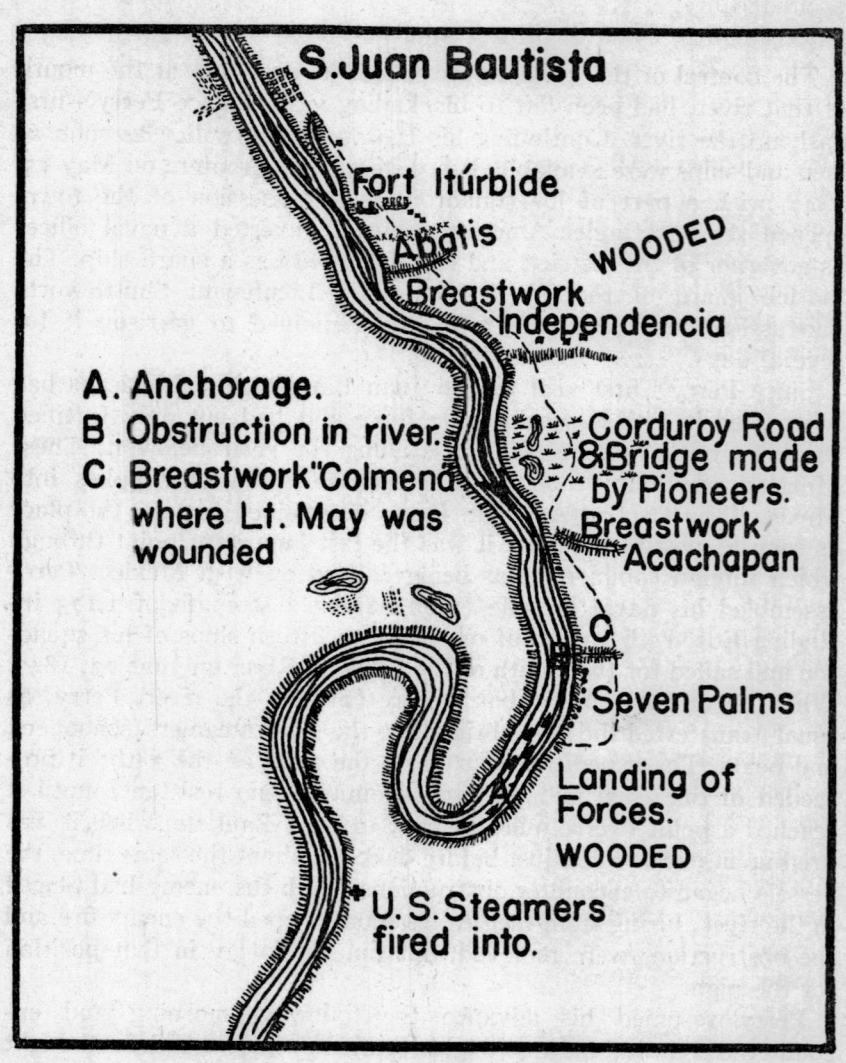

```
S. Juan Bautista
  Fort Itúrbide
  Abatis
  Breastwork         WOODED
  Independencia

A. Anchorage.
B. Obstruction in river.
C. Breastwork "Colmena"      Corduroy Road
   where Lt. May was         & Bridge made
   wounded                   by Pioneers.
                             Breastwork
                             Acachapan

                             Seven Palms

                             Landing of
                             Forces.
                             WOODED

      U.S. Steamers
      fired into.
```

SECOND TABASCO EXPEDITION

The steamers proceeded up the river for about a mile. There they encountered the enemy's main works, defended by about three hundred men. The steamers opened fire, and, when the naval brigade approached, the Mexicans retreated. The expedition then moved on up the river with the brigade marching under the support of the vessels. About 4 P.M. they reached the city and found it defended by about four hundred Mexicans, who promptly retired upon the approach of Perry's superior force. Perry then occupied San Juan Bautista with his naval brigade and took possession of the available public quarters. By this time the Navy had become very efficient as land forces; the officers and men of Perry's brigade showed considerable enthusiasm over being a small army. The expedition had been able to brush aside about fourteen hundred Mexicans in the brief operations. Perry destroyed the works that defended the town as well as all military stores that he found.

The enemy retreated but not far enough to make the task of holding the place an easy one. Perry garrisoned San Juan Bautista with about 300 sailors and 115 marines and re-embarked the remainder of the brigade aboard vessels lying in the river. They held the town without being molested by the enemy until the night of June 25 when about 150 Mexicans attacked but were repulsed without loss to the Americans. Small bands of Mexicans hung around the town and made it necessary for the garrison to keep constantly on the alert. On June 30 a force of 500 Mexicans was reported at the village of Temulty, about three miles from San Juan Bautista. Commander Bigelow with a detachment of 240 men from the brigade went to look for the reported enemy. Bigelow's detachment was ambushed by the Mexicans, who poured musketry fire into the column on both flanks until his artillery got into action and drove off the Mexicans. Bigelow attempted to pursue the fleeing Mexicans but was unable to engage them again. On hearing the firing of the encounter, two steamers tried to go up the river to support Bigelow; both grounded, however, and did not arrive until after the engagement was over. They landed a detachment which marched to the village of Temulty but found Bigelow's detachment had gone. They returned to the steamers without meeting the enemy. This engagement was the end of hostilities in that vicinity.

After leaving a garrison supported by some of the small steamers at San Juan Bautista, Perry rejoined the squadron with most of the vessels of the flotilla. The danger from Mexican soldiers was found to be of minor importance compared to the dreaded yellow fever which soon broke out in the garrison. Perry had anticipated this difficulty, and, according to his plan, the garrison was again withdrawn late in July. As proof of the terribly unhealthful conditions, thirty-six of the *Mississippi's* sixty-six marines were sick on July 22 when they left the town. By this time, however, Perry's control of the coast and the situation in the interior of Mexico prevented the Mexicans from again building up a strong force on the Tabasco River.

## Marines with Scott's Army

As previously noted, Congress proposed that the war should be fought—at least on shore—by short-time volunteers. Congress well knew that the first contingent of one-year volunteers would be due for discharge early in 1847 but made no provision for their replacement, in spite of the fact that the President and the War Department had strongly recommended at the beginning of the session meeting in December, 1846, that immediate provision be made for the replacement of these men. After considerable political play and other delays, Congress finally authorized (March 30, 1847) the raising of ten new regiments and gave the Marine Corps a modest increase of twelve company officers and one thousand enlisted men. But many delays occurred before the new regiments reached the theater of operations.

Almost immediately after taking Vera Cruz, Scott took up the advance on Mexico City in order to get his troops out of the yellow fever zone. Santa Anna moved his army from San Luis Potosi to stop Scott's advance on Mexico City. Scott's army encountered the Mexicans at Cerro Gordo soon after entering the mountains, brushed them aside with little difficulty, and continued the advance. He pushed on to Puebla where he rested and reorganized his army. He had lost many men in the siege of Vera Cruz and in the Battle of Cerro Gordo. Still more had been lost or made ineffective by disease and the rigors of campaign. Worst of all, the enlistments of 3,700 men were about to expire, and only enough of them to make one small company could be persuaded to extend their enlistments. After sending the men due for discharge to the rear, Scott found his army reduced to a little over seven thousand men. To advance farther into Mexico with his much depleted forces, Scott believed to be out of the question; there was nothing left for him to do but to remain in Puebla until fresh troops could arrive. Fresh troops did not begin to arrive in Mexico until June, and none reached Puebla until July 8. But the addition of these troops gave Scott only slightly more than eight thousand effectives while more than two thousand were sick.

Shortly after the increase in the strength of the Marine Corps had been authorized, it began recruiting and made the authorized increase of officers. Many delays followed: the organization of a marine contingent for duty with Scott's army was not ordered until May 21, 1847. Then the Secretary of the Navy directed the formation of a marine regiment composed of the newly-allowed enlisted men and the marine detachments from the Home Squadron. By this time the naval forces had gained almost complete control of the eastern coast of Mexico, and Scott's army was considered the place for all dependable troops. The marines for his army were organized into a skeletonized regiment, with the expectation of adding volunteers and marines from the squadron after arriving in Mexico. Lieutenant Colonel Samuel E. Watson was placed in command, with Major Levi Twiggs second in command; both were veterans of the War of 1812 and rather advanced in years for such assignment. Major William Dulany also joined and was the only one of the field officers to survive the war. The regiment was assembled at Fort Hamilton, near New York. With the exception of a small contingent of experienced noncommissioned officers and practically every available officer of the Corps, the regiment was made up of recruits. All posts in the United States were cut down to a small sergeant's guard as had been done during the Florida Indian wars.

The regiment, having had little or no training, sailed for Mexico within three days after it was organized. It arrived at Vera Cruz July 1 and went into camp on the beach north of the city. Shortly afterwards Brigadier General Franklin Pierce (later President) arrived at Vera Cruz with 2,500 troops of the new army. Watson reported his regiment to Pierce for duty. Commodore Perry, who had succeeded to the command of the Home Squadron, was very reluctant to give up his marines for duty with the army. They were at the time nearly all ashore, forming garrisons at Tabasco, Laguna, Frontera, and Alvarado. Perry disregarded the Navy Department orders, as far as possible, and sent only such marines as were readily available—only twenty-eight marines and one officer who were still on board ships near Vera Cruz. The marine detachment of the *Germantown* was temporarily detached to Watson's unit but was transferred to Tampico before the marine regiment left for the interior of Mexico.

### THE MARCH TO PUEBLA

On July 16 Pierce's brigade with Watson's marines attached marched to join Scott's army at Puebla. The route was then infested with guerrilla bands and irregular Mexican troops. Watson had not been given sufficient men to fill out his regiment and was forced to reorganize it into a battalion. Pierce assigned the marines as the rear guard. On the first day of the march they had many difficulties trying to move long wagon trains with horses that had not been properly trained. As Pierce reported it, the first day was taken up trying to move the wagon train through sand, which was at times hub deep, and most of their energy was expended in breaking horses and trying to persuade balky teams to go on. On the second day they encountered steep and difficult hills and received a report of a strong guerrilla band ahead. The excitement among these inexperienced warriors may well be imagined. Pierce sent forward the marine battalion, with two pieces of light artillery in support, to drive away the supposed enemy, reported to be five hundred strong. The romance soon fell flat, however; they found not the least sign of an enemy. The next three days passed in a downpour of tropical rain, with the camps at times under water.

On the twenty-first the column reached the National Bridge over the Antigua River where serious difficulties threatened the column. As they approached the bridge, the marines repulsed a minor attack on the rear of the column. About one hundred fifty Mexicans were discovered in a strongly entrenched position on a high hill covering the main span of the bridge. A rapid flanking movement by one of the infantry regiments, supported by a few rounds from the artillery, drove off the enemy. By the end of the next day the column had reached the battlefield of Cerro Gordo, where it again had a minor encounter with a guerrilla band. The troops were not allowed to forget for very long at a time that they were in the enemy country. They had six contacts with the enemy before reaching Puebla on August 6. The marines found Scott's army making final preparations for the advance on Mexico City. The marine battalion was attached to the 4th Division under General Quitman and brigaded with the Second Pennsylvania Volunteers with Watson in command of the brigade.

### The Advance to Mexico City

With no further increases to his army in sight, Scott made every possible man available for field duty and on August 8 practically abandoned his line of communication and left his base guarded by a few sick and ineffectives. As was then said, he drew the sword, threw away the scabbard, and started for Mexico City to obtain what was then demanded—a conquered peace from the Mexican Government.

Santa Anna and his government during all the delay had exerted every possible effort to raise and equip a new army and to fortify not only the approaches to, but also the city of Mexico itself. The total Mexican strength in the vicinity of Mexico City was approximately 32,000 men. Scott had not more than twelve thousand effectives. His army advanced, knowing that retreat was impossible and that there was nothing left to do but to conquer or die. Their approach to Mexico City was through a maze of lakes and marshes, over causeways, and in the face of strongly fortified positions, held by greatly superior enemy forces. A series of turning movements gradually led Scott's army to a position about fifteen miles south of San Agustin. The Mexican army, having been turned out of its main defensive works to the east of the city, promptly shifted to a position between Scott and the city, where they soon prepared other elaborate defensive works.

Scott's advance on Mexico City was made more difficult by a rugged, almost impassable lava flow of about five miles in diameter, called the "Pedregal," lying almost directly between his army and the city. Scott fought several battles and skirmishes before he had cleared this strong natural obstruction, but the marines together with Quitman's entire division remained in reserve—guarding the trains at San Agustin. Soon after getting past the difficult Pedregal, Scott's army engaged the Mexicans in the battle of Cherubusco—his troops showing an almost unbelievable fighting spirit. At one stage of the battle Quitman was called upon to put in one of his brigades, but, much to the disgust of the marines, Shield's brigade was chosen and they were again left to guard the accursed wagon train.

Believing that his army was too much disorganized and tired out for further immediate operations, Scott inadvisedly made an armistice with the enemy, and with N. P. Trist, a special representative of the State Department, accompanying him, tried to make a treaty of peace with the Mexican Government. The negotiations failed completely; it was then more apparent than ever that the Mexican Army would have to be completely crushed and Mexico City captured before the desired peace could be obtained.

Relying upon erroneous information that El Molino del Rey, a strongly fortified group of buildings lying about three miles southwest of the city, contained a gun foundry, Scott determined upon its capture. On September 8, by a series of assaults and after suffering casualties as high as 30 per cent by some of his best troops, he captured the position, wrecked its defenses, but immediately evacuated it. During these operations Watson's entire brigade was still kept in reserve. By this time Scott's army had been reduced to slightly more than seven thousand combat troops. He was still faced with at least three times that number of Mexicans. His next move seems to have been considerably debated in a council of war after which, against the best advice, Scott announced his decision to storm and capture the Castle of Chapultepec.

## THE STORMING OF CHAPULTEPEC

The marines at San Agustin were at last permitted to move from that position to San Angel, just south of Mexico City, on the day of the Battle of El Molino del Rey. On the night of September 11 they advanced to Tacubaya, about one mile south of Chapultepec, in readiness to take part in the assault. Not only were they to be given a chance to show their strength, but they were given the task of assaulting the castle from its most difficult approach. Chapultepec stands on a volcanic promontory rising nearly two hundred feet above the plain. There are very steep slopes on its east and south sides but more gentle slopes on the west and north.

It was during the battle of Chapultepec that the fighting spirit of the American army probably reached the highest pitch of determination and willingness to do or die that it has ever attained. Some of its troops had been repulsed during the attack on Molino del Rey and had left a considerable number of helpless wounded comrades on the field. The Mexicans had sallied and ruthlessly killed these men in sight of the American army. This tended to steel the Americans' nerves and determination, and made them, of course, more determined not to be repulsed and, it has been claimed, caused many of them to retaliate against the acts of the Mexicans. The marines, of course, knew all these things and that many of the troops present had come off victorious in upward of a dozen battles. Watson's battalion was thus put on the spot, as never before, to make good or die.

The general plan for taking the castle was to attack it from the west and south simultaneously, with the support of all available artillery, which was, of course, far too meager for the task at hand. The castle had been provided with a series of outer works, in addition to its close defenses. It was held by approximately seven hundred Mexicans whom Santa Anna refused to reinforce because he believed no more troops were necessary for its defense. Scott hoped to force the Mexicans to evacuate Chapultepec by a vigorous bombardment and a mere threat to assault it. He had all available artillery placed in position while the infantry moved forward ready for any contingency. Quitman's division advanced part way to the enemy's position to support a battery of artillery. Scott's artillery bombarded the castle intermittently throughout the day of September 12. It did considerable damage to the enemy's defenses and played havoc with their morale, but the Mexicans did not yet show any signs of giving up the fight. Quitman sent Major Twiggs with a detachment of marines forward to make a reconnaissance and to induce the enemy to disclose their positions. The detachment drew a heavy fire from both artillery and musketry and, having accomplished its mission, retired. The Mexicans, thinking that they had repulsed the marines, came out of their works and followed them. They soon came under the fire of Quitman's main line and promptly retired.

The bombardment having failed, Scott determined to assault the castle the following day. In addition to the other difficulties for the attackers, the castle was surrounded on the southern side by a high wall and by a series of strong works, placed well down the sides of the hill. Part of Quitman's troops were organized into special storming and pioneer parties, that were to advance for special missions along with the main attack. Six such storming parties were formed by Quitman; two were commanded by marine officers while some of the others contained marines as well as soldiers. A storming party under Major Twiggs, consisting of 120 men, was expected to play a leading part in the assault on the southern side of the castle.

The batteries advanced to the closest possible positions during the night, and the troops moved up in support. Pillow's division was ordered to encircle the castle from the west and north, where the going was easier and considerable cover was available; Quitman's division was ordered to assault it from the south and east where the hill was very steep and defended by the strongest works. Quitman, with the marine battalion leading, took up the advance in the early morning of September 13 along a causeway road passing to the east of the castle. When the head of the column reached a position about three hundred yards from the enemy's outer works, the leading troops were forced to leave the road by the fire of a battery of artillery, shooting directly down it, and by a heavy musketry fire from the enemy's advanced positions. On Quitman's orders, Watson halted the marine battalion under the cover of a ditch at some old buildings; some of the storming parties accompanying it halted in the same position. Two volunteer regiments that marched across the field to the left reached the enemy's outer defenses. The marines in their sparsely covered position were subjected to a heavy artillery and musketry fire. They suffered a considerable number of casualties and expended most of their ammunition while waiting. The officers and men became impatient with the delay, but Watson would not permit them to advance unless ordered to do so by Quitman. Major Twiggs, apparently with the intention of advancing alone with his storming party, exposed himself in front of his unit and was immediately killed.

The encircling troops under Pillow had considerable difficulty and had to be reinforced by part of Worth's division. With that help they soon scaled the walls and engaged the Mexicans in hand-to-hand fighting. Meantime, General Smith's brigade was advancing on the right of the marines with the mission of cutting off the retreat of the Mexicans. The enemy fire to the front of Quitman's division then began to slacken, and he finally ordered an assault. The marine battalion and the accompanying storming parties resumed their advance. When the assault started, the Mexicans began to break rapidly.

### Terrett Gets Loose

Captain George H. Terrett with part of Company C of marines (seven officers and about thirty-six men), who had been in a more advanced position during the halt, had taken up a vigorous attack against the enemy without orders from anyone. They assaulted the Mexican battery which had been playing havoc with them during the halt and took it with little difficulty. Knowing nothing of Quitman's orders to assault the castle, they took up a vigorous advance in front of all the troops, passed to the west of the city and continued on toward the northwestern gate.

The remainder of Quitman's division, including the rest of the marine battalion, moved rapidly to the base of the hill, became intermingled by units, but "swept on like a flood" as an eyewitness put it, to the crest of the hill and into the castle. As the marine battalion charged into the castle gates they discovered a group of Mexicans in a wood on their left. After a few shots from the marines the Mexicans threw down their arms and "begged most piteously for life." Twenty or thirty were taken prisoners.

In the meantime Terrett with his little command was making history for the Marines. After capturing the enemy's battery, they advanced north a few hundred yards where they were joined by Magruder's battery of two light guns, just in time for a few effective artillery shots to repel an attack by a large group of lancers, who were forming to charge them. The lancers took to flight and were seen no more during the battle. Terrett lost several men, picked up a few more scattered ones on the battlefield, and continued a vigorous advance. When about halfway up the road to the northwestern gate, he encountered a large enemy group, which he estimated at one thousand, holding a strongly fortified position. Terrett advanced within fifty yards of the enemy trenches, but finding the going too heavy, he detached part of his little command, turned the enemy's left flank, causing them to retire. With only about twenty of his little force remaining, Terrett took up a hot pursuit. He lost four more marines but continued to pursue the enemy with the utmost vigor. Upon approaching the San Cosme gate, he was joined by Lieutenant U. S. Grant with about twenty soldiers, who were also well out in front of their division in hot pursuit of the fleeing Mexicans. The two detachments, acting as a unit, captured the gate and entered the city. They were thus the first Americans to make an entry. They held the gate for about fifteen minutes and were then ordered by General Worth to retire from their very exposed position and join his command.

Worth had taken time to reorganize his troops after the assault on Chapultepec and had not arrived as early as the dashing Grant. Worth ordered Terrett to report his marines to one of the brigade commanders who in turn had them report to Major Hunter of the Eleventh Infantry. Under Hunter's command these marines attacked and captured a picket position at Los Huertas and remained there the next two days. The exploits of this group of marines were without doubt among the most spectacular of the Mexican War. Terrett, First Lieutenant John D. Sims, and Second Lieutenant Charles A. Henderson (son of the Commandant) were later breveted for their heroic conduct. What remained of Terrett's detachment rejoined the marine battalion after Mexico City had been captured.

## To the Halls of Montezuma

Quitman also took time for a hasty reorganization of his troops before advancing along the Chapultepec causeway to the southwestern gate of the city. During the brief pause they had time to look out across the city of Mexico; the roofs of the houses were black with people watching the engagement; beyond the National Plaza they saw the end of their crusade—the Halls of the Montezumas. The marine battalion was hastily reorganized and received a fresh supply of ammunition when it returned to the foot of the hill. It then advanced towards the city to support a battery which was firing on the enemy's outer defenses.

Quitman did not feel that he had yet been given an opportunity to win his part of the military glory. Despite the fact that Scott had ordered him only to make a serious threat against the southwestern gate, he was determined to take up a vigorous pursuit of the enemy and enter the city if possible. He borrowed part of Pillow's troops and, with the mingled units only hastily reorganized, he vigorously pursued the enemy. When about halfway to the city his men were held up by a battery in a strong position to the right of their line of march. The determined assailants then advanced from arch to arch of the aqueduct toward the main fortifications and the strong temporary field works which defended the gate.

Three hundred yards north of the gate along the wall of the city stood the formidable citadel surrounded by walls and a wet ditch and strongly manned. It was recognized as a serious obstacle to the taking of the city from that direction. In spite of its flanking fire, in the face of heavy fire from the front and the other flank, Quitman's troops stormed the gates of the city. Several times Quitman personally led the assault. The attacking troops succeeded in entering the city but made little further advance. The enemy reinforced their lines and forced Quitman to retire to the vicinity of the gate. The Americans' ammunition began to give out; hence the firing ceased. The Mexicans grew bold and counterattacked. They were driven back but attacked again and again; each time they were repulsed, but were seemingly not discouraged. Nightfall put an end to the fighting. Quitman's division, including the marine battalion, spent the night digging in where they were and preparing for another assault.

Scott threw his remaining troops into the advance against the San Cosme gate. By 4 P.M. Worth's leading troops arrived at that gate, shortly after it had been temporarily taken by Terrett and Grant. Worth's advance was delayed for a while until artillery could be brought up and troops maneuvered against the flanks of the enemy's position. The attack was then successful and at 6 P.M. Worth's troops forced their way into the city. The army spent the night reorganizing its depleted forces and preparing for perhaps more difficult fighting the following day. At the first sign of daylight Quitman's troops were at the point of opening fire when a white flag and an invitation to enter reached Quitman. Santa Anna with his remaining forces had evacuated during the night and retired toward Guadelupe Hidalgo.

Quitman was compensated for his having been given little opportunity to win military glory by being allowed to enter the city first. His division fell in for the triumphal entry. The general, on foot and wearing only one shoe, led the march. Behind him followed the mud-spattered and blood-stained troops with little attempt at military formation. They marched through the citadel grounds which they had expected to have to take with as much exertion as they had made against Chapultepec. They then moved on to the plaza, where they formed in line to render honors to General Scott upon his entry into the city. They raised the American flag over the National Palace—"The Halls of Montezuma"—and the marines cleared it of robbers and thieves, who had flocked in after Santa Anna had evacuated. The marines then settled down in their colorful cross-belted uniforms, patrolling that historic edifice as if it were part of their daily routine. The rest of the troops gazed in "profound exultation" at the long pinkish facade and the endless balconies, while the people looked silently at the American troops. A bystanding foreigner remarked "They are all and each of them heroes." An admiring poet wrote:

> Light up your homes, O fathers,
> For those young hero bands,
> Whose march is still through
>     vanquished towns
> And over conquered lands,
> Whose valor, wild, impetuous
> In all its fiery glow,
> Pours onward like a lava-tide,
> And sweeps away the foe!

Although the last important engagement of the war had been fought, Scott's army had still to remain in Mexico City for several months while the slow process of peace negotiations went on and a few minor military operations took place. Santa Anna resigned from the presidency and with a few of his scattered forces attempted to attack the small American garrison protecting a large number of sick in Puebla. He was not successful, however, and again left the country.

### Supporting Manifest Destiny

The State of Yucatan maintained a nominal independence during the Mexican War and on repeated occasions declared its neutrality, but our naval commanders were convinced that too much dependence could not be placed on such assertions and proceeded to watch the more important ports of that part of Mexico as well as the other ports. One of Yucatan's principal ports of entry was the town of Carmen, lying at the entrance of a large lagoon called "Laguna de los Terminos." In December, 1846, Perry with the *Mississippi* and three small vessels arrived off Carmen. He embarked a landing force on the smaller ships, took them in tow of the *Vixen,* stood in towards the town of Carmen, and demanded its surrender. The show of force proved sufficient. The town surrendered and the enemy abandoned all of their defenses. The landing forces went ashore, destroyed the fortifications, took away all powder that was found, and withdrew for other operations in that part of Mexico, leaving the *Vixen* and *Petrel* to guard the entrance to the lagoon.

Little further attention was paid to that vicinity until the more important ports along the eastern coast of Mexico had been brought under complete control. In May, 1847, Perry again visited the lagoon and found a considerable amount of contraband trade had grown up. He landed with a force of sailors and the marines from the *Mississippi* and *Scorpion* and took possession of the town and island with appropriate ceremony. Perry detailed Commander G. A. Magruder as naval commander of the port and governor of the vicinity, furnished him a small garrison of marines and sailors, and opened the port under American control.

The nominal independence and neutral status of Yucatan placed that state in direct communication with the American government. On several occasions Yucatan requested the assistance of American armed forces to protect the white inhabitants from the depredations of Indian tribes. As the war progressed, the idea of "manifest destiny" began to take a strong hold upon the imagination of the American people. Our government began to take steps looking to the control of the Isthmus of Tehuantepec, then considered the best route of interoceanic communication. Provision for the United States to control the isthmus was not made a part of the Treaty of Guadelupe Hidalgo, but there were urgent demands that our transit rights be secured and the treaty changed accordingly.

These and possibly other reasons led to the establishment of a considerable garrison of marines both at Laguna and at Alvarado. An additional battalion of marines, under Major John Harris, was organized at New York in March, 1848, and sent to Mexico to reinforce Perry's squadron on the Isthmus of Tehuantepec. It arrived at Vera Cruz, however, after the armistice had been concluded March 5, 1848, and was sent to garrison Alvarado and Laguna. The marine battalion with the army at Mexico City passed to the command of Major William Dulany upon the evacuation of Colonel Watson soon after the capture of the city. Watson died at Vera Cruz on the way back to the United States. Dulany's battalion was transferred from Mexico City to Vera Cruz, soon after Harris' arrival, and also went to Alvarado. The marines at Alvarado and Laguna were organized into a regiment under Dulany, who made his headquarters at Alvarado. The regiment garrisoned those two places until after the treaty of peace was ratified on May 30, 1848.

The Second Battalion at Laguna made itself thoroughly comfortable in the Mexican barracks at that place and also built temporary quarters. Apparently they expected to occupy that part of Mexico for some time. The First Battalion was evacuated from Alvarado to Pensacola in June, 1848, but the other battalion remained at Laguna nearly two months longer. On July 14 orders were issued for the return of the marines that remained in Mexico to the United States. The battalion at Laguna was transferred to Boston, Norfolk, and New York on some of the smaller ships of the squadron and on a chartered vessel; Laguna was evacuated on July 26, 1848.

## Chapter VI
## THE MEXICAN WAR—OPERATIONS IN THE WEST

### Operations in California

In addition to being at odds with Mexico, our government felt considerable anxiety as the Mexican War approached lest Great Britain should take advantage of chaotic conditions in Mexico to extend her possessions along the western coast of North America. A British squadron was known to be operating in the eastern Pacific; it was commonly thought that its purpose was not only to strengthen the British claim on Oregon but also to establish a claim over California, if an opportunity presented itself.

For some years prior to the outbreak of the Mexican War our Navy had maintained a small squadron in the Pacific. As early as June, 1845, the Navy Department decided to reinforce this squadron and sent Commodore John D. Sloat with the *Savannah* to the Pacific station. At the same time the Navy made plans to increase the squadron as ships became available. Sloat's orders, which had been given him as "secret and confidential," indicated the anticipated course of events in California. They directed him, upon receiving news of the outbreak of war, to "employ the forces under his command to, the best advantages," to take possession of Yerba Buena (San Francisco), and to take or blockade such other ports on the western coast of Mexico as his forces would permit. Further instructions to take and hold Monterey and San Diego and to occupy Los Angeles, if forces were available, were sent to Sloat as soon as war was declared. Sloat did not receive these orders, however, until after he had heard of the outbreak of war and therefore acted, at first, under his previous instructions.

In addition to having the Pacific Squadron keep in close contact with the situation in California, President Polk had three agents, in whom he appears to have had great confidence, carrying on activities in California under his own secret instructions. Captain John C.

Frémont, Topographical Engineers, U.S.A., had been sent to California with a small detachment of troops on an "exploring and scientific expedition." Frémont's activities were received with an air of mysteriousness by the Californians, who concluded that he was attempting to foster a revolution against the Mexican Government. General Castro, the Mexican commander in California, moved against Frémont who was encamped near the present site of Sacramento. Frémont, to avoid a conflict, retreated to the north.

The American consul at Monterey, Thomas O. Larkin, was also acting as Polk's confidential agent. His exact instructions are not known, but he was undoubtedly watching the situation, keeping the State Department informed about developments, and using his influence to prevent, if possible, any other country than the United States getting possession of California.

The third mysterious character, First Lieutenant Archibald H. Gillespie, U.S.M.C., had been detailed as a special agent of the State Department and as an executive agent of the President several months prior to the outbreak of the war. In October, 1845, he had been called into conference with Secretary of State Buchanan and later with President Polk and given some secret instructions which he was to deliver verbally to Larkin at Monterey and to Frémont wherever he could be located. In addition to his verbal instructions he was given written dispatches to carry to Larkin and some orders in cipher for Commodore Sloat. Gillespie memorized and then destroyed the instructions to Larkin; those to Sloat were a duplicate of orders carried by Commodore Stockton on the *Congress,* which was sailing around Cape Horn to join the Pacific Squadron.

Gillespie made his way to Vera Cruz, thence to Mexico City, traveling as a business man. He was delayed for some time at the latter place by a revolution in the vicinity but finally reached Mazatlan where he reported to Commodore Sloat, who had arrived on his new station and taken command of the Pacific Squadron. Gillespie did not divulge his secret instructions to Sloat, but on the day following Gillespie's arrival Sloat sent the *Cyane,* Commander S. F. Dupont, to take him to California. The *Cyane* sailed via the Sandwich (Hawaiian) Islands, apparently to conceal Gillespie's mission, and arrived at Monterey April 17. Gillespie delivered his instructions to Larkin and after some preparation started out to overtake Frémont, who was reported to have left California by going north. After an extremely hurried and hazardous trip through the rugged northern country, infested with hostile Indians, whom he encountered at times, he found Frémont on May 7 at Klamath Lake. Whatever the secret instructions to Frémont were we do not know, but he reversed his course and returned to California with Gillespie. Gillespie and Frémont then engaged in activities apparently designed to separate California from Mexico, much to the discomfiture of our naval commanders who were present and trying to maintain a neutral position. There is evidence that the two secret agents had an intimate connection with the declaration of independence of California at Sonoma, when the so-called Bear Republic was proclaimed by a group of Americans. Their activities in that connection are not a part of this brief account of the naval conquest of California. But it is necessary to mention them as they increased the problems of the Navy.

Sloat was still lying in the harbor of Mazatlan when he received the first definite information of Taylor's battles on the Rio Grande. Sloat was very hesitant, however, of taking any definite action; apparently he bore in mind Commodore Jones's experience in 1842. On June 5, 1846, he sent the *Levant* to Monterey but he himself remained behind, awaiting further news of the situation. The information which he already had was apparently conclusive that war existed, but Sloat refused to leave or take any definite action until he learned of the blockade of Vera Cruz. Then he finally sailed (June 7) on the *Savannah* for Monterey. He reached Monterey July 2, found the *Cyane* and *Levant* already there, and learned that the *Portsmouth* was in San Francisco Bay.

## The Capture of Monterey

Instead of taking immediate and vigorous action Sloat again hesitated, paid official calls on shore as if nothing unusual had happened, and delayed action until further pressure was brought to bear on him. He received more definite information about the activities of the British squadron, acquired all information known to Larkin, and learned something about the activities of Frémont and Gillespie. Finally, being persuaded to act, Sloat organized a landing force of 165 sailors and 85 marines from all his ships present. Under the command of Captain William Mervine of the *Savannah,* the troops landed in the early morning of July 7. Mervine demanded the surrender of Monterey, but the Mexican commandant refused on the ground that he had no authority to surrender. Mervine proceeded to take possession of the town and, with appropriate ceremonies, raised the American flag over the custom house. Most of the sailors from the squadron returned to their ships as soon as the town had been taken, but the marines, under Captain Ward Marston, U.S.M.C., remained on shore and established a regular garrison. Upon taking possession of Monterey, Sloat published a proclamation to the effect: that California had become part of the United States; that the people would be protected in all of their property rights; and that they were permitted to remain as neutrals or depart. He also announced provisions for temporary government and for the collection of custom duties. The Californians seemingly acquiesced; most of the foreigners appeared quite jubilant.

Sloat notified Commander John B. Montgomery of the *Portsmouth* of the action he had taken and directed Montgomery to take possession of Yerba Buena. In order to insure communications between that place and Monterey, Sloat appointed Purser D. Fauntleroy as captain of a company of dragoons, made up of volunteer sailors and marines from the ships present and of American citizens who volunteered for the duty. Fauntleroy not only kept up the desired communications but also reconnoitered a considerable part of the country. On July 17 he went out to take possession of and raise the American flag over the mission at San Juan. He found Frémont already in possession of San Juan, however, and returned to Monterey with him two days later. Shortly afterwards a detachment of Fauntleroy's dragoons established a garrison at the mission and recovered a considerable quantity of guns and powder, which had been hidden there by General Castro during his hasty retreat to the south.

### Capture of San Francisco

When Montgomery received Sloat's orders, he landed with seventy sailors and marines at 8 A.M., July 9, took possession of Yerba Buena, raised the American flag over the customs house, and had his ship salute the flag with twenty-one guns. He then published Sloat's proclamation that the United States had taken possession of California. After completing the above-mentioned acts and formalities, the landing force, with the exception of Lieutenant Henry B. Watson, U.S.M.C., and fourteen marines, returned to the *Portsmouth.* Watson was appointed military commandant of the garrison ashore, which included a newly organized militia unit as well as the marines. The marine detachment was later increased to twenty-six; Watson continued on duty as commandant until the following November. He immediately set about strengthening his position by converting his barracks into an improvised blockhouse and building a fort in which he mounted a small gun from the ship. Watson named his little fort, Fort Mervine. The *Portsmouth* also supplied Watson with muskets and ammunition for arming a newly organized militia. Weapons were so scarce, however, that it was necessary to gather up all that were available in the vicinity. Watson sent out expeditions to procure them wherever they were reported. The ships of the squadron furnished arms, ammunition, and supplies to Frémont and Gillespie for the California Battalion, which they organized from volunteers.

Marston made his position at Monterey more secure by mounting some guns ashore in an improvised fort, which he garrisoned by marines and sailors. On July 15 Commodore Stockton arrived on the *Congress* and reported for duty. Sloat had been at sea more than the regular period of duty and was old, sick, and highly nervous over the situation for which he was responsible. He gladly turned over command (July 23) to the younger and more aggressive Stockton, who appears to have been itching for action. Upon the arrival of the *Congress* its marine guard, under Lieutenant Jacob Zeilin, joined the garrison at Monterey but withdrew just prior to the ship's sailing for San Pedro on August 1. The marine detachments of the *Savannah* and *Cyane* remained on duty at Monterey for several weeks.

San Francisco Bay was believed secure by the end of July, and the naval forces began to send expeditions inland. Lieutenant J. S. Missroon of the *Portsmouth* took a patrol to Fort Sutter, up the Sacramento River. Lieutenant J. W. Revere went to Sonoma, took command of the American forces at that place, and held it for nearly four months. During the night of August 14 a reported advance of California insurgents alarmed the garrison at Yerba Buena; an additional detachment of twenty-five men from the *Portsmouth* landed to reinforce it. The danger soon passed, however, and the detachment was reduced to its previous size. During September, Stockton made Second Lieutenant William A. T. Maddox, U.S.M.C., commandant of the Northern Department of California with headquarters at Yerba Buena. The marines and sailors from the *Portsmouth* continued to help garrison Fort Mervine until November 26, when the *Portsmouth* was withdrawn for duty elsewhere. The marine detachment from the *Warren* relieved them. During December the *Savannah* and *Dale* were in San Francisco Bay; their marine detachments helped to garrison San Francisco and participated in some expeditions sent into the interior. The most important of these was an expedition composed of fifty sailors and marines from the *Savannah*, sent out on November 22 under Commander Joseph B. Hull of the *Warren* for temporary duty at San Jose.

### First Taking of San Pedro and Los Angeles

Having gained control of northern California, Stockton sailed (July 30) on the *Congress* from Monterey to capture San Pedro. He reached Santa Barbara on August 4, landed a few men, and took possession of that place. On the following day he landed a larger force, including the ship's band, and raised the American flag over the town with proper ceremonies. Stockton left Sergeant Watson, with a detachment of fifteen marines to guard the town, and proceeded on his way to San Pedro where he arrived on August 6. The remainder of the marine detachment of the *Congress* under Zeilin landed (August 7) and took possession of San Pedro. The marines were soon afterwards reinforced by a detachment of sailors. Stockton immediately began to make preparations for an advance on Los Angeles. He landed artillery and other equipment and organized a battalion of marines and sailors with Zeilin as adjutant. In the midst of these preparations came representatives from Castro to treat with Stockton who refused all concessions but unconditional surrender. All preparations having been completed, Stockton took up the march on Los Angeles (August 12) with a force of 350 men. Frémont, who was operating from San Diego with 120 volunteers, joined Stockton near Los Angeles the next day; their combined force marched into the city. The *Cyane* had been ordered to participate in the operation but had been becalmed en route from San Diego and did not arrive at San Pedro until August 15. Its marine guard landed the following day and joined Stockton's forces at Los Angeles. Stockton's battalion took possession of Los Angeles without resistance and with the usual ceremony, including the publication of a proclamation.

Stockton immediately set about organizing a government for California. He appointed Frémont military commander of the North and made Gillespie military commander of the South. In slightly over two months California had apparently been conquered; all known organized enemy forces had either laid down their arms or had been dispersed. Even the Mexican Government announced that California had been lost. The battalion from the squadron remained in Los Angeles until early in September. Leaving Gillespie with a company of volunteers to hold that city, Stockton then re-embarked his forces and sailed for Monterey. He called at Santa Barbara en route and withdrew the marine detachment, which he had left there during the previous month.

### The Capture of San Diego

In the meantime Frémont and Gillespie with the California Battalion had been sent on the *Cyane* to take San Diego and cut off the retreat of Castro, who was reported to be attempting to escape into Mexico. Frémont had reported to Stockton at Monterey with his volunteer troops, and Stockton had mustered them into the United States naval service, prior to leaving for San Pedro. Frémont was then promoted to major and Gillespie to captain. Gillespie was made adjutant of the battalion. The *Cyane*, bearing Frémont's battalion, reached San Diego July 29. Lieutenant Stephen T. Rowan, executive officer of the *Cyane,* with a few sailors and the marine guard landed, took possession of the town without resistance, raised the American flag, and published Sloat's proclamation. Frémont landed part of his battalion, shortly afterwards, and the remainder on the following day. The marines under Maddox remained ashore a few days to help garrison the town and then returned to the *Cyane.*

The situation at San Diego was by no means as peaceful, however, as it first appeared. Frémont reported on July 31 that Castro, who apparently thought the town was held only by a few marines, planned to attack the garrison on the night of July 31. The *Cyane* landed one hundred additional men under Rowan late in the afternoon to reinforce the garrison. Castro did not attack, however. Rowan returned to the ship three days later leaving the marine detachment on duty ashore until August 9 when it, too, was withdrawn. The *Cyane* sailed for San Pedro to assist Stockton. A few days after the taking of San Diego, Frémont marched with 120 men of his battalion to help Stockton take Los Angeles, leaving Gillespie with 48 men to hold San Diego. Frémont attempted to gain contact with Castro's forces but they successfully evaded him. After the *Cyane* had left, Castro again threatened to attack the little garrison at San Diego. Gillespie organized the citizens of the town into a militia company to assist him in the defense; Castro retired into lower California without molesting the town. Frémont returned to San Diego from Los Angeles August 18 but left part of his troops at San Luis Rey. Gillespie had by that time provided mounts for his detachment of volunteers. He marched for Los Angeles a few days after Frémont's return, arrived there on August 31, and assumed his position as military commander. Frémont returned to northern California by sea, with the remainder of his battalion, to take up similar duties.

## The Revolt of the Californians

The conquest of California was by no means as complete as Stockton and Frémont had supposed. The main forces of the Californians had merely been broken up and had not really been defeated. The provisions made for garrisoning the country as a whole and Los Angeles in particular were hopelessly inadequate. Most of the Spanish population resided in the vicinity of Los Angeles, and it was there that disaffection against the newly formed military government soon began to show itself. Gillespie's position was particularly difficult. His ability as an officer and leader of men under field conditions could not of course be questioned, but he does not appear to have been successful in dealing with the temperamental civil population of California. One historian even accused him of being a petty tyrant and, by his methods, of causing the rebellion. Gillespie's soldiers were not all that could be desired. When they settled down to a garrison routine in Los Angeles, where wine and *aguardiente* were always plentiful, they began to cause him a great deal of trouble by their drunkenness.

Shortly after assuming his duties in charge of the military government, Gillespie drew $20,000 from the *Congress* for military expenditures and took it to Los Angeles. This fact became known, and a group of adventurers began to plot to get this money. Rumors also began to come in of groups of Californians assembling and threatening to attack Gillespie's little garrison. He arrested a number of the leaders of these factions and attempted to deport some of them. Opposition continued to grow, and, on the night of September 23, a band of Californians under Cervula Varela attacked his garrison; Gillespie easily repulsed them. This action, however, had the effect of unifying the Californians in a determination to resist the control of the United States; large numbers of them flocked to the leadership of Jose Maria Flores, to whom they looked for leadership after the retirement of Castro. Flores succeeded in stirring up the Californians by issuing bombastic and violent proclamations accusing the American forces of all manner of cruelties to the native population. Flores with 300 or 400 followers soon began a more or less systematic siege of Gillespie's garrison.

Some foreigners rallied to his support, and he was able to get his habitual drunkards under control and restore discipline in his command. At the time the siege began, his little garrison numbered only fifty-nine men, and his supply of ammunition was very low. The enemy was able to collect some artillery which had been hidden after Castro retreated; Gillespie had some abandoned guns which he could use only after drilling out the spikes and mounting them as field pieces on oxcarts, and improvising ammunition for them. His situation was hopeless from the beginning. In spite of the heroic defense made by the little detachment, the Californians gradually tightened their siege, and Flores' force continued to grow. He demanded an unconditional surrender on the 25th, but Gillespie refused. During the next two or three days they parleyed over terms for Gillespie to give up while the Californians continued to make minor attacks on Gillespie's position, which he had fortified in every possible way. Gillespie warned Flores that a direct assault would only result in a large number being killed; the Californians hesitated to storm his position. Gillespie sent a messenger to Stockton describing his predicament and attempted to play for time until assistance could arrive.

He held conferences with the enemy under flags of truce and was finally able to have a direct contact with Flores, who strongly manifested his desire for Gillespie's force to withdraw from the vicinity. The conferences led to an armistice on August 27. The Californians then proposed that Gillespie be permitted to retire with the "honors of war" but under circumstances that would have put him in a dangerous position had the Californians violated the terms of the agreement. Gillespie, of course, rejected such terms. Coming down from the north in an attempt to raise the siege, Captain Watson with twenty-five volunteers was captured on August 28. Gillespie's position grew more difficult because of the lack of water, and his officers began to feel that they must find the easiest way out of the situation. On the 29th Gillespie came to terms with the enemy and exchanged some prisoners. On the following day he marched to San Pedro, taking every precaution against possible treachery on the part of the Californians. Learning that the enemy were planning to violate their agreement, he transferred his troops aboard the *Vandalia*, which was then lying at San Pedro.

### Stockton's Return to Southern California

Stockton had gone to San Francisco upon hearing that the Walla Walla Indians had gone on the warpath. Frémont, who was in the vicinity and who knew some of these Indians, succeeded by his personal influence in pacifying them. Gillespie's messenger did not reach Stockton until September 30 when he was occupied with the Indians. He immediately despatched the *Savannah* to San Pedro to support Gillespie and ordered Frémont to report with part of his force to San Francisco for transfer to the same duty. When Frémont reported, he embarked upon the *Sterling*, and that ship together with the *Congress* sailed for southern California on October 15 to assist in putting down the revolt of the Californians. Soon after sailing, they met a ship from Monterey with news that the garrison at that place was in serious danger of being attacked. Stockton put into Monterey with the *Congress*, landed an additional force of two officers and fifty men, including the marine detachment of the *Cyane* under Lieutenant Maddox, and more ordnance stores, then immediately resumed his voyage to San Pedro.

### Mervine's Defeat

In the meantime the *Savannah* arrived at San Pedro on October 7 and learned from Gillespie of his being driven from Los Angeles. Captain William Mervine of the *Savannah* appears to have been over-anxious to get revenge against the Californians. He made hasty plans for a rapid advance upon Los Angeles and early the following morning landed a force of three companies of sailors, the marine detachment, and Gillespie's company from the *Vandalia*. A few Californians were waiting for him on shore, but after a few shots they retreated; the landing and taking of San Pedro proceeded without further resistance. Eighty additional men from the *Savannah* landed soon afterwards and the expeditionary force then totaling 310 was organized for the advance on Los Angeles. The marines under Captain Marston formed the advance guard, while Gillespie's riflemen deployed as skirmishers to protect the flanks of the column.

Mervine's expedition soon encountered minor resistance which Gillespie's men brushed aside. As the column moved on, small groups of enemy on all sides occasionally fired on the flankers. Twelve miles from San Pedro the column halted (at 2 P.M.) for a rest. Unaccustomed to marching, the men were practically exhausted. They saw a group of sixty Californians driving the cattle from the surrounding country. Gillespie's riflemen drove the enemy off but could still see them on the near-by hills. After a further short march the force went into camp; they were harassed throughout the night by mounted men, who repeatedly fired a few shots and rapidly withdrew. Mervine sent out a number of patrols in useless attempts to capture the elusive enemy.

The column again took up the march the following morning and soon encountered about 200 of the enemy in position across the road. When Mervine's main body got within range, the enemy began firing on it with a cannon. Mervine deployed and drove the enemy from the position. Before the enemy field piece could be taken or forced to retire, however, it had played considerable havoc with Mervine's main body. He soon saw that the enemy moved too fast for him even to catch up and ordered a retreat.

The expedition withdrew to the place, where it had camped the previous night and, after holding a council of war and taking care of the wounded as best they could, resumed the retreat on San Pedro. The enemy attempted to take possession of the hill lying between Mervine and his ships, but the commanding position was secured by Marston with his marines. Gillespie's company formed the rear guard during the retreat. The enemy harassed the force all the way back to San Pedro. Fauntleroy, making use of his experience with his famous dragoons, fortunately had landed with two pieces of artillery from the *Vandalia* and taken up a position to help cover the retreat. Mervine immediately re-embarked his forces, including Gillespie's troops, and gave up San Pedro in spite of the fact that Fauntleroy and Gillespie volunteered to remain ashore and hold the place. Mervine had made up his mind that the best place was aboard ship until Stockton arrived.

The situation for the volunteer garrison at San Diego was also reported as being very critical. On October 14 Mervine sent a detachment of two officers and thirty-five men from the *Savannah* and fifteen of Gillespie's volunteers under Lieutenant George Minor, U.S.N., on the whale-ship *Magnolia* to help hold San Diego.

Stockton arrived at San Pedro on October 26, took stock of the situation, and pursued his usual vigorous policy in an effort to restore the control of the United States. He ordered Gillespie's detachment to proceed with muffled oars and take every other possible precaution to surprise the enemy, land at 4 o'clock the following morning, and cover the landing of the battalion from his ships. Gillespie's troops, for some reason, failed to make the landing on time, but the sailors and marines, who were already in their boats, promptly went ashore to retake San Pedro. They encountered only a few scattered enemy and once more raised the American flag. Stockton then landed field pieces and strengthened the position ashore to withstand an attack. Flores, with a force of approximately 1,800 Californians, was reported in the general vicinity.

Stockton soon discovered, however, that another advance on Los Angeles was not practicable under the existing circumstances. The enemy had driven practically all the cattle and horses from the vicinity, and the open harbor of San Pedro was not a suitable place to leave ships with most of their personnel away. In order to have a secure anchorage and in the hopes of providing cattle and horses for an advance on Los Angeles, Stockton decided to move his base of operations to San Diego. The landing force ashore, including Gillespie's volunteers, was again withdrawn. The small garrison at San Diego was reported to be in a state of siege. Stockton transferred a detachment of twenty marines and seven Colt riflemen from the *Savannah* and Gillespie's volunteers aboard the *Congress* and sailed for San Diego on October 31. The *Congress* grounded a number of times, trying to enter San Diego Bay, but it succeeded in putting ashore the detachment from the *Savannah* and Gillespie's troops, and then withdrew to deeper water. The garrison in San Diego was relieved just in time, because its food supplies were completely exhausted—all the cattle and sheep of the vicinity had been driven off by the enemy. Fortunately some friendly Indians brought in some cattle a few days later. A supply of horses and cattle for the forces ashore was provided by sending forty miles down the coast, an expedition which brought back 90 horses and 200 head of cattle. The sailors from the *Savannah,* who had been besieged, went aboard the *Congress* to recuperate.

San Diego having been secured, Stockton then tried to locate Frémont, from whom he had not heard for some time. He returned to San Pedro on the *Congress* on November 4, took the *Savannah* from there, and sailed farther up the coast with the two ships. They met the *Sterling* on November 10 and apparently got news from Frémont. The *Savannah* went on to Monterey, and Stockton on the *Congress* returned to San Diego. He immediately began to organize, equip, and train an expeditionary force to retake Los Angeles. Late in November he landed practically all available men from the *Congress,* placed them in camp, and began training ashore. The enemy in considerable force remained in the vicinity but did not dare attack the garrison nor its patrols, which went out from time to time to gather food and other supplies.

### Helping Kearny

In the midst of preparations for the advance on Los Angeles, Stockton received news that General Kearny, who was marching from Fort Leavenworth to California, had arrived in Warner's Pass, about fifty miles east of San Diego. Gillespie, with twenty-six of his volunteers, Lieutenant Beale, U.S.N., and about ten sailors were sent to meet Kearny, report the situation to him, and return with him to San Diego. They met Kearny at Warner's Ranch (Warner's Hot Springs) on December 5 and found that he had only 100 dragoons and 8 or 10 other officers and men, including the famous scout, Kit Carson. They started for San Diego but soon received information that a force of Californians was near the Indian village of San Pasqual, through which it was necessary for the column to pass. They halted for the night at Santa Isabel Ranch and advanced the following morning for a daylight attack. They were at first following a ridge road with part of the dragoons acting as advance guard, with Gillespie's volunteers next in order, followed in turn by the main body and the train. Most of the Californians were well mounted, while Kearny's dragoons had only a few animals, which were almost exhausted by long marches.

Kearny encountered the enemy in a narrow valley, deployed behind a small stream. The advance guard charged; the enemy withdrew for a short distance; the advance guard pursued them and became separated from the main body by some distance. Catching them in this disadvantageous position, the Californians turned back, and a desperate hand-to-hand battle followed. The advance guard was driven back, seemingly in utter confusion, but the arrival of the main body saved the day. Kearny was able to retain control of the battlefield. The Americans lost nineteen killed and about fifteen wounded, including both Kearny and Gillespie. They buried the dead, improvised ambulances for the wounded, and resumed the march the following morning. They sent messengers to Stockton but afterwards discovered that they had been captured by the Californians. Stockton, however, heard from an Indian that Kearny had been defeated and immediately began to organize a relief column.

Kearny succeeded in reaching San Bernardo Ranch (a few miles south of the present town of Escondido), where he again encountered an enemy force estimated about 180. He took up a defensive position on a hill, but the Californians managed to drive off all his animals and capture his train and stores. The Californians did not assault Kearny's position, but surrounded it and held him in position. The situation was desperate. The Americans had no water, and their only remaining food was mule meat. Kearny did not dare to try cutting his way out. Beale, Kit Carson, and an Indian made their way out of camp at night, got past the enemy, who were in position on the San Diego road, and after two nights' traveling (hiding in the daytime) reported the situation to Stockton on the morning of December 9. A relief expedition of 215 sailors and marines, under Lieutenant Gray, U.S.N., and Zeilin, started out almost immediately and reached Kearny's camp on December 11. The enemy kept out of the way; Kearny and the relief column marched into San Diego next day.

## DIFFICULTIES IN THE NORTH

Frémont's efforts to assist in restoring American control over southern California failed on practically every turn. His first plan was to disembark at Santa Barbara, provide himself with horses and cattle, and move overland against the Californians around Los Angeles. He found that Santa Barbara had been captured by the Californians; he knew from past experiences that if he drove them out they would take all the cattle and horses with them. He therefore returned to Monterey and after considerable delay succeeded in providing himself with horses and began the march (about November 15) into southern California, leaving northern California almost wholly unprotected.

Discontented Californians around San Francisco Bay began to band together to take advantage of any situation that might arise. In December, Lieutenant W. A. Bartlett, U.S.N., and five sailors were out purchasing a supply of beef. An enemy group of thirty, under Francisco Sanchez, captured and carried them away to a camp in the mountains. The captors offered Bartlett and his men in exchange for Captain Weber of the Volunteers, who had previously been in the Mexican service. Montgomery refused to listen to such a proposition and immediately organized an expeditionary force to operate against the Sanchez group.

The expedition, consisting of two volunteer companies and the marine detachment of the *Dale,* all under Captain Marston, marched (December 29) on Santa Clara where Sanchez had been reported. Marston encountered Sanchez with about 120 men on January 2, 1847. After a brief skirmish the Californians were driven back and retreated into the Santa Cruz Mountains. On the following day Sanchez returned under a flag of truce, presented the Californians' complaints to Marston, who, thinking he saw some justice in their case, granted them an armistice, pending full settlement of the difficulties.

Lieutenant Maddox, who had been sent out from Monterey with a force of fifty men to operate against the Sanchez group, came face to face with another force of Californians near by, but Marston learned of the contact and extended the armistice to include those forces as well. Marston was later severely criticized by Montgomery for not destroying the Californians while he had the opportunity instead of parleying with them. Later events proved, however, that Marston had not made a serious mistake; Sanchez returned his prisoners and unconditionally surrendered his entire group. Marston's force returned to San Francisco, which he, with the marine detachments of the *Dale* and *Warren,* helped to garrison.

## The Second Conquest

Stockton at San Diego spent the remainder of December in mobilizing, training, equipping, and assembling supplies for a force of every available man, with which he was determined to reconquer the Californians. His immediate objective was to retake and hold Los Angeles. The *Portsmouth* and *Cyane* had been ordered from San Francisco to San Diego so that all their available men could take part in the expedition. Stockton improvised a train, largely of ox-carts, for carrying ammunition and other stores. After several months of fighting in various parts of California, the clothing of most of his men was worn out, and a large portion of them were reduced to wearing shoes made of canvas. After assembling all possible men and stores the expedition was finally ready to march, but in the coldest time of the year.

As finally organized, the expedition totaled approximately 600 men, including 60 dragoons of Kearny's expedition, 50 of Gillespie's volunteer company, all available sailors and marines from the *Con-*

*gress, Cyane,* and *Portsmouth,* which remained in San Diego harbor, part of the marines and some sailors from the *Savannah* who had been on detached duty at San Diego since the first of November, and nearly one hundred drivers, herdsmen, and Indians. The marines of the force were organized into a separate detachment under Zeilin, who also acted as adjutant of the expeditionary force. The entire naval contingent was commanded by Lieutenant Rowan, while General Kearny acted as commander of troops; Stockton reserved for himself the position of commander in chief and governor of California. Several hundred head of cattle had been collected for the principal item of food during the operation. Their care and protection as well as the protection of the train was one of the most difficult tasks on the long march, which proceeded without interruption by the enemy until January 7, 1847.

The horses drawing the ammunition and store carts soon began to give out; it became necessary for the men not only to draw part of the artillery but at times to help pull the carts, and always, of course, to help pull them up the hills. In spite of the very trying conditions of the march, Stockton reported that the men maintained a high spirit of cheerfulness and showed an excellent morale. The line of march was about 140 miles in length and over what is now approximately the route of the hilly inland highway between Los Angeles and San Diego. Groups of the enemy were seen from time to time, but they made no attempt to delay or attack the column. Flores and his officers, who had all previously signed a parole, were very nervous over their predicament. On January 1 they sent representatives to Stockton, offering to make an armistice until the difficulties could be settled between the United States and Mexico. Stockton refused to grant them any consideration whatsoever and pushed belligerently on with his nondescript but determined force.

## The Battle of San Gabriel

During the night of January 7-8 Stockton learned that the enemy had taken up an ambush position on the hills between his camp and the San Gabriel River. Before marching the following morning, they made every possible arrangement for the battle which appeared inevitable. Stockton marched to the right around the ambush position and, when he arrived upon the plain approaching the San Gabriel River, formed his troops into a square with the train and cattle in the center. The Californians had successfully defeated Kearny and had caused the failure of Mervine and Stockton in their two attempts to retake Los Angeles from San Pedro by capturing or driving off their beef cattle, horses, and trains. Stockton knew that Flores would attempt to repeat his previous tactics; hence he took every precaution to protect his supplies. An advance guard covered the front of the square; the marines and three companies of sailors under Zeilin protected its right flank; two companies of sailors covered the left flank; while Gillespie with miscellaneous detachments covered the rear and formed the guard of the day. As the formation approached San Gabriel, they saw the enemy with a strength of about 600, formed in three divisions, on the hills beyond the river about two miles away.

Stockton's cumbrous formation pushed steadily toward the enemy. Lieutenant H. B. Watson with the marines of the *Portsmouth* reinforced the more exposed left flank of the square during the advance. The enemy attempted to drive a band of wild horses against the front of the formation but failed. Upon reaching the river, the advance guard, acting as skirmishers, mounted, forded the stream, and pushed on toward the enemy, who were in position only 600 yards away. The Californians opened fire both with small arms and artillery but did little damage. Stockton's artillery unlimbered at the rear edge of the stream to return the fire, but he ordered them to cross the river first. They did this immediately and then opened fire. The dragoons and sailors on the front of the square reformed beyond the river and took up an assault on the enemy's position. The awkward formation of a square filled with carts and cattle continued its advance in the face of an incessant fire, which fortunately had very little effect.

Zeilin's detachment reinforced by two pieces of artillery deployed to the right. Stockton's artillery fire by that time began to show considerable effect upon the enemy—one shot made a direct hit upon a gun. An enemy group attempted to turn the right flank of the square; Zeilin quickly redisposed his marines, and the Californians, seeing their plans blocked by his maneuvers, retreated across the river. Another group then attempted to attack the left side of the square but were successfully repulsed by the sailors. Stockton then redisposed his troops to drive the enemy from the heights in front of the formation. The troops formed in line, charged the heights, and, after a few minutes' resistance, the Californians retreated. A few of them rallied and attacked the rear of the square but were repulsed by Gillespie's detachment. Others rallied under the protection of their artillery, but the accurate fire of Stockton's field pieces soon drove them from their new position. Stockton celebrated his capture of the enemy's position by having his band play "Hail Columbia" and "Yankee Doodle" in commemoration of the anniversary of the glorious battle of New Orleans. Stockton's forces lost during the day's operations only two killed and nine wounded; both Rowan and Gillespie were wounded.

## THE RECAPTURE OF LOS ANGELES

Stockton camped for the night near the battlefield, being careful to provide safety for his animals under the banks of the river. The enemy fired upon his camp during the night but did little damage. At daylight the following morning Zeilin with thirty marines went out on patrol, looking for the enemy and for provisions. They returned at sunrise, having found neither. At 9 A.M. the column resumed its march, and, after advancing about six miles, encountered the enemy deployed upon a hill which effectively blocked the line of march. The enemy opened an ineffective artillery fire. Stockton's field pieces replied, while his column continued the advance. The Californians opened up with more artillery; Stockton placed his battery about six hundred yards from them and returned an effective fire which drove them back. His artillery then directed an effective fire on the California infantry; it promptly retired toward Los Angeles. The fight has been commonly called the Battle of La Mesa. Kearney's forces pursued to a point within three miles of the town, where they again camped for the night. The losses for the day were only one killed and five wounded.

Kearney resumed the march about 10 A.M., January 10 and entered Los Angeles without further resistance. He marched through the main street of the town with the band playing. Gillespie again hoisted over the government house the same flag which he had been forced to haul down when he gave up the city in September. Stockton in reporting his victorious operations stated:

> I have thus truly exhibited to you, sir, sailors, (who were principally armed with boarding pikes, carbines and pistols, having no more than 200 bayonets in the whole division) victorious over an equal number of the best horsemen in the world, well mounted and well armed with carbines, pistols, and lances.

Most of the California troops dispersed or became insubordinate to their leaders. Flores fled with about 100 men into Mexico, leaving Andres Pico in charge of the remaining scattered forces. Pico retreated to Cahuenga ranch, near San Fernando, where he met (January 12) Frémont, who was marching from Santa Barbara to Los Angeles. The Californians offered peace; Frémont made an armistice with them without consulting Stockton. On the following day Pico's followers surrendered to Frémont under the terms of the so-called "Treaty of Cahuenga." They gave up all of their arms, promised to abide by the laws of the United States, and were allowed to return to their homes. The insurrectionists had practically dictated the terms under which they would lay down their arms despite the fact that most of them had broken the parole which they had previously signed. They surrendered under almost exactly the same terms that Stockton had rejected on January 1. Stockton, however, later approved Frémont's acts.

## THE ARMY TAKES OVER CALIFORNIA

Shortly after the second taking of Los Angeles, army units began to arrive in California. Stockton saw that his naval forces could soon withdraw for duty elsewhere. Stockton in his capacity as commander in chief appointed Frémont governor of California. Frémont with his battalion took over Los Angeles and vicinity, and Kearny withdrew to San Diego with his dragoons. Rowan withdrew the naval landing forces to San Pedro and then took them on a whale-ship back to their ships at San Diego.

Soon after the naval forces returned to San Diego, they received a report that General Bustamante was marching north to California with an army of 1,500 men. Stockton went down the coast 120 miles below San Diego, landed, stationed some of his men, marched inland, and found out after considerable investigation that the report was not true. His landing force re-embarked and returned to San Diego. Stockton then went again to San Francisco Bay and turned over the command of the squadron to Commodore W. B. Shubrick, who had arrived on the *Independence*. Stockton then made his way overland to Washington.

A battalion of Mormons arrived overland at San Diego January 29 and helped to hold that place. The marines from the *Congress* also helped to garrison San Diego at various times during February and March, 1847. A battery of army artillery arrived at Monterey, January 20 with necessary material to fortify that place as well as San Francisco. These soldiers relieved the sailors at Monterey, and the latter returned to their ships, but marines continued on duty there. Maddox's volunteers were discharged shortly afterwards. Gillespie with his volunteers went back to Monterey after the insurrection. He was relieved from duty with the California Volunteers March 1, 1847, and ordered to report overland to Washington. He was later breveted major in recognition of his outstanding services. The *Columbus* with Commodore James Biddle soon afterwards joined the squadron at Monterey. The first contingent of a New York volunteer regiment arrived to help hold Monterey and San Francisco.

The marines and sailors from the ships of the squadron continued on various duties around San Francisco Bay during the first six months of 1847. They helped to garrison San Francisco, and for a short time a detachment protected Sonoma against Indian attacks, while another one was stationed for a time at San José. The number of marines on shore in that vicinity was gradually reduced as the ships went south for duty along the Mexican coast. The marines from the *Dale* under Lieutenant Robert Tansill were the last to withdraw from duty in California.

## Operations on the Coast of Mexico

While the landing forces from the Pacific Squadron with the aid of a few other troops were engaged in the conquest of California, that squadron also carried on a more or less effective blockade of the principal Pacific ports of Mexico. Sloat left the *Warren* blockading Mazatlan when he left there in June, 1846, for California. After the *Cyane* had taken Frémont's battalion to San Diego, where it also left its marine guard, that ship relieved the *Warren* on the coast of Mexico. The tasks performed by this little vessel during the following few months are almost unbelievable, but its marines were on detached duty from the ship, and its exploits could hardly be considered a part of this history. The *Cyane* was recalled to California to assist in putting down the revolt. It arrived in time to take part in the march on Los Angeles which completed the conquest of California.

For various reasons the commander in chief of the squadron did not press the war against the western coast of Mexico for some time after the Californians were subdued. The personnel of most of the ships needed rest, and the weather conditions along the western Mexican coast were not suitable for landing force operations during the late spring and summer months. The *Portsmouth* went south early in 1847 to keep up the blockade. Montgomery demanded the surrender of San José on March 29, but the Mexican commander refused. A landing force of 140 men including the marines from his ship captured the place on the following day. San Lucas was taken a few days later. After it had refused to surrender, a landing force of ninety marines and sailors captured La Paz on April 14. All three towns were taken without resistance. The *Cyane* and *Independence* relieved the *Portsmouth* in April; it returned to California.

Commodore Shubrick, on the *Independence*, took charge of operations and shifted his attention to the mainland. He was unable to blockade an important port with a single vessel and, therefore, kept both the *Cyane* and *Independence* at Mazatlan until additional forces arrived. During the late spring and summer of 1847, various ships of the squadron took their turn in blockading the principal ports along the coast.

Shubrick, finding that more extensive operations were necessary to make an effective blockade of that Mexican coast, made plans for operations designed to close several ports as soon as weather conditions would permit. Preparatory to this, he concentrated most of the ships of the squadron in the vicinity of Monterey and San Francisco and put the crews through a period of intensive training ashore for landing force operations. After that training Captain E. A. F. Lavallette, in command of the *Congress, Portsmouth,* and *Dale,* sailed early in August for the Mexico coast to establish the most rigid blockade possible over its principal ports. The remainder of the squadron under Shubrick followed in October. Shubrick's plan, as reported to the Secretary of the Navy, was to blockade certain minor ports and to capture and hold the larger ones with garrisons of marines; the operations were to progress south beginning with Guaymas and San Lucas. The entire squadron rendezvoused off Cape San Lucas late in October, and operations began in earnest to close all the principal ports.

### Operations at Guaymas

In the meantime the *Portsmouth, Congress,* and *Independence* had carried on a considerable operation against Guaymas. These ships had arrived off Guaymas October 17 and immediately began preparations to capture the place. They placed heavy artillery on two small islands in the harbor, while the ships took position for bombarding the town and covering landings. A demand for the surrender of the town met with a flat refusal. The ships and the guns on the islands began (October 20) a bombardment of the town. After about an hour's firing the Mexicans ran up a white flag and evacuated the place; most of the inhabitants also left. The marines from the *Portsmouth* under Watson went ashore next day and raised the American flag; the marines from the *Congress,* assisted by a detachment of sailors, landed and destroyed the fort. The landing forces returned to their ships for the night and went ashore again the following day to protect the American consulate and other foreign property in the town.

Late in the afternoon reports reached the naval commander that a large force of Mexicans were approaching for a night attack. Four additional companies of seamen, two of which were armed as artillery, hurriedly landed to meet the situation. The troops were disposed for the defense of the town and remained in readiness for attack throughout the night. Reports of deserters from the enemy's force, received the following day, indicated, however, that its strength had been greatly exaggerated, and that the Mexicans were in no condition to make an attack on the Americans. The situation at Guaymas was turned over to Montgomery, commanding the *Portsmouth;* the landing forces from the other ships withdrew to their ships, which sailed for Mazatlan. The marines and sailors from the *Portsmouth* also withdrew from Guaymas October 24, after having gathered up all arms that could be found in the town and having secured the valuable property of foreigners.

The *Portsmouth* was relieved at Guaymas by the *Dale* on November 8 in order to make the larger ship available for more important operations elsewhere. The enemy strength in the vicinity of Guaymas was then reported to be about one thousand. For a time a few occasional shots from the *Dale* induced them to remain at a safe distance from the town. The American flag was kept flying over an island in the harbor. On November 17, however, it was learned that they had returned in considerable strength. Commander T. O. Selfridge landed with a force of sixty-five marines and sailors, encountered about three hundred Mexicans in the town, and after a brief attack supported by fire from the *Dale,* drove the Mexicans out. Selfridge was the only one of the American landing force wounded in the fight, but the enemy suffered a loss of thirty killed and wounded. First Lieutenant Robert Tansill, commanding the marine detachment of the *Dale,* was later made brevet captain for gallantry and meritorious conduct during this operation. The small force from the *Dale,* being insufficient to garrison the town, withdrew to its ship which again attempted to control the town by its gunfire. The victory had a decided general effect, however; the Mexicans were forced to abandon some of their operations in lower California as a result of not being able to control Guaymas.

The *Dale* continued its hold on Guaymas by lying close in and keeping the town covered with its guns. Toward the end of January, 1848, the village of Cochori, situated on the coast about nine miles east of Guaymas, was found to be held by a small Mexican force. The Mexicans, by means of a guard boat, had effected a kind of blockade over Guaymas. Lieutenant E. M. Yard, then commanding the *Dale,* determined to drive the enemy from Cochori and undertook a night operation during the early morning of December 30. Part of the marine detachment under Orderly Sergeant Ramsdale and a detachment of sailors, fifty men in all, under Lieutenant T. A. M. Craven, started out to capture the village. Craven went in boats to within three miles of Cochori, landed, and proceeded overland to surprise the enemy while his boats awaited orders off shore. Ramsdale with his marines advanced directly on the village, with the intention of overpowering the picket guard, while Craven with the sailors made a turning movement to approach the village from the opposite side. The sailors were the first to be discovered, but as soon as the alarm was given, the marines promptly overcame the pickets, killing two and capturing one. The sailors then closed in on the enemy. Part of the Mexicans fled, but their commanding officer and seven others were taken prisoners. Some arms, ammunition, and other equipment were captured. The landing force then returned in their boats. One of the boats proceeded along the coast and captured the enemy's guard boat and crew.

During the following month the *Dale* controlled most of the eastern coast of the Gulf of California by sending boat expeditions south along the coast and by operating with a chartered schooner for a distance of about fifty miles northward. Its crew made landings at Guaymas from time to time to determine conditions. On March 15 the marines under Tansill with a company of sailors again attacked the enemy at Cochori and drove them from the village. The *Dale* with similar operations continued to control Guaymas and the coast on each side of it for some distance until news of the armistice was received. On May 1 the marine guard under Tansill established a garrison on shore, where it remained until June 24 when news was received that the treaty of peace had been signed.

## Supporting the Army at La Paz

La Paz was permanently occupied by two companies of New York volunteers, under Lieutenant Colonel Burton, who had been sent down from California in 1847. Burton's general mission was to maintain American control over Lower California. This was found to be a difficult undertaking because Mexican military activities could easily be supported from across the gulf. During the early stages of the operations in the Gulf of California, the Navy did not have sufficient ships in those waters to cut communications between lower California and the rest of Mexico.

The *Dale* went to La Paz to support Burton's detachment. During November an outbreak against American control, led by Manuel Pineda, assumed considerable proportions. Pineda attacked Burton's force at La Paz a number of times during November and December but was each time repulsed. These attacks occurred at about the same time that Heywood's garrison at San José was also being attacked by another group of insurgents. The attacks against La Paz ended with the timely arrival of the *Cyane* early in December. That vessel remained in support of Burton's detachment, and the *Cyane's* marines helped to hold La Paz until February, 1848. Burton was reinforced on March 21 by the arrival of Colonel Mason, with 150 additional troops from California, and no further naval assistance in that vicinity was needed.

## Operations at San José

The *Congress* and *Independence* had arrived off San José during October, 1847. On November 2 part of the marine detachment and five seamen from the *Independence* were sent from San José on a boat expedition against an enemy band, reported at Todos Santos, a few miles west. They were later reinforced by twenty additional marines and three officers, but they encountered no enemy and returned on November 8.

A combined detachment of marines from the *Cyane, Congress,* and *Independence* and four passed midshipmen, under command of Lieutenant Charles Heywood, U.S.N., of the latter ship, then went ashore on November 8 to garrison San José, taking provisions for a month, a light artillery piece, and an ample supply of ammunition. The ships sailed away the following day, leaving Heywood with his marines to make the best of the difficult situation. Heywood was able to recruit twenty more or less dependable volunteers. With the assistance of the midshipmen, he fortified an old mission in which his troops were garrisoned in preparation for the siege which appeared imminent.

On November 19 a force of 150 Mexicans, mostly Yaqui Indians, appeared at San José and demanded the surrender of Heywood's force. Heywood of course refused. The Mexicans then began a systematic attack, which they continued intermittently throughout the night. They withdrew a slight distance at daylight. The following night they again besieged the marines and tried to rush them but were driven off by deadly musketry fire. When one party of Yaquis was trying to rush the garrison on one side, another attempted to scale the other sides of the building with ladders. The marines repulsed the attackers, and the scaling parties promptly retreated. The situation was somewhat relieved the following day by the arrival of an American whale-ship which the Mexicans apparently mistook for a man-of-war. The Mexicans withdrew and marched away on the La Paz road, firing a few shots at the Americans as they left the town.

The Mexicans continued to threaten the San José garrison but did not again attack it for several weeks. The *Portsmouth* arrived off San José and reinforced Heywood's garrison with sixteen marines and thirty-three sailors. The sailors returned to the ship a few days later, but the marines under Lieutenant Watson helped to garrison the town until December 21. On November 22, a force of Mexican cavalry captured two midshipmen and six others while they were out of the garrison. The *Portsmouth* left San José early in January, 1848. Shortly afterwards the Mexicans resumed military operations in that part of Lower California. The storeship *Southampton,* which had arrived at San José, rendered some assistance to Heywood and went to La Paz with a request that the *Cyane* come to the support of the garrison. Before relief could be received, however, a Mexican force, estimated at three or four hundred men, began a determined attack upon the garrison. Heywood then had only twenty-seven marines, ten sailors, and twenty Californians. In addition to their other troubles they had on their hands fifty women and children who had taken refuge in the mission. On the following day the Mexicans closed in for a systematic siege. They kept it up for more than a week. However, the Mexicans did not dare to storm the garrison. Heywood with the marines made several sorties and drove off parties of the enemy. This made the Mexicans more cautious. By February 10 the enemy had gained control of most of the town, including a near-by church. From it they were able to deliver a deadly fire into the mission. Two days later they got control of Heywood's source of water supply; he dug for water but found none. By February 14 their water was practically all gone; the situation was indeed desperate. On that afternoon, fortunately, the *Cyane* hove in sight. Although it was too late to render assistance that day, the besieged men were greatly cheered because they knew Dupont would not be long in coming to their relief. Dupont did not dare to venture a night attack on the crafty Yaquis but landed early the following morning with 102 officers and men. Supported by a fire from the ship, they commenced a systematic advance to drive the Mexicans from the town. As they approached the mission, Heywood with the marines sallied and helped open the way for their advance. The Mexicans were completely routed, despite the fact that they had more than three times the combined strength of the Americans. This ended the long series of sieges, which Heywood and his heroic garrison had been subjected to by the fierce Yaqui Indians. In all of the operations the garrison had lost three killed and four slightly wounded.

On the same day that Heywood was liberated, the New York volunteers from La Paz attacked the Mexicans at San Antonio and liberated the two midshipmen and six men who had been captured from the San José garrison. The *Cyane* continued to support the San José garrison during the following month. Landing forces of sailors and marines from that vessel went out as patrols against the enemy in the vicinity. One patrol captured twenty Mexicans. Additional troops from California began to arrive. Two hundred volunteers with heavy artillery reached San José on April 30, relieved Heywood's garrison and a landing force from the *Cyane*. The volunteers established a strong post and encountered no further difficulties. The marines and sailors from the squadron then returned to their ships. All organized Mexican resistance in Lower California had ended.

## Mulejé

The little village of Mulejé, just across the gulf from Guaymas, had, in the meantime, been the center of activities in Lower California. Forces for the occupation of that port were not available during the initial stages of the war. Our naval forces learned near the end of September, 1847, that the Mexicans were crossing the gulf in considerable numbers and landing at Mulejé. The *Dale* went there to investigate conditions and found Mulejé occupied by a considerable force of Mexicans and a Mexican schooner lying in the mouth of a near-by creek. A boat expedition of fifty men under Lieutenant Craven captured and took the schooner out to sea without meeting serious resistance. Commander Selfridge of the *Dale* then sent an officer ashore with a flag of truce to treat with the inhabitants of Mulejé. In the meantime he had placed the broadside of his ship towards the village and had prepared a landing force of marines and sailors to go ashore. The attempt to negotiate with the Mexicans only resulted in insults; the marines and two companies of sailors immediately started ashore. Under cover of fire from the ship, which drove the enemy from the shelter of the village, the landing force advanced and pursued the Mexicans who retreated into the jungles and hills and disappeared. The men from the *Dale* attempted to pursue, but the enemy ambushed them. Since little more could be accomplished by attempting to fight Indians in the brush, the landing force returned to the ship, having acquitted itself with great coolness and bravery. The enemy had completely abandoned the village, but the *Dale* did not have forces available to occupy it; furthermore, it was needed for more important tasks elsewhere. A few days later the *Dale* went up the coast to the Bay of Loreto. The marine guard and a company of sailors went ashore and, while operating under the protection of the ship's guns, captured several pieces of artillery. In order to accomplish the dual task of controlling Mulejé and Guaymas, Selfridge transferred part of his crew to a chartered schooner which kept guard over Mulejé, while he blockaded Guaymas with the *Dale*.

## OPERATIONS AT MAZATLAN

The control over the important port of Mazatlan by the Pacific Squadron was more or less intermittent during the spring and summer of 1847. Part of Shubrick's general plan, when he shifted his activities south, was to occupy and garrison permanently Mazatlan. The *Congress, Independence,* and *Cyane* arrived off the town on

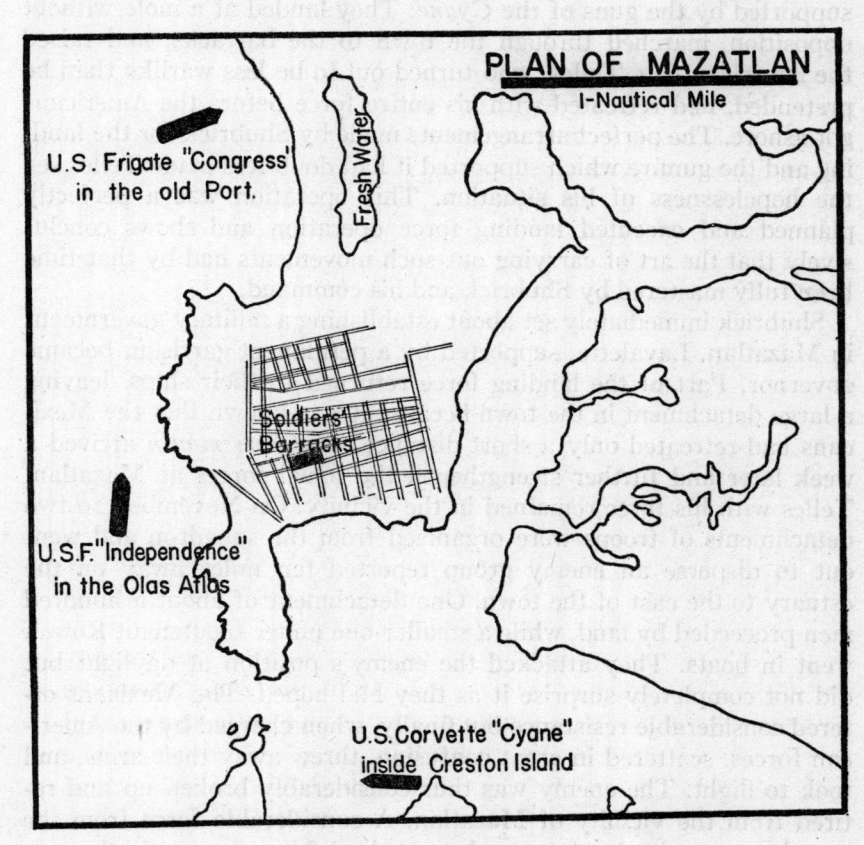

### PLAN OF MAZATLAN
1-Nautical Mile

U.S. Frigate "Congress" in the old Port.

Fresh Water

Soldiers' Barracks

U.S.F. "Independence" in the Olas Atlas

U.S. Corvette "Cyane" inside Creston Island

MAZATLAN HARBOR

November 10, 1847. Colonel Rafael Telles was then reported to be holding the town with an estimated strength of from nine to twelve hundred men. During the night after his arrival Shubrick placed his three ships as indicated on the accompanying sketch.

The positions of his ships were such as to permit a converging fire on all parts of the town. Captain Lavalette of the *Congress* went ashore the following morning with a flag of truce and delivered a demand to surrender the town. Telles very indignantly tore up the demand.

An elaborate landing operation of six hundred sailors and marines supported by five field pieces had been arranged; additional boats were furnished by the *Erie,* which had just arrived. The landing force, under the direct command of Shubrick, assembled near the *Cyane,* formed in three lines of boats, and proceeded into the harbor, supported by the guns of the *Cyane.* They landed at a mole without opposition, marched through the town to the barracks, and raised the American flag. Telles, who turned out to be less warlike than he pretended, had retreated with his entire force before the Americans got ashore. The perfect arrangements made by Shubrick for the landing and the gunfire which supported it had doubtless made Telles see the hopelessness of his situation. This operation was a perfectly planned and executed landing force operation and shows conclusively that the art of carrying out such movements had by that time been fully mastered by Shubrick and his command.

Shubrick immediately set about establishing a military government in Mazatlan. Lavalette, supported by a permanent garrison, became governor. Part of the landing force returned to their ships, leaving a large detachment in the town because it was known that the Mexicans had retreated only a short distance. The *Portsmouth* arrived a week later and further strengthened the naval forces at Mazatlan. Telles with his force remained in the vicinity. On November 20 two detachments of troops were organized from the squadron and went out to disperse an enemy group reported ten miles away on the estuary to the east of the town. One detachment of about a hundred men proceeded by land, while a smaller one under Lieutenant Rowan went in boats. They attacked the enemy's position at daylight but did not completely surprise it as they had hoped. The Mexicans offered considerable resistance but finally, when charged by the American forces, scattered in great confusion, threw away their arms, and took to flight. The enemy was thus considerably broken up and retired from the vicinity of Mazatlan. A considerable force from the squadron remained ashore and garrisoned Mazatlan until the war was over. The marines from the several ships were used largely in garrisoning not only this port but the several other ports along the Mexican coast, which had been captured in the above-mentioned operations. Captain Zeilin of the *Congress* and Lieutenant W. W. Russell of the *Independence* with practically their entire marine detachments were on garrison duty at Mazatlan during the closing months of the war. The marines from the *Portsmouth* and the *Savannah* also did short tours of garrison duty at Mazatlan.

After the signing of the armistice in April, 1848, until the conclusion of the treaty of peace on May 30, the Pacific Squadron occupied itself only with the holding of Mazatlan and Guaymas and in blockading San Blas. The *Ohio*, with Commodore Thomas ap C. Jones, of Monterey fame, joined the squadron on May 7. He later took over the command of the squadron from Shubrick. Its final act in the Mexican War was performed by the squadron June 17, when the last of the troops evacuated Mazatlan. The American flag was replaced by the Mexican flag and saluted with twenty-one guns.

## Conclusion

During the Mexican War the Pacific Squadron was called upon to perform one of the most unusual and difficult tasks that a small squadron of ships has perhaps ever undertaken. It was entirely out of communication with its own government and received practically no supplies from home. It was provided with no special equipment or personnel for operations ashore, yet it successfully carried out extensive field operations in the face of almost unsurmountable difficulties. At first inexperience and ignorance of local conditions caused a number of mistakes, but the personnel of the squadron showed great aptitude in adjusting themselves to conditions that were entirely foreign to their usual mode of life; they also hardened themselves to withstand the most trying marches and campaigns in difficult, almost barren country. As the war progressed they mastered the technique of that particular kind of warfare and acquitted themselves in a highly commendable manner. The determination shown by beleaguered garrisons such as Gillespie's in Los Angeles and Heywood's in San José cannot help but call forth our greatest admiration. The planning and executing of the campaigns and individual operations were on several occasions beyond criticism. Not only did they learn well the character of the enemy country and deal successfully with it, they learned so thoroughly the qualities of the enemy that they seemed to know just how to deal with a class of troops who were lacking in certain military qualities even though at times they showed exceptional ability, bravery, and disregard for their own safety and comfort.

## Distribution of the U. S. Marine Corps, August, 1847

| Station | Commanding Officer | Officers | Enl. Men |
|---|---|---|---|
| Headquarters, Washington, D. C. (incl. Marine Bks. & Navy Yd.) | Col. Comdt. Archibald Henderson | 11 | 176 |
| Boston, Mass. | Capt. A. N. Breevoort. | 1 | 49 |
| Brooklyn, N. Y. | Lt. Col. Samuel Miller. | 4 | 190 |
| Gosport, Va. | Major John Harris | 2 | 29 |
| Pensacola, Fla. | Capt. Francis C. Hall. | 1 | 21 |
| Philadelphia, Pa. | Capt. Job G. Williams. | 1 | 21 |
| Recruiting—at four cities | | 5 | 13 |
| Three Receiving Ships | | 1 | 51 |
| Home Squadron—eight ships* | | 3 | 82 |
| Pacific Squadron: | | | |
| Razee *Independence* | Capt. James Edelin | 2 | 47 |
| Frigate *Savannah* | Capt. Ward Marston | 2 | 38 |
| Frigate *Congress* | 1st Lt. Jacob Zeilin | 1 | 46 |
| Sloop *Portsmouth* | 1st Lt. H. B. Watson | 1 | 21 |
| Sloop *Cyane* | O. Sgt. E. D. Forrest | — | 22 |
| Sloop *Dale* | 1st Lt. Robert Tansill | 1 | 18 |
| Sloop *Preble* | Orderly Sergeant J. Culp | — | 23 |
| Brazil Squadron—two ships | | 1 | 58 |
| African Squadron—four ships | | 1 | 88 |
| East India Squadron—Flagship *Columbus* | | 3 | 62 |
| On the Lakes—Steamer *Michigan* | | — | 12 |
| Preparing for Sea—two ships | | 2 | 73 |
| On five other vessels | | 4 | 117 |
| Mexico—Marine Battalion | Lt. Col. Samuel E. Watson | 22 | 334 |

*Marine detachments of ships of the Home Squadron temporarily served on ships of the squadron in Mexican waters or ashore in Mexico.

## Chapter VII

### THE MARINES SEE THE WORLD

DURING the period between the close of the Mexican War and the outbreak of the Civil War the United States Navy and its auxiliary, the Marine Corps, again participated in the world-wide affairs, in which they had been involved in the years preceding the Mexican War. This period of American history, in addition to its many other characteristics, was one of ever-expanding foreign commerce and of building a merchant marine that ranked high in comparative size and was second to none in efficiency. The primary function of the Navy was to support our expanding commerce and to protect the lives of Americans and their property, particularly in the parts of the world that were torn by internal dissension or political revolutions, or were in the process of being subjugated by other foreign nations. At no other time, perhaps, in the history of the American Navy has it participated in operations so far-flung as during the period covered by this chapter. The marines attached to naval vessels were called upon to perform a great variety of duties, extending from duty in Nicaragua to elaborate ceremonies with Perry in Japan and from suppressing the African slave trade to desperate fighting operations in the storming of forts at Canton.

After the close of the Mexican War the Corps came in for its usual postwar let down and readjustment. The number of officers, having been hopelessly inadequate for war purposes, was, fortunately, not reduced, but the enlisted strength was cut by approximately one thousand men. The reduction entailed considerable hardship, especially among the noncommissioned officers who in many cases were reduced in rank to fit in with the new organization. Peacetime duties were resumed in the various home stations after the withdrawal of the regiment from Mexico. Ship detachments, many of which had been reduced in size or discontinued because of the duty in Mexico, particularly those of the Home Squadron, were increased to their usual strength or re-established. The Navy grew considerably during this period; steam vessels gradually replaced the older sailing frigates and other sailing vessels. This resulted in an ever-increasing demand for marines at sea. By 1855 more than half of the Corps was again at sea, and a few years later a still greater proportion. The President authorized two hundred additional marines to be enlisted during 1856 and in April, 1857, 240 more to be sent to sea as replacements for landsmen. In September, 1858, a further additional allowance of 232 marines was made for filling up the ship detachments of the vessels ordered on an expedition to Paraguay. All these increases were maintained throughout the remainder of the period.

The following table shows the distribution of the Corps at about the middle of the period:

### DISTRIBUTION OF THE MARINE CORPS
### November, 1855

| | Brig. Gen. Comdt. | Majors | Captains | First Lieuts. | Second Lieuts. | Sergeants | Corporals | Musics | Privates | Aggregate |
|---|---|---|---|---|---|---|---|---|---|---|
| H.Q., Washington, D. C. | 1 | 3 | 2 | 3 | 4 | 11 | 4 | 36 | 72 | 136 |
| Navy Yard, Washington, D. C. | | | 1 | | | 2 | 2 | 2 | 22 | 29 |
| Brooklyn, N. Y. | | 1 | | 4 | 2 | 7 | 7 | 7 | 75 | 103 |
| Charlestown, Mass. | | 1 | | | | 4 | 2 | 2 | 69 | 78 |
| Gosport, Va. | | 1 | 1 | | | 4 | 3 | | 33 | 42 |
| Philadelphia, Pa. | | 1 | | 3 | | 6 | 2 | 3 | 50 | 65 |
| Portsmouth, N. H. | | | 1 | | | 5 | 3 | 2 | 32 | 43 |
| Warrington, Fla. | | | 1 | | | 5 | 2 | | 47 | 55 |
| Pacific Squadron | | | 1 | | 2 | 8 | 14 | 10 | 120 | 155 |
| Home Squadron | | | 1 | 1 | 2 | 6 | 10 | 15 | 79 | 114 |
| Mediterranean Squadron | | | 1 | 1 | 2 | 7 | 11 | 6 | 104 | 132 |
| Brazil Squadron | | | | 1 | 2 | 4 | 7 | 4 | 63 | 81 |
| Africa Squadron | | | 1 | | 1 | 4 | 7 | 6 | 58 | 77 |
| East India Squadron | | | | 3 | 1 | 9 | 11 | 9 | 116 | 149 |
| On Receiving Ships | | | | 2 | | 6 | 8 | 2 | 90 | 106 |
| On the Lakes | | | | | 1 | | 1 | 2 | 11 | 15 |
| Practice Ship, Annapolis | | | | | | | 1 | 2 | 6 | 9 |
| | 1 | 7 | 10 | 18 | 17 | 88 | 95 | 108 | 1047 | 1389 |

### WITH PERRY TO JAPAN

One of the most interesting experiences of the marines during this period of world-wide adventure was that with Perry's squadron during his famous visits to Japan. On several occasions during the first half of the nineteenth century, a number of nations had made unsuccessful attempts to induce Japan to reopen her doors to foreign commerce, after having secluded herself as a hermit nation for nearly two hundred years. As the middle of the century approached, conditions became rather chaotic in Japan, and changes from the old order of things were very much needed. Many American whalers and a few trading vessels ventured into the western Pacific during the preceding decade. Several vessels had been wrecked on the coast of Japan, and the Japanese had treated their crews with unusual severity. Our growing commerce, after having forced an entrée into China, was anxiously looking for new outlets of trade and for coaling stations. This urge, no doubt, had considerable influence on our government in bringing about the carefully planned expedition to Japan to negotiate a suitable treaty for the protection of our nationals and for the opening of certain ports for our trade.

In 1852 the President and the Secretary of State began to make definite plans for such an expedition. Commodore Matthew C. Perry, who had served in the Navy since 1809, was selected to command the East India Squadron. Some of the new steam vessels were ordered to that squadron, which, thus augmented, was ordered on an expedition to Japan. The six larger vessels of the squadron had marine detachments ranging in strength from twenty to fifty men, with an aggregate of about six officers and two hundred marines. Major Jacob Zeilin was ordered to the squadron as senior marine officer and went out with Perry on the *Mississippi*. Tremendous preparations were made for the expedition, not only by Perry and his accompanying staff of scientists and other experts but by many other persons interested in the expedition. The proposed methods for dealing with the Japanese were designed to impress them as much as possible, and all arrangements were made with that end in view.

Perry proceeded to his new station by way of the Cape of Good Hope and shortly after arriving at the squadron base, Hong Kong, began to make final arrangements for the great adventure. He went first to the Luchu Islands, where he did considerable exploring and gave his squadron a period of thorough training, including the drilling of marines on shore. On July 2, 1853, with the steamers *Susquehanna* (flagship), the *Mississippi,* and the sloops of war *Saratoga* and *Plymouth*, he sailed for Yedo (Tokyo) Bay. He arrived at the mouth of the bay on the morning of July 8 and steamed up the bay against wind and tide—greatly to the astonishment of the Japanese. Japanese officials at Uraga tried to persuade Perry to leave immediately and carry on his negotiations through the Dutch at Nagasaki. Perry, carrying a letter from the President of the United States, not only insisted on delivering it in the vicinity of Yedo but took the position that it would be delivered only with proper ceremony to one of the highest officials of the land. After considerable argument over matters of rank and respect due the American flag, arrangements were finally made for Perry to land and deliver the President's letter.

The landing was made an event of all possible display and pageantry both by the Americans and the Japanese. Before going ashore Perry moved his steamers into position for covering the landing place by gunfire if necessary. A guard of honor of three hundred officers, sailors, and marines had been organized to accompany Perry. One hundred marines under Major Zeilin were the first troops to land. They immediately formed lines on both sides of the route from the boat dock to a temporary building which had been erected for the reception. One hundred sailors came next and extended the lines towards the reception hall. Two bands accompanied the landing party. Perry came last with a large staff, personal bodyguards, pages, and other trappings indicative of his great importance. The Japanese had more than five thousand troops drawn up along the shore to do proper honor to the occasion. As soon as Perry and his staff had landed, the military escort headed by the marines marched with him to the appointed place for the reception. After an elaborate ceremony and the rendering of appropriate honors, Perry with his escort withdrew and returned to the ships.

After telling the Japanese officials that he would return early the following year for their decision and to negotiate a treaty with them, Perry left Japan July 17. He went back to the East India Station, making some surveys and explorations while en route. Affairs in China were very chaotic, and the protection of American interests in that vicinity absorbed most of his attention for several months. Perry was determined, however, to let nothing deter him from carrying out his original mission in Japan. Early in 1854 his suspicion was aroused by Russian and French naval officers who had mysteriously sailed from Hong Kong; he decided to return to Japan as soon as possible. This time he ordered every available ship of the squadron, eight in all, to rendezvous at the Luchu Islands. From there he again sailed for Yedo on February 7. After some delay by storms he was again back in Yedo Bay. A repetition of the Japanese efforts to induce him to leave that vicinity and receive his reply at Nagasaki greeted him. Failing that, the Japanese insisted that he anchor his vessels farther out to sea; this Perry refused to do. He demanded that another meeting take place as near Yedo as possible. When the Japanese authorities insisted that it take place farther down the bay, he began moving his squadron towards Yedo; the Japanese officials then promptly agreed to meet him at Yokohama.

Perry's second meeting with the representatives of the Mikado

LANDING OF COMMODORE PERRY AT YOKOHAMA, JAPAN, MARCH 8, 1854

The *Hartford* and *Tennessee* at Close Quarters
(Marines at Great Gun in Center of Picture)

was even more elaborate than the first. This time, with his increased number of ships and personnel, Perry was able to land with an escort of five hundred officers and enlisted men, including every available marine. Perry with his escort in twenty-seven boats proceeded to the shore with all possible ceremony and display. The marines were again the first to land and, together with the rest of the troops, rendered military honors to the commodore as he passed by them on his way to the place appointed for the meeting. During Perry's absence the Japanese Government had been given ample time to think the situation over, and, after considerable hesitation upon his return, the Japanese representatives accepted a treaty which granted certain valuable rights to Americans in Japan. The treaty provided for two open ports as coaling stations, for places of safety for American seamen shipwrecked along the coast of Japan, and in addition contained a number of other provisions.

Completing certain provisions of the treaty caused some delay; during this time the American squadron concerned itself largely with trying to impress the Japanese with the superiority of our civilization. Valuable presents were exchanged, including a miniature railway equipment and telegraph apparatus, presented by the Americans to the Japanese. The native wrestlers gave demonstrations of their art; the marines went ashore to drill and greatly impressed the Japanese with their discipline and the precision of their exercises. Friendly relations were promoted by elaborate receptions and banquets on board Perry's vessels. This great diplomatic success made by Commodore Perry effected the opening of Japan to the outside world and marked the beginning of a new era for that nation. The marines of the squadron, dressed in one of the most showy uniforms ever worn by the Marine Corps, did their bit by making the military displays more colorful and impressive to the Japanese and thereby contributed materially to the success of the undertaking.

Revolution followed Perry's visit to Japan and led rapidly to the modernization of that country. The changes took place, however, with many internal difficulties and struggles. Vessels of the East India Squadron frequented Japanese waters throughout this unsettled period, and on a few occasions, when the necessity arose, landing parties of marines and sailors guarded American officials and other Americans.

### Supporting Trade in China

The East India Squadron with the exception of certain vessels, which returned to the United States with Perry, went back to its regular station along the China coast. In addition to numerous difficulties with various European nations attempting to seize every possible advantage, China was torn by the great Taiping rebellion. The American squadron co-operated with British and French vessels in the protection of their nationals, but its principal mission continued to be that of protecting the ever-increasing American trade in the Far East. As during the earlier period, when Caleb Cushing was in charge of American affairs in China, there continued to arise in the vicinity of Canton as well as around Shanghai difficulties which required action by the East India Squadron.

While Perry was on his second visit to Japan he left the sloop *Plymouth* at Shanghai to look after American interests. Revolutionary forces occupied the full attention of the Imperial troops in the vicinity, leaving the foreign settlements no means of protection except that provided by themselves. On the evening of April 4, 1854 the *Plymouth* received a signal from Americans ashore asking for protection. A detachment of sixty sailors and marines from that vessel promptly landed, and later on the same evening additional men reinforced it. The detachment guarded the American Mission during the night. This mission, together with the other foreign settlements, was being encroached upon by the Imperial troops; vigorous action was necessary. Commander Kelly of the *Plymouth* joined his troops with a similar force of 150 sailors and marines from British vessels, some English volunteers, and a number of volunteers from American merchant vessels. By means of a flanking movement and a vigorous frontal attack they soon threw the Chinese troops into a disorderly retreat and cleared the foreign settlement. Part of the *Plymouth* landing force remained ashore, guarding the American consulate and mission until June 15.

The steam frigate *Powhatan* put in at Shanghai during March, 1855, and found conditions again very unsettled. The commander took no definite action, however, until May 19, when the marine guard of forty-one men under First Lieutenant James H. Jones went ashore. The guard remained for two days and then returned aboard ship and sailed from that port. The records do not show the particular reason for this landing nor any of the details of the operation.

### Storming the Forts of Canton

Protection of Americans and their commerce in the vicinity of Canton continued to be one of the principal concerns of the East India Squadron. The sloop *Portsmouth* (Commander Foote) was lying off Whampoa on October 22, 1856, when it received a communication from the American consul at Canton that American interests were in imminent danger. Early the following morning Foote sent a landing force of five officers and seventy-eight enlisted men, including Second Lieutenant William W. Kirkman with eighteen marines, in boats to Canton. This little landing force proved entirely inadequate to protect the American settlement and on October 27 a detachment of sailors and marines from the *Levant* was sent to assist the *Portsmouth*'s landing force. Commodore James Armstrong arrived on his flagship, the steam frigate *San Jacinto*, November 12, sent Brevet Captain John D. Simms with twenty-eight marines from that ship as additional reinforcements for the detachments at Canton, and ordered Simms to take command of the entire force.

At the request of the Chinese commissioner Yeh (November 16), who promised protection, the American and French guards at Canton began to withdraw. The landing forces from the *Portsmouth* and the *San Jacinto* returned to their ships, leaving only a small guard from the *Levant* to protect the American consulate. It was arranged for the *Levant* to lie off Canton as a ready refuge for the consul and other Americans.

On the same day a sounding boat sent up the river by Commodore Armstrong was fired upon by one of the barrier forts of Canton, and a sailor was killed, while in the act of heaving the lead. French and Portuguese boats had frequently passed the same forts without being molested. Armstrong determined to force respect for the American flag by retaliatory measures. As the *San Jacinto* drew too much water to go up the Canton River, Armstrong transferred all of its crew to the *Portsmouth* and *Levant,* except those absolutely necessary to take care of the ship. While engaged in preliminary arrangements for an attack, the boat of Commander Foote of the *Levant* was also fired upon by the barrier forts, but no damage was done except to raise the ire of that temperamental officer. Armstrong transferred his broad pennant to the *Portsmouth* and arranged a combined landing force of nearly three hundred to storm the offending forts. Late that afternoon small steamers towed the *Portsmouth* and *Levant* up the river, and the *Portsmouth* began an intensive bombardment of the forts. The *Levant,* unfortunately, was grounded before getting within range, but the *Portsmouth* kept up a vigorous fire with shell and grape, expending about seven hundred rounds before darkness put an end to the day's activities. The *Portsmouth* was hulled a number of times but suffered no serious damage; the only casualty of the day was one marine wounded. They spent the following night in getting the

*Levant* afloat and the next three days preparing for more decisive action. Meanwhile Armstrong was attempting to adjust matters by negotiations.

Because of ill health, Armstrong withdrew to his flagship and left the more impetuous and daring Foote in command at Canton. A communication from the commodore to Foote indicated that the negotiations were not progressing satisfactorily and gave Foote authority to proceed with punitive operations—even to the extent of landing and destroying the forts. This authority seems to have been very much to Foote's liking, judging from the character of his daring exploits which followed in rapid succession during the next several days.

In the early morning of November 20 Foote began operations with great determination. Both the *Portsmouth* and *Levant* were then in suitable firing positions to cover two of the forts. A landing force of 287 officers, sailors, and marines, supported by four howitzers, pulled away in three columns for storming operations under cover of a bombardment by the two vessels. The Chinese forts at first vigorously returned the naval gunfire but were soon silenced. The sailors of the landing force and the squadron marines under Simms landed and advanced on the nearest fort. They passed through a village in the rear of the fort, where they brushed aside some resistance and continued their attack. When within effective range the storming party took up a destructive musket fire which soon had its effect. The Chinese garrison fled; the marines shot down some forty or fifty of their fleeing adversaries. The marines then occupied the fort and raised the American flag. Some of the fort's fifty-three guns were manned by the landing force. The nearest fort opened fire on them. Simms with the marines then returned to the village, which had been reoccupied by Chinese soldiers and again drove them away, this time into the rice fields where the muddy ground made further pursuit very difficult. Simms ordered his men to retire; the Chinese, mistaking this movement for a retreat, followed with two thousand or more soldiers. The marines then turned on the advancing enemy with a deadly fire that soon caused them to break and flee. Simms then returned to the fort.

A force of four or five thousand Chinese troops then came out from Canton, only four miles away, and made three assaults on the Americans, but each time the deadly musketry of the marines and the fire from the howitzers repulsed them. The final repulse turned into a complete rout. A part of the landing force under

Simms held the fort without difficulty during the night. The remainder had returned to the vessels.

At three o'clock the following morning the next barrier fort up the river began firing on the *Portsmouth*. Simms with his landing force embarked in boats and lay off, preparatory to another landing. Three hours later both vessels opened a vigorous fire on the three remaining forts. For a short time the forts briskly returned the fire. In the meantime a small steamer towed the landing force into position for storming operations against the next fort, called "Fiddlers Fort." One of Simms' boats was raked by a shot from a 64-pounder and most of the occupants were killed or wounded. The landing force proceeded ashore without other serious difficulty; in the face of artillery fire they advanced across ditches waist-deep and successfully stormed Fiddlers Fort, with the additional loss of only Private Thompson, who was severely wounded by a rocket. Corporal McDougal, the standard bearer of the marines, planted the first American flag on the walls of the fort in the face of more than a thousand Chinese soldiers. Simms soon captured the fort and promptly turned a number of its guns on the next fort, called "Center Fort," which returned a vigorous fire. The marines spiked the remaining guns, burned their carriages, and systematically destroyed the other equipment of the fort. In the meantime Foote prepared for an assault on the remaining forts.

Simms with the marine detachments then advanced in the direction of Canton to storm the Center Fort. He moved along the river bank for a time under cover of an embankment in an effort to draw the Chinese in the fort from their guns. While carrying out this maneuver he encountered a breastwork mounting seven guns, which he attacked and captured and then turned the guns on the enemy. The Chinese promptly counterattacked, but the marines repulsed them with little difficulty. Simms left Lieutenant William W. Kirkland with part of the marines to hold the breastworks with orders to withdraw later after destroying the guns. Simms took the remainder of his men to join a navy landing force, in further offensive operations.

An island fort next stood in the way of Foote's destructive advance towards Canton. The ships bombarded it while the boats embarked the marines and sailors from their position near Fiddlers Fort. Under cover of the fire of the *Portsmouth* and the *Levant*, the landing force successfully landed on the island and, with little difficulty, captured the fort there. The marines' standard bearer, McDougal, again was the first to raise the American flag over this fort, which proved to be a well-built structure with thirty-eight guns. The landing force immediately set about a systematic destruction of the enemy's materiel, including as usual the spiking of the guns. The eventful day ended in an artillery duel between the remaining Chinese fort and the ships, supported by the fire of the howitzers of the landing force and the guns from captured Fiddlers Fort. The enemy fire was silenced as darkness approached, but Foote was not yet ready to give the Chinese any respite.

Early the following morning preparations were underway for the storming of the last of the barrier forts. The landing force was again in its boats and advanced towards that fort, under the fire of the ships' guns and the fire from Fiddlers Fort. As the boats were unable to get close to the shore, the assaulting parties were forced to wade a considerable distance. But, they successfully stormed and captured the fort, which they found armed with twenty-eight guns. The Chinese again counterattacked but were promptly repulsed with heavy losses. Foote then set about completing the destruction of all of the forts; this required several days. The outer granite walls, which were several feet in thickness, were systematically mined and demolished. Foote had most of the guns rolled into the river and burned or otherwise destroyed the other equipment. A spark, knocked from a stone by a crowbar accidentally, set off a charge of fifty pounds of powder which had been placed for demolition purposes. The explosion killed and wounded several of the mining party.

In the series of daring operations a few hundred men of the East India Squadron defeated, on every turn, a force of approximately five thousand Chinese and lost only seven killed and twenty-two wounded, during the actual fighting. The Chinese losses were at least ten times that number. The four forts contained approximately 168 cannon, the larger of which was $8\frac{1}{2}$-inch caliber. The expenditure of ammunition by Foote's vessels ran into thousands of rounds. When the work of demolition was finally completed, the *Levant* and *Portsmouth* with the squadron landing force returned to the regular squadron anchorage, a short distance down the river at Whampoa. The vigorous measures were entirely successful in that they induced Imperial Commissioner Yeh to apologize for the firing on the American flag. No further hostile acts against Americans were—for the time being—committed in that vicinity.

Prior to the middle of the nineteenth century all of the relations between foreigners and the Imperial Chinese Government were conducted through Canton—the Emperor thus successfully avoiding direct contact with foreigners. As alien influence grew more powerful, it became more insistent that the Imperial Government receive western representatives in the usual manner at Peking. In 1859 the point was made one of considerable issue. The ministers of France, Great Britain, and the United States were temporarily located at Shanghai, while pressing arrangements to be received in Peking. The British, in their efforts to force the issue, suffered a disastrous reverse in an attempt to capture or destroy the Chinese forts at the mouth of the Peiho River. The American Minister, employing more pacific means, was permitted to go to Peking, where, together with the Russian Minister, he was reluctantly received.

The British reverses caused the Chinese to become more aggressive toward all foreigners and to commit a number of indignities against them around Shanghai. The steam frigate *Mississippi* arrived off the near-by port of Woosung in July, 1859, and, upon the request of the American consul, sent its marine detachment and sixty sailors to Shanghai, where they guarded the American interests until early in August. The outbreak of the Civil War greatly curtailed our naval activities along the China coast as well as in the rest of the Far East.

## In the Fiji Islands

The marines again had exciting contacts with the savages of the South Sea Islands during this period. The severe lessons which Commander Wilkes taught the Fiji Islanders during his famous exploring expedition apparently were forgotten after a few years, for they resumed their mistreatment of American traders who ventured into that part of the Pacific. The sloop of war *John Adams*, while making a cruise among the South Sea Islands looking after the protection of American interests in general, received information, while at Samoa, that American residents and shipwrecked seamen in the Fiji group were being seriously mistreated by the natives. In accordance with his general mission, Commander Boutwell proceeded with the *John Adams* first to Nukulau, in the Fijis, where he arrived on September 12, 1855. He at once landed the marine detachment and a few sailors under Lieutenant John L. Broome of the Marine Corps; Broome made a demonstration in a number of places on the island for moral effect and then returned to the ship. Boutwell then proceeded to Viti Levu where he again landed a small force to bring King Tui Viti to his ship for the purpose of negotiating a treaty with Tui and exacting some adjustment for damages his people had inflicted on American property. The King was brought aboard the *John Adams*. He promised to require his people to respect American property and accept the treaty. Boutwell then moved on to the island of Ovalau where he remained about a month, carrying out his usual mission. He returned to Viti Levu, where it was reported to him that the King had not afforded protection to Americans as he had agreed to do. Boutwell decided to repeat the lesson given by Wilkes in the earlier days. He landed a small expedition, burned the town of Butia, and returned to the ship. On the following day he took a landing force and went to the town of Lassalassa, where he encountered considerable resistance from the native warriors. He had reinforcements brought from the ship and fought it out with the natives, giving them a thorough chastisement and burning two more of their villages. These retaliatory measures had the desired effect in the Fijis for about three years. Then, another similar retaliation was necessary.

Two American citizens were killed in the summer of 1858 on the island of Waya. The act was reported to Commander Arthur Sinclair of the sloop *Vandalia*, when he arrived in the Fiji group some months later. Sinclair fitted out an expedition of about sixty marines and sailors and placed them aboard the American schooner *Mechanic*, which had a shallower draft than his vessel, and sent them to Waya on October 6. Lieutenant C. H. B. Caldwell, U.S.N., who landed with the detachment at Waya, demanded that the murderers be turned over to him. Their chief not only refused but assumed a very hostile attitude towards the Americans. While the parley was in progress, about three hundred Fiji warriors gathered around; the situation looked serious for the little group of Americans. Caldwell and his determined band, however, were by no means overawed by this show of force but were determined to avenge the murder of their countrymen. A pitched battle ensued in which the natives were completely routed. Caldwell then returned (October 16) with his expedition to the *Vandalia*.

### Early Interventions in Nicaragua

Early in 1852 the marines had their first of a series of contacts, extending over nearly three quarters of a century, with the turbulent republic of Nicaragua. They went ashore at San Juan del Sur (Greytown) on February 5 and assisted in extinguishing a serious conflagration which was sweeping the town. During the following year they returned for diplomatic reasons. Greytown had sprung up as the eastern terminus of the transit route across the Isthmus of Nicaragua, which assumed great importance during the California gold rush days. Greytown at the time was in a sort of no man's land, located between the territories of the Mosquito Confederation, Nicaragua, and Costa Rica. The unsettled conditions in the locality prompted Commander John Hollins of the sloop

*Cyane* to land his marine detachment for the protection of American property on March 11, 1853. After the danger had somewhat passed, two days later, he withdrew it.

Not long afterwards the American Minister to Nicaragua, Borland, went ashore at Greytown and became involved with the local officials. He was forcibly detained and not allowed to return to his ship. The affair was reported to the State Department; Hollins was directed to return to Greytown and demand reparation for the insult to the American Minister, as well as reimbursement for some damages that had been inflicted upon American property. Hollins made his demands upon the local authorities, but they did not reply promptly. He then made a public declaration that, unless his demands were immediately complied with, he would land a force and if necessary bombard the town. On July 12, after waiting three days for a reply and receiving none, he sent his marine guard and fifteen sailors under two officers ashore to seize any arms and ammunition found in the town. They took possession of three field pieces and several muskets, destroyed a quantity of powder, and returned to the ship. Still having received no reply to his original demands and after having furnished boats for the removal of property and persons to those who desired the services, Hollins bombarded and destroyed most of the town—without any loss of life, however, as the natives had fled. When the bombardment ceased in the afternoon, Hollins again sent a landing force ashore and destroyed the town. The Nicaraguan Government demanded reparations for Hollins' severe acts, but, as that government had previously refused to accept any responsibility for American losses in Greytown, our government refused to acknowledge any rights of reparation.

## Interventions on the Isthmus of Panama

In 1846 the United States Government negotiated a treaty with Colombia, then called New Granada, by which our government guaranteed the neutrality of the Isthmus of Panama and the security of the isthmian transit. As the result of chaotic conditions on the Isthmus and in accordance with the provisions of the treaty, our naval forces made a long series of interventions, which did not cease until several years after Panama had become a separate nation and the Panama Canal had been constructed. Not long after the treaty was signed, gold was discovered in California, and gold seekers rushed westward over every possible route. Their most popular route from the Atlantic coast was by steamer to Colon, thence across the Isthmus, and then by another vessel from Panama. The transit, as made at first, was up the Chagres River as far as possible and then by trail to the Pacific coast. General political chaos in New Granada and the presence of disorderly elements along the line of transit caused considerable concern to the American authorities. When available, one or more vessels of our navy were generally retained in the vicinity during this early phase of isthmian transit.

The possibility of constructing a railroad across the Isthmus soon appealed to American promoters, who with great difficulty built such a railroad between 1850-1855. Travel across the Isthmus greatly increased. The construction work had attracted a great many laborers, who were left without employment when the job was finished; the disorderly elements on the Isthmus were thereby greatly increased. In April, 1856, while three shiploads of American passengers were making the transit, a serious riot occurred in which the native officials joined the rioters; a number of Americans were killed and about fifty were wounded. The rioting did not stop until the *St. Mary's* arrived at Panama on June 18. That small vessel, not having sufficient men to land and cope with the situation, and the government of New Granada refusing to act, Commander Bailey of the *St. Mary's* determined to do all in his power without resorting to a landing. He had a landing force stand by in boats, when ships were in port, and made other show of force. As a result of such measures a semblance of peace was restored for the time being. Rioting broke out again about three months later, but fortunately both the *St. Mary's* and the *Independence* were present. Commander Mervine, fearing serious consequences, promptly landed a force of 160 marines and sailors under Captain Addison Garland, U.S.M.C., who established a camp at the railroad station at Panama, in order to protect the transit facilities from attacks by the several hundred insurgents in the vicinity. By means of parades and other demonstrations Garland made a considerable show of force with his little battalion. Within three days the situation had sufficiently cleared up for the troops to be withdrawn. A similar naval force landed about a month later to protect the transit of the passengers and cargo of an American ship.

The transit situation was more or less critical for several years thereafter, and one or more of our naval vessels remained on the scene for prompt intervention if necessary. In September, 1860, a band of negroes started an insurrection in the vicinity of Panama and attacked the city. A British naval vessel landed a force for the protection of its nationals; the captain of the *St. Mary's* promptly followed suit by landing a force of sailors and marines from his ship to guard the railroad station at Panama. Conditions gradually improved after the loyal forces had defeated the rebels. The landing force from the *St. Mary's* withdrew October 8. These interventions on the Isthmus of Panama were only the beginning of a series, the accounts of which will be found in later chapters.

### Suppressing the African Slave Trade

By the beginning of the nineteenth century the anti-slave movement had made considerable headway in England; in the United States, it was then thought that it was only a question of time until slavery would come to an end. The importation of slaves into the United States had been made illegal early in the century; continued agitation against the slave trade resulted in the enactment of a law by Congress in 1820, which made slave-carrying on the high seas an act of piracy. The United States Navy, prior to 1842, had an occasional vessel along the African coast, attempting in a feeble way to run down slave ships. The insistence of the United States that vessels under our flag should not be searched upon the high seas by foreign men-of-war, complicated the situation. When closely pressed by a man-of-war, many slavers took refuge under the American flag. In an effort to stop the slave trade near its source, Great Britain had been keeping a squadron of various strength along the western coast of Africa. Looking to a solution of some difficulties between the United States and Great Britain and more effectively to suppress the African slave trade, the Webster-Ashburton treaty was agreed to in 1842. That treaty provided that the United States keep a squadron of at least eighty guns along the western coast of Africa to operate in conjunction with a more powerful British Squadron against the slave traders, who at times were reported to have had as many as three hundred vessels.

In conformity with the Webster-Ashburton treaty, our Navy, from early in 1843 until the outbreak of the Civil War, maintained along the African slave coast a squadron varying from two to seven vessels. During this period most of the vessels of the Navy, as well as a majority of the naval officers and junior marine officers, together with a substantial proportion of enlisted men of the Corps, took their turn at this trying duty. The usual base of the squadron was the Cape Verde Islands; the cruising ground extended more than three thousand miles along the inhabited part of the African coast. In addition to those extensive operations and also in compliance with the above-mentioned treaty, in which the United States agreed to use its influence to suppress the slave trade wherever found, the vessels of our Brazil Squadron carried on extensive operations against slavers in the waters of Brazil; our Home Squadron carried on similar duty in attempting to prevent the landing of slaves in Cuba. The details of the far-flung anti-slave operations are too numerous to warrant even a brief mention.

The task of the African Squadron was, of course, an extremely difficult one. The British, as a rule, maintained two or three times as many ships on duty suppressing the slave trade as did the United States; yet the trade continued to thrive, despite the fact that a considerable number of slave vessels were captured from time to time and the negroes returned to Africa. In addition to the suppression of the slave trade, the American squadron was expected to support the extensive movement of returning freed negroes from the United States to Africa; colonies had been established for them in Liberia. The squadron was never really successful in its operations until steam vessels were placed on that duty, because the slavers were able to avoid slow sailing ships. After the advent of steam, however, the trade was practically stopped, particularly during the last few years preceding the Civil War. In 1860, for example, our West African and Home squadrons captured twelve slave ships and freed more than three thousand slaves. The duty of the marines during all of these operations varied from boarding parties, sent on vessels suspected of being slave ships, to expeditions ashore in which they occasionally found both adventure and excitement.

The uncivilized tribes along the coast were accustomed to attacking and plundering undefended vessels and, on certain occasions, had murdered members of American crews. Commodore Perry, while in charge of the squadron, landed in Liberia in November, 1843, with a force of seventy-five sailors and marines to investigate reported murders of Americans. The native chiefs all vigorously denied the responsibility. Nevertheless Perry was convinced of the guilt of the inhabitants; he took three of them as hostages and burned their villages. He made several other landings during the following month, to establish relations with a number of native chieftains. In each of these visits Perry was heavily guarded by a landing force of marines and sailors. His attempts to fix the responsibility for depredations against American vessels proved quite difficult—one tribe would always accuse some other tribe.

While engaged in a parley with a chieftain called "King Ben Crack-O" of the Berribee tribes, Perry became somewhat peeved over the king's obvious lying; the two engaged in a hand-to-hand encounter; and the king attempted to drag Perry towards the place where he had left his arms. Perry was more than a match for him, however, and held his ground. When they separated, the king was still obviously bent upon starting a real fight. As he was leaving the room a sergeant of marines shot him, and some other marines jabbed him with bayonets. He was then bound and carried away by Perry's party. Then a general fight started between the natives of the village and Perry's landing force. The Africans soon fled, and Perry had the torch applied to their village. While retiring to their boats, the Americans were fired upon from the woods. They turned upon the Berribees and drove them back a safe distance before re-embarking in their boats. On the following day Perry with a landing force of sailors and marines destroyed several more villages of the same tribe. Perry's rather severe measures appear to have produced considerable respect for Americans along that part of the African coast. The African Squadron was less active under Perry's successors, who only on rare occasions resorted to operations ashore. The last landing operations from the African Squadron took place in 1860, in what is now Portuguese West Africa, when the marines and sailors from the sloop *Marion* went ashore to guard American lives and property.

### With the Brazil Squadron

After a number of years with only occasional cruises by our naval vessels to lower South America, that area was made a regular cruising station, and our squadron in the area designated the Brazil Squadron. For several years after its establishment, the commodore of the squadron was called upon to carry out a number of diplomatic missions in countries with which we had not yet exchanged regular representatives. The Brazil Squadron formed part of the world-wide protection that our navy attempted to furnish for our ever-expanding foreign trade. The duties of the squadron were, on the whole, more or less peaceful, but, on several occasions, it made armed interventions. For a number of years after declaring their independence from Spain, the countries in that part of South America were in an almost constant state of civil strife.

Reports of revolutionary activity in the vicinity of Buenos Aires in 1833 brought Commodore Woolsey with his flagship to support the *Natchez*, which at the time was the only American naval ship in the vicinity. Woolsey found conditions very unsettled, and on October 31 landed a force of forty-three officers, sailors, and marines under Commander Isaac McKeever, whom Woolsey had designated as officer in charge of American affairs in Argentina. McKeever's force stayed in Buenos Aires until conditions had become more settled, then (November 15) withdrew.

Some twenty years later McKeever was again on the Brazil station as commander in chief of the Squadron. Revolution again broke out at Buenos Aires; McKeever, who was at the time at Montevideo, sent the marine guard of his flagship, the *Congress,* under Captain Algernon S. Taylor, to the scene of the disturbance. McKeever then conferred with the senior naval officers of other countries and with foreign representatives. They agreed upon joint action for the protection of foreigners in Buenos Aires—at the time practically in a state of siege.

The marine detachments of the *Congress* and the *Jamestown* were placed aboard a small American steamer and transported into the inner harbor of Buenos Aires. Boats, supplied by a British naval vessel, then (February 3, 1852) took them ashore. They formed a guard for the American representatives in the city as well as for certain large American commercial interests. British and French landing forces were also disposed about the city for the protection of other foreign interests. While engaged in their protecting mission, a small detachment of marines had a skirmish with a band of pillagers and, before it was over, killed four of the band. This vigorous action helped materially to restore order in the city. A provisional government was finally able to regain control. The marines were withdrawn about ten days after they had landed. Another disturbance in Buenos Aires occurred during the following September. A marine guard from the *Jamestown* guarded the American consulate for a number of weeks.

## Landings in Uruguay

The revolutionary fever spread soon afterward to the neighboring republic of Uruguay, where lives and property of all foreigners became seriously jeopardized. The commander in chief of the Brazil Squadron kept one vessel in immediate readiness at Montevideo, the center of the revolutionary activity. The *Germantown* was on that duty during the summer and autumn of 1855. An overthrow of the government of Uruguay by revolutionary factions appeared imminent to Commander William F. Lynch of the *Germantown,* and on August 28 he sent his marine detachment ashore to guard American lives and property. The revolutionary movement ended almost at once, however, and the marines returned to their ship the following day. Another revolt broke out in Montevideo during November. The marines from the *Germantown* under First Lieutenant Augustus S. Nicholson, together with landing forces from naval vessels of three other countries, guarded the different consulates and the customs house during the closing week of November.

Conditions grew worse on November 27 and additional men from the *Germantown* temporarily reinforced Nicholson's marines. Nicholson prevented the massacre of a body of insurgents, who had given up their arms and surrendered to government troops, by interposing himself and some of his men between the two factions.

Three years later revolution again broke out in Montevideo. Flag Officer French Forrest, commanding the Brazil Squadron, stood by to take care of American interests with the *St. Lawrence* and *Falmouth*. Forrest made arrangements with the British naval commander for a joint landing force to protect the nationals of the two countries. On January 2, 1858, the marine guard of the *St. Lawrence*, under Brevet Major John G. Reynolds, went ashore as the American contingent of the joint operation. Reynolds guarded the American consulate and the customs house until January 27. The British landing force was then increased and assumed the responsibility for protecting American interests.

### Enforcing Respect in Paraguay

A strong naval demonstration was made necessary soon afterwards by certain hostile acts of Paraguay. In February, 1855, when the U.S. Steamer *Water Witch* was making a survey of the Parana River, which at the particular place was the boundary between Paraguay and Argentina, it was fired upon by a Paraguayan fort. One of the crew was killed, and the vessel was forced to retire from its mission. There had also been considerable mistreatment of American citizens in Paraguay, and the property of some had been seized. Congress took cognizance of these hostilities and authorized President Buchanan to "adopt such measurees and use such force as in his judgment may be necessary and advisable." Acting upon that authority, Buchanan sent a commissioner to adjust the difficulties and augmented the Brazil Squadron to the then powerful fleet of two frigates, two sloops of war, three brigs, twelve armed steamers, and two armed storeships, carrying in all 2,500 men, including about three hundred marines. The squadron was especially well equipped for landing force operations. The show of force on the coast of Paraguay and sending part of the steamers up the Parana River as far as the capital were sufficient to induce the government of that country to adjust difficulties and thereafter respect the American flag.

## With Other Naval Squadrons

In addition to the activities with the African, Brazil, and East India squadrons, the marines had considerable experience during the period with the other squadrons of the Navy. The Mediterranean Squadron had been maintained with slight interruptions since the wars with the Barbary corsairs. During the period of this chapter the strength of the squadron varied from one or two vessels to as many as seven. Its activities were especially important during the several revolutions which swept Europe in 1848. None of the vessels, however, became engaged in any actual belligerent operations. The Home Squadron had a greater field of activity than its name indicates, as its cruising area was from the Newfoundland banks to the mouth of the Amazon. It was concerned primarily with unsettled political conditions in the Caribbean area and around the Gulf of Mexico. In 1851 a rebellion against Spanish rule was raging in Cuba. Sympathy for the rebels aroused a great many adventurous Americans. American organizations attempted to aid the Cubans in various ways. At times vessels of the Home Squadron were kept busy enforcing neutrality in Cuban affairs.

Our only other squadron, the Pacific Squadron, continued its far-flung operations in the Pacific Ocean. From its usual base at Valparaiso its vessels cruised extensively in the South Seas and along the west coast of South and North America. With the exception of the experiences in the Fiji Islands the duties of the marines with the squadrons were more or less routine. Incident to their experiences with the Pacific Squadron as well as with the several other squadrons of the Navy, it is very evident that the marines during this period of our history quite thoroughly saw the world.

## Indian Fighting

The few available marines were kept too busy going to sea to assist very greatly in suppressing Indian uprisings as they had in the period preceding the Mexican War. During the 1850's, however, the Indians around Puget Sound were showing considerable hostility to the early inhabitants; for the purpose of furnishing protection for that isolated settlement, the sloop of war *Decatur* was kept stationed in the vicinity of the village of Seattle. On January 26, 1856, upon receiving report that Indians in large numbers were in the woods surrounding the town, a landing force from the *Decatur*, including its marine detachment, went ashore to protect the inhabitants. The troops were supported by the fire of a howitzer, which they had taken with them and by the ship's battery in the fight which followed. The little naval force attacked the Indians and within about half an hour drove them to the northward of the town. They then renewed the attack in the same direction and kept up the fight six hours longer. After suffering severe losses, the Indians finally gave up and retired during the night.

## Suppressing Domestic Disturbances

The marines stationed in Washington, D. C., had a warlike experience without leaving their home station. On June 1, 1857, while elections were in progress and the issues were unusually bitter as the results of the activities of the "Know-Nothing" Party, a gang of hired roughs and bullies of the cult of "Plug-Uglies" arrived in Washington from Baltimore, at the behest of the "Know-Nothing" leaders, and began to interfere seriously with the election. They even took possession of voting places and prevented further voting. The civil authorities, helpless to deal with the situation, were in need of a military force. The mayor called upon the President; he promptly ordered a company of marines to restore order in the city.

The "Plug-Uglies," armed with all sorts of weapons, including a brass cannon, were parading up Pennsylvania Avenue when two companies of marines from the Washington barracks marched up behind them and reported to the mayor for duty. At the request of the mayor the marines formed in a line near the City Hall, while the rioters threatened and insulted them in every conceivable way. The "Plug-Uglies" hauled up their cannon, pointed it at the military formation, and demanded that the marines return to their barracks immediately, or the cannon would be fired into their ranks. When Captain Tyler, in command of the marines, heard their demand, he immediately ordered a detachment to advance and capture the cannon. The situation was quite tense. General Henderson, who, dressed in plain clothing, had mingled with the mob, forced the muzzle of the cannon around so that it no longer aimed at the marines. Henderson warned the rioters of the seriousness of their acts and told them that the marines' pieces were loaded with ball cartridges and if necessary they would be ordered to fire. A number of rioters then fired their pistols at Henderson; fortunately, he suffered no harm. As a platoon of marines charged to capture the cannon, the rioters fired upon them and then retreated. Later they attacked the marines in a vain attempt to recapture the cannon.

In the midst of the fight one of the rioters, at a distance of only a few feet, aimed his pistol at Henderson; fortunately, a marine struck the rioter's arm with his musket and knocked the loaded pistol to the ground. The general personally seized the culprit and marched him off to the mayor. The rioters fired a number of pistol shots at the marines who, in obedience to Henderson's orders, held their fire for some time in spite of the danger to themselves. Finally when one marine was shot in the cheek and several others were struck with stones, they could be restrained no longer and opened fire on the rioters. Their officers stopped the firing as soon as possible, but the rioters, who had retired for some distance, continued to fire. Tyler then prepared his whole battalion for fighting; the rioters took to their heels and fled. Order was finally restored. A part of the marines were then sent to the railroad station to prevent the arrival of other disorderly gangs from Baltimore.

One of the frequent yellow fever epidemics of those days was raging at different Atlantic ports during the summer of 1858. Some government buildings on Staten Island were used as pest houses for yellow fever patients, taken from incoming vessels. The citizens of the island seriously objected to the practice and determined to destroy the buildings. On the night of September 1 they succeeded in burning part of them. The *Susquehanna,* which had recently returned from the fever-infested Nicaraguan coast, had left several patients as well as a quantity of stores on Staten Island. The naval authorities received information on the following day that the mob would probably continue its operations that night. A detachment of sixty-five marines from the barracks at the New York Navy Yard and from the *Sabine* were sent to occupy and protect the government buildings on Staten Island. The rioting continued for another week; the disorderly elements attempted to force their way into the area occupied by the marines by using battering rams and other instruments but failed. As a result of the assistance given by the marines, order was finally restored.

### Capturing John Brown

In the fall of 1859 John Brown, the militant leader of the abolitionist movement, after a tempestuous career elsewhere, established himself at Harper's Ferry and began to induce negro slaves of the vicinity to revolt against their masters. With a number of followers, including some ex-slaves, he had taken possession of the United States arsenal at Harper's Ferry and obtained arms and ammunition for his band. The situation was too serious for the local civil officials or even the Governor of Virginia to deal with. Federal assistance was requested. The Navy Department ordered all available marines in Washington to the scene of the disturbance. Ninety were assembled and placed under First Lieutenant Israel Green, who proceeded (October 18) to Harper's Ferry by rail and reported to the senior officer of the Army, Colonel Robert E. Lee.

Considerable fighting had already taken place between Brown's insurgents and some volunteer troops under Lee. The marines relieved the volunteers inside the arsenal grounds, but, in the meantime, Brown had established a stronghold in the engine house. The morning after the arrival of the marines, Green was ordered to prepare a special storming party with suitable equipment to break into Brown's fortress. Lieutenant J. E. B. Stuart, U.S.A., acting as Lee's aide, approached the engine house with a demand for Brown to surrender, while Green and his storming party of marines stood by ready to attack. Brown refused to surrender under the terms offered; Stuart gave the signal for Green to attack. The marines attempted to break open the door with a sledge hammer, but, failing at this, used a ladder as a battering ram and forced it open. Green led his storming party in and soon personally encountered Brown, just too late to prevent him from firing a shot which killed one of the marines. Green struck Brown with his sword, knocked him down, and stabbed him. This put an end to further resistance. Brown soon recovered from his wounds sufficiently to be removed to Charles Town. He was escorted there by Green's detachment of marines.

### Death of Archibald Henderson

Brigadier General Archibald Henderson, who had been Commandant of the Marine Corps since October 17, 1820, died while still in that office on January 6, 1859, at the mature age of 76. It will be recalled from an earlier chapter that he first distinguished himself in 1815 while in command of the marine guard on the *Constitution* during the celebrated action of that vessel with the *Cyane* and *Levant*. His illustrious service during the Florida Indian War has also been mentioned. Henderson can, without doubt, be given credit for giving the Marine Corps its first national reputation. During his administration many customs and traditions grew up, the maintenance of which had much to do with the shaping of the later colorful history of the Corps and of its devotion to duty. During his thirty-nine years as Commandant of the Marine Corps, with untiring effort he supervised in great detail its affairs with remarkable ability and foresight. The volumes of letters from him to officers of the Corps and their letters to him express a spirit of intimacy and confidence that is rarely equaled in such organizations. He was not only able to manage the internal affairs of the Corps but always maintained the closest possible relations with the Navy

Department and with the civil officials of the Government. He seldom missed an opportunity, in the face of continual discouragement, to promote the interests of the Corps even though it entailed great personal sacrifice. With his passing, the leadership of the Corps fell to weaker hands, and for a number of years it did not enjoy the national reputation that it had gained during his administration and has enjoyed during the past several decades.

General Henderson was succeeded as Commandant of the Marine Corps by Lieutenant Colonel John Harris, who was given the rank of Colonel Commandant. Harris was then well along in years and had served forty-five years as an officer in the Marine Corps. He was a veteran of considerable distinction in two major wars and of the Florida Indian War. He had had a great variety of peacetime duty, both on vessels of the Navy in various parts of the world and at the several regular posts of the Marine Corps. His advanced age as well as his lack of any particular ability, however, seriously handicapped him as well as the entire Corps during his tenure of office.

## Life in the Marine Corps

As this period of the Corps's history drew to a close, the days of wooden ships and iron men in the American naval service were beginning to pass; living conditions for marines were becoming much less severe than during the early years of the nineteenth century. The Marines continued to enjoy an excellent reputation within the naval service; the reputation in the country at large, which they had won during the Florida Indian Wars and the Mexican War, was maintained throughout this period by the exceptional services they rendered on several occasions. The country was not yet, however, inclined to be in the least military-minded; it still looked to volunteers and to the militia as its main fighting force in time of war. The average marine was better provided for in his pay and allowances than he had been previous to the Mexican War. The uniforms that he wore during this period were perhaps the showiest that the Marine Corps has ever had.

A general tendency toward a less severe treatment of unfortunate individuals, who, in one way or another, had offended some law or regulation, swept the country during this period. It had its effects in the naval service; more humane punishments were adjudged for offenses. The brutal practice of flogging with the cat-o'-nine-tails was used in exceptional cases only—usually for such serious offenses as desertion. The sentence to wear a ball and chain continued to be common, but long periods of confinement were not usually resorted to. Punishments in some cases, such as for direct disobedience of orders, were even milder than are now considered necessary for the maintenance of discipline.

The routine duties of marines ashore and at sea continued about the same as during the earlier years of their history; marine guards were continued at all principal navy yards and stations. As the government in Washington became more thoroughly established and other means for guarding public buildings and property were gradually developed, there was less tendency to call upon the marines for miscellaneous guard duties. Routine duties at sea were still very similar to those of the Continental Marines and to those in the early years of the Marine Corps. Marines were considered the shock troops for landing operations; they continued to perform the duties of sharpshooters, on elevated positions on warships, to support or repel boarding parties. It was not yet considered one of their normal battle functions to man a division of guns on board ship. Their importance as the mainstay of discipline during battle and at other times had been somewhat lessened because a higher type of men then enlisted in the Navy and an ever-growing percentage of the Navy's personnel were native-born Americans.

The Marine Corps was suffering under handicaps similar to those of the Army at the time, in that most of the higher ranking officers of both services were too old for active duty. With this condition still in existence the country was swept into the Civil War. The Marine Corps for that reason, in addition to many others, was prevented from giving its largest possible usefulness to the country during that great emergency.

## Chapter VIII
## THE CIVIL WAR

THE services rendered by the Marine Corps to the cause of the Union during the Civil War were not so outstanding in several ways as they had been in previous wars. The Corps was increased only slightly, and during most of the war it was under the leadership of an old man of none too great ability. The other senior officers of the Corps were also too old for field service. The Corps functioned almost exclusively as detachments on vessels of the Navy and on only a few occasions attempted to fight on shore. Small detachments of marines repeatedly distinguished themselves in battle, while handling great guns on board naval vessels. The few attempts at placing hurriedly organized battalions of marines into operations ashore resulted in but little success. The Civil War period of the Corps's history was probably the lowest ebb of fighting efficiency that the organization has ever reached in time of war. The reasons for this are made evident by a study of the difficult conditions which faced the Corps.

### PERIOD OF DISINTEGRATION

The Marine Corps approached the Civil War considerably under its authorized strength, having, as of January 1, 1861, both in officers and enlisted men, an aggregate of only 1,892. Its officers varied in age and experience from young, newly-appointed second lieutenants to a sprinkling of veterans left over from the War of 1812. Most of the officers, other than the younger first lieutenants and the second lieutenants, were veterans of the Mexican War, in which many of them had rendered distinguished service. The field officers of the Corps at the outbreak of the Civil War were without exception too old for field duty, and none of them left their home stations during the entire Civil War. The records do not show the ages of these senior officers, but from their length of service it is evident that all of them had attained the age of sixty years and upwards.

During the period of uncertainty from the time of the election of Abraham Lincoln until he took the oath of office, the military services, as well as other branches of the Federal Government, went through a period of disintegration. Officers in all branches of the service of the United States, who were from the South or whose sympathies were strongly in favor of the South, began to resign and offer their services to the southern states. The Buchanan administration, obviously sympathetic to the South, accepted these resignations without question and apparently bade the officers concerned Godspeed. The Marine Corps went through as great a disintegration in comparison as any branch of the service. About half of its captains resigned, including such officers as George H. Terrett, who had so distinguished himself in the fighting at Mexico City, and four other captains, who had been breveted for their service in the Mexican War. In the first lieutenant grade nearly two-thirds resigned, including such officers as John D. Simms who, it will be recalled, had not only been breveted for his services in the Mexican War but had shown an outstanding fighting spirit in the storming of the Barrier Forts at Canton, China. Several other officers who had been breveted for distinguished service in the Mexican War also resigned, as did nearly half of the second lieutenants. The field officers of the Corps, with one exception—Major Henry B. Tyler, the Adjutant and Inspector—remained faithful to the flag. The Commandant himself seems to have wavered somewhat during this period as is indicated by the fact that he gave a letter of recommendation to one of the resigning officers, who, it was evident, was offering his services to the South.

The enlisted men of the Corps with very few exceptions stood by the colors. There are few records even of desertions or requests for special discharges for the purposes of joining the Confederacy.

With the coming of the new administration on March 4, 1861, the policy of accepting resignations from the regular services to go to the South was abruptly ended. Thereafter officers who attempted to resign found that their names were either stricken from the rolls by order of the President or—by his special authority in time of war—that they were summarily dismissed.

It having become evident to the new administration that a military organization could not function in time of war with all the senior officers in or approaching their dotage, Congress enacted a law which provided that officers who had served over forty years or were physically disabled could retire. A few months later Congress further provided that the President—at his discretion—could retire officers of over forty-five years of service or over sixty-two years of age. For some reason the provisions of the latter law were not promptly carried out in the Marine Corps, and the officers in the upper grades continued to occupy the more important positions until more than a year later. Then they began to be forced into retirement to make room for younger men.

## Reorganization

The problem of reorganizing the Corps and expanding it for war purposes after losing nearly half of its officers was no small one. Thirty-eight new officers, most of whom had had no military experience, were appointed early in 1861. Congress authorized an increase of 28 officers and 750 enlisted men in the strength of the Corps in July, 1861, making an allowed aggregate strength of only slightly over three thousand, which was not further augmented by Congress during the war. The President, however, under the authority of an act of Congress of 1849, which empowered him to substitute marines for landsmen on vessels of the Navy, authorized two increases of five hundred marines each in 1861. At no time during the war did the aggregate strength of the Corps exceed 3,900. With the rapid expansion of the Navy and the ever-increasing calls for marines for its larger vessels, the Marine Corps was always handicapped by insufficient personnel. It was able only to maintain a few marines in the naval shore establishments, provide marine detachments for some of the naval vessels, and, during short periods, maintain small battalions of marines on field duty. During the last two years of the war the number of naval vessels having marines had grown so large that marines were available only for vessels of the Navy and its regular shore establishments. Repeated calls for marines far in excess of those available could not be supplied. As during the War of 1812, the Navy on some occasions employed soldiers to take the place of marines. The lack of foresight and the failure of the Government to expand the Marine Corps to a sufficient strength to perform its normal wartime duty were doubtless due to the policy of using volunteer troops almost exclusively.

## Confederate Marines

The officers of the Corps who joined the Confederacy, with few exceptions, became part of the Confederate Marine Corps which was organized in 1861. These officers did not fare as well at the hands of the Confederate government as did those officers of the regular Army of the United States who gave their services to the Confederate Army. Most of them served in the Confederate Marine Corps during the war at approximately the same grade they had had at the time they resigned from the Marine Corps. The Confederate marines performed the usual Marine Corps duties for the Confederate Navy. They formed a number of detachments for Confederate naval vessels. A battalion of Confederate marines took an inconspicuous part in several land operations in Virginia during the war. Useless to say, none of the officers who resigned from the Corps at the outbreak of the Civil War were ever allowed to return.

### HELPING THE ARMY

The United States Army suffered a similar disruption during which it lost nearly 30 per cent of its officers to the Confederacy. These officers were given high positions and wide authority in the Confederate Army and promptly organized it into a formidable force. The regular Army of the United States in the meantime continued to disintegrate until some time after Lincoln became President. It was very much weakened in the general vicinity of Washington, where disorder was so prevalent that the few available marines in Washington were called to its support. On January 5, 1861, forty marines and an officer took over the garrisoning of Fort Washington, fourteen miles south of the capital, on the banks of the Potomac. A short time afterwards a similar detachment of one officer and thirty-nine marines was sent to garrison Fort McHenry at Baltimore. These marine detachments helped to hold these important military stations until soldiers could be made available for their relief. Another detachment of marines went with some artillery troops from New York on the first relief expedition to Charleston, S. C., to reinforce Fort Sumter, sailing from New York January 7, on the *Star of the West*. That vessel was forced to retire, however, and returned to New York without having landed the troops on board. Marines were kept on the alert in both Washington and New York and were assigned definite tasks in the event of serious riots by Confederate sympathizers, which were at the time greatly feared.

### LOSS OF THE SOUTHERN NAVAL ESTABLISHMENTS

During the period of disintegration the Navy lost most of its shore establishments in the southern states. One of the greatest of these losses was that of the navy yard at Pensacola. It was then the only well-developed naval station on the Gulf of Mexico. Florida was one of the first states to secede. As early as January 12, 1861, a large armed force of Floridians, assisted by disloyal employees at that naval station, forced its surrender. In order to prevent its capture, the marine detachment regularly stationed at the navy yard was transferred to one of the Union vessels present and sent to New York. The Florida troops soon afterwards gained control of Pensacola's defending forts with the exception of Fort Pickens on an island near the entrance to the harbor; they also captured large quantities of military stores in the vicinity. A relief expedition consisting of a small naval squadron was sent to reinforce Fort Pickens early in April, 1861. The squadron had about 110 marines with it. These marines under Lieutenant John C. Cash together with some Union soldiers landed and held the fort until a large garrison of soldiers was provided. Fort Pickens remained in the hands of the Union forces throughout the war.

While these incidents were taking place around Pensacola, the only remaining naval station in the South which had a marine barracks—Norfolk—was being seriously threatened by Virginia forces. Soon after the secession of Virginia (April 17, 1861) the authorities of that state made plans and provided troops for the seizing of the navy yard at Norfolk. A total of eleven naval vessels, including some under construction—a part of which were almost completed—and a few older vessels together with vast quantities of naval ordnance and stores were in the navy yard. The Navy Department had ordered its commandant to evacuate all the ships and ordnance stores to a safer location, but he delayed doing this until it was too late. When the danger of losing the important station with all its material began to appear imminent, the Secretary of the Navy dispatched Captain Hiram Paulding on the *Pawnee* with one hundred extra marines from Washington to reinforce it. Paulding picked up 250 volunteers in addition at Fortress Monroe but arrived too late; Virginia troops had already collected in considerable numbers and were momentarily expected to attack the almost undefended naval station. The commandant had begun taking desperate measures.

Some hours prior to Paulding's arrival with reinforcements, the commandant, believing that it was impossible to hold the yard any longer, had begun scuttling the vessels. Paulding, upon his arrival, did not approve of the desperate action that had been taken, but, thinking that the naval property could not be saved from the hands of the Virginians, joined in the destruction. The Union naval forces carried out a systematic destruction of all government property in the vicinity, which could not be evacuated readily by their vessels. The *Pawnee* and the *Cumberland* were first taken out of the danger zone. All of the principal buildings and the vessels which could not be removed were set on fire; efforts were made to spike or otherwise partially destroy the hundreds of guns which were stored in the yard. Small arms and other infantry equipment were damaged and together with the ammunition thrown overboard. About 125 marines, including the regular detachment from the navy yard under Colonel James Edelin, the guards from the *Pennsylvania* and *Cumberland*, and those who had arrived on the *Pawnee*, took part in the work of destruction. All the principal buildings were set on fire, and the Union personnel was evacuated to the vessels remaining afloat. But the work of destruction proved ineffective; the Virginians came in and saved many of the most important shops and buildings. Edelin's marines, however, succeeded in completely destroying their barracks before leaving them. They and the receiving ship detachments were then transferred to Washington.

## The Navy Prepares

At the outbreak of the Civil War the active vessels of the Navy were scattered in the several distant squadrons. The Buchanan administration made no effort to redispose them to meet the national emergency. Soon after March 4, 1861, fifteen steam vessels were ordered home from the various foreign stations, leaving only three ships away from the United States. Reserve ships were hurriedly placed in commission; suitable commercial crafts were altered for war purposes; and an extensive shipbuilding program was undertaken. As additional vessels were placed in commission, more and more marines were called to sea duty. As the war progressed towards its close, the number of vessels in the Navy carrying marines had so greatly increased that the greater part of the Marine Corps was absorbed into the crews of naval vessels.

It soon became manifest that the great task for the Navy in the suppression of the rebellion was to isolate the Confederacy by establishing an effective blockade of its coast from the mouth of the Chesapeake to the Rio Grande. In order to accomplish this, in addition to the essential naval operations on the Atlantic, it was necessary to carry on extensive joint operations with the Army to seize and hold important forts along the Atlantic seaboard and prevent their use by the Confederates. During some such operations marines were used as landing forces. In spite of the fact that extensive experience in the Mexican War had demonstrated the importance of having naval landing force units with special training in that type of warfare and the fact that the marines were particularly suitable for such duty, only a single battalion of marines was ever available during the Civil War to support the fleet. Their normal functions in such operations were assumed by detached forces of the Army.

## The Battle of Bull Run

In response to cries for action by the press and people of the North, the Union Army in the vicinity of Washington, which consisted of five infantry divisions and miscellaneous other troops totaling approximately 35,000 under the command of General McDowell, ventured out of its defenses in an effort to defeat the rapidly growing Confederate Army scattered in various places south and southwest of Washington. McDowell's army set out in high hopes, stimulated by the war cry of "On to Richmond." It was not in reality an army at all but rather a hastily assembled mob of untrained recruits.

The Marine Corps attempted to do its small part and hastily threw together a battalion of 12 officers and 336 marines under Major John G. Reynolds. The battalion was composed almost entirely of raw recruits, many of whom had just received their arms and equipment and some had never even had a gun in their hands before taking the field. Two veteran officers and several juniors, who were almost as inexperienced as the raw recruits, led the hastily organized companies. Commandant Harris sent the unit forth to battle with "feelings of great anxiety lest" it should fail to sustain the good reputation of the Corps. Despite its many deficiencies it marched off on the afternoon of July 16, 1861, and joined the long column of McDowell s army as a part of the First Brigade of the First Division. The march to the field of battle was so hurried that not only the marines but many other units were almost completely exhausted before getting into action.

Colonel Porter, commanding the First Brigade, assigned the marines to support a battery of artillery; while taking up a position, they were exposed to a galling fire. The battalion managed to get into position, but the fire was so heavy that they were promptly driven back. Their officers rallied them three times and urged them back into their positions. Finally, when the general rout of the Union Army began, the marines joined in with the rest of the retreating raw and inexperienced troops, in spite of the efforts of their officers to further rally them. Considering their inexperience, however, and the disastrous turn of the battle, many of the marines and their officers conducted themselves in a commendable manner.

As the retreat continued, the units of the Union Army became badly mixed. Reynolds gathered up the marines along the line of retreat, collected them at the long bridge across the Potomac as best he could, and brought the remnant of his scattered battalion back to the marine barracks in the city. The losses to the battalion amounted to forty-four. The Marine Corps felt very much chagrined at the failure, and Harris in a letter to Gideon Welles remarked that, "it was the first instance recorded in its history where any portion of its members turned their backs to the enemy." The Marine Corps, however, like the Union Army, was sadder and wiser for its unfortunate experience and set about making a better military organization.

## HATTERAS INLET

The first naval expedition undertaken against a Confederate port was made in August, 1861, against Hatteras Inlet, where it was reported large quantities of war material were being smuggled into the Confederacy by English blockade runners. A joint expeditionary force, having about one thousand soldiers under General Butler and several naval vessels under Commodore Silas H. Stringham, was fitted out at Hampton Roads and sailed for the North Carolina coast. The expedition arrived off Hatteras Inlet and found that both sides of the entrance had been fortified. Weather conditions being unfavorable for a large landing operation, the marine detachment of the *Minnesota,* commanded by Captain William L. Shuttleworth, was transferred to the *Harriet Lane* and, together with 250 regulars, landed through the surf in special boats, most of which were destroyed in beaching. With the aid of supporting naval gunfire, they succeeded, after a four-hour engagement, in capturing Fort Clark which protected the eastern side of the inlet. The weather continued unfavorable for further landing operations. Fort Hatteras, on the other side of the inlet, however, was forced to surrender three days later. The naval vessels bombarded it, then a landing force under General Butler stormed and captured it. The forts on both sides of the inlet were permanently occupied by Union forces and held during the remainder of the war. This deprived the Confederacy of one of its most important ports.

## OPERATIONS AT PORT ROYAL, S. C.

Soon after the successful campaign at Hatteras Inlet, plans were formulated for other joint operations of the Army and Navy to seize additional positions farther south along the coast and thereby control important Confederate ports. A force of about 15,000 volunteers and other troops, commanded by General W. T. Sherman, were assembled at Hampton Roads, where they joined forces with the augmented South Atlantic Blockading Squadron under Flag Officer S. F. DuPont. Dupont, who had had considerable experience with Marine landing forces attached to the Pacific Squadron during the Mexican War, was anxious to have a specially trained battalion of marines. The desired unit of three hundred marines was assembled and placed under Major Reynolds. After being equipped with the .58-caliber rifle muskets, they were embarked on the *Pawnee* as part of the joint expedition. In order to provide more comfortable living conditions and not have the battalion on one of the main firing ships of the squadron, DuPont later transferred Reynolds' marines to the chartered vessel *Governor*.

The expedition left Hampton Roads on October 29, 1861, with the transports carrying the expeditionary force following the naval vessels. They encountered a storm off Hatteras, which proved rather disastrous for the battalion of marines on board the *Governor*. That steamer was separated from the rest of the ships and, on the night following the second day out, was considerably damaged by heavy seas. For a time the ship was able to maintain enough steerage way to heave to in the storm. Damage to her smokestacks and steam pipes later reduced the working of the engine to only a small part of the time. By the following morning further damage, including a broken rudder, left the ship practically out of control.

Two small naval vessels answered the *Governor's* call for relief, but the heavy seas prevented them from giving any material assistance. The frigate *Sabine* later arrived, took the distressed vessel in tow, and attempted to rescue the marines by transferring them to the *Sabine*. Thirty marines were thus rescued, but the towing cables were parted by the plunging of the vessels. Further attempts at rescuing were abandoned, but during the night the *Governor* was again taken in tow. On the following morning several attempts were made to rescue the marines by small boats. This proved to be very hazardous as the sea was still running high, making it extremely dangerous to approach the *Governor* on account of the guards over her side wheels. Finally the rescue boats had to lie off and haul aboard marines, who had jumped into the sea. All of the marines were saved, with the exception of one corporal and six privates who were either drowned or crushed. Reynolds was not willing to give up to the elements; by exerting every effort he managed to save nearly all of the arms, part of the accouterments, and about half of the ammunition of his battalion from the sinking transport. The marines, however, lost practically all of their other equipment and clothing. For forty-eight hours they fought to keep the *Governor* afloat but, despite their efforts, it went down. Once aboard the *Sabine* the marines were well cared for, re-equipped and clothed, and even the losses in men were made good by the marine detachment of the *Sabine*, which at the time was under orders to return to its base at Hampton Roads.

In the meantime DuPont's squadron had proceeded toward Port Royal, S. C., and on November 7 attacked the Confederate batteries on Bay Point and on Hilton Head Island. Both batteries were silenced after a bombardment of four hours. The Confederates abandoned Fort Walker on Hilton Head. Commander C. R. P. Rodgers went ashore with the marine detachment and a company of seamen from the *Wabash* and occupied it until General Sherman could disembark his troops. The Confederates also abandoned the fort on Bay Point; a navy landing force soon occupied it.

During December, 1861, the marines from the South Atlantic Squadron participated in several minor engagements and reconnaissances on shore. The marines from the *Savannah* landed on Tybee Island, Georgia, and made a futile attempt to attack a Confederate fort which protected Savannah. A few days later the marine detachment of the *Dale* went on board the small steamer *Isaac Smith* in St. Helena Sound (between Port Royal and Charleston, S. C.) and steamed up the Ashepoo River. They made two landings; during one they drove a small detachment of Confederates from their position and burned their quarters. Some two weeks later, the same marines went up the South Edisto River, which flows into St. Helena Sound, and had another engagement with a small Confederate detachment.

The *Sabine*, with Reynolds' battalion of marines on board, reached Port Royal after the Confederate forts had fallen. The battalion landed at Bay Point and became part of the regular garrison of the fort at that place. DuPont's squadron established a base at Port Royal, from which it carried on blockading operations against Savannah and Charleston and gradually extended its control down the Florida coast.

On February 23, 1862, in accordance with DuPont's orders, Reynolds embarked his battalion on board the transport *McClellan* and joined (March 2) the naval forces off Amelia Island. He left a detachment of fifty marines under Lieutenant C. A. Stillman at Bay Point. DuPont had planned for Reynolds' battalion to land and occupy the town of Fernandina. The *McClellan* then proceeded to Fernandina on the 6th but, finding the town already occupied by Union troops, did not land the battalion. The marines returned to Hilton Head two days later and reoccupied their former quarters on Bay Point.

On March 17 Reynolds' marine battalion embarked on the steamer *Bienville* and proceeded to St. Augustine, Florida, taking along its complete camp equipment in anticipation of garrisoning that city. In the meantime, however, the Confederate forces had evacuated St. Augustine, and a landing force of marines and sailors from the *Mohican* and the marine detachment of the *Wabash* under Major Isaac T. Doughty had occupied the city. Again Reynolds' battalion was not landed, as the Army had sent all the troops necessary to garrison the city. DuPont, seeing no further need for retaining a marine battalion with his squadron, reluctantly sent it to Washington on board the *Bienville* on March 25. The battalion as well as the marine detachment of the *Wabash* were highly commended for the excellent manner of performing their duties during these operations with the South Atlantic Blockading Squadron.

## THE CAPTURE OF NEW ORLEANS

In addition to the North and the South Atlantic Blockading Squadrons, the Western Gulf Blockading Squadron was organized early in 1862. It established its base in Mississippi Sound, which had been used by the British as a base during their attack on New Orleans in 1815. Captain David G. Farragut was given command of the new squadron and ordered to co-operate with an army expeditionary force of approximately 18,000 troops, under Major General Benjamin F. Butler. Butler's objective was to close the mouth of the Mississippi and to capture and hold New Orleans. That city was defended by Fort Jackson and Fort St. Philip which lay several miles below the city and were powerfully armed with 116 guns and mortars. Fort Jackson was in turn supported by a strong battery on the opposite bank of the river. They together covered a chain and hulk barrier across the river which protected a flotilla of Confederate gunboats in the river between the Union vessels and New Orleans.

Farragut's task to force his way past the forts was one of the most difficult that has ever confronted an officer of the American Navy. He made plans for every possible contingency and thoroughly trained and equipped his squadron for the precarious operation. He spent more than a month in making the final preparations, which included such details as camouflaging the sides of the ships with daubs of mud and whitewashing their decks to aid vision during the anticipated night attack. On April 16 Farragut's squadron moved up the river into a preliminary position, just out of the range of Fort Jackson. The plan of co-ordination with the army called for the ships to force their way past the forts to quarantine, a few miles farther up the river, where Butler's troops would join them by coming in through a bayou which connected with the Gulf a short distance eastward. On April 18 twenty Union mortar boats began a five-day bombardment of Fort Jackson. This did considerable damage to that stronghold. Attempts by the Confederates to return the fire did little damage to the Union vessels, but fire-rafts sent down the river caused some annoyance. During the night of the 20th two Federal gunboats daringly went under the muzzles of the Confederate guns and made a breach in the chain and hulk obstruction across the river. At 2 A.M. on the 24th, the squadron, in three divisions, got under way to fight its way past the forts. The first division, consisting of eight vessels with the *Cayuga* in front, led the advance with the specific mission of attacking Fort St. Philip, on the east bank of the river above Fort Jackson. The center division, consisting of three large vessels led by Farragut in person on the *Hartford*, followed and paid particular attention to Fort Jackson.

The remaining division followed generally Farragut's lead. The fire of the attacking vessels kept down the fire of the Confederate forts. Fire rafts towed by the Confederates, however, played considerable havoc, even setting the *Hartford* on fire. The Confederate ram *Manassas* succeeded in ramming some of Farragut's vessels. After passing the forts, a Confederate squadron was encountered, but before daylight nine of its vessels, including the dreaded *Manassas*, which had been driven ashore, were destroyed. During this phase of the operation twelve of Farragut's vessels carried marine detachments varying in size and having in all 7 officers and 326 marines. While passing the forts, these marines served as gun crews on some of the ships; on others, they helped to keep down the fire of the Confederate forts with their galling rifle fire. They were highly praised, not only by Farragut, but by a number of his captains, for the manner in which they bore themselves and the gallantry with which they fought during the hazardous night battle.

After most of the ships had successfully passed the forts, the marine detachment of the *Hartford* was sent ashore to the quarantine station, captured it, took a considerable number of Confederate prisoners, and raised the United States flag. Farragut sent word to Butler to land his army. On the following day Farragut moved up to New Orleans, silencing two batteries below the city while en route. From his position on the swollen river, Farragut controlled all of the streets as well as the only land approach to the city.

On the morning following the arrival at New Orleans a detachment of thirty marines, under Lieutenant J. C. Harris, landed and marched through the crowds of excited people, who threatened them in every conceivable way. But, the marines, showing their highly developed discipline, marched calmly with measured steps to the United States mint. They surrounded the mint, took possession of it, lowered the Confederate flag, and replaced it with that of the Union. In the meantime Farragut had demanded the surrender of the city. The Confederate commander refused but agreed to evacuate immediately in order to save the inhabitants from the danger of an attack. On April 29 all of the marines of the squadron were landed and formed into a battalion of four companies under Captain John L. Broome, U.S.M.C., from the *Hartford*. The battalion proceeded to the custom house, about a mile distant, and took possession of it after forming a line to protect its approaches. Broome raised the United States flag and left the *Richmond*'s detachment of about fifty marines to hold the building and protect the flag.

Broome then marched the remainder of his battalion, which had been joined by a detachment of seamen with two howitzers, to the city hall—located about a half mile from the squadron near the center of the city. By this time the Confederate troops had entirely evacuated the city; the streets were filled with excited mobs, who abused and threatened the marines but did not venture to attack them. Broome's battalion surrounded the city hall while a detachment of marines occupied the building and hauled down the Louisiana flag; but, according to a previous agreement with the city officials, they did not replace it with the United States flag. During that afternoon the marine battalion, with the exception of the detachment at the custom house, returned to the vessels of the squadron. Butler's army began to arrive at New Orleans on May 1, and the last of the marines withdrew from the city. With the exception of a detachment of eighteen marines, under First Lieutenant McLane Tilton, which was stationed at Pilot Town, Louisiana, from June until December, 1862, the remainder of the marines of Farragut's squadron continued on their regular duties aboard his vessels.

### The Attacks of the *Merrimac*

The marines on the *Cumberland* and *Congress* at Hampton Roads came in for more than their share of losses in the fatal attacks of the Confederate ironclad *Merrimac* on those two vessels, which proved most vulnerable to attack by a more modern vessel, protected by armor and having rifled guns. On March 8, 1862, when the *Cumberland* and *Congress* together with several other Union ships were lying peacefully in Hampton Roads and more or less unprepared to give battle, the *Merrimac,* supported by some small steamer gunboats, steamed out of the Elizabeth River and headed for the *Cumberland*. The *Merrimac* passed the *Congress,* exchanged a few broadsides with that ship, and left it to the supporting Confederate gunboats. It then bore down upon the *Cumberland* from off its bow.

The *Cumberland* was unable to swing to use its broadside guns and opened the battle with a few forward guns which could bear. The *Merrimac* opened with a heavy shot, which raked the foredeck of the *Cumberland*, killing or wounding nine marines who were assembled in formation. Fortunately, not all of the marine detachment was so dangerously exposed; some of the marines were manning the four after guns on the gun deck. The *Merrimac*, from its advantageous position, continued to rake the *Cumberland*, producing a scene of indescribable carnage and destruction on the older wooden vessel, but the few shots fired by the *Cumberland* made practically no impression against the armor-protected Confederate vessel. After about fifteen minutes of destructive fire with seven-inch rifled guns against the helpless *Cumberland*, the *Merrimac*, under full steam, crashed into the *Cumberland* with her ram, making a terrible hole underneath the water line but breaking her own ram. The two vessels then separated and turned broadside to each other. In spite of having suffered so severely during the first stages of the action, the *Cumberland* poured three broadsides into the *Merrimac*, which, even at the range of two hundred yards, had little effect other than shooting away the flagstaff and riddling the smokestack. Shots from the Confederate vessel went through the sides of the *Cumberland* as if they were paper. In spite of the punishment his ship had received, Lieutenant Morris refused to surrender. During this stage of the fight, the marines and others armed with rifles on the upper deck of the *Cumberland* fired into the *Merrimac*'s gun ports and inflicted a number of casualties. The *Merrimac* regained its old raking position on the bow of the *Cumberland*, which was sinking and unable to swing into a new firing position. The *Cumberland* was soon sinking rapidly, but her gun crews continued to fight until almost the last minute when they took to their boats at the stern or jumped overboard as the vessel went down. The ill-fated vessel lost nearly one-third of its crew, including approximately twenty marines. Captain Charles Heywood (later Commandant of the Marine Corps), in charge of the marine detachment, was afterwards breveted major for his gallant and meritorious services during this historic encounter.

The Confederates then proceeded to attack the equally helpless *Congress*, which had slipped its moorings and, knowing its probable fate, headed for the shore and ran aground to avoid being sunk. The destruction inflicted upon the *Congress* was soon almost equal to that which had been meted out to the *Cumberland*. The commander of the *Congress*, however, seeing that it was utterly hopeless to continue the fight, surrendered; but the Confederates were prevented from taking control of the *Congress* by the fire of Union troops on the near-by shore. The crew of the *Congress* was rescued in various ways by Union troops, but the ship was set on fire with hot-shot and incendiary shells from the *Merrimac*. The marine detachment of the *Congress*, consisting of one officer and forty-nine marines, did their part in the hopeless fight by firing the midship, spar-deck guns in addition to performing other battle duties.

The other Union vessels attempted to come to the support of the *Cumberland* and the *Congress*. Three of the larger ships ran aground, but fortunately the *Merrimac* could not get within effective range because of the shallow water. By 6:30 P.M. the tide was falling and the danger of grounding induced the *Merrimac* to withdraw for the night. The *Monitor* arrived from New York shortly after dark. The historic battle between the two ironclads took place the following morning. The *Merrimac* was not completely defeated in the battle but withdrew and never again ventured out to fight. It was soon afterwards effectively blockaded in the Elizabeth River by Fort Wool and a number of Union naval vessels.

Demands for action by the press and the insistence of the Government at Washington finally forced the Army of the Potomac to attempt a determined advance on the Confederate capital. McClellan moved that army to the peninsula between the James and York Rivers and attempted to advance on Richmond from the southeast with his flanks protected at first by naval vessels on those rivers and, as he advanced farther, by small vessels on the Chickahominy and Pamunkey Rivers. A number of naval vessels under Goldsborough supported McClellan throughout his advance towards Richmond and rendered notable services during the disastrous withdrawal from the campaign. Several of Goldsborough's vessels carried small marine detachments, which performed the usual duties of marines aboard smaller vessels of the Navy. The later Union military operations in Virginia were mostly far inland and no direct naval support was possible. The ships in the Chesapeake Bay area thereafter devoted most of their efforts to blockade operations.

There was some nervousness at the beginning of the campaign lest the *Merrimac* escape from Norfolk and interrupt the operations. This danger was soon eliminated, however, by the capture of Norfolk (May 10), thus cutting the *Merrimac* off from its home port. Having no place to go and not daring to attempt a run past the Union vessels and fort, it was beached and destroyed by its own crew.

Norfolk and vicinity was evacuated by the Confederates on May

9, 1862, and on the following day General Wool occupied the city with Union troops from Fortress Monroe. Shortly afterwards Wool's troops took over the town of Gosport and the navy yard. Goldsborough was anxious for naval forces to reoccupy the important naval establishments of Fort Norfolk and the navy yard, but Wool refused to turn them over to naval control unless so ordered by the President or Secretary of War. On May 24 the necessary orders for their return to the Navy were issued. In the meantime a detachment of two hundred marines, under Captain Charles G. McCawley, had been organized for the purpose of taking over and policing the navy yard. McCawley's marines took possession of the navy yard on May 25 and again raised the United States flag. The occupation was made without resistance (contrary to some previously written accounts) as it was at the time under the control of General Wool's troops.

## The Attack on Charleston

After the successful operations at Port Royal Sound, the Union Army advanced to within sight of Charleston but in May, 1862, abandoned further attempt and withdrew to its base, fifty miles to the rear. President Lincoln and the Secretary of the Navy, Gideon Welles, were of the opinion that the capture of Charleston would be a great moral victory and (early in 1863) ordered Admiral DuPont of the South Atlantic Squadron to make every effort to capture it. By this time several monitors had been completed and were ordered to Charleston to force their way by the outer forts and bombard the city. Several preliminary attacks against the forts were followed by a determined attack on April 7, in which seven monitors participated. This battle demonstrated that this new type of vessel could not successfully operate against powerful forts armed with heavy artillery. DuPont's efforts were not satisfactory to Washington, and Rear Admiral John A. Dahlgren was placed in command of the squadron with orders to make a more determined attempt to capture Charleston.

Three thousand Union troops under General Gillmore were brought up from Hilton Head and took part in a combined attack on July 6. Gillmore's troops landed on the south end of Morris Island and with the support of naval gunfire advanced towards the entrance of Charleston harbor to take Fort Wagner, which protected the channel on the south side. The attack failed; the monitors had made little impression on the fort. The combined operation went on for two months; the squadron was in action twenty-five times; the army was reinforced by a battalion of marines from the squadron; but still the fort held out.

Another battalion of three hundred marines, for service with the South Atlantic Squadron, was assembled in New York in early August, 1863. It was placed under command of Major Jacob Zeilin and reported (August 10) to Dahlgren at Charleston. Dahlgren ordered all available marines from the squadron and the newly-arrived battalion organized into a regiment under Zeilin. The regiment conducted special training for landing force operations and went ashore on Morris Island soon afterwards. Zeilin was dissatisfied with his troops since most of them were untrained recruits and, being ill, was transferred aboard the *Wabash* and later relieved. In the meantime Lieutenant Colonel J. G. Reynolds was ordered to command the unit, which had been reduced to a battalion. The siege of Fort Wagner was then being carried on by sapping operations, under the cover of army artillery and naval gunfire. Heavy guns were also emplaced for firing on Fort Sumter. These guns, together with those of the naval vessels, fired several thousand shots at Sumter and reduced it to a mass of ruins, with practically all of its guns out of commission. Fort Wagner was finally taken, and, Sumter apparently being ready to fall, operations were planned for the taking of the latter by a boat expedition, consisting of the marine battalion and a navy landing force.

### Repulse by Fort Sumter

The boat expedition to capture Fort Sumter, commanded by Commander Thomas H. Stevens, was organized into five divisions, and preparations were begun for a night attack. Four of the divisions were composed of sailors and marines from the vessels of the squadron, while the fifth was made up entirely of marines from Morris Island under Captain McCawley. Each division consisted of slightly over one hundred officers and men and was embarked in five or six boats. Some monitors supported the landing force which was to be towed as far as possible by a tug and then to be cast off to drift with the tide towards the fort.

The plan proceeded with some confusion; the night was extremely dark, and the orders were not clear. McCawley's division had been ordered to cover the fort with rifle fire, if necessary, while some of the advance divisions effected a landing. Later they were to follow the leading troops ashore. The towing tug for some reason turned about without casting off the boats and threw the expedition into considerable confusion. The leading division made for the island, however, and in spite of a challenge by a Confederate sentry, surprised the garrison. Several boatloads got ashore and began scaling the outer defenses of the fort. The other Confederate forts in the vicinity soon began firing on the expedition. The garrison at Fort Sumter was by this time thoroughly alert and held off the division which had landed, while the falling shells threw the entire expedition into confusion. McCawley's boats got separated in the darkness. Part of them pushed on to the island; some of his marines landed and joined the leading division. By the time McCawley with part of his boats was within sight of the fort, he met several boatloads of retreating troops. After making a vain effort to induce them to return to the attack, he, too, retired from the action together with the boats, laden with marines, which were directly under his command.

The landing parties that had successfully got ashore soon found themselves in an impossible situation. The Confederate garrison made an heroic defense, and the assailants, having no means at hand to scale the walls, were unable to close with the enemy. They were, in the meantime, subjected to musketry fire and grenades by the enemy's garrison and to the artillery fire from the surrounding forts. The naval troops that were unable to land gradually made their way back to the flagship. Lieutenant Commander E. P. Williams, who was captured, claimed in his report that the other landing parties could have landed easily if they had promptly rushed to the shore as he did. However, with every Confederate fort in the vicinity able to concentrate their fire on Fort Sumter, the attempt to capture it under the circumstances does not appear to have been particularly advisable. The marines who were made prisoners of war were exchanged about one year later. Several marine officers received brevet ranks for their gallant conduct in the attack on Fort Sumter.

The Federal Government by this time saw that the taking of Charleston would be such an extremely difficult task and the probable losses so great that it would not be worth the sacrifice. The efforts to take the city were called off, and it remained in Confederate hands until near the close of the war. A close blockade of the port was continued from a temporary naval anchorage in the lee of Folly Island. The marine battalion which had been stationed on Morris Island was transferred to the southern end of Folly Island and went into camp in support of the naval vessels anchored there. Sickness and transfers to marine guards of the fleet rapidly reduced its strength. The battalion continued on that duty, however, during the remainder of 1863, but early in 1864 it was broken up into detachments and sent on other duties.

The number of vessels in the Navy had mounted steadily since the outbreak of the war, and, by the end of 1863, marines were serving on about ninety naval vessels. The number of marine detachments at sea continued to grow until it reached considerably over one hundred, absorbing practically the entire enlisted personnel of the Marine Corps, with the exception of small detachments at the navy yards and stations. It was then impossible to organize any permanent land force of marines. Temporary detachments were formed by combining marine guards of several vessels for special duty ashore.

## With the Mississippi Flotilla

While the Army was reorganizing after the disastrous Battle of Bull Run and the Atlantic Squadron was carrying on the operations referred to above, the Union Army in the West, with the support of a flotilla of gunboats, was beginning to make progress by means of expeditions up certain rivers. By the time General U. S. Grant, in command of the Army of the West, was prepared to advance up the Cumberland and Tennessee rivers, seven river gunboats were available to assist in the operations, and a number of others were in process of construction at St. Louis. The first contingent of marines to be assigned to this flotilla consisted of one second lieutenant and twenty-seven marines and joined the flagship of the flotilla, the *St. Louis,* on January 31, 1862. These river gunboats supported Grant's army in the successful attacks on Fort Henry and Fort Donelson.

The flotilla next shifted its activities to the Mississippi where it aided General Pope in the capture of New Madrid, Mo., and Island Number 10 in April, 1862. The Union Army then advanced south while the naval vessels pushed down the Mississippi and captured or occupied post after post along the river, as the Confederates were forced back or retreated. A Confederate flotilla attempted to stop the advance of the gunboats on May 10, 1862, at Fort Pillow but failed. The Union gunboats followed the Confederate vessels to Memphis, attacked them on June 7, and destroyed three of them. The remainder of the Confederate flotilla retreated south. The city of Memphis surrendered to Commodore Davis, commander of the Union flotilla. For more than a year thereafter strong Union naval and army forces were driving south from Memphis and north from New Orleans in an attempt to cut the Confederacy in two. This was not accomplished, however, until July, 1863, when Vicksburg was finally taken after a long campaign by two river forces combining their strength with a powerful Union army. Marines served on some of the larger vessels of the river forces throughout the campaign of separating the Confederate States.

## The Defense of Gunpowder Bridge

During the siege of Petersburg and Richmond in the summer of 1864, Lee dispatched a corps, commanded by General Early, to move down the Shenandoah Valley and threaten Washington with the hope that this move would cause the withdrawal of part of Grant's army and relieve the pressure against Lee's hard-pressed position. Early's corps swept into Maryland and to the very outskirts of Washington, without meeting serious resistance. By this time, however, sufficient Federal troops had arrived from Virginia to defend Washington. Early's cavalry raided a large part of Maryland and cut Washington off from the north and east. Military units of every description were hastily thrown together in an effort to re-establish communications with Washington. Major Gilmor with a detachment of Confederate cavalry had burned the railroad bridge over Gunpowder Creek between Baltimore and Havre de Grace, and the no less important bridge at the latter place was in imminent danger.

In order to assist in re-establishing and maintaining railroad communication between Philadelphia and Baltimore, the commandant of the navy yard at Philadelphia ordered a naval detachment consisting of all available sailors and marines to Havre de Grace on July 11. The marines were formed into a battalion under Captain James Forney. The detachment arrived at Havre de Grace and reported for duty with the irregular forces which had been assembled at that place. The marines, supported by the naval howitzers, took over the protection of the long railroad bridge over the Susquehanna. The naval detachment later protected the work of reconstructing the Gunpowder River Bridge and repelled a Confederate attack against that important link in the railroad. With their assistance communication with Baltimore was soon restored. The danger having passed, the naval detachment returned to Philadelphia on July 18. Forney was later awarded a brevet rank of major for meritorious services during the operation.

## The Attack on Mobile

For various reasons no attempt was made to capture Mobile until the summer of 1864. The entrance to Mobile Bay was defended by two forts—Gaines on the western side and Morgan on the eastern side, close to the navigation channel. The entrance was also heavily protected by torpedoes (mines). The ironclad ram *Tennessee* and a few small gunboats were stationed in Mobile Bay as part of its defending force. The strength of the forts and their positions made their reduction by bombardment practically impossible. Farragut determined to use tactics similar to those he employed at New Orleans—run by the forts and reduce them from the rear. His force of eighteen ships made their way past Morgan (August 5) from which they received considerable punishment but suffered no serious damage. The squadron was then exposed to the danger of torpedoes but, in spite of considerable confusion, made its way into Mobile Bay with the loss of only one vessel. During this phase of the operation the marines on the larger ships served as crews of the great guns. Several marine gun crews were cited for the gallant manner in which they carried out their duties.

Soon after the vessels got out of the danger of the torpedo fields and forts, they were vigorously attacked by the *Tennessee* and its supporting gunboats. The *Hartford* drove off the gunboats, but the *Tennessee*, which was so heavily armored that the Union gunfire had practically no effect on it, proved a formidable adversary. In addition to its very effective gunfire against Farragut's ships, the *Tennessee* repeatedly attempted to ram different Union vessels. Several of them in turn attempted to ram the *Tennessee*. These maneuvers continued until one of Farragut's monitors was able to get a position at short range astern of the *Tennessee* and, by pounding away with 11-inch shots for more than half an hour, did enough damage to the gallant Confederate to cause the wounded commander to surrender. The marines on the *Lackawanna* were able to furnish substantial protection to their ship during its fight with the *Tennessee* by effective delivery of small-arms fire through the gun ports of the enemy vessel. This prevented the *Tennessee's* guns from being served. Major Heywood, later Commandant of the Corps, was breveted Lieutenant Colonel for his gallant and meritorious conduct in this battle.

## The Broad River Expedition

By the end of 1864 the Navy had succeeded in closing nearly all the Confederate ports to foreign shipping and by this means was slowly strangling the Confederacy into submission. Sherman made his historic march from Atlanta to the sea during the closing months of 1864. After leaving Atlanta, he abandoned his line of communication, with the intention of re-establishing a new one with a base on the Atlantic coast when the march was completed.

In order to facilitate Sherman's arrival at the coast, the South Atlantic Blockading Squadron, assisted by the Union troops in the vicinity of Port Royal, S. C., organized an expedition to advance up Broad River for the purpose of first cutting the Charleston and

Savannah railroad and then moving to meet Sherman. A naval brigade was organized from vessels of Admiral Dahlgren's squadron. It consisted of a battalion of sailors acting as infantry, another as artillery, and a third battalion of 182 marines drawn from twelve different ships of the squadron. First Lieutenant George G. Stoddard, the only marine officer with the squadron, took command of the battalion while its three companies were officered entirely by noncommissioned officers. The brigade of sailors and marines was hurriedly assembled at Bay Point on November 26, 1864, and given two days' hasty training before it embarked for the hazardous undertaking. The only army troops available were negro regiments and some depleted regiments of New York volunteers.

The expedition embarked on seven small vessels, and, after some delay caused by fog, the naval brigade reached Boyd's Neck on the western bank of the river about twenty miles away. The marine battalion landed first and covered the landing of the rest of the brigade. The expedition then took up the march on Grahamville but was stopped by the Confederates when about five miles from Boyd's Neck. The army contingent of the expedition, also organized as a brigade, arrived in the afternoon and assumed the lead in the attempted advance to the west. On the following day with the army brigade still leading, they advanced a short distance west and encountered a considerable Confederate force in an entrenched position at Honey Hill. The marine battalion was thrown into the front line on the extreme Union right to help develop the enemy's position. The Union advance was soon definitely stopped, and the Confederates counter-attacked during the afternoon. As the Union army brigade was driven back, the marines retired in order to avoid being outflanked. The entire Union force gradually withdrew to the position where it had camped the first night, entrenched itself, and remained there until December 6, awaiting a more favorable opportunity to cut the railroad.

They made a second attempt to reach the railroad by advancing to the northwest. The expedition re-embarked on its vessels to be transported as far up Tullifinney Creek as navigation would permit. Low tide soon stopped the vessels, but the troops shifted to boats and continued their advance up the creek a short distance farther. The army troops landed first this time and took up the advance on a road running parallel to the creek about a mile to the west of it. The naval brigade followed with the marine battalion protecting its right flank. They again encountered the enemy and fought a skirmish with them on December 6. They drove back the

Confederate advance troops to within about one mile of the railroad but were again definitely stopped.

The naval brigade as well as army troops again dug in and remained in position for several days facing the Confederates, who seemingly had again prevented them from carrying out their mission. Union forces next made a determined local attack with the marine battalion in front supported by the navy artillery. They hoped to drive back the Confederates sufficiently to permit the clearing of a field of fire through the dense woods so that the navy guns could bombard the railroad. The operation was successful, and, as soon as the field of fire was cleared, the marines withdrew to their regular defensive positions and the artillery subjected the railroad to a destructive fire. The Union force remained in position until December 26, when the naval brigade withdrew. The marine battalion went to Bay Point; the naval units disbanded and returned to their regular vessels. The Confederates were still in possession of the railroad and no material assistance had been given to Sherman's army.

Stoddard's little marine battalion had lost a total of 23 killed, wounded, and missing during the several skirmishes with the Confederates. Although no great results were accomplished by the expedition, the naval brigade acquitted itself in such a manner as to demonstrate that it could fight ashore as gallantly as its men had fought during the purely naval operations. Stoddard, the only officer with the battalion, except on a few occasions when naval officers voluntarily aided him, managed to control the battalion in such a commendable manner that he was breveted captain for his gallant and meritorious services in the battle of Boyd's Neck and in the so-called battle of Tullifinney Cross Roads.

## THE REDUCTION OF FORT FISHER

By December, 1864, the only remaining Confederate port open to occasional blockade runners was Wilmington, N. C. The entrance to that port was via the Cape Fear River, the mouth of which was strongly defended by Fort Fisher on the eastern side and a small fort on the western side of the entrance. Its great importance to the Confederate army led Grant and the Union navy to make a determined effort to capture it. Such an operation had been considered previously, but a large enough army expeditionary force to operate with the Navy had theretofore not been available. A force of approximately 6,500 soldiers under Generals Butler and Weitzel was assembled at Hampton Roads early in December, 1864, for a joint expedition to capture Fort Fisher and close the last Confederate port. The North Atlantic Blockading Squadron, with Rear Admiral David D. Porter in command, was augmented to more than fifty vessels and assigned to the same task.

Porter bombarded the fort with nearly six hundred guns to cover a landing by the army a few miles north of the fort. The troops were to attack it by land. The army did not arrive in time, however, to land under cover of the first day's bombardment. The bombardment was repeated on Christmas Day; the army landed with little difficulty at some distance from the fort and advanced within a few hundred yards of it. The two army generals, finding the face of the fort towards them not yet demolished, refused to make the planned assault and retired to their vessels—much to the disgust of the naval forces. During this first attack on Fort Fisher the marines on the large vessels of Porter's fleet served mostly as crews of great guns. They were highly commended by a number of commanding officers for the efficient manner in which they handled their guns during the bombardment. About the only casualties to the marines of the fleet were due to the explosion of guns. Second Lieutenant Jones Pile was killed in this manner on board the *Juniata*. Some other marines were casualties for the same reason on other vessels. The army sailed back to Hampton Roads where its generals were relieved. The force was slightly augmented and reorganized and placed under the command of General Terry. The role of the marines in the second and successful attack against Fort Fisher was of an entirely different nature and a greater test of their courage.

Eight thousand soldiers were provided for the next attack, and more complete plans were made for co-operation between the fleet and the landing forces. On January 13, 1865, Terry landed his entire force to the northward of Fort Fisher while the naval forces under Porter bombarded the fort. Terry spent the following day reorganizing and consolidating his position while the fleet again carried on a bombardment in a special effort to destroy that part of the fort facing the soldiers. It was planned to make a determined naval assault on the sea face of the fort in order to create a diversion from Terry's troops, who were to advance from the north and storm it. Sixteen hundred sailors and four hundred marines were landed from the fleet and hastily organized into units to make the secondary attack. The sailors were armed with cutlasses and pistols and were expected to assault the fort in the then prescribed manner for "boarders." The marines with their muskets and rifles were ordered to get into firing position near enough to the parapets to keep down the Confederate small-arms fire, to cover the assault of the sailors, and, after the sailors had closed on the enemy, follow them in the assault.

Neither the marines nor the sailors were accustomed to this kind of operation. Neither had been given the slightest training in it. Furthermore the plan was very poorly understood; hopeless confusion resulted. One detachment of the marines under First Lieutenant Louis Fagan advanced as skirmishers to a previously prepared line of rifle pits and took up the fire against the enemy. The remainder of the marines, who had been hastily organized into a four-company battalion after they landed, attempted to advance to another line of rifle pits and other cover nearer the forts, where they would be able to keep down the fire of the Confederate infantry and thus cover the assault of the sailors. In the meantime the several divisions of sailors advanced via the flank along the beach, and their leading units attempted to assault before the marines got into positions to support them. The leading waves of sailors were driven back by the time the two most advanced companies of marines had occupied their supporting position. The rear companies of marines retreated with the retiring sailors and never reached the firing position.

In the final reports of the operation some naval officer claimed that the marines failed to carry out their part of the plan, and for that reason the sailors' assault failed. Captain L. L. Dawson, who commanded the marine battalion, claimed, on the other hand, that he did not have time to place his men into firing positions before the leading naval units started their assault. There were no doubt many mistakes made—one being the use of cutlasses to storm a fort. All blame, however, was lost sight of in the outcome of the operation. The naval landing force had created a decided diversion by their assault. The Confederates in the fort thought it the main attack and shifted most of the troops to that side of the fort while Terry's forces advanced against the northern face which was left with little protection. Terry's assaulting groups, showing the highest order of dash and courage, swept into the fort and soon had possession of part of it and were graually advancing when the fight ended by the Confederate garrison surrendering at 10 P.M. The failures of the naval forces were soon lost sight of when a number of naval and marine officers succeeded in rallying a considerable body of men, who helped keep up the fight during the remainder of the day. About half of the marines were reassembled and they, with a portion of the sailors, joined Terry's troops and assisted in holding a sector until the fort surrendered. Three marine captains and five first lieutenants of the battalion were commended for their bravery and breveted to the next higher rank for the heroic parts they played during the attack. The Federals captured Wilmington soon afterwards and virtually ended blockade running.

## Capture by the *Alabama*

The rapid growth of the West, which continued in spite of the Civil War, created a growing demand for the establishment of permanent naval facilities on the Pacific Coast. Early in the 1860's the construction of the first Pacific navy yard was begun on an arm of San Francisco Bay near Vallejo, California. It has since been given the name of Mare Island. In spite of the urgent need for marines in carrying on the Civil War, a detachment of 112 officers and marines under Major Addison Garland was organized at the Brooklyn Navy Yard early in November, 1862, for duty in California. The detachment, plus replacements for the Pacific Squadron, sailed on the Pacific Mail steamer *Ariel* to Aspinwall (Colon) for transfer across the Isthmus to Panama and thence by steamer to its new station.

Off the coast of Cuba on December 7, the *Ariel* was overhauled by a war vessel flying the U. S. flag. When within half a mile distance, however, the ship hauled down that flag and ran up the Confederate flag, and shortly afterwards fired a shot across the bow of the *Ariel,* forcing her to heave to. The armed vessel proved to be the famous Confederate cruiser *Alabama,* and the *Ariel,* having no means for defense, surrendered. The Confederates placed a prize crew on board the *Ariel,* removed $9,500 in cash found on board, and took the arms from the marines. The relations between Garland and the Confederate prize officer were most cordial in spite of the delicate situation. At the request of Captain Semmes of the *Alabama,* the marines continued to act as sentinels over the spirits room to prevent members of the prize crew from over-indulging themselves. Semmes agreed that the marines should be paroled and allowed to proceed on their way subject to later exchange as prisoners of war. Arrangement was made for the vessel to be ransomed for $261,000; it was then allowed to proceed on its voyage. Garland's detachment went on its way and arrived at Mare Island December 27, and, while still on parole, established a permanent Marine Corps post at that place, which has since continued as one of the Corps' regular shore stations.

## Marines at Cairo and Mound City, Illinois

Shortly after the outbreak of the Civil War, the Navy began the development of a flotilla of armed vessels to operate on the rivers of the Middle West. The part played by these vessels during the war is noted above. Cairo, Illinois, was selected as the base for the river flotilla, and its development began during 1862. A marine guard of 4 officers and 88 enlisted men transferred from Headquarters, Washington, during November of that year for maintaining the usual naval station guard at Cairo and furnishing detachments for a few of the vessels of the flotilla. A detachment of one officer and thirty-eight marines went aboard the *Black-Hawk,* flagship of the flotilla. A sergeant's guard was maintained at various times on one or two of the river vessels. The Cairo detachment was maintained throughout the remainder of the war; its strength was augmented to 158 officers and men during the spring of 1864. In May of that year it was removed to Mound City, Illinois, a few miles to the north of Cairo, where practically all naval property had been placed.

## Suppressing the New York Draft Riot

Opposition to the war in the northern states was a serious handicap to the Federal Government and at times made the outcome appear quite uncertain. Certain peace societies were especially active against continuing the war. The volunteer enlistments proved ineffective; a draft law was put into operation in 1863. The activities of organizations opposing the war became particularly intense just before Lee's invasion of the North during that year. There appears to have been a concerted plan to end the war favorably to the Confederacy by these two moves. The peace plan collapsed, however, with Lee's defeat at Gettysburg and Grant's capture of Vicksburg, but arrangements for a violent demonstration against the war proceeded in New York City. When the draft law went into effect, serious rioting lasting several days followed. The civil government almost completely broke down; the inhabitants lived in mortal terror. The Governor of New York, being more or less sympathetic with the peace movement, exerted himself very little towards restoring order. Union troops in the vicinity were too few to handle the situation, and other troops were summoned.

A naval brigade was organized at the Navy Yard, Brooklyn, under Lieutenant Commander R. W. Meade. A two-company battalion of about 180 marines under Captain J. C. Grayson joined the brigade. It proceeded to the city hall, and Grayson's battalion was distributed in different localities, where they kept the streets clear and assisted the police in making arrests and otherwise keeping down the rioters. The marines also patrolled the more disorderly districts and guarded public buildings and property. The rioting continued for more than a week with a loss of two million dollars worth of property. It was stopped only after the temporary suspension of drafting in the city. The naval brigade withdrew on July 20, having won for itself in the meantime the approbation of the city authorities as well as that of the orderly element of the people.

### ZEILIN MADE COMMANDANT

John Harris' service as the Commandant of the Marine Corps came to an end with his death on May 2, 1864. During his tenure of office he appears to have had many difficulties with the other senior officers of the Corps. Harris persisted in keeping one of the field officers in an inactive duty status even in time of war. The most competent of his field officers—at least the one to whom was entrusted the most important assignments during the war, Lieutenant Colonel John G. Reynolds—Harris had court-martialed on more or less trivial charges. Gideon Welles, Secretary of the Navy, confided to his diary after attending Colonel Harris' funeral that, "his death gives embarrassment as to a successor. The higher class of marine officers are not the men who can elevate or give efficiency to the Corps. To supersede them will cause much dissatisfaction. Every man who is overslaughed and all of his friends will be offended with me for what will be deemed an insult. But there is a duty to be performed." His diary discloses a few days later how the "duty" was performed. Acting upon the authority of a retirement law passed in 1862 and with the approval of the President, he retired all of the officers of the Corps senior to his own choice and on the following day, June 9, appointed Major Jacob Zeilin as Colonel Commandant of the Marine Corps.

Zeilin had entered the Corps as an officer October 1, 1831, and had had a great variety of experiences as a junior officer at sea and ashore. He had served with considerable distinction with the Pacific Squadron in the Mexican War and participated in a number of actions during the conquest of California and in the operations along the west coast of Mexico. He had been breveted major for his gallant conduct in the battles of San Gabriel and La Mesa near Los Angeles, California. He was later fleet marine officer of the Pacific Squadron and in 1852, as senior marine officer of the East India Squadron, he accompanied Perry on his famous expedition to Japan. Although a major at the time, he voluntarily commanded a company of marines in Reynolds' battalion during the Battle of Bull Run. In August and September, 1863, he commanded a battalion of marines which took part in the siege of Fort Wagner, S. C. At the time he was chosen as Commandant of the Corps, he was serving as commanding officer at the Marine Barracks, Portsmouth, N. H.

## Morale and Losses

The Marine Corps suffered serious breaks in morale and loyalty as did both the Union and Confederate armies during the Civil War. Desertions in the Union Army ran very high during doubtful periods of the war; and, after serious reverses, large numbers of men and officers alike left the Army without authority. After the Battle of Antietam, for example, the Union Army was reported to have had thirty thousand on unauthorized absence. The Confederate Army suffered staggering losses from desertions, especially during the closing months of the war when it was becoming more evident that defeat was inevitable. In the Union Army the desertions were far more numerous among the regular troops than in the state and volunteer units.

The desertions from the Marine Corps approximately kept pace in percentages with those of the regular army, yet were somewhat different in that maximum desertions by marines occurred during the closing year of the war. The total number of desertions for the years 1861-65 inclusive was approximately equal to the maximum strength that the Corps reached during the period. Desertions during the first year of the war were only 300, less than the average for the prewar years, but they gradually rose to 993 in the last year of the war.

Useless to say, losses by desertion were several times those suffered from battle. The total number who were killed or died of wounds was only 77, while 257 are reported to have died from disease and other causes. The number of losses due to wounds which did not prove fatal is unknown, but 131 were reported wounded, not fatally. A total of forty is shown in the records as missing or absent.

## Résumé

The greatest combat service performed by the marines during the Civil War was on vessels of the Navy, while acting as gun crews in battle, and especially during several bombardments of Confederate forts. It has been noted that as the war progressed, the number of marine detachments at sea continued to grow until there were more than one hundred such contingents, and that sea duty absorbed the greater part of the enlisted strength and most of the junior officers of the Corps. Of the performance of their duties at sea, no criticism in any of the records has been found by the writer.

When they attempted certain land operations, they gave no better account of themselves than did navy landing forces under the same circumstances. On the few occasions when battalions of marines were formed from marine detachments of the fleet for services ashore, invariably they were hastily thrown together and more hastily rushed into battle with practically no training for such duty and very little opportunity even to organize themselves into proper tactical units. The battalions formed out of the regular shore establishments were almost as hastily thrown together, and, according to reports of officers who commanded each of them, were untrained recruits and, for that reason, did not give an account of themselves such as had always been expected and rendered by Marines prior to the Civil War.

## DISPOSITION OF U. S. MARINE CORPS
### (1864)

| | Col. Comdt. | Col. | Lt. Col. | Major | Capt. | 1st Lt. | 2d Lt. | Sgts. | Cpls. | Music | Privates |
|---|---|---|---|---|---|---|---|---|---|---|---|
| H. Q., Washington, D. C. | 1 | | | 1 | 4 | 1 | 6 | 13 | 3 | 60 | 185 |
| Navy Yard, D. C. | | | | 1 | 2 | | | 6 | 4 | 2 | 86 |
| Brooklyn, N. Y. | | | | | 2 | 2 | 2 | 12 | 12 | 7 | 182 |
| Charlestown, Mass. | | | | | 1 | 3 | | 13 | 17 | 3 | 139 |
| Gosport, Va. | | | | | 1 | 1 | 2 | 9 | 7 | 5 | 92 |
| Philadelphia, Pa. | | | | | 3 | 1 | 1 | 10 | 9 | 4 | 154 |
| Portsmouth, N. H. | | | 1 | | 1 | 1 | 1 | 10 | 5 | 2 | 52 |
| Mound City, Ill. | | | | | 1 | | 2 | 11 | 9 | 5 | 95 |
| Pensacola, W. Fla. | | 1 | | | 1 | | | 4 | 4 | 2 | 77 |
| Mare Island, Calif. | | | 1 | | 2 | 2 | 1 | 10 | 7 | 6 | 119 |
| On board six Receiving Ships | | | | | | 1 | | 10 | 15 | 2 | 161 |
| Mississippi Squadron (*Black Hawk*) | | | | | | 1 | | 2 | 2 | | 24 |
| Pacific Squadron | | | | | | | | | | | |
| *Lancaster* | | | | | 1 | | 1 | 3 | 4 | 2 | 42 |
| 5 other ships | | | | | | 2 | 1 | 7 | 12 | 4 | 87 |
| West Gulf Squadron | | | | | | | | | | | |
| *Hartford* | | | | | 1 | | | 3 | 4 | 2 | 49 |
| *Constellation* | | | | | | 1 | | 2 | 3 | 2 | 34 |
| *Richmond* | | | | | | | 1 | 3 | 4 | 1 | 39 |
| 19 other ships | | | | | | 1 | | 24 | 38 | 9 | 271 |
| East Gulf Squadron | | | | | | | | | | | |
| 12 ships | | | | | 2 | 2 | | 14 | 27 | 6 | 183 |
| So. Atlantic Sqdn. | | | | | | | | | | | |
| 20 ships | | | | | | 2 | | 24 | 45 | 10 | 290 |
| No. Atlantic Sqdn. | | | | | | | | | | | |
| *Colorado* | | | | | 1 | 1 | | 3 | 4 | 2 | 39 |
| *New Ironsides* | | | | | | 1 | 1 | 3 | 4 | 2 | 37 |
| *Wabash* | | | | | | | 1 | 3 | 3 | 2 | 51 |
| *Powhatan* | | | | | | 1 | | 3 | 4 | 2 | 40 |
| *Minnesota* | | | | | 1 | | | 3 | 4 | 2 | 48 |
| 33 other ships | | | | | | 2 | | 38 | 66 | 10 | 438 |
| Potomac flotilla | | | | | | | | | | | |
| *Don* | | | | | | | | 1 | 1 | 2 | 13 |

## Chapter IX

## MARKING TIME IN THE GILDED AGE

THE Marine Corps from the close of the Civil War to near the end of the century, during what has been called "the Gilded Age" by a number of eminent historians, had an existence that was quite the opposite to the bustle and hurry which the country as a whole was then experiencing in making its gigantic strides in developing the West. The Corps underwent no noticeable period of demobilization as is commonly the case after major wars because no substantial increase had been made in its personnel during the war. Our comparatively large navy, which was kept in commission for a number of years following the war, required approximately the strength of the Corps which it had at the end of the war. The Marine Corps settled down to its routine peacetime duties with very little reorganization. A large number of navy vessels bearing marines were sent back to their foreign stations, which in some cases were reorganized to meet the new conditions. The regular shore stations continued about the same as during the war.

The period from 1865 to 1898 proved to be the least active the Corps has ever experienced. It marked time not only in regard to its number of belligerent experiences, but in many other ways it was hampered and its services minimized. Its strength, after a few years, was gradually reduced to less than it had been since the outbreak of the Mexican War. There was very little change in its officer personnel, who during the period grew old with practically no promotions; the enlisted men as well had very little opportunity for advancement. On several occasions there was a serious break in their morale. Yet the Corps carried on as best it could under the circumstances and at least maintained its continuity until such time as its services were again required for bigger things. For the convenience of the reader the experiences of the Marine Corps during this period are grouped according to the nature of the duties performed or the tendencies that were manifested, and no effort has been made to present the incidents in strict chronological order.

## Experiences at Sea

Service at sea was of paramount interest to the Corps during this period. Our navy at the close of the war was the most powerful in the world. However, most of its iron-clad and turreted vessels were of hasty wartime construction and did not hold up even as well as the prewar wooden vessels. The Navy in general deteriorated for nearly twenty years after the war, simply wearing out its old equipment. The foreign squadrons were re-established, mostly with new names and new cruising areas. The European Squadron alone was assigned to the eastern hemisphere; the South Atlantic area was turned over to the new squadron by that name, and the South Pacific Squadron was established, particularly for the purpose of patrolling the west coast of South America and a portion of the South Seas. The old East India Squadron was renamed the "Asiatic Squadron." There was some rearrangement of the squadrons and their stations as the period progressed. Almost immediately after the war substantial quotas of vessels were sent back to the foreign stations, and the Marines to some extent resumed their far-flung foreign experiences of which they had had so many in the years preceding the Civil War. The principal mission of the foreign squadrons was to protect American lives and property and especially to support American shipping, which, because of forces over which the Navy had no control, progressively declined during the period.

The European Squadron was re-established with ten vessels and, like its predecessor, made its principal cruising ground the Mediterranean. Its strength varied from that number as its maximum to as few as three vessels, according to the needs. It did a great deal of calling at various ports to show the American flag and make the usual rounds of official calls and entertainments. The most outstanding of its experiences was in 1882 when the entire squadron, which then consisted of only three vessels, was at Alexandria, Egypt.

Egypt at the time was nominally independent, but because of foreign indebtedness was partially under the dual control of Great Britain and France. A patriotic move against foreign influence was led by Arabi Pasha, and the Khedive was powerless to protect foreign rights. France declined to participate in a military intervention, and Great Britain undertook it alone. The British fleet bombarded Alexandria, which was controlled by Arabi, on July 11,

1882, and set fire to the city; this bombardment brought about great disorder and insecurity to the large foreign population. A detachment of seventy-three marines from our squadron, under Captain H. C. Cochrane, assisted by Lieutenant L. W. T. Waller, together with about sixty sailors, promptly landed to assist in restoring order and to prevent further spreading of fires. Their primary object, however, was to protect the American consulate and American interests. Soon afterwards the British landed about four thousand troops; other foreign forces also took part in the occupation of the city. Quiet in the city having been restored, the American sailors from the squadron returned to their ships on the 15th and a part of the marines on the 20th; the remaining detachment under Lieutenant Frank L. Denny withdrew on the 24th. The British soon afterwards sent an army into Egypt from Suez; it captured Cairo and put an end to Arabi's rebellion.

The South Atlantic Squadron was re-established with eight vessels in 1866 and took over the duties formerly carried on by the old Brazil Squadron. The new squadron was gradually reduced and for a number of years consisted of only two vessels. In the Southern Pacific a squadron was formed about the same time with seven vessels; the number was gradually reduced to three. In 1877 the South Pacific Squadron was discontinued as a separate organization, and its cruising area was made a part of the regular Pacific Station. The squadrons which had normal cruising areas in the southern hemisphere and in the tropics carried on a great variety of duties in which the marines performed their usual functions. They together with the sailors participated in several landing operations which were in the nature of interventions and forerunners of the greater interventions which occurred in the following century and are discussed hereafter.

The Asiatic Squadron was established with a strength of twelve vessels soon after the close of the war and resumed the routine duties formerly carried on by the East India Squadron. The vessels remaining in home waters were at first assigned either to the North Atlantic or North Pacific Squadrons. They participated in all manner of operations, from assisting Arctic explorers to interventions in the unsettled countries in Latin America. Twenty-four marines on the *Alliance* had extensive experience in the polar seas, when that vessel was attempting to locate the lost Arctic explorers in the region north of Norway in 1881. Another small detachment of marines was on the *Alert*, with Commander W. S. Schley's three vessels which went in 1884 to the relief of the Greeley Expedition, lost somewhere in the region west of Greenland. The *Alert* had been presented by Queen Victoria for the use of the expedition, because Greeley was in turn seeking the lost Sir John Franklin. The expedition successfully located Greeley with six survivors on Cape Sabine and brought them back to the United States.

Down in the tropics one of the principal services rendered by the marines was the landing of a detachment from the *Kearsarge* under First Lieutenant George D. Bates on Navassa Island, located south of the eastern end of Cuba. An American company, engaged in the removal of guano from the island, was having difficulties with its negro laborers; the trouble seriously endangered the lives of the Americans present. Bates landed with his detachment on June 2, 1891, quickly restored order, and protected the Americans and their property. The difficulties were adjusted by the twentieth of the month, and the marines were withdrawn.

### Protecting Seals in the Bering Sea

During the same year a special detachment of marines, in addition to those on the several vessels of the Pacific Squadron, assisted in an effort to put a stop to the wholesale destruction of seals in the Bering Sea. Seal poachers of various nationalities, principally British, were promiscuously catching seals on the high seas and without regard to the breeding season. The practice, if allowed to continue, would have meant almost the complete extinction of those valuable fur-bearing animals. Prior to our purchase of Alaska from Russia in 1867, the seals had been somewhat protected by Russia's asserting exclusive jurisdiction over a large part of the northern Pacific. This claim was somewhat supported by certain treaties between Great Britain and the United States, and our Congress claimed that upon our purchasing Alaska the jurisdiction over Alaskan waters passed to the control of the United States. A long diplomatic controversy between the United States and Great Britain relative to sealing followed. The two nations finally agreed to arbitrate the dispute, and, pending a permanent settlement, a *modus vivendi* was agreed to on April 15, 1891. By this arrangement the naval officers of each nation were empowered to seize and detain anyone engaged in sealing and turn them over to their own governments for prosecution. Pending final settlement only enough seals for the use of the natives were to be killed. Great Britain sent three vessels into the Bering Sea to patrol part of the area, while the United States made similar arrangements. Our navy chartered a small steamer called the *Al-Ki* and placed a detachment of three officers and forty marines under Captain H. C. Cochrane on board at Mare Island, California; that vessel, together with the *Thetis*,

BRIGADIER GENERAL JACOB ZEILIN
1864-1876

COLONEL CHARLES G. MCCAWLEY
1876-1891

MAJOR GENERAL CHARLES HEYWOOD
1891-1903

MAJOR GENERAL GEORGE F. ELLIOTT
1903-1910

COMMANDANTS OF THE MARINE CORPS

CAPTAIN MCLANE TILTON, CORPORAL BROWN, AND PRIVATE PURVIS WITH THE FLAG THEY CAPTURED FROM A KOREAN FORT, 1871

*Mohican, Alert,* and *Marion,* commanded by Commander C. S. Cotton, were ordered to the troubled area. Two revenue cutters later joined in the duty.

Before starting out to patrol the area, however, both nations advised all parties interested of the action that was being taken. As a result only four vessels suspected of seal poaching were found during the long period of widely scattered patrolling operations, carried on by the vessels of the two countries. The *Al-Ki* with Cochrane's marines on board was made a prison ship for the offenders and was stationed at Unalaska. Two offending American vessels, the *La Ninfa* and the *Ethel,* were captured and their crews transferred to Cochrane on the *Al-Ki.* Cochrane placed prize crews of marines on board and towed the vessels twelve hundred miles to Sitka, where he turned them over to the American authorities. The *Al-Ki* on August 15 left Sitka for Unalaska where it remained until October 5, by which time the weather was so generally stormy that sealers were not likely to venture forth. Cochrane's marines were able to supplement their meager sea rations by seining for fish and by obtaining vegetables and fruit ashore. The crew of the *Al-Ki* proved to be rather unruly and on several occasions were at the point of mutinying; but the support of Cochrane's marines helped the captain to keep them at their tasks. The marine detachment of the *Alert* boarded several suspicious vessels and in some cases warned them to leave the waters of Alaska. Cochrane and his marines returned to Mare Island on October 14.

The protection of the seal industry was later ruled on by arbitration but the decision was unsatisfactory to the United States and proved ineffective. The problem was not solved until 1911, when a convention was agreed to by Great Britain, Russia, Japan, and the United States prohibiting their nationals from sealing at sea in the disputed area.

## The *Virginius* Affair

Shortly after the declaration of a republic in Spain in 1873, the *Virginius,* an American vessel, was captured at sea by a Spanish war vessel and taken into Santiago, Cuba, where it was promptly condemned for engaging in a filibustering expedition to Cuba; fifty-three of its passengers and crew were summarily executed. The act was obviously a gross violation of American rights on the high seas; the executions had no legal basis. Feeling ran high in the United States; strained relations followed between the two countries; and the United States mobilized a substantial fleet under Admiral Porter at Key West. During the long period of the negotiations which followed, however, the personnel of the fleet were given extensive training ashore. Colonel Heywood, the fleet marine officer, was able to assemble ten companies of marines for field exercises ashore. This was their first opportunity since the Civil War for such training. The difficulty was finally settled by Spain's proving that the American registry of the *Virginius* was fraudulent.

Two years afterwards President Grant, as part of his preparations for a possible intervention in Cuba in behalf of revolutionists, again assembled the fleet at Key West and gave the Marines another opportunity for training in larger units. Contrary to the usual American diplomatic policy, Grant consulted with the European powers regarding intervention. He received no encouragement, so he dropped the matter. This incident was just another preliminary to the actual intervention which occurred some twenty-three years later.

## INTERVENTIONS IN LATIN AMERICAN COUNTRIES

### URUGUAY

Political conditions in most of the Latin-American countries continued to be chaotic, as they had been during the years preceding the Civil War. Uruguay, in particular, continued to be a troublesome locality. Another revolutionary outbreak occurred in 1868, and armed vessels of six different foreign countries stood by in the harbor of Montevideo. The military garrison which normally guarded the city turned against the constituted authority; the latter promptly requested, through the American consul, protection for the Loyalist factions and for the customs house. The authorities made similar requests of the representatives of other countries present. The Americans and several other powers agreed to make a combined landing for the protection of the city. Five vessels of the South Atlantic Squadron (*Guerriere,* flag-ship, *Quinnebaug, Shamokin, Kansas,* and *Wasp*), commanded by Rear Admiral Charles H. Davis, took part in the operation.

The American part of the combined landing force which went ashore in the early morning of February 7 consisted of several officers, fifteen marines, and thirty sailors from the *Guerriere.* An Italian admiral was the senior officer present and took command of the combined expedition. The show of force ended the revolution. Upon the governor's request the foreign forces withdrew to their ships. A short time afterwards, however, serious trouble again occurred. The governor was assassinated by some of the opposing faction, and his followers proceeded to retaliate by killing thirty or forty of the rebellious party. Davis had left Montevideo, leaving behind the *Kansas* and the *Wasp*. Fifty officers and men from those vessels landed on February 19 and guarded the American consulate and the customs house until the 27th, when they withdrew upon the request of the President of Uruguay.

## MEXICO

Some two years later our Navy again found it necessary to come to the aid of ineffective local authorities at Guaymas, Mexico. A piratical gang on the steamer *Forward*, flying the San Salvador flag, had put into that port, robbed the customs house, forced foreign merchants to pay contributions, and compelled the American consul to give them a supply of coal. The U.S.S. *Mohican*, Commander W. W. Low, was at Mazatlan and, upon hearing of the incident, set out to run down the pirates. Upon reaching San Blas a few days later, Low learned that the *Forward* had gone to Boca Teacapan. He arrived off that place the following morning (June 17, 1870), disembarked a landing force of marines and sailors into six boats, and dispatched them up the river to locate the piratical steamer.

The landing force from the *Mohican* had proceeded twenty-five miles when they learned from a fisherman that the *Forward* was aground fifteen miles farther up the stream. They located the pirate vessel at 7:45 P.M. and immediately took possession of it without difficulty, as only six of the crew were on board. As they had approached the vessel, a boat had been sighted making for the shore loaded with others of the pirate crew. Some of the Americans took up pursuit. They received a heavy fire from ashore which killed one and wounded two. The landing force later discovered that the pirates had taken their cannon ashore and with their available small arms had prepared to defend themselves. Lieutenant Brownson, U.S.N., in command of the expedition, finding that it was impossible to remove the *Forward*, accomplished his mission by setting fire to the vessel in a number of places (including the coal bunkers) and then returned to his ship.

## HAITI

Another of our periodic interventions in the affairs of Haiti occurred in 1888. An American steamer had been seized by a Haitian war vessel, taken to Port au Prince, and condemned by a prize court. Rear Admiral Stephen B. Luce was sent to Port au Prince with the *Galena* and *Yantic*, carrying a small expeditionary force of marines. His orders were to retake the captured American vessel, if necessary, to procure its release. He arrived at Port au Prince on December 20 and through the American Minister notified the Haitian authorities of his mission. The mere show of force was sufficient, and the ship was released.

## Argentina

For a number of years after the American naval intervention of 1852, affairs in Argentina were sufficiently stable to cause no great concern to the American authorities. Revolution again broke out, however, in the province of Buenos Aires in July, 1890, and marines from the *Tallapoosa* landed in July to protect the American consulate and the residence of the American Minister.

## Chile

In the near-by republic of Chile, the relations of that country with the United States were severely strained about one year later, when a mob attacked a liberty party from the U.S.S. *Baltimore* at Valparaiso, killing two American bluejackets and wounding eighteen. A revolution was in progress there at the time, and the attack was caused by the mob's thinking that the United States was aiding the opposing faction. Some of the ill feeling was caused by a guard of thirty-six marines and as many sailors, under the command of Captain William S. Muse, U.S.M.C., which had been maintained ashore for some time guarding the American Legation. The riot naturally caused a tremendous outburst of feeling in the United States; many clamored for war. Relations continued to be strained for some time afterward, but the American authorities handled the situation calmly and efficiently in spite of further violent attacks on Americans by the Chileans. The two governments finally came to an agreement by Chile's paying an indemnity and permitting the political refugees who had been lodged in the American Embassy to be removed to an American naval vessel.

## Isthmus of Panama

Securing the transit of the Isthmus, in compliance with the treaty of 1846 with New Granada, exacted far more attention than did all the difficulties in the rest of the Spanish-American countries combined. Even during the Civil War our naval vessels were usually stationed in the vicinity and kept a close watch over the transit. Throughout the period, disorders, riots, rebellions, and insurrections recurred at frequent intervals on the Isthmus. Soon after the close of our Civil War, Colombia requested that the United

States assist her in maintaining sovereignty over the troubled area. The request was flatly denied, and our duties thereafter became somewhat more restricted.

In April, 1873, a serious squabble occurred between the political factions on the Isthmus; the leader of the rebel faction captured and imprisoned the governor of Panama and set up a provisional government of his own. The Colombian troops in the vicinity refused to recognize the new government and proceeded to attack its forces. Admiral Steedman arrived on his flagship, *Pensacola*, about that time and made all necessary arrangements with the American consul and a group of American citizens for intervening upon a prearranged signal. The signal was forthcoming that very evening, and a landing force went ashore from the *Pensacola* to furnish the necessary protection for the railroad property. Conditions in the city of Panama grew more dangerous to the foreigners, and upon their request a detachment of marines and sailors went ashore from the *Tuscarora* and *Pensacola,* guarded certain places in the city, and strengthened the guard over the transit facilities. Only a show of force was necessary. In a few days the usurping faction agreed to lay down its arms. Peace was thus restored and our naval landing forces withdrew after having been ashore ten days.

The same faction which had caused that trouble again grew dissatisfied with their treatment, raised another armed force of several hundred men, and began an attack on the city on September 23. They kept up an almost continuous fire day and night for the following ten days, but the loyal troops in the city held them off. The danger to the transit grew worse, however, and a landing force of 110 sailors and marines again went ashore from the *Pensacola* to guard the railroad property and furnish train guards. This force was augmented the following day by some additional marines and sailors, and guards were also placed over the American consulate and several American residences. As an added precaution in the protection of the transit, a detachment went to Mamei, the halfway point on the railroad across the Isthmus. The following day a detachment from the *Benicia* and some additional men from the *Pensacola* went to reinforce the Americans. Conditions had again improved by October 4, and our troops gradually withdrew.

During the next few years conditions on the Isthmus were somewhat less turbulent; nevertheless, one or more American vessels were kept stationed in the vicinity. The commanders of these vessels used their influence on several occasions to maintain peace and managed to avoid armed intervention for several years. Revolutionary outbreaks continued to occur but they did not again interrupt the transit of the Isthmus.

## THE EXPEDITION OF 1885

By the close of 1884 the French Canal Company had begun making considerable progress in digging an isthmian canal and had brought many thousands of unruly laborers into the already turbulent locality. A complete collapse of the government of Colombia occurred during the following year; the United States found it necessary to make an intervention on the Isthmus which resembled in magnitude those made in a number of other Latin-American countries in the twentieth century. The Colombian Government withdrew all of its regular troops from the Isthmus to combat revolution elsewhere and left only the local police to protect that part of the country from the unruly mobs.

At the recommendation of the American Minister, several naval vessels were promptly ordered to Colon and Panama. The President of Panama soon announced his inability to protect the transit, and the railway officials requested our protection. The *Alliance* was the first vessel to arrive at Colon, where it went alongside the dock on January 18, 1885, and sent its marines ashore to guard the railway property. It was forced to leave almost immediately, however, in compliance with its sailing orders, and conditions rapidly grew worse. A rebel leader as usual soon appeared, this time Aizpuru, and began to organize the disorderly elements for his own purpose. By March 16 the rebels under Aizpuru had gained control of both Panama and Colon as well as the entire railroad. The *Galena* soon arrived at Colon, and its marine detachment under Second Lieutenant Charles A. Doyen went ashore to guard the American consulate. Soon afterwards Doyen's detachment was reinforced by sailors from the *Galena*. Serious rioting occurred at Panama, and a British naval vessel sent seventy men ashore to protect the railroad at that place.

Soon after the Colombian troops were withdrawn from Colon, Pedro Prestan, a Haitian negro, organized a force of radicals and took possession of the town. A few local troops from Panama attempting to regain control defeated Prestan; but, before they could get his faction out of Colon, he set the town on fire in a number of places, and the greater part of it was destroyed. By this time Aizpuru felt strong enough to declare himself governor of Panama. The situation by this time was plainly beyond the control of a few small landing parties from vessels of the Navy.

## McCalla's Expeditionary Force

Upon learning of the burning of Colon, our government immediately ordered a substantial expeditionary force mobilized for duty on the Isthmus. By order of the Secretary of the Navy all shore stations in the eastern part of the United States and vessels which were not ordered to Panama were stripped of their marines for this duty. A battalion consisting of 10 officers and 212 marines was assembled in New York, under Lieutenant Colonel Charles Heywood, and sailed for Panama on April 3. Another battalion of 15 officers and 250 marines, commanded by Captain John H. Higsbee, together with a naval battalion and hastily improvised artillery detachments, sailed from New York four days later. Commander B. H. McCalla, who had been designated to take command of the entire expeditionary force in Panama, was in charge of this contingent. The expeditionary force was increased by transferring the company of marines from Florida direct to Colon on board the *Tennessee*.

By this time several additional naval vessels had arrived on each side of the Isthmus and had begun to take prompt action to control the situation. The *Shenandoah* landed a battalion, consisting of one company of marines, two companies of sailors acting as infantry, and one armed as artillery, at Panama. They immediately placed strong guards on the railway property. Shortly afterwards another landing force went ashore at Colon from the *Tennessee* and *Swatara;* they immediately provided for protection at that end of the railroad and organized strong train guards protected by improvised armored cars. Under the protection thus provided, the transit was promptly reopened.

Heywood's battalion arrived on April 11 and was immediately transferred to Panama to take over the guarding of that city from the personnel of the Pacific Squadron. One of its companies and a detachment of sailors were placed on detached duty at Matachin. These measures enabled the railroad to re-establish its regular train service. Most of the city of Panama was still under control of the revolutionary forces and feared that it might suffer the same fate as Colon. The American commander refused to recognize Aizpuru as the rightful ruler of the city, and Aizpuru immediately set about stirring up violent feelings against the American forces. The remainder of the American expeditionary force arrived on April 15, and McCalla assumed command of all the forces ashore.

The marines were organized into a so-called brigade of two battalions, under Colonel Heywood. Higsbee's battalion, which was the last to arrive, took over the guarding of various positions in the vicinity of Colon, thus relieving a number of detachments from naval vessels. McCalla organized a special railway battalion for the protection of trains. This battalion, which was made up of one company of marines and two sections of Gatling guns manned by sailors, furnished train guards for several trips daily between Colon and Panama. The additional marine detachments were stationed at various towns along the railroad. Heywood made his headquarters in Panama and was given command of all troops in that locality. Although the safety of the transit was thereby secured, other difficulties remained.

The danger to the city of Panama was made worse by Aizpuru's erecting barricades in the streets. The railroad docks were close to the city. If the city were burned they would probably burn also, and the transit would be seriously hampered. The Colombian Government had regained some strength and was able by this time to make troops available for duty at Panama. Their arrival at Panama, however, would probably result in a battle for the possession of that city. On April 20 a report was received at Panama that a force of Colombian troops had embarked at a near-by port. Thereupon McCalla ordered Companies B and D of the Second Battalion of Marines, at Colon, to Panama as reinforcements. These companies were further reinforced by a Gatling gun and a howitzer with navy crews and formed into a provisional battalion. The battalion guarded the main approaches to the city each night. Panama was further reinforced by a detachment of marines from the *Shenandoah*, and McCalla made plans for a systematic occupation of the city if conditions grew worse.

The rebels continued the erecting of barricades, which tended to make the planned American occupation more difficult. Aizpuru threatened to seize the telegraph office. Seven hundred Colombian troops were reported to be approaching Panama. Admiral Jouett, senior naval officer present, fearing a repetition of the Colon disaster, ordered the city to be occupied by the American forces. Two more companies of marines from Colon together with some naval contingents were brought over to reinforce Panama. The protecting of Colon was again taken over by landing forces from naval vessels.

As the State and Navy Departments did not approve of the occupation of Panama, they ordered it evacuated as soon as possible and turned over to the dominant force. This, of course, left the situation very embarrassing for McCalla. But, before he could withdraw from such a situation, he found himself in the midst of still more difficulties.

During the night following the occupation of Panama some minor riots occurred among the citizens, and, purely for moral effect, one of the American units fired a Gatling gun over the tops of the houses of the city; a few excited sentinels fired a few shots. McCalla, in the midst of the excitement which followed, had Aizpuru arrested, held him overnight, and forced him to agree to take his force of some five hundred men out of the city. On the following day McCalla made an agreement with Aizpuru in which the latter agreed to protect the foreigners in the city, permit no fighting within its limits, and allow no more barricades to be erected. McCalla in turn agreed to evacuate. He did this by stages soon afterwards. Panama was reoccupied by Colombian troops three days later without resistance.

In the meantime the marine detachments holding the railway stations in the interior shared to some extent in the exciting situation. A serious riot occurred between some Jamaicans and Colombians at Paraiso station, and a company of marines rushed to the scene. The riot had subsided, however, by the time the marines arrived, and their only duties were to take care of the wounded and prevent interference with the transit.

Soon after the arrival of the Colombian troops at Panama the American forces began to withdraw from the Isthmus, the ship detachments being the first to leave. McCalla's forces gradually withdrew to Colon. A part sailed for the United States on May 7, and the remainder were gradually removed from the country. By May 21 only a small detachment of marines from the *Shenandoah* remained to guard the trains. The Colombian troops took over that duty on May 25, and, with the addition of several reinforcing units which had arrived, they were able to control the situation on the Isthmus.

Conditions remained relatively quiet in the vicinity until 1888, when the French Canal Company disastrously collapsed and all work ceased, leaving many thousands of unemployed laborers on the Isthmus. Our naval vessels closely watched the situation for some time, but we made no other armed intervention until after the period discussed in this chapter.

### NICARAGUA

The severe lesson taught the inhabitants of southeastern Nicaragua by the rather violent retaliatory measures of Commander Hollins appears to have been remembered for a number of years afterwards. The filibuster, William Walker, had caused some annoyance in the vicinity from about 1855 to 1860, but the United States did not find it necessary to make a military intervention. Several landings for the protection of Americans and their property were made, however, from American naval vessels during the closing years of the nineteenth century. One of the periodic revolutions of that turbulent republic was in full swing during the summer of 1894. The *Columbia* and *Marblehead* were kept stationed in the waters of the east coast of that country to look after American interests. At the request of the American consul at Bluefields, the marine detachment of the *Marblehead*, commanded by First Lieutenant Franklin J. Moses, and a company of sailors landed early in July and provided protection for about one month. The force was approximately doubled on July 31 by the addition of the marine guard and a company of seamen from the *Columbia*. The combined landing forces withdrew one week later. A small landing force was sent ashore from the *Alert* at Bluefields in May, 1896, under similar conditions. The *Alert* remained in the vicinity for some time and had occasion to send a landing force ashore to protect the American consular agent at San Juan del Sur about two years later.

### Surveying Expeditions

During the early part of the period the Navy undertook a series of surveys to determine the best location for an inter-oceanic canal. A number of routes across the Isthmus of Panama were examined and also the route which has been more seriously considered in recent years across Nicaragua. A detachment of three officers and sixty marines assisted in the survey of the Darien route in 1870.

### Activities in Eastern Asia

### In Japan

For a number of years following Perry's expedition to Japan, that country was intermittently torn by civil wars, and there were periods of violent outbreaks against all foreigners. On a number of occasions one or more ships of our Navy were sent to the treaty ports for the protection of Americans and particularly American representatives. Outbreaks against foreigners occurred during the period of our Civil War when only the *Wyoming* was on the Asiatic Station. An American ship was fired on by the forts on the Straits of Shimonoseki, and, on approval of the American Minister, for retaliation the *Wyoming* bombarded the forts and fired upon some Japanese vessels, sinking one of them and blowing up another.

Immediately after the war more ships were made available on the station, and in 1867 Admiral Bell with several large vessels remained along the coast of Japan for the special purpose of protecting the American Minister. On May 1 of that year the marine guards of Bell's vessels supplied a special escort of honor as well as protection to the American Minister, Mr. Van Valkenburgh, at Osaka. At this time civil war was in progress in Japan between the forces of the Mikado and some of the remaining shoguns, the former attempting to regain his imperial powers which had been usurped by the latter several hundred years previously.

In 1868 two new treaty ports were opened, Osaka and Hiogo. Some display of friendliness was made initially at the former place but very shortly considerable hostilities developed towards foreigners. A detachment of Japanese troops attacked the foreign residents and among others seriously wounded one of the crew of the U.S.S. *Oneida*. A joint naval operation was immediately undertaken on February 1 by the foreign vessels of war present. A detachment of sailors and marines from the *Oneida* took part and helped to guard the foreign settlement until February 8. Assurance was then given by the Mikado, who had succeeded in reasserting his powers, that foreigners would be protected; thereupon the landing forces were withdrawn. Hostility towards foreigners, however, did not cease, and early in April, 1868, the foreign naval commanders at Yokohama formulated a plan for the protection of their nationals. This plan called for the landing of a joint force under an American commander to operate as suggested by the American Minister. Under the plan, twenty-five marines from the *Monocacy* and *Iroquois* took part in the guarding of foreigners at Yokohama between April 4 and May 12. A detachment of marines from the Asiatic Squadron guarded the residence of the American Minister to Japan at Yedo and at other places during the greater part of 1868.

## Fighting Savages in Formosa

The American bark *Rover*, engaged in a regular inter-island trade in the western Pacific, was wrecked on the southeastern end of the island of Formosa. Early in 1867 a report came to Rear Admiral Bell, Commander of the Asiatic Squadron, that her crew had been murdered by the semi-savage inhabitants of the island. Bell sent the *Ashuelot* to verify the reported atrocities and, if possible, to punish the offenders. The local authorities of Formosa expressed a willingness to give satisfaction but delayed repeatedly and finally claimed that the offenders belonged to savage tribes who were not obedient to their laws. Commander John C. Febiger of the *Ashuelot*, believing the situation too much for him to handle, returned and reported the situation to Bell. Bell then proceeded to Formosa with his flagship, the *Hartford*, and the *Wyoming*. He called at Taka where several foreigners agreed to aid him in his operations.

Bell determined to put a landing force ashore on June 13, 1867, to punish the offending savages. He landed a force of nearly two hundred, including forty-three marines commanded by Captain James Forney, the fleet marine officer. The landing force located a band of savages on some hills about two miles from the landing beach and advanced to attack them. The Formosans resorted to the tactics commonly used by the American Indians, firing and retreating without being seen. In spite of being ambushed several times, the landing force pursued the savages until 2 P.M. They halted and the savages attacked them. Lieutenant Commander McKenzie led a company of the naval forces against the savages but was himself ambushed and received a wound from which he soon afterwards died. The men of the expedition were entirely unused to such experiences. In addition to the punishment inflicted by the savages, several of the Americans suffered severe sunstrokes and by 4 P.M. the entire force was practically exhausted. Commander Belknap, in charge of the expedition, decided that it was time to withdraw, and the expedition returned to their ship considerably worsted by the enemy and heat. Bell, thereafter, contented himself by burning a number of huts, driving some of the natives into the interior, and otherwise punishing them.

### Protecting Americans in China

During the Gilded Age disorder and chaos continued in the Chinese Empire pretty much the same as they had existed there in the years preceding the Civil War. Outbreaks against foreigners continued; hence the Asiatic Squadron, as soon as it was re-established in 1866, found it necessary to take protective measures for Americans and their interests. The American consul at Newchwang was assaulted by Chinese, and Bell sent the *Wachusett*, Commander Robert Townsend, to protect the consulate. That vessel arrived on June 20, 1866, and immediately sent a landing force of fifty marines and sailors ashore to determine the situation. The Chinese local authorities were willing to assist in bringing the assailants to punishment but were afraid to arrest their leaders. Townsend was unwilling to let the culprits go unpunished and sent a force of one hundred marines and sailors ashore on the 25th to bring back the leader of the gang, one Sword Rack Hoo. Townsend saw to it that the offenders were brought to trial and punished, but, upon leaving, removed the consul to Chefoo. On July 14 Townsend arrived at Tung Chow Foo and, in his characteristic way, escorted by an armed detachment of one hundred sailors and marines, paid a visit to the authorities. He then went to Shanghai. Shortly after his arrival there a serious fire broke out; he landed a part of his crew to assist in its extinction.

During the Sino-Japanese War of 1894 conditions in China became even more chaotic than usual, and Rear Admiral Charles C. Carpenter of the Asiatic Squadron was ordered to give every possible protection to American interests. A Japanese army advanced on Peking; during the excitement that ensued, anti-foreign riots frequently occurred. The American Minister at Peking, Colonel Charles Denby, requested the protection of a marine guard for the legation. The marines of the *Baltimore*, under Captain George F. Elliott (later Commandant of the Marine Corps) were selected to furnish the protection. They were transferred to a small steamer at Chefoo, proceeded to Taku, and then went by rail to Tientsin. Elliott found the *Monocacy* at that place, and, his progress to Peking being interrupted by an edict of the Emperor forbidding any foreign troops to be in the Chinese capital, he reported his detachment aboard that vessel. In spite of the Emperor's edict the Admiral ordered Elliott to go unescorted to Peking to confer with Denby and make arrangements for a legation guard, if one were needed. Because the Japanese were operating in that part of China, twenty-five thousand Chinese troops lined the railroad between Tientsin and Peking and permitted no trains to be run. Captain Elliott, undaunted, proceeded on horseback and reached Peking, a distance of eighty miles, in two days. Peace negotiations between the belligerent countries were opened a few days later, and Elliott returned to Tientsin. With his detachment of marines he rejoined the *Baltimore* at Nagasaki, nearly six months after having left that vessel.

### THE PUNITIVE EXPEDITION TO KOREA

The American sailing ship *Surprise* was wrecked off the eastern coast of Korea in 1866. Its crew was kindly treated but taken across the Yalu River and turned over to the Chinese. Another American sailing vessel, the *General Sherman*, entered the Han River soon afterwards, over the objection of the local officials, and went far up the river on the high spring tide. The water suddenly dropped and left the vessel stranded. The Koreans set it on fire by means of a fire raft and, when the crew came ashore, massacred them. A number of French missionaries had suffered a like fate, and the French determined upon retaliation. A French force attempted to land and storm some Korean forts but was defeated and driven off. Korea was at the time nominally part of the Chinese Empire, but in reality the government of China exercised very little control over it. Our government determined to send a mission backed up by a strong naval force to Korea in an effort to adjust difficulties, obtain some assurance for the protection of Americans and, if possible, open up the country to American trade. Our minister to China, A. A. Low, was entrusted with the mission. Escorted by Rear Admiral John Rodgers, Commander of the Asiatic Fleet, with his flagship the *Colorado*, together with the *Alaska, Benicia, Monocacy*, and *Palos*, Low proceeded to the western coast of Korea where the squadron anchored off the mouth of the Han River, May 19, 1871. While awaiting the arrival of some officials of the country whom Low had asked to see, Rodgers sent the *Palos* and four steam launches to make a survey up the river. The surveying party returned four days later without having been molested. Communications were established on the 30th, but with officials of inferior rating and without credentials, and Low would not recognize them as proper representatives of the Korean Government.

Desiring to examine further the approaches towards Seoul, Rodgers sent out a second surveying detachment on June 1 consisting of the *Monocacy* and the *Palos* and four boats. After proceeding a short way up the river, borne along by the swift current caused by very high tides, the expedition sighted a fort which appeared to be manned with at least a thousand men and flying a flag which indicated the command of a general. Without the least warning a single shot was fired from near the flag, and many guns of the fort immediately thereafter opened fire upon the American boats and ships. The *Palos* and *Monocacy* returned the fire and soon drove the fort's garrison to the shelter of the hills and ravines in the rear. Before the vessels could stop their onward rush with the tide, the expedition was carried around the bend of the river where it faced another fort. Expecting a hostile reception from it, they promptly opened fire. This fort did not return the fire, and no Koreans were seen. The *Monocacy* had struck a rock in the meantime and was leaking rather badly. Seeing no further signs of the enemy, the Americans ceased firing and returned to the fleet anchorage. The gunnery of the Koreans was very poor; only two men were wounded—one of these accidentally by the recoil of a howitzer. None of the boats were hit.

Rodgers and Low waited ten days to give the Korean officials ample time to apologize for the hostile acts of the fort. They then determined to carry out a punitive expedition against the forts in order to force the respect of the Korean officials and to aid in obtaining the desired treaty. In accordance with Rodgers' plan for the operation, the *Monocacy* and *Palos* were assigned to support a land attack on the forts. All available members of the crews of the *Colorado, Alaska,* and *Benicia,* together with twenty-two boats, were organized into a landing force of 651 men besides the boats' crews. The sailors were organized into a battalion of infantry and a battery of seven light howitzers, while the 105 marines of the squadron, commanded by Captain McLane Tilton, were organized as the shock troops of the force. Commander H. C. Blake commanded the entire expedition while Commander A. L. Kimberly was in charge of the landing force. The supporting vessels were ordered to silence the forts before the landing force went ashore.

The expedition got under way during the forenoon of June 10 with the *Monocacy* leading. Some steam launches and the *Palos* towed the boats in which the landing force had embarked. The *Monocacy* successfully silenced the first fort and breeched its walls. The Koreans attempted to return the fire for a short time only and then fled. The landing force reached the shore at a position which outflanked the fort and where the fort could not fire on them. The landing place, however, proved to be a wide tide marsh in which the men and artillery bogged down. They reached solid ground after considerable difficulty.

The marines, acting as skirmishers, led the formation; the sailor battalion and howitzers followed. The force reached the first fort without further difficulty. The remainder of its garrison fled upon their approach; the marines took possession of the fort before the rest of our troops arrived. The fort proved to be a semicircular redoubt, mounting fifty-four guns. The marines formed the outpost to protect the remainder of the forces which remained for the night in the captured fort. Early the following morning the expedition completed the destruction of the fort and burned several houses near-by which had been used by the Korean soldiers. At 5 A.M., the landing force marched on the second fort, about three miles away, with the marines again leading the main body. The marines reached that fort, found it abandoned, and promptly occupied it. They found the fort armed by fifty or sixty small brass cannon, which they threw down a cliff into the water. Two companies of sailors arrived in time to assist in the destruction of the fort.

Tilton's marines again led the advance towards the next fort in line, scouting and clearing the line of march of the few remaining enemy. After going about one-half mile along a deep ravine, they were fired upon from a high hill off to their right. The marines immediately formed a line of skirmishers, advanced up the hill, and soon cleared it of the enemy. From that ridge a still stronger detachment of the Koreans was seen on the next ridge but were out of range for small arms. A howitzer was brought up and fired a few effective shots. The enemy then retreated. The marines, still acting as the advanced guard, again resumed the advance on the last and most important fort—a circular redoubt which they called the "Citadel."

## Storming the Korean Citadel

When the leading units reached a position about one-third of a mile from the Citadel, they halted for a brief rest to permit the remainder of the expedition to close up and form for assault. In the meantime a considerable number of the enemy had been left to the flank and the rear. As a precaution against attack from that direction, Commander Kimberly left two companies of sailors in positions to protect the remainder of the troops. While preparations were being made for the assault on the main fort, a company of sailors went out on a separate mission to destroy an abandoned enemy battery. After a brief rest and having gotten into a deployed formation, the force again moved forward with the marines covering the front with a line of skirmishers deployed at one yard intervals. The marines were able to reach the cover of a ridge within 150 yards of the enemy's main position before their advance was checked. They held the ridge until the remainder of the troops had closed up on them; both sailors and marines then prepared for some determined fighting.

There was another ridge at a distance of only thirty yards in the direction of the enemy which offered excellent cover, but the advance to it was entirely exposed and within effective range of the enemy. Tilton determined to reach that ridge by a quick and determined rush. This he succeeded in doing in a very few seconds with a loss of only one marine. From their new position within 120 yards of the enemy, they opened fire with their rifles. This fire was obviously very destructive to the Koreans, as forty or fifty of them were later found dead in the redoubt and were undoubtedly killed during this phase of the fighting. Part of the Korean losses, however, were no doubt caused by their fearless but foolish exposure of themselves. They fought with their bodies from their waists up exposed above the parapet and sang melancholy songs, apparently to keep up their courage. After about four minutes of destructive fire the Americans resumed the assault. At first small parties of marines made their way across the next ravine under the cover of the fire of the remainder; then groups of sailors charged, showing themselves as dashing and courageous as the marines.

The advancing groups were greeted with exclamations of defiance and with showers of stone hurled from the parapet. One of the first assaulting parties to enter the redoubt was led by the heroic Lieutenant McKee, U.S.N., "who fell pierced with a bullet in a hand-to-hand struggle on the rampart" and died soon afterwards. His death was almost immediately avenged by Lieutenant Commander Schley, later of Spanish-American War fame, who dashed over the parapet with a storming party closely behind McKee and killed the Korean who had shot his brother officer. Desperate hand-to-hand fighting then became general all along the line. The marines and sailors rushed into the Citadel over the walls and soon drove out the enemy. Private Hugh Purvis ran to the flagstaff which bore the enemy flag over the fort and loosed its halyards. A second or two later he was joined by Corporal Charles Brown who tore down the enemy's flag. These two marines were the outstanding heroes of the battle. Both were awarded the Congressional Medal of Honor for their heroic acts.

In all of the desperate fighting as well as in some of the preliminary operations, only three of the Americans were killed, including one marine, while ten in all were wounded. The latter were promptly cared for and evacuated to the *Monocacy,* lying in the stream. Forty-seven standards and 182 cannon were captured in the Citadel. It was systematically destroyed. Its guns were spiked and thrown into the river; some of the walls were thrown down. The Americans then disposed themselves for their own security within the Citadel, which they renamed Fort McKee after the gallant officer who had fallen. They placed the artillery to command all the approaches and established a line of outposts by men bivouacking on the near-by hills. Early the following morning the landing force re-embarked on board the *Monocacy;* the marines acting as rear guard were the last to withdraw. The *Monocacy* then took the expedition back to the fleet which was anchored some ten miles down the river.

Throughout all the operations ashore the *Monocacy* had given all possible support to the landing force by furnishing ammunition, supplies and provisions, by taking care of the wounded, and by furnishing supporting gunfire whenever possible. That vessel prevented any enemy movement along the river which might have interfered with the landing operations. The success of the expedition was significant in that it demonstrated that the marines and sailors had lost none of their dash and ability in planning and executing an operation, which they had shown repeatedly during the closing months of the Civil War. The sought-for treaty was not, however, immediately secured, but the severe lesson given the Koreans appears to have had considerable lasting effect. A treaty was negotiated about ten years later by Commodore Shufeldt by means of deliberations carried on with the aid of the great Chinese Viceroy, Li Hung Chang.

Marines and sailors from the Asiatic Fleet again landed in Korea during the Sino-Japanese War, 1894-1895. The Japanese forces were operating in Korea as well as in China. They reached Seoul, the Korean capital, in June, 1894, and overthrew the existing weak government. The American Minister to Korea called upon the U.S.S. *Baltimore* to furnish protection for our consulate in Seoul as well as for missionaries and other foreign residents. Captain George F. Elliott, who commanded the marines on the *Baltimore*, was given a detachment of about fifty marines and sailors and ordered to land at Chemulpo, the seaport of the Korean capital, proceed to Seoul and furnish the desired protection. Elliott preferred to march with his marines while the sailors for his detachment went up a river in boats. Elliott's detachment remained in the Korean capital, guarding the American Legation and forming other protective missions, until the following September. Detachments from different vessels of the Asiatic Fleet maintained a legation guard in Seoul until April, 1896, when it was discontinued for a time.

## Peacetime Routine

The general distribution of the Corps underwent very little change during this long quiet period. The number of its shore stations varied from eight to eleven. Garrison duty consisted mainly of routine guarding of navy yards and naval property. The largest Marine post seldom exceeded two hundred men, and there was practically no opportunity for anything more than the mere fundamentals of military training. The number of marine detachments at sea was comparatively large, varying from sixty or more soon after the close of the war to approximately half that many in the early 1890's. The Corps was filled with new officers during the war, and only enough of the prewar officers remained to fill the more senior ranks. There was an almost complete stagnation of promotion throughout the period. As the Spanish War approached some thirty-three years later, several of the officers taken in during the Civil

War were still captains, while others with approximately the same length of service filled the higher grades of the Corps. Francis H. Harrington, for example, who had entered the Corps in 1864, was promoted first lieutenant five years later, made captain in 1884, and was still in that grade in 1897. The enlisted strength at times was less than 2,000 thus making the opportunities for advancement of enlisted men almost as slow as that for officers. Approximately half of the enlisted personnel was assigned to vessels of the Navy.

There seems to have been little effort made to digest the lessons in military tactics learned during the Civil War and teach them to the personnel of the Corps. Being a marine or a soldier in those days was a practical kind of profession, learned only by experience and by personal contact with older men. Practically the only books available on tactics and strategy until near the close of the period were foreign publications. Upton's and Wagner's works on tactics and related subjects then became the standard. Not many marine officers, however, took the study of their profession seriously.

The serious study of the military profession by marine officers probably did not begin until after the adoption of a regular examination prior to promotion in 1891. The first regular officers' school, the School of Application, was opened soon afterwards at the Marine Barracks, Washington, for newly commissioned officers. By the close of the period it had made substantial progress in the systematic teaching of the military profession to at least most of the junior officers of the Corps. A few of the older officers showed exceptional ability in some particular field and became recognized as authorities. The great majority, however, continued to be "practical soldiers" and considered such study not particularly worth while. No effort was made until near the close of the period to provide courses of instruction in military subjects for enlisted men. Systematic instruction in rifle firing was not undertaken until about the middle of the period but thereafter rifle marksmanship made notable progress. The fact should not be forgotten, however, that in those days even the learned profession of medicine was practiced after listening to lectures for a few months, and the other learned professions practiced with similar lack of training.

## Morale and Discipline

Judged from the reports of inspections made by the Commandant of the Corps throughout the period, the morale of the organization was usually good despite discouraging circumstances. Some of the southern posts were extremely unhealthful and had violent outbreaks of yellow fever. When one considers the living conditions at some of the posts—in dilapidated barracks and even on board old discarded hulks of naval vessels—the little pay and allowances which were even further reduced and the exceedingly meager rations allowed, there is little wonder at breaks in morale such as occurred in 1872 when the ranks of the Corps as well as the Army and Navy were seriously decimated by desertions.

The types of punishment employed in the maintenance of discipline, like those applied to civil offenders, became somewhat more humane during this period. The practice of many courts-martial of awarding solitary confinement on bread and water or diminished rations was disapproved of in 1882 by the Navy Department as being unnecessarily severe in most cases. The inflicting of extra guard duty as a punishment was at the same time strictly forbidden. The common use of irons and ball and chain as a means of punishment continued, however. Corporal punishment had of course been abolished previously.

Typical court-martial sentences for various offenses were: for drunkenness and deserting his post without being relieved, a sentry was tried by summary court-martial, found guilty, and sentenced to be confined for two months and to lose three months' pay amounting to fifty-four dollars; an enlisted man found guilty of desertion by a general court-martial was sentenced "to be confined for one year in such place as the Hon. Secretary of the Navy may designate, to have fastened to his left leg a chain four feet long, to which is to be attached a ball weighing twelve (12) pounds, to do general police duty during the term of confinement, to forfeit ten dollars per month of his pay (amounting to one hundred and twenty dollars) during such confinement, to be dishonorably discharged from the U. S. Marine Corps." (The Secretary mitigated this sentence by remitting the ball and chain.)

### Aiding the Civil Power

During the years following the Civil War while the country was experiencing many growing pains, there were periods of violent strife between capital and labor during which the maintenance of law and order became too great a task for the civil powers, and even at times too great to be handled by the military forces under the control of the governors of the various states. In addition to labor troubles, riots of different kinds, particularly in New York, made it necessary for Federal troops to be called out. There were also several occasions of national disaster which necessitated the use of Federal troops to aid the civil authorities. Marines were called out several times for such duty.

Shortly after the close of the Civil War, Cuba was in the throes of one of its many rebellions against Spain. Sympathy for the Cubans ran high in some parts of the United States, where many aided the rebels. Such aid at times took the form of filibustering expeditions which our Federal Government was, of course, required to prevent if we maintained a neutral position. In July, 1869, it was reported to the Federal authorities that a band of filibusters had assembled on an island off the eastern end of Long Island. A detachment of fifty Brooklyn Navy Yard marines, commanded by First Lieutenant James B. Breese, went on the revenue cutter *Mahoning* to the island. They surrounded the filibusters' camp, captured 125, and turned them over to the civil authorities.

Poor fire protection that existed in our growing cities resulted in a number of great fires; during several such fires the marines were called out to assist in any way possible. On July 4, 1866, a large portion of Portland, Maine, was swept by fire and a period of lawlessness and suffering in the city followed. Two companies of marines under Lieutenant Colonel James H. Jones were hurriedly sent there from the near-by Portsmouth, New Hampshire, Navy Yard. They remained in the city for almost a week doing all manner of duty in connection with restoring order and relieving suffering. They received the thanks of the city for their services. A similar great fire swept a portion of Boston on November 9, 1872; the marines from the barracks in that city promptly turned out and rendered all possible assistance. Another serious fire broke out in Boston on May 30, 1873, and the marines from the navy yard, as well as from two naval vessels present, again assisted in restoring order.

During the early part of the period covered by this chapter marines were repeatedly called upon to assist the Federal and other authorities in the enforcement of the revenue laws. The marine barracks in the Brooklyn Navy Yard were adjacent to a center of illicit liquor making and selling, commonly termed "Irishtown." The violators of the law were too strong for the revenue officers and other available civil authorities. Beginning in 1867 marines were called out on a number of occasions to assist in determined raids to enforce the revenue laws. Four companies of marines furnished moral support to the revenue officers during the first of these raids. In March of the following year marines seized and destroyed a number of illicit distilleries in Irishtown. Early in November they were again called out for the same purpose and met considerable resistance by a mob sympathetic to the law breakers. The mob stoned the marines, compelling them on two occasions to charge the rioters in order to carry out their original duty. During one of the periodic outbreaks of disorder in January, 1871, a large detachment of marines went out and occupied fourteen legitimate distilleries to protect the workmen. During the following July they were again called upon to break up serious street fighting in the lawless district. Their timely arrival and a few effective shots promptly dispersed the mob. Similar outbreaks took place in Irishtown during the next few years on several other occasions, and the marines assisted in enforcing the law.

During a severe cholera epidemic in 1892 numerous ships arrived in New York with cases of the disease on board. Marines were called from the navy yard and ships in the vicinity to guard a large Quarantine camp established at Sandy Hook. Their most outstanding aid to the civil power, however, was rendered during the serious labor riots which occurred in 1877.

## Supressing Labor Riots

The most serious railroad strike which has ever occurred in the United States reached its climax in July, 1877, and resulted in a complete tie-up of railroad transportation in nine states. Federal forces were freely used to help keep order, particularly in the general vicinity of Philadelphia and Baltimore. A battalion of marines under Lieutenant Colonel Charles Heywood was organized at the marine barracks, Washington, and ordered to go by special train to Baltimore, one of the strike centers. Some difficulty was experienced in obtaining an engineer for the train but after one was finally procured, it proceeded cautiously, particularly over bridges, and stopped at numerous stations for the latest news of the situation. The train finally arrived at the Camden railroad station. The marines dispersed a mob that had gathered around the station and cleared all of the approaches to it. Without being molested, they then marched around the city as a show of force. Separate detachments guarded freight depots and protected railway bridges and work shops. Some army troops assisted in patrolling Baltimore and with the aid of the marines restored some semblance of order.

Heywood's battalion then moved on to Philadelphia where rioting was also serious. They were forced to detrain by the railroad track's being torn up near the outskirts of the city. The marines marched into Philadelphia and drove the mobs from the more important railroad properties. Soon after their arrival in Philadelphia they were joined by a part of the Third Artillery. The combined force

Marine Guard of the U.S.S. *Galena*, 1885

Marine Corps Uniforms of the Gilded Age

Uniforms of the Civil War Period

performed various duties in connection with maintaining order and protecting railroad property.

Serious labor trouble then broke out at Reading, Pennsylvania, and Heywood's battalion moved to that place by special train on August 1. Conditions in both Baltimore and Philadelphia had been very trying on the men of the battalion, but at Reading they found conditions much more pleasant. The only duty that they were required to perform was to parade and otherwise show themselves. They were exceptionally well cared for by the city authorities while at Reading. The disturbance subsided by August 13; Heywood's battalion went back to Washington.

A second battalion of marines was organized on July 26 under Lieutenant Colonel James Forney with officers and men drawn from Norfolk, the monitor fleet, and the North Atlantic Squadron. Its first duty in helping to control labor rioting was to take over the guarding of the Washington Arsenal and replace the regular soldier garrison, which had gone to one of the strike centers. Forney left a small detachment to guard the arsenal and moved the remainder of the battalion to Baltimore. The railroad company made a determined effort on July 30 to reopen railway transportation to the west of Baltimore. Twenty-five trains were made ready; each was furnished a guard of marines from Forney's battalion and escorted to the western limit of the strike area. The trains all reached Martinsburg, West Virginia, safely, and the marines convoying them were then assigned to trains returning to Baltimore. Forney's battalion also performed various duties around Baltimore, such as protecting grain elevators and wharves, until August 15 when it was ordered to Washington, where Heywood's battalion had already arrived from Reading.

While the two battalions were in Washington, an occasion was made of so many marines being in one place (actually only about 350), and they were marched in review, in spite of their having nothing but fatigue uniforms, up Pennsylvania Avenue and past the Navy Department. During the period of the railroad strikes considerable apprehension prevailed lest the strikers attempt to seize the arms from the United States arsenals. Marine detachments assisted in guarding Frankfort Arsenal and Watervliet Arsenal for about one month.

In 1894 prolonged railroad strikes occurred in California, and a detachment of marines from the Mare Island navy yard assisted regular army troops in guarding the United States mail. This was a forerunner of the spectacular guarding of the mails by the Marine Corps on two notable occasions since the World War.

## Exposition Guards and Memorable Parades

While the records of the Corps throughout this comparatively long period of reaction are rather lacking in incidents that would tend to bring the Corps to the notice of the country, a few occasions did arise when it was able to make a public display and attract favorable attention. During the Universal Exposition at Paris in 1878, Lieutenant B. R. Russell, one other officer, and twenty-nine marines sailed to France on the *Constitution* and acted as guards over American exhibits. This was the first of a long series of expositions at which our marines have appeared as part of the regular military-naval show. Another exposition was held in Paris in 1889; Captain H. C. Cochrane, one other officer, and thirty marines acted as exhibit guards. The detachment was highly commended for services rendered, and Cochrane was made a Chevalier of the Legion of Honor.

A battalion of marines took part in the four hundredth anniversary Columbian parade in New York, October 12, 1892. Another battalion participated in the dedication of the Columbian Exposition at Chicago soon afterwards. A detachment of marines served as guards through that exposition which was formally opened May 18, 1893. The Marine Band, during that period as at present the official band of the President of the United States, was adding to its reputation under the leadership of John Philip Sousa.

## Uniforms and Equipment

The marines continued to wear the uniform of the Civil War period until 1875, when many substantial changes were made, most of which indicated a strong French influence. In 1892 changes were again made and many of the present characteristic details appeared. A helmet, strongly suggestive of German influence, was made part of the unifom. All the service uniforms provided were blue, but during the summer months uniforms of white cloth were worn on fatigue and while off duty. The Marine Corps insignia, substantially the same as that now in use, was adopted in 1868.

The Marine Corps was issued a new breech-loading, rifled musket in 1870 which so pleased General Zeilin that he reported that there was nothing left to be desired in the military equipment of the marines. That musket continued to be used until the latter 1880's when it was replaced by the Springfield rifle, model 1884, caliber .45, which was, in turn, used until the end of the century. The Lee straight-pull rifle (6 millimeter) was used by the marines in Cuba during the Spanish-American War. The United States magazine rifle, caliber .30 (Krag-Jorgenson) was adopted in 1900 and used by the marines in the Philippine Insurrection. The Krag-Jorgenson was thereafter the principal arm of the Corps until the Corps adopted, in 1908, the new Springfield rifle, caliber .30, model 1903, which has continued in use by the Marines until the present time.

The only weapons besides small arms used by the Marines were the Gatling gun and the Hotchkiss revolving cannon, which they adopted in the 1890's. They then considered these rapid-fire weapons the most destructive pieces of ordnance that infantry could use. They were the forerunners of the present machine gun and the 37-millimeter cannon.

The sword with the Mameluke hilt, which had been carried by Marine officers for many years prior to the Civil War, had been replaced in 1859 by a sword with a basket hilt—the same as then used by infantry officers. The sword with the Mameluke hilt, now carried by Marine officers, was readopted in 1875.

### Commandants of the Corps

Jacob Zeilin, who was made Commandant of the Marine Corps during the Civil War, continued in that office until he retired November 1, 1876. Charles G. McCawley, a veteran of both the Mexican and Civil Wars, was selected as his successor and given the rank of Colonel Commandant, which was the statutory rank of the position. As indicated in this chapter, McCawley's long tour of duty, which did not terminate until 1891, was quite uneventful and in many respects a period of "marking time." McCawley was retired for age on January 29, 1891, and Charles Heywood was selected as Colonel Commandant of the Corps. Heywood had seen long service with the Marines since receiving his original commission in 1858. He had had the usual rounds of sea and garrison duty as well as considerable active service both ashore and afloat during the Civil War, in addition to his connection with various other happenings recounted in this chapter. He served as commandant until October, 1903. During his tenure of office the Corps finally began to climb to a position of considerably more prominence in the public service. He was one of the most capable leaders that the Corps has ever had. Under his guidance the organization made many outstanding advances, the most of which, however, were made during and shortly after the Spanish-American War.

The long period of postwar general decay of naval materiel was finally brought to a close by beginning the construction of a new navy in 1883, when four cruisers were appropriated for. Thereafter the building of new ships continued without interruption and by the outbreak of the Spanish-American War the Navy had a respectable force of modern vessels. Substantial detachments of marines, usually fifty or more with two officers, were assigned to the new larger ships.

The period of the Gilded Age was one of the most uneventful in the history of the Marine Corps. The little organization carried on with the grim determination to make the best of discouraging circumstances. The country had no interest in its affairs and like the regular army it was thrust aside in the rush of national development. On a few occasions, however, the marines gave a fair account of themselves and even showed a brilliant dash reminiscent of their high fighting spirit in the Corps's earlier history. The conduct of those who took part in the retaliatory affairs in eastern Asia caused a burst of pride in the otherwise discouraged organization. The marines did their part in helping to maintain order during several of the most violent outbreaks of lawlessness that have occurred in our history. They had a taste of Latin-American intervention, which anticipated their most important duties so far during the present century. In some way—it is difficult to tell how—they avoided that "dry rot" which often takes hold of a military organization during long periods of peace. This was manifest by the fact that when war came, at the end of the period, the organization was soon back again into its old fighting spirit.

## Chapter X

### THE WAR WITH SPAIN AND OPERATIONS IN THE FAR EAST

THE long period of a small stabilized Marine Corps, which had existed with little change in strength since the Mexican War, came to a dramatic end upon the approach of the Spanish-American War. The organization, which had been more or less suppressed, within a few brief months burst into a place of considerable prominence in the service of its country. In less than ten years the Corps grew to nearly four times its previous strength. Its personnel had many thrilling belligerent experiences from Cuba to the capital of the Celestial Empire. With the rapid expansion of the Navy incident to the War with Spain, the number of marine detachments at sea was greatly increased. A battalion of marines made the first landing in Cuba and established an advanced naval base for the Atlantic Fleet operating against the Spanish Fleet. Soon after the outbreak of the insurrection which followed closely our taking possession of the Philippines, four battalions of marines were hurried off to the Far East, where they participated not only in the operations against the insurrectos but also played an important part in the relief expedition to Peking, China, in 1900.

The Navy of the United States had been modernized as a result of a building program begun in 1884 and, by the outbreak of the War with Spain, it was believed to be fully prepared for the emergency. The growth of the Marine Corps did not keep pace with that of the Navy for a number of years, as no additional marines were allowed until June, 1896, when the Corps was increased by five hundred men, making the then authorized strength 93 officers and 3,574 enlisted. Actually this number was not yet attained. When the war came on, the Corps's strength was only 77 officers and 2,900 men. The Corps at the time was distributed at fifteen different shore stations on both coasts of the

United States, and its personnel were serving on thirty-five regular ships of the Navy in addition to five receiving ships.

As a result of extremely slow promotion since the Civil War, all of the field officers of the Corps and the senior captains were veterans of that war and were generally too old for active field duty. The profession of arms was still a practical one; little theoretical education was considered necessary. However, the veteran officers of the Corps made up for their lack of theoretical education by their knowledge gained by long years of service in peace and war. Practically all the junior officers were graduates of the Naval Academy and many of them had had several years of experience as officers. The Corps was fortunate, however, in having a number of well-suited officers for making the rapid expansion and carrying on the far-flung operations which the Corps undertook during the next few years and in which the Marines made a brilliant record.

## Preparing for War

The Navy began its preparations for war several months before the actual outbreak. A number of converted vessels were made a part of the Navy; several of these carried marine detachments. Soon after war was declared, the Atlantic Fleet was concentrated near Key West and the Asiatic Fleet at Hong Kong. Both were put into the best possible condition for wartime operations.

In the midst of these preparations and at a time of intense feeling, not only between the Spanish authorities and the Cuban patriots but also between Spain and the United States, our Consul General Fitzhugh Lee at Havana suggested that it might be advisable to send American war vessels to that port for the protection of our citizens. The battleship *Maine,* Captain Sigsbee, was promptly dispatched to Havana harbor where it was received by the Spanish authorities with a pretense of friendliness but actually with intensely hostile feelings. The ship was mysteriously blown up on the night of February 15, 1898, and went down with a loss of 260, including 28 marines.

Among the surviving marines was Private William Anthony who, in spite of the violent explosion, the lights of the vessel being extinguished, its compartments filled with smoke, and the vessel itself rapidly sinking, made his way below deck to Captain Sigsbee, reported conditions, and accompanied Sigsbee to the quarterdeck. For calmly performing his duty in the face of great confusion and imminent danger, Anthony was highly commended by the Marine Corps and the Navy and became a national hero.

The declaration of war with Spain was made on April 21 at the urgent insistence of public opinion, instigated by an excited press, and as a result of a finding that the explosion which caused the destruction of the *Maine* came from outside of the vessel. The Marine Corps then set about in earnest to prepare organizations for fighting ashore and additional detachments for vessels of the Navy. A temporary increase in the Corps of 24 officers and 1,640 enlisted men was authorized by Congress on May 4, 1898. In the meantime orders had been issued to assemble every available marine in the eastern part of the United States at New York and organize them into a battalion for service in Cuba. Posts and receiving ships were stripped of marines. Within a very few days, the 23 available officers and 623 enlisted men were organized into a battalion of five rifle companies and an artillery company with Lieutenant Colonel Robert W. Huntington as battalion commander. Transportation was made available after some delay and the battalion was sent to the fleet base at Key West, to be in readiness for duty in Cuba.

## With Dewey at Manila

Meanwhile the Asiatic Squadron at Hong Kong was completing its final preparation and being reinforced with additional ships and provided with extra ammunition. Commodore George Dewey left Hong Kong with his squadron on April 25 for the Philippines with orders to destroy the Spanish squadron which was reported to be somewhere in the waters of Luzon. After vainly seeking the enemy vessels at several other places he boldly steamed into Manila Bay under cover of darkness in the early morning of May 1. The enemy vessels were sighted off Sangley Point, near Cavite, at daybreak, and Dewey's squadron boldly closed on them. The engagement which followed proved most disastrous to the Spanish, while the Americans suffered practically no losses. By a series of five runs past the stationary Spanish ships in which Dewey's ships engaged the enemy at effective range, the Americans wrecked most of the Spanish vessels. Ammunition was by then running low, and the squadron drew off for breakfast without knowing definitely that it had already inflicted great damage on the almost helpless Spanish squadron. Dewey returned to the scene of action a few hours later and destroyed the remaining Spanish vessels. All except one of Dewey's seven fighting vessels carried marine detachments, which performed their usual functions of manning secondary batteries during the engagement.

The Spanish authorities at the Naval Station, Cavite, surrendered the navy yard and arsenal the following day, and on May 3 a detachment of marines from the U.S.S. *Baltimore* under First Lieutenant Dion Williams landed, took possession of the station, raised the American flag, and established the necessary guard for the protection of what proved to be a valuable naval base for Dewey's squadron. The Spaniards also surrendered the defenses on Corregidor Island, and the Governor of Manila agreed that there would be no firing on the American vessels.

Dewey kept most of his vessels stationed at Cavite while awaiting the arrival of additional ships and army expeditionary forces which were absolutely essential to the control of the situation. Manila was still held by about thirteen thousand Spaniards but an insurrection against their rule was being carried on by the Filipinos. Our army did not begin to arrive until the end of July, when two thousand American troops landed and occupied Manila. Although more American troops became available in the Philippines, the insurrectionists also became stronger. Our government did not choose to recognize the insurgents, and the situation became very delicate. The insurgents insisted upon occupying Manila when it was given up by the Spaniards; this was prevented however by the close co-operation of Dewey and the army commander. Finding themselves left out, the Filipinos under Aguinaldo began brewing an insurrection against the United States. The participation of marines in this phase of our colonial difficulties is discussed later.

### Huntington's Battalion at Guantanamo Bay

For some time after the declaration of war there was a great uncertainty and alarm along our Atlantic seaboard because a Spanish squadron, under Admiral Cervera, had sailed from Spain with its destination unknown; all manner of conjectures were made as to where it would next appear. Efforts were made to intercept the squadron off Porto Rico but it was not encountered. Finally it was reported by a patrol vessel off the north coast of South America. Nothing more was seen of the Spanish squadron for a time, but it was suspected of having gone to Santiago. Commodore Schley with a cruiser squadron sailed from Key West on April 26 to Cuban waters; two days later some of his vessels sighted the enemy ships inside of Santiago harbor.

Our fleet established a close blockade off Santiago harbor and on June 3 made an heroic but futile effort to prevent the escape of the enemy vessels by sinking the collier *Merrimac* in the narrowest part of the channel. Rear Admiral W. P. Sampson, in command of all the Atlantic Fleet, then undertook to reduce by bombardment the forts protecting the entrance to the harbor. The probable long stay of the fleet in Caribbean waters prompted Sampson to find a

OFFICERS OF THE GUANTANAMO BATTALION, 1898

Marine Detachment under Lieutenant Dion Williams, Cavite, P. I., 1898

sheltered bay to use as an advance base for his vessels. He selected Guantanamo Bay, lying about forty miles to the east of the entrance to Santiago Harbor.

Huntington's battalion of marines, which had been in camp at Key West for more than a month undergoing field training, was selected to help capture the proposed base. It re-embarked on the *Panther* on June 7 and started for eastern Cuba. In the meantime, Commander Bowman H. McCalla of the *Marblehead* had been detailed by Sampson to take Guantanamo Bay. He first entered it on June 5 with his own vessel accompanied by the *St. Louis* and the *Yankee*. His vessels bombarded and destroyed a Spanish blockhouse on the hill near Fisherman's Point, at the inner end of the channel leading into the harbor. They then had a skirmish with the Spanish gunboat *Sandoval,* which retreated into the inner harbor. On the early morning of June 10 McCalla landed a detachment of forty marines from the *Oregon* and twenty from the *Marblehead;* they protected a reconnaissance of the proposed position on Fisherman's Point for Huntington's Battalion and then returned to the ship.

The *Panther* arrived in Guantanamo Bay at about 1 P.M., June 10, and soon began landing Huntington's marines. Before the day was over four companies with camp equipment and a considerable quantity of stores were ashore. As a supposed precaution against yellow fever, they burned the native shacks in the vicinity. What appeared to be the most appropriate camp site was the top of a hill, where the old Spanish blockhouse had stood. Huntington renamed the site McCalla Hill in honor of Commander McCalla. The location proved to be greatly exposed to enemy approaches through the thick brush from all sides except that towards the bay. Huntington's marines vigorously set about entrenching the camp and established the usual outposts. During the first twenty-four hours ashore the worst enemies proved to be the tropical heat, which overcame a number of men during the strenuous work of moving ashore, and the swarms of mosquitoes which came out of the brush surrounding the camp. More serious enemies, taking advantage of the exposed position, were soon to be reckoned with.

In the later afternoon of the second day the Spaniards attacked one of the outposts and killed two marines, who were at the time on patrol. Huntington promptly reinforced the outpost from the main camp but failed to locate the enemy. Soon after nightfall the camp was subjected to a series of minor attacks from the surrounding thickets, each attack causing a general alarm. At about 1 A.M., June 12, the Spaniards made a more determined attack on three sides of the camp at the same time. Early the next morning an outpost of Company D, under First Lieutenant W. C. Neville, which was about to be relieved, was vigorously attacked by the Spaniards. Sergeant H. C. Smith was killed and three other marines wounded. These experiences were sufficient to demonstrate the weakness of the position.

On the morning of the 12th the camp was moved towards the bay to lower ground, and the hill was made the main defensive line; this should have been the layout from the beginning. The Spaniards continued to attack, but less effectively, on the following night; the marines lost their sergeant major, Henry Good. The Spaniards made still another attack during the following evening but were repulsed with little difficulty. It was becoming apparent, however, that something more than a mere defense of the position was necessary.

## THE ATTACK ON CUZCO WELL

By that time it had been ascertained that the Spaniards had between five and eight hundred regular troops and a few hundred guerrillas in the immediate vicinity and probably several thousand in the region surrounding Guantanamo Bay. Their only water supply in the immediate vicinity was Cuzco Well, about six miles southeast of the marines' camp and near the coast. Huntington decided to take the offensive, drive away the Spaniards, and cut off their water supply. The marines were reinforced by a detachment of about seventy Cubans, under Colonel Tomas, who arrived just in time to take part in the operation.

During the forenoon of June 14, Companies C and D, commanded at first by Captain W. F. Spicer, and about fifty Cubans under Tomas set out through the hills to attack the Spanish at Cuzco Well. Again the tropical heat proved too much for some of the unseasoned marines, and several of them, including Spicer, had to be taken to the coast. They were placed on board the *Dolphin*, which was moving east along the shore, ready to furnish gun support against the Spanish positions. Captain G. F. Elliott, later Commandant of the Marine Corps, succeeded to the command of the expedition. When within about three miles from the enemy position, Elliott sent a platoon of Company C, under First Lieutenant L. C. Lucas, and about half of the Cubans to make a turning movement to the left in the hope of cutting off some of the enemy's pickets. The Spanish soon discovered the maneuver, however, and their outposts promptly retreated, spreading the alarm to their main body near the well. A high hill which lay between Elliott's main body and the Spanish apparently dominated the enemy position. Part of the remaining marines and the rest of the Cubans immediately occupied the hill but were heavily fired upon at long range from the valley. Lucas with his detachment then rejoined the main body.

As soon as the firing was heard at the marine camp, Lieutenant L. J. Magill, who, with fifty marines, was on outpost duty in the direction of the firing, immediately set out to join in the battle. First Lieutenant J. E. Mahoney, with another detachment, was ordered to march to the scene of the conflict. Meanwhile, Elliott extended his lines along a semicircular ridge facing the Spanish positions; a long-range, rifle-fire fight ensued. An assault of the enemy's position was made almost impossible by the intervening chaparral. Elliott sent a signal to the *Dolphin* to shell the enemy positions, but that vessel mistook the intended target and fired in the direction of Lieutenant Magill's platoon, forcing him to take cover behind a ridge. The shell fire, however, caused the Spaniards to break cover and present a more favorable target for the marines.

### Sergeant Quick

The problem of stopping the interfering fire from the *Dolphin* was solved by Sergeant John H. Quick, who heroically placed himself in plain sight of the vessel, but in danger of the falling shells, and signaled for the fire to be stopped. Magill then attempted to advance a skirmish line but was again stopped by the resumption of the shell fire from the *Dolphin*, which was not yet aware of the actual situation. The Spaniards, however, had enough of it by 2 P.M. and began to retreat. The marines continued to fire mostly at long range for another hour at the retreating enemy—by this time estimated at about five hundred.

The Spanish force escaped with the exception of an officer and seventeen privates, who were captured. A platoon of Company B advanced (at 3:15 P.M.) from the ridge to the evacuated Spanish position, burned a house, and destroyed Cuzco Well. Again the heat proved more deadly than the long-range enemy bullets; only one marine was wounded in the entire operation, while a number were overcome by heat. The Spanish losses were variously estimated from five, according to Elliott's report, to sixty killed and one hundred and fifty wounded, according to the reports of Spanish prisoners. The Cubans lost two killed and two wounded. A few Spanish guerrillas remaining in the vicinity were gradually driven out by the Cubans and marines. The retreating Spaniards reported that they had been attacked by ten thousand Americans. Elliott's detachment marched back to camp at 5 P.M.

The aggressive operation proved entirely successful. In spite of the fact that there were several thousand Spanish soldiers in the vicinity, the marine camp at Fisherman's Point was subjected to no further annoyance. Two companies and a detachment of Cubans went into the country west of Guantanamo Bay to attack some enemy forces on June 25 but did not make contact with them. Patrols also went out in various directions to keep in touch with the situation but no other belligerent operations occurred.

## At Manzanilla

The Marine Battalion abandoned its camp on August 5 and embarked on the *Resolute,* which had been specially fitted out as a marine transport, and four days later, accompanied by several naval vessels, sailed for the Isle of Pines. Upon passing Manzanilla, Captain C. F. Goodrich, U.S.N., the senior officer present, diverted the battalion to capture that port, which at the time was already blockaded by American vessels and hemmed in by Cubans on the land side. Goodrich demanded the surrender of the Spanish garrison; the commander refused because his military code precluded surrender "except as the sequence of a long siege or other military operations." The naval vessels opened fire upon the town and the marines prepared to land and make a flanking attack against the Spanish position. Everything was in readiness for landing on the morning of August 13, but just as the boats for the marines were called away, a message was received that a peace protocol had been signed and an armistice proclaimed. It later became known that the Spanish commander had a message ready to send out to the American forces offering to surrender the city.

The movement to the Isle of Pines was abandoned and soon afterwards Huntington's battalion was ordered north. It arrived at Portsmouth, New Hampshire, on August 26 and went into camp on Seavey Island in the navy yard. It remained in that camp until September 21. When it became obvious that the war was over, the battalion was demobilized and its personnel redistributed to their regular stations. It was the only expeditionary unit of marines used during the Spanish-American War.

## Operations At Santiago

Soon after Huntington had completed his little war with the Spanish around Guantanamo Bay, the Atlantic Fleet made the deciding stroke of the war on July 3, by completely destroying Cervera's fleet, which attempted to escape from Santiago harbor. An army expeditionary force of seventeen thousand men had been brought to the vicinity for the purpose of landing and encircling

Santiago Bay to force the Spanish fleet into the open or destroy it. General Shafter in command of the force landed his troops some twenty miles to the eastward of Santiago at Daiquiri. By July 3 he had defeated the Spaniards on the battlefields of El Caney and San Juan and had Santiago, as well as the Spanish army, definitely in his grasp. It was obviously time for Cervera to act if his fleet was to be saved. Furthermore, he had been ordered by the Governor General at Havana to effect an escape.

## The Naval Battle of Santiago

Although faced with certain destruction, the Spanish Squadron began a dash from Santiago harbor during the forenoon of July 3. As each vessel made its way out of the crooked and dangerous channel into the open sea, the terrific fire of the American fleet greeted it. Cervera, hoping to escape to the wesward, had each of his ships turned immediately in that direction and steamed close to the shore. The Americans hotly pursued and poured a destructive fire into them. One by one the Spanish ships were either sunk by their adversaries' gunfire or were run ashore by their own crews. The loss of its fleet proved to be a knockout blow to the tottering Spanish Empire; the result of the war was then a foregone conclusion.

The part played by the marines in this decisive naval victory was largely that of carrying on their usual duties while aboard warships. On the *Brooklyn,* for example, a guard of sixty-nine marines operated six-pounders, one-pounders, and Colt automatic guns in addition to a number of auxiliary assignments during the battle. On the *Oregon* the marines furnished eight six-pounder gun crews in addition to performing other duties. On the *Indiana* a guard commanded by Captain L. W. T. Waller manned several one-pounders from which they fired five hundred shots in sixty-five minutes. Judging from the reports of Commodore Schley and a number of captains of vessels, the marines played no inconspicuous part in delivering the effective gunfire which destroyed the Spanish squadron.

The survivors from the Spanish vessels were picked up by American boats, and about 750 of them, including Admiral Cervera and 52 other officers, were transferred to Portsmouth, New Hampshire, on the *St. Louis*. Later nearly one thousand more were sent to the same place on the *Harvard*. The marines of the Portsmouth Navy Yard, under Colonel James Forney, furnished the necessary guard for a concentration camp for the prisoners until they were sent back to Spain in the following September.

## Operations in Porto Rico

Immediately after Cervera's squadron had been disposed of and Sampson's fleet had definitely obtained control of the sea, other military objectives were sought. General Nelson A. Miles, who had just arrived off southern Cuba with reinforcements, was assigned, with the support of five naval vessels, to make an attack on Porto Rico. The principal Spanish force on the island was reported to be at San Juan, on the northern coast. Miles chose Ponce, on the opposite coast, which town was reported to be held by only three hundred Spanish soldiers, as his point of landing. Ponce surrendered to the American forces without resistance. A detachment of marines commanded by First Lieutenant H. C. Haines participated in the occupation of Ponce in the early morning of July 28, 1898, when the American flag was for the first time raised over the island. Haines with his few marines guarded certain government buildings and set up a Colt automatic gun on the roof of the customs house for its protection. The army under General Miles arrived about two hours later and not long afterwards relieved the marines.

On the opposite side of the island, on August 8, a naval detachment from the *Cincinnati* was ashore guarding the lighthouse at Cape San Juan. It was attacked during the following night but, with the aid of searchlights and gunfire from the *Cincinnati*, drove off the Spaniards. Early the following morning First Lieutenant John A. Lejeune, with thirty-seven marines from the *Cincinnati* and a navy landing force of approximately the same strength from the *Amphitrite,* landed to assist in covering the withdrawal of the lighthouse guard and to protect a number of refugees, who had congregated around it. Lejeune accomplished his task without resistance. A naval station with a marine barracks, having a garrison of two officers and forty marines, was established at San Juan, October 26, 1898. The post remained a regular shore establishment of the Marine Corps for a number of years thereafter.

## Occupation of Cuba

In accordance with the terms of the treaty of peace between the United States and Spain, as the Spanish troops withdrew from Cuba the United States Government became responsible for the protection of life and property and was required to occupy the island and set up an emergency government. A few marines took part in the task. A naval station was established at Havana, and a guard of four officers and seventy-five marines went there in December, 1898. The marines performed their duties from on board the *Reso-*

*lute* until April of the following year, when they were given quarters ashore. The detachment continued on duty at Havana until the following August, when it was withdrawn because of an outbreak of yellow fever.

### THE CORPS WINS ITS SPURS

The many long delays incident to preparing military forces for operations in Cuba and the promptness with which a battalion of marines was raised and dispatched to the theater of operations resulted in a great deal of favorable publicity for the Marine Corps from the very beginning of the war with Spain. The calm demeanor of Private Bill Anthony on the sinking *Maine* focused attention on the Marines, who managed in various ways to stay in the limelight throughout the war. Their being the first to land on Cuban soil and the first to raise the American flag over the island seemed to be particularly gratifying to an impatient press always demanding action. The performance of the marine battalion, while ashore around Guantanamo Bay, was for the time being the focal point of war news. When Huntington's battalion came home it was triumphantly received in keeping with the spirit of the time and marched down Pennsylvania Avenue to the tune of *A Hot Time in the Old Town Tonight*. It passed in review before President McKinley in the south portico of the White House. The publicity given and the reputation won aided materially in a rapid expansion of the Corps soon after the war and in a great enlargement of its fields of activity.

### THE TAKING OF GUAM

The island of Guam, one of the Ladrone, or Marianne, Islands, lying far out in the Pacific, was taken over by American forces as a mere incident of the larger operations in the Philippines. The U.S.S. *Charleston*, convoying six troop ships to the Philippines, stopped at Guam on June 20, 1898, for the purpose of disarming the Spanish forces. The *Charleston* entered the harbor, leaving the troop ships outside. It soon sighted old Fort Santa Cruz—abandoned some years previously—and upon orders from Commander Henry Glass opened fire with three-pounders. After firing twelve shots, no fire having been drawn from the fort, the *Charleston* ceased firing.

Shortly afterwards a Spanish officer came out from Piti, the landing place on the inner end of the harbor, and apologized to Glass for not returning the "salute," which he had fired. Glass told the Spanish officer and his three attendants that the firing was not a salute but a hostile act since war existed between Spain and the

United States. This was the first inkling that the Spanish authorities of Guam had had of the existence of war. The Spaniard was made a prisoner of war but immediately paroled and sent to the Spanish governor, Juan Marina, to notify him of the existence of war and convey to him a demand to come aboard the *Charleston* for a conference with the American commander. Marina refused to come. On the following day Glass sent an ultimatum to him demanding the surrender of the islands. A landing force consisting of thirty marines from the *Charleston,* under Lieutenant J. T. Myers, together with two companies of Oregon infantry from one of the troop ships, was prepared to go ashore to enforce Glass's demand, if necessary.

In the meantime Lieutenant William Braunersreuther, U.S.N., had gone ashore at Piti as Glass's representative to deliver the ultimatum and to receive any communication from the Governor. After considerable hesitation the Spanish authorities complied with the demands and ordered the Spanish troops to report themselves with their arms and equipment to Piti for surrender. Marina together with three other Spanish officers constituting his staff were then made prisoners of war and taken on board the *Charleston*. They and the remainder of the Spanish prisoners were later transferred to the *Sydney,* one of the troop ships, and taken to the Philippines.

Without waiting for the Spanish garrison to report, Glass proceeded to take formal possession of Guam in the name of the United States. He had the American flag raised over Fort Santa Cruz, while the bands on board some of the transports, which had come into the harbor, played the National Anthem, and the *Charleston* fired the national salute. Four o'clock in the afternoon being the time set for the Spanish garrison to report itself, Braunersreuther, accompanied by a landing force consisting of sixteen sailors and thirty marines under Myers, went ashore at Piti to disarm the Spanish soldiers and bring them out to the ships. The remainder of the Spanish military forces—a company of native Chamorros—were left on the island. The *Charleston* left Guam the following day without establishing any form of American government, because the Secretary of the Navy had ordered the convoy to hurry on to Manila and had given Glass no instructions relative to establishing an American government.

### Kelton's Battalion in Guam

Guam, controlled only by such improvised government as was agreed to by the inhabitants, was left to shift for itself for several months thereafter. It formally passed to the possession of the United States by the Treaty of Paris, which was ratified some time afterwards. The U.S.S. *Bennington*, Captain Taussig, went to Guam late in January, 1899, and, on about February 1, raised the American flag over the governor's palace at Agana. The *Bennington* sailed from Guam (February 20), leaving an inhabitant as acting governor. Several other navy ships called at the island during the succeeding months, but made no change in its status.

A battalion of 4 officers and 119 marines, which had been organized under Major Allen C. Kelton for duty in the Philippines, sailed from New York in June, 1899, on the U.S.S. *Yosemite*, via the Suez Canal, Singapore, and Manila, and arrived in Guam, August 7. The force was sent to garrison a naval station to be established there. The new order of things which came into being produced most friendly relations with the Chamorros. The officers of the battalion were assigned to various civil positions for administering the newly established government. Captain R. P. Leary, U.S.N., assumed the position of acting governor on the same day that Kelton's battalion arrived and immediately set about trying to improve living conditions. Leary made Kelton public works officer with the immediate task of improving the sanitation and water supply of the island. This was a serious need because of an epidemic of typhoid fever that was raging.

During the first few months of naval government, procurement of food was particularly difficult as the natives were afraid to enter into contracts for supplying the American forces. They attempted to raise part of their food but failed. Arrangement was made a few months later for passing Army transports to call at Guam with supplies at least once a month; this greatly improved the food situation. Like other pioneers the marines suffered many hardships, but by hard and patient work they installed a sanitary water supply, built roads, erected a sawmill and an ice plant, and improved general sanitation.

Guam has, ever since, been one of the regular stations for marines. Its garrison has varied from a small company to a full strength battalion. The marines in Guam have carried on many civil functions in addition to their military duties, which at times included fortifying the island with artillery capable of repelling naval vessels. The marines in Guam have carried on many of the duties of coast artillery—a type of soldiering they are not commonly called on to perform. The potential value of Guam as a naval base has been much disputed but up to the present nothing very permanent has been done for its development as such or for its defense. With the abrogation by Japan of the pact of the Washington Conference, we are again free to fortify the island as we see fit.

### Landing At Port Olongapo, P. I.

The marines of the Asiatic Fleet began to be drawn into the war against the rebellious Filipinos. A large rifled gun was discovered in position near the mouth of the Kalakan River, at Port Olongapo on Luzon, by our naval forces. A joint naval and marine landing force operation was undertaken on September 23, 1899, for the purpose of capturing or destroying the gun. A detachment of about thirty-five marines from the *Baltimore, Concord,* and *Charleston,* commanded by Captain J. T. Myers and assisted by a few sailors, undertook the task. The attack was supported by gunfire from the vessels. The landing met with considerable resistance but was successful. A part of the marines remained at the boat landing to protect the boats and to cover a raiding party with long-range rifle fire while it destroyed the gun. The purpose accomplished, the landing force withdrew to the ship without suffering any loss.

### Marine Battalions in the Philippine Insurrection

During the early months of 1899 the rebellious Filipinos continued to gain strength; hence it was necessary that Dewey's naval base at Cavite be given better protection. Dewey cabled on March 9, 1899, for a battalion of 250 marines to be sent to garrison Cavite. A battalion under Colonel P. C. Pope was organized and sent to San Francisco about a month later. It sailed on an Army transport and arrived in the Philippines on May 23. Pope took over the guarding of Cavite, but his strength proved insufficient for the task, and, in the following July, Dewey's successor, Rear Admiral Watson, requested an additional battalion to reinforce the garrison. The Second Battalion was accordingly organized with 14 officers and 350 marines under Major George F. Elliott, at the Marine Barracks, New York, sent overland to Mare Island, California, and transferred to Manila, where it arrived on September 21. A few days later it relieved a detachment of Infantry at the Naval Station, Cavite. This placed that important base and general vicinity entirely under naval control; the garrison consisted of 30 officers and 916 marines. Posts were established at various outlying localities for the better protection of the naval base. With the additional marines, operations were also undertaken in conjunction with the Army.

## Attack on Novaleta

Early in October, 1899, the Filipino insurrectos were active in Cavite province, especially in the vicinity of the naval base. The army commander planned a series of strokes against them. Marines from Cavite participated in one of these operations. General Lawton, in command of the area, formed a column at Bacoor, a few miles east of Cavite on the mainland, to drive the insurrectos out of Imus. He sent other forces along the coast to the west from Bacoor to strike the enemy at Cavite Viejo and Novaleta. Lawton's troops advanced on Imus (October 3) and had a skirmish near Siran.

About one hundred marines and twenty-four sailors from Cavite and from the *Baltimore,* under Captain H. C. Haines, U.S.M.C., took part in this preliminary operation. A battalion of 20 officers and about 360 marines, under Lieutenant Colonel Elliott, soon afterwards made a direct frontal attack on the insurgents at Novaleta, located southwest of Cavite. In this attack the marines were supported by gunfire from the U.S.S. *Petrel*. An army column attacked Cavite Viejo at the same time, while another one advanced on Novaleta from a direction that outflanked its defenses. The country was so difficult that Elliott found it necessary to divide his force into two small columns—the left column commanded by Captain Haines and the right one by Captain B. H. Fuller. Elliott's marines encountered Filipino outposts in the early morning of October 8.

As soon as the *Petrel* learned that the supporting army column was in position for its part of the attack, that ship commenced firing on signal from Elliott and covered the marines' advance along what amounted to a causeway. With the support of the naval gunfire Elliott's marines advanced about one mile in spite of the bad condition of the terrain—swampy ground and tidewater runs. They brushed aside occasional resistance for a time but later encountered heavier fire and were held up. By that time the marines were able to deploy somewhat and with their effective rifle fire dislodged the insurrectos from the concealed positions from which they had flanked several marine units. The marines then resumed the advance; some of them waded muddy rice fields while others forced their way through the difficult chaparral. When they were within about 250 yards of the enemy's main entrenchments, they found a dyke and a line of old rifle pits, under cover of which they were able to reorganize their somewhat mixed up units. They then opened an effective fire upon the enemy position, but the Filipinos returned it with equal vigor.

A group of wounded marines, left in the rear, were fired upon by Filipinos. This made it necessary for a detachment of twenty men from the firing line to go back to protect the wounded. The front line marines kept up fire against the enemy's position for a time; the part of their line which had favorable ground to its front charged and gained a footing within the Filipinos' defenses. The enemy's entire line then gave away, but some of the Filipinos continued to fire on the advancing marines from huts in the rear. In the meantime the army column had struck the flank of the Filipino line, and the rebel forces practically all fled or concealed their arms and pretended to be friendly. Elliott's marines suffered eleven wounded, one of whom afterwards died, in this, their first real battle with the Filipinos.

After the successful completion of the above operations, the army shifted its main effort to the north of Manila and withdrew a large part of the troops from Cavite province. This left the naval station at Cavite with fewer troops to protect it. Two hundred or more marines were kept constantly on outpost duty south of the station for a time, leaving the main station none too well protected. Admiral Watson asked for another battalion of marines. The Third Battalion, consisting of 15 officers and 325 enlisted men under Major L. W. T. Waller, collected from a number of posts on the east coast of the United States and from Mare Island, California, arrived at Cavite, December 15.

### Capture of Vigan

Heretofore, the operations against the Filipinos, in which the marines participated, had been confined to the southern part of the island of Luzon; in the fall of 1899 a concerted effort to crush the insurrection on the island was carried out by several army columns pushing north across it. The more westward of these columns, under General Young, was advancing along the west coast of Luzon, pursuing a force under Aguinaldo. Vessels of Watson's squadron co-operated with Young on several occasions.

In order to support Young's advance and to protect the Spanish and other inhabitants of Vigan, near the northwestern corner of the island, fifty marines under Captain Dion Williams and a naval detachment from the *Oregon* joined in the operations ashore. Supported by the gunboats *Callao, Samar,* and the battleship *Oregon,* the naval detachment landed (November 26, 1899) and marched with the marines leading on Vigan—a distance of about three miles.

The taking of the town proved to be more of a reception than a military operation. Representative officials met Williams and gladly turned over the town to the American authorities; most of the inhabitants greeted them joyously. As it had been reported that insurrectos were still in the vicinity, an outpost was established for the protection of the command, and patrols went into the interior to locate the enemy. The naval detachment took over more than a hundred Spanish prisoners and put them aboard the *Oregon* for transfer to Manila. A company of infantry arrived two days later. The naval force, upon being assured by Lieutenant Colonel James Parker, U. S. Infantry, who had accompanied it, that the infantry company could hold the town until Young's column arrived, withdrew to its ship.

### Draper At Subig Bay

In accordance with an agreement made between the naval commander in chief and the military governor of the Philippines, the naval forces gradually took over the entire jurisdiction of Cavite peninsula as well as the area surrounding Subig Bay, northwest of Manila, which was to be developed as a naval base. In December, 1899, a detachment of 117 marines from Cavite, under Captain H. L. Draper, went to Subig Bay, occupied Olongapo, and cleared the surrounding country of the insurgents and robbers. The situation for the little marine outpost was made somewhat difficult as the only available water supply was at some distance in Bataan Province. On February 16, 1900, the Filipinos attacked a small water party from Olongapo and killed two marines. A relief party hurried out and rescued the party without further losses.

The enemy group which had attacked the marines retired to Morong. Draper was determined to punish them at the earliest possible moment. He took practically all of his men the following day and went to Morong but found none of the Filipino rebels. However, he did locate some of their ammunition in houses which he proceeded to burn. On February 23, Draper went out again with a hundred marines to Benictican, where the water party had been attacked. The *Nashville* shelled the town; the marines then entered but found no insurgents. Draper burned the village but provided homes for its peaceful inhabitants in Olongapo.

Early in March, with a detachment of forty-five marines, Draper continued his campaign by proceeding on the *Nashville* to Bogac to assist in an attack on that place. He landed and covered the town on one side while an army detachment marched up the beach, entered Bogac on the other side, and captured the town. Draper sent out numerous other combat patrols against the insurgents, whom they encountered and fought on several other occasions. The rebel resistance was gradually overcome, however, and, within three months, law and order was somewhat restored; a system of municipal government was set up under Draper's supervision.

An additional company of marines was sent to Olongapo in March, 1900. A new marine post was established at Port Isabela near by. The marines in the Subig Bay area were increased by still another company soon afterward. The detachments at Cavite and Olongapo established several additional outposts. The brigade of slightly less than one thousand was thereafter disposed in thirteen different detachments, including five lighthouse guards. Its active field operations were interrupted during the summer of 1900 by the transfer of more than half of its men to China for participation in the operations against the Boxers. The experiences of the marines in China are discussed at the end of this chapter. During the absence of the expedition to China all outposts were withdrawn, as there were only sufficient men to guard the two naval stations and the necessary lighthouses.

Early in June, 1900, Admiral Remey, who had succeeded to the command of the Asiatic Fleet, requested an additional battalion of marines to replace those transferred to China and to guard the naval establishments, which army troops were still protecting. A small battalion was organized at Washington under Major W. P. Biddle and hurried off to the Philippines, but conditions in China were so serious that it went there instead. The Fifth Battalion of marines was organized about a month later and rushed to the Far East, but it, too, was diverted to China as part of the expeditionary force. At the request of the commander in chief of the Asiatic Fleet, the Sixth Battalion was in turn raised for duty in the Philippines, but only two of its companies ever reached the Asiatic Station.

## The First Real Brigade

On September 28, 1900, the Secretary of the Navy ordered all marines with the expeditionary forces in China except the legation guard to be transferred to Cavite and relieve the Army at that place. About one thousand marines went from China to the Philippines during October, 1900, and helped to form the first real marine brigade with an aggregate strength of 1,678. It was organized into two regiments of two battalions each, a fleet marine battalion which could be called from the vessels of the Asiatic Fleet, and two companies of artillery. Most of the First Regiment went to Olongapo for duty, while the Second Regiment and Brigade Headquarters were stationed at Cavite. Two small additional posts at advanced naval bases were established near the extreme southern end of the Philippine Archipelago—a detachment of one hundred marines at Port Isabela on the island of Basilan and a detachment of fifty at Polloc, on Mindanao.

With the increased strength of marines in the Manila area, the Navy took over the governing of the country along the coast on both sides of Cavite Peninsula and the area around Subig Bay and exercised the usual functions of military government. Most of the responsibility for the local government in the area fell upon marines and marine officers. The commanding officer of each district was also its military governor. Detachments were placed in several additional towns in Cavite Province. In addition to their other duties the marines guarded the military prison for Filipinos which was established at Olongapo under the general jurisdiction of the Army. For about one year after the marine expeditionary force returned from China, the First Marine Brigade concerned itself largely with matters of guarding naval bases and administering military government in the several districts noted above.

### WITH WALLER IN SAMAR

The island of Samar had for some months been a veritable hotbed of insurrection. On September 28, 1901, Company C of the Ninth Infantry, stationed at Balangiga, was caught unawares while in the mess hall eating dinner; they were massacred by the Moros. A vigorous campaign against the rebellious Moros of the island promptly ensued.

The Navy did its part in the campaign by patrolling around the island and by sending small gunboats up the rivers to co-operate in various ways with the troops ashore. A battalion of marines, fourteen officers and about three hundred enlisted men under Major Waller, was withdrawn from Cavite and sent on the U.S.S. *New York*, to take part in the campaign. It arrived at Catbalogan, Samar, on October 24 and was soon afterwards sent through the straits between Samar and Leyte to Basey, where Waller disembarked his headquarters and two companies and relieved some units of the Ninth Infantry. The remainder of the battalion, under Captain D. D. Porter, U.S.M.C., went to Balangiga, where it relieved a detachment of the 17th Infantry.

The situation in the vicinity was very tense because of the massacre and other recent happenings; hence the measures prescribed for crushing the insurrection were somewhat retaliatory. Porter was given orders to scout the surrounding country and clear it of the treacherous enemy by expeditions which were admittedly punitive. Also, orders were issued to destroy food supplies that might fall into the hands of the insurrectos. Every precaution was taken by the marines to avoid being surprised. Waller from his post at Basey entered upon similar aggressive operations. All marines in Samar were under Brigadier General Jacob M. Smith, U.S.A., who was in command of a military district which included the island. The area assigned to the marines included practically all of the southern end of Samar.

Porter at Balangiga sent strong combat patrols each day into the interior, and on two occasions his men joined in patrols sent by sea to make landing operations. The patrolling into the interior revealed many indications that there were large numbers of insurgents in the vicinity, but the patrols failed to make contact with any group. A detachment under Waller on the *Vicksburg* with part of the troops from Balangiga went east along the southern coast and landed in the face of some resistance by the Filipinos in Quinapundan Bay. They made several similar landings; each time they were fired upon intermittently by the enemy but were unable to engage the insurrectos, who fled upon their approach. Waller then returned to Basey. He sent out a strong patrol to a near-by village, which had been smuggling rice to the insurrectos; the patrol captured two suspected smugglers and burned the village. Other strong combat patrols succeeded in clearing the vicinity of Basey of insurrectos, who, according to the reports, took refuge in a strongly fortified position on a cliff several miles inland on the Sohoton River.

For several days in early November vigorous patrolling and raiding operations went on from each of the marine stations in southern Samar. On November 5, Waller went out and attacked a strongly fortified position to the east of Basey and succeeded in driving off the insurgents with little difficulty but lost two marines during the operation. In several other raiding expeditions Waller killed a number of insurgents and destroyed considerable quantities of enemy supplies. Porter continued to harass the enemy in the vicinity of Balangiga. Many of the patrolling expeditions found equipment of all kinds which had been taken from the ill-fated company of the Ninth Infantry. Nearly all of the patrols were fired upon, but it was difficult to force the enemy to make a stand. Although all of the raids were extremely trying to the marines, they were beginning to have a decided effect on the enemy.

## The Attack on the Sohoton Cliffs

As a result of the continual harassing by the marines along the southern coast of Samar, the Moros fell back from that region and occupied their highly developed cliff defenses along the Sohoton River. Some of the cliffs reached a height of two hundred feet and were almost vertical. They were of porous volcanic rock, which could be easily dug out, and the insurgents had made caves in them as places of final retreat. These were reached by numerous bamboo ladders and by trails which were cut along the face of the cliff and protected by bamboo guard rails. To add to the protection of the position, tons of boulders were suspended in baskets, ready to be released on assailants below. The approach to the position was either up the river, from which the attacker would have to scale the cliffs, or over difficult trails—if indeed such could be located—or through the well-nigh impenetrable jungles. According to Waller's best information, the Moros had spent at least three years in preparing these cliffs for defense. The Moros considered them as impregnable last retreats. Obviously, the moral effect of dislodging the enemy from such a position would be great. The indomitable Waller was not to be stopped by the extremely difficult proposition of storming the enemy's last retreat.

Waller decided upon the Napoleonic maneuvers of concentration on the battlefield. He sent two columns, one under Porter and one under Captain H. I. Bearss, to march through the jungle on the enemy's position. Waller with a third detachment started up the river some time later in boats. The two marching columns joined (November 16) and halted for the night on the left bank of the river below the first of the cliffs, after having carried out their usual harassing tactics against the enemy, while making the march. Waller's boat expedition arrived on the river some two hundred feet below and established communication with them.

Because of a misunderstanding between Waller and Porter, and the fact that Porter thought it impossible for the boats to proceed farther without almost certain destruction, Porter and Bearss moved out alone early the following morning without waiting for Waller to join in the attack. After advancing through the brush for a short distance, they struck a well-defined enemy trail on the bank of the river. Along this trail they saw the usual traps, bows, spears, and other indications that an enemy's camp was near by. A number of bamboo guns were found a little farther along. One of them had a burning fuse. Acting Corporal Harry Glenn promptly rushed to the gun and pulled the fuse before the gun fired. No actual enemy had yet been seen. As the head of the column came over the crest of the cliff, the marines sighted a camp which they rushed but found empty—fires still burning, the food cooking indicated that the enemy had just fled.

The column pushed on; as the point reached the next higher cliff, it discovered two other camps on the opposite side of the river about 150 yards away. The enemy were busily preparing food or cutting bamboos in each camp and were perfectly unaware of impending danger. Porter carefully closed up his column, brought up a Colt automatic gun which was being transported by native carriers, and placed it and his men in position for a telling stroke upon the enemy's camps. After about ten minutes of preparation and upon Porter's signal every available weapon opened fire. The Moros were completely surprised and routed, and before they could flee thirty of them were killed.

After systematically destroying the enemy camps on the left bank of the river, Porter led his marines down the cliff and, by means of two small dugout canoes and a raft, crossed the river, and began scaling the cliffs on the opposite bank. By using the bamboo ladders and other facilities provided by the enemy, which they had not taken time to destroy in their precipitant retreat, the marines gradually made their way up the cliffs. Their progress was hindered only by two volleys fired by the fleeing enemy. The marines then destroyed the camps at the top of the cliff from which they had routed the Moros. By capturing the cliff they had accomplished a feat considered impossible by the Moros and had taken from them their last rallying place.

By this time the marines were pretty well used up as a result of their intensive campaign, which they had been carrying on for nearly three weeks; their experiences during the previous three days had been particularly exhausting. They were out of rations, and many of them were barefooted, but all were in high spirits because the main force of the Moros had been disposed of. The marines returned to their camp at Basey on November 19. Gunnery Sergeant John Quick, who had distinguished himself in the fighting around Guantanamo Bay, Cuba, three years previously, and Corporal Glenn were the outstanding enlisted heroes of the affair. Captains Bearss and Porter received a well-earned but long-delayed recognition for their heroic services by being awarded the Congressional Medal of Honor in March, 1934. The awards came after Bearss had been for a number of years on the retired list as a Colonel and Brigadier General and only three years before Porter's retirement as Adjutant and Inspector of the Marine Corps.

After a few days' rest at Basey, Waller again resumed his vigorous operations against the Moros. He sent out three separate expeditions late in November to further harass the enemy in the general vicinity of the cliffs along the Sohoton. He also sent a boat expedition up the river with supplies for his troops. The expedition established a base about eight miles up the river. Small columns marched up on each side of the river at the same time to attack the enemy wherever found. The column on the right bank of the river was commanded by Captain Robert H. Dunlap and the one on the left by Porter. Dunlap's column was particularly successful in its operation in that it located an enemy powder mill, where crude weapons of many kinds were also being made. The Moros fled upon his approach, and Dunlap destroyed not only the munitions plant but a number of camps as well. Porter's column, on the other hand, encountering difficult trails, apparently lost its way, and did not find the river until it had passed the rendezvous—the supply camp—nearly seven miles. The net result of these operations, in addition to the scoop made by Dunlap, was to drive more of the insurgents from the general vicinity by destroying a number of their camps and cutting off their food supplies.

## The Ill-fated March Across Samar

The next task undertaken by Waller's battalion was merely a reconnaissance, looking for a trail across the island along which a telegraph line could be constructed from Basey to the east coast. In spite of the fact that it neither expected nor encountered any organized enemy resistance, the obstacles of nature which Waller's marines encountered proved far more deadly than the Moros and their many contrivances. The effort resulted in a disaster never to be forgotten in the annals of the Marine Corps.

Before attempting the march across the southern end of Samar, Waller shifted a picked detachment by boats to the east coast. After making some preliminary investigations, he decided to start from Lanang, at the mouth of the river by that name, on December 28, 1901, and work up that river as far as possible, then march by a trail, which he hoped to find, to a point on the Sohoton River somewhere in the vicinity of the cliffs which his troops had recently stormed. In addition to Waller the detachment consisted of Captains Porter and Bearss, Lieutenants A. S. Williams and Frank Halford, fifty marines, one officer and a few soldiers of the Seventh Infantry, two native scouts, and thirty-three native carriers.

The expedition started up the Lanang in boats, which they found necessary to abandon at the end of the second day because of impassable rapids. The Seventh Infantry detachment took the boats back to Lanang. On the following day Waller followed a trail which repeatedly led back and forth across the river. As the river was swollen, it was always difficult to cross. By the end of the day the detachment was well into the rugged mountains. The march became more and more difficult. The men had to cross and recross the river and climb up over difficult ledges. Because of the winding of the river, sometimes almost in circles, little progress could be made to the westward. By the end of the third day the trail was lost entirely; by the end of the fourth the hardships of the march began to tell on the men. Although they had marched more than twelve miles along the stream, they knew that they had progressed only about one third of that distance in the desired direction. Waller discovered that his meager supply of rations had been reduced by some members of the party thoughtlessly throwing away the hard bread which had been somewhat damaged.

During the next day the party pushed on to the crest of a ridge, climbing the river bed which had become very steep. Shortage of food necessitated a cut to half rations and only two meals a day. Fatigue was beginning to be very noticeable on many of the men. The search for a trail leading towards the Sohoton still proved futile. They finally found a stream leading to the northwest which they thought flowed into the Sohoton, but, much to their disappointment, they discovered that it joined a large river flowing back towards the east. It could be none other than the Siribao, which flowed back to the eastward.

By the afternoon of January 2 the rapidly vanishing food supply and the condition of the men made the situation very serious. No food whatsoever had been found along the line of march. They built rafts in the hope that the detachment could go down the Siribao on them, but no raft could be constructed that would bear the weight of even one man. Waller, believing that the shortest way out of the difficulty was to push on to the westward, picked out Halford and thirteen marines who were in the best condition and started out the following morning in a determined effort to get through and send back a relief party.

Porter was left in command of the remainder of the detachment with orders to rest his men and follow slowly along the trail which Waller carefully marked. Waller again followed up a river. His maps and papers had all been destroyed; it was impossible to build a fire; and the ration was reduced to one meal of raw food. Waller sent a native messenger back to Porter with orders to try another raft. After a short march the following morning Waller's little band fortunately came upon a clearing where bananas, coconuts, potatoes, and a number of native vegetables were growing. A trail from the clearing led into a more distinct trail along which, after about five minutes' walk, they saw native houses.

The messenger who had been sent to Porter returned to Waller's camp with Bearss and Corporal Murphy, who had made their way up from Porter's camp. Waller said in his official report that Bearss had left Porter "about an hour and a half back" and also stated that he sent a second native messenger with detailed instructions to Porter, which Porter never received. On Bearss' statement, that judging from conversations, Porter intended to follow, Waller made no further effort to get the all important message through to Porter's detachment. This, as future developments showed, was a fatal error. Waller left a message for Porter in a tin can on a pole, but since Porter advanced no farther he did not find it.

Luck had decidedly turned in Waller's favor while disaster confronted Porter. Waller, pushing on to the west, soon came upon a settlement and impressed a native who knew the trail to Basey to act as his guide. In the late afternoon of January 4 the weather cleared; Waller's little band joyously recognized in the distance the cliffs of the Sohoton. The guide led them back over part of the trail and up a river which they had previously followed. They soon reached the Sohoton, which they followed down, continuing their march until seven or eight o'clock. Resuming the march early the next morning, they soon found themselves again on familiar ground and, by mere accident, met Dunlap, who had come up from Basey to build a supply camp while awaiting their arrival. Waller and his men immediately got in Dunlap's boats and in the early afternoon of January 6 were back in Basey.

Waller's first thought was to send a relief expedition back to Porter. A group of fresh men started out the following day. In spite of his worn-out condition Waller, himself, set out on the following morning with another party of fresh men to overtake and accompany the relief column. He continued on the trail for nine days searching for Porter, even going back as far as the place where he had originally left him and, after again undergoing untold hardships and finding no trace of Porter's detachment, returned to Basey on January 17. Completely exhausted and ill, he was at once sent to the hospital.

### Exhaustion and Starvation

Porter had attempted to follow Waller on the day following their separation. He met Waller's messenger and in accordance with the message again attempted the construction of a raft but could find no wood that would even float. During that afternoon he tried to communicate with Waller by means of a native carrier who returned without delivering the message. Porter then decided to retrace the trail to Lanang and ask for a relief party to be sent out for his detachment, the most of whom were unable to march. He chose seven marines who were in better condition—among them was Sergeant Quick—and with six natives in addition set out (January 3) for Lanang. He left Williams in charge of the remainder of the detachment with orders to follow as the condition of the men would permit.

Porter's return to Lanang was made under difficulties many times greater than those during the march into the interior. Food was almost totally lacking. Terrific downpours of rain filled the streams, making it next to impossible to follow down their banks or cross them repeatedly as was necessary. In spite of all difficulties Porter finally reached Lanang on January 11 and reported the situation to the army commander at that place. A relief expedition was at once organized to go for the remainder of Porter's men, but it was unable to start for three days, because of the swollen condition of the river. Even after it started it made little progress. The relief party soon found four men whom Porter had left behind a day or two before he reached Lanang.

Undoubtedly the most trying task of the whole unfortunate affair fell to the lot of Williams, left in charge of the weakest men of the expedition—the ones, of course, to become the actual casualties. The full circumstances of his attempts to extricate these exhausted men from the midst of a tropical jungle is too pitiful to recount. Without food, yet realizing that starvation was certain if they remained in camp, Williams slowly followed Porter's trail, leaving men behind one by one to die beside the trail when it was no longer possible for them to continue. One man went insane. As a last resort, to save some of the stronger men, Williams sent ahead nine marines under Sergeant Dooley to save themselves and to impress upon any rescuing party the desperate straits of the remainder. To make matters even worse for Williams some of his native carriers became mutinous; at one time some of them attacked him with bolos, while others stood by and permitted it. After having left ten marines to die along the trail, he was finally met by the relief expedition and taken back to safety.

## Waller Carries On

These unfortunate and trying experiences did not end the fighting experiences of Waller's battalion in that difficult theater of operations. After a brief rest the stronger of the men were again in the field and resumed their harassing tactics against the Moros. On January 16 a detachment of three officers and forty-six marines was sent to garrison Quinapundan, near the southeast corner of the island. While patrolling into the interior from there, Sergeant MacSwiney was killed.

During the occasion of the ill-fated march across Samar, and on several occasions thereafter, the native guides and carriers in various ways turned upon the marines and attempted to murder them. Waller somewhat impetuously, though with the sanction of his immediate commander, had some of these natives tried and shot. An outcry against the act resulted in trials by court-martial of Waller and several other officers. Despite the fact that all were acquitted, the unfortunate circumstance blighted Waller's otherwise brilliant career and finally stood in the way of his being made Commandant of the Marine Corps.

Waller's battalion was withdrawn from Samar and returned to its regular station at Cavite, March 2, 1902, after having been relieved by a detachment of soldiers. The affairs of the First Marine Brigade settled down to a more nearly normal peacetime routine. It continued for some time to occupy the towns in Cavite Province and to guard lighthouses in different parts of the Islands. A detachment of eight marines guarded for some time the light in San Bernardino Straits. During 1903 the bulk of the Brigade was shifted to Olongapo, a more healthful and agreeable place to live. It was maintained as a ready expeditionary force for use of the naval commander in chief or to support the army. Its civil functions, as well as the number of posts it maintained, were gradually reduced until, by 1906, the marines were all at the two main stations, Cavite and Olongapo, with the exception of a small detachment still at Polloc. The Brigade was gradually reduced during the succeeding years and in April, 1914, was disbanded as such. Since then, Cavite and Olongapo have continued as regular peacetime stations of the Marine Corps.

## In the Boxer Rebellion

The Manchu Dynasty had been gradually losing its hold on the people of the Celestial Empire throughout the greater part of the nineteenth century, largely on account of humiliating defeats in the foreign wars and the ever-growing authority of foreigners in China. As that century grew to a close, the position of the Manchus was particularly difficult; they were faced with the proposition either of continuing to protect the foreigners or of shifting to the popular anti-foreign position in order to continue in power. Anti-foreign riots became quite common during the latter 1890's, and a number of foreign missionaries were massacred with the approval of local officials. The Imperial Government refused to take action.

These difficulties, as well as other anti-foreign outbursts, led to the establishment of legation guards in Peking by the foreign powers. An American legation guard established in November, 1898, consisted of eighteen marines taken from the *Boston, Raleigh,* and *Baltimore* under First Lieutenant Robert McN. Dutton. A guard of thirty marines from the same vessels was placed over the American consulate in Tientsin soon afterwards. After conditions at both places had improved during the succeeding months, both guards withdrew March 15, 1899, and returned to their ships.

### Guarding the Legation

Anti-foreign feeling among the Chinese continued to grow, however, with the Imperial Government showing less willingness to oppose it. By May, 1900, conditions in Peking were almost desperate for the foreign population, in spite of the efforts of the Powers to persuade the Imperial Government to provide protection. An American legation guard of forty-eight marines and three sailors from the *Oregon* and *Newark,* under Captain John T. Myers, landed at Taku and proceeded with some other foreign troops to Peking, where they arrived on May 31, just before the city was encircled by the Boxers—a popular militia organization with a strong anti-foreign attitude.

Conditions grew worse in Peking during the following months, and the foreign legations requested permission to increase their guards. The Imperial Government, which by this time was openly siding with the Boxers, flatly refused. The foreign ministers then called upon their naval forces off Taku for further protection. Vice Admiral Sir Edward Seymour responded to the call and organized an international force of about two thousand men, including a detachment of 112 American sailors and marines under Captain B. H. McCalla, U.S.N. The force advanced from Tientsin towards Peking but encountered considerable resistance; Tientsin in the rear fell into the hands of the Boxers. Seymour's force, unable to reach Peking, retired fighting its way back towards Tientsin. It engaged in a number of battles with the Chinese and lost about 25 per cent of the personnel. Twenty-five of McCalla's detachment were wounded and three were killed in action. During Seymour's last encounters with the Chinese he captured a strong position in which he remained until rescued by another relief column.

## THE DEFENSE OF THE LEGATIONS

In the meantime the foreigners in Peking and its environs were likewise faring badly. Plans for the defense of the foreign legations were agreed upon early in June. Captain Newt Hall with a detachment of American marines was placed on guard over a Methodist mission at some distance from the legation compound. They made every effort to protect the native Christians, who were being massacred by the Boxers. The Imperial Government, becoming openly hostile, demanded that the foreign legations leave for Tientsin. This the foreigners refused to do since there was no assurance that they would be protected en route.

The German Minister was killed in a riot on June 20. A German detachment, while attempting to recover his body became engaged in a severe fight with some Chinese. Foreign women and children then moved into the English Legation while Hall and his charges repaired to the legation compound. Thereafter, firing upon foreigners became quite general. On June 24 serious fighting began on the walls surrounding the legations. The Germans repulsed the first Chinese attack. Then the marines under Myers established a position behind a barricade, and the Germans occupied a position several hundred yards in their rear facing in the opposite direction. Some Chinese soldiers attempted to rush the marines' position but were driven back in great confusion and with considerable loss. They did not repeat the experiment. The sector assigned to the marines was too large for the small force to defend; hence it was necessary to reinforce them each day with small detachments of Russians, Germans, and English. During the closing days of June fighting was almost continuous. Some of the Allies evacuated a large section of the wall during a heavy Chinese bombardment on July 1, but at the insistence of Myers, promptly reoccupied it before the Chinese discovered that it had been left undefended.

The Chinese next succeeded in building a tower on the wall which threatened to make the position of our marines untenable. Myers was given the task, with the support of a few foreign troops, of capturing the tower by a night attack. The carefully planned maneuver completely surprised the Chinese, who fled down the wall several hundred yards to their next barricade. Two marine privates were killed, and Myers was wounded in the fight. During the remainder of the siege the Chinese became more cautious and resorted principally to sniping, while the Allies busied themselves in strengthening their positions along the wall. An armistice, agreed to on July 16, lasted until the relief column arrived.

## The Capture of Tientsin

Meanwhile the American Government, having become thoroughly alarmed, ordered the commander in chief of the Asiatic naval station to render all possible assistance to the legations in Peking. Rear Admiral George C. Remey, then in command, ordered all available marines in the Philippines sent to Taku, China, to be in readiness to march to Peking. Similar orders went out to certain army units in those Islands. The first contingent of marines to reach Taku was a detachment of 7 officers and 131 enlisted men commanded by Major Waller. He started from Taku to Tientsin in the afternoon of June 20 by train. He reached a point within twelve miles of his destination, sent the train back, and bivouacked for the remainder of the night.

The only other foreign force in the vicinity, with the exception of a few in Tientsin, who were being besieged and in great danger, was a detachment of about 450 Russians. In co-operation with the Russian troops, Waller pushed on towards Tientsin and reached the edge of the city early the following morning. There, they encountered serious resistance and after about two hours' fighting, in which Waller lost three killed and seven wounded, the marines together with the Russians were forced to retire. They retired to the positions where they had bivouacked the night before—the marines performing the difficult task of rear guard during the retreat.

Some allied reinforcements, mostly Russians and English, arrived on the night of the 22nd; this brought the total force up to approximately 2,000. Waller joined his little force with a British naval detachment under Commander Craddock. In the early morning of the 24th, the augmented allied force again reached Tientsin. After overcoming considerable resistance, they entered the city and relieved the beleaguered foreigners. Waller lost one killed and three wounded in the day's fighting. The force rested for about twelve hours and then pushed on to the relief of the Seymour expedition, which was then being besieged in an arsenal about eight miles beyond Tientsin. The relief was accomplished without resistance, and the combined forces returned to Tientsin, June 26. McCalla, who had been wounded three times, turned his naval detachment over to Waller and returned to his ship.

The Chinese were still holding the position from which they

succeeded in driving back Waller and the Russians about one week before. The Russians alone again attacked it but were repulsed. Two officers and forty marines, together with a British naval detachment, then reinforced the Russians, and the combined forces (about 1,800) drove the Chinese (estimated at 7,000) from their strongly fortified position. Waller strikingly reported the experience of the marines thus far in his own colorful language as follows:

"Our men have marched 97 miles in the five days, fighting all the way. They have lived on about one meal a day for about six days, but have been cheerful and willing always. They have gained the highest praise from all present, and have earned my love and confidence. They are like Falstaff's army in appearance, but with brave hearts and bright weapons."

The situation was still very difficult for the Allies; the Boxers and other Chinese forces were still in possession of the native walled city of Tientsin, and their strength was growing much faster than that of the allied forces. Additional allied troops were soon forthcoming, however. The French and the British sent some native colonial troops. The Russians and Japanese added a few more troops during the next fortnight. The next American troops to arrive were the Ninth Infantry (less one battalion) and the First Regiment of Marines—the two having a combined strength of about one thousand men. With the arrival of these reinforcements the long-delayed plans to capture the walled city were immediately undertaken.

### The Storming of the Walled City

A more or less co-ordinated attack was agreed upon for the early morning of July 13. The city was bombarded, principally by Russian artillery, during the preceding night. The marines who had just arrived from the Philippines were grouped with the Ninth Infantry, both under the command of Colonel R. L. Meade, U.S.M.C., whose organization was in turn brigaded with the Royal Welsh Fusiliers and a British naval force, all under the command of Brigadier General Dorward of the British Army. Plans for the attack were very vague, and the existing reports of what followed are not clear. It is therefore difficult to reconstruct an account of the fighting which took place during the two succeeding days. It appears, however, that General Dorward's mixed command attacked the walled city along its south side, while a Japanese force operated on Dorward's right.

The advance to the attack was made both to the front and the flank over a practically flat plain which in places was marshy, and the only cover from fire was occasional grave mounds and dikes.

The advance of the American and British forces was hotly contested by the Chinese, and casualties were quite heavy on both sides. The allied force reached the wall and occupied it in some places, but as night approached the situation was still so uncertain that the troops withdrew to a more sheltered night position. They vigorously resumed the advance the following morning; the signal for the attack was the blowing open of the south gate. The Allies were then everywhere successful. The enemy in the rear of the proposed advance to Peking had been eliminated but much remained to be done before another relief column could be started.

The fighting around Tientsin, in which the marines had participated thus far, was the most desperate of the entire campaign. The casualties to the Marine Corps personnel were particularly heavy, but they took their losses as veterans, and throughout the remainder of the campaign still kept up that fighting spirit which the Corps had demonstrated in similar difficult campaigns throughout its history. A number of officers of various positions in the organization won distinction which marked them throughout their careers in the Marine Corps.

### The Advance on Peking

The resistance of the Chinese as far as Tientsin had been completely crushed, but still there were too few allied troops to undertake the relief of Peking. More of our army troops arrived from the Philippines late in July, accompanied by Major General Chaffee, U.S. Volunteers, who took command of the American forces. On August 3 a troop of the Sixth Cavalry, a battery of light artillery, the Fourteenth Infantry, and another battalion of marines joined the allied forces. Their strength by that time was approximately 18,600, and the advance began immediately. The railroad to Peking had been almost completely destroyed. It was necessary to use a fleet of junks to transport the supplies and ammunition up the Pei-ho River, which approximately paralleled the line of march. The weather was extremely hot and dry, and most of the troops were unused to field conditions. The suffering was intense, and many more casualties resulted from the heat than from acts of the enemy.

The allied force encountered its first resistance on August 5 but brushed it aside before the American troops got into the action. On the following day, however, at Yang Tsun, where the force met with more serious resistance, the Americans took part in the attack. The marine regiment was assigned to support Reilly's battery and their principal part in the affair was to drive off a Chinese cavalry attack by several well-aimed volleys. They also helped to capture two villages during the day, suffering no casualties except those caused by the heat. In spite of the trying conditions, the march continued at the rate of about twelve miles per day. Very few of the marines, as compared to the other troops, fell out on account of the heat. By the 12th the column was well on its way to Peking. The Japanese contingent captured, with little difficulty, Tungchow, the last stronghold before Peking.

## The Capture of Peking

It was agreed among the allied commanders that on the 13th only a short march would be made and the troops given a rest before attempting to capture Peking, then only a few miles away. Much to the surprise of all the other Allies, heavy firing was heard in the direction of Peking early on the 13th. It was soon learned that the Russians had violated their agreement and had pushed on alone in an attempt to capture Peking. The American forces, upon receiving the news, resumed the advance and joined the Russians who had captured one of the gates of Peking. By 3 P.M. the Russians and some Americans, including two companies of marines, had fought their way to the wall of the Tartar City and were within sight of the American Legation. The Japanese, in the meantime, had captured the native city in the face of considerable resistance. Late in the afternoon the legations were reached and the siege raised.

On the following day the Allies attacked the Imperial City itself. Marines led one of the attacking columns in the initial stage of the attack. Others took up a position over the Chien Men Gate and cleared the way for artillery to come into action. Shortly afterwards, two other companies of marines took up firing positions in a pagoda, while a battalion gained a favorable firing position on the wall and delivered an effective rifle fire against Chinese troops in the Imperial City. The Chinese were gradually driven out; the Imperial Court fled from Peking, leaving the country practically without a government. Peking was looted first by the retiring Chinese troops, and then by the foreign troops who did a systematic job of it. Order was not restored in the vicinity until weeks later. After the fighting was over the marines moved into the Tartar City. They remained in Peking until September 28, when they were evacuated to ships and later to the Philippines. A guard for the American Legation was established by the Army.

## Chapter XI
## SUPPORTING THE FOREIGN POLICY

In addition to making the United States a Far Eastern power by taking possession of the Philippine Islands, the Spanish-American War also led to a greatly increased interest in the Caribbean area. Diplomatic arrangements had finally been made for the construction of the Panama Canal and that, in turn, led to the policy of asserting naval supremacy in that general area. The Monroe Doctrine was greatly extended and as a result of several far-reaching corollaries thereto, the most important of which were made by Theodore Roosevelt, a considerable degree of control was assumed over several countries in the Caribbean area, ostensibly for the purpose of preventing certain European countries from intervening in violation of the Doctrine. This led to outright military and political interventions in several of the smaller countries. Then, too, by the Platt Amendment our government had obligated itself to maintain an orderly government in Cuba. Woodrow Wilson's policy of refusing to recognize governments which came into being as a result of violence was undertaken to discourage revolution and further extended our efforts to maintain peace in neighboring countries.

The far-reaching changes in our foreign policy created new missions for the Marine Corps and for more than three decades the organization found itself continually engaged in one or more extensive military interventions in the countries of the Caribbean area. The employment of marines as an aid in carrying out the foreign policy gave them a place of greater importance in their service to the country. The Corps necessarily went through a number of expansions and changes, and by the time we entered the World War it was a vastly different organization as regards size, scope of duties, and functions than during the long period of peace preceding the War with Spain.

The activities of the Marine Corps in Cuba, Santo Domingo, Haiti, and Nicaragua were so extensive as to warrant an entire chapter recounting the Marines' activities in each of those countries. Their actions of a similar nature but less extensive, together with the general development of the Corps between the War with Spain and the World War, are treated of in this chapter.

## Panama

Revolution, riots, and political disturbances continued to occur during the closing years of the nineteenth century on the Isthmus of Panama, but no further actual military interventions were made until after the War with Spain. It will be recalled from a previous chapter that our obligations for maintaining peace on the Isthmus had been assumed more than fifty years before by a treaty with New Granada. When it was determined that the United States would dig the Panama Canal, our interests in that locality took on an entirely new aspect, and the use of force thereafter was for other purposes.

The next serious disturbance on the Isthmus that necessitated actual landing-force operations was during a revolution in 1901 when one of the factions cut the railway telegraph wires and threatened the train service to such an extent that the railroad officials refused to run trains without American protection. A force of 12 officers and 233 enlisted men, including the marine detachment from the *Iowa*, landed at Panama on November 24, and a smaller force was put ashore from the *Machias* at Colon. The train service was promptly reopened under their protection. The landing forces furnished strong train guards for all passenger trains. The situation, however, soon became further complicated by the arrival at Colon of several hundred Colombian troops, with the declared intention of bombarding the place and driving out the Liberal forces. Our forces ashore were reinforced by detachments from other vessels. American and other foreign officials succeeded in persuading the Colombian commander to call off the intended attack and the situation at Colon was relieved.

Fighting along the railroad broke out again between the two contending factions, but arrangements were made with them to suspend their battles and allow the trains, still being guarded by American naval personnel, to pass without danger. This arrangement continued for several days and on November 28 Captain Perry, of the *Iowa*, used his influence to bring about a settlement of difficulties. He called a conference with the contending leaders, and a plan was worked out whereby the Colombian general (Alban) was to show great indulgence to the rebel faction under de la Rosa, who could then gracefully surrender. The American forces took control of Colon for a brief period prior to the entry of the Colombian troops in order to assure the safety of the town. The rebel forces surrendered their arms to our landing force, which then marched out to meet the Colombian troops, escort them into Colon, and turn the city over to them. The train guards were continued for a few days, but normal conditions were soon restored and the last of the landing forces withdrew on December 4.

The peace, brought about by the above arrangements, did not prove at all satisfactory to the Liberal forces. They assembled a substantial land force and two improvised naval vessels near Panama early the following year and announced their intention of taking the city. Complications soon arose over the use of the American-owned railroad by the troops of the contending factions. Some armed encounters took place near the railroad, but no actual intervention was necessary to protect the transit. The scene of trouble next shifted to a place about one hundred miles to the westward.

A force of Liberals numbering some five or six hundred men threatened to take possession of Boca del Toro, the shipping port of the United Fruit Company, held by a few government troops. The company, being unable to load its bananas because of the Liberal interference, complained to the American authorities, who promptly dispatched the *Machias* to the locality. Upon the arrival of the *Machias*, Commander McCrea found the Liberals approaching to attack the town. McCrea warned them that he would not permit the use of artillery and promptly sent a small landing force ashore to protect the American consulate and our citizens. The Liberals started an attack early the following morning, and it was soon evident that the little government garrison would be overcome. At the request of the Liberal leader, McCrea used his influence as a peacemaker. He called a conference of the contending leaders on board his vessel and arranged for a cessation of hostilities and terms of peace whereby the government troops were allowed to lay down their arms and leave without being made prisoners. Boca del Toro was guarded in the meantime by a landing force from the *Machias* including some additional sailors and marines, until it could be turned over to the control of the Liberal troops who guaranteed protection for American interests.

No sooner had this arrangement been completed than two Colombian ships arrived bearing a force of nearly one thousand troops who insisted on retaking Boca del Toro. Negotiations similar to the above followed. This time the Liberals were allowed to leave, taking their arms and equipment with them. American marines and sailors again

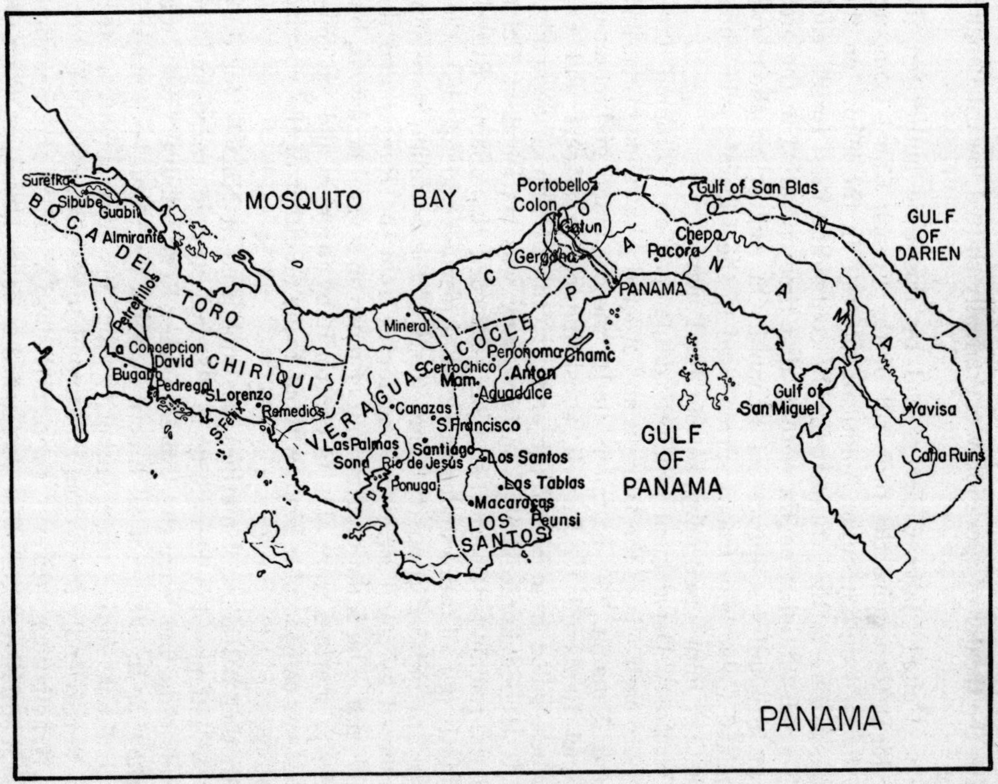

MAP OF PANAMA

protected the town during the transfer of authority. The peace arrangements again proved to be very ineffective and both factions continued to operate in the general vicinity. Both increased their forces on the Pacific coast south of Boca del Toro and soon afterwards the theater of operation was gradually shifted toward Panama City.

The United States Congress had by this time authorized the President to acquire the property of the French Canal Company and by that authorization American interests in the affairs on the Isthmus were further stimulated. The contending local forces, each with a substantial strength, were at that time operating in the area about fifty miles southwest of Panama. On August 30 about two thousand Colombian troops surrendered to the Liberals, who then, with their improvised navy, set out for Panama.

Our Navy Department promptly despatched an additional naval vessel to each side of the Isthmus and ordered a battalion of marines sent to Panama. The battalion, under the command of Lieutenant Colonel Benjamin R. Russell, consisting of 17 officers and 325 marines, sailed from New York and arrived at Colon on September 22. It landed immediately; one company was stationed at Colon and the remainder of the battalion proceeded to Panama. Russell promptly put all trains under an escort of marines and guarded other important railroad property. The efforts of the battalion were supplemented by small naval landing forces from the *Ranger* and the *Cincinnati*. The situation grew rather tense on several occasions, but Russell's marines were able to control it by firmness and, on some occasions, considerable bluff, without firing on either of the warring factions.

Another battalion of marines was mobilized at Norfolk for duty on the Isthmus, but conditions in Panama soon improved and the battalion did not leave the United States. Rear Admiral Casey was at the time in charge of all American naval forces on both sides of the Isthmus. Acting upon authority from his government, he tendered his friendly services in an attempt to restore peace in Colombia. Negotiations, however, proceeded slowly, and in the meantime several situations arose that threatened to cause hostilities along the railroad which each side, as usual, desired to use for transporting troops. The Liberal revolt was gradually brought under control after several thousand additional Colombian troops arrived on the Isthmus. Casey's peacemaking efforts finally had results in November, and according to arrangements the Liberal forces laid down their arms and were given their freedom. Colombian troops took over the protection of the trains; Russell's battalion of marines withdrew from Panama on November 17. As a result of the then recent developments of medical science and for the first time in our history, American troops had been able to operate in that sickly tropical climate with very few cases of malaria or yellow fever.

### INDEPENDENCE OF PANAMA

Early in 1903 the Hay-Herran Treaty was negotiated between the United States and Colombia. It provided that the United States pay ten million dollars for a canal zone concession and a quarter of a million dollars as an annual rental. The concession which Colombia had made to the French Canal Company was due to be forfeited in the near future, and the Colombian Government, knowing that we had offered forty million dollars for the French property, attempted to delay the settlement of the matter until the French were forced to forfeit. The United States Senate promptly ratified the Hay-Herran Treaty, but the Colombian Congress stalled for time in various ways and finally adjourned on October 31 without taking action on the treaty. President Theodore Roosevelt, being especially interested in the matter, grew very impatient with Colombia, as did also the energetic representative of the French Canal Company—Colonel Bunau-Varilla. Bunau-Varilla was actively instigating a revolution in Panama and arranged with the revolutionary leaders for the disposal of the French Canal property in a manner satisfactory to him.

The revolutionary faction sent Dr. Amador to the United States as their representative to seek aid for a new revolution. Amador appears to have made very little progress, and Bunau-Varilla went to Washington to use his influence. He made what appeared to be casual calls on the President and Secretary of State and drew his conclusions as to what they would do in the event of a revolution in Panama. He advanced $100,000 to the support of the revolution and assured its leaders that they would have the protection of the United States within forty-eight hours after it started. For his services to Panama he demanded and received from the revolutionary leader full powers to negotiate a treaty with the United States. Amador returned to Panama and according to arrangements was expected immediately to start the revolution. He wanted more assurance of American protection, however, which was promptly given him by Bunau-Varilla. Acting solely on reports contained in newspapers that the *Nashville* had left Jamaica with sealed orders, the latter positively assured Amador that the ship was en route to Colon, where it did arrive two days later, and the revolution was started by a declaration of independence in Panama City.

With what was at least an uncanny foresight for coming events President Roosevelt had some two weeks previously directed the Navy to have ships within easy distance of the Isthmus and several ships had sailed for the general vicinity. On November 2, when the outbreak was imminent in Panama, the Navy Department sent the following instructions to three ships in the vicinity:

Maintain free and uninterrupted transit. If interruption is threatened by armed force, occupy the line of railroad. Prevent landing of any armed force with hostile intent, either Government or insurgent at any point within 50 miles of Panama. Government force reported approaching the Isthmus in vessels. Prevent their landing if, in your judgment, the landing would precipitate a conflict.

At daylight the morning of November 3 Colombian gunboats carrying between four and five hundred troops arrived at Colon. The *Nashville* was present but had not received the above-mentioned orders and permitted the Colombians to land. It received the Navy Department's orders two hours later, however, and Commander Hubbard immediately went ashore to carry out his assigned mission. He found that the railroad company had refused to transport the Colombian troops to Panama, but that the generals commanding the troops had gone to that city. Late that afternoon the news of the revolution reached Colon. Hubbard refused to permit the Colombian troops to use the train to Panama. Colonel Torres, their immediate commander, made many dire threats as to what he would do if not permitted to carry out his "duty." Hubbard immediately transferred a part of his crew ashore to protect the Americans and took up a firing position near the town with his ship. The Colombian troops surrounded Hubbard's landing force, making his situation somewhat critical, but nothing happened.

Torres offered to withdraw from the town into the near-by country providing the *Nashville* would withdraw its landing force. Hubbard agreed as his little force was outnumbered about ten to one. He withdrew his men only to discover early the following morning that the Colombians had withdrawn to the edge of the city only, where they occupied some buildings. They refused to complete their withdrawal upon the demand of Hubbard, who again sent his landing force ashore and reoccupied a position at the railroad station. Torres marched his troops back into Colon, and the *Nashville* resumed its firing position off the town. The Colombians became decidedly less belligerent, however, and before the day had passed the Panamanians, well supplied with French Canal Company money, persuaded Torres to re-embark his troops and return to Cartagena.

WALLER WITH OFFICERS OF THE SECOND REGIMENT MARINES, PANAMA

Hiram I. ("Hiking Hiram") Bearss
Hard-Fighting Marine of the Old School

Major General John Twiggs Myers (Retired)
Hero of Peking, and Always a Model Marine Officer

An expeditionary battalion of marines had been assembled in Philadelphia in anticipation of trouble and sailed on the U.S.S. *Dixie*, October 25, for the Caribbean. The *Dixie* was in Kingston, Jamaica, on November 3, and while there received the Navy Department orders quoted above. The vessel arrived at Colon early in the afternoon of November 5, and, upon receipt of signals from ashore that the situation was extremely critical, Major John A. Lejeune, in command of the Marine Battalion, promptly landed with two of his companies. The naval officers on duty in Colon had not yet learned of the withdrawal of the Colombian troops which had taken place a few hours previously. Lejeune with his marines relieved the *Nashville's* landing force in Colon. The remaining Colombian troops upon the Isthmus had by this time gone over to the new Republic of Panama. Comparative quiet was soon restored in Colon and vicinity. Upon assurance that the police force in Colon was sufficient for its protection, the marines were withdrawn from the city at noon on November 6 and went back on board the *Dixie*.

The revolution in Panama had been accomplished largely by Colombian troops turning revolutionist and by the work of a revolutionary party, organized under the guise of "city firemen." Two Colombian gunboats which remained faithful to the government fired a few shots on the city and retired. The Navy Department learned of this and ordered the *Nashville* to send a battery across the Isthmus to compel the cessation of the bombardment. The ship was, of course, too busy at the time with affairs in Colon to comply. The situation soon quieted down on the Pacific side of the Isthmus. The independence of the Republic of Panama was recognized by our State Department on November 6. The *Boston* arrived at Panama the following day and carried out the instructions heretofore quoted, and which were also carried out by several ships on the Atlantic side. Since all Colombian troops in the immediate vicinity had been eliminated and our naval vessels would not permit others to be landed, there was little chance for the Colombian Government to regain its control over Panama.

A number of other American naval vessels arrived on both coasts of Panama during the next ten days and joined in the patrolling of the waters of that country. The commander of our Caribbean Squadron attempted to make a peaceful settlement of the whole affair by calling a conference between certain Panama officials and General Reyes of Colombia on board his flagship on November 17. No agreement was reached but the independence of Panama was made more secure by the Colombian general being advised that our naval forces would not allow his troops to enter Panama. The near-by Colombian ports which were suspected of having troops were kept under observation by our naval vessels.

A treaty was made with Panama on November 18, giving the United States all of the desired canal rights on the same terms as had formerly been proposed to Colombia. This treaty superseded the Treaty of 1847, and thereafter all of our interventions made in Panama were to assure a stable government in that country, to protect the construction of the canal and the operation of the railroad. The only route by which Colombia could send a large body of troops into Panama entered Panama at the extreme eastern end of the Isthmus. The strategic points which appeared to command this route were Real de Santa Maria and Yaviza. The Panamanian Government was asked by the naval commander to garrison these two places, but to make sure of their security Rear Admiral Glass, Commander of the Pacific Squadron, sent an expeditionary force on November 14 to establish a strong observation post at each. The *Wyoming* and the *Boston* were ordered to transport the troops via the Gulf of San Miguel and up the Tuira River to their positions. Captain Smedley D. Butler with his company of marines was sent from Colon and went aboard the *Boston* as part of the expeditionary force. The initial contingent of troops for the new posts started inland on December 15, under Lieutenant Miller, U.S.N., and Butler followed with his company of marines two days later. Eighty additional men from the *Boston*, including its marine detachment under Captain J. M. Salladay, were sent to the observation positions a few days later. The Navy Department apparently did not approve of establishing posts quite so strong in that part of Panama, and all except twenty-nine marines from the *Boston* remaining at Yaviza were soon withdrawn.

Lejeune's battalion on the *Dixie*, in the meantime, had been used as a reserve at Colon. Small detachments were placed on shore for short intervals to carry out special missions. An advanced detachment of the battalion was sent to Empire to establish a camp on December 8; the rest of the battalion followed on the 16th.

Another battalion of marines, consisting of 11 officers and 300 enlisted men under the command of Major Louis C. Lucas, was mobilized at Philadelphia and sailed on November 9 for Guantanamo Bay, Cuba, where it was held in readiness for duty in Panama. It was transferred to Colon on December 21 and was later removed to Bas Obispo. Both it and Lejeune's battalion were housed in the buildings of the French Canal Company.

Pursuant to further orders from the Navy Department, two additional battalions of marines with a combined strength of 635 officers and enlisted men, were assembled at Philadelphia and sailed on the *Dixie* December 28 for duty in the Republic of Panama. Brigadier General Commandant George F. Elliott, with the necessary brigade staff, accompanied this expeditionary force and later assumed command of all marines in Panama and organized them into a provisional brigade of two regiments.

The troops on the *Dixie* arrived at Colon on January 3, 1904. The Second Battalion, First Regiment, under Major Eli K. Cole, moved to Empire for station and duty. The First Battalion, Second Regiment, commanded by Major James E. Mahoney, was transferred to Bas Obispo and quartered with Lucas' battalion.

While on duty on the Isthmus the Marine Brigade concerned itself largely with becoming familiar with the country. Numerous scouting parties went out with the object of studying the surrounding area and gathering data for topographical maps. They thoroughly reconnoitered and mapped all of the trails in the vicinity and located the principal terrain features. They devoted considerable time to making reconnaissances and studies for the defense of the Canal and the City of Panama.

The marine post at Yaviza remained in position until January 11, 1904, when it was relieved by Panamanian troops and returned on board the *Boston*. A ship of the Pacific Squadron was for some time thereafter stationed in the Gulf of San Miguel to maintain contact with some Panamanian troops that had taken up a position at Boca de Cupe. By the middle of January the new Republic of Panama had an army of only about 850 men. It is rather improbable that this force could long have held out against the Colombian Army without the constant support of the United States. Colombia did not give up the struggle immediately but made several efforts to get troops into Panama to reassert her authority.

A number of reports indicated that late in January, 1904, several detachments of troops were about to move into Panama from Colombia. While the naval vessels were closely watching both coasts of the country, Lejeune with his battalion made a reconnaissance to the eastward of the Canal Zone to head off any forces advancing through the interior and to locate strategic positions for occupancy in the event of a determined invasion by the Colombian troops. Lejeune was determined not to remain on the defensive if the Colombian troops invaded the Canal Zone.

Relations between the United States and Colombia became less tense during February, 1904; our diplomats had apparently in some way offered satisfaction to Colombia. By the end of that month there was decidedly less indication of Colombia's determination to invade Panama, and by the middle of March all troops which had been held in readiness for that purpose were sent back into the interior, and the Colombian Government announced that it would send no expedition against Panama.

The Marine Brigade remained encamped on the Isthmus until February 14, 1904, when part of the First Battalion and all of the Second Battalion, Second Regiment, were withdrawn and transferred on the *Prairie* to Guantanamo Bay, Cuba. General Elliott was detached from the brigade on February 16 and proceeded to Washington to resume his duties as Commandant of the Marine Corps. Headquarters and the Second Battalion of the First Regiment were withdrawn on February 25 and sailed on the *Dixie* for Philadelphia. The First Battalion of that regiment remained on duty in the Canal Zone. The marines remaining continued to reconnoiter the surrounding country and went for considerable distances into Panamanian territory. They were retained in the country as a stabilizing force and for use in any contingency. The necessity for their presence was evident before many months had passed.

The Panamanian Army under the leadership of General Huertas was practically in a state of mutiny in November, 1904. Huertas, who evidently was planning to secure control of the government, formed a plot to seize Amador, who by this time had become President of Panama, and some of his cabinet. Amador learned of the plot and asked the American Minister, John Barrett, to support him with the marines at Empire. Barrett refused but warned Huertas in no uncertain terms that the American forces would intervene if he attempted to carry out his suspected plot. Several ships of the Pacific Squadron arrived at Panama about this time and Rear Admiral Goodrich, in charge of all American forces in the vicinity, ordered Company A of the marine battalion moved in the early morning of November 17 to Ancon Hill, in the Canal Zone but just outside the city and overlooking it. At the request of Amador, Goodrich then also ordered the company of marines to maintain order in Panama. Arrangements were made for direct communication between the Panamanian officials and Lejeune, who kept the remainder of his battalion in readiness at Empire for immediate movement into Panama.

Considerable excitement prevailed in the city; Huertas issued a proclamation stating his position, while Amador demanded his resignation. This Huertas refused to do but agreed to retire, however, after he had been offered five hundred dollars a month retired pay. Most of the people appeared to be for Huertas. Panamanian troops demanded their discharges, and they were expected to mutiny at any moment. After much discussion it was finally decided to disband the troops, and Amador requested that the marines be brought into the city until this could be accomplished. His wishes were not complied with, but the marine battalion was kept in its state of readiness. The police force from Colon came over to assist in keeping order. The army was disbanded a short time afterwards under the threat of using the marines, if necessary, to assure its men being peacefully mustered out.

Lejeune's battalion was relieved late in 1904 by a battalion of 12 officers and 486 marines under Lieutenant Colonel Thomas A. Wood. Wood's battalion was reduced about a month later to a detachment of 4 officers and 165 marines—the remainder being placed aboard the *Dixie*. A new detachment of 8 officers and about 200 marines under Major C. G. Long took over the duty in Panama in December, 1905. This detachment was reinforced by a battalion of 17 officers and 400 enlisted men under Lieutenant Colonel J. E. Mahoney on May 28, 1908, and used as a reserve force by the American Minister during the elections held shortly afterward. Mahoney's battalion was withdrawn on July 6 and returned to the United States.

Elections were again held in Panama during the summer of 1908 and an additional force of marines, consisting of 19 officers and 706 enlisted men under Colonel Eli K. Cole, was sent there to augment the permanent battalion and to help maintain order during the elections. Detachments were stationed at Camp Diablo, three miles out from Panama on the railroad; at Camp Elliott, near Bas Obispo; and at Mount Hope and Mindi, both near Colon. During these elections the marines remained in their assigned stations with special trains standing by for quick transportation to any point on the railroad where trouble might arise. After completing this duty Cole with his detachment sailed from Colon for the United States on July 31.

A marine battalion remained on duty in Panama with an average strength of about fifteen officers and four hundred enlisted men until January 21, 1914, when it was withdrawn and transferred to duty with the Marine Expeditionary Brigade at Vera Cruz, Mexico. During the last few years of their stay in Panama the marines served as a stabilizing force against local disturbances and as advanced base troops to be used by the Navy in the Caribbean area. The battalion was away from its regular station on expeditionary duty to Nicaragua during part of 1912.

The necessary appropriation was made by Congress in 1913 for the erection of permanent quarters for a marine battalion at Ancon.

The project was held in abeyance for several months and it was later decided not to keep permanently a large marine post in the Canal Zone. A small marine detachment was later stationed at Coco Solo, a submarine and air base, near Colon, where a regular detachment is still maintained.

The Army began to take over the defense of the Canal Zone with the arrival of the Tenth Infantry at Colon on October 4, 1911. The Army's strength on the Isthmus has been gradually increased, other branches added, and it now has a substantial force on guard over the canal.

## In Readiness for Mexico, 1913

Near the close of President Taft's administration, revolutionary activities in Mexico had divided the country into a number of factions and civil war was in progress in several parts of the country. In February, 1913, Francisco Madero, who had been made president as a result of a revolution, was in turn deposed by a revolutionary faction led by General Huerta. Madero and his vice-president were murdered soon afterwards under circumstances which strongly placed the blame on Huerta, who shortly thereafter had himself proclaimed President of Mexico. The chaotic conditions which resulted from the revolution and the attendant danger to American lives and property prompted our government to take several preliminary steps for possible military intervention in Mexico and for evacuating Americans from danger zones.

The Army ordered additional troops to Galveston and vicinity where transports were held in readiness. The Navy disposed several war vessels at the principal ports on both coasts of Mexico. As part of the precautionary measures and under orders from the Secretary of the Navy, the Marine Corps on February 20, 1913, assembled a brigade consisting of approximately 72 officers and 2,097 enlisted men under Colonel Lincoln Karmany, at Philadelphia and Norfolk, from which ports the marines were transferred by the army transport *Meade* and the U.S.S. *Prairie* to Guantanamo, Cuba, where they went into camp and held themselves in readiness of any emergency. The brigade was never called into active service but busied itself in various kinds of field training until it returned to the United States in two contingents on May 2 and June 1, 1913.

## Intervention in Mexico, 1914

The concern of the United States Government and the precautionary measures taken in connection with the revolutionary and chaotic conditions in Mexico during 1913 proved to be only a minor preliminary to the drastic action which followed. Woodrow Wilson had become President of the United States and along with his other ideas of progressive and liberal government, he had a keen desire to help the great mass of Mexican people. It was quite apparent that the hoped-for reforms, which had sprung up during the brief reign of Madera, had been at least for the time being terminated by the seizure and control of the government by the reactionary Huerta. Prior to Wilson's administration revolutionary governments had been recognized whenever in our opinion they were capable of controlling the situation. Growing out of his desire to promote social progress in Mexico and other motives, Wilson evolved a new doctrine and announced a policy of refusing to recognize governments in Latin-American countries which had come into power by other than constitutional means. The principle was, in effect, an extension of the Monroe Doctrine. It would have worked, probably, much better had it been applied initially to a weaker prospect than Huerta, who was already in substantial control of the Mexican situation and had been recognized by a number of countries. Wilson's refusal to recognize Huerta naturally placed the Mexican president in a position of having little desire to please the United States. But if Huerta were to be deposed, it was up to Wilson to devise means to overthrow him. Economic as well as diplomatic pressure was applied and as the months went by relations between Huerta and our government became more strained. Finally by a more or less unimportant indiscretion on the part of Mexican officials a crisis was precipitated.

In conformity with Wilson's policy naval vessels were stationed at a number of Mexican ports early in 1914. Fighting was going on in the vicinity of Tampico between two of the contending Mexican factions. On April 6, while a boat from the U.S.S. *Dolphin* was at a boat landing at Tampico for the purpose of obtaining supplies, some of the sailors who accompanied it together with the paymaster of the *Dolphin* were arrested by an officer of Huerta's forces and promptly confined. The Americans were released soon afterwards but no apology was offered. Such apology, by a gun salute to its flag, was thereupon demanded by the United States. Huerta avoided compliance and offered substitute apologies that were unsatisfactory. In spite of being warned by American diplomatic representatives that his non-compliance would probably lead to armed intervention, Huerta still demurred. Wilson asked Congress for authority to use the armed forces to enforce respect for the American flag. In the meantime the situation was aggravated by reports that the German steamer *Yperanga,* bearing large quantities of arms and ammunition for Huerta's troops, was due to arrive in Vera Cruz in the near future and that complete arrangements had been made for the prompt despatching of the munitions into Mexico.

During this period of excitement and strained relations the Navy Department was making extensive plans and disposing its forces for armed intervention. Practically every vessel in American waters was ordered to Mexican ports and even certain decommissioned ships were ordered placed in an active status.

The Marine Corps was called upon to make a maximum effort with its peacetime strength in preparation for the emergency. The First Advanced Base Brigade had been practically on a war basis during the preceding winter; it had participated in extensive joint maneuvers with the fleet at Culebra Island and after the conclusion of the maneuvers it was held in readiness either on board transports or in camps ashore at Gulf ports. Brigade Headquarters and the First Regiment had been sent first to Pensacola and thence to New Orleans on board the *Hancock,* while the Second Regiment had gone to Pensacola after the conclusion of the winter maneuvers. Part of the Second Regiment, on board the *Prairie,* spent most of the month of March off Vera Cruz. The battalion of marines formerly stationed in Panama had been placed on several vessels of the Atlantic Fleet in January and kept in the same vicinity. When the crisis following the Tampico incident was reached, Headquarters and part of the First Regiment was on board the *Hancock* en route from Tampico to Vera Cruz. Part of the Second Regiment was still on board the *Prairie* at Vera Cruz. The remainder of the regiment, from its camp at Pensacola, was hurried on board the U.S.S. *Mississippi* for transfer to Vera Cruz.

While these preparations were being made on the East Coast, the *Pittsburgh* took 260 marines from Mare Island, Calif., to San Diego to stand by, and several vessels were ordered to different ports on the west coast of Mexico. The Fourth Regiment of Marines was mobilized at San Diego, placed on board three vessels of the Navy early in April, and went down the west coast of Mexico. The greater part of the regiment, on board the *South Dakota,* lay off Acapulco for several weeks while another detachment, on board the *Jupiter,* stayed at Mazatlan and other ports for some time. No American forces landed on that coast during the subsequent operations in Mexico.

Rear Admiral F. F. Fletcher, in immediate command off Vera Cruz, was initially ordered on the early morning of April 21 to "take the Customs House immediately and prevent the delivery of arms and ammunition." While preparing his landing forces to carry out these orders Fletcher notified the Mexican authorities, including

General Maas, in charge of the local National troops, and the commanding officer of San Juan de Ulua, of his intentions. He warned them that if his troops were fired upon, his naval vessels would return the fire.

The first troops to land were marines of the Second Regiment on the *Prairie*, followed closely by a part of the marines who had come up from Panama. They landed on the principal pier of the port without resistance, promptly occupied the cable station near by, securing communication with the United States, dispatched a company to hold the electric power plant a few hundred yards to the west, and covered the approaches to the pier from the same direction. Colonel W. C. Neville, in command of the regiment, then advanced his main body along a street between the city and the railroad terminal for a distance of about one half mile. At about noon the head of his column was fired upon for the first time by the Mexicans. The marines continued to make some advance in spite of the resistance and early in the afternoon a detachment took the roundhouse—a strong position lying just west of the city. During the first night ashore the marine regiment held a position with Major Berkeley's battalion on the line, extending from the western edge of the city northward towards the beach, while Major George Reid's battalion of fleet marines, which had landed later, held the left of the line.

In the meantime several battalions of seamen had begun to land and operate on the left of the marine regiment. One naval battalion seized the customs house, the post office, and the railway terminal. The bluejackets then advanced into the city for a few blocks where they too were fired upon, principally from windows and housetops. The initial landing was made with less than eight hundred men, of whom about five hundred were marines. Early in the afternoon the *Prairie* fired upon a cavalry detachment, seen on the sand hill to the west of the city, and drove it off. When resistance began to be encountered, Captain W. R. Bush, Naval Brigade commander, asked for strong reinforcements. When they were arriving during the afternoon and landing alongside the pier, they were fired upon by Mexican troops, who had taken up a position in a building occupied by the naval school, situated about two hundred yards south of the pier. The fire was promptly returned by one-pounders carried in the bows of some of the boats, and the *Prairie* fired a few 3-inch shells into the building and silenced the hostile fire. The augmented naval landing force took over a sector in the heart of the city on the left of the marine regiment during the afternoon. By the end of the first day the entire force had been able to clear only about one half of the city of the various Mexican forces.

Admiral Fletcher took personal command ashore during the night and landed additional troops. Several more detachments of marines from the fleet landed and, together with ship detachments already ashore, were formed into a provisional regiment under Major Catlin, Fleet Marine Officer. Catlin's regiment was tentatively designated as the Third Regiment and was assigned to support the Second Regiment. The two under the command of Neville, early the following morning, resumed the difficult task of clearing their sector of the city of irregular Mexican forces, who were holding up their advance largely by sniping from the windows and the tops of buildings.

The *Hancock* with Headquarters, First Marine Brigade, and the First Regiment on board, arrived during the forenoon of April 22. The Brigade Commander, Colonel John A. Lejeune, immediately took command of all marines ashore. The First Regiment under Colonel C. G. Long landed at 1 P.M. With the aid of the additional units Lejeune's brigade was able to extend its sector to the left towards the center of the city and pursue more vigorously the process of mopping up the rather determined Mexican resistance. By the end of the second day the Marine Brigade had cleared an area from three to five blocks deep across its front, which due to the heavy Spanish construction was easily defended. The marines again halted their advance during the night, took up a defensive line, and heavily patrolled the area in their rear.

The Naval Brigade landed substantial reinforcements during the first night and the second day. It too had encountered substantial resistance. Admiral Badger, commanding the Atlantic Fleet, arrived on the second day with five additional battleships, all of which promptly landed troops, including their marine detachments that were sent to reinforce the Marine Brigade. While attempting to clear their part of the city, the sailors were subjected to a great deal of sniping from the windows and roofs of the houses. A regiment of seamen, while marching in close formation, was fired upon by a number of Mexicans from the windows of the naval school. But for the prompt firing by the *Chester, Prairie,* and *San Francisco* with three-, four- and five-inch guns upon the building, which very soon riddled its upper story, the situation might have been quite difficult for the troops, caught totally unprepared for the encounter. The Naval Brigade cleared its sector of the city during the second day's operation.

The First and Second Marine Regiments resumed the advance and cleared the remainder of the city in their sectors on the third day. Practically every building had to be searched in order to be sure that it contained no snipers. Firearms, found in the possession of the population, were confiscated. All except the outskirts of the city had been cleared by noon, and the troops were able to go into billets for a much-needed rest. They established strong outposts along the sand hills which were located just west of the city and extended northwestward to the sea. The fleet regiment of marines was in reserve during the day's operation.

During the rest of the operations in Vera Cruz little more fighting took place, and commanders were mostly concerned with shifting troops to better positions for their comfort and protection. The remainder of the Second Regiment and a battalion of three batteries of artillery arrived on the *Mississippi* from Pensacola on April 24 and were added to the marines ashore. Reid's battalion of fleet marines was sent on the following day to the city waterworks at El Tejar, some ten miles by rail from Vera Cruz. Additional outposts were established at Vergara, near the coast and about two miles west of the city, and at a near-by pumping plant. By the end of the fourth day Fletcher had a total force of nearly seven thousand ashore. In addition to his headquarters he had a naval brigade of nearly 200 officers and approximately 3,760 sailors while the Marine Brigade had a strength of 96 officers and 2,373 enlisted men.

Another regiment of marines consisting of 33 officers and 861 enlisted men finished its mobilization at Philadelphia on April 22 and sailed the following day on the *S.S. Morro Castle* for Vera Cruz where it arrived on the 29th and joined the Marine Brigade. It soon afterwards took the place of the fleet marine regiment which was sent back to the vessels of the fleet. The ship detachments at El Tejar were relieved by a battalion of this regiment commanded by Major J. H. Russell on April 30.

Prior to the beginning of the landing operations, the *Utah* was ordered to sea to meet the *Yperanga* but was recalled to Vera Cruz where its crew took part in the landing operation. It was not necessary to seize the *Yperanga* as the captain volunteered to place his ship practically in the custody of the American forces. It stayed at Vera Cruz for several weeks and was later reported to have landed its arms and ammunition at another Mexican port.

For several months prior to the actual landing of American forces at Vera Cruz, the Army had been preparing for intervention in Mexico. A considerable force of troops had been concentrated near the Mexican boundary and a reinforced brigade had been held in readiness near Galveston. This organization, commanded by Brigadier General Frederick Funston, embarked on April 23 and sailed for Vera Cruz the following day. Funston was ordered by the War Department to relieve the naval landing forces at Vera Cruz with his brigade and was specifically instructed not to extend the limits held by the American forces on April 26. Funston arrived at Vera Cruz with the first of his troops on the 28th and had debarked most of his brigade by the 30th. With a few remaining troops still en route, he had an aggregate strength of 4,067. Fletcher formally turned over command of the city to Funston on April 30, and all of the regular fleet personnel including marine detachments returned to their ships. The Marine Brigade with an aggregate strength of 3,141 was assigned to duty under Funston. Colonel L. W. T. Waller arrived at Vera Cruz May 1 and superseded Lejeune in command of the brigade.

The expeditionary force at Vera Cruz then settled down for months of "watchful waiting" for the development of affairs in Mexico. The command was gradually and systematically reorganized for its own defense and comfort. Every precaution was taken to improve sanitary conditions; the city was given perhaps the most thorough cleaning up that any Mexican city had ever seen. The buzzards, which had habitually lived on the garbage thrown into the streets, were forced to move elsewhere. The marines continued to hold the right brigade sector which included about two-thirds of the outpost line, which extended from southeast of the city along the row of sand hills to the beach northwest of the city, and in addition they maintained a battalion, supported by a battery of artillery, over the waterworks at El Tejar.

There were occasional rumors that Mexican troops were being concentrated in the vicinity to attack Funston's forces. Most of the reports proved to have no foundation in fact but one force of undetermined strength appeared at the outpost line of El Tejar and demanded the immediate surrender of Russell's battalion. Russell's call for reinforcements from Vera Cruz caused considerable excitement, and a column was sent scurrying to the relief of the supposedly beleaguered garrison, only to arrive at El Tejar, after a few hours' marching and train ride, to find that the danger of a Mexican attack had vanished. The experiences at Vera Cruz were very valuable to the marines as it gave them considerable training in handling larger units and seasoned the troops for the more belligerent experiences, which were to follow in rapid succession in other countries of the Caribbean area and elsewhere.

During the stay of American troops at Vera Cruz, practically the entire American Navy remained on duty at various Mexican ports on both the east and west coasts. The Fourth Regiment of Marines, on different vessels of the Navy, remained on the west coast of Mexico until July 3 when it returned to San Diego, California, and was placed in camp on North Island.

Wilson's refusal to recognize Huerta resulted in the latter being unable to obtain foreign financial support. Our government favored his principal opponent Carranza, who gradually grew in strength while Huerta's support lessened. On July 15 Huerta fled the country. Plans were soon afterwards made to withdraw the expeditionary force from Vera Cruz, but due to the rise in prominence of another revolutionary leader, Pancho Villa, the situation became considerably confused, and the evacuation was delayed. It was finally carried out on November 23, 1914. The original purpose of the intervention, to exact an apology, apparently had been lost sight of, as none was ever made. However, the intervention probably furthered the overthrow of Huerta's reactionary government and helped to establish the liberal government which after more years of uncertainty appears to have restored peace and started Mexico on the road to greater development and social progress.

### Expansion of the Corps

The Marine Corps during the first century of its existence had never exceeded a total strength of three thousand. With the coming of the new order of things, ushered in by the war with Spain, the organization was more than tripled in strength by a series of seven increases made every two or three years up to 1916. This rapid expansion of the Corps together with additional allotments to the higher ranks of both officers and enlisted men, assured a liberal flow of promotions to all ranks. The increases in strength were made upon the repeated urgent requests by the Commandant of the Corps in order to provide sufficient personnel for the ever-enlarging functions of the Marines throughout the world.

The Marine Corps, like many other groups of our national life, underwent a decided broadening in its intellectual scope. The profession of arms had theretofore been considered as having to do with matters purely practical that could be learned only by experience. Many of the Corps' officers, and for that matter the leaders in many other walks of life, were men of rather limited schooling. The new order of things not only insisted that officers have a liberal education before being commissioned but also gradually evolved a system of professional training for its officers and specially selected noncommissioned officers. By this process the military profession was brought more in line with the learned professions.

The wartime duties of the Corps, which had been theretofore

limited almost exclusively to duty as riflemen, became somewhat more complex with the development of new weapons of warfare. Several additional weapons as well as new instruments were added to the equipment of the Marines. They began to employ machine-gun, artillery, signal, and specialized advanced base units in order to be ready for the more complicated situations of warfare. The organization in the minds of some of its officers had necessarily become a kind of small army with a variety of weapons requiring special training. Advances in naval gunnery tended to make the service of the marines at sea more technical and consequently required more thorough training for both officers and enlisted men. Sufficient training and experimentation in aviation was started by the personnel of the Marine Corps to enable them quickly to develop a substantial aviation force during the World War.

Greater progress was made in rifle shooting than ever before. The groundwork was laid and a system of instruction perfected which made the Corps probably the best shooting military organization in the world. By means of local and national matches, efficiency in rifle shooting was further increased. The Marine Corps National Match Team won repeatedly during the period just preceding the World War.

## New Foreign Stations

In addition to enlarging the number of Marine Corps posts within the continental limits of the United States with the growing personnel of the Corps, several new foreign stations were established. Temporary contingents of marines had encamped at various times on the site of the newly acquired naval station at Guantanamo Bay, Cuba. A battalion camped there late in 1903 and another one for a short time during the following spring. A small regular garrison was established at the naval station in November, 1906, and was gradually enlarged to a company post, which has since been maintained.

Some new stations were also established in the Pacific. A marine detachment of about fifty officers and men was stationed at Honolulu in March, 1904. After the development of the naval station at Pearl Harbor the detachment increased in strength and moved into new barracks at the station in July, 1914. A naval station was also established in Samoa in 1904, and the question arose as to whether or not it should have the usual contingent of marines. It was settled by detailing a senior noncommissioned officer in charge of a native constabulary called the "Fita-Fita," which in addition to its other duties furnished guards for the naval station.

Early in 1904 the Pacific Cable Company was completing its line across the Pacific and building a relay station on Midway Island, located about twelve hundred miles northwest from the Hawaiian Islands. The construction company had a force of rather unruly laborers, principally Japanese, who in addition to the other trouble they caused, insisted on killing the birds for their valuable feathers. For the purpose of maintaining order and of preventing the extermination of the bird life on the island, a detachment of twenty marines, commanded by Second Lieutenant Clarence S. Owen, was sent to Midway early in May, 1904, and established what was perhaps the most lonely and isolated post that the Marines have ever known. Owen succeeded in carrying out his mission only by confiscating all firearms on the island. Due to the extreme isolation of the post, men were not allowed to remain very long; the detachment as a whole was relieved from time to time. This duty continued until the construction was completed, and the troublesome laborers removed in March, 1908. The detachment was then withdrawn.

### Legation Guard at Seoul, Korea

An unusual mission for the Marines was the assignment of a company of one hundred men and three officers as a legation guard at Seoul, Korea, early in 1904. For a number of years previously both Russia and Japan had been contending for control of the Hermit Kingdom. The Korean Government was too weak to assure protection for our legation. Considerable property had been acquired by Americans in Korea, including the Seoul Electric Company. A group of Korean soldiers, without due provocation, attacked one of its electric cars, did some damage and injured the conductor. The presence of the American marines, who arrived at the Korean capital soon afterwards, served to restrain such attacks on Americans and their property.

Soon after the conclusion of the war with Russia, Japan extended her control over Korea to the extent of making it practically a dependent state. By November, 1905, control of Korean foreign affairs had been assumed by Tokyo, and, there being no longer any necessity for maintaining a diplomatic post in Korea, it was closed on the 28th of that month. The marine detachment had been transferred to the First Regiment of Marines in the Philippines a short time before.

### China

The Legation Guard—a company of the Ninth Infantry—which had been maintained at Peking since the Boxer Rebellion, was relieved by a detachment of one hundred marines commanded by Captain Harry Lee on September 12, 1905. The post was increased to 125 the following year and since that time has been given several small increases. It has since been maintained and had a strength of more than five hundred in 1938.

The unsettled conditions in China, incident to the transition from the old autocratic government to a more democratic one, which began with the overthrow of the Manchu dynasty in 1911, made it well-nigh impossible for local authorities, even when they were willing, to protect foreign lives and property. These conditions led to many armed interventions by foreign powers. In some of these, American forces participated jointly with other foreign forces. The vessels of our Asiatic Fleet were kept on duty at various important Chinese ports, watching the development of the situation and ready to furnish protection to Americans and other foreigners. A great many minor landing force operations were made from vessels of the fleet, in which marines as well as sailors participated. Unsettled conditions which began in 1911 have continued up to the writing and have necessitated military interventions by the United States by forces varying in size from small detachments to a reinforced brigade of marines.

Among the earliest of these interventions in which the marines participated was one at Hankow in October, 1911. The marine detachment of the *Helena* in addition to some small detachments of sailors was kept ashore for several weeks, guarding the American Consulate, the Standard Oil plant, and the power and light company. Early in November the marine detachment of the *Albany* landed at Shanghai and protected the office of the commercial cable company for a few days.

The Commander in Chief of the Asiatic Fleet, in order to have available a stronger land force, arranged for a battalion of marines from the First Brigade in the Philippines to be sent to China. Fifteen officers and 360 enlisted men under Major Philip M. Bannon went from Olongapo on the *Rainbow* to Shanghai in October, 1911. The battalion remained on board the *Rainbow* at Shanghai and at other Chinese ports during the following winter. A company of marines from the Philippine Brigade was also sent to reinforce the Legation Guard at Peking. That guard was further reinforced by one of the companies of Bannon's battalion in December. With these additional troops the legation was considered sufficiently protected at least for the time being.

Early in March, 1912, however, fighting between Chinese factions in Peking again endangered the foreign legations. The marines prepared the American Legation compound for a state of siege, erected barricades and provided other defenses. At the urgent request of the American Minister the Fifteenth Infantry, on duty at Tientsin, sent a detachment of 6 officers and 229 soldiers to Peking as reinforcements. When they arrived on March 3, most of the soldiers were placed on guard over four American missions, lying outside the legation compound. The remainder of Bannon's expeditionary battalion at Shanghai also went to Peking and on March 10 relieved the Infantry detachment, which returned to Tientsin. The Legation Guard thus reinforced was kept at a strength of more than five hundred until early in May when conditions quieted down. Two companies of the expeditionary battalion were then transferred back to vessels of the Asiatic Fleet and resumed the status of a floating reserve force.

Even the marines of the faraway station in Guam were drawn into the troubled areas in China. Thirty-six of them, under Second Lieutenant Harry Schmidt, were placed on board the *Supply,* the regular station ship for Guam, and sent to the China coast to join the Asiatic Fleet. Schmidt and his Guam marines were landed at Chefoo for a few days during November to protect American interests. The smaller vessels of the Navy, which did not carry marines, made a number of landings with small detachments on similar missions. During the remainder of 1912, general conditions improved somewhat, but it was again necessary on several occasions to land sailors and marines from the *Albany* and the *Rainbow* at Shanghai for the protection of American interests.

### Aiding the Civil Power

During the early years of the twentieth century the Marine Corps was again called upon several times in great emergencies or catastrophes to come to the aid of the civil power. The most notable occasion was at San Francisco during the great earthquake and fire in April, 1906. All available army and navy personnel was rushed to the scene of the catastrophe. Among the first to arrive and go on duty was the marine detachment from the naval training station on Yerba Buena Island in San Francisco Bay. A battalion of marines from Mare Island arrived a few hours later and together with other available marines took over the control of a substantial area of the city. The marines helped to preserve order, rescue people from burning buildings, prevent fires, guard private as well as public property, and provide shelter and relief for the many thousands of refugees.

More pleasant and less serious duties were assigned to the marines for creating military effect on a number of occasions. The custom had grown up in the previous period of having marine guards at national and international expositions. They frequently guarded national exhibits and took part in military parades. A detachment was sent for that purpose to the Pan-American Exposition at Buffalo, New York, in 1901. Another battalion was on duty for a number of months at the Louisiana Purchase Exposition at St. Louis, Missouri, in 1904. Organizations of marines repeatedly rendered honors to distinguished personages at Washington and elsewhere.

## Marines Taken Off Ships

The Marine Corps received a bit of a shock to its pride in October, 1908, when President Theodore Roosevelt issued an executive order describing its duties and omitted all reference to its service on board vessels of the Navy. There had never been a time in the history of our Navy when marines had not served on practically all of its larger vessels and, as far as they had ever been able to ascertain, their services had been held in high esteem. It appears that certain influential naval officers had conceived of a new duty status for marines at sea—that of accompanying the fleet on transports as expeditionary units, ready for all manner of landing operations, instead of the traditional mission which they had had since Revolutionary days. In compliance with the executive order and upon the demand of Commandant Elliott that they be removed *en masse*, if they were to be deprived of duty afloat, more than two thousand marines were transferred ashore and their vacancies filled by an equal number of naval personnel. The country voiced itself rather emphatically against the change, and Congress made known its desires by including in the next naval appropriation bill the proviso that none of the appropriations therein for pay of the Marine Corps could be expended unless the marines were returned to duty on board vessels of the Navy. Not only were the marines returned to all the ships from which they had been taken but several additional vessels were given marine detachments.

## Advanced Base Force

The doctrine of an expeditionary force of marines equipped to seize and hold temporary naval bases and to accompany the fleet in any distant adventure in time of war began to take form early in this century. The idea appears to have had its origin in our Navy's experiences at Manila Bay and at Guantanamo Bay, Cuba, during the Spanish War. As early as 1902 special training was undertaken in advanced base operations. An advanced base regiment was organized and carried on training with the fleet at Culebra, Virgin Islands, during the following winter. Training in the use of guns and submarine mines to defend naval bases was initiated. The idea gradually came to be accepted that such duty was one of the major missions of the Corps. Special instruction and training was undertaken by marine units during the succeeding years when the Corps's personnel was not otherwise fully occupied with urgent duties—particularly expeditionary duty. The training and equipping of an advanced base brigade had made substantial progress by 1914 but due to the several expeditions to Caribbean countries and the World War, that particular kind of training was discontinued for a number of years. It was revived, however, some years after the World War and its further development will be discussed in a chapter to follow.

## Chapter XII

## UNDER THE PLATT AMENDMENT IN CUBA

THE Island of Cuba was formally transferred to the possession of the United States on January 1, 1899, in accordance with the terms of the Treaty of Paris which formally ended the War with Spain. Our government then announced its plan to make Cuba free as soon as it was ready to set up a government of its own. Under the leadership of Major General Leonard Wood it was given three years of preparation and pronounced ready for nationhood. The United States was not unmindful, however, of its obligation under the Treaty of Paris as well as its moral responsibility for the success of the experiment. In order to guard against possible failure by the Cubans in governing themselves, a plan was devised which practically made Cuba a dependency of the United States. The provisions of this plan, expressed in what was known as the Platt Amendment, were set forth in the Army Appropriation Bill of March 2, 1901. The third clause of the amendment is of special interest to this study and reads as follows:

That the government of Cuba consents that the United States may exercise the right to intervene for the preservation of Cuban independence, the maintenance of a government adequate for the protection of life, property and individual liberty, and for discharging the obligations with respect to Cuba imposed by the Treaty of Paris on the United States, now to be assumed and undertaken by the government of Cuba.

The amendment was submitted to the Cuban Constitutional Convention for consideration, and, in spite of the objections of the Cubans, upon the insistence of our government, it was made a part of the Cuban constitution. During the first four years of independence, when the government was practically non-partisan, Cuba managed to conduct its own affairs in such a way as to cause no major interference by the United States. Thereafter, as the result of failures of Cuba to maintain a stable government and in accordance with provisions of the aforesaid arrangement, United States forces were stationed in Cuba on several occasions for the purpose of restoring an adequate government throughout the island.

As the end of Cuba's first presidential administration approached, two political parties, with decidedly conflicting points of view, sprang up. The Moderate Party formed under the leadership of the first president, Tomas Estrada Palma, while the much stronger Liberal Party sprang up under the leadership of José Miguel Gomez. After the elections held in December, 1905, under the control of the Moderates, that party announced that its candidates had been elected practically everywhere, despite the fact that the Liberal Party was known to be much stronger in most parts of the country. The Liberals were especially dissatisfied with the results because they were unable to secure any of the coveted government positions and in August, 1906, they rose in open revolt.

The Cuban military forces at the time were very weak and consisted mainly of rural guards scattered in small detachments throughout the island. They were too weak in any locality to suppress the Liberal uprising, even if they had all been enthusiastic supporters of the government—many of them were not. The Liberal revolt, started in the vicinity of Havana and in Santa Clara province, soon developed considerable strength in the extreme western province of Pinar del Rio. The rural guards in these vicinities were none too loyal to the Cuban Government. The central government called out two thousand veterans to reinforce the guards and succeeded in putting down the revolt in western Cuba and in Matanzas Province. The insurgents in Santa Clara, where Gomez, the recently defeated candidate for president, had an immediate following of nearly one thousand armed men, continued to grow rapidly in numbers. There were obviously only two logical alternatives for the Cuban Government: either to crush completely the rebellious party or turn the government over to it. Instead, the government tried to make terms with the insurgents and at the same time began to look longingly to the United States for assistance.

The insurrectionists grew rapidly in strength during early September and extended their activities over a number of provinces. Their disorderly conduct and destruction of property owned by American sugar companies caused many complaints to the American Legation in Havana. President Theodore Roosevelt assumed the attitude that we should intervene only as a last resort and then only after being "absolutely certain of the equities of the case and needs of the situation." Upon the request of President Palma, however, Roosevelt sent the U.S.S. *Des Moines* and *Tacoma* to Cuban ports, but with specific instructions only to "protect American lives and property if endangered." In order to force the United States to intervene, the Cuban president announced his intention of resigning and leaving Cuba without an organized government.

Thus far no special move had been made for the mobilization of American forces for intervention in Cuba. A battalion of marines, however, had been placed on board the *Dixie* in June for service in Caribbean waters. It was augmented in strength during July and again in September by adding 2 officers and 110 marines. The *Dixie* arrived in Cuban waters with the battalion on board on September 12, when the Cuban trouble reached a crisis. By that time Roosevelt appeared to be of the opinion that military intervention was inevitable. He directed that naval ships be prepared to sail for Cuba and that all available marines be sent to Havana as soon as they could be made ready. The Navy Department promptly dispatched a number of vessels to Cuban waters, where they arrived at various ports within the next ten days. A battalion of four hundred marines, with necessary equipment for field service, was mobilized at each of the navy yards at Norfolk and Philadelphia. The Norfolk battalion sailed September 16 on board three cruisers for Havana, and the Philadelphia battalion followed two days later on the *Minneapolis*.

Eight thousand insurgents were reported just outside of Havana on September 13. The Palma government was panic-stricken and urgently requested the immediate landing of American forces for its protection. Chargé d' affaires Sleeper, who appears not to have been conversant with Roosevelt's intentions, acceded to the request and directed the landing of an American force at Havana. A battalion of 6 officers and 124 sailors and marines, under Lieutenant Commander M. L. Miller, went ashore from the *Denver*, hoisted the American flag over "La Fuerza" fortress, and encamped in front of the president's palace. A few hours later, before report of the landing had been received by the State Department, Sleeper received instructions that no armed forces should be landed under any circumstances unless so ordered by that department. In spite of Palma's protests, Sleeper ordered the landing force to withdraw the following morning.

Although the landing had been made contrary to the wishes of the State Department, its effects on the situation at Havana and throughout Cuba proved very beneficial. Representatives of the revolutionary faction around Havana immediately issued orders that

all hostilities cease and offered to bring in all insurgent generals, turn in their arms, and disband their soldiers. It also greatly relieved the situation in Havana by ending the fear of invasion of the city by the insurrectionists. The *Dixie*, with the battalion of marines on board, arrived at Havana September 16, augmented the available American force, and helped greatly to relieve the tense situation.

While conditions in the vicinity of Havana were improving, the insurgent faction became more active in Santa Clara. The western part of that province was especially rich in sugar plantations owned by influential American interests. General instructions had been given to naval commanders authorizing them to make landings in case of serious threats to American interests. On September 14 the commanding officer of the *Marietta* at Cienfuegos notified the Navy Department that, unless otherwise directed and in accordance with demands of owners of sugar plantations, he would send landing forces ashore to protect American interests at Hormiguero and Soledad. He sent two officers and thirty-one men to the Soledad estate in the late afternoon of that day, just in time to protect the properties from a threatened attack by insurgent groups. The detachment, fully armed with rifles and machine guns, was under strict instructions to avoid engagements if possible.

The situation in the vicinity of Cienfuegos was so threatening that the commanding officer of the *Marietta* strongly urged additional forces sent there. The Secretary of the Navy immediately complied with the recommendation. On September 15 a second landing force from the *Marietta*, two officers and thirty-five sailors, under Lieutenant J. V. Klemann, U.S.N., went ashore at the urgent request of the manager of the Constancia sugar plantation to protect it from anticipated attack by the insurgents.

In spite of efforts to prevent outrages against American property, the violations continued in that general vicinity. Further requests for protection—many of which were in the nature of demands—poured into Washington and were complied with by the administration as rapidly as forces could be made available. On September 18 a detachment of fifty marines commanded by First Lieutenant W. E. Parker, went ashore from the *Dixie* at Cienfuegos to guard the Constancia sugar plantation. Twenty-five marines under Second Lieutenant R. L. Shepard landed from that ship to help guard the Soledad plantation. Major A. W. Catlin, in command of the marines on the *Dixie*, transferred his headquarters, four officers and one hundred and twenty-five marines, to the Hormiguero sugar plantation. The remainder of the *Dixie* battalion, twenty-five marines, went aboard the *Marietta* for temporary duty, and the

*Dixie* left Cienfuegos. Catlin's battalion took over the guarding of American property both at Soledad and Constancia, relieving the naval detachments from the *Marietta* which returned to their ship.

On September 25 the Cuban Central Railroad was reported in danger of destruction by the insurrectionists at Palmira. A landing force of four officers, twenty-two marines and sixty-four sailors, commanded by Klemann, went ashore from the *Marietta* at Cienfuegos and proceeded to Palmira to protect the railroad. A part of the detachment went back to its ship the same day and, after the danger was over, the remainder returned a few days later. A similar danger arose to the Cuban Central Railroad at Sagua la Grande on September 21. Klemann with thirty-two marines and sailors again landed, proceeded by rail to that place and prevented the destruction of the railroad. A detachment of two officers and fifty-one marines from Catlin's battalion relieved Klemann's force and established a regular post at Sagua la Grande.

Roosevelt paid little attention to the Cuban Government's request for intervention but sent a special commission headed by William H. Taft, then Secretary of War, to investigate matters and render all possible aid. The commission arrived in Havana on September 19 and immediately arranged a truce between the two factions. Our government refused to take sides in the matter as it believed favoring one side might lead to a general resistance on the part of the Cuban people against the United States. After some investigation, Taft's commission decided to re-establish the Liberals in control in the towns which had been taken from them as the result of the last elections. Palma took this as a signal to carry out his previously announced intentions of getting out. He refused to co-operate, even temporarily, by appointing a cabinet composed of both factions. By September 24 military intervention appeared inevitable, and Taft suggested to Roosevelt that more ships be made available and troops mobilized for an active intervention.

## THE ARMY OF CUBAN PACIFICATION

In anticipation of possible intervention, the War Department prepared plans for organizing and transporting to Cuba an expeditionary force of eighteen thousand men. The principal difficulty of the plans was the fact that transports had to be procured from commercial steamship companies. The War Department believed that any preliminary arrangements for ships would become known and would embarrass the efforts being made by the President to bring about the settlement of affairs in Cuba without the use of the armed forces. As soon as Roosevelt decided that an army of pacification would be sent to Cuba to support a provisional government, the War Department on September 29 ordered six thousand men mobilized at Newport News for that duty. The expeditionary force, with an actual strength of 333 officers and 5,064 enlisted men, sailed for Cuba on a number of vessels between October 7 and 11.

The Marine Corps had been called upon in the meantime to furnish two additional battalions from its shore stations for duty in Cuba. The troops were assembled within thirty-six hours after orders were issued, but lack of water transportation caused considerable delay in transferring them to Cuba. One of the battalions assembled at Boston under Lieutenant Colonel F. J. Moses and sailed on the *Prairie* on September 30. The other was ordered to assemble at Havana under Major Edward R. Lowndes. A part of it sailed from Norfolk on board the *Texas*, October 1, while other marines were sent by mail steamers from Key West and New Orleans. The remaining troops to complete the battalion started from San Juan, Porto Rico, on the *Dixie* but never joined the organization. An additional battalion of marines, composed of marine detachments from six ships of the Atlantic Fleet which had not been ordered to Cuban waters, arrived in Havana on October 1 on board the *Kentucky* and *Indiana*.

Palma persistently refused to co-operate with any plans suggested by Taft and resigned, effective September 28, in spite of urgent requests by both Roosevelt and Taft to continue in office until his relief could be arranged. The Cuban Congress was called to consider Palma's resignation but the Moderates refused to attend and, there being no quorum, no official action could be taken. Cuba was thus left without a central government, whereupon Roosevelt directed Taft to land American forces and establish a provisional government.

The two battalions of marines from Philadelphia and Norfolk had remained on board ships in Havana Harbor and had been organized as the First Regiment under command of Lieutenant Colonel George Barnett. Captain A. R. Couden, commanding the *Louisiana*, was the senior officer present in Cuban waters and, as such, was in command of all Navy and Marine Corps operations in the vicinity. The marine regiment as well as all other marines on ships in Havana Harbor prepared for immediate landing upon receipt of the above-mentioned orders from Roosevelt.

Just prior to his relinquishing office, Palma requested that an American guard be placed over the Cuban Treasury. Second Lieutenant G. M. Kincade and thirty marines were sent ashore for that purpose on September 28. On the following day a provisional government was established and approximately two thousand marines landed at Havana. A part of them went to Camp Columbia, seven miles away, while the First Regiment, with a strength of about five hundred men, fully equipped and supplied with tentage and other field equipment, left by train for Cienfuegos. Barnett's regiment arrived at Cienfuegos during the forenoon of September 30 and occupied the town. Barnett took command of all naval forces in the vicinity. On October 1 he sent one officer and fifty marines to relieve the naval detachment at Constancia, two officers and seventy-five marines to occupy Soledad, and a company to occupy Santa Clara. Shortly afterwards detachments of one officer and twenty-five marines each from the First Regiment occupied Arriete, Santo Domingo, and Esperanza. Detachments of eleven marines each were sent to San Marcos and Caunao. These small detachments were disposed primarily for the purpose of protecting the railroad. Some used storehouses and railway cars when available for living space while others camped in tents. Barnett had armored railway cars equipped for use in case of emergency. Small detachments from the regiment later went to occupy Trinidad, Manicaragua, Cruces, and Ranchuelo.

The arrival of the marines in Santa Clara was just in time to prevent serious disturbances by several thousand insurrectionists operating in that province. Conditions rapidly returned to normal under the protection of the marines. The protective system was extended to other parts of the Island.

On September 30 a detachment of 5 officers and 151 marines under Captain W. C. Harllee was sent by naval vessel from Havana to Nuevitas where it arrived on October 3 and disembarked the following day. Harllee camped on the beach while awaiting transportation and on October 5 went by rail with 2 officers and 102 marines to Camaguey and occupied that town. Second Lieutenant R. L. Denig with the remainder of the detachment remained at Nuevitas. Another company of marines commanded by Captain Wirt McCreary left Havana on September 30 on the *Tacoma*, landed at Tumas on the southern coast of the island on October 3 and occupied Sancti Spiritus.

Colonel L. W. T. Waller was designated by the Commandant of the Marine Corps to command all marines in Cuba and directed to organize them into a provisional brigade. He arrived at Havana on October 1 and after various conferences with the naval commanders and the American Commissioners, established his headquarters at

## UNDER THE PLATT AMENDMENT IN CUBA

Camp Columbia and organized a brigade of marines with the following units and commanders:

*First Regiment:* Lieutenant Colonel George Barnett
  First Battalion (4 companies), Maj. T. P. Kane
  Second Battalion (4 companies), Maj. D. Williams
  Third Battalion (3 companies), Maj. E. R. Lowndes
  Fouth (or separate) Battalion (3 companies), Maj. A. W. Catlin

*Second Regiment:* Lieutenant Colonel Franklin J. Moses
  First Battalion (6 companies), Maj. W. C. Neville
  Second Battalion (3 companies), Capt. W. N. McKelvy
  Third Battalion (4 companies), Capt. P. M. Bannon

Conditions in Pinar del Rio and Havana Provinces continued to cause considerable concern. By order of Taft who had been made provisional governor, a detachment of 4 officers and 207 marines was sent from Camp Columbia on October 3 to occupy the town of Pinar del Rio. A company of marines commanded by Captain Logan Feland was stationed at Guines.

Several detachments also occupied additional threatened points in eastern Cuba. Two officers and fifty marines landed October 11 at Baracoa and established a regular station. A detachment commanded by Captain H. C. Reisinger landed at Santiago, went by rail on October 23 to Guantanamo City, and furnished protection for American lives and property in that vicinity.

Additional detachments were soon required in the western provinces. Bejucal was occupied by a detachment of two officers and fifty marines on October 19, and a detachment of one officer and twenty-five men was sent to Nueva Gerona on the Isle of Pines on the 22nd. Other small detachments went out for special purposes and occupied other towns for short periods of time. A reserve force of marines was formed at Havana under Major W. C. Neville, by landing several marine detachments from naval vessels in the harbor.

The battalion which had sailed on the *Prairie* arrived at Havana October 6 and was added to the brigade reserve at Camp Columbia. A part of Lowndes' battalion also arrived at Havana October 8 and joined the reserve. The Marine Brigade reached its maximum strength on October 27 with about 100 officers and 2,800 marines. The following table shows the approximate distribution of marines by stations on that date:

| Station | Officers | Enlisted Men |
|---|---|---|
| Camp Columbia | 50 | 1133 |
| Pinar del Rio | 5 | 207 |
| Bejucal | 2 | 50 |
| Guines | 3 | 103 |
| Santo Domingo | 5 | 100 |
| Sagua la Grande | 1 | 50 |
| Santa Clara | 3 | 87 |
| Ranchuelo | 4 | 101 |
| Cruces | 1 | 50 |
| Hormiguero | 6 | 182 |
| Arriete | 1 | 25 |
| Palmira | 2 | 78 |
| Constancia | 3 | 50 |
| Cienfuegos | 13 | 267 |
| Caunao | .. | 11 |
| Soledad | 1 | 51 |
| Casilda | 1 | 25 |
| Sancti Spiritus | 3 | 98 |
| Camaguey | 3 | 110 |
| Nuevitas | 2 | 48 |
| Guantanamo | 2 | 47 |
| Baracoa | 3 | 31 |
| Nueva Gerona | 1 | 25 |
| Manicaragua | 1 | 25 |

The results of the occupation of Santa Clara Province by a regiment of marines were soon quite noticeable. At first the number of insurgents continued to grow but this was probably due to their hopes of being rewarded for laying down their arms. When the marines arrived at Camaguey there was reported to be twelve hundred insurrectionists in the vicinity. Conditions quieted down immediately, and most of the rebel forces turned in their arms in accordance with an agreement, hereafter mentioned. About fifty drunken rebels terrorized the town soon afterwards, but the marines under Harllee promptly disarmed them and sent them away. This action was much appreciated by the people of Camaguey but caused some hostility on the part of the Liberal leaders. Harlee, thereafter, allowed the insurgents to enter the town only under his prescribed conditions.

The insurrectionists at Palmira removed the civil officials and installed officers of their own and attempted to remove the government telegraph operators. Barnett took a hand in the affair; Consul General Steinhart investigated it and with his assistance order was eventually restored. At Guines the insurgents, after giving up their arms, did not disperse as they had agreed and caused considerable disturbance. The Rural Guards and the former insurgent officers were able, however, to bring the situation under control. There was considerable feeling against the police at Guines which was allayed by Feland's disarming them. Guines continued to be a source of trouble for some time. Since Feland had so successfully controlled the situation from the beginning, he was left in charge at Guines by special request of responsible Cuban officials. The situation at Pinar del Rio quieted down after the insurrectionists had been disarmed. No further serious trouble was experienced in any of the troubled areas of the Island.

Taft had little difficulty in persuading most of the insurgent leaders to disband their groups and turn in their arms. He decreed that the militia also be disarmed temporarily. The latter undertaking proved more difficult to accomplish. In spite of many difficulties, however, disarmament of all troublesome factions was nominally accomplished in about two weeks. A disarmament commission, headed by Brigadier General Frederick Funston, who had been assigned to command the Army Expeditionary Force, was formed to receive and account for all arms turned in. A great many rifles, revolvers, and machetes, as well as ammunition, were turned in to the marine officers in charge of collecting stations. The disarming of the rebels appears to have resulted in only the worst weapons being turned in. It was necessary for the marines to hunt up a considerable number of machine guns, belonging to the Cuban Government, which had been hidden from the commission.

The army units which had been ordered from Newport News began landing in Cuba, October 10. In spite of all the activities carried on ashore in the meantime, by the marines and sailors, and the fact that at least a dozen naval vessels were in Cuban waters, the Secretary of War in his report of 1906 without any apparent intention of being humorous stated that "the Army landed without opposition." The command of the American forces in Cuba, including all Marine Corps personnel on the island, passed to the control of General Funston on October 10. Funston was relieved from command three days later by Brigadier General J. Franklin Bell.

At the urgent request of the Commandant of the Marine Corps, the marines on duty in Cuba were transferred back to their ships of the fleet or returned to the United States as rapidly as their duties could be assumed by army units. On October 13, soldiers were sent to Santa Clara and Sagua la Grande and relieved the marines at those places soon afterwards. The Eleventh Cavalry relieved the marines at Pinar del Rio on October 18, and other soldiers relieved those at Camaguey on the 27th. The marines of the *Louisiana, Virginia,* and *New Jersey* were returned to their ships from Camp Columbia on October 12. Nearly six hundred officers and enlisted men of the Marine Corps were returned to the United States about ten days later. Arrangements were made with General Bell to withdraw all marines, except one thousand, and reorganize those remaining as the First Provisional Regiment. By November 1, the reduction had been carried out by returning the remaining marine detachments to their ships and by transferring other marines to their regular stations in the United States. Waller was detached (November 1) leaving Lieutenant Colonel Franklin J. Moses in command of marines in Cuba.

After the reorganization of the Army of Cuban Pacification, following the arrival of the Army Expeditionary Force, and the reduction of the marine strength in Cuba, the First Provisional Regiment occupied regular stations on December 1, 1906, as indicated by the following table:

| Station | Unit | Comdg. Officer | Off. | Enl. |
|---|---|---|---|---|
| Camp Columbia | Hq. & other units | Col. F. J. Moses | 22 | 287 |
| Manzanillo | 1st Bn. Hq. & Co. B | Maj. T. P. Kane | 5 | 74 |
| Santo Domingo | 3d Bn. Hq. & Co. I | Maj. A. W. Catlin | 3 | 54 |
| Guines | Det., Co. H | Capt. L. Feland | 3 | 33 |
| Nuevitas | Co. H | Capt. G. C. Thorpe | 3 | 77 |
| Sancti Spiritus | Co. D | Capt. W. McCreary | 3 | 93 |
| Palmira | Co. E | Capt. D. D. Porter | 4 | 44 |
| Hormiguero | Det., Co. E | Lt. H. S. Green | 1 | 21 |
| Isle of Pines | Det., Co. H | Lt. R. Tittoni | 1 | 25 |
| San Marcos | Det., Co. I | Sgt. B. E. Stingle | — | 8 |
| Trinidad | Co. K | Capt. P. S. Brown | 3 | 91 |
| Lajas | Co. L | Capt. C. S. Hill | 4 | 101 |
| Baracoa | Co. M | Capt. H. C. Davis | 3 | 52 |

The troops of the Army of Pacification carefully carried out the policy of President Roosevelt to avoid friction, whenever possible, and to help the Cuban people in every way to settle their difficulties. The American troops carefully avoided the exercise of actual force but kept themselves in readiness to support the recognized Cuban authorities.

It appears that most writers on this intervention in Cuba have failed to give the Marine Corps full credit for its accomplishments. It will be noted from the above remarks that the pacification of the island and the disarming of many of the rebellious factions was completed before the Army arrived. Although the marine strength in Cuba, after its reduction to a provisional regiment, was considerably less than that of the Army, marines continued to carry out a full share of the duties. Their strength was less than one-fifth of the Army of Pacification on August 31, 1907; they were occupying eleven stations to the soldiers' eighteen. On October 1, 1907, the marines were distributed as follows:

| Station | Strength Off. | Enl. |
|---|---|---|
| Headquarters, Havana | 8 | 5 |
| Camp Columbia | 10 | 317 |
| Nuevitas | 3 | 67 |
| Manzanillo | 3 | 77 |
| Sancti Spiritus | 2 | 70 |
| Palmira | 2 | 71 |
| Santo Domingo | 3 | 79 |
| Trinidad | 2 | 60 |
| Lajas | 3 | 70 |
| Baracoa | 2 | 50 |
| Nueva Gerona, Isle of Pines | 1 | 25 |
| Total | 39 | 891 |

The problem of Cuban pacification proved more difficult and long drawn out than was initially anticipated. Taft was relieved as Provisional Governor (October 13, 1906) by Charles E. Magoon, who was much less successful in the conduct of Cuban affairs and whose record has been subjected to much criticism by Cuban writers. The setting up of a properly constituted self-government for Cuba was greatly delayed by the decision to take a new census of the population before proceeding with the registration of voters. The results of the census were not completely tabulated until March, 1908. The local elections were not held until May and the general election until August 1. In the meantime Roosevelt had announced the provisional government would end February 1, 1909, and on that date the Liberal government under Gomez, as president, was installed and took full control.

With the exception of Lajas which was abandoned on March 3, 1908, the marines continued to occupy the stations held in October, 1907, until the Army of Pacification began to withdraw. The posts occupied by marines on the Isle of Pines, at Hormiguero, Baracoa, Manzanillo, Sancti Spiritus, Trinidad, and Palmira were abandoned in December, 1908, and the troops from them were concentrated at Camp Columbia. Seventeen officers and 378 marines from those interior posts returned to the United States on the *Prairie*, sailing from Havana, January 1, 1909. The remaining stations occupied by the marines were abandoned and the troops transferred to Camp Columbia early in January. The last of the First Provisional Regiment—21 officers and 405 marines—left Cuba on the 23rd. The army units were withdrawn between January 9 and April 1, 1909. Upon the withdrawal of the marines from Cuba, Major General Thomas H. Barry, U.S.A., commanding the Army of Cuban Pacification, highly commended them for their performance of duty while under his command.

### The Negro Rebellion—1912

After the withdrawal of the Army of Cuban Pacification in 1909 there was an observable change in the policy of the United States towards Cuba, in that enonomic considerations assumed more and more prominence. A so-called preventive policy was adopted by the State Department, which assumed a constant and critical watchfulness of affairs in Cuba with the idea of controlling situations before they led to the necessity of military intervention. This policy was continued, with some variation, for approximately fourteen years.

The politics of the Cubans began to sink lower and lower into unbelievable depths of inefficiency and corruption. Scandal, graft, crime, bribery, and nepotism were everyday affairs until a climax was reached under Machado and violent revolution followed. These tendencies caused considerable concern to our government, which on several occasions, intervened diplomatically and narrowly avoided military intervention. The situation was particularly acute in 1912, when a public land scandal was rapidly followed by an agitation of the veterans of the Spanish War to dismiss from the government service all Cubans who fought against the cause of independence. The veterans were induced to modify their demands only by our threat of armed intervention.

A still more serious problem arose almost immediately afterwards in Oriente Province, in eastern Cuba, growing out of a negro agitation for the right to organize a political party on racial lines. This had been specifically forbidden by the Moruá law, passed two years before, designed for the express purpose of suppressing a negro party. The movement to form such a party had been led for several years by Evaristo Estenoz, who always insisted on using the word "colored" to designate his organization. The Estenoz movement assumed a decidedly belligerent attitude in May, 1912. Armed bands of negroes arose in Havana, Santa Clara, and Oriente Provinces while serious outbreaks occurred in the vicinity of Guantanamo and Santiago. The leaders of the movement attempted to prevent its degenerating into a mere race riot, but it soon became greatly feared that such was its marked tendency. By May 20 it had developed into an armed insurrection of considerable force.

The possibility of a black republic at our door seems to have considerably frightened our government and our people as well as the whites in Cuba. Secretary of State Knox was not willing to wait for the Cuban authorities to try to put down the revolt, as Roosevelt had done before intervening in 1906. The American Minister to Cuba, Mr. Beaupré, became very much concerned about the whole affair. He did not appear to have been in on the secret, that the revolution was fomented by the President of Cuba for political purposes, as some writers have claimed. The promptness of the action taken by the United States is partially explained by the urgent demands for the protection of American-owned copper mines, railroads, and sugar properties in Oriente Province. Estenoz deliberately set about to force an intervention in the hopes that his "colored" party would be recognized by the United States as it unfortunately had been by Governor Magoon in 1908.

The negro revolt was at first somewhat widespread but the Cuban forces were soon able to stamp it out except in Havana and in Oriente Province. The situation was complicated in Havana by a strike of stevedores and lighter men, which threatened to cut off the food supply of the city. Estenoz was reported to have issued an order (May 29) to his followers that if the Moruá law had not been repealed by June 1, railroad bridges, telephone and telegraph lines, and other American property should be destroyed; and further if the law were not repealed within the following fifteen days, to begin killing all whites encountered, irrespective of nationality.

Beaupré took the reports of the future plans of the rebels very seriously and apparently believed they indicated the probable course of events. He recommended that battleships be ordered to Key West with a large force of marines on board and that a gunboat be stationed at Nipe Bay. He advised the State Department that Havana was in serious danger of a negro revolt. The situation reached a climax on June 2 when the consulate at Santiago reported that La Maya, a town of four thousand inhabitants, had been burned by the rebels.

In the meantime American-owned corporations, also greatly alarmed over the situation, were urgently requesting protection of their Cuban properties. Measures for their protection were promptly initiated. As early as May 23 the State Department had requested a force of marines and all near-by naval vessels to be sent to Guantanamo. The *Prairie* was immediately ordered to take the First Provisional Regiment of marines to Cuba and the *Nashville* was ordered from Santo Domingo City and the *Paducah* from Santa Cruz, Cuba, to Guantanamo. The flagship and the Third and Fourth Divisions of the Atlantic Fleet, nine battleships, were ordered to take a regiment of marines on board and proceed to Key West. A gunboat was ordered to Nipe Bay. The War Department ordered five thousand soldiers made ready. Knox advised the Cuban Government on May 29 that, if the situation were not brought under control, United States troops would be landed.

The First Provisional Regiment mobilized at the Navy Yard, Philadelphia. Contingents with a total strength of 32 officers and 777 marines arrived from the several marine barracks, hospital detachments, naval prisons, and receiving ships of New York and the New England States within twenty-four hours after receiving orders. The regiment, commanded by Colonel Lincoln Karmany, with all equipment and expeditionary stores, finished embarking on the *Prairie* by 7:30 P.M., May 23. It sailed immediately and arrived at Guantanamo Bay, Cuba, on the 28th and went into camp.

Another regiment of marines, consisting of 40 officers and 1,252 enlisted men under Colonel James E. Mahoney, assembled at New York and Hampton Roads, embarked on ships of the Atlantic Fleet, and went to Key West to await further orders. Its First Battalion was sent to Guantanamo Bay on June 5 and the Second Battalion to Havana on the 10th. The latter unit took no part in the operations ashore which followed. All marines in Cuba were organized into a provisional brigade under Karmany, who established his headquarters at Guantanamo Bay, where it remained during the entire intervention.

In addition to having marines and naval vessels sent to Cuba, Knox insisted that the Cuban armed forces give every possible protection to American property. He requested the Cuban Government to station strong armed forced at Daiquiri, Firmeza, and at El Cobre and made similar requests for guards to protect American interests at other places. These requests for stabilized guards made the situation more difficult for the Cuban commanders who wanted all available troops to run down the rebel bands. The situation was relieved by the marines taking over the guarding of various American properties, relieving the Cuban troops to operate in the field. President Gomez protested at first against sending marines into the

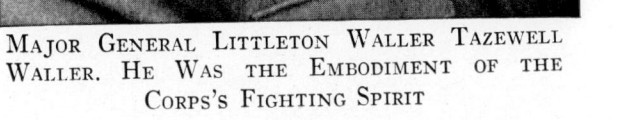

Major General Littleton Waller Tazewell Waller. He Was the Embodiment of the Corps's Fighting Spirit

Colonel Lincoln Karmany (Retired) In His 56th Year of Service

Marine Corps Uniforms, 1912

Marine Corps Uniforms, 1900

interior of Cuba but later saw the advantage of having his troops relieved of guard duty in the towns and on plantations. He then welcomed the marines and was willing to co-operate with them in every possible way and expressed great gratification for the assistance they rendered. The co-operation of Gomez was partially procured by assuring him that the marines would be used only for the protection of American property and would not actively intervene in the affairs of Cuba.

As previously noted, Estenoz wanted to force a military intervention by making the American property owners believe that their Cuban possessions were in great danger of being destroyed. He did not at first intend to do any serious damage. The situation got beyond his control when one of his bands under the leadership of Isidoro Carrera burned the American-owned sugar mill at La Maya. Gomez was of the opinion that Estenoz had gone too far with his plot and asked the Cuban Congress for martial law in Oriente. The request was promptly granted. The rebels next threatened to burn the sugar plantations at Belona. Their forces grew rapidly around Santa Cecilia where Estenoz threatened to burn the sugar company's property. The rebels soon afterwards burned the railroad station and two stores, set fire to the cane fields at Correra Larga, and burned several houses at Palma. Numerous negro bands were threatening havoc in the vicinity of El Cobre and Siboney. It appeared high time for vigorous action.

Urgent requests for the protection of American properties in the general vicinity of Santiago were made to the Commandant, Naval Station, Guantanamo Bay. The Daiquiri Mines near Siboney were reported damaged by the revolutionists; Company A of the First Regiment embarked on the *Paducah* (May 30) and proceeded to the vicinity. It did not land, however, until June 7 when it occupied El Cobre, Puerto Sal, and Hermatanas. The *Paducah* remained in Santiago Bay in close support. One company proved to be insufficient to furnish all the desired protection. The marine detachment at the naval station at Guantanamo Bay and 50 marines from the First Regiment were sent to reinforce the Santiago area. The forces in that district were further strengthened on June 8 by sending 125 additional marines to El Cobre and 60 to Siboney. On the night of June 9-10 a detachment of marines at El Cuero was attacked by rebels, who were repulsed without loss to either side. Lieutenant Colonel John A. Lejeune went to Santiago on June 10 to take command of all marines in that district. Lejeune made his headquarters in Santiago and later placed marine detachments at Ocana, Firmeza, and the Aguadores Railroad Bridge.

Conditions at Manzanillo were reported very threatening at the time the First Regiment landed at Guantanamo Bay. The Central Teresa Sugar Company requested the protection of naval forces. Company H (Captain Frederick L. Bradman) re-embarked on the *Prairie* at Guantanamo Bay on June 1 and proceeded to Manzanillo Bay where it remained for some time watching the situation, but nothing serious happened in that vicinity. The *Prairie* returned to Guantanamo Bay, July 12, and the company of marines was used for other duties.

The remainder of the First Provisional Regiment remained in camp at Guantanamo Bay until June 5 when most of its remaining troops moved into the interior. Three companies under Lieutenant Colonel Lewis C. Lucas went to the general vicinity of Guantanamo City. They were split up into several contingents and occupied Guantanamo City, Soledad, San José, Los Canos, Santa Cecilia, San Justo, Isabel Estate, San Antonio, Romelie, and San Carlos. The two companies of the Second Regiment remaining at Guantanamo Bay were later sent to reinforce the marines in the Guantanamo district.

Early in June reports began to be received of increased rebel activity in Oriente. Sagua was reported burned (June 8) and according to reports rebel forces threatened to attack Mayari. The *Nashville* arrived at Nipe Bay the next day and after investigation reported that the situation was not as critical as had been claimed but recommended that additional forces be sent to the vicinity. The Spanish-American Iron Company urgently requested a force to be landed at Nipe Bay to protect what it alleged was an eight million dollar investment. The marine detachment from the *Missouri* occupied Baracoa on June 9. Fifty-four sailors from the *Nashville* and *Paducah* commanded by Lieutenant E. P. Finney, U.S.N., landed at Preston, Nipe Bay, on June 10 and proceeded by rail to Woodfred to guard some mines, the Spanish-American Iron Works, and other American property. This small force was relieved two days later by the marine detachment of the *Ohio* (Captain R. S. Hooker), which had been hurriedly sent there from Guantanamo Bay on the *Eagle*. Hooker's detachment and the *Missouri* detachment were relieved early in July by Company E of the Second Regiment.

The mission of the marines stationed at various places in Oriente Province was principally that of occupying towns and guarding mining property, sugar plantations, and railroad bridges to prevent their destruction by the rebel faction. They also relieved Cuban troops from guard duties, leaving the Cubans free to run down the rebel groups. The marines also guarded the railroads and trains in the occupied areas. They put into operation a regular system of train guards between San Pré and San Luis. The railroad company later showed its appreciation for the protection afforded by sending in a claim for transportation furnished the marines while acting as guards on the trains. Such payment was recommended by the naval authorities only for transportation furnished when the guarding of the railroad property was not directly concerned.

As usual during interventions of this kind, many requests were received for the protection of lives and property of other foreigners. Protection had been afforded British subjects by the Army of Cuban Pacification (1906-1909); it was again requested by the British Government. The Brazilian Government made a similar request to the State Department, while many foreigners made such requests direct to Naval and Marine Corps commanders in Cuba. Upon request of the State Department the Brigade Commander issued the necessary orders (June 30) to give British nationals the same protection as Americans.

By the middle of June the situation in the vicinity of Santiago quieted down to some extent. General Mendieta, who had command of all Cuban forces in Oriente, established his headquarters at San Luis, and his troops had numerous engagements with the rebellious negro groups in the vicinity. The Cuban forces attacked and dispersed a large rebel band near Juragua on June 12. Two days later a force of Rural Guards made a surprise attack on a rebel camp twelve miles north of Daiquiri and another guard detachment had a successful contact with the rebels near San Luis. Rebel activity in the vicinity of Santiago had increased again by June 19, and it was considered advisable to reinforce the marine garrison at El Cuero by sending the marine detachment of the *Mississippi*. Estanoz' total armed following on June 20 was believed to be about 1,800. He was reported to have a band of 700 near San José and threatening to attack the marines. The rebels also threatened to attack the marines at El Cuero but made no attack at either place. A group of one hundred rebels was reported between El Cuero and El Cobre. A Cuban force was sent against it.

The units assigned and the number of troops at each station in this district as well as the other parts of Cuba were as shown on the following table:

### DISTRIBUTION OF FIRST PROVISIONAL BRIGADE—CUBA
(As of July 1, 1912)

| Organization | Station | Strength |
| --- | --- | --- |
| Brigade Hdqrs. and other troops | Guantanamo Bay | 260 |

### DISTRICT OF SANTIAGO

| Organization | Station | Strength |
|---|---|---|
| Co. A, 1st Regt. | El Cobre | 88 |
|  | Puerto Sal | 11 |
|  | Hermatanas | 4 |
| Co. C, 1st Regt. }<br>Co. B, 2nd Regt. } | Ocana | 94 |
| Co. A, 2nd Regt. | El Cuero | 123 |
| Co. C, 1st Regt. | Firmeza | 52 |
| Co. B, 2nd Regt. | Aguadores Bridge | 39 |

### DISTRICT OF GUANTANAMO

| Organization | Station | Strength |
|---|---|---|
| Co. B, 1st Regt. | Soledad | 75 |
| Co. B, 1st Regt. | San José | 25 |
| Co. C, 2nd Regt. | Guantanamo | 62 |
| Co. E, 1st Regt. | Los Canos | 50 |
|  | Santa Cecilia | 52 |
| Co. F, 1st Regt. | Isabel State | 42 |
|  | San Antonio | 26 |
|  | Romelie | 26 |
|  | San Carlos | 13 |
| Co. G, 1st Regt. (artillery) | Belona | 69 |
| Co. G, 1st Regt. | West Belona | 9 |
|  | Arroyo Piedra | 10 |
|  | Manantial | 9 |
| Co. D, 2nd Regt. | San Luis (La Union) | 53 |
|  | Esperanza | 57 |
| Co. B, 2nd Regt. | Juragua Iron Co.'s Pier, Santiago | 15 |
| Co. E, 2nd Regt. | Baracoa | ½ company |
|  | Mayari | ½ company |

NOTE: Organizations not shown above were aboard vessels of the Atlantic Fleet.

The Cuban Government offered general amnesty to all rebels who would surrender by June 22. Many began turning themselves in on the 19th. Estenoz with a large group continued to annoy the vicinity of Soledad and San José. He was reported killed (June 26) in an engagement at Miraca near Nipe Bay. The report was later confirmed, and his body brought to Santiago (by the Cubans) for identification and exhibition for the benefit of all rebel sympathizers. Some of the remaining rebels began to break up into smaller groups and take to the hills. Many returned to their homes without arms while others surrendered to the Cuban authorities. The Cuban forces continued to have successful engagements with the rebel groups and by the end of June had succeeded in breaking their resistance. A few remaining rebels, in small bands, continued to pillage in the more remote parts of the province. Ibonet, the second most important rebel leader, was reported between San Luis and Guantanamo with his group on July 13. He was defeated soon afterwards and driven into the hills to the north. Cuban forces continued to pursue him but he held out against them for some time.

By the middle of July the general condition of lawlessness in the mining area near Santiago appeared to be at an end. The Cuban Government began to withdraw its troops from Oriente Province, leaving three thousand to handle the situation. By July 20 refugees were everywhere returning to their homes, and from all indications confidence was restored. There was no further need for marines to remain in the interior of Cuba.

The actual withdrawal of the marines from Cuba and the naval vessels from Cuban waters had already begun. The marines on the battleships at Havana returned to the United States early in July. The Secretary of the Navy ordered (July 12) the gradual withdrawal of marines from the Guantanamo district, turning over all posts and stations to the Cuban troops as they could be made available. Cuban troops relieved the marines at San Antonio and Romelie, while the post at Soledad was abandoned. Evacuation of the Guantanamo district was effected by July 23, the troops withdrawing to Guantanamo Bay.

The district of Santiago was evacuated in the same general manner, and this was completed on July 23. The marines at Nipe Bay and Baracoa withdrew to Guantanamo Bay, leaving the *Petrel* stationed at Nipe Bay to furnish temporary protection. All marines in Cuba were concentrated at Guantanamo Bay by July 24. Evacuation to the United States had begun a few days before by the sailing of 7 officers and 217 marines on the *Cyclops* for their regular home stations. Another contingent of 280 sailed on the *Lebanon* August 2 for stations in the New England States. The *Prairie* evacuated the remainder of the expeditionary force, 22 officers and 284 marines, to stations in the Middle Atlantic States.

The Marine Corps was able to settle down to peacetime routine duties for a short breathing spell before entering upon a long period of continuous field duties, which began early in 1914 with an expeditionary brigade going to Vera Cruz, Mexico, and continued until the withdrawal from Haiti in 1933. The operations carried out by the brigade of marines under Karmany in Cuba during 1912 showed that they had learned much since their previous experiences with the Cuban Army of Pacification. The reports submitted by Karmany and his staff are convincing proof that he was master of the situation and knew what was going on at all times. The reports of the previous occupation indicate considerable confusion and lack of knowledge of what was going on and why. The increased efficiency during the second operations was no doubt due to experience in the meantime and to the unquestioned ability of Colonel Karmany.

### The Sugar Intervention, 1917-1922

Although Gomez, with the somewhat passive assistance of the marines, had been able to put down the negro rebellion in Oriente in 1912, his victory did not have the effect that he had hoped for—uniting the country strongly behind him. Due to a split in the Liberal ranks, the Moderates again gained control of the government in 1913. The Liberals were reunited during the next presidential election, but again the Moderates were in control of the election machinery, and the Liberals were everywhere counted out. The Liberals, still under the leadership of Gomez, took up arms even before a new election, which had been ordered, could be held. Our State Department issued a warning to the Cuban people that: it would support only a legally constituted government in Cuba; it would not countenance unlawful and unconstitutional acts; and would hold the leaders of any revolt responsible for the injuries done to foreigners and their property.

The warning had little effect on the rebellious Liberals. Gomez marched on Havana and forced President Menocal to flee. The Liberal revolt grew in strength in central Cuba and many of the garrisons of government troops in the eastern provinces went over to the Liberals. The government troops took possession of both Santiago and Guantanamo and turned those cities over to the Liberals. Revolt broke out in the west but was finally put down by the government troops. Following these successes, Menocal was able to muster sufficient force to invade Santa Clara, the center of the Liberal revolt, and on March 7 captured Gomez with most of his followers. The United States was at the point of declaring war on Germany; its subsequent acts were largely influenced by that factor.

The rebels in eastern Cuba resorted to deliberate destruction of American property and other means of frightening Americans, in the hope of bringing about a speedy intervention. Their depredations promptly caused a flood of requests for protection by American property owners. The maintenance of the supply of sugar was of vital interest to the Allied nations, whom we were at the point of joining. Several sugar mills were closed down in eastern Cuba because of rebel activities and threats.

A division of our battleships was sent to Guacanayabo Bay early in February to be in readiness to protect the sugar production. Additional naval vessels were sent to the vicinity of other important sugar centers in readiness for intervention. Several American corporations having properties in eastern Cuba grew more insistent for protection. The American consul at Santiago recommended immediate intervention (February 22, 1917) in order to prevent great damage to American property. An expeditionary force of marines was again ordered to be made available. A six-company battalion was organized from troops of the First Brigade of Marines at Port au Prince, Haiti, and transferred to Cuba on March 4.

The first actual step towards armed intervention was made primarily to protect the water supply of the naval station at Guantanamo Bay. The water was taken from springs near Guantanamo City, transported by train to Caimanera and then sent by water barge to the station. The water supply was seriously threatened by the rebel forces, who began a systematic burning of near-by cane fields. Rebel forces in the general vicinity continued to increase and become more menacing. Interested American parties protested to the Commanding Officer, Naval Station, and requested protection. That officer decided to act immediately, reported his intentions to the Commander in Chief of the Atlantic Fleet, and on the afternoon of February 25 sent a detachment of 220 marines, made up of the marine guard of the *Montana* and the marines regularly on duty at his station, to Guantanamo City to occupy the town and to prevent the destruction of American property.

The protective measures provided in the vicinity of Guantanamo City soon proved to be insufficient. On March 9 it was reported that the rebels were sending a force to blow up the railroad bridge between San Luis and Ermita Plantation. The Seventh Company of marines, which had arrived at Guantanamo City from Haiti a few days previously, was sent to protect the bridge and to guard the plantation. The 51st Company, which had been doing patrol duty in Santiago, was transferred (March 22) to Guantanamo City.

As previously noted, several battleships had been sent to Guacanayabo Bay to be near important sugar plantations. The plantations were given some protection by the Cuban authorities but on February 12 the Rural Guards withdrew from the property of the Francisco Sugar Company, leaving it with no protection except that which the company could provide. The manager of the company reported (February 25) that conditions were very serious in that vicinity and urgently requested the landing of one hundred marines to protect the sugar mills and plantation. A provisional battalion of marines was organized under Captain C. H. Lyman from the marine detachments of the *Connecticut, Michigan,* and *South Carolina.* The battalion landed on February 25 at the sugar company's wharves on the north shore of the bay and proceeded to the mills and plantation eleven miles inland. It furnished protection to American property and lives in the vicinity but was unable to prevent cane fires on the surrounding plantations.

Locally interested parties greatly feared that if the marines were withdrawn, after once having landed, more serious destruction of property would follow. However, the force was reduced by withdrawing part of the marines a few days later and further reducing the number on March 8, leaving one ship's detachment to guard the property until March 17, when it too withdrew. In the meantime another marine detachment had been sent (March 3) to guard the Rio Cauto Estate, twenty miles northeast of Manzanillo, where serious losses at the hands of the rebels had been reported. The 55th Company of marines from Haiti took over the guarding of the estate about March 10 and sent a detachment to guard the San Francisco Estate. It remained only a few days and was relieved by Cuban troops soon afterwards. The battleships, which had been in the vicinity for more than a month, left for Guantanamo Bay on March 20 and 21. The Cuban forces were able to restore a semblance of order in that vicinity and the 55th Company, the last of the marines ashore in that part of the island, withdrew on March 23.

Conditions around Santiago had not yet become so menacing as in other parts of the country. One or more naval vessels had been kept stationed there since the outbreak of the revolution. Early in March the Liberal forces occupied the town but were unable to hold it. The Liberal Acting Governor of Oriente, José Marcía Muñoz, advised (March 8) Admiral Belknap, the commander of our naval forces in the vicinity, that the Liberal troops could no longer protect Santiago and requested that an American landing force be sent ashore for its security. Belknap agreed, provided all Liberal troops withdraw from the city, and at the same time informed them that they would not be allowed to return unless they delivered their arms to the American forces. A force of 7 officers and 113 men then landed from the *San Francisco.* It was later reinforced by detachments from the *Olympia* and *Machias* and by the 43rd and 51st Companies of marines from Haiti. The marines guarded and patrolled the city and protected valuable American properties in the immediate vicinity.

Outbreaks in eastern Cuba continued for some time; fighting took place between the insurgents and the government troops on several occasions. The rebels continued to destroy cane fields and commit other outrages. Many inhabitants from the rural districts took refuge in the towns. On March 19 the Aguadores Railroad Bridge was found to be on fire, and a guard was sent from the *San Francisco* to prevent its complete destruction. Belknap received repeated requests for the protection of near-by mines. A large group of insurgents was reported in the vicinity of El Cobre mines (March 20) and, to meet the situation, the 43rd Company was sent to Daiquiri to guard the Spanish-American iron mines and La Playa ore docks. The marine detachment of the *Olympia* was sent to guard the El Cobre mines, which prior to that time had been under the protection of a daily guard sent from the *Baltimore*. The *Olympia* sent guards each night to protect the Aguadores Railroad Bridge. The 43rd Company continued to guard the various mining properties in the vicinity until May 24 when it was transferred to the United States.

Along the northern coast of Camaguey and Oriente Provinces, especially around Nipe Bay and Nuevitas Bay, there were still many valuable American properties. That part of Cuba had its part of the general disorder and destruction of property and gave forth its share of outcries for protection. Small naval landing forces were sent ashore at Nuevitas, San Geronimo, and Banes to protect American property. The situation in the vicinity, nevertheless, continued to grow worse, and several engagements took place between the rebels and the regular Cuban forces. By March 20 the rebels were especially strong around Nipe Bay, where they held up trains, robbed stores, and attacked the town of Nipe Bay. The *Machias* was there at the time and had a small landing force ashore but was unable to control the situation. Her few marines and sailors were able to protect only the towns, while the surrounding country was left to the mercy of the rebels.

The 55th Company was transferred to Nipe Bay (March 31) and established posts at Preston, Felton, Woodfred, and Manati. A detachment from that company later went to Baracoa. The government troops finally dispersed the rebel bands in that part of the country, and the situation began to improve. The *Machias* had withdrawn the last of its landing parties by April 11, leaving the 55th Company to take care of the situation. The detachments of that company continued to occupy the above-mentioned place until the company was withdrawn May 25 and transferred to more important duties in France.

The duties performed by the marines in Cuba during the Sugar Intervention were purely for the defense of American lives and property. They influenced the general situation only by guarding the towns and other important places, leaving the regular Cuban troops free to operate against the rebels. The marines had begun a gradual withdrawal from the Guantanama District when the 24th Company returned to its regular stations at Guantanamo Bay on March 28. The Seventh and 51st Companies left early in April, leaving only the 17th Company in the interior of Cuba. Although the main force of the rebels had been broken, they were still operating in small bands, and the situation was by no means under control. Due to the need for troops in the World War, however, the last of the marines were withdrawn from the Guantanamo district (May 23) and returned to the United States.

Cuba entered the World War on the side of the Allied nations soon after the entry of the United States. The question of food for the Allies was then of pressing importance; they could ill afford to have the Cuban sugar supply interrupted by the activities of a few roving bands, probably instigated by German agents. Our government decided (July, 1917) to send a regiment of cavalry to the sugar producing part of Cuba as a stabilizing force. The necessary plans and reconnaissances were made by army officers, but it was later decided in a White House conference that an army regiment could not be spared and that a regiment of marines should be sent instead. The Cuban Government agreed to co-operate with its troops in Camaguey and Oriente Provinces—the center of the sugar industry. The army plans were turned over to the Marine Corps for execution.

Pursuant to the plan again to send marines to Cuba, the Seventh Marines was organized at Philadelphia under Lieutenant Colonel Melville J. Shaw in August, 1917. They were transferred to Cuba and encamped at Guantanamo Bay, where they underwent a period of two months' training. Late in October some of the companies occupied important centers in the sugar-growing district. The 37th and 72nd Companies, organized as a provisional battalion, under Major Frank Halford, were stationed at Camaguey. The 59th and 86th Companies went into camp at San Juan Hill, just outside of Santiago, where the Headquarters of the regiment moved early in November. The 90th Company was sent to Engenio Confluente near Guantanamo City. The remainder of the regiment moved into the interior early in November, two companies going to San Juan Hill and the 93rd Company to Central la Union and San Luis. The regiment was re-enforced by two companies from Quantico, which joined the force at San Juan Hill late in November. The 94th Company was sent to Bayamo (December 11) for regular station, in compliance with the request of the American Minister and the approval of the Cuban Government.

The assignment of marines to the above-mentioned places remained practically unchanged during the following years. They were engaged primarily as a stabilizing force. They carried on their usual training and made long practice marches for moral effect, visiting different parts of the provinces in which they were stationed but engaged in no military intervention. During December, 1917, the marines in Cuba were increased to a brigade by the addition of a brigade headquarters and the Ninth Marines and designated as the Third Brigade. Colonel James E. Mahoney, who arrived with his headquarters at Guantanamo Bay on December 24, took command. The Ninth Marines, which had been organized at Quantico under Lieutenant Colonel F. L. Bradman, arrived with Mahoney. The Ninth Marines and Brigade Headquarters remained in camp at Guantanamo Bay until July 31, 1918, when, with the exception of two companies which joined the marine detachment at that place, they were transferred to Galveston, Texas, for duty.

On November 8, 1918, the First Marines (Colonel Thomas C. Treadwell), which had remained in Philadelphia since the outbreak of the World War, arrived at Guantanamo Bay for advanced training. The marines in Cuba were again organized into a brigade under Treadwell and designated the Sixth Marine Brigade. The Second Machine Gun Battalion, commanded by Major Julian C. Smith, joined the Brigade at Santiago (January 26, 1919) and was stationed at Camp San Juan.

Treadwell's brigade began to withdraw from Cuba in May, 1919. The Second Machine Gun Battalion was transferred first to Guantanamo Bay and in June returned to the United States. The First Regiment and Sixth Brigade Headquarters were disbanded and the personnel transferred during June. The Seventh Marines remained in Cuba and continued to occupy approximately the same stations until August, 1919, when the marine force in Cuba was reduced to a two-company battalion stationed at Camaguey. The remainder of the regiment assembled at Guantanamo Bay and returned to the United States. The occuption of Camaguey continued until February 6, 1922, when the battalion withdrew to Guantanamo Bay and was absorbed into the garrison at that station.

Cuba, during the ten years following the last occupation by marines, was governed most of the time by a fairly strong but notoriously corrupt government. That, together with several years of prosperity, made for sufficient internal stability to obviate the necessity of military intervention under the Platt Amendment. The depression of 1929, however, started a serious turn of affairs which came near a revolution in 1932. The explosion was postponed for a time by repressive measures, amounting to a reign of terror, imposed by President Machado. A revolutionary faction sought the intervention of the United States where, in the meantime, considerable public opinion was growing which demanded a revision of our policy towards Cuba. The revolutionists overthrew Machado. Provisional governments followed in rapid succession. The United States made a treaty of general relations (1934) with one régime, which, among other things, abolished the Platt Amendment and brought to an end the American protectorate over Cuba which had existed for more than thirty years.

A number of precautionary steps were taken by our naval forces during the latter revolutionary period in Cuba, which looked only to the protection of American lives. A number of vessels were kept in Cuban waters during the period, and a battalion of marines was kept on board a vessel ready for use during part of the period but never landed on Cuban soil.

## Chapter XIII

### OCCUPATION OF THE DOMINICAN REPUBLIC

Our right of mediation in the affairs of Latin-American countries was further extended and intervention in the Dominican Republic was justified by President Theodore Roosevelt in his corollary to the Monroe Doctrine, which asserted that since the United States did not permit other countries to intervene for the protection of the rights of their nationals, it became our duty to intervene for their protection. The Dominican Government had for some time been heavily indebted to a number of foreign creditors, principally European, and had pledged its custom duties as security for the indebtedness. The country was practically bankrupt in 1904, and its European creditors were urging definite action to protect their interests.

Roosevelt proposed a financial supervision under the general direction of the United States. He suggested, in effect, that the United States should act as a kind of receiver in bankruptcy, looking after the interests of all creditors. His plan was drafted into a protocol and submitted to the Senate, which, after some delay, refused to ratify it. Roosevelt, nevertheless, by a mutual working agreement with the Dominican Republic, set up the supervision, and a few years later the Senate agreed to the installation of a general receiver of customs under the protection of the United States, which was to continue until the bonded foreign indebtedness had been paid in full. The arrangement worked very well for a few years until interrupted by internal Dominican disorders.

Such disorders or even foreign intervention was nothing new in the history of the Dominican Republic. Ever since the overthrow of Spanish rule in 1844, its history had consisted largely of a continual round of internal disorders, wars with Haiti, attempts by Spain to reconquer the country, financial exploitation by foreign capitalists and occasional intervention by other countries. During President Grant's administration it was only by the Senate's rejection of a treaty of annexation that Santo Domingo missed becoming a part of the United States. Like the people of some of its sister Latin-American republics, the people of Santo Domingo were lacking in political capacity. The country was usually under the control of dictators, who managed by various means to establish themselves in power.

Financing the government was made more difficult by the expense of putting down, or of trying to put down, insurrections which occurred at frequent intervals. The expense of combatting rebellion was particularly heavy for a number of months following the assassination of President Cáceres in November, 1911. Eladio Victoria was elected as Cáceres' successor, by compulsion of the army, but some of the other political leaders refused to acknowledge him as President and started a revolt. The customs service was interrupted, particularly along the Haitian border, where the rebels captured and held several forts.

In an effort to help adjust the difficulties during the following year, the United States sent two commissioners, supported by the Second Provisional Regiment (750 marines under Colonel Franklin J. Moses) on board the U.S.S. *Prairie,* to Santo Domingo City (Ciudad Trujillo). The Commission with its supporting troops was fully prepared to re-establish the lost customs houses for the government and to protect other customs houses, if necessary. The marines were placed practically under the command of the Commission, to co-operate "as fully as circumstances render possible in complying with their requests, and in furthering a successful solution of their mission." Moses' regiment (with the exception of one company on board the U.S.N.A. *Caesar* off Sanchez and Monte Cristi) remained on board the *Prairie* at Santo Domingo City during the negotiations which continued for nearly two months. The Commission, with the moral support of the marines supplemented by a threat to withhold all customs money, reached an agreement with the revolutionist leaders and succeeded in persuading the objectionable President to resign. The Dominican Congress elected (December 1, 1912) Monsignor Nouel, the Archbishop of Santo Domingo, as Provisional President for two years. The regiment of marines withdrew from Dominican waters and returned to Philadelphia.

The Archbishop was given every possible moral support by the United States. The revolutionists ceased their open warfare for the time being but later refused to co-operate with the central

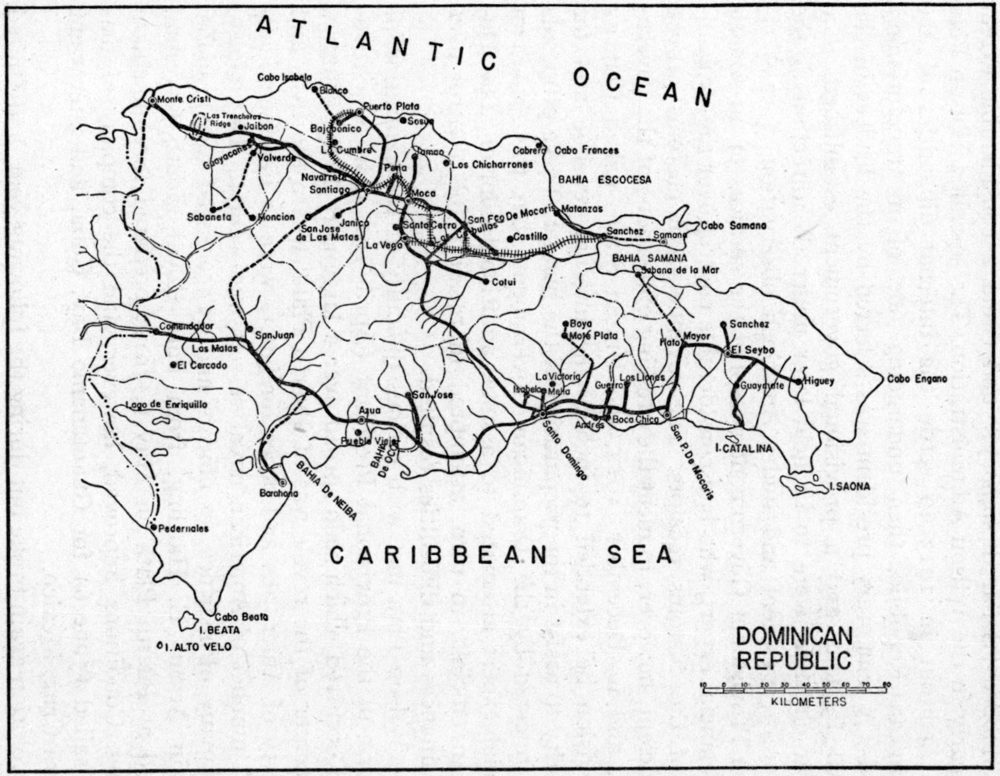

MAP OF THE DOMINICAN REPUBLIC

government unless certain impossible demands were fulfilled. Nouel thereupon declined to serve as president any longer and in March, 1913, left for Europe.

The policy of the United States Government towards the Dominican Republic and other countries of the Caribbean area, which had been dubbed "dollar diplomacy," underwent a considerable extension early in the Wilson Administration. The so-called Wilson Plan was tried out in 1913 to settle the internal difficulties of the Dominican Republic, then undergoing one of its revolutionary periods. A temporary president was selected by the leaders of the several factions and a provisional government established. The regular elections were to be held later under the direction of the temporary president and under American observation.

The Provisional Government accepted the services of an American financial expert, who had considerable control over the expenditure of the customs receipts. The revenue from customs proved insufficient, however, to meet the pressing obligations of the government, and in December, 1914, the United States asked that its supervision be extended to include the internal revenue and for authority to assist in the preparation of the budget. These proposals were rejected by the Dominican Government; but the American financial expert attempted to assume additional control. The Dominican officials, in turn, attempted to reassert full control over their finances and difficulties resulted.

The Wilson Plan met with serious difficulty at the expiration of the term of the Provisional President (April, 1914), when a revolution occurred which soon spread over a large part of the country. The center of the revolt was at Puerto Plata, where the lives and property of Americans and other foreigners were in imminent danger. A number of American naval vessels were sent to the vicinity. A company of marines (3 officers and 125 enlisted men), under Captain Arthur E. Harding, from Port Royal, South Carolina, arrived at Puerto Plata on May 6, 1914, prepared for immediate landing. Conditions improved, however, and the company of marines sailed (June 6) for Guantanamo Bay, Cuba, and later went to Vera Cruz, Mexico.

Revolution again broke out during the following year, and United States naval forces were stationed at various ports of the Dominican Republic. The Fifth Regiment of Marines, under Colonel Charles A. Doyen, sailed on board the U.S.S. *Hancock* from Guantanamo Bay and arrived at Puerto Plata on August 15, 1915. A few days later the regiment went to San Pedro de Macoris and from there to Santo Domingo City, where it remained until October 12. Captain E. W.

Eberle, U.S.N., (senior naval officer present in Dominican waters) had, by that time, with the support of the regiment of marines and other naval forces, been able to persuade the leaders of the revolution to disband their forces.

Combatting revolutions in the Dominican Republic led to continual excessive expenditure for its army, whose support was assured "only at the cost of a disastrous financial and political concession." William J. Bryan, Secretary of State at the time, took the position that our government should vigorously back the existing Dominican Government and hold all leaders of opposing factions personally responsible for their pernicious revolutionary activities. He initiated a far-reaching policy of maintaining a responsible government in the Dominican Republic, of giving the Dominican people the opportunity to develop its resources, and of putting an end to graft and waste in its government. He notified the President of the country of his intention and made ready a naval force to support his demands.

Resistance against the wishes of the United States by the Dominican Government grew rapidly during the early part of 1915; Dominican political conditions showed no improvement. Bryan further demanded (in November) that a financial adviser, designated by the United States and having broad powers, be immediately appointed and that a Dominican constabulary be established under American officers. The Dominican Government refused to agree to this, and political conditions in the country went from bad to worse.

Desiderio Arias, a leader of one of the rebellious factions, took advantage of a political disturbance in Santo Domingo City and occupied one of the city's forts with a band of followers. Arias' force was soon sufficiently augmented by malcontents from the government faction joining it, to assure him control of the city. Jiminez, who had been elected president under the Wilson Plan, unable to muster sufficient force to stop Arias, left the city. Arias proceeded further, by persuasion and coercion, to have the congress initiate the impeachment of Jiminez. The United States offered military support to Jiminez, which he at first agreed to accept but later flatly rejected.

The American Minister, W. W. Russell, anticipating that any intervention by the United States might precipitate violent reaction against our citizens in the Dominican Republic, asked (May 3, 1916) that additional naval vessels be sent to Dominican waters for their protection, particularly at Puerto Plata, Macoris, and Sanchez. Two destroyers were ordered to each of those towns and two additional naval vessels were sent to Rear Admiral William B.

Caperton at Port au Prince, Haiti, who was at the time in command of naval forces in both Haitian and Dominican waters.

A brigade of marines, consisting of the First and Second Regiments and an artillery battalion, was engaged, at the time, in putting down disorders and attempting to restore peace in the adjoining Haitian Republic. The marines of that brigade were the only ones immediately available for duty in the Dominican Republic. The Sixth and Ninth Companies, commanded by Captain F. M. Wise, were sent from Port au Prince on the *Prairie* to Santo Domingo City to be in readiness for a military intervention.

The government forces led by Jiminez were at the time making a feeble effort to re-establish control over the Dominican capital. The American naval and diplomatic authorities held a conference with Arias but, being unable to persuade him to come to any reasonable terms, determined to take the necessary steps at least to assure the protection of the American Legation and of Americans and foreigners in the city. In anticipation that an actual landing at any point would arouse considerable hostile feelings in all parts of the country, they called for additional troops to be used as reinforcements and landing forces at other important ports, particularly at Puerto Plata, Macoris, and Sanchez.

The *Prairie* and the *Castine* were the only American naval vessels present at Santo Domingo City on May 5 when, due to the disorder in the city and the fighting of the two contending factions, a landing of troops could no longer be postponed. The commanding officer of the *Prairie*, the senior naval officer present, in accordance with his instructions and after a conference with Russell, decided on immediate armed intervention. The two companies of marines from the *Prairie* landed and went to protect the American Legation, while the marine detachment of the *Castine* landed to guard the Haitian Legation. A detachment of about 130 sailors also landed and seized Fort San Geronimo, which they held as a base for the forces ashore. The city proper, however, was not entered at that time. There was an estimated force of several hundred rebels, well supplied with ammunition, holding the city. The weaker government forces in the vicinity had very little ammunition and could not be counted upon materially to assist the landing forces had they become engaged with Arias.

The American forces being unable to cope with the situation, Caperton ordered the Fourth Company from Port au Prince on the *Culgoa* and 150 marines from the naval station at Guantanamo Bay on the *Hector* to Santo Domingo City. At the request of Jiminez the Americans planned an attack, to be supported by the fire of the *Prairie* and the *Castine,* to drive the rebels from the city. Jiminez later refused to accept the aid of the Americans and called off the attack. It was obviously too great a task for the little American force alone to undertake the capture of the city. They resorted rather to bluff and persuasion.

The situation became less tense for a time; the *Culgoa* delayed until it could go to Cap Haitien for an additional company of marines. The *Culgoa* then brought both companies to Santo Domingo City, where they landed at Fort San Geronimo. Admiral Caperton, who had arrived on May 12, took direct command of the operation. The marines from Guantanamo joined the forces ashore at Santo Domingo City on the following day. Caperton, after a consultation with Russell, demanded the immediate surrender of all rebel forces and the disarming of all persons in the city. He warned the rebel leaders that, if his demands were not complied with by 6 A.M., May 15, he would occupy the city and disarm them by force. Arias and other rebel leaders, with about two hundred followers including a group of released convicts, evacuated the city in the early morning of May 14.

In accordance with his previously announced plans, Caperton took over the city. Major Newt H. Hall, who had arrived with Caperton, entered the city over the north wall with the battalion of marines and occupied its most important points. A battalion of sailors from four naval vessels present joined in this operation. While no resistance was encountered, there was considerable indication that the occupation was greatly resented by the inhabitants.

Shortly after his leaving the city, the Dominican Congress started impeachment proceedings against Jiminez. Being unable to retain his power and unwilling to call upon the American forces for help, he resigned his position, leaving the government in control of his cabinet, which remained in the city. A long struggle over the selection of a provisional president followed between Caperton and Russell on the one hand and the Dominican authorities on the other. The Americans knew that if the Dominican Congress elected a president, he would undoubtedly be the highly undesirable Arias; they, therefore, made every effort to forestall such action. They deemed it advisable to delay the selection of a president until order could be restored.

In the meantime plans had been made to land American troops at the other leading ports of Santo Domingo as soon as possible. At the request of the Dominican Government, however, the landings were delayed for several days even after troops had arrived at the different ports, to permit a Dominican commission to ascertain whom the country desired as president. In the meantime Colonel T. P. Kane, with three additional companies of marines, arrived at Santo Domingo City, reinforced the troops ashore and assumed command. Arias with his followers repaired to Santiago, which had for some time been his principal place of support. Disorder continued throughout the country. On May 30 Caperton ordered the troops, which had been waiting at several ports, to land.

## Taking of Puerto Plata

The marine detachments from the *Rhode Island* and the *New Jersey* were at the time on board the *Salem,* supported by the *Sacramento,* at Puerto Plata. Commander R. C. Bulmer, of the *Sacramento,* in accordance with orders from Caperton, notified the acting rebel governor, Rey, that it was his intention to land a force and occupy the town. Rey strongly protested against such action by the American forces and declared his intentions to resist the landing to the utmost. By parades and other means, Rey managed to stir up considerable anti-American feeling. Two forts defended the town; both were occupied by the rebels. Bulmer notified all foreigners of his intentions and advised them either to come aboard his vessel or otherwise get out of danger.

Early in the morning of June 1, under the cover of a bombardment of the forts by supporting naval vessels, a small battalion consisting of the two marine guards and a naval detachment (about two hundred men under Major Charles B. Hatch) effected a landing in the face of heavy rifle fire. With the sailors leading, the battalion had headed for a slightly sheltered cove, landed and made a charge on one of the forts, which it soon captured together with the surrounding high ground. The rebels, occupying positions which gave them considerable shelter, continued to fire on Hatch's battalion. A few well-aimed shots from the *Sacramento*'s 4-inch guns, however, soon drove the rebels from their shelter and ended their resistance. The only casualties to the landing force was a marine slightly wounded and Captain J. H. Hirshinger, U.S.M.C., mortally wounded while yet in one of the boats. The landing force soon gained control of the town, and the rebels retreated to the south.

## The Landing at Monte Cristi

The *Panther* with the marine detachment of the *Louisiana* arrived at Monte Cristi on May 25, and its commander, Harris Lanning, attempted to negotiate peaceful settlement with the rebel leaders. The towns in the vicinity were under the control of the rebels but were fairly peaceful and quiet. Lanning's efforts to persuade the former governor to resume his office and the acting rebel governor to retire proved futile. In accordance with his orders from Caperton, Lanning notified the rebel governor of his intention to land and occupy the town. The rebels retired. The *Louisiana*'s marines and a detachment of sailors landed early in the morning of May 26 and occupied Monte Cristi without resistance. A part of the troops occupied the fort while others advanced through the town and took possession of it. After that had been accomplished, the rebels saw how small the American force was and immediately began threatening to drive it out. They were expected to attack on June 3; the town was highly excited. The landing party was reinforced by all available men from the ships, about one hundred in all; but the rebel attack did not materialize.

Taking advantage of the extra troops ashore, Captain F. M. Wise with about sixty marines made a reconnaissance towards the ferry and waterworks on the river south of the city. Much to his surprise, he encountered the rebels between the river and the city. Their outpost promptly retired but soon afterwards they charged Wise with their main body. The marines attempted to stop them with rifle fire which was not immediately effective; but Wise brought his machine guns into action, and the rebels fled almost immediately. The position being too exposed to hold with such a small force, Wise returned to the fort in Monte Cristi. Our landing forces encountered no further resistance by the Dominican rebels in that vicinity. Arias with his main force at Santiago continued to incite the rebels throughout northern Santo Domingo; Lanning strongly recommended that Santiago also be occupied.

The rebel forces continued to grow rapidly throughout most of the country, particularly in the northern part. It became obvious that the small landing forces ashore at Monte Cristi and Puerto Plata were not even strong enough to hold those places, let alone take the field against Arias' forces. Caperton requested substantial reinforcement of troops; the Fourth Regiment of marines was ordered from San Diego via New Orleans to report to him in Santo Domingo. A battalion of sailors landed at Santo Domingo City and took over the holding of that place, relieving Kane's marines, who recently had been reinforced by Major R. H. Dunlap's marine battalion of artillery and the Fourth and Sixth Companies. Kane left on the *Memphis* (June 8) to reinforce the landing forces in northern Santo Domingo, where, by virtue of his rank, he assumed command of all marines ashore. He landed two companies to reinforce Hatch's battalion at Puerto Plata and proceeded to Monte Cristi with the remainder of his forces and landed. Kane with the two detachments held Monte Cristi until the Fourth Regiment arrived, when he joined in the advance into the interior.

Caperton and Russell continued to negotiate with the different factions and managed to delay the selection of a provisional president. Conditions in the northern part of the country quieted down to some extent but by the middle of June grew worse again; fighting broke out in several localities.

## The Fourth Regiment

The Fourth Regiment, under Colonel J. H. Pendleton, arrived at Santo Domingo City on June 18, and Pendleton took command of all naval forces ashore. He proceeded with his regiment to Monte Cristi, where he arrived three days later. Caperton authorized all commanders ashore to establish martial law, whenever in their opinion they considered it necessary. Pendleton landed his regiment and immediately began to make arrangements for an advance on Santiago, which, together with Moca and La Vega, he had orders to occupy if he considered such action necessary.

The preparations for an advance into the heart of the rebel area with a considerable force caused great excitement throughout the country. Many influential Dominicans advised against such a move and tried to delay its execution. The preparation for the invasion proceeded, however, and in the early morning of June 26, Pendleton left Monte Cristi with a column of 33 officers and 800 marines, leaving 5 officers and 230 men at Monte Cristi to hold that place. Another column, consisting of the Fourth and Ninth Companies, started from Puerto Plata for Navarette, where they were to join Pendleton's column and help take Santiago. Pendleton, upon arriving at Navarette, planned to shift his line of communication to the railroad from Puerto Plata and abandon his communications with Monte Cristi. Pendleton's column covered about twenty-four kilometers during the first day's march without meeting any resistance. From the point where the regiment camped during that night, a ridge called Las Trencheras, could be seen about three kilometers farther east, crossing the line of march. It was soon discovered that this commanding position was entrenched with two lines of resistance and held by a considerable force of rebels. The situation demanded the driving of the rebel force from the position as soon as possible before they could be reinforced.

## Las Trencheras

Pendleton had a single battery of artillery placed in position to cover the first line of trenches, while a machine gun company was placed to cover it from a flanking position. The regiment was deployed in line (early June 27) and, under cover of the supporting fire, worked up to an effective firing position. The advance was soon temporarily stopped by heavy fire from the rebels' front line. There appears to have been some lack of co-ordination at first between the two battalions; but that was soon overcome by the energetic efforts of Major Dunlap, acting chief of staff for Pendleton. Dunlap not only caused unity of action between the two battalions but assumed command of some front line units and led them to the final assault which, ending in a bayonet attack, quickly drove the rebels from their first defensive line.

The enemy retired to a second line of trenches higher up the ridge from which the marines easily drove them with their rifle fire. The attack was the first experience of marines advancing with the support of modern artillery and machine guns. Las Trencheras had been for many years considered impregnable. On it the Dominicans had successfully defied the Spaniards in the 1860's. Its capture was a great moral victory for Pendleton. In this rather extensive engagement the marines lost but one killed and four wounded.

## On to Santiago

The column resumed its march the following morning but was delayed by impassable roads and the necessity of repairing bridges that had been destroyed. One battalion was left temporarily at Trencheras to protect the line of communication. Despite the many difficulties, Pendleton succeeded in advancing about fifteen kilometers and camped in a well-protected position. The rebels attacked the camp during the night but were driven off with severe losses and, while retreating, ran into one of the marine outposts and were again punished severely. The Dominicans did not again attempt night operations against Pendleton's marines. The battalion which had been left to guard the line of communication rejoined the regiment on June 29. The column pushed on for a few more kilometers against resistance offered by the rebels who had been driven out of Las Trencheras.

During the following day more bad roads and destroyed bridges delayed the march but the column reached Jaibon. On June 30 they fought two battles, losing only one marine killed. They spent the next two days in bringing up troops and supplies from the rear. All communications with Monte Cristi were then abandoned and the regiment became, in Pendleton's words, a "flying column." The situation was quite delicate until a new line of communication could be established over the railroad from Navarette. Contrary to Pendleton's hopes that serious engagements in which men were wounded might be avoided, the regiment again became engaged on July 3 with a considerable force of rebels at Guayacanas in which one marine corporal was killed and eight marines wounded. Pendleton resumed the march the following day, taking care of the wounded as best he could on top of the motor trucks and in some Ford cars which accompanied the column. He reached Navarette without again becoming seriously engaged, established communication with Major H. I. Bearss's battalion, and successfully evacuated his wounded by rail to Puerto Plata.

## The Puerto Plata Column

On June 26, the Fourth and Ninth companies of marines, leaving their base at Puerto Plata protected by the ships' detachments, advanced by rail on Navarette. It was necessary to protect the train's movement at times by an advanced guard on foot. The detachment halted for the first night at Terez and established the necessary protection against the enemy—then reported to be only two miles ahead. During the second day they drove the enemy from two successive positions and advanced the train a short distance. The detachment reached a railroad bridge during the forenoon of the 28th just in time to save it from destruction by a fire started by the retreating rebels. Bearss arrived that night with the *New Jersey* detachment of marines and took command of the detached force—then styled the "railroad battalion."

On the following day the enemy was again encountered on a ridge pierced by a railroad tunnel. The battalion attacked the position by the unusual maneuver of sending a detachment through the tunnel to cut off the retreating enemy; but the rebels retreated too quickly to be caught and fled towards Santiago. They made no further resistance of any consequence. Bearss's battalion reached Navarette and joined Pendleton on July 2. A great deal of work had become necessary for the railroad battalion to maintain communications with the rear and repair damaged bridges ahead of the train. The 24th Company of marines came by rail from Puerto Plata and joined the consolidated column on July 5.

## The Occupation of Santiago

Resistance of the rebels by this time was almost completely broken. A peace commission came out from Santiago to meet Pendleton on July 5 and accepted Caperton's demand for the occupation of the city. The Dominicans, nevertheless, tried to delay the entry of Pendleton's troops into Santiago. Fearing that any delay might result in giving the demoralized rebels a chance to reorganize, Pendleton pushed his column closer to the city on the afternoon of July 5 and marched up to a position overlooking it early the following morning. This movement took the Dominicans completely by surprise, and they immediately made arrangements for the marines to enter the town peacefully. Pendleton's forces occupied Santiago including Castillo and Fortaleza San Luis (outlying forts) that afternoon. The occupation of Santiago admittedly was a much tougher proposition than had been anticipated, but much to the credit of all concerned, it was successfully accomplished. A number of both officers and enlisted men were later rewarded for their heroic and distinguished conduct during the operation.

The repeated defeats of the Dominican rebels had greatly demoralized them, and for a time they were inactive. A number of rebel bands gave up and turned in their arms and ammunition. The efforts to obtain a government that would comply with the wishes of the American authorities were continued. The Dominican Congress refused to delay longer and on July 25 elected Dr. Francisco Henriquez y Carvajal temporary president for a period of six months. The American controlled customs service extended its control to include the internal revenue. Payments from both sources to the Dominican Government were suspended on August 18, thus holding a whip over the newly elected president and greatly restricting his running the government. Carvajal submitted a treaty to the American authorities on September 20 acceding to practically all their demands, except the control of a native military force by American officers. The State Department rejected Carvajal's proposition; the Dominican President refused to make further concessions and attempted to call a general election in November. Since it was known that the result of such an election would most likely be against the American wishes, and the new government would probably be under the influence of Arias, the State Department recommended that more drastic steps looking to a stable government in the country be taken.

In the meantime the marines in the Dominican Republic had occupied the towns of which they had previously taken possession and extended their control over several additional important centers of population. The towns of Moca, La Vega, and San Francisco de Macoris, lying generally to the southeast of Santiago, were occupied by permanent detachments of marines during July. They established two posts along the northern shore of Samana Bay. In addition to collecting the arms which were turned in by rebels, large reconnaissance groups of marines went to various parts of the country, not occupied by permanent detachments. Patrols rounded up certain troublesome leaders. One patrol operation resulted disastrously to the marines. While attempting to arrest Roman Batista, a notorious rebel leader, Captain Low and First Sergeant Atwood were killed by Dominicans who had rallied to Batista's aid; Batista also was shot during the affray which ensued.

The distribution of the marines, organized by that time (October 31) as the Second Brigade, was as follows:

| Place | Officers | Men |
|---|---|---|
| Santiago | 13 | 514 |
| Santo Domingo City | 22 | 520 |
| Moca | 3 | 79 |
| Navarette | 1 | 60 |
| Puerto Plata | 1 | 98 |
| Monte Cristi | 1 | 98 |
| San Francisco de Macoris | 2 | 125 |
| Sanchez | 2 | 100 |
| La Vega | 1 | 82 |
| La Cumbre | 1 | 62 |
| Total | 47 | 1738 |

### Establishing Military Government

Military government throughout the Dominican Republic was proclaimed on November 29 by Captain Harry S. Knapp, U.S.N., who had just assumed command of our naval forces in Dominican and Haitian waters. His proclamation, which had been drawn up in the State Department and approved by President Wilson, declared that the purpose of the occupation was to establish good government, peace, and prosperity to the country; and that the United States had no intention of assuming permanent control over it. Knapp, by virtue of his rank and position, became Military Governor. He immediately put into effect vigorous measures, such as forbidding the possession of firearms and establishing strict censorship, to restore peace in the country. Knapp at first intended that most of the civil government should be conducted by Dominican officials but, due to the refusal of the cabinet members to continue in office and his inability to persuade other qualified Dominicans to replace them, he found it necessary to fill all of those important positions with American officers. The problems of financial control and relations with the United States were obviously solved for the time being by the drastic method of resorting to military government.

On the whole the Dominicans submitted peacefully to the new order of things. Many of them felt that it was the only logical solution to their difficulties. A few leaders, however, held out against the Military Government and caused some difficulty for the marines during the succeeding months. This was particularly true at San Francisco de Macoris and vicinity, where Governor Perez refused to submit.

The situation in that town was rather delicate for the little marine garrison under First Lieutenant E. C. Williams, who was opposed not only by the followers of Perez, but also faced the possibility of having the hundred criminals confined in the Fortaleza released and armed to join the rebellious forces. The fort had not yet been taken over by the marines, but had been left under the control of a small body of native troops. The situation had apparently preyed on Williams' mind, and when he received the order to establish military government, during the evening of November 20, he immediately attacked and captured the fort with a mere handful of men, performing one of the most daring exploits in the history of the Marine Corps.

With only a dozen men immediately available, he rushed the gate of the fortress; but before he could reach it eight of his party were wounded by the rifle fire of the defenders. With the four remaining men Williams pressed on, threw himself against the door, just as it was being closed by the Dominicans, and forced an entry. His death was narrowly averted by the prompt action of Drummer Schovan who, when Williams' pistol had jammed, jumped in front of him and grabbed the rifle of a Dominican who was attempting to fire at Williams from a distance of only about four feet. Once inside, Williams and his men killed two of the guards and within a very few minutes had control not only of the fort but also of the one hundred prisoners. Another detachment of marines of Williams' garrison had, in the meantime, taken possession of the police station. Williams later received the Congressional Medal of Honor for his prompt and heroic conduct.

Perez, at San Francisco de Macoris with some two hundred followers, was in the meantime acting almost as rapidly as Williams—in getting out of the town by train. His escape into the country, however, and his having a considerable number of well-armed followers caused considerable concern to the other near-by marine garrisons. The marines at Sanchez were promptly relieved by a naval landing force and started by train to the center of the trouble. At approximately the same time, sixty marines left La Vega by train on the same mission. Both experienced delays en route; the marines from Sanchez were derailed and forced to march part of the way. Shortly after the reinforcements had arrived at San Francisco de Macoris, its defenses were improved and several strong patrols started after Perez and his followers. The patrols had several contacts with Perez, whose force they gradually broke up and drove to the south.

## The Military Government

The central government of the country was administered in the face of many difficulties. The officers who filled the cabinet positions all had long careers in the naval service but were of course quite unaccustomed to running the executive departments of a strange country, with whose political conditions and internal problems they were none too familiar. Pendleton was initially placed in charge of the Departments of War and Navy, Interior, and Police. Colonel R. H. Lane was for a considerable time the head of the Departments of Foreign Relations, Justice, and Public Instruction. Other departments were administered by naval officers of the Military Governor's staff. The departments having to do with more technical affairs, such as Exchequeur and Commerce, Public Works, and Sanitation were gradually placed under naval staff officers with special qualifications along those particular lines. Some of the customs houses were supervised by officers of the Navy Supply Corps.

The lesser officials and clerks who had been serving the Dominican Government were, as a rule, willing to carry on their duties, particularly since arrangements were made for the immediate resumption of their salaries, which had been suspended for some months. The Dominican judiciary generally remained at their posts and with the aid of the marines, and later the Guardia, carried on their normal functions. The relations between the inhabitants and the occupying forces, as in any military government, was a matter of special arrangement. A system of provost courts and eventually a provost department, covering the entire country, was developed. The provost department maintained a special office in each of the more important towns where the marines were stationed and in the provincial capitals. The provost marshals were the representatives of the Military Government and they alone dealt directly with the inhabitants. The provost personnel had a wide range of duties, particularly before the Guardia was fully organized.

## Disarming the People

In the Dominican Republic, most of the male inhabitants were in the habit of going about armed in some manner. The problem

MARINE PATROL AT SAN PEDRO DE MACORIS, D. R.

MARINES WITH PACK TRAIN, SEIBO, D. R.

JOSEPH H. (UNCLE JOE) PENDLETON (RETIRED)
BELOVED LEADER OF MARINES IN NICARAGUA, DOMINICAN REPUBLIC, ETC.

of completely disarming the civil population, which had already been started, proved to be one of the most difficult tasks of the Military Government and the Marine Brigade. The local officials, in co-operation with the agents of the Brigade Commander and the representatives of the provost department and later the Guardia personnel, did most of the actual collecting of arms. In some localities, however, the local officials resisted the process and, in extreme cases, it was necessary to resort to a house-to-house search and use pressure methods in order to induce the giving up of arms. The process was very slow and the disarming was never more than partially completed. But, during the first year and a half under the Military Government, approximately 53,000 firearms and 14,000 cutting weapons were collected. Firearms were reissued to well-selected and responsible individuals for their own protection and to those entrusted to assist in maintaining law and order.

After the initial campaign and the application of the necessary force for the establishment of military government throughout the country, the Second Brigade's duty was to provide the necessary force to support the Military Government. The marines were distributed at important towns throughout the country, particularly in civic and economic centers, in places of political unrest and in bandit-infested areas. Due regard was had in their distribution for the protection of the American-operated customs houses. The country was divided into two military districts—Northern and Southern—separated by an east and west mountain range. Each district was garrisoned by a regiment of marines, supported by certain auxiliary troops. The worst trouble center was in the eastern part of the country, where considerable activity by the marines operating against bandit groups continued until as late as 1922.

## Combatting Lesser Groups

The breaking up of the Perez group was only the beginning of a long series of similar operations which lasted for about six months before the resistance of organized groups—with claim of political character—was overcome and a degree of order established in the country. At the beginning, some of the groups were of considerable strength; but in time they were either captured, persuaded to give themselves up, killed off, or broken up into smaller groups. At first the operations against them partook somewhat of the nature of guerrilla warfare; after a time, they became little more than policing operations. Initially, the tactics was to send out one or more marine patrols to the reported localities of bandit activity in an attempt to contact the bandits and run them down. The operations were too numerous, however, to give an account of more than a few typical cases; a hundred patrols went out and fought a score or more of engagements during the first half of 1917.

## Chacha and Vincentico

One of the more important of the earlier operations took place during January, 1917, in Macoris Province. Several detachments of marines under Lieutenant Colonel Bearss had a hard-fought skirmish with a bandit group, led by Chacha, at Consuelo and drove the bandits north into Seibo Province. The marines lost contact with the group for several days, but in a series of rapid marches they searched practically the entire eastern part of the country. About ten days after the fight at Consuelo, one of the marine detachments again succeeded in engaging Chacha: one marine was killed and another wounded. This encounter led to negotiations which resulted in Chacha giving himself up. Only three of his band surrendered with him, however, and the remainder carried on under an equally troublesome leader—Vincentico Evangelista.

The marines continued to disarm the inhabitants, as opportunity presented, and engaged in an intensive campaign against banditry, keeping the bandits on the move to prevent them from augmenting their forces. The vigorous activities of the marines under "Hiking Hiram" (Colonel Bearss) were reminiscent of their operations in the Philippines many years before under that officer. Several companies of marines continued operations in Macoris Province for a number of weeks; they had several minor engagements with bandit groups but made no decisive gains. During the latter part of March, however, they obtained fairly definite information as to the whereabouts of Vincentico's group in Seibo Province. A detachment of marines under Captain R. S. Kingsbury moved against them. Kingsbury encountered the bandits (March 1917), who had grown unexpectedly bold and dared to attack him. The marines killed about fifteen out of forty and wounded a number of others including Vincentico.

The affair proved a deterrent to banditry for some time. Vincentico's band was again located in a mountain stronghold during the following June. After negotiations he agreed to surrender with more than two hundred of his followers; all but about forty were disarmed and liberated, while Vincentico and the remaining ones were held for their crimes. Vincentico was killed a short time afterwards, while attempting to escape.

In the meantime the marines were attempting to run down other bandit groups. A large combined patrol of marines and some of the newly established Guardia located and attacked (in April) a strong bandit position at Las Canitas, in western Santo Domigo. After a fight lasting seven hours, they succeeded in driving out the enemy, killing nine and wounding several times that number. Only two marines were wounded.

With the surrender of Vincentico, bandit activities subsided very substantially during the remainder of 1917 and conditions became apparently almost normal. The Commandant of the Marine Corps in his annual report in October of that year stated that, "all the bandit leaders have been captured or killed and their followers dispersed"—a conclusion somewhat premature in view of what followed.

## Banditry

From the very beginning, the marines had to contend with outright banditry, which had long existed in the Dominican Republic. Prior to 1918 a large part of the resistance to the American forces was from bands of varying size to which at least some semblance of political or patriotic motive could be credited. The last of such groups, however, were practically eliminated by the end of 1917 and during the remainder of the occupation most of the difficulty of the Second Brigade as well as of the Guardia was with lawless bands which existed for no other purpose than plunder, pillage, and racketeering. In addition to the more or less normal number of such individuals, this class of criminals was considerably augmented by jail deliveries which took place during the more recent revolutions and at the beginning of the American occupation. During the time that the United States was at war with Germany, there was every indication that some of the banditry was instigated by German agents, who doubtless in some instances supplied arms and equipment to lawless groups. It also appears most likely that some of the propaganda, designed to arouse animosity against our forces, was under German direction.

That the Dominican lawless elements were accomplished brigands is evidenced by the fact that it took the combined efforts of the Marine Brigade and the Guardia, pursuing a more or less continuous and vigorous campaign against them, more than five years to bring them successfully under control. In some parts of the country conditions were so bad, at times, that it was necessary to assemble the peaceful inhabitants into towns for protection as the countryside was practically being laid waste. On some occasions, the bandits were so bold as to attack marine patrols, especially when they could ambush them without any great danger to themselves. Many of the trails over which the marine patrols moved were in hilly and heavily wooded country and practically walled in with brush and Spanish bayonet. The bandits were accustomed to lie in wait along such trails and suddenly open up on patrols with a heavy fire at short range, accompanied by a great deal of yelling to boost their own courage and frighten their adversaries. It was quite difficult, as a rule, to gain definite contact with a bandit group, and when they were encountered every effort was made, both day and night, to follow them. Marine patrols were usually small and often in command of noncommissioned officers. A number of small groups of marines, moving on parallel trails at times, went out to sweep an entire area.

The hardships involved in carrying on such campaigns in infested tropical countries, especially during the rainy season, is difficult for the uninitiated to imagine. Malaria and dengue, especially, wore down the effective strength of the marines. The patrolling, which took place almost continuously, was nearly all on foot, as mounts were only available for about one-fifth of the men. The danger to patrols was increased by the fact that each patrol sent out was usually quite small. At times several groups operated in conjunction, at varying distances apart, in order to gain contact with bandit groups. This practice was carried on, even at the risk of having small patrols completely wiped out by greatly superior groups of bandits. Marine patrols during 1918 had more than a hundred skirmishes with bandit groups of all sizes and with varying degrees of success. Some of these amounted only to the exchange of a few long range shots, while others developed into substantial skirmishes with considerable loss to each side. Nearly all of the combat operations during this phase of the occupation were in Seibo and Macoris Provinces.

## Bandit Contacts

Obviously it would be impracticable to describe more than a few of the encounters which took place between the marines and the Dominican bandits. Brief mention only is made of the more important engagements. One of the more difficult operations was undertaken in January, 1918, by a combined Guardia and marine patrol into the mountainous region of western Santo Domingo against the camp of one of the notorious bandit groups, led by Dios Olivorio. The maneuver necessitated a march of about 250 miles and the climbing to the top of a mountain range. The expedition failed to surprise the bandits, however, and most of them fled at its approach; only a few were captured and their camp destroyed. Such contacts were infrequent during the first half of 1918, however, but the bandits became more active from July to October.

One of the tightest places that a combined group of the Guardia and marines got into was near Hato Mayor during July, when Captain C. F. Merkel with such a patrol was attacked from three sides while making camp in a horseshoe-shaped valley. Merkel's men gradually fought their way out of the pocket by advancing up the hills against the bandits. The fight lasted about twenty minutes; the bandits fled leaving behind eight killed and two wounded. One marine and two of the Guardia were wounded in the affray.

### Rushforth's Gallant Stand

A most desperate fight by marines took place near Manchado on August 13, 1918. A corporal's patrol of four marines was ambushed while rounding the turn of a trail and crossing a stream. A large group of bandits had practically surrounded them. The marines fought valiantly, killing and wounding a number of their assailants, as one by one, they were in turn cut down. Finally, only Private Rushforth remained, who, in spite of many wounds, desperately carried on the hopeless fight. A severe machete wound in the right hand made it impossible to offer further resistance. Fortunately, he then spied his own horse near by, ran and jumped upon it, and escaped. While riding away, he was followed by a shower of bullets, one of which struck the horse in the neck and another passed through part of the saddle wounding Rushforth in the hip. Rushforth at last reached safety in spite of several bleeding wounds which bore indisputable proof of a horrible adventure. For his heroic conduct in the desperate fight Rushforth received the commendations of his superiors up to and including the Secretary of the Navy. The lack of witnesses to the affair alone debarred him from receiving the Congressional Medal of Honor which was undoubtedly deserved for such heroic conduct.

A patrol of nine marines and two officers escaped disaster two days later, only by prompt and vigorous action. They were surrounded just after dark, while eating supper in a native house, and fired upon from out of the darkness on three sides. By running out of the house quickly, deploying at wide intervals, and vigorously returning the fire, the marines drove off their adversaries after about five minutes of rapid-fire fighting.

During September and October a number of marine patrols participated in similar encounters. One of the more outstanding of these occurred on October 24 when two small patrols, under Captain W. C. Byrd, went to attack a reported bandit camp in the mountains near

El Seibo. The bandits were completely surprised, and after firing a few shots, scattered and ran away. A few hours later the patrols, which had been combined into one, were ambushed while crossing a difficult wooded stream. Prompt fire from a machine gun drove the bandits away, and the marines escaped without casualties.

During the closing months of 1918 there was comparatively little activity by bandits. Some of the banditry during that year, as well as later, was encouraged by the payment of tribute to bandit leaders by sugar plantation owners to deter them from burning their cane fields. Early in 1919 Rear Admiral Thomas S. Snowden relieved Knapp as military governor. According to an eminent State Department critic, Snowden was not so successful in dealing with the Dominican people because he held himself aloof and was not in close contact with the situation. This, together with the fact that the Dominicans were unable to obtain any definite promise for evacuation of the country, alienated a number of the political leaders and possibly added to future difficulties.

## Guardia Nacional Dominicana

It will be recalled that the policy of the State Department demanded a responsible government in the Dominican Republic, which would assure an opportunity for the people of the country to develop its resources and put an end to graft and waste in government. It also insisted on a financial supervision and the establishment of a constabulary under American officers. No steps had been taken for the organization of the Guardia prior to the declaration of military government. It, therefore, fell to the lot of Admiral Knapp to actually establish such an organization after his authority had been firmly established with the aid of the brigade of marines. After considerable preliminary study of the subject had been made, plans were formulated and the Secretary of the Navy on March 17, 1917, directed the Military Governor to proceed with the establishment of the organization.

Previously there had been a poorly organized "army" in the country and a militia called the "Guardia Republicana." In the Dominican Republic there was no such thing as political parties, held together by definite ideas, as we are wont to picture them. Personalities alone controlled politics; political leaders at the head of armed bands often clashed in civil wars. Our policy not only demanded that this state of affairs be stopped but insisted that the setting up of an armed force, which could be used to perpetuate a leader in power, must be prevented. The American Government decided that an *army* was not what was wanted, but rather, a *na-*

*tional police force* capable of maintaining law and order in the ordinary sense and able to cope effectively with organized resistance against the government. Knapp decided first of all to dissolve the older military organizations and then have the personnel, who had served therein—those who were suitable—join the new military organization.

The Military Governor on April 7, 1917, ordered the establishment of a national police force under the name of "Guardia Nacional Dominicana." He set aside one-half a million dollars for its maintenance during the remainder of that year and placed its direction under the Commanding General of the Second Brigade. The Guardia was actually organized on May 1, 1917, and its first assignment was to take over the frontier guard duty along the Haitian boundary. Its initially allowed enlisted strength was 1,234 but only about 60 per cent of that number were recruited at the outset. Its strength was brought up to about 1,200 men early in 1918 and remained near that number until shortage of funds forced a reduction to only 346 enlisted men in February, 1921.

In accordance with the announced policy, the officer in command of the organization, as well as all of the other officers of higher rank, were to be taken from the regular personnel of the United States naval service. Authorization for American naval personnel to accept employment under the Dominican Government was not allowed, however, until February of the following year, when an act was approved, which was substantially the same as a previous law, authorizing the acceptance of such employment in Haiti. Practically all of the officers during the first few years of the organization were officers or noncommissioned officers of the Marine Corps. The usual officer strength of the Guardia was about eighty. There was little difficulty in filling the ranks of the organization, but obtaining Dominicans of sufficient reputation and education for officers proved very difficult. All of the old political caste shunned the organization for several years, and men who would take commissions were seldom acceptable.

As initially organized, the Guardia, like the Second Brigade, had its northern and southern departments divided by the range of mountains running across the country. Each department was in turn divided into districts; each province was assigned a company as its garrison. The companies were in turn divided among the more important towns of the province with the company headquarters in the provincial capital. The primary function of the organization was to protect life and property and suppress organized lawlessness. Under proper supervision, the Guardia arrested violators of the law and brought them to justice. It maintained a frontier guard along the Haitian-Dominican boundary, to prevent smuggling and to enforce immigration laws. Locally, when called upon, it co-operated with other departments of the government as well as with the municipal police.

From the very beginning the organization was beset with many difficulties. The politicians, who had refused all co-operation with the Military Government, and many other leading citizens looked upon it merely as part of the Military Government and, as such, an instrument of oppression. They *really* disliked it because it prevented them from carrying out their usual activities—exploiting the people. The mass of the Dominican people were disposed to look upon the Guardia with favor; but even they, at times, were turned against it by the propaganda and leadership of the politicians. The enlisted men were as a rule very faithful followers of their officers and the organization was at least safe from mutinies such as occurred in similar organizations of native troops run by Marine Corps personnel in other countries.

The Dominicans proved their courage in many a skirmish with bandit groups; there is only one known case where they were defeated in such an encounter. Soon after the withdrawal of part of the marines from Santo Domingo, when we entered the World War, the newly recruited Guardia took the field to assist the marines in fighting the bandits and from the beginning gave a reasonably good account of itself.

There has been some criticism of the Guardia throughout its history. On one occasion its commandant, who had been commended very highly by a previous Military Governor, was not so well thought of by his successor. Commanders of the organization changed in rapid succession during the early months of its existence and, as a rule, they attempted to conduct its affairs in addition to having a full assignment of duties with the Marine Brigade. According to the opinion of one Military Governor, there appears to have been some mistaken ideas as to the real function of the Guardia. Its critics, even as late as 1919, said that it was attempting to be an army instead of a police force. There is no doubt as to its slowness in developing into a strong enough force to control organized lawlessness.

Most of the contacts made with bandit groups were by marine patrols during the years of bandit activity. By November, 1921, however, the Guardia had reported 122 bandit contacts in which it killed or wounded 320 bandits in addition to bringing to justice more than 2,500 criminals of all descriptions. The Guardia aided substantially in disarming the population by bringing in several thousand firearms and other miscellaneous weapons. Its total casualties, while fighting the bandits, were probably greater than those of the Second Brigade. The activities of the Guardia after it developed sufficiently to assume all of its normal functions are discussed below in conjunction with the further activities of the Marine Brigade.

## Increase in Banditry

Despite all the efforts that had been made, control of banditry was far from realized by the beginning of 1919. With the World War off its hands, the Navy Department determined to make a strong concerted effort to put an end to banditry in Santo Domingo. The Fifteenth Regiment of Marines and an aviation squadron were sent to reinforce the Second Brigade, augmenting it to a strength of about 3,000, in hopes that with the additional troops the bandits could in some way be brought under control. The Fifteenth was used at first to reinforce the other regiments in their respective areas. On July 1, 1919, the Eastern District was formed, and the Fifteenth not only took over the duty of garrisoning its principal towns but, with the aid of about half of the Third Regiment, entered upon a vigorous patrolling campaign in Seibo and Macoris Provinces, which it kept up with considerable success during the remainder of the year.

There seems to have been a revived political significance to some of the bandit activity during 1919 and the remainder of the time that it continued. Certain political leaders were prevented from carrying out their designs by the prolongation of military government, and they, to some extent, encouraged bandit groups. The marines succeeded in gaining only an occasional effective contact with the outlaws during the first five months of the year. During the remainder of the year, however, by means of vigorous patrolling, supported often by planes, they had engagements with bandits every few days and managed to run a considerable number to cover, kill some, land others in prison, and break those remaining up into smaller groups. Contacts more commonly took place at houses in different parts of the country with small groups, or at camps in remote mountain regions. In the year 1919 the marines had more than two hundred separate contacts and, in various ways, disposed of several hundred outlaws. The Guardia, still none too effective as a constabulary force, did not contribute materially to this campaign of exterminating bandits.

## Contacts

The typical contacts of that year were similar to those previously made. The bolder groups of bandits still dared to ambush marine patrols. It was usually necessary, however, for the marines to run them down in order to bring on an effective engagement. One of the most successful encounters for the year was made by a patrol under Captain Byrd, during February in eastern Santo Domingo. Acting upon what proved to be very reliable information, Byrd struck a camp of about sixty bandits in an unusually difficult mountain fastness, killed twelve of them and captured a considerable supply of their arms and ammunition. Some two months later, by a sheer stroke of luck, First Lieutenant D. G. Oglesby, with a patrol of about twenty marines, succeeded in striking three bandit camps and had as many successful contacts all in the same day.

At times during the year several bandit groups united and formed substantial forces. A marine patrol under Second Lieutenant F. H. Biebush struck such a force in May, succeeded in killing twelve or fifteen bandits and broke it up. The aviation squadron succeeded in bombing and machine-gunning several bandit groups during the year, in addition to furnishing a great deal of information to the ground troops, thereby bringing the Dominican guerrilla warfare somewhat up-to-date in military technique. The aviation squadron was stationed for some time on a large sugar plantation at Consuelo but moved to Santo Domingo City in 1920. Reports as to the Brigade's accomplishments for the year vary and, in so far as they pertain to the number of bandits disposed of, are probably mere estimates. Three or four marines were killed and at least twice that many wounded.

## Peace at Last

Throughout 1918 and 1919, with the exception of the two troublesome eastern provinces, the country was enjoying a safer and more peaceful existence than it had ever experienced. The Military Government carried on its many functions with little difficulty. It introduced a number of social reforms and sought by all possible means to improve economic conditions and the public health situation. American control made substantial progress in the development of the Dominican Republic in a number of other ways. It had a system of roads constructed which brought the important parts of the country much closer together. Enrollment of school children increased from 18,000 to nearly 100,000 with a hundred per cent improvement in average daily attendance. The country grew rich during the period of war prices on sugar and other commodities; ample revenue was available for carrying on the governmental activities. In 1920, however, the postwar depression and a collapse in the price of sugar hit the country particularly hard. The Government was forced to discontinue much of its public work. A foreign loan was impossible because of the uncertainty of the continuance of the occupation. Arrangements for the eventual evacuation of the country by the American naval forces met with many difficulties.

In December, 1920, President Wilson directed the Military Governor to announce that the time for withdrawal had arrived. The political leaders of the country continued to stand by their determination to accept only an unconditional withdrawal. Our government naturally did not want all of its accomplishments, which had been so painfully attained, completely cast aside, and the country to return to its previous state of chaos. No successful agreement for withdrawal was reached until March, 1922, when a tentative plan was formulated for the Military Government to continue until the public works program, then in progress, had been carried out and the training of the Guardia completed. Arrangements were made soon afterwards for the establishment of a provisional government over which the Military Governor would retain only a measure of military and financial control.

While the long negotiations for a plan of eventual withdrawal were being discussed, the Second Brigade continued its support of the Military Government and its attempts to exterminate the bandits. The strength of the Brigade was allowed gradually to run down during the latter part of 1919; two companies from each of the regiments were disbanded. By the first of July, 1920, the strength of the brigade was down to approximately 120 officers and 2,000 enlisted men. Most of the marines serving in Santo Domingo had been enlisted during the World War; many, who expected to serve only in France, had been retained in Santo Domingo long after the close of the War. This condition together with the many hardships led to some dissatisfaction, which had a noticeable effect on the morale of the command.

## Further Troubles

The gradual reduction of the strength of the occupying force proved rather untimely. With the coming of the depression and the easing of censorship over speech and the press, the politicians succeeded in stirring up considerable ill-feeling against the Military Government. Even the obviously beneficial reforms, designed for the best interests of the country, were often received with disfavor.

The more radical leaders even agitated revolution. Admiral Snowden and the Brigade Commander, Brigadier General Logan Feland, became somewhat alarmed, and asked for a substantial increase in the number of marines in the country. As the unrest continued to grow during the fall of 1920, the brigade of marines increased its patrolling in an effort to keep down disorder. A decided fall in wages and employment further complicated social problems. Despite its handicap, lack of funds and men, the Guardia gave a reasonably good account of itself during this rather critical period. Both the marines and the Guardia continued their efforts to disarm the population and by the middle of 1921 had collected a total of nearly 53,000 firearms in addition to many thousands of cutting weapons. Despite the seemingly little permanent good that the occupying force was accomplishing, it cost the American Government, for the fiscal year 1921, more than $7,500,000. Contacts between marine patrols and bandits decreased in number and had almost ceased by September, 1921. There was then estimated to be not more than two or three hundred active bandits left in the country. Most of them were operating around the sugar estates in the eastern part of the country against which they occasionally made forays from their mountain hideouts in the region south of Samana Bay. They were encouraged to some extent by political agitators, who, on some occasions, were believed to have supplied them with equipment and clothing.

## THE CORDON SYSTEM

A new system was initiated late in October, 1921, in a more or less desperate attempt to rid the eastern part of the country of bandits. It was successful in gathering in bandits but resulted in violent opposition on the part of the inhabitants. By March of the following year, under the direction of Colonel W. C. Harllee, a series of nine roundups had been made in which a considerable force of troops participated. A cordon of troops in each drive surrounded a large area of the country and practically every male inhabitant, against whom there was any possible suspicion of banditry, was collected and held for identification. The system of identification was not designed to be very agreeable to suspicious characters. It was usually carried out at night; the bandits, in some cases, were identified by a locally notorious woman whose identity was kept carefully concealed. She and other persons who knew many of the bandits were sometimes placed in darkened tents, while the suspicious characters under a glaring light were placed in the open in front of the tents. Before being held as a bandit, the suspect was identified as such by a majority of the secret observers. The number of men collected in the drives varied from 150 to about 576, and a hundred or more bandits or their accomplices were identified in a single drive. The series of drives and the trials which followed netted more than six hundred convictions for banditry or some form of implication therein.

The cordon system was discontinued on account of the violent protests of innocent inhabitants. The patrol system was re-established and resulted in several contacts and heavy casualties to the bandits. The cordon system doubtless served, more than any method previously used, to terrorize the bandit element and their accomplices. It probably had much to do with their wholesale surrender, and the practical cessation of banditry during the two months that immediately followed.

## Dominican Co-operation

Soon after the last of the roundups, the marines unexpectedly started another *coup de main* against the remaining bandits. They formed five groups of Dominicans, gave them a special course of training in shooting and the tactics of patrolling and, in conjunction with numerous marine patrols, the Dominicans took the field against the bandits. The Dominicans succeeded in having six effective contacts with the outlaws which still further tended to convince the remaining ones that their Robin Hood profession was no longer worth while.

The more or less sudden successes against the bandits were made possible partly by the change in attitude of the Dominican people towards the Military Government, the Marine Brigade, and the Policia Nacional, brought about by the formulation of definite plans for the restoration of a free Dominican government. The new brigade commander, Brigadier General Harry Lee, also made a determined effort to overcome the hostile feelings of the Dominicans towards the marines by indoctrinating all members of his command with the principle of extreme fairness to all of the inhabitants and of avoiding all suggestion of friction with them.

Following closely the effective campaigns against banditry, which was for the first time almost completely whipped, the outlaws still at large were given a limited and final opportunity to surrender themselves, be disarmed, and, in some cases, paroled, pending investigation of their past records. Despite the fact that no immunity was offered them where heinous crimes were involved, and practically none for ordinary misconduct, the bandits surrendered themselves almost to the last man, and banditry definitely ceased in the entire country on May 31, 1922, on which date the offer for amnesty expired. A number of bandit leaders and subchiefs, together with their followers who had surrendered, were given suspended sentences of from fifteen to twenty years during good behavior.

## The Policia Nacional Dominicana

By the time the bandit problem was solved, arrangements for the re-establishment of a provisional government were well under way and the early withdrawal of the occupying force was being considered. A tremendous effort was made to raise the efficiency of the Guardia (renamed the "Policia Nacional Dominicana") to enable it to control the country after the withdrawal of the marines. Recovery from the depths of the depression had begun and funds were again available to recruit the Guardia back to its full strength. Suitable Dominican officers, then obtainable, were trained and, under the supervision of American officers, gradually took over many positions. The Policia began to take over some of the garrisons which the marines had held for several years and the process of concentrating the marines into a few important cities was started in June, 1922. As this process went on, the Policia, in accordance with orders from the Navy Department, was given more and more of the police and constabulary duties, which had been performed by Marine Corps personnel since the establishment of the Military Government. All civil duties were turned over to the Policia, and the Provisional Government took control of the country on October 21, 1922. By the end of 1922 the strength of the Policia was again over 1,200, and its training was progressing very satisfactorily under its last marine commandant, Colonel Richard M. Cutts.

In the meantime the Second Marine Brigade had been completely reorganized. The Third and Fifteenth Regiments were disbanded on August 1 and their personnel transferred to the Fourth Regiment and the newly re-established First Regiment. At the time the Provisional Government took control of the country the marines had been concentrated in Santiago, Puerto Plata, Santo Domingo City, San Pedro de Macoris, and Chicharones. Friction between the forces of occupation and the Dominican people had practically ceased. In slightly more than one year, more progress had been made, in restoring law and order, than during all the previous years of the intervention.

During the remainder of the occupation the Second Brigade functioned as a potential reserve in support of the Policia and never again took the field or exercised any control over the Dominican Government. The Brigade concerned itself mostly with the training of its own personnel, which was carried on principally at two training centers—located near Santo Domingo City and near Santiago. The post at Chicharrones was abandoned in May, 1923, leaving only four cities garrisoned by marines. San Pedro de Macoris was evacuated on April 10, 1924, and during the final months of the occupation marines were stationed only in Puerto Plata, Santiago, and Santo Domingo City. Aviation Squadron One continued as part of the Brigade until July 18, 1924, when it returned to the United States.

After acting as Military Governor since December 5, 1922, General Lee became Military Governor on April 18, 1923, and held that position in addition to that of Brigade Commander. He served as Military Governor until the new constitutional government was inaugurated July 12, 1924.

Shortly after the re-establishment of a regular government in the Dominican Republic, the Second Marine Brigade began its withdrawal. As a fitting part of the ceremony transferring control over the Government to the Dominican authorities, the American flag over Fort Ozama was lowered and the Dominican flag raised in its place. The First Regiment was disbanded and its personnel transferred to the Third Battalion, Sixth Marines (Regiment) and to casual companies. The newly formed battalion went to Guantanamo Bay, Cuba, for temporary duty on July 18. Lee then turned over command of the remaining troops to Cutts and returned to the United States. The remainder of the marines withdrew gradually and went to both coasts of the United States. The contingent, transferred to San Diego, California, was reorganized as the Fourth Marines and has continued in existence. Since March, 1927, it has been stationed at Shanghai, China. The last marines, a company left behind to assist in closing out supply and administrative affairs, withdrew September 16, 1924.

An accurate appraisal of the permanent good to the United States as well as to the Dominican Republic of the more than eight years of military occupation of the latter country by a brigade of marines averaging approximately 2,000 men throughout the period is not easy to make. The occupation was, for some time, detrimental to our relations with other Latin-American countries, who deemed our interference uncalled for and highly imperialistic. The United States spent vastly more in restoring a stable government and in rectifying the finances of the Dominican Republic than the latter's foreign debt amounted to at the beginning of the intervention. Some advantages accrued to us no doubt by the maintenance of the Monroe Doctrine during the critical period of the early years of the World

War. While our efforts were unappreciated at the time, they have undoubtedly resulted in more cordial relations with the Dominican Republic. The incidental value to the Marine Corps of the more than eight years of accumulated experience in military government and field service should not be minimized.

As to the permanent benefits of the occupation which accrued to the Dominican Republic, some of them were aptly summarized in General Lee's final report:

The occupying force assumed control of a state rife with revolution, banditry, ungoverned and mismanaged. We left a state enjoying peace, and with a loyal and well-developed military force, with fine roads, many schools, a fine military hospital, and, in short, with every promise for a future of stable government under Dominican rule.

With the exception of a bloodless revolution in 1930, when General Raphael Trujillo, the Commander of the Dominican Army, seized control of the government and has since then been president of the country, peace has been maintained. The military force, developed by marine officers, has been enlarged and kept in a high state of efficiency; but, contrary to our original wishes, it is now doubtless used to maintain a dictator in power. The program of public works and road building has been continued. The school system which was established has continued with some increase in the enrollment of pupils. Economic and social conditions made tremendous improvement during and after the intervention. The sanitary and public health measures initiated by the Military Government have been continued, and "Ciudad Trujillo," the capital of the Republic, (renamed January 9, 1936) is now one of the cleanest cities in Latin America. Law and order is being maintained under a strong central government backed by efficient military and police forces.

## Chapter XIV

## TWENTY YEARS IN HAITI

THE foreign policy governing our relations with Haiti closely paralleled that applied to the Dominican Republic. Haiti also had its difficult financial problems and was even more given to violent revolutions than its sister republic. The same broad, somewhat idealistic program for the maintenance of stable governments in the Caribbean area, sponsored by the Wilson administration, was applied to both countries. The United States Government feared that continual disorder in either would lead to complications with European states. The intervention in Haiti by American naval forces began a few months prior to that in the Dominican Republic, but because of the long period of diplomatic intervention, at times backed by armed forces which preceded the military occupation, and the fact that our forces did not withdraw from Haiti until 1934, the experience of the Marine Corps in Santo Domingo is presented first.

### FINANCIAL DIFFICULTIES

Haiti's financial difficulties, like those of Santo Domingo, were of long standing; most of them grew out of over-extended loans, principally from France. Despite the fact that the country was already heavily in debt, it was able to borrow 65 million francs from American, French, and German bankers in 1910. At that time the bankers established the Banque Nationale, a privately owned institution, to act as the government treasury and to receive and have custody over all government funds. In addition to its foreign obligations Haiti had a large internal and floating debt which increased rapidly after 1912. Successive issues of bonds had been made to pay the expenses of successful revolutions. The finances of the Haitian Government were further complicated by its failure to pay interest on the guaranteed bonds of the National Railroad Company. The Haitian debt was secured by specific liens on the customs duties.

Practically all sources of income had been pledged by 1912, and the government had no funds for current expenses except a fixed sum advanced each month by the bank which usually recouped itself at the end of the fiscal year from the surplus remaining after preferred obligations had been paid.

In August, 1914, the bank, in the hopes of forcing American control over the customs service, refused to make further advances and gave as its reason that no balance would remain at the end of the fiscal year. This left the government in a desperate financial condition and soon led to its overthrow. Rumors reached the bank that the government was about to seize the bank's gold reserve. The National City Bank of New York, which had been supporting the Banque Nationale, arranged with the State Department for the secret transfer of a part of the gold to New York. The U.S.S. *Machias,* with a detachment of sixty-five marines, under Major C. B. Hatch, arrived at Port au Prince on December 17, 1914; $500,000 in gold was taken from the bank secretly and escorted by Hatch's marines on board the *Machias,* which sailed for New York immediately.

Throughout Haiti's colonial history its social stability had gradually grown more precarious because of an increasing proportion of negro slaves who, by the end of the eighteenth century, outnumbered the combined white and free colored population nearly ten to one. The French Revolution started a series of violent outbreaks in Haiti. Unspeakably bloody racial wars, revolts against the French, foreign invasions, and attempts of the French to reconquer the colony practically wiped out all semblance of civilization. For more than a hundred years the country had been in a state of political chaos, ruled by negro military chiefs or petty monarchs who by armed force gained control and maintained themselves in power for varying periods. General conditions had improved very little, and revolutions became even more frequent in the early years of the present century. Every ruler of the country from 1886 to the beginning of the American intervention in 1915 was either overthrown or killed in office—some of them maintaining their rule for only a few months.

## Policy of the United States

Intolerable conditions in Haiti and the pressure of foreign creditors caused considerable concern to our State Department, which had embarked upon a policy of more or less supervision over the turbulent Caribbean countries—a policy already being applied in the Dominican Republic. The Roosevelt corollary to the Monroe Doctrine was also applicable to Haiti, and the danger that some Euro-

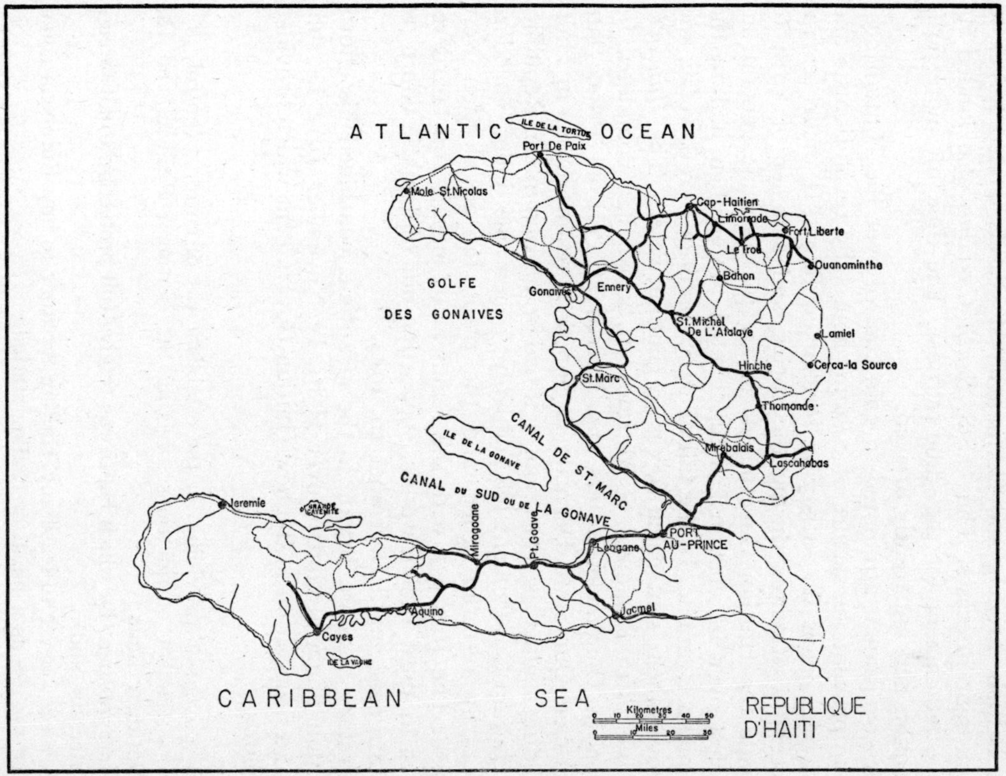

Map of Haiti

pean country might make a determined intervention was even more imminent. Minor military interventions by various foreign powers, who landed small forces to protect their nationals during disturbances at Port au Prince and Cap Haitien, had repeatedly taken place. During revolutionary disturbances in Port au Prince in January, 1914, British, French, and German naval vessels landed forces to protect their interests. The U.S.S. *South Carolina* also landed its marine detachment for the same purpose. The time for more positive action had apparently arrived.

Our government attempted to gain control over the Haitian customs to prevent the seizure of customs houses by revolutionists and to provide means for satisfying foreign creditors. It made several unsuccessful attempts during the spring and summer of 1914 to persuade the Haitian Government to accept the same general supervision over its customs as the United States then had in the Dominican Republic. In the fall of 1915 conditions grew worse, and our government sent naval forces to Haitian waters. The *Hancock*, with the Fifth Regiment of Marines on board, had completed its mission in Dominican waters and arrived at Port au Prince late in October. Our State Department hoped to restore order in Haiti by holding a supervised election, as it had in the Dominican Republic. The Haitian Government fell suddenly; a new one under Theodore temporarily restored order, and the plans for an election were dropped. The *Hancock* with the regiment of marines on board remained in West Indian waters, supporting our diplomatic efforts to maintain peace until December 16, 1914.

Secretary of State Bryan, in the meantime, continued his efforts to obtain financial control over Haiti. In November 1914 he submitted a proposition to the new Haitian Government which provided as follows:

(1) A convention providing for the establishment of customs control,
(2) A settlement of questions affecting the National Railway and the National Bank,
(3) An agreement by which Haiti was to give full protection to all foreign interests, and
(4) A pledge never to lease any Haitian territory to any European country for use as a naval or coaling station.

The plan was declined by Haiti, but, without pressing the matter particularly, Bryan continued his efforts. He sent a commission to Haiti in the hope that it might be able to work out some plan for solving the Haitian problem. The commission accomplished nothing, nor did a special representative, Paul Fuller, sent to Port au Prince about two months later. It was then apparent that no Haitian Government would voluntarily submit to as much control as our State Department desired. The solution to the problem was found only after a reign of terror in the Haitian capital and by strong military intervention.

## THE REVOLUTION OF JULY, 1915

A revolution to overthrow the Theodore government started in northern Haiti early in 1915 under the leadership of Guillaume Sam. It gained control of the country in a few weeks and made Sam president on March 4, 1915. Another revolution began almost immediately in the north under the leadership of Dr. Rosalvo Bobo. Sam imprisoned some two hundred leading citizens whom he suspected of complicity with Bobo. Many others took refuge in foreign legations in order to avoid arrest. The common people turned against Sam's government because of its system of enforced military service —none too gently administered. Revolution broke out in the capital and the disaffected element, led by the refugees, besieged the presidential palace. President Sam directed General Oscar, in charge of the political prisoners, to kill all of them if the revolutionists succeeded in driving him from the palace. The President made his escape into the French Legation, adjoining the palace grounds. Oscar then massacred 167 of his prisoners. The furore of the populace knew no bounds. Oscar fled to the Dominican Legation but was dragged from it by the mob and killed (July 27). On the following day a mob dragged Sam from his hiding place in the French Legation and literally tore him to pieces in the streets of Port au Prince. All government and authority ceased to exist, and the city was at the mercy of the infuriated mob.

Our government watched the development of the Haitian situation with increasing concern. As early as June, 1915, the U.S.S. *Washington* went to Haitian waters for protecting American interests. France sent a naval vessel, which landed a small force of sailors at Cap Haitien, to protect her consulate on June 19. A landing force from the *Washington* went ashore at Cap Haitien on July 9 to guard a radio station. The troops remained ashore until July 27 when Rear Admiral Caperton, commander of the cruiser squadron, learning of the revolutionary activities at Port au Prince, withdrew his forces and proceeded on the *Washington* to the Haitian capital. The U.S.S. *Eagle,* in the meantime, had arrived at Cap Haitien and sent a party ashore for the protection of the French Consulate, which had been violated by a revolutionist band.

## Landing at Port au Prince

When Caperton arrived at Port au Prince on July 28, he received orders from the Navy Department to effect a landing at once to protect American and foreign interests, to advise the French and English authorities that their interests would be protected by the Americans, and further to request the representatives of those nations not to land troops. Late that afternoon a naval regiment, commanded by Captain George Van Orden, U.S.M.C., and composed of one battalion of three companies of sailors and a two-company battalion of marines, landed from the *Washington* at Bizotan, about two and a half miles southeast of the city, and entered that place at about dusk. By midnight the forces had occupied important positions in the city of Port au Prince. They encountered no resistance except occasional sniping and soon restored order.

## The First Brigade of Marines

Caperton at this time had only three comparatively small vessels at his disposal, and his only available troops, other than their regular crews, was one expeditionary company of marines. Soon after learning of the chaotic state of affairs at Port au Prince, Caperton called upon the naval station at Guantanamo Bay, Cuba, to send all available marines on the *Jason* to his assistance and requested that a regiment of marines be dispatched from the United States. The 24th Company of Marines from Guantanamo arrived at Port au Prince in the late afternoon of July 29 and was promptly added to the forces ashore. Five companies of the Second Regiment of Marines, under Colonel E. K. Cole, sent from Philadelphia on the *Connecticut,* reached Port au Prince on August 4. By that time the State Department had decided to make a determined effort to restore law and order in Haiti. It being evident that a still larger military force would be necessary to control the situation, Caperton requested an additional regiment of marines. A brigade of marines, under Colonel L. W. T. Waller, was organized for duty in Haiti.

The Bobo revolution proceeded in spite of the American intervention. The revolutionary forces continued their march from the north on Port au Prince. In an effort to restore peace in the city, an emergency committee of Haitians was formed for the purpose of disarming all soldiers and civilians. The committee collected many arms and placed them under guard in the palace. On July 30 the first serious clash occurred between Caperton's forces and a disorderly faction; two American sailors and several Haitians were killed. The French warship *Descartes* insisted on sending a landing force ashore for the protection of its consulate but promised not to interfere with the activities of the American troops. A number of Haitian soldiers, who claimed to have given up their arms, still insisted on maintaining their organization. Their appearance in various parts of the city caused considerable uneasiness. The committee of Haitians initially worked in co-operation and complied with the wishes of Caperton but later attempted to act on its own initiative. Many influential citizens advocated the formation of some form of provisional government. The arrival of the Second Regiment (August 4) greatly eased the tense situation; Bobo's troops assumed a decidedly more peaceful attitude and promised to disarm.

Caperton, being still none too sure of the situation, recommended on August 5 that vigorous action be taken to restore peace in the country. He extended his control by occupying Fort Nationale at Port au Prince with a force of marines and sailors. He ordered all Haitian soldiers whose homes were not in Port au Prince to leave the city at once. Some hesitated and were promptly arrested. A few resisted; a conflict resulted and two Haitians were killed.

### Bobo Continues to Resist

In the meantime the situation was growing more complicated by the revolutionary movement in the north. Cap Haitien formed a committee of safety to assist our landing forces in maintaining order. Some two thousand troops—Bobo sympathizers—were forbidden to enter the city without giving up their arms. Bobo, at first, appeared conciliatory and, after a conference with the American authorities, called upon his generals to turn over their arms to the Americans, but very few arms were actually turned in. One company from the Second Regiment was sent on the *Connecticut* to Cap Haitien where it landed on August 6 to augment the forces already ashore. The situation still showed no improvement and two companies of sailors from the *Connecticut* were added to the forces ashore. The influence of Bobo made it impossible to form a civil government in northern Haiti free from his domination, and on August 12 Admiral Knapp established military government at Cap Haitien.

There were two likely candidates for the presidency of Haiti—Bobo, who had a strong "caco" following, and Sudre Dartiguenave, a member of the Haitian Senate. The United States Government was anxious to see a man selected who would co-operate with its efforts to restore peace. In accordance with instructions from Washington, Caperton notified the Haitian Congress that only a government that could control the situation would be recognized, and that the United States expected to control the customs as well as have some control over the finances of the country. Dartiguenave let it be known that he and most of the congressmen were willing for the United States to intervene as necessary and would permit the Americans to control the customs. He expressed the opinion that no government could stand in Haiti without the aid of the United States. Before an election was held the United States announced its intention of maintaining a force in Haiti only long enough to restore order. Dartiguenave agreed to accept and support Bobo, if Bobo were elected president, but Bobo bluntly stated that he would neither accept nor support Dartiguenave as president.

Bobo's troops then became active in opposition to the efforts to restore peace. His followers in the vicinity of Grande Riviere refused to give up their arms and caused considerable disturbance. Some troops of the deposed government attacked St. Marc but were successfully repulsed by a committee of safety. Bobo's party and other oppositionists controlled a revolutionary committee at Port au Prince. Anticipating that Dartiguenave would be elected, the revolutionists ordered Congress dissolved and threatened to use force against its meeting but were prevented by marines from sealing the doors of the assembly room. Caperton then promptly dissolved the committee and announced that he would consider the committee an enemy of the United States if it attempted in any way to act against his policy. In order to make additional force available, Caperton had the *Castine* and *Eagle* placed alongside the wharf and part of their crews landed to augment his forces in Port au Prince. During such a state of affairs the Haitian Congress met the following day and elected Dartiguenave president. Dartiguenave expressed his appreciation for the co-operation of the American forces and assured everyone that his was a free election.

## The Cacos

It soon became evident that the principal resistance to the intervening forces would come from a somewhat pugnacious element of the population called "cacos." The cacos were the descendants of the more warlike type of negroes who had run away from slavery and lived in the mountains. They were, among other things, professional soldiers, ready to support any revolutionary movement which would pay them for their services. They were organized in bands under irresponsible and lawless leaders and were greatly feared by all Haitians. For some time they had practically controlled politics. The government in power usually paid tribute to them in order to retain their support. If not so rewarded, the cacos usually turned to some revolutionary leader whom they helped to put in control of the government and kept him there as long as they received pay. They were especially strong in the more mountainous regions and in the north. Some of the caco leaders announced that they would not support Dartiguenave and demanded Bobo for president. Organized bands of these people proved quite formidable enemies; the marines in Haiti carried on a considerable campaign in order to break their power and waged a second, more serious, campaign against them during the caco revolt in 1918-1920.

## The Occupation of Haiti

Caperton's mission was made more definite by instructions from the Navy Department to assist in carrying out the State Department's plan for the re-establishment of responsible government in Haiti. The remainder of the First Brigade of Marines arrived at Port au Prince on August 15, and Waller took command of all American forces ashore. He sent Colonel Cole with the Headquarters and the First Battalion of the First Regiment to Cap Haitien. The remainder of the Brigade was stationed at Port au Prince.

There were some disturbances in different parts of the country shortly after the election of the new president, and additional marines were sent to occupy important places. A company supported by the U.S.S. *Eagle* was sent (August 17) to occupy the town of Leogane, about twenty miles west of Port au Prince, to further secure the capital and its food supply. Another company was sent on board the *Castine* for the same purpose and occupied St. Marc, on the coast northwest of Port au Prince. Port de Paix on the north coast was among the first localities to show hostility to the Dartiguenave government; its inhabitants appeared ready to join the cacos. The cacos around Cap Haitien were very much dissatisfied with the turn of events and were reluctant to give up their usual activities and turn in their arms. When Cole arrived there with his troops, he took command of all American forces in northern Haiti, including a detachment from the *Nashville* which had landed on August 12.

The task assigned to the Brigade was again considerably enlarged on August 18 by orders from the State Department to take over the ten principal customs houses and use the funds collected thereat for organizing and maintaining a constabulary, initiating a program of public works to relieve unemployment, and supporting the Dartiguenave government. The Nineteenth Company of marines occupied Port de Paix on August 25 to secure that place and protect its customs house. The Twelfth Company occupied Petit Goave and Miragoane, and the Seventh Company occupied Gonaives a few days later to assist in taking over the customs houses. Cayes was occupied by the Fourth Company on September 15 and Jacmel by the Seventeenth Company on the following day for the same purpose. A three-battery battalion of Marine Corps artillery, sent from the United States to reinforce Waller's brigade, arrived at the end of August. Waller sent one battery to Cap Haitien and assigned the other two to Port au Prince. The First Brigade then (September, 1915) had a strength of 88 officers and 1,941 enlisted men.

### Fighting the Cacos

With the exception of minor disorders and the occasional sniping at marine patrols, the occupation of Haiti by the American forces had been accomplished without resistance. The cacos had instinctively feared and distrusted the white man since the days when the French tried to reconquer and return them to slavery. This, together with the fact that they could no longer look to the Haitian Government for support and had no prospect of income from another revolution, caused them to become rebellious and for a time stoutly to resist, in their own crude and ineffective way, the American occupation. Some of their leaders parleyed with our officers for a time and made various promises to turn in their arms and cease their usual warlike activities. It was soon learned, however, that they had no such intention and that their strength, particularly in northern Haiti, was far greater than had been originally estimated.

The marines' first encounter with a group of cacos occurred near Gonaives. Early in September a group of about two hundred cacos approached that town and greatly terrified the inhabitants. The company of marines there was immediately reinforced by a landing party from the *Castine*. The cacos made no aggressive move but continued to increase in numbers and shut off the normal flow of food supplies into the town. However, on September 18, a marine patrol exchanged a few shots with a band of about seventy-five. Major Smedley D. Butler took command of the forces at Gonaives a few days later and initiated one of his usual vigorous campaigns to rid the vicinity of the harassing force of cacos. Butler undertook to re-establish the water supply, railroad connections, and the flow of food supplies into the town, all of which the cacos had stopped. At the same time he carried on negotiations with the caco leader, Rameau. Butler went out with a patrol, sent other patrols to near-by places, and had several minor clashes with caco groups. Rameau then promised to withdraw his forces. Butler re-established communications to Ennery by proceeding with a guarded train and the necessary repair equipment to reopen the railroad. Conditions were restored to more nearly normal in that part of the country only to become even more menacing along the northern coast.

### The Campaign in the North

The cacos in the general vicinity of Cap Haitien began preventing that city from obtaining its usual flow of food supplies from the interior in early September. Cole, being none too sure as to what course of action to take, remained inactive. A detachment of marines from Cap Haitien was finally sent out and forcibly re-established communications by rail to Grande Riviere on September 18. The cacos were greatly excited by that move but made no attack on the American forces. Cole parleyed with the caco chiefs, who with their band had practically encircled the city to the south. He attempted to persuade the cacos to turn in their arms but accomplished little. He then tried to impress them with a show of force and ordered some strong patrols of marines to march into the interior and back on short circular routes.

The patrols, which had to pass through caco outpost lines, had some exciting experiences. The first to go out, after an argument with a caco outpost commander, was allowed to pass without molestation. The chief of the caco band showed his disapproval of such leniency, however, by having the subordinate's head chopped off with a machete. Next day when another marine patrol of five squads, commanded by Captain F. A. Barker, attempted to pass the caco line, it was fired upon. Captain Chandler Campbell was on patrol with six squads of marines near by when the firing started. He marched to Barker's assistance, while another patrol of marines hurriedly started out from Cap Haitien in the direction of the firing. The latter patrol was fired upon by Cacos before it reached Barker's detachment and two marines were wounded. The combined detachment was soon surrounded by a great number of excited cacos who began firing from all sides and wounded four more marines.

Campbell's patrol, coming to Barker's assistance, also became engaged and four of his marines were wounded. As the fight developed, Cole had a landing force from the *Connecticut* take over Cap Haitien and started with the remainder of his marines to join in the fight. The cacos were finally driven off. They showed unusual bravery during the fight but manifested little sense of the danger they were exposing themselves to. Their total losses must have been quite heavy as forty of them were found dead in the area where the skirmishes occurred.

Cole then determined to make a more vigorous effort to bring the cacos to terms. He marched out early in the morning of September

27 with five companies of marines to drive the cacos from their main headquarters at Quartier Morin. He captured the town after a slight skirmish and left a marine garrison to hold it. On the following day detachments of marines and sailors made circular marches through the country south of Cap Haitien, where the marines had fought two days previously, but encountered no resistance. The flow of food supplies into Cap Haitien was re-established.

The remainder of Haiti was comparatively quiet during this period. Some disturbance by the cacos was reported at Petit Riviere, and one-half of a company of mounted marines went out from St. Marc to protect the town. That detachment became engaged with a caco group and Sergeant John Platt was killed—the first marine killed in Haiti.

### Waller Takes Charge

When Colonel Waller at Port au Prince learned of the situation in the northern part of the country, he determined to take personal charge of operations there. He obtained a substantial allotment of Haitian funds for paying off caco leaders who would agree to desist from their usual practices and for rewards for turning in arms. In a conference with some of the principal caco leaders, he obtained a written agreement from Morency and Petion to give up their arms and disband their groups. October 5 was set as the date to deliver their arms at Quartier Morin. The leaders were probably sincere in their promises but their followers had begun to scatter and most of them did not comply with the agreement. Several hundred rifles were turned in, however.

Waller then took the Eleventh Company of Marines and proceeded to Fort Liberte on the *Nashville*. From there they marched to Ouanaminthe on the Dominican frontier. Ouanaminthe had been the starting place of most Haitian revolutions. It was at the time garrisoned by nearly four hundred poorly armed loyal Haitian troops, most of whom were practically naked and all near starvation. They were more than delighted to give up their arms and receive in exchange transportation back to their homes, some clothing and a small sum of money. Waller returned to Cap Haitien and soon afterwards to Port au Prince leaving the company of marines to garrison Ouanaminthe and Fort Liberte. During his short trip he collected more than a thousand rifles.

Waller's negotiations, however, were not entirely successful, as a considerable number of cacos were known to be holding their arms. Those who refused to disarm, by the conditions of the offer made them, were thereafter considered as bandits with no legal rights. The difficult task remained of running down the remaining cacos who had their hangouts in more or less developed strongholds in the wild mountainous region lying generally to the south and southeast of Cap Haitien. The operations which finally eliminated them for a time were carried out in two phases—the first, a reconnaissance operation and the latter, a concerted drive against their strongholds.

### Butler's Reconnaissance

In order to build up a stronger force of marines in close proximity to the caco country, part of the Thirteenth Company was moved to Grande Riviere, the Fifteenth Company (Captain W. P. Upshur) was sent to Fort Liberte and the Eleventh Company concentrated at Ouanaminthe. A detachment of the Thirteenth Company under Lieutenant Thomas E. Thrasher next pushed deep into the bandit country, occupied Bahon and was joined soon afterwards by the remainder of the company. Cole, accompanied by Butler and some additional troops, moved his headquarters to Grande Riviere. Several strong patrols took various routes through the caco country in search of bandits and their strongholds.

Butler, accompanied by several other officers with a mounted detachment of about forty marines, made a six-day reconnaissance of about 120 miles through the mountainous caco country and had an interesting contact with a large band of cacos, described by him as follows:

After dark evening of twenty-fourth (October) while command was crossing river in deep ravine suddenly fired upon from three sides by about four hundred cacos in bushes one hundred yards from fort. One horse killed, fought our way forward to good positions and remained there for night surrounded by cacos who kept up continuous but poorly aimed fire. We returned fire only when necessary to repel their actual advance towards us. Owing to our good position no men or horses injured during the night. At daybreak three squads in charge of Captain Upshur, Lieutenant Ostermann and Sergeant Daly which had been covering our position during the night, advanced in three different directions, surprising and chasing cacos in all directions. Eight cacos killed and ten wounded, this number verified. Many more reported. Private Fredericks slight flesh wound left arm. Upshur and Ostermann advancing from two directions captured Fort Dipitie with a total of thirteen marines putting garrison to flight. Demolished and burned fort; all three squads burned all houses from which fire had been coming. Swept clear the district within one mile of all cacos.

Captain William P. Upshur, First Lieutenant Edward A. Ostermann and Gunnery Sergeant Dan Daly awarded Congressional Medals of Honor for their part in this engagement.

The detachment went through almost indescribable hardships but succeeded in obtaining much valuable information which proved useful in the final drive of the campaign.

## Capture of Fort Riviere

By the end of October preparations were well advanced for a determined campaign. Waller, acting under Caperton's orders to take vigorous measures to suppress the cacos, rejoined the field forces in the north and made his headquarters at Le Trou. The cacos made a night attack against Le Trou shortly afterwards, but the marines successfully repulsed them after a twenty minute fight. The cacos left thirty-two dead behind; the marines pursued and accounted for several more. Only one marine was wounded during the several encounters.

Strong marine patrols pushed deeper into the caco country, searched out bands wherever they could be located, and captured and destroyed their forts. This phase of the campaign extended into November. Most of the cacos succeeded as a rule in escaping before the marines drove home an attack. Marine patrols were having contacts with the cacos practically every day, inflicting considerable losses on them and keeping them on the run. The cacos were driven gradually into their last retreat—Fort Riviere, an old French fort, located in the mountain region about eight miles south of the town of Grande Riviere, constructed of masonry and believed by the cacos to be impregnable. In the meantime different detachments of marines were gradually closing in on the fort in an effort to cut all avenues of retreat. The marines were also obtaining valuable information for the final drive, designed to crush the caco resistance.

Several detachments approached the fort from different directions during the night of November 17. The Thirteenth Company from Bahon was assigned the task of attacking the east side of the fort under the cover of its own automatic rifle fire. The *Connecticut*'s marine detachment on the left of the Thirteenth Company was assigned the task of advancing against the south side, while the Fifteenth Company, accompanied by Butler, advanced from the west to assault the fort and enter it through an opening so narrow that only one man could pass at a time. A detachment of sailors from the *Connecticut* had the job of preventing the escape of the cacos over a trail leading north.

Upon a whistle signal from Butler at about 7:30 A.M. all units

The Marine Corps Regimental Flag

FORT RIVIERE, HAITI, AFTER ITS CAPTURE BY THE MARINES, 1915

FORT RIVIERE, HAITI. MARINES ON THE WALLS AFTER THE CAPTURE

advanced to the attack—three of them under cover of the fire of Benet automatic rifles. This took the cacos completely by surprise; some of them attempted to escape over the walls only to be shot down by automatic rifle fire. The Fifteenth Company soon reached the opening and Sergeant Ross L. Iams, followed by Private Samuel Gross, volunteered to enter first. They were followed as closely as possible by several squads; a hand-to-hand encounter ensued; fighting with rifles, bayonets, machetes, clubs, and rocks continued until the last caco had fallen. More than fifty cacos including several important leaders were killed. The attacking marines suffered only a few bruises and scratches. The first two marines to enter the fort and Butler were awarded the Congressional Medal of Honor. Butler brought up a ton of dynamite and had the walls of the fort demolished; it has never since been used by a military force. The destruction of Fort Riviere with its entire garrison broke the resistance of the cacos.

The report of the Cacos' losses at Fort Riviere as well as in several other engagements proved too bloody for Secretary of the Navy, Josephus Daniels, who upon hearing of the results directed that thereafter operations against the cacos be carried on with less bloodshed. Operations, except those necessary to protect the inhabitants and for the marines' own defense, were discontinued. Fortunately, however, the Secretary's order was issued after the campaign had been successfully terminated.

### End of the First Caco War

Haiti gradually assumed a state of peace such as it had not known since a black rebellion overthrew the rule of the French near the close of the eighteenth century. The Marine Brigade, gradually reduced to 100 officers and 1,667 enlisted men at the end of 1915, garrisoned the following towns and cities: Port au Prince, Cap Haitien, Miragoane, Grande Riviere du Nord, Gonaives, Petit Goave, Fort Liberte, Le Trou, Limonade, Jacmel, Cayes, Jeremie, Ouanaminthe, and Port de Paix. The garrisons varied in size from nearly 600 at Port au Prince to 33 at Limonade and exercised a degree of military government in the vicinity of each occupied town. Patrolling, for the purpose of protecting the inhabitants from the depredations of the remaining cacos, who had reverted to outright bandits and were preying upon the population for a living, continued for a number of months. Patrols still had occasional contacts with bandit groups which, after the disastrous defeat at Fort Riviere, were usually quite small. Approximately six minor skirmishes occurred during December, 1915, each resulting in one or more casualties for the cacos but none to the marines. Similar incidents continued during January of the following year. Banditry gradually decreased and after a few more months it was for a time practically eliminated.

A feeble effort to start another revolution was made in Port au Prince early in January, 1916; a barracks occupied by the marines and the provost marshal's building was fired upon by a small revolutionary band. The troublemakers were promptly run to cover. The affair was undoubtedly a protest against the Dartiguenave government which was being maintained by the intervening force.

The organization of the Gendarmerie—more fully discussed below—had proceeded far enough by February 1, 1916, for Caperton to issue a proclamation that, thereafter it would assume all military and police duties throughout the country and that the Marine Brigade would be used only for its support. This change in administering the country was accomplished within a few days by 1,300 *gendarmes*, reinforced by about 400 rural guards, assuming civil control throughout Haiti. Peace at last had replaced the continual round of revolutions and lawlessness. Caperton reported:

Brigandage and pillaging stopped. Complete order everywhere exists. Peasants now have feeling of security and are planting their farms. General feeling of relief throughout the country and contentment with American occupation and intentions except amongst few discontented politicians. Government and people eagerly awaiting American action on treaty and introduction of American capital.

The marines had scarcely finished their vigorous campaign of crushing the troublesome cacos in Haiti when they were called to other theaters of operation. The 24th Company was relieved by a small detachment, withdrawn from St. Marc, and returned to its regular station at Guantanamo Bay to resume protection of that important naval base. As noted in the preceding chapter our intervention in Santo Domingo was initiated early in 1916 and that emergency, which Admiral Caperton also had to contend with, necessitated a military force which was most readily available from Haiti. Two companies of the First Brigade were dispatched to Santo Domingo City in April and nearly half of the remaining marines in Haiti followed in May. The number of garrisons in Haiti was reduced to ten and the strength of those remaining materially diminished.

During August, 1916, the marines and *gendarmes* made a concerted drive to capture one of the principal caco leaders still at large. Less than one thousand marines remained in Haiti by October when orders were issued to withdraw half of that number. It was then deemed necessary that some marines remain until the Gendarmerie had been further trained and developed. Waller returned to the United States in November. Cole took command of the Brigade, which then consisted only of a headquarters, a constabulary detachment, the greatly reduced Second Regiment, and a few auxiliary troops. Just prior to our entry into the World War, three additional companies of marines were withdrawn from Haiti and went to help form the Fifth Marines, which was sent to France as part of the first American contingent. By this time, with peace in Haiti almost restored and the Gendarmerie of sufficient strength to perform the ordinary military police duties, the marines, reduced to about 600 in number, began to concentrate in Port au Prince, Cap Haitien, and Ouanaminthe. Upon the urgent request of the brigade commander, however, the strength of the brigade was later increased by about 300 men.

## Gendarmerie d'Haiti

At the time of the election of the President of Haiti in August, 1915, Secretary of State Lansing submitted to the Haitian Government, through the chargé d'affaires at Port au Prince, certain alterations and additions to the treaty which had been proposed a year previously. They provided among other things for the establishment of a constabulary under American control and for the co-operation of the United States in the sanitation and public improvements of the country. The new government of Haiti was to be recognized only upon acceptance of the proposed treaty. The treaty was signed by Haiti on September 16. By orders of the Navy Department Caperton proceeded with plans early in October for the creation of a constabulary and recommended a strength of 55 Marine Corps officers and 1,530 *gendarmes*.

Pending the treaty's final ratification and proclamation a *modus vivendi* was agreed to (November 29) by plenipotentiaries of the two countries, putting the treaty into effect immediately. The difficulty of its being a violation of the Constitution of the United States for personnel of the Marine Corps to be in the employ of a foreign government without the consent of Congress was immediately encountered. This obstacle was overcome by having a number of officers and marines placed in an *acting* capacity, and the organization of the Gendarmerie proceeded. Officers detailed by the Brigade Commander drew funds from the nearest customs house and set about enlisting and training the personnel for the new military police force. As organized at first, the Gendarmerie had 12 sections of 28 men each—a total of 336, including noncommissioned officers.

The legal position of the officers of the newly formed organization and their means of maintaining discipline was initially on rather unsteady grounds. Cases of serious breach of discipline were tried by provost courts, maintained under martial law in different parts of the country by the occupying forces. The *gendarmes* at first were dressed in Marine Corps clothing and were supplied with whatever equipment was available. Waller was initially in charge of the newly created organization but, due to his many other duties, most of the early experimental work and planning was carried on by subordinate officers who later had much to do with the finished organization. Butler was appointed the first regular chief of the Gendarmerie and assumed the position shortly after the close of his campaign against the cacos.

### Early Experiences

Since the revolution of July, 1915, local government had been weakened even more than formerly and in many parts of Haiti had almost ceased to exist. The Gendarmerie took over military and police duties in all 109 departments in February, 1916, and assumed practically all the functions of the former local officials. It had, in the meantime, been given some practice in performing its duties at various places, usually in the towns occupied by the marines.

Scarcely had the Gendarmerie entered upon its new duties in the old caco country than it was subjected to a series of attacks by caco groups, who had maintained some control of that part of the country for more than a hundred years and therefore looked upon the *gendarmes* as invaders of their domain. A *gendarme* patrol was ambushed near Thomonde, within a few days after its arrival in the area, and a corporal was killed. Shortly after arriving at Cerca la Source, a garrison of ten *gendarmes* was attacked while asleep; two *gendarmes* were killed, one wounded and the others fled. The American officer and his orderly, aroused by the conflict, in turn attacked the cacos, killing four and driving off the remainder. The cacos attacked the post at Lamielle, a patrol of seven *gendarmes* under an American officer, and another post during the next three days. The *gendarmes* stood their ground sufficiently well to show the cacos that they could not easily be driven out.

Due largely to the lack of vigilance on the part of the inexperienced *gendarme* sentries, five hundred prisoners in the National Penitentiary at Port au Prince (May 30, 1916) rushed and overcame the entire guard and escaped. Other *gendarme* detachments in the city and marine patrols killed or rounded up the prisoners, a part of whom attempted to escape into Santo Domingo. The entire penitentiary guard showed a decided lack of courage in the affair. Nine were court-martialed for cowardice and desertion and sentenced to long periods at hard labor.

Establishing the Gendarmerie on a firm legal basis proved to be a rather long-drawn-out affair. The treaty signed in September, 1915, was not ratified by both countries until the following March and not proclaimed until May 3. A law was enacted by our Congress in June, authorizing the assignment of Navy and Marine Corps personnel for duty with the Haitian Government. Many details regarding salaries, manner of appointment, numbers to be employed, further definition of legal status and authority, and of organization were worked out in August by executive agreement between the two governments. The Gendarmerie, with legally appointed American officers receiving pay from the Haitian Government, was established September 1, 1916, with ninety-five officers and enlisted men of the Marine Corps attached. A medical service for the Gendarmerie was established under medical officers and enlisted men of the Navy.

## Organization and Administration

For purposes of administration the Gendarmerie d'Haiti was divided into four geographical departments and into eighteen districts which in turn were divided into subdistricts, communes and rural sections. The Chief of the Gendarmerie, whose headquarters was at the capital, was given the rank of major general and his second in command, who acted also as chief of staff, was made a brigadier general. An administrative staff for the headquarters of the organization was also provided. The four departments were in charge of department commanders with the rank of colonel. The eighteen districts, each having a company as its normal garrison, were commanded by captains. Each district in turn usually divided its *gendarmes* into small detachments for the subdistricts, which were normally under the command of lieutenants. A combined pay and supply department extended its services throughout the organization. The medical service also had many duties in connection with health measures for the entire population.

Initially, all of the officers with the rank of captain and above were taken from the commissioned ranks of the Marine Corps and the lieutenants were drawn from its enlisted men. After a few years Haitian officers were gradually taken into the organization and several of the enlisted men of the Marine Corps rose to the rank of captain. The aggregate strength of the organization during the American intervention varied from its small initial allowance of acting officers and a few hundred enlisted men to approximately 2,700 officers and men in 1925. Thirty of its officers at that time were commissioned officers in the Marine Corps, 82 were marines, and 53 were Haitians. It also had 16 officers and enlisted men of the Navy Medical Corps. When it was known that the occupation was soon to be terminated, renewed effort was made to qualify suitable Haitians to take over all positions and be ready to carry on after the American withdrawal.

## Duties

The Haitian Gendarmerie performed a great variety of duties. It was trained as a military force and was ready to oppose groups of outlaws. It exercised all the normal police functions, both local and national. It preserved order and protected the rights of individuals and property. *Gendarmes* supervised the distribution of all arms and ammunition, the public lands, travel and traffic, and weights and measures. It was their duty to prevent smuggling, collect vital statistics, enforce sanitary regulations, exercise control over prisons, enforce harbor and docking regulations, and, for several years, they were largely responsible for the development and maintenance of the roads and telegraph lines of the country. In times of national emergencies they had plenary control.

The lower ranking officers particularly were required to have an extensive knowledge of their numerous duties. A subdistrict commander, for instance, was practically a chief of police, was expected to know the laws of the country, and of course had to be familiar with its language. The rural police, who functioned in the smaller subdivisions of the country, were under his control. He was adviser without full authority over numerous civil officials and over local communal assemblies. One subdistrict commander, Faustin Wirkus, made a considerable reputation for himself by his several years of rule over the Island of Gonave, where he was commonly referred to as the "White King of Gonave." Other subdistrict commanders were equally successful and left a lasting good influence behind them.

## Training Haitians

In order to make a constabulary that could eventually be turned over to the full control of the Haitian Government, the Haitianization of its officer personnel was undertaken as early as 1916. Ten young men were selected from better families and given a course of instruction in an attempt to fit them to become officers in the Gendarmerie. The attempt was a failure, however, as the American instructors did not understand the Haitian psychology, and the candidates did not adapt themselves to military discipline—a common fault of the members of the ruling class of the country, which largely accounted for their inability to control their own affairs. All the candidates became disgruntled for various reasons and one by one resigned. The training of Haitian officers was postponed until the organization became more experienced and efficient.

The Gendarmerie officers experienced great difficulty in trying to make ignorant and usually diseased Haitian negroes into efficient soldiers and policemen. By actual blood tests it was found that 95 per cent of the *gendarmes* had syphilis and that a very high percentage in addition had hookworm and other enervating diseases. Men in such condition did not have the vitality to maintain the alertness required of a soldier. They almost invariably fell asleep when on post, even while standing in the broiling hot sun. The condition was gradually overcome by systematic medical treatment and, when freed of disease, the Haitian became quite reliable in the performance of his duties.

An affair which left a lastingly bad impression occurred on June 19, 1917. The President issued a decree dissolving the legislature. It was customary for a member of the cabinet to deliver such a decree, but on this occasion the President requested the chief of the Gendarmerie, General Butler, to deliver it. Butler, accompanied by a number of *gendarmes*, went to the legislature and personally delivered the decree to the presiding officer of a joint assembly of both houses. The legislators were quite outspoken against the procedure. The *gendarmes*, on two occasions, thinking that it was about time to start shooting, loaded their rifles, but each time unloaded them at Butler's orders. After much confusion the decree was finally read and the legislature dissolved. The affair obviously did not help to promote good feelings between the Haitians and the American forces.

## Road Building

One of the greatest difficulties that faced the Marine Brigade in its efforts to restore peace in Haiti was the almost total lack of means of communication. There had been a fairly complete system of roads when Haiti was a French colony, but they, like many other improvements, had been allowed to deteriorate, and they had grown up in brush until most of them were all but impassable.

For instance, vehicles from Port au Prince could reach only the near-by towns. Soon after the occupation, road construction and repair were initiated under marine officers and considerable progress was made. The building of roads as well as other public work was undertaken to relieve unemployment, which was the cause of much disorder. Road construction was turned over to Haitian civil officials late in 1915 but afterwards taken over by the Gendarmerie. The Gendarmerie controlled it until 1919 when the job was taken over by Haitian Government engineers. By December, 1917, it was possible to travel by automobile from Port au Prince to Cap Haitien and by 1922 nearly four hundred miles of new road had been constructed and about two hundred miles of old road repaired. The work continued throughout the occupation and by 1930 a road system of approximately one thousand miles was in use.

A public health service was something new to Haiti. Measures for the improvement of the health of the country were initiated soon after the occupation began. The medical service of the Gendarmerie operated, in addition to its other duties, a public health service which maintained a number of hospitals and free clinics. The *gendarmes* enforced regulations for public sanitation and carried out a number of projects in sanitary engineering. Since one of the purposes of the intervention was to make the country more stable and prosperous, a number of steps were taken with this end in view—first by marines, later to some extent by the Gendarmerie and finally by special agents. Irrigation projects were carried out by repairing old facilities and constructing new ones. The newly constructed roads greatly facilitated trade. The public school system was extended and improved. The public works projects and general improvements were made possible by the additional funds derived from the more efficient customs service under American control.

## The *Corvée*

The peaceful conditions that had existed throughout Haiti for more than two years, created the general impression that all elements of the population were more or less satisfied with the new order of things. Such was not the case, however; the old ruling class, who had made careers of politics—the only successful career available—found nothing much open to them. Their usual method for gaining power had been to start a revolution. The marines, and later the *gendarmes,* in their vigorous efforts to open up means of communication throughout the country, made use of the *corvée*— legally enforced free labor on the public highways. Camps, which provided food and some amusement, were maintained with Haitian funds for the men while working on the roads. So long as the *corvée* was carried out reasonably and near their own homes, the Haitians did not object to the system.

In an effort to open up a road across the entire country, a considerable number of Haitians were transported some distance from their homes and required to work for several weeks. It was the duty of local officials either to collect a road tax from all men in their communes or to require them to report for road work. Some local officials misappropriated the taxes they had collected and made up the difference by requiring other men to work overtime. Road construction was chiefly under the supervision of *gendarmes,* who in some instances were guilty of accepting bribes for release from road work. Sometimes they even embezzled funds provided for feeding and entertaining the *corvée* workers. The *corvée* system proved to be particularly irksome to the peasants, especially when they were taken from their own communes to work on the main highways. Being compelled to work under such conditions naturally made the average Haitian dislike those making him do it—the marines and the *gendarmes*. Instead of being regarded as friends to the Haitians, which was the real purpose of the intervention, many marines and the *gendarmes* were looked upon by the Haitians as tyrants. The *gendarmes* no doubt were somewhat overbearing in the use of their authority, as Haitian officials have always been.

## The Caco Revolt

Resistance to the *corvée* manifested itself strongly in the east central part of the country; several outbreaks occurred at Jacmel during June, 1918. A *gendarme,* sent to notify the Haitians to report for road work, was severely beaten. A patrol, in turn sent to the vicinity, was ambushed and one of its members killed. Other less striking incidents occurred which indicated that dissatisfaction about the *corvée* was becoming general. Colonel A. S. Williams, U.S.M.C., Chief of the Gendarmerie at the time, acting in accord with the opinion of other authorities, ordered the *corvée* discontinued except where men were worked in their own districts and in cases of emergency. The order appears to have been misconstrued by a few zealous subordinates, who were anxious to open up roads to their garrisons. In the east central part of the country the *corvée* was continued for a time in the face of growing resistance. A system of paid road gangs was set up in the hopes that the employment provided would offset the discontent.

## Charlemagne Peralte

Disgruntled politicians—the "outs" at the time—seized upon the discontent caused by the *corvée* and used it to foment an insurrection. The rebellious movement found a leader in the person of Charlemagne Peralte, a caco chief, who had been under arrest for some time but recently had escaped to the hills. He organized groups of bandits and forced many peasants to join his aggregation. The rebellion grew rapidly in strength as well as in violence; it terrorized most of northern Haiti, causing the peasants to flee to the towns for protection, abandoning their land and thus producing serious shortages of food supplies. The revolt assumed some of the characteristics of the revolutions which had previously occurred in the country. While Charlemagne's followers probably never exceeded three thousand, at any one time, the movement at its height involved indirectly nearly one-fifth of the entire population.

Charlemagne launched a series of attacks on the Gendarmerie in October, 1918, apparently with the object of enhancing his reputation by successful encounters. He picked Hinche as his first place to attack and moved (October 15) against it with three groups. The *gendarmes* at Hinche fortunately knew that the bandits were coming and were prepared to receive them. A group of seventy attacked the garrison but within twenty minutes were driven off, leaving twelve dead behind. The other two groups remained at a safe distance. This was the first serious engagement for the Gendarmerie, but the Haitians behaved themselves exceedingly well and demonstrated their dependability.

The bandits rapidly increased their activity in the vicinity of Hinche. A group of sixty burned the *gendarme* barracks at Maissade and escaped without serious punishment, on November 10. The *gendarmes* in the area, upon being reinforced, carried out more active patrolling against the bandits. During January, 1919, strong patrols of *gendarmes* and marines, operating in the disaffected area, had several successful contacts with large bandit groups, killed a number of bandits and captured some of their arms, provisions and horses.

The revolt continued to grow. Early in February a *gendarme* patrol encountered a band of about two hundred bandits and defeated them. A number of caco bands were ravaging some parts of the country. Small detachments of marines were sent to the infested areas to hold the towns and relieve the *gendarmes* for field operations against the bandits. The revolt of the bandits became so serious that the Gendarmerie alone could not cope with it. The Chief of the

Gendarmerie made a much belated request (March 16) for the full co-operation of the Marine Brigade to help suppress the uprising. Numerous transfers of marines to other duties during the unrecognized development of a grave situation had reduced the strength of the brigade to only 37 officers and 831 enlisted men. Four additional companies were transferred (March 25) to Haiti from the Seventh Regiment at Guantanamo Bay, Cuba, and the marines went to the aid of the Gendarmerie.

### The Marines Take the Field

To help cope with the situation in the disaffected area, a company of marines was sent to St. Michel, one to Mirebalais, two to Hinche, and two to Las Cahobas. The company of marines normally stationed at Ouanaminthe was moved down into the midst of the bandit areas to Thomonde. Detachments of these larger garrisons were sent in turn to occupy about twenty-five smaller towns. Small detachments were also sent to several towns outside of the troubled area. The marines again relieved the Gendarmerie in a number of other towns to permit the *gendarmes* to take the field against the bandits.

From two to half a dozen engagements with the cacos occurred monthly during the first half of 1919. The first Gendarmerie officer lost was Sergeant Maskoff of the marines who died of wounds received in action on March 21. Maskoff's detachment of Haitians carried on the fight without his leadership in a commendable manner and brought his body back with them. Major John L. Mayer, U.S.M.C., while leading a large marine patrol on April 4, was killed in an encounter with some five hundred bandits near Hinche. The failure of Mayer's successor to fight to a finish with the cacos caused them to claim a victory over the marines. The cacos increased their activity; several engagements followed in rapid succession. No particular progress was made, however, in putting down the cacos until later in the year.

### Attack on Port au Prince

During July, August, and September the marines and the Gendarmerie carried on an intensive campaign against the bandits in which there were approximately eighty skirmishes. On October 7 Charlemagne made his greatest bid for fame and fortune: he sent three hundred of his followers to attack Port au Prince. They were joined by some of the lawless element of the city. But the marines and *gendarmes,* warned of their coming, easily drove them out of the city and pursued them back to their hideouts.

In the operations in general there appears to have been considerable confusion and lack of co-ordination between the marines and the *gendarmes*. Through lack of knowledge of each other's activities and not recognizing each other, marines and the Gendarmerie patrols fired upon each other on more than one occasion; this resulted in the death of a number of marines and *gendarmes*. Apparently there had been a tendency to discount the seriousness of the caco revolt and to suppress information about it. Without attempting to place the blame on anyone, along the chain of command from the policy-making powers of our Federal Government down to commanders in the field, the fact remains that there was serious blame somewhere for the turn of events in Haiti. A great deal of criticism resulted.

The enlisted personnel situation in Haiti was in the same unfortunate state as it was in Santo Domingo at about the same time. Most of the men had been enlisted for the World War and were dissatisfied over their retention in the tropics long after their comrades, who, in their opinion, had far more glorious experiences on the fields of France, had been discharged. This, together with the fact that the vast expansion of the Marine Corps during the World War made it necessary for many officers with very little experience to be placed in responsible positions, led to one breach of discipline in the midst of the other difficulties of putting down the caco revolt. As the weary campaign dragged on, however, it more or less unexpectedly reached a brilliant climax in one of the most daring exploits in the history of the Marine Corps.

## Hanneken and Charlemagne

Captain Herman H. Hanneken of the Gendarmerie, then a sergeant, U.S.M.C., conceived a clever plan for capturing or killing Charlemagne Peralte. He had one of his own trusted *gendarmes* join the cacos and become a "secretary," while he managed to have a Haitian civilian, in whom he reposed special confidence, made the "general" of a group of cacos. Both succeeded in gaining the confidence of Charlemagne and other bandit leaders. The "general" maintained a caco camp of his own at Capois which was attacked several times by *gendarmes* under Hanneken's careful supervision in order to make the rest of the cacos believe in the loyalty of the group. Hanneken led one of the attacks and had a report given out that he was wounded in the affair and actually went about for a time with his arm in a sling to lend credence to the report.

Hanneken, working through his two agents, succeeded in arousing the ambition of Charlemagne to make a concerted attack on the town of Grande Riviere and even arranged for the place that Charlemagne himself would remain, awaiting the results of the battle. It was also arranged for the garrison at Grande Riviere, which had been reduced to entice the bandits to attack, to be reinforced by marines just in time to meet the attack. Hanneken and his lieutenant (Corporal William R. Button, U.S.M.C.) blackened their faces and with twenty *gendarmes* carefully dressed themselves in old civilian clothes so as to appear like cacos, yet well armed and well supplied with ammunition.

The disguised group started to the place where Charlemagne had planned to be. They successfully passed many bandits, who were on their way to attack Grande Riviere, without arousing suspicion. Hanneken learned just in time from one of his agents that Charlemagne had changed his mind and was hiding on the top of a distant hill, awaiting the results of the battle to be brought to him by a caco detachment. Hanneken then determined to reach Charlemagne's hideout by impersonating with his men a caco group, bearing tidings of victory to their chief.

Led by the *gendarme* who had been acting as secretary to the cacos and who knew their countersign, Hanneken and his followers set out to find Charlemagne. The secretary went ahead and told Charlemagne that a detachment had come bearing news of victory. Charlemagne directed the messengers be brought to him. The secretary went back and informed Hanneken that there were six lines of outposts before the bandit chief could be reached. Hanneken and his party pushed on without the slightest hesitation. The first outpost received the glad news with a great deal of excitement and let them pass. The countersign, aided by Hanneken's pretense of great exhaustion in order to avoid talking, got them past the second outpost of about forty cacos. The third and fourth lines were passed without much difficulty, but a few casual remarks between the *gendarmes* and the bandit groups began to make Hanneken's situation appear somewhat precarious. The bandit in charge of the fifth outpost drew his revolver on Hanneken who, by pretending to be utterly exhausted, succeeded in staggering past him. The bandit leader then grabbed Button, who was just behind. Button tore himself away and by some skillful answer to the bandit's question, "Where did you get such a nice looking rifle?" (referring to Button's automatic rifle) avoided a conflict and the patrol passed on toward the last outpost where about 250 cacos formed the immediate bodyguard of Charlemagne.

Hanneken and the secretary finally reached the last outpost; the secretary pointed out Charlemagne standing beside a fire only fifteen paces away. The bandit chief suddenly became suspicious, and his men began to get their arms ready. The moment to strike had come. Hanneken promptly shot Charlemagne while Button opened fire with his automatic rifle on the group of cacos standing guard. In the fight thus begun, the bandit headquarters guard was dispersed with ten killed, including their chief. Hanneken remained at Charlemagne's camp until daylight, repelling several caco attacks during the night. In order to make sure that he had killed the real bandit chief, Hanneken took Charlemagne's body back to Grande Riviere for identification.

In the meantime the cacos had made their attack on Grande Riviere and had been disastrously repulsed. On his way to Grande Riviere, Hanneken had several successful encounters with retreating bandit groups. He reached Grande Riviere with Charlemagne's body at 9 A.M. and reported the operation as though it were a perfectly routine affair. Both Hanneken and Button were rewarded with Congressional Medals of Honor "for extraordinary heroism and conspicuous gallantry and intrepidity in actual conflict with the enemy." Button died of malarial fever soon afterwards. As a further recognition of his heroism and ability, Hanneken was soon afterwards made an officer with the rank of second lieutenant, near the top of that grade in the Marine Corps, and is now (1938) a major.

## A New Start

During the closing months of 1919 the Marine Brigade in Haiti underwent a considerable reorganization under its new commander, Colonel John H. Russell. The duration-of-the-war marines were relieved from duty in Haiti as well as in Santo Domingo and replaced by marines serving on regular enlistment. They kept the cacos on the move by a continuation of the previous program of patrolling against them. Russell reorganized the Brigade, improved the conditions under which the marines lived, and prepared for a period of more active operations which he hoped would put an end to banditry. The Eighth Regiment was formed under Lieutenant Colonel L. McCarty Little, who was also placed in charge of the theater of active operations early in January, 1920.

After the killing of Charlemagne, banditry declined rapidly in the north. The leadership of the cacos fell to Benoit Batraville, a native of Mirebalais District, and thereafter the country in that vicinity and the mountainous region to the east became the center of banditry. At the height of his power, Benoit controlled more than 2,500 men—mostly in central Haiti. Many more, however, were engaged in banditry and more or less subject to his control.

The new plan of campaign against the bandits was to keep their groups on the run by relays of patrols; fresh patrols were to relieve tired ones which had been following cacos for some days. It was hoped by such tactics that the bandits would be unable to reorganize, rest, or provide themselves with food and be forced to give up. The bandit area was carefully mapped and divided into squares for use in disseminating information and directing operations. The Brigade Commander and the Central Haitian Government both launched a campaign of propaganda and promised amnesty to bandits who surrendered themselves.

Banditry had reduced the cultivation of the soil in central Haiti to practically nothing more than an occasional garden. This not only made it difficult for the bandits to feed themselves but compelled the marines and *gendarmes* operating against them to transport their food into the area. With the aid of the newly developed road system and the use of several "sub-chasers," together with a newly arrived marine airplane squadron and the wide use of radio sets, a system of communication and supply was developed which contributed greatly to the success of the campaign that followed. The Marine Brigade had a strength of 83 officers and 1,261 enlisted men and the Gendarmerie an aggregate strength of about 2,700 at the beginning of the series of drives which practically eliminated banditry from the country.

## The Campaign of 1920

The marines and *gendarmes* started a campaign early in January, 1920, which they relentlessly kept up for six months. They had nearly two hundred encounters with bandit groups of various size; practically all remaining bandits were killed, captured, or surrendered themselves. A bold but, as it developed, indiscreet move on the part of the bandits played into the hands of the combined forces early in the campaign. About three hundred bandits entered Port au Prince on the night of January 14-15 by sneaking into the city in small groups and meeting at designated places. Considering the fact that practically none of them had watches and were strangers in the city, their plan was remarkably well executed until they were discovered by the defenders. The bandit groups were promptly met by marine and *gendarme* patrols who also sent out detachments to cut off the cacos' retreat. Before the encounter was over more than half of the bandits were killed, wounded, or captured while only two marines were wounded.

The "debacle," as the bandits called it, proved very disheartening. It, together with the harassing patrolling that was carried on against them, caused some 3,200, including several well-known leaders, to surrender during the remainder of January and February. Every effort was made to provide employment for those who surrendered, to encourage them to make an honest living and desist from banditry.

Among the more important engagements during March was the attack on Benoit's main camp, held by a band of about three hundred, which resulted in the scattering of the band in all directions. Patillon, the leader of the bandits in northern Haiti, surrendered soon afterwards. A few of the encounters proved somewhat disastrous to the marines and *gendarmes*. In one instance a small combined patrol, led by Lieutenant Lawrence Muth (Sergeant, U.S.M.C.), was ambushed and completely surrounded by Benoit's band on Mont Michel. Muth was killed and another marine wounded but with the aid of an automatic rifle the two remaining marines and the *gendarmes* fought their way out, killed ten bandits, and brought their fallen comrades back to Las Cahobas. The partial success of the bandits was immediately counteracted by twenty-one patrols going into the area and pursuing the bandit group until they had killed twenty-five more of them.

### Perkins vs. Benoit

A striking success, second only to that of Hanneken, was scored against the bandits during May by Captain Jesse L. Perkins with a patrol of one other officer and twenty-eight marines, resulting in the surprise and capture of Benoit. Acting upon reports as to the location of the bandit leader's camp, Perkins struck a small outpost which fired a few shots on his patrol and fled towards what turned out to be the main camp. Perkins sent all except three of his men to follow the fleeing bandits while he with the three went as fast as they could over a short cut to the bandit camp in the hope of surprising Benoit before he could escape. The camp was surrounded by a strong natural protection of large rocks. Perkins was fired upon by a number of rifles as he approached. His little group, led by Sergeant Passmore with an automatic rifle, disregarded the rifle fire, rushed into the camp, and almost ran into Benoit who fired at a range of only ten feet and was himself immediately shot down by Passmore. The remainder of the bandits, taking cover behind the rocks, continued to fire on the four marines but were driven off when the remainder of the patrol under Lieutenant Edgar G. Kirkpatrick reached the scene.

The loss of a much respected chief proved discouraging to some of the lesser leaders and during the first half of June thirty-five

MAJOR GENERAL SMEDLEY D. BUTLER (RETIRED)
HE STOLE THE SHOW

MAJOR GENERAL WILLIAM P. BIDDLE
1911-1914

MAJOR GENERAL GEORGE BARNETT
1914-1920

MAJOR GENERAL JOHN A. LEJEUNE
1920-1929

MAJOR GENERAL WENDELL C. NEVILLE, 1929-1930

COMMANDANTS OF THE MARINE CORPS

surrendered. Both the marines and the *gendarmes* continued their vigorous patrolling. A number of other chiefs surrendered, and by the end of June organized banditry had been all but eliminated. Only a few small scattered groups remained—mostly mere bands of thieves. The *gendarmes* in the bandit area had worked in close conjunction with the marines during the 1920 campaign and had contributed much to its ultimate success. Nearly two thousand bandits were reported killed during the two years of rebellion as compared to only about 250 in the first campaign against the cacos. During the last ten months of the revolt about eleven thousand outlaws were reported captured or surrendered. The marines lost seven killed and ten wounded; twenty-seven Haitians in the Gendarmerie were killed and forty-five wounded. The new Brigade and Gendarmerie commanders had been able to regain what had been lost by the inaction and indecisions of their predecessors, though at a price of much criticism from certain newspapers, which had suddenly grown sentimental over the Haitian bandits.

### The End of Caco Resistance

The Marine Brigade as well as the Gendarmerie continued an active patrolling program in central and northern Haiti during the remainder of 1920 but had only a few minor encounters with bandit groups, which, with one or two exceptions, were composed of only a few men. The marines continued to garrison a number of towns throughout Haiti. The duty of policing the country was gradually shifted back to the Gendarmerie, which also took over the less important posts from the marines. Conditions grew better throughout the disaffected area during the remainder of 1920. By 1921 people were in general carrying on their usual occupations, and a constant flow of provisions was coming into the towns.

The Gendarmerie suffered a considerable loss of prestige by allowing the caco revolt to get beyond its control. It had not stopped the movement in its early stages and the marines did most of the fighting which finally put down the rebellion. Most of the people still distrusted the *gendarmes* because they were prone to use their authority, as Haitian officials always had, to impose upon and exact tribute from them—in spite of the efforts of American officers. For a long time the people were unwilling for the country to be left to the unlimited control of the Gendarmerie, but the distrust was eventually overcome.

## More Normal Conditions

The few remaining bandits in the mountain regions of central Haiti were gradually run down during 1921. At the beginning of the year it was estimated that there were about three dozen small groups still in existence. Most of these groups were eliminated by a series of patrols during the spring of that year; by October banditry as it had existed for more than a hundred years definitely ceased. Along with the elimination of banditry there occurred a decided reduction in petty thievery and other minor crimes throughout the country.

With the return of more peaceful conditions and knowing that an early withdrawal from the country was not being considered, the Marine Brigade settled down to a more nearly peacetime routine, improved its living conditions, provided recreation for its personnel, and initiated training programs. It was maintained at an average strength of about fifteen hundred during 1922. For several years thereafter it varied between twelve hundred and fourteen hundred men. The number of garrisons was reduced to eighteen in July, 1921. Several more posts were withdrawn during the following year, and by July, 1923, the Brigade was concentrated at Port au Prince and Cap Haitien, with one company at St. Michel. By this time the Brigade was comfortably housed and living under satisfactory sanitary conditions. Patrolling was continued, but with a friendly motive to keep the marines familiar with the country. Colonel T. P. Kane took command (March 29, 1922) of the Brigade but was relieved after a short tour of duty by Brigadier General B. H. Fuller.

## Russell—High Commissioner

Conditions continued to improve throughout Haiti; the people, with the exception of the professional politicians, appeared quite satisfied with the new order of things. The Gendarmerie continued to improve in efficiency as well as in reputation; a beginning was made for its eventual Haitianization. A number of the newspapers in the United States assumed a critical attitude towards the manner of conducting the occupation of Haiti. Their criticism led to a board of investigation by high-ranking naval officers and to extensive hearings by a Senate committee. The findings of both were generally favorable to the marines but certain weaknesses were pointed out—the most important of which were the lack of unity of command and lack of co-operation on the part of the several agencies attempting to improve conditions in Haiti.

In order to eliminate these faults Brigadier General John H.

Russell, who had had extensive experience in the country and had been quite successful in dealing with many of its problems, was appointed High Commissioner (February, 1922) with the rank of Ambassador. Russell acted as the diplomatic representative of the United States, supervised and directed the work of treaty officials, and as senior officer present exercised authority over the Marine Brigade as well as over the Gendarmerie.

Louis Borno, who had theretofore been somewhat of an obstructionist to the American policy, was elected president by the Council of State. Immediately after his inauguration, however, he abandoned his previous tactics and co-operated with the American officials. The financial difficulties of the Haitian Government were satisfactorily worked out under American supervision. The Government had ample funds from the increased returns of its customs receipts to carry on a number of public projects. Improvement in sanitation and public works was especially noteworthy. The standard of living of the people was generally raised, and the school system throughout the country was greatly improved with emphasis placed on vocational training.

## Peace at Last

The period from 1922 until 1929 was one of practically uninterrupted peace and progress. Public work and road-building projects continued throughout the period, many reforms were made and the country on the whole shared in the general prosperity. The Gendarmerie was reorganized and enlarged several times until it reached a maximum strength of over 2,700. The number of departments was increased to five. The rural police system under Gendarmerie direction was extended (1924) to cover the entire country. As the Gendarmerie grew and assumed more control, the Marine Brigade was reduced until only slightly more than five hundred remained—acting only as a reserve to support the Gendarmerie during an emergency. A few additional Haitian officers were added to the Gendarmerie, but Haitianization made very little progress until near the end of our occupation. Its command was changed in May, 1927, in order to bring it back into line with the ideas of the High Commissioner.

Many Haitians felt that, since it was the country's only military force, the name "Gendarmerie," which is suggestive only of police functions, was not suitable. The name "Garde d'Haiti" was accordingly given it in November, 1928; that name was considered more appropriate as the Garde had wide political and administrative functions as well as military and police duties. The Lighthouse

Service was included as one of its functions in 1927. It maintained a telephone service and operated a number of radio stations throughout the country.

## Disturbances of 1929

Since the beginning of the American occupation the Haitian people had had very little opportunity to express their wishes concerning who should run the government. The politicians of the "outs" were not at all satisfied with the state of affairs and were constantly on the lookout for an opportunity to make trouble for the existing administration. The coming of the world-wide depression caused considerable unrest and furnished a fertile field for conspiracy. Politicians succeeded in creating unrest in the southern peninsula during August, 1929, but this was successfully allayed by friendly visits of American officials.

In order to induce students to attend the Central School of Agriculture, scholarships were awarded, practically all of which were in the hands of city students. It was decided to give part of the scholarships to country boys, thus reducing the number available for the former, who thereupon went out on a strike. Disgruntled politicians seized on the opportunity to foment a general strike of students and government employees and succeeded in persuading the customs house employees in Port au Prince to join the students in the strike. The two groups together with the ever-ready mob element created considerable disturbance on the streets of the city, and the situation looked quite menacing. The government declared martial law, extensively patrolled both Port au Prince and Cap Haitien, put into effect a curfew order in both towns, and arrested a few of the leaders. The situation, for the time being, was brought under control.

The agitators soon extended their activities to the country districts which were less effectively policed, and disorder spread to a number of localities. The troublemakers succeeded in organizing a strike of school children at Cayes, in which the stevedores joined. A detachment of one officer and forty-five marines went there from Port au Prince and temporarily restored order. Reports that the strike leaders had smuggled arms into the country added to the tenseness of the situation. When it was feared that the disaffected peasants were about to march on Jacmel, additional *gendarmes* were sent to that place on the *Galveston*. Reinforcements for the Garde were rushed to Leogane and Petit Goave, and additional provisions were made to maintain order in the troublesome cul-de-sac region lying to the eastward of Port au Prince. The general situation looked so threatening that martial law was again declared on December 4 and the Garde placed under the command of the Brigade Commander. Russell cabled for reinforcements from the United States, and the First Provisional Battalion of Marines was dispatched on December 7 from Hampton Roads.

The stopping of seasonal emigration from the Cayes District, the drop in the price of coffee, and other conditions aroused the suspicions and animosity of the ignorant country people, who, under the influence of agitators, formed a mob of about fifteen hundred and started towards the town of Cayes. A detachment of about twenty marines on December 6, armed with rifles and automatic rifles, met the mob, armed only with machetes, clubs, and stones, and would not let them enter the town. Their spokesman demanded the release of some prisoners. The request was refused; the peasants began to advance towards the marines. The marines at first fired over the heads of the mob, stopping them temporarily. The mob again resumed its advance; the marines held their fire until one of the leaders was in their midst with the mob following closely. It was not until then that the marines opened fire, killing six and wounding twenty-eight of the mob, which promptly dispersed.

Similar mobs gathered at two other places in the general vicinity; but, by the rare judgment shown by the Garde officers in charge, the mobs were handled without the necessity of firing on them. The wave of disorder collapsed suddenly on December 8, and conditions quickly became normal throughout the country, leaving responsible officials in the position of having been unnecessarily alarmed over conditions. The whole affair was decidedly nerve-racking to all of the Americans concerned as well as to the Garde. It served to show, however, that the Garde had grown to be a thoroughly dependable organization which could be relied upon in such national emergencies. Many efforts to disaffect its members by means of propaganda had failed, and in all of its 108 far-flung outposts its colors were kept flying throughout the period of disorder.

In order to provide for such contingencies in the future, each of the five Gendarmerie Departments of the country, in addition to the Twelfth Mobile Company at Port au Prince, provided for a reserve for immediate use in the event of serious disorder in other departments. The battalion of marines, which had been dispatched from the United States so hurriedly, was diverted to Guantanamo Bay, Cuba, when the disorder ceased and soon afterwards returned to the United States. Despite the fact that the situation had been successfully dealt with and no serious results had followed, it served to attract attention and led to the appointment of a Presidential Commission to investigate conditions and make recommendations with a view of helping to determine the future policy of the United States in its relations with Haiti. However, some changes in our policy had already been contemplated.

## THE FORBES COMMISSION

The Commission headed by the Honorable W. Cameron Forbes, after making a study of conditions in Haiti during March, 1930, recommended among other things: a rapid Haitianization of all services then under American control; a Minister to supersede the High Commissioner; the recognition of a temporary president and of a regular president, provided he was fairly elected; a gradual withdrawal of the marines, to be arranged for between the two governments; and a modification of the existing treaty, providing for less intervention in Haitian affairs.

Eugene Roy was selected and became temporary president. After regular elections were held, the National Assembly chose Stenio Vincent as president. General Russell resigned on November 12, 1930, and Dana G. Munro assumed the duties of American Minister four days later. The carrying out of the recommendations of the Forbes Commission proved to be quite a long-drawn-out affair. The Haitianization of the treaty services had been going on slowly for some years; about one-third of the officers of the Garde were Haitians. Haitianization was immediately stepped-up in the Garde without waiting for a definite agreement. The Central Department was turned over to a Haitian officer in December, 1930, and the proportion of Haitian officers in the Garde was gradually increased to more than half.

The withdrawal of the Marine Brigade presented some difficulty. It was finally determined that American officers should not be left serving in Haiti without protection and that the complete turning over of the Garde to Haitian authorities should be accomplished before withdrawing the Brigade. A treaty was agreed upon in 1932, which abrogated the provisions of the treaty of 1915 pertaining to the Garde, and a protocol was signed to speed up Haitianization. The treaty and protocol remained unratified for some time, but an executive agreement, made on August 7, 1932, provided for the complete Haitianization of the Garde by October 1, 1934, and for the withdrawal of the Marine Brigade within thirty days thereafter. Prior to this agreement, however, thirty-eight new Haitian officers were made. A class of fifty Haitians was started at the Military School to train sufficient officers to relieve the remaining Americans. The complete military force of Haiti, including the Coast Guard and rural police, at the time it was turned over to complete Haitian control on August 31, 1934, had a strength of 199 officers and 3,000 enlisted men and rural police. Colonel Demosthenes P. Calixte, who had served many years with the organization, was made its first Haitian Commandant.

## THE WITHDRAWAL

After the disturbances of 1929, the Marine Brigade took no further part in Haitian affairs. Its strength remained at approximately eight hundred—mostly in Port au Prince, with a small force in Cap Haitien. The marines performed garrison duty, carried on the usual routine of troop training and held themselves in readiness for any further emergencies. The Haitianization of the Garde progressed more rapidly than was anticipated by the agreement, and its full control was turned over to Haitian officers two months earlier than the date originally set. The First Marine Brigade evacuated Haiti at the conclusion of impressive ceremonies and in the midst of an outburst of friendly feeling by the populace on August 15, 1934.

The intervention in Haiti proved by far the longest and in some ways the most eventful of the Marine Corps's experiences in Latin-American countries. There is an interesting parallel between its experiences in Santo Domingo and in Haiti. In both countries the Marines succeeded in a relatively brief campaign in restoring order and in each, after a period of relative peace, a revolt occurred which required more effort to subdue than did the original pacification. These two revolts occurred at approximately the same time and were each probably instigated, to some extent, at least in their initial stages, by German agents during our participation in the World War. They both occurred at a time when the Marine Corps was greatly extended and its enlisted ranks as well as its officers' grades filled with inexperienced and relatively untrained men. The ultimate result in both Haiti and Santo Domingo appears to have been successful from the standpoint of the United States as well as the countries concerned.

## END OF MILITARY INTERVENTIONS?

The withdrawal of the marines from Haiti, according to our present avowed foreign policy, marked the end of a series of similar military interventions in Latin-American countries that had continued with only brief periods of interruption since the turn of the century. So long as the present good-neighbor policy and treaties now in force continue, marines will not again be called upon to perform such duty.

## Chapter XV
## INTERVENTIONS IN NICARAGUA

THE policy of the United States in its relations with Nicaragua has been governed by the Monroe Doctrine, by the desire to maintain stable governments in the countries of the Caribbean area, and by our interests in interoceanic transit and canal rights. Nicaragua like several other Latin-American republics has been highly unstable politically since its separation from Spain. It has had more than its share of revolutions, interference by filibusters in the early days, and foreign capitalists from the California gold rush days, when Commodore Vanderbilt maintained an extensive transit across the country, to recent ventures of fruit, sugar, and mining companies. It was in Nicaragua that the Marine Corps was called upon to make its latest and most extensive intervention in the affairs of any foreign country.

It will be recalled that several minor naval interventions or retaliatory actions took place in that country during the nineteenth century; but this chapter is concerned with the more recent interventions. For sixteen years prior to 1909 José Zelaya, a Liberal, had not only been able to control Nicaragua but attempted to extend his domination over some of the neighboring republics; he was a constant troublemaker for several Central American countries. A revolution to overthrow Zelaya started in eastern Nicaragua during the fall of 1909, and the attention of the United States was strongly attracted when he executed two Americans who had been serving with the rebels. The revolutionary forces at that time were strong enough to warrant the assumption that they could control the country. Secretary of State Knox broke off relations with the Zelaya government and declared that the revolutionists more nearly represented the Nicaraguan people. Zelaya, no longer able to maintain his power, resigned December 20, 1909, in favor of Dr. José Madriz.

In order to have a ready force available to deal with any turn of events in Nicaragua, a regiment of 750 marines under Colonel James E. Mahoney was sent from Philadelphia early in December, 1909, to the western coast of Nicaragua. It remained on board ship at Corinto until March, 1910, when it was withdrawn to Panama. At Bluefields, however, our naval forces took a more decisive stand, which favored the rebels, who, under General Juan Estrada, were at the time in possession of the town. Madriz' troops, supported by the small Nicaraguan gunboat *Venus,* moved on Bluefields to attack the revolutionary force. The *Venus* had cleared New Orleans a short time before as a commercial ship. The U.S.S. *Paducah* was at Bluefields with definite orders to protect American and foreign lives and property.

The *Venus* prepared to bombard Bluefields and support an attack of the Government troops. The commanding officer of the *Paducah* refused to let the *Venus* fire, for the reason that there were no rebels in the town and that it would endanger American and foreign lives; furthermore he would permit no fighting in Bluefields. His position was supported afterwards by the United States Government on the ground that the *Venus* was not properly a man-of-war. The *Paducah* sent a landing force ashore to protect American and other foreign interests on May 19.

A larger force was needed to control the situation, and upon request for more troops two companies of marines, under Major Smedley D. Butler, were sent from the Canal Zone to Bluefields where they arrived on May 30 and went ashore the following day. Butler with his marines continued the protection until early the following September when he returned to Panama. The Nicaraguan Government forces, as a result of the American action, failed to take Bluefields. Estrada's forces later moved on Managua and overthrew the government. In an effort to restore stability to the country, the United States, represented by Thomas C. Dawson, arranged for the formation of a temporary government and provided for the election of a regular president.

The Conservative Party, which came into power, soon developed a number of contending would-be leaders who fought among themselves for control of the country. Promises made the United States by one of the leaders were promptly repudiated by his successor. Feelings grew particularly intense between the contending groups early in 1911; riots and vandalism prevailed throughout the country. Adolfo Diaz was made president in May, but almost immediately his rule was seriously menaced by a Liberal plot culminating in the blowing up of Loma Fort, which dominated the city of

Managua, killing sixty people. A few days later a magazine in the city was also blown up. A filibustering vessel with a cargo of arms was reported en route to the western coast to aid the rebellious Liberals. One or more United States naval vessels stayed at both Corinto and Bluefields during this uncertain period.

Nicaragua, like some other countries of the Caribbean area, was beset with financial difficulties. Our State Department attempted to carry out a supervision of its finances similar to that which it had undertaken in the Dominican Republic. A convention to effect a measure of American control was agreed to in June, 1911, but our Senate refused to ratify it. Some New York banking interests after consulting with the State Department made arrangements with the Nicaraguan Government for short-term loans which served to carry it over for a time.

Continued strife within the Conservative Party and other disturbing influences caused Diaz to announce that a friendly military intervention by the United States was necessary to restore order; he proposed an amendment to the constitution permitting such intervention. General Mena, in control of the assembly, had himself elected president for the next term and General Emiliano Chamorro came back as chief of the army. Mena soon started a new revolution. He had previously taken possession of large quantities of arms and ammunition belonging to the government and placed them under his own control in Masaya. He left Managua with several hundred followers and, by additional recruiting around Masaya and with the use of his munitions, soon had a substantial and well-armed force. To further strengthen his position, he went over to the Liberals under Zeledon and their combined forces soon represented a formidable rebellion. Within ten days after leaving the capital, Mena returned with an army and besieged it. He kept Managua under artillery fire for several days but was unable to capture it. He sent a part of his supply of arms and ammunition to outfit a Liberal uprising at Leon—the center of Liberal influence in the country—and raised a considerable force in that vicinity. Diaz sent a force of Honduran mercenaries against Leon but they were severely handled by the Liberals.

## THE INTERVENTION OF 1912

Meanwhile, at the urgent request of the American Minister to provide for the safety of our Legation, one hundred sailors from the U.S.S. *Annapolis* at Corinto proceeded to Managua on August 3, 1912. Shortly afterwards President Taft consented to the sending of additional troops into Nicaragua. A battalion of about 360 officers

and marines under Major Butler was hurriedly transferred from Panama to Managua to reinforce the Legation Guard. The rebels had bombarded Managua intermittently between August 11 and 14 but, upon the arrival of Butler's battalion, withdrew towards Masaya. At the request of the governor and our consul at Bluefields the *Tacoma* landed a detachment of sailors and marines to protect Americans and other foreigners.

Revolutionary activities in the general vicinity of the capital continued despite the presence of our forces. The rebels interrupted the railroad to Corinto several times. On August 20, Commander Terhune, who had been in command of the American forces at Managua, started by special train with forty sailors and ten marines to return to his ship at Corinto. He was stopped by a mob at Leon, who took his train away from him. He started back to Managua and marched about twelve miles before being picked up by a wood train which took his detachment back to the capital. More determined efforts were initiated to re-establish communications with Corinto; Butler with part of his battalion on board two trains started back to Corinto with Terhune to reopen the railroad. After repairing numerous breaks in the tracks and some bridges, they reached Corinto two days later and Butler returned to Managua.

A regiment of about 30 officers and 750 marines under Colonel Joseph H. Pendleton was assembled at Philadelphia and sent via the Canal for duty in western Nicaragua. Several naval vessels were also ordered to the western coast of the country.

The situation was still critical both for the Nicaraguan Government and the American forces when Rear Admiral W. H. H. Southerland arrived (August 28) with the *California*. He promptly took charge of the situation and sent ashore the marine detachment and a battalion of nearly three hundred sailors from the *California* and a landing force from the *Denver*, all under Terhune, to keep the railroad open. Butler, who had come down to Corinto with fifty marines, took part in the advance which, after repairing the railroad track and several bridges, reached Leon September 1. Detachments had been stationed at the four principal towns along the way to prevent further damage to the railroad, and Terhune had about three hundred men in Leon. In the meantime, Southerland, learning that the insurrectos were pressing hard a small garrison of government troops at San Juan del Sur about 120 miles down the coast from Corinto, sent the *Denver* to that port. It landed a force of twenty-five sailors from the remainder of the crew to protect a cable station and American interests.

## Neutralizing the Railroad

By this time Southerland had received more definite instructions. He decided to open the railroad its entire length to Granada, deny its use to the rebellious Liberals, and impress the rebels with the hopelessness of their cause. He was determined not to permit the fighting of Nicaraguan factions to interfere with the railway traffic. Pendleton arrived at Corinto with his regiment on September 4. He hurried one battalion to Leon, followed with the remainder of his troops the next day and, after leaving the First Battalion in Leon, reached Managua on September 6. In the meantime the *Colorado* had arrived and added 250 sailors and its marine detachment to the forces ashore as further protection for the railroad and to help hold Leon. By the end of the first week in September Southerland had secured the railroad as far as Granada and was preventing the rebel forces from using it.

In compliance with instructions from Washington, Southerland issued a proclamation to the Nicaraguan people (September 11) that his forces were acting under orders not to permit: railroad transportation of munitions of war or armed bodies the bombardment of any unfortified place; the inhumane treatment of prisoners; any acts of wanton barbarity; or any act not in strict accord with the rules of civilized warfare.

## The Relief of Granada

The relief of the old aristocratic city of Granada was the next concern of the American forces. The rebels at Masaya and Granada had reduced those cities almost to a state of starvation in addition to imposing other terrors incident to their lawless operations. Nicaraguan troops were facing the rebels under Zeledon at Masaya but were making little effort to drive them away from the railroad. They were apparently waiting in the hope that the marines would do the job for them. Southerland, anxious to avoid any conflict if possible between his forces and Nicaraguans, urged action, and the Nicaraguan troops made a half-hearted effort to drive off Zeledon. On September 13, Southerland decided to push an American force, escorting a large quantity of Red Cross supplies, through to the relief of Granada. Pendleton started by rail with a force of marines and a detachment of sailors. They passed the government troops investing Masaya, but the rebel leaders insisted on holding a conference before permitting the train to pass through their lines. After the loss of two days in conferences the rebel leader agreed to let the marines pass. Butler's battalion then proceeded but was fired upon by artillery, and a band of rebels attempted to ambush his train as it was passing through Masaya. The marines promptly drove off the rebels but Butler withdrew his train. Zeledon denied responsibility for the affair but would not again permit trains to pass his position.

Not far from the western edge of Masaya the railroad passes through a cut. The rebel forces, by holding the hills on each side of the cut, completely commanded the railroad. Pendleton reinforced Butler's battalion with a battalion of marines under Major McKelvy and a battery of artillery and notified the rebel leader that his forces would attack the next morning if the rebels had not evacuated the positions which controlled the railroad. Zeledon refused and the marines prepared for an attack on the morning of September 19. Zeledon then agreed to let the train pass without firing upon it. Butler's train again started through Masaya but was fired upon by a group of irresponsible rebels and three or four marines were slightly wounded. The marines promptly returned the fire and in a few minutes killed fifty-six and wounded seventy rebels. Butler stayed in Masaya that night and proceeded towards Granada the next day.

After some further delays Butler reached Granada with the relief supplies on September 22 and Mena turned the city over to him. Pendleton reached Granada that day with an additional battalion of marines. Mena's forces were at first restricted to the garrisons where they had barricaded themselves, but after some negotiations Mena agreed to surrender, if given safe passage out of the country, and give up his troops to be disarmed and paroled. The Nicaraguan Government agreed to fairly liberal terms of surrender and the rebels were disarmed by Pendleton's marines. Butler, in full charge of Granada, restored law and order. The gratitude of the inhabitants, who had been at the mercy of their vindictive enemies for several weeks, was unbounded and freely and frankly expressed—especially by the women of that city.

### The Storming of Coyotepe Hill

About eight hundred rebels continued to hold the positions which dominated the railroad and commanded the city of Masaya. Zeledon stubbornly refused all offers for peaceful settlement. Pendleton withdrew part of the marines from Granada, past the rebel position, in order to have them in a position to drive out Zeledon. A battery of artillery came up from Leon to Managua to be in readiness for an attack.

The State Department at the request of the Nicaraguan Government directed our forces: to assume full responsibility for keeping the railroad open throughout its length; to control all towns along it which were not held by Nicaraguan Government forces; and further, not to permit any rebellious troops to menace the railroad by occupying threatening positions—apparently a direct order to dislodge Zeledon from his position at Masaya. The Nicaraguan forces made another feeble attack against Zeledon's position and subjected it to an ineffective four-day bombardment, but with no results. The attempts only encouraged the rebels, who considered the higher of the two hills—Coyotepe, a strong natural military position—impregnable. Rebel activities continued to cause much annoyance to the American forces at other towns along the railroad, particularly at Leon. Southerland then planned to put an end to the affair at Masaya, strengthen his hold on the railroad, completely occupy Leon, and send troops to make marches to a few important places in the interior as a show of force.

Butler's battalion and two batteries of Marine Corps artillery moved into a covered position west of Coyotepe Hill during the night of October 2-3. Pendleton offered Zeledon a last chance to evacuate the position and surrender himself and his army before the American forces should attack and drive him from it; Zeledon refused. The marine artillery bombarded the position intermittently throughout the day, inflicting considerable damage, but the rebels still refused to give up. There appeared nothing left to do but storm Coyotepe.

Under cover of darkness, in the early morning of October 4, Pendleton moved his troops, consisting of the First Battalion (McKelvy), Third Battalion made up of two companies of marines and a company of sailors from the *Annapolis* (Butler), and a battalion of sailors from the *California*, into positions east of the hill. McKelvy's battalion took position in the center, the *California* battalion on the right, and Butler's mixed battalion on the left. Some Nicaraguan troops had agreed to take part in the assault, but none were in position; the attack proceeded without them.

The rebels on Coyotepe were strongly entrenched and protected by barbed-wire entanglements. Pendleton's troops made a vigorous assault and completely overran and captured their position. The marines in the center led the advance and suffered the greater losses. The rebels were taken completely by surprise by the swiftness of the blow and, after a few minutes resistance with Pendleton's forces closing in on them from two directions, fled into Masaya. The battle lasted only thirty-seven minutes. The Nicaraguan troops finally joined in the battle, after learning the results of the attack on Coyotepe, and attacked Masaya. Butler occupied Masaya soon after the federal troops had finished with the remaining rebels, and restored order. The Americans lost four killed and fourteen wounded during the battle while the rebels had sixty killed and an unknown number wounded.

## The Occupation of Leon

The disastrous defeat at Masaya proved very discouraging to the Liberal forces still holding Leon. They were the next to be dealt with in carrying out Southerland's plan. The troops at Leon under Lieutenant Colonel C. G. Long were increased to nearly twelve hundred and on December 6 started operations to gain complete control of the city and dispose of the rebel forces. The rebels were disorganized and largely out of control; their leaders agreed to turn over the city to the Americans. When Long began the occupation of the city by advancing into it from the east, some drunken irresponsible rebel soldiers, engaged in looting and shooting up the town, attempted to resist the advance. In the fight that followed one marine and two sailors were killed and two marines and one sailor wounded, while nearly fifty of the rebels were killed before they were driven from Leon.

A few minor encounters between the American forces and the Nicaraguan rebels occurred at other places before the rebel strength was completely broken. A marine detachment at Chichigalpa, attempting to seize some arms and bombs, was fired upon by a mob of rebel soldiers and irresponsible individuals. Before the fight thus started was over, five marines were wounded and thirteen Nicaraguans killed and several wounded. The rebels evacuated Chinandega on October 6; the American forces thereafter maintained order at that place. Some of the rebels, driven from Leon, retreated towards Managua. A company of marines was sent out to La Ceiba to help the government troops intercept them. The rebel bands either surrendered or broke up and scattered, many leaving the country. A number of their leaders were given passports. The Nicaraguan Government extended amnesty to all rebels who would give up their arms by Ocober 11.

The landing force at Bluefields remained ashore until after the rebel forces had been completely crushed in western Nicaragua and until conditions had improved sufficiently for them to withdraw on October 13.

## The End of the Revolt

Conditions throughout Nicaragua rapidly became normal after the middle of October, and Southerland made plans to withdraw part of his forces. Prior to withdrawing, however, he determined to make some demonstration of his support of the central government by sending troops to a few important towns off the railroad. Pendleton, with an expedition of sailors and marines accompanied by a small detachment of Nicaraguan troops, marched to Matagalpa and back to Managua. Another such expedition went out under McKelvy. All measures taken during the intervention by our naval forces were either upon the direct request of or with the approval of the Nicaraguan Government, which repeatedly displayed deep gratitude for the assistance given in putting down the Liberal insurrection. The Liberal portion of the population, of course, was not so enthusiastic about our actions.

The American naval forces began to withdraw early in November; Southerland left Pendleton in charge with orders to carry out his general policy. Pendleton withdrew with part of his regiment and Butler's battalion on November 21, leaving Long at Leon with one battalion and a company of marines at Managua under Captain R. O. Underwood as a legation guard. Long's battalion withdrew January 16, 1913, leaving only the Legation Guard of 4 officers and 101 marines. A naval vessel was kept for some time at Corinto as a support for the Legation Guard.

## Growing Unrest

The Conservatives maintained themselves in power in their customary manner by controlling elections, leaving no other way for the Liberals to regain control than by revolution. The Liberals began to create disturbances again in 1921 but made no considerable headway against the existing government. They succeeded only in embarrassing it financially and creating a certain amount of political unrest. Marine detachments from two vessels reinforced the Legation Guard at Managua during January, 1922, when conditions were particularly menacing. The detachments were relieved during the following month when the Guard was permanently increased.

In the following May, a band of dissatisfied Conservatives seized the Loma fortress. The American Minister promptly informed them that any firing upon the barracks of the marines or upon the city would result in immediate intervention by American forces. The troublemakers surrendered when offered liberal amnesty, and peace was restored. Liberal outbreaks occurred in other parts of the country, but the Nicaraguan Government succeeded in quelling them. However, it was all too evident that the Conservative Government could not continue to control the country without the presence of the Legation Guard of marines and the attendant threat of reinforcements to any extent necessary. The United States nevertheless agreed to withdraw the small detachment but delayed doing so until a Nicaraguan constabulary under American supervision could be established. The Legation Guard was finally withdrawn at the insistence of our State Department, early in August, 1925.

## The Return to Chaos

The worst civil war in the history of Nicaragua broke out soon after the withdrawal of the Legation Guard. Despite the fact that the departure of the marines had been considerably delayed to permit the creation of a constabulary, that organization was still in its infancy and unable to control the country. A coalition government, with Carlos Solorzano as president, had just come into power, but it proved to be a house divided against itself. General Chamorro, the disappointed Conservative candidate, executed a *coup d'etat* in October, 1925. He seized the Loma, forced the president to eliminate all Liberals in the government, had himself elected president, and then forced Solorzano to vacate. The United States as well as some Central American countries refused to recognize Chamorro. Dr. Juan Sacasa, the legal vice-president of the country and a Liberal, went to Washington and tried to persuade our government to intervene. The Liberals started a revolution on the east coast in May, 1926, but were suppressed by Chamorro's troops.

Acting under Navy Department orders to protect American lives and property, yet remain strictly neutral, a landing force of marines from the *Cleveland* occupied Bluefields and maintained it as a neutral zone from May 6 to June 5. Another Liberal revolt broke out in August. It was soon suppressed in the west; but under the leadership of General José Moncada, the Liberals gained control of several towns in the east. A landing force of about two hundred marines and sailors from the *Galveston* again made Bluefields a neutral zone. The marines from the *Rochester* later took over Bluefields and maintained it as a neutral zone until the end of November. Several naval vessels were kept in Nicaraguan waters watching developments.

At the insistence of the United States Chamorro held a conference with Liberal leaders at Corinto during October, in an attempt to make a peaceful settlement of affairs. At the request of both factions, a detachment of sailors and marines from the *Denver* guarded the conference and provided for the safety of the delegates. The factions were unable to agree; hostilities were resumed. Chamorro, believing his situation impossible, withdrew, and Adolfo Diaz was again elected president by a proceedings of doubtful constitutionality. The United States recognized Diaz, but not until he had asked its help to protect American and foreign lives and property. The Liberal revolt, receiving substantial supplies of arms and ammunition from Mexico, continued to grow. Its leaders were so hopeful of success that they could not be persuaded to make terms with Diaz.

## Neutral Zones

Revolutionary activities were seriously interfering with the foreign fruit, lumber, and mining companies in eastern Nicaragua. They strongly urged the protection of the United States. The system of neutral zones, which had been used in Bluefields a few months previously, was perfected and several such zones were established by American landing forces. A neutral zone was understood to be a proscribed region, the safety of which was threatened by the contending factions. Certain localities were taken under control for the purpose of protecting the lives, property, and interests of Americans and other foreigners. No fighting was permitted within the zone; all armed forces were required to withdraw, usually within twenty-four hours, or turn in their arms and ammunition. In each neutral zone civil administration was left to the faction in local control unless some American interference was necessary to enforce neutrality.

Eastern Nicaragua was at the time but slightly developed. Roads did not exist and vehicles were practically unused. All travel and transportation was by water or over trails. Whenever the Liberal or rebel forces needed transportation, they seized foreign-owned boats. The owners protested against such seizures; the government of Nicaragua agreed to permit American protection. Secretary of State Kellogg recommended the landing of naval forces at Puerto Cabezas and other necessary places to furnish the desired protection.

The Liberal forces won a decisive victory over the government forces in the vicinity of Rio Grande and Pearl Lagoon, late in December. A landing force battalion from the *Rochester* went ashore at Rio Grande on December 22 and established a neutral zone. As soon as the zone became effective part of the battalion force withdrew, leaving 130 sailors and marines to maintain neutrality. Sailors and marines from the *Cleveland* and the *Denver* established another neutral zone at Puerto Cabezas shortly afterwards. In addition to these protective measures, several small United States naval vessels were watching conditions along the eastern coast of Nicaragua, supporting the forces on shore or affording such protection as their limited strength permitted. They made practically every port on that coast a more or less effective neutral zone. The Liberals protested that our activities were not entirely neutral and that we were hindering their operations.

By the end of December the available forces of the Special Service Squadron were overextended in their efforts to provide protection. The squadron commander requested the assistance of a battalion of marines. The Second Battalion, Fifth Marines, under Lieutenant Colonel James J. Meade, at the time camped at Guantanamo Bay, Cuba, was promptly sent to Bluefields where it arrived on January 10, 1927. In the meantime the marine detachment of the *Denver* had established a neutral zone at the entrance to Pearl Lagoon, and about one hundred sailors and marines from the *Cleveland* had set up another such zone at Prinzapolka. Meade's battalion disembarked at Bluefields, proceeded up the Escondido River to Rama, where it established a neutral zone in the midst of a Liberal stronghold, and declared the waters of the Escondido River also neutral. The rebels managed to move most of their troops above Rama, however, and prepared to march west. Meade's battalion remained at Rama until January 18, when it withdrew, leaving its 51st Company to maintain the neutral zone. The battalion was transported via the Panama Canal to western Nicaragua where the Liberal movement to overthrow the Diaz government was rapidly growing.

## Moncada Moves West

General Moncada, with greatly augmented Liberal forces, had marched west early in January, 1927. The British and Italian envoys in Managua pointed out the imminent peril to their subjects. A landing force of 175 sailors and marines from the *Galveston* went (January 6) from Corinto to Managua to establish a legation guard. Several additional foreign powers asked protection for their nationals. Our State Department continued to back the Diaz government in spite of its waning strength. Meade's battalion arrived at Corinto late in January and went to Managua to take over the Legation Guard and relieve the landing force from the *Galveston*.

The Liberals gained control of Chinandega February 7, after defeating its garrison of nearly three hundred government troops, and interrupted the railroad service between Corinto and Managua. It was reopened two days later, but the commander of the Special Service Squadron set about to make the railroad throughout its entire length a neutral zone. On February 19 a rifle company and a machine-gun platoon from Managua went to Leon to guard the railroad. Landing forces from the *Milwaukee, Raleigh,* and *Galveston* at Corinto established guards ashore and sent detachments to Chinandega, to assure the uninterrupted operation of the railroad.

Two hundred additional marines from vessels of the Scouting Fleet arrived at Corinto on February 21 and reinforced the garrisons at Chinandega and Leon. On the twenty-third, the 77th Company of marines occupied the Loma at Managua, at the request of President Diaz.

## Civil War

The Liberal revolt continued to gain strength, and the government forces were substantially reinforced. Moncada defeated a federal force at Muy Muy, and many of its soldiers went over to his side. February ended with Moncada facing Matagalpa. Neither of the contending factions attempted decisive operations during March. Our government continued to support the Diaz government and on February 25 sold it three thousand rifles, two hundred machine guns, and three million rounds of ammunition.

Larger forces were obviously needed to maintain the increasing number of neutral zones and to meet the requests for protection of foreigners and their property. The remainder of the Fifth Regiment of Marines and an aviation squadron were ordered to Nicaragua. Brigadier General Logan Feland was sent to take command of all our forces ashore in western Nicaragua. In the meantime, a company of marines occupied Granada and extended the neutral zone to that end of the railroad. Following an attack on our consular agent at Matagalpa early in March by a group of unknown persons, a detachment of 125 marines was sent there. The federal forces concentrated at Matagalpa for a final effort to stop the advance of the Liberals. Upon the arrival of the Fifth Regiment and the aviation squadron, they in conjunction with other naval forces established garrisons at a number of additional towns along the railroad. There were then fourteen such garrisons and the neutrality of the railroad was assured. By the middle of March American naval forces ashore in Nicaragua, including those holding neutral zones in the east, numbered about two thousand. They had so far had no conflicts with the Nicaraguans.

At the end of March, the main bodies of the contending Nicaraguan forces were facing each other about twenty miles east of Matagalpa. The government troops had the far greater strength, but the Liberals were more ably led. There was little indication that either side could impose its will upon the other. The general conditions of the country at the time were described by Henry L. Stimson:

> The long-continued disorder and violence had also produced a general disintegration in the social fabric of the country; semi-independent bands of marauders were taking advantage of the situation to plunder even the

settled districts. Our minister had reported to Washington that a general condition of anarchy was probably approaching.

The time had apparently come for action if further disaster were to be avoided. At the suggestion of the State Department President Coolidge requested Stimson, formerly Secretary of War, to go as his personal representative, with broad powers, to Nicaragua to see if some plan could be worked out to put an end to the conflict.

### The Stimson Mission

While awaiting the arrival of Stimson, the contending factions came to no decisive blows. The marines at Matagalpa established a neutral zone (April 17) when it was reported that the Liberals were about to attack the town. Stimson made a thorough investigation into affairs—first consulting with our own diplomatic and naval officials and then interviewing Nicaraguan leaders. He concluded that the military situation was practically a stalemate, and that the soldiers of both armies, being largely conscripts, had deserted in great numbers and turned outlaws, adding to the disorder of the country. The people were generally sick of the war and looked favorably on an American intervention. Even the Liberals, who had reason to be somewhat bitter, were willing to trust their future to a fair election and a nonpolitical constabulary under American control.

President Diaz on April 22 submitted a proposal that indicated his willingness to concede a great deal for the common good and suggested:

1. Immediate general peace and delivery of arms simultaneously by both parties into American custody.
2. General amnesty and return of exiles and return of confiscated property.
3. Participation in the Diaz cabinet by representative Liberals.
4. The organization of a Nicaraguan constabulary on a nonpartisan basis, to be commanded by American officers.
5. Supervision of 1928 and subsequent elections by Americans who would have ample police power to make effective such supervision.
6. A temporary continuance of a sufficient force of American marines to secure the enforcement of peace terms.

The plan anticipated that Diaz would remain in office until after the elections proposed for 1928. Stimson's next step was to arrange, with considerable difficulty, a conference with Moncada.

## The Tipitapa Conference

The main bodies of the contending factions were then facing each other about forty miles northeast of Managua; Moncada threatened to contain the government forces with part of his army and move on Managua with the remainder. Major M. B. Humphrey with a few marines started out May 2 to find Moncada and bring him back, if possible, for a conference. Humphrey located Moncada, who, in spite of the obvious danger of passing numerous enemy forces, came with Humphrey as far as Tipitapa where a conference was arranged with Stimson. The conference was held in the afternoon of May 4, and, after an informal talk lasting only thirty minutes, they reached an agreement. Moncada accepted all of the President's suggestions, after Stimson had obligated the United States to supervise the proposed elections and to carry out a general disarmament, including the forcible disarming of all who refused to turn in their arms—an arrangement applying to the elements, particularly among the Liberals, who had a leaning towards banditry. Moncada later secured the co-operation of practically all of his followers. The plan was approved by President Coolidge. An armistice, which had been put into effect during the negotiations, was continued while the arrangements to bring about peace were carried out.

## Disarmament

The Tipitapa Agreement had wider implications than were realized at the time. Certain parts of the country had been in a state of anarchy for years and were at the mercy of marauding bands. If all armed forces were disarmed and a constabularly formed to control the country, there would obviously be an interval of considerable time before the new military force could hope to be sufficiently organized and trained to control the country. Moncada warned Stimson of this apparent difficulty, and Stimson by implication assumed the responsibility for the American forces to maintain order until the proposed constabulary was capable of doing so. Future events proved this obligation to be an extremely large order for our marines to undertake and under the circumstances well-nigh impossible to accomplish. At the request of both Diaz and Moncada, eight hundred additional marines were sent to Nicaragua to assist in carrying out the greatly extended duties. In spite of its having over four thousand marines in China, besides those already in Nicaragua and Haiti, the Marine Corps was able to collect enough men on the east coast and from Haiti to organize the Eleventh Regiment for duty in Nicaragua.

The first task of the Second Marine Brigade (as the occupying force was called after March 26) was, in accordance with Stimson's agreement, to disarm both armies. In order to prevent a clash between the two armed forces, a part of the Fifth Regiment took up a defensive line along the Tipitapa River, covered the withdrawal of the Federals, and prevented the Liberals from passing that line until disarmament was completed. The Nicaraguan Government authorized the payment of ten dollars for each rifle or machine gun; an arms commission consisting of three marine officers carried out the disarming. Nicaraguan paymasters were on hand to make payment. Detachments of marines took the arms into custody and saw them safely convoyed to Managua. The rebel forces turned in a total of 3,704 rifles, 31 machine guns and more than one and a half million rounds of ammunition, while the Federals turned in approximately 11,000 rifles, 308 machine guns and over four million rounds of ammunition.

It was not definitely known at the time just how completely disarmament had been carried out. Augusto Sandino, a Liberal leader of doubtful motives who had been with Moncada, refused to disarm and left with about 150 followers for the Honduran border. Other smaller groups also left with their arms. These rebellious elements formed the nucleus of outlaw bands, against whom the intervening forces carried on continual warfare for more than five years.

## Policing Nicaragua

The magnitude of the task of restoring peace in Nicaragua, maintaining law and order, and developing a strong constabulary was, at first, only vaguely appreciated by the American and Nicaraguan authorities. With several thousand additional demobilized troops turned loose upon the disorderly country, it did not of course immediately become peaceful. While performing their mission of maintaining peace and protecting the lives and property of foreigners, the marines, still stationed mostly along the railroad, soon began to clash with the disorderly elements. A railroad patrol from Leon was fired upon by a revolutionary band on May 14. The marines returned the fire and the band fled. Another more serious clash occurred two days later at La Paz Centro, where a band of outlaws estimated at about three hundred entered the town at night and began shooting it up. Captain R. B. Buchanan, in charge of the marine garrison, engaged the outlaws in a street fight and, before they were driven off, Buchanan and Private Jackson were killed and two other marines wounded.

Garrisons next pushed out to the more important towns, off the railroad. A company plus a machine-gun section went to Rivas and a similar garrison to Juigalpa. A detachment marched on May 21 from Leon to occupy the town of Esteli. The Eleventh Regiment (Colonel R. C. Berkeley) arrived on May 19; most of its troops initially helped to garrison the town along the railroad. The country was divided into districts, each occupied by a battalion. In order to prevent serious disorder, it was soon found necessary to occupy a number of smaller towns with detachments of a squad or more, which functioned as outposts of the larger garrisons. By the end of May marine posts had been established as far north as the general line Somotillo, Esteli, and Jinotega with outposts as far as San Rafael. Small posts protected the lines of communication extending south.

Little definite information of conditions was yet available. Sandino was thought to have retired northward. At the end of May, with about two hundred followers, he was reported near Ocotal; little was known of his intentions.

Early in June a detachment of about fifty marines under Major H. C. Pierce marched from Matagalpa northwest through what later developed into the bandit country. Pierce established a garrison at Ocotal, restored order, and marched south via Telpaneca and Esteli. Ocotal was soon reinforced and became one of the more important garrisons of the country. Sandino was reported attempting to augment his forces at Telpaneca where his band was committing minor depredations; a marine garrison was sent there on June 13.

## REDUCTION OF FORCES

After the arrival of the Eleventh Regiment and with several naval landing forces still ashore, the Second Brigade reached a strength of approximately 3,300 early in June. It was scattered in forty-three different garrisons, in addition to those along the eastern coast. The aviation squadron engaged in making extensive reconnaissance flights and helped to keep up communications.

Despite the fact that the Second Brigade had yet made but little progress in carrying out its mission—the policing of the country scarcely begun and the constabulary a mere embryo—a movement was set on foot to withdraw part of the marines. General Feland began making plans as early as May 24 for a partial withdrawal and expressed the belief that order could be maintained with half the number of marines then in Nicaragua. The Special Service Squadron approved the withdrawal of one of the aviation squadrons, and the Commandant of the Marine Corps recommended the taking out of more than half the marines, leaving only the Fifth Regiment,

TYPICAL MARINE MOUNTED PATROL, NICARAGUA

BULL CART MEETING MARINE TRANSPORT PLANE

MARINE PATROL ON THE COCO RIVER

MAJOR VICTOR F. BLEASDALE WITH TYPICAL FIELD EQUIPMENT IN NICARAGUA

less one battalion, an aviation squadron, and a constabulary detachment of forty-six—a total of only 1,377. The force was actually reduced by nearly one thousand men by the end of June, and a number of the smaller garrisons were discontinued.

## Guardia Nacional de Nicaragua

The proposition of establishing a Nicaraguan constabulary under American officers was first considered in an extensive study in 1923. The beginnings of the organization were finally made under the supervision of a former Philippine constabulary officer a short time previous to the withdrawal of our Legation Guard in 1925. As the result of the chaotic conditions which followed, the constabulary made little progress. The forming of an effective constabulary under American officers was one of the most important stipulations of the Stimson Agreement. In anticipation of a definite arrangement, President Diaz (May 8, 1927) requested the appointment of American officers to instruct and command the Guardia Nacional. Lieutenant Colonel R. Y. Rhea took charge (May 12) of what remained of the old Guardia and began its reorganization. Other marine officers detailed to the organization initially occupied themselves with organizing civil guards, to maintain order in towns not garrisoned by marines. The first enlistment in the new Guardia was made on May 24. The first company, three officers and fifty enlisted men, was organized in Managua late in June, and after a few days' training went to Ocotal where it arrived in time to take part in the defense of that town five days later. Two other companies were soon organized and began training in Managua.

The sending of the first Guardia unit to the more lawless part of the country indicates that initially the policy was to use the organization to help restore law and order in the turbulent parts of the country. The completed organization and the full functioning of the Guardia was at first only vaguely visualized. It was initially planned to assign only about thirty or thirty-five officers and enlisted men of the Marine Corps to the Guardia, which was to have a strength of approximately one thousand enlisted men. Lieutenant Colonel Elias R. Beadle was selected as its first regular Jefe Director (with the rank of general of brigade) and assumed that position on July 12, 1927. The Nicaraguan Government had not yet enacted the necessary laws to form the organization, but Diaz authorized the enlisting of six hundred men and the appointment of 6 per cent of that number as officers.

## Rise of Banditry

While optimism was being entertained apparently by every one in control of the occupying forces, Sandino and other leaders were developing organizations of bandits, augmented by forced recruitment and other means. Only slight knowledge of the strength or whereabouts of these bandit groups was yet available, but on July 2 the commander of the Special Service Squadron directed that the forces ashore "inaugurate operations as soon as possible to disarm Sandino and his band."

Plans were immediately formulated to send an expedition from Matagalpa into Nueva Segovia. Some acting *guardias* were organized to accompany the force, for political reasons. After some difficulty in organizing its supply and transport, the expedition, under Major Oliver Floyd with seven officers, seventy-five marines and seventy-four *guardias* with more than two hundred animals, began the march on July 15. It was anticipated that the garrison at Ocotal would operate from the west while Floyd, entering Nueva Segovia from the south, would, with the support of the aviation squadron, soon crush Sandino's band.

## Sandino's Attack on Ocotal

Scarcely had a detachment of marines under Captain G. D. Hatfield and a company of forty-eight *guardias* under Captain G. C. Darnall settled themselves in billets in the town of Ocotal, when they were attacked by a greatly superior bandit force. Sandino had unexpectedly and by various means raised five or six hundred armed men in addition to having many sympathizers in Ocotal. He had learned of the expedition sent against him and determined to strike a decisive blow before it arrived. He approached Ocotal on the evening of July 15, carrying extra rifles for recruits (residents of Ocotal) who were expected to join him at the last minute.

But for the vigilance of the sentry in front of the walled Spanish house, in which the marines were billeted, Sandino would have surprised the garrison. The alarm was given; the marines were soon at their stations but completely surrounded by the outlaws who had filtered into the town and by armed inhabitants, thoroughly familiar with the situation. The Guardia garrison was also attacked, but the two organizations were separated and could support each other only by rifle fire. The initial stage of the fight lasted from about 1 to 3 A.M., when Sandino called off the attack, only to launch another an hour later which continued until after 8 A.M. He then sent a flag of truce demanding surrender and threatening complete destruction if the marines refused. Hatfield sent a reply to Sandino that marines did not know how to surrender and informed the bandits that he would commence firing again as soon as their flag of truce was out of the way.

The fight was resumed. At about 10 A.M. two marine planes arrived from Managua and, upon signal from the ground, took part in the fight with their machine guns until their ammunition gave out. Five planes with bombs as well as machine guns again attacked the bandits early in the afternoon, and the outlaws retired. Sandino got the worst of it in attempting to attack well-armed troops protected by thick-walled Spanish houses. The marines lost one killed and one wounded and the Guardia three wounded, while Sandino's casualties were variously estimated from fifty to three hundred killed—mostly by bombs. The bandits scattered towards the east and were lost track of for the time being.

Sandino's bold stroke was not considered at the time to have any great significance; it was believed that his repulse had been disastrous to his cause and that his strength would soon rapidly melt away. Rear Admiral David F. Sellers, the new commander of the Special Service Squadron, visited Nicaragua soon after the battle and after extensive investigations concluded that conditions were gradually returning to normal, and that a reduction of the forces ashore and the number of vessels in Nicaraguan waters was justified. The Guardia, with a strength of approximately 230, was contemplating taking over the policing of the entire country. President Diaz was not at all disturbed about conditions. The reduction of the Marine Brigade proceeded about as planned, and by the end of July it had about 1,700 men.

The whole question of military intervention in Nicaragua and particularly the use of our armed forces, as contemplated by the Stimson Agreement, drew extensive criticism on the administration from Congress, from the press, and also from a number of Latin-American countries. Several prominent members of the Senate Foreign Relations Committee were outspoken against the whole affair. The furnishing of about 4,100 marines for a brigade in China had taken nearly all marines from the regular stations in the United States and necessitated using a great many marines from vessels of the fleet. The urgent need of marines for other duties influenced the decision to withdraw part of those from Nicaragua as soon as the disarmament had been completed.

## Reinforcing Nueva Segovia

The Ocotal affair decidedly stimulated the movement of troops into that vicinity. Floyd, with fifty mounted marines of his column, rushed into Ocotal. A company of marines was hurried out of Managua in trucks to Dario to march from there to Ocotal, and a part of another company started for Nueva Segovia. Floyd moved east from Ocotal a few days after his arrival with a detachment of about 110 marines and *guardias* to operate against Sandino. He had encounters with bandit groups at San Fernando and near Santa Clara. He then pushed east via the San Albino Mines to Quilali, in the eastern part of Nueva Segovia, and returned to Ocotal without having encountered another bandit. He found the country generally deserted—the inhabitants probably in hiding. Banditry under Sandino's leadership appeared to those in authority to be eliminated.

The forces ashore in eastern Nicaragua were placed under the Second Brigade early in August. By that time the situation in the entire country was believed to be practically under control. Sellers reported that in his opinion only routine duty probably would be necessary in the future. Garrisons were redistributed on the basis of approximately 1,200 marines. Posts were established at Somoto and Pueblo Nuevo, south of Ocotal. Feland left the Brigade (August 24), considerably reduced in strength, to the command of Colonel L. M. Gulick.

Sandino proved to be a demagogue of the highest type. He was a master of propaganda and managed to use the Ocotal affair to his advantage: it served to attract attention of communistic and other radical elements in Central America, Mexico, and even in the United States; and it made Sandino a central figure to rally around. Considerable sums of money were raised, some even in the United States, and turned over to him for the purpose of providing military equipment and maintaining an armed force. Within a few months Sandino had several thousand followers and an actual armed force of nearly a thousand men. All this went on, however, without the knowledge of any responsible American official. Upon the retirement of Feland from Nicaragua the control of our military forces passed to weaker hands, and the Jefe Director of the Guardia, failing to grasp his proper mission, persistently withheld all except a small proportion of his men from the troubled area.

## The Bandit Offensive

The marines garrisoned some of the more important towns in the bandit area but, having insufficient strength to do otherwise, practically remained on the defensive, providing a few safe localities. Patrolling, largely for purposes of supply and communication, was carried on; as conditions grew worse patrols counted themselves lucky when they escaped being ambushed. Scarcely had the additional troops under Floyd left Nueva Segovia, when the bandit groups resumed their belligerency. The marines at Somoto had two encounters with bandit groups during September; a group under Sandino attacked the Guardia and marine post at Telpaneca. The marine posts in the bandit area were then reinforced sufficiently to carry out a few offensive operations.

The marine aviation squadron under Major Ross E. Rowell frequently patrolled the bandit area and was an aggressive and effective force against the bandits during the closing months of 1927. While flying over the bandit country, a plane crashed near Quilali. Its crew was seen to leave the wreck by aviators in another plane. A ground patrol hurried out to rescue them but encountered a group of about three hundred bandits, whom they repulsed only after three *guardias* were killed and a number of bandits killed or wounded. Another such patrol, looking for the lost aviators, engaged a bandit group near Quilali on October 27 and, with the aid of supporting planes, drove off the bandits. The lost aviators were never found, but it was definitely determined some months later that they had been captured and killed by Sandino's orders.

Bandit forces continued to grow during the remainder of 1927; marine patrols in northern Nicaragua had about twenty contacts with them—usually the marines were ambushed. Lawlessness broke out in the east; a bandit gang attacked a town of the Bragman Bluff Lumber Company and killed the *commandante*. A marine patrol from Puerto Cabezas drove them off. The *Tulsa* landed reinforcements at Puerto Cabezas. Sellers had been kept in the dark, by lack of sufficient reports, until about the middle of October, when he learned of the alarming conditions and hurried back to Nicaragua. Two hundred additional marines were sent from the States with all possible dispatch. Rowell's aviators confirmed persistent reports that Sandino had concentrated a force of several hundred troops at a fortified camp in eastern Nueva Segovia. The situation was beyond the control of our reduced forces, but further disasters happened before the unpleasant fact would be admitted.

### Fighting Around Quilali

In spite of his shortage of men, overlooking the many difficulties of supplying field forces in the wild jungle country and greatly underestimating Sandino's ability and forces, Gulick determined to attack the bandit stronghold. He assembled a detachment of about 150 marines and 7 *guardias* with 213 animals and a number of *muleros* at Jinotega under Captain Richard Livingston. The expedition set out December 21, with a long exposed column, through wild and undeveloped country, to attack Sandino. A second detachment of about sixty marines and *guardias* under First Lieutenant M. A. Richal marched east from Pueblo Nuevo to join Livingston at Quilali, in southeastern Nueva Segovia. When Livingston was within one mile of Quilali (December 30), he was ambushed by a large bandit group and, before the bandits could be driven off, five marines were killed, twenty-three wounded—six seriously, including Livingston—one *guardia* killed and two wounded; many of the supplies and animals were lost by the scattering of the pack train.

Shortly after noon of the same day, Richal's detachment, which was a few miles west of Quilali, was ambushed by another large group of bandits who were driven off after a twenty-minute fight with a loss of only one marine wounded. While attempting to make his way into Quilali two days later, Richal was again ambushed by about four hundred bandits. After a fight lasting one hour in which one marine was killed, Richal himself seriously wounded, and three other men wounded, they drove off the bandits and killed about thirty of them. A relief column, supported by planes, came out from Quilali the following day and returned with Richal's detachment.

The combined force remained in Quilali, awaiting evacuation of the wounded. A landing field was prepared by demolishing part of of the village, and First Lieutenant C. F. Schilt, by making a number of landings and take-offs in a very restricted space, successfully evacuated the wounded to Ocotal. Schilt was awarded the Congressional Medal of Honor for his daring feats. Captain R. W. Peard took command of the marines in Quilali and started to San Albino Mines—a more suitable base for operations against Sandino's camp on El Chipote.

The resistance of the bandits had been far greater than Gulick expected; in the hope of bettering the situation, or at least in getting the marines at Quilali out of the difficult situation without further losses, he sent additional detachments into the bandit area. About one hundred marines from Matagalpa marched to Ocotal, while a similar detachment from Managua went there by trucks and marching. With all marines that could be made available, Major Archibald Young set out from Ocotal to join forces with Peard. Reinforcements from the south, which arrived the following day, overtook Young, and the combined detachment joined with Peard soon after Peard reached San Albino. With more than three hundred marines in the heart of the bandit area and others en route to reinforce them, the critical situation was relieved for the time being.

The marines from San Albino and a group of planes attacked Sandino's camp on El Chipote on January 14, 1928. The ground troops succeeded in driving back an important outpost while the aviators inflicted considerable damage in the main camp with bombs and machine guns. With some additional reinforcements of *guardias* and marines, Young initiated a slow but systematic advance on the bandit camp. He sent several detachments to operate against it and at the same time cut off its ways of escape. After several trying days in the jungle, Young reached Sandino's camp on January 26, only to find it deserted. His further patrolling operations failed to locate the bandit group.

### Reinforcing the Second Brigade

No sooner had news of the ambush of Livingston's column reached Washington, than plans were set on foot to send the Eleventh Regiment back to Nicaragua. The first contingent to leave, with General Feland, who, in spite of poor health, had been ordered back to command the Brigade, and the Commandant of the Marine Corps, Major General J. A. Lejeune (obviously much concerned about the situation), hurried off from Charleston on three cruisers via the Canal to Corinto where it arrived on January 15. The remainder of the regiment arrived shortly afterwards. In the meantime three hundred marines and one hundred sailors from the Special Service Squadron were landed to help guard the railway. The Eleventh Regiment under Colonel Robert H. Dunlap was initially stationed at the larger towns along the railroad, vacated by their garrisons being sent into the bandit country.

The situation was made even more tense, while awaiting the arrival of reinforcements, by a mutiny of the *guardias* at Somotillo. The Guardia officers, supported by two marines, fought the mutineers, killed four of them, but five escaped with their arms to Honduras. A marine detachment rushed to Somotillo, the following day, and restored order.

It was then (January, 1928) estimated that the bandits had a fairly well-organized force of nearly fifteen hundred armed men in northwestern Nicaragua. They were resorting mostly to ambushes with an occasional attack on towns held by small garrisons.

## The Northern Area

The part of the country in which most of the bandits were located was made a special military zone, the Northern Area, placed under the command of Dunlap, and, as rapidly as possible, reinforcements were sent into it to restore order. The movement to the north was slow, as means of communication and for forwarding supplies for the troops were practically nonexistent. Improvised bull-cart and pack trains with the occasional use of Fokker transport planes—the first of which had just arrived in Nicaragua—had to be used. Dunlap planned to occupy additional towns and initiate a vigorous system of patrolling, to run down the bandit groups. Sandino was given one more chance to surrender before the marines started a new campaign.

It required more than a month to transport the necessary supplies, establish the new garrisons in the Northern Area, and fit out the troops for field operations. Approximately 750 more marines went into Nueva Segovia in addition to those sent to the adjoining parts of Esteli and Jinotega, which were also infested with bandits. Wherever possible, landing fields were developed near garrisons to facilitate communications. An additional aviation squadron was added to the Brigade.

While waiting for the arrival of additional forces, the marines in the bandit country carried on the campaign against Sandino. They engaged a number of bandit groups during the latter part of January and in February. In most of the contacts the marines successfully avoided casualties but inflicted considerable losses on the bandits and succeeded in breaking up some of their groups. A surprise concentration of about 350 bandits ambushed (February 27) a patrol of thirty-five marines under First Lieutenant E. F. O'Day convoying an empty pack train at Bromaderos in southern Nueva Segovia. The bandits surrounded the marines and contained them until the following day when a detachment of nearly one hundred marines under Captain William K. MacNulty came out and drove the bandits off. The marines lost five killed and eight wounded in the skirmish but, with the aid of the relief column, inflicted severe casualties upon the bandits.

Banditry spread into the coffee district around Matagalpa, where the marines were promptly sent to protect a number of American and foreign-owned ranches. By March, 1928, the bandits began to move only under cover of darkness and avoided contact. They kept themselves as a rule somewhat dispersed and formed in larger groups only for some particularly sudden stroke.

## Development of the Guardia

The Guardia had not developed as rapidly as expected. Except for the company which had been sent into Nueva Segovia, its personnel was occupied in more or less routine police duties in the peaceful parts of the country. An agreement was made with the Nicaraguan Government in September, 1927, to provide more specifically for the Guardia's administration and control. The agreement provided, among other things, that it should be the sole military and police force of the country. Beadle was unwilling to use the Guardia as a military force and insisted that it should have a long period of training before taking the field against organized outlaws. Nicaraguan officials were perfectly willing for the marines to fight the bandits but refused to co-operate.

The failure to support the intervening forces was made an issue by Sellers, who insisted that the President order all subordinate officials to co-operate with the marines. Diaz issued such an order, but its results were negligible. Under the leadership of the conservative Chamorro, the passage of the election law, agreed to by the Stimson Agreement, was effectively blocked. The American authorities wanted the marines relieved of all police duties, leaving them to act as a reserve force and to carry on necessary military operations as they had done under similar circumstances in Haiti and Santo Domingo. The Nicaraguan Congress refused to do anything for the Guardia. However, it was given an authorized strength of 43 officers and 1,136 enlisted men by presidential decree, late in 1927. After the Quilali affair the *guardias* in the bandit area were temporarily increased; a few of them were used in the operations against Sandino at El Chipote. After the Eleventh Regiment occupied Nueva Segovia, most of the *guardias* were withdrawn from the Northern Area. Thereafter for several months they were used almost exclusively in the more peaceful parts of the country.

## Neutralizing Nueva Segovia

By the time the Eleventh Regiment had accumulated sufficient supplies and equipment in the Northern Area, actively to take the field, the more thickly settled parts of that department were practically neutralized; the bandits retreated to the more inaccessible regions to the east and southeast or into Honduras. It was believed desirable to drive Sandino and his followers from the country, if possible, prior to the general election which the Americans had agreed to supervise. The brigade was further reinforced by marine detachments from battleships. A drive against the bandits was made in southern Nueva Segovia early in March, but with no decisive results. Contacts with bandit groups had by this time become very difficult, because the bandits were always able to evade the marines.

It was learned that the bandits were accumulating supplies in the rugged region of eastern Nueva Segovia and in near-by Jinotega. Early in April several marine detachments, sent into the area, thoroughly covered it in an operation lasting about ten days. Bandits were sought out wherever there was a chance of locating them, and all known accumulations of supplies were destroyed. Combat patrols were kept in the field throughout the bandit areas, but only a few relatively unimportant contacts resulted during March and April. The destruction of bandit supplies tended to break up the groups and no doubt caused many of them to quit. The marines drove others still farther into the interior but thereby enlarged the bandit area and necessitated far-flung operations, in the face of almost impossible difficulties, in order to break their strength. Many of the bandits retreated into the almost uninhabited area of north central Nicaragua—accessible only over a few trails during the dry season and along the larger rivers.

## The Eastern Area

Since the end of the civil war in 1927, there had been little difficulty in maintaining order in the eastern part of Nicaragua. That region was only sparsely inhabited by the peace-loving Mosquito Indians and had no roads; communications were almost exclusively by sea, across the lagoons, on the rivers, and, during the dry season, over trails. About one hundred miles west of Puerto Cabezas lies a rich gold-mining area which had tempted operators for more than fifty years. It contained a few mines in operation at the time of the latest intervention.

Driven out of western Nicaragua, several seasoned groups of bandits under Sandino started towards the gold-mining region. Reports of the movement caused considerable uneasiness throughout eastern Nicaragua. Early in April a marine patrol started to the mining area from Puerto Cabezas to protect it from bandits, then reported along the Coco River to the northwest. Another patrol went up the Coco River to Waspuc, at the junction of the river by that name with the Coco, to prevent the bandits from going up the Waspuc to the mining area. Before the two patrols could reach their positions, Sandino raided the La Luz Mine, in the southwestern end of the mining region, and destroyed most of its plant. He then proceeded to the northeastern end of the region, raided the property of the Neptune Mine, and retired to the northwest with his loot.

The entire eastern half of the country was practically undefended; the bandits were free to go wherever they liked. Both the commander of the Special Service Squadron and Feland took measures to protect eastern Nicaragua. Additional marines were provided for the purpose by landing detachments from several vessels and by sending 160 marines from the Eleventh Regiment through the Canal to Puerto Cabezas. The Eastern Area was formed with headquarters at Puerto Cabezas to cope with the situation in the eastern half of the country. Plans were made to contain the bandits in the north central area for a time and later drive them from their retreat.

## The Advance from the East

The marine patrol, sent from Puerto Cabezas to the mining area, heard many frightful reports of Sandino's operations. Thinking his little force too small to deal with so many bandits, the officer in charge took the patrol back to its base. Two patrols of over fifty men each went into the area early in May, and thereafter denied it to the bandits.

Persistent reports of bandit activities along the Coco, to the north of the mining area, led to the sending of stronger patrols up that river in the hope of contacting the bandits, or at least to protect the inhabitants. Captain M. E. Edson, in charge of the marines along the Coco, moved up the Waspuc River to the Indian village of Musawas, located not far from the northern edge of the mining area. He defeated a small bandit group on the way. Edson exchanged his boat equipment with Captain W. W. Walker of the marine detachment stationed at Neptune Mine for animals and started southwest after a bandit group. Failing to find the bandits, he joined forces with Captain H. D. Linscott, who had gone out from La Luz Mine with a patrol on the same mission.

Linscott with the two detachments moved across country to Bocay, then reported to be Sandino's headquarters and the center of bandit activity. They found Bocay completely deserted, due to reports that marines were coming up the river from Waspuc. In the meantime patrols from the Northern Area had pushed out to the eastern edge of Nueva Segovia, further to restrict the area open to the bandits. An aviation detachment which had been assigned to the Eastern Area aided greatly in keeping contact with the marines, operating at great distances from their base at Puerto Cabezas.

The coming of the rainy season made the trails almost impassable, and Feland decided to stabilize the advanced line of the Eastern Area. The detachment under Linscott was shifted to Cuvali, about forty miles southwest of La Luz, on the trail to Matagalpa, to keep the bandits west of that place. Two small detachments of marines held the mining area.

## OPERATING IN THE JUNGLES

Aviators from Managua located a force of bandits at Poteca, farther up the Coco from Bocay. The commanding officer of the Northern Area maintained that the place could not be reached from Nueva Segovia, but Major H. H. Utley, the Eastern Area commander, agreed to try to send marines up the Coco River. Before that could be undertaken, however, one hundred additional men and supplies for thirty days had to be brought up the Coco to Bocay from Puerto Cabezas—a distance of nearly 350 miles, up a swollen river, past many difficult rapids and part of the way in small dugout boats, poled by Indian crews. Edson was given command of the expedition to Poteca.

After nearly two weeks of preparation and with only part of his men available, Edson started up the river from Bocay. He lost most of his supplies passing the Callejon rapids but pushed on without them, expecting to live off the country or be supplied by planes. He soon found his way blocked by a strong bandit outpost on the river but skillfully outflanked it and drove off the bandits. In this battle he lost one marine killed and three wounded. It later developed that he had destroyed Sandino's main outpost which protected his camp at Wamblam, a few miles east of Poteca. Edson pushed on to Sandino's camp, from which the bandits had fled, leaving most of their stores. He reached Poteca on August 17.

In the meantime Walker at Bocay heard that the bandits were holding Garrobo at the headwaters of the Bocay River. He proceeded up that river for about a week, against the difficult current, and occupied the place on August 31. Garrobo was the most remote and inaccessible post that the marines of the Eastern Area occupied. It was twenty-six days' travel up the rivers from Cape Gracias. The marines from Poteca, Garrobo, and Cuvali patrolled still farther into the uninhabited regions to the southwest. The operations carried on by these detachments of marines in such a wild, inaccessible region, where food was often only available by killing wild animals, and men had to continue on the trail in spite of illness, demonstrated the highest order of courage and fortitude in those who took part. Edson continued his operations farther up the Coco throughout the remainder of 1928, reaching as far as Santa Cruz, which frequently had been visited by patrols from the Northern Area.

## Activities in Western Nicaragua

About twelve hundred marines continued to occupy the Northern Area for the remainder of 1928 with strong garrisons in the principal towns, assuring order therein and maintaining relatively peaceful conditions in the surrounding country by means of patrols. The bandits had been broken up into small groups or had gone east with Sandino. Some groups, however, continued to terrorize different localities; obviously, these were outlaws for the main purpose of making a living. They carefully avoided a contact; the marines rarely were able to see any of them and averaged only two or three contacts per month during the remainder of 1928.

During May, 1928, when the marines in the Eastern Area were driving the bandits from the gold-mining region, several patrols from the Northern Area went into the new bandit region to the east. One of these, led by Captain Robert Hunter, left Quilali and marched several days northeast from Santa Cruz. Hunter's patrol chanced to encounter a large bandit group—apparently on its way back from the east—on May 13. The bandits, for the first time in several months, put up a substantial battle; before they could be driven off, one marine was killed and one wounded. Hunter, mortally wounded, died a few days later.

In the summer of 1928 more than sixteen hundred self-confessed bandits turned themselves in and accepted amnesty, offered by Admiral Sellers. During the closing months of the year, occasional patrols from the Northern Area, sent into the more uninhabited regions to the east, co-operated with the advanced troops of the Eastern Area, operating from Poteca, Garrobo, and Cuvali. By the end of 1928 it was evident that Sandino was exercising little control over the other bandit leaders, who were operating on their own, for what they could make out of it.

## Supervising Elections

The obligation under the Stimson Agreement to supervise elections during November, 1928, in spite of widespread banditry, proved to be no slight undertaking. About fifteen hundred additional sailors and marines and a number of army officers, headed by Brigadier General Frank R. McCoy, were brought into the country during the summer and given special training, prior to registering the voters and supervising the elections. Nearly all the marines and many of the sailors were taken from the battleships of the United States Fleet in order to provide the necessary personnel. The men on election duty were dispersed in small groups to hundreds of towns throughout the country; many of them required protection. The Nicaraguan Congress refused to pass the desired election laws; it was necessary to proceed with the elections under a presidential decree. With the aid of all available personnel of the Second Brigade and most of the Guardia Nacional, both the registration of voters and an election were peacefully carried out for the first time in the history of the country. The result was a sweeping Liberal victory, in which General Moncada was elected president.

## The Militant Guardia

The Guardia, in the meantime, continued to develop. Beadle held fast to his policy of first taking over the police of the more orderly parts of the country, leaving the suppression of banditry to the marines. *Guardias* gradually took over the towns along the railroad and in the southern departments. During May, 1928, the Guardia began the organizing of units for policing eastern Nicaragua. By July 1 it had an aggregate strength of more than thirteen hundred and by the end of the year more than two thousand but still had very few men in the bandit-infested regions.

There was an ever-growing feeling in the Second Brigade that at least a part of the Guardia should be helping to suppress banditry. It was quite evident, however, that its strength should be further increased before it could, unaided, maintain order throughout the country. Moncada, soon after taking office, indicated a lack of confidence in the Guardia by proposing a corps of volunteers (all Liberals, of course) to help the marines fight the bandits—a duty which both Feland and Sellers felt should be performed by *guardias*. Friction developed between Beadle and the other American officials over the proper manner of auditing the Guardia accounts and other matters. Beadle resigned and the way was made clear for the organization to assume a larger role.

Colonel Douglas C. McDougal was appointed Jefe Director of the Guardia Nacional on March 11, 1929, and immediately began putting into effect many sweeping changes. He acknowledged the Guardia's mission to be military as well as police and reorganized it accordingly. He organized a battalion of *guardias* in Managua and, after giving it a short course in field training, sent it to Jinotega, to be distributed in that department to carry out field operations against bandits. Within a few weeks after McDougal took office, Moncada promoted him to the rank of major general.

The Guardia was reorganized into five areas: the Central Area, covering generally Matagalpa and Jinotega, became effective June 1, and the Northern Area, which included the remainder of the bandit country, on June 11. By the end of July the Guardia had seventeen stations with 609 men in the Northern Area; seventeen with 414 men in the Central Area; and fifteen with 257 men in the Eastern Area, which comprised generally the eastern half of the country. The more settled southwestern part of the country, where the two remaining areas were located, was thereafter more lightly policed. *Guardias* took over a number of marine stations scattered throughout the bandit-infested regions.

## A Stalemate

By the beginning of 1929 it was becoming more and more evident to all concerned that the marines in Nicaragua had been called upon to perform an almost impossible task, in the face of difficulties over which they had no control. They were expected to maintain order—taken to mean the eradication of banditry—without any control over the civil population, on whom they were almost entirely dependent for information, co-operation, and support. Neither the people nor their officials stood behind the marines in their attempt to put down lawlessness. The bandits were able to intimidate the people into telling the marines nothing about the bandits' movements and to keep them informed of all the movements of the marines. The bandits were able to hide their weapons and disguise their identity, almost at a moment's notice, and pass as peaceful citizens. Notwithstanding all of their vigorous efforts, officers conducting the campaign were practically unanimous in the opinion that the military situation had reached a stalemate. So long as the people would not assist the marines, the bandits could continue to operate in small groups and carry on their depredations in spite of everything the marines could do. The shifting of *guardias* into the bandit area was acclaimed as a probable solution to the difficulty, as they could control the civil population and force them to co-operate if necessary.

Moncada was inaugurated President of Nicaragua January 1, 1929. Shortly afterwards he manifested his willingness to support a policy which would permit the Guardia to assume its full duties as rapidly as it could be prepared, leaving American forces to protect American and foreign property and help to preserve order, only where the *guardias* were unable to do so. Sellers then approved a reduction of the ground forces of the Brigade to 2,500 men, and the marines from a number of naval vessels were withdrawn. After the reduction, the marines maintained seventeen posts and had approximately 1,200 men in the bandit-infested areas.

By the beginning of 1929 banditry had become definitely localized. Several bandit leaders, such as Ortez, Salgado, and Diaz, were operating in their favorite areas, carrying on thieving operations, extorting money from property owners, and avoiding contacts with the marines.

The Nicaraguan volunteers, operating usually with marine patrols, started a campaign along the Honduran frontier, which had become a favorite locality for bandits, as they could retreat into Honduras when closely pressed. Joint operations of marines and volunteers were carried on for several months with varying degrees of success. They had a number of contacts with bandit groups, but such operations did not put an end to banditry.

## The Guardia Further Expands

The increased strength of the Guardia and its taking over a number of posts in the bandit area and along the railroad permitted the withdrawal of marines from a number of stations and a further reduction of the Brigade. By the end of April, 1929, it was evident that the uninhabited north central section of the country, into which the bandits had been driven during the previous year, was no longer a bandit hangout. The advance posts which had been pushed into that area were withdrawn. The Eastern Area, then commanded by the author, gradually withdrew all of its posts along the Coco River and thereafter held the mining area as its most western line. The number of marines in the area was reduced to 230. A further reduction was made in the Brigade early in August by the withdrawal of the Eleventh Regiment, whose duties were taken over by the Fifth Regiment. The Northern Area was reduced to about one-half of its previous strength; all but ten of its posts were taken over by *guardias*. By the end of August there were about two thousand marines left in Nicaragua. The number of posts in the bandit country was further reduced in early autumn, when *guardias* took over several additional posts.

## Mutiny Again

In the meantime the Guardia sent approximately one thousand men into the bandit-infested areas. It was rapidly gaining experience in field operations and, in spite of an occasional breach of discipline, was becoming a dependable field force. The entire garrison at Telpaneca mutinied on October 5 and killed its commanding officer, Second Lieutenant Lewis H. Trogler, a sergeant in the Marine

Corps. The act was perpetrated under the leadership of a Guardia first sergeant and was disguised as a bandit attack. The circumstances did not come to light until after a second mutinous act (noted below) by the same men. Second Lieutenant Charles J. Levonski, a sergeant in the Marine Corps, with some additional men was sent to Telpaneca to take command. Affairs went normally for two weeks.

In the meantime, the leader of the mutiny had been transferred to Ocotal. Rumors reached the garrison at Telpaneca that the above-mentioned first sergeant had been executed for his mutinous acts. This prompted a second mutiny of the garrison, which was still made up of substantially the same men. The mutineers confined their two American officers, looted the town and started for Honduras, taking the officers as prisoners—fearing to kill them until they had got beyond reach of marine patrols. Levonski fortunately found out that some of his new men had been forced to join the mutiny and, by dint of good luck, the two officers, at the rear of the column, were guarded by men who were still loyal at heart. The officers escaped into the brush with these faithful men before the mutineers missed them and managed, after many trying adventures, to reach safety. Telpaneca had been immediately reoccupied by a detachment of marines, and steps were taken to protect Guardia officers. The mutiny probably grew out of personal and political motives and was dismissed as a sporadic outbreak.

Two Guardia officers were murdered early in 1930 under circumstances which closely resembled mutiny. Captain Edward Selby (First Lieutenant, Marine Corps) was shot and killed by a sentry while returning to his camp on the night of March 9. About a month later a Guardia corporal took a machine gun from its defensive position, turned it on the officers' quarters at Jicaro and killed Captain V. H. Dartt.

Despite these unfortunate affairs, the Guardia continued to improve, and its patrols were soon able to hold off many times stronger groups of bandits. Banditry was more or less sporadic, and by small groups, during early 1930, but Guardia patrols succeeded in having half a dozen contacts each month with the outlaws. On three occasions the bandits grew bold enough to attack small Guardia garrisons, apparently to discourage the new Nicaraguan force, but each time were repulsed. The Guardia had made sufficient progress by the middle of the year to take over more of the military duties in the bandit areas. It was given every opportunity to show its ability; the marines were purposely held in the background to permit it to gain experience and prestige. It was at last well on its way toward being a national military force.

There was another outburst of interest in favor of Sandino during May, 1930. As the result of propaganda among radical organizations, a large sum of money was collected in New York and elsewhere to finance his return to Nicaragua, after a period of retirement in Mexico. He came back to his old hiding place, in the mountains of Jinotega, re-established some control over several bandit groups, and even gained the support of a few civil officials. Banditry again increased throughout the Northern and Central Areas, and *guardias,* with renewed efforts, had a dozen or more contacts with bandits each month during the remainder of 1930. A mutinous plot at Somoto was discovered by Captain G. A. Williams (First Lieutenant, Marine Corps), aided by a loyal member of the Guardia, in time to prevent serious trouble.

### THE MARINES IN RESERVE

The Second Brigade remained at approximately the strength it had after the withdrawal of the Eleventh Regiment until March, 1931. It then further restricted its activities by withdrawing from all towns along the railroad, except Managua and Corinto, and by turning over two additional garrisons in the Northern Area to *guardias.* Marines continued some patrolling against the bandits, however, and were kept in close support of their officers, serving with the Guardia, as a safeguard against mutinies. The marines in the Eastern Area were further reduced and held only La Luz and Neptune Mines and Puerto Cabezas until April, 1930, when they were all withdrawn. Several additional marine posts were withdrawn, and the Brigade was reduced to slightly over twelve hundred marines, with only 236 remaining in the Northern Area.

### MARINE AVIATION

While the ground troops of the Second Brigade had greatly decreased in strength and activity, the aviation squadron continued to carry on its usual military missions with the Guardia. During the year ending June 30, 1930, its planes had made 1,275 military flights and a total of nearly 5,000 flights with more than 5,900 hours in the air. They had fought the bandits on five different occasions, using both machine guns and bombs. They rendered invaluable service in keeping up communications with remote Guardia posts, delivering mail and emergency supplies and evacuating the wounded.

## The Guardia Carries On

As the Marine Brigade stepped aside, the Guardia became more and more active in its operations against banditry. The bandits continued to operate in several groups, which Guardia patrols managed to keep pretty well on the run. In the Northern Area they drove some groups into Honduras and others into the less inhabited region of eastern Nueva Segovia. In the Central Area most of the bandits were driven to the north. Marines occasionally assisted by holding garrisons while the *guardias* took the field. Occasionally one or two marines, acting as automatic riflemen, accompanied Guardia patrols. On one or two occasions, the few remaining marines in Nueva Segovia took part in combined operations in an effort to drive the bandits out of some particular area. Late in 1930 the Guardia undertook the first of a series of operations with its troops of the Central and Northern Areas operating jointly. Several patrols from each area took the field and attempted to comb the area along the Coco River, while the marines held part of their posts and helped patrol the Honduran border. The Guardia was having an ever-increasing number of encounters with bandit groups.

The coffee-picking season of 1930 approached with its usual difficulties. The foreign property owners strongly insisted on protection. The Guardia was carrying on extensive field operations, at the time, and did not have personnel to guard the coffee crops. Upon the urgent demand of the owners, the marines established garrisons on as many as six plantations and maintained active patrolling throughout the coffee district until the spring of 1931.

Throughout 1931 the Guardia continued its efforts to put an end to banditry. At times, it seemed to be making progress; at other times, however, no definite betterment of the situation was discernible. It had a dozen or more contacts with bandit groups nearly every month. The bandits usually kept out of the way but occasionally grew bold and attacked towns held by small Guardia garrisons. Late in the year, Sandino made one last desperate effort to stage a comeback. He managed to accumulate a considerable quantity of arms and ammunition, mostly from Honduras, and for a time banditry increased to three or four times its usual proportions.

More than a thousand *guardias* were stationed in Nueva Segovia (the bandits in that department were reported to have increased to approximately 1,500), leaving the remainder of the country policed by only 650 men. Drives against the bandits in Nueva Segovia scattered them into other parts of the country. Some more determined groups made their way into the theretofore more peaceful parts of the country—Leon and Chinandega. They attempted to disrupt the railway service in November, but a concerted drive, by *guardias* and some other Nicaraguan military forces, defeated them several times and eventually forced them to give up the effort. They attempted it again early in 1932, but with no results except loss of prestige by Sandino.

During the rise in banditry the outlaws again invaded eastern Nicaragua. They established themselves on the upper Coco around Bocay and created considerable disturbance down that river. Pedro Blandon made his way as far east as the banana plantations of the Standard Fruit Company, near Puerto Cabezas. Some of his followers ambushed and killed Captain Harlan Peffley, in charge of a Guardia detachment that was attempting to drive them off. Reinforcements from Puerto Cabezas came out, drove the bandits from the banana plantations, and inflicted heavy losses on them.

The Guardia reported 141 contacts with the outlaw groups during 1931.

## The Marines Concentrated

The marines of the Second Brigade were drawn into the campaign against the bandits during the period of increased activity. On December 31, 1930, a patrol of ten marines under Sergeant Arthur Palrang went out to repair a telephone line east of Ocotal. In spite of its obviously having no combat intentions, the patrol was surrounded and vigorously attacked by a large group of outlaws. Eight of the marines were killed; the two remaining, both wounded, managed to save themselves by hiding. This sudden and savage stroke was apparently made in the hope that such a disaster would create a demand in the United States for the immediate withdrawal of all marines from Nicaragua.

Despite the increase in banditry, the State Department—yielding perhaps to the insistent demands for a cessation of what was styled imperialism in Latin-American countries, and influenced by the fact that the Guardia had at least demonstrated its ability to put up a substantial fight against the outlaws—announced (in February) the policy of withdrawing all marines from outpost duty and reducing the strength of the Brigade to approximately one thousand. After May 12 only those marines serving with the Guardia were stationed outside of Managua.

During 1932 the main effort of the American authorities was to shift the responsibility for maintaining order to the Nicaraguan Government. At the urgent request of the Americans, the Guardia was gradually augmented in strength until it had approximately 267

FIELD UNIFORMS AND EQUIPMENT, NICARAGUA

MAJOR GENERAL LOGAN FELAND
OUTSTANDING LEADER IN THE WORLD WAR AND IN NICARAGUA

officers and 2,240 enlisted men. Banditry continued, and the Guardia had approximately 160 contacts with groups of outlaws in 1932. The Brigade, with the exception of the aircraft squadron, acted as a reserve while the aviation unit continued in full support of the Guardia. The bandits, who had lost all semblance of centralized control, were operating in small independent groups. Despite its otherwise substantial growth in efficiency, the Guardia had several mutinies or attempted mutinies during the year. Levonski was killed in a mutiny of his detachment in eastern Nicaragua during April; his garrison joined the bandits and returned with them to attack the town where it had been stationed. Gunnery Sergeant Edward H. Schmierer, at the time acting as a Guardia officer, was killed in a mutiny at San Isidro on June 30.

### THE EARTHQUAKE

The marines assisted in conducting the congressional elections during the fall of 1930 and also the general elections of 1932 when Dr. Juan Sacasa was elected president. On March 31, 1931, Managua suffered a severe earthquake, followed by fire which completed the destruction of most of the city. Approximately one thousand were killed. Great confusion followed, and the marines, then commanded by Brigadier General F. L. Bradman, took control of the situation. They helped the *guardias* to enforce martial law, furnished guards for the city, helped to keep down looting, and established many first-aid and food centers. The emergency continued for several weeks until the city could be somewhat reconstructed.

### THE TURNOVER

Despite the fact that the job of restoring order in Nicaragua had not been completed, the Hoover administration was determined to put an end to the intervention as soon as possible. Banditry continued throughout the last six months of the occupation. The *guardias* vigorously carried on against it and had 96 contacts during that brief period. As late as December 26, 1932, a group of bandits, estimated at 250, attempted to prevent the running of trains on the new Leon-El Sauce Railroad and attacked a train carrying about sixty *guardias*. In the battle which ensued three *guardias* were killed and three wounded; the bandits suffered about thirty killed before being driven away.

The problem of turning over the Guardia to Nicaraguan officers presented some difficulties. A new president was due to take office at the time the American forces had been ordered to withdraw. It was obviously necessary to give the Nicaraguan officers some experience in their positions if the Guardia were to continue functioning efficiently. Initial steps had been taken as early as 1930 to make available junior officers for the Guardia, by running a military academy which had graduated several classes, by the time the marines withdrew from the country. More experienced men were needed for the higher positions. In order to provide a list of those acceptable to the incoming president, Colonel C. B. Matthews, the Jefe Director of the Guardia, requested each of the two candidates for president to prepare a list of those desired to fill all higher positions in the Guardia with the exception of the Jefe Director and the chief of staff. It was agreed that Moncada would appoint, as officers, the list submitted by the successful candidate in the presidential election to be held early in November. By this arrangement all officers would have at least a few weeks as understudies to officers of the Marine Corps, prior to assuming the full responsibility of office. In accordance with the arrangement Anastacio Somoza was appointed Jefe Director of the Guardia, and other high-ranking positions were filled.

As the time approached for actual transfer of control, the American officers in the outlying districts turned over their commands to the Nicaraguan officers and retired to Managua. The commands of the districts nearest to the capital were the last to be turned over, and the process was completed on December 31. Sacasa was sworn in as president on January 1, 1933, and the last of the American officers retired from the Guardia Nacional the following day and withdrew from Nicaragua along with what was left of the Second Brigade.

## Conclusion

Since the beginning of the last intervention in Nicaragua, the American naval forces had lost 32 killed in action; 15 died of wounds, 24 of disease; 41 accidental deaths including those in aviation accidents, while 24 died of other causes. They carried on a continuous warfare against the Nicaraguan bandits for two years with little support from the Guardia and had about 150 engagements of various importance. They closely supported the Guardia during its development period in 1929 and 1930 and, after the Guardia had demonstrated its ability to carry on the war with the bandits, retired to a position in reserve. Under the leadership of officers of the Marine Corps, the Guardia Nacional had approximately 510 encounters with bands of outlaws. It lost nearly 200 killed or wounded in action and estimated that it killed more than a thousand bandits, in addition to wounding, capturing, or driving out of the country many more.

At the time of the American withdrawal from Nicaragua officers of the Marine Corps turned over a well-organized military force numbering approximately 2,650 to the Nicaraguan Government. In addition to its regular military and police functions the Guardia had a well-organized medical department with facilities ranging all the way from a general hospital to those for rendering first aid in isolated localities. It also had an efficient legal department, a military academy, and a communications system which reached nearly every Guardia station, either by wire or radio.

If an appraisal be made of the results of the last intervention in Nicaragua by taking the Stimson Agreement and checking off its stipulations as fully or partially complied with, the results as a whole would be found satisfactory; but not all of the conditions could be claimed as having been fully complied with. Certainly it can be said that the American forces left the country in a better condition politically. A series of fair elections were held—wholesome demonstrations of fairness in politics. Economic conditions had not substantially improved. The country was still backward in many ways and almost completely lacking in communications. For those reasons in addition to others, lawlessness will probably continue until the country has been more fully developed.

The advantages and disadvantages which have accrued to the United States as the result of the intervention have been the subject of considerable controversy. The additional cost of maintaining naval forces ashore in Nicaragua and naval vessels in Nicaraguan waters, over and above what the cost would have been if they had been performing the usual duties of peace, amounted to several million dollars. The intervention caused considerable indignation throughout Latin America as being uncalled-for interference and was subjected to a great deal of criticism in the United States. These influences and other considerations ultimately led to the adoption of the "good-neighbor" policy and to more or less repudiation of such interventions. The Marine Corps gained a great deal of experience in certain types of field operations. While the task of restoring law and order was not carried to completion, the final results may prove as enduring as those of other interventions in which the mission apparently was more fully carried out.

## List of Commanders and Directors in Nicaragua
### Commanders of Second Brigade

Brigadier General Logan Feland..........Feb. 21, 1927 to Aug. 23, 1927
Colonel Louis M. Gulick...............Aug. 24, 1927 to Jan. 15, 1928
Brigadier General Logan Feland..........Jan. 16, 1928 to Mar. 26, 1929
Brigadier General Dion Williams........Apr. 18, 1929 to June 4, 1930
Brigadier General Frederic L. Bradman...June 26, 1930 to Nov. 26, 1931
Brigadier General Randolph C. Berkeley..Nov. 25, 1931 to Jan. 2, 1933

### Jefe Directors
#### Guardia Nacional de Nicaragua

| Name | Guardia Rank | Dates of Service |
|---|---|---|
| Lt. Col. Robert Y. Rhea | Brig. Gen. | May 12-June 29, 1927 |
| Major Harold C. Pierce | Major | June 30-Jul. 10, 1927 (Actg.) |
| Lt. Col. Elias R. Beadle | Brig. Gen. | Jul. 11 1927-Mar. 10, 1929 |
| Col. Douglas C. McDougal | Maj. Gen. | Mar. 11, 1929-Feb. 5, 1931 |
| Lt. Col. Calvin B. Matthews | Maj. Gen. | Feb. 6, 1931-Jan. 1, 1933 |

## Chapter XVI
## THE WORLD WAR

THE World War was by far the greatest experience in the history of the Marine Corps. In the five foregoing chapters the activities of the Corps in support of a rather aggressive foreign policy, from the turn of the century until 1935, have been discussed. This chapter deals with the activities of the organization in the war: its routine duties at home; its augmentation and training; and its miscellaneous duties throughout the world during the war, excepting the part it played with the American Expeditionary Force in France, discussed in the following chapter. The strength of the Marine Corps increased approximately seven and a half times during the war; it continued not only to perform all of its regular duties, which had greatly expanded and, therefore, required many times more personnel, but it also furnished a substantial force for duty with the Army which aided materially in the ultimate Allied victory.

### THE NATIONAL DEFENSE ACT

From the outbreak of the World War in 1914, it gradually became more and more evident that the United States would eventually be drawn into the conflict. No definite step was made by way of military preparation, however, until the summer of 1916 when, after considerable delay (August 29), the so-called "National Defense Act" was approved. It provided for substantial increases in all branches of our military and naval services. The authorized personnel of the Navy was greatly increased, and a gigantic building program was initiated. The allowed strength of the Regular Army was augmented to 220,000 and that of the National Guard to 450,000, but the Act provided that the increases should be made in five annual increments which, of course, greatly restricted immediate preparation for entry into the world conflict. The Act authorized an increase in the Marine Corps from 344 officers and 9,921 enlisted

449

men to 597 officers and 14,981 enlisted men and gave the President authority, in the event of a national emergency, to further increase the Corps to 693 officers and 17,400 enlisted men. The passage of this Act marked the beginning of the expansion and preparation of all branches of our armed forces which continued until the close of the war.

At the time of the passage of the National Defense Act, the Marine Corps had an actual strength of 354 officers and 10,727 enlisted men. Its personnel was distributed in twenty-five posts and stations in the United States—mostly at naval shore activities—eight permanent foreign stations, thirty-two detachments on board vessels of the Navy, and a small brigade of marines in both Haiti and Santo Domingo. Notwithstanding the existence of a world-wide conflagration into which we were expecting to be drawn, the Marine Corps set about its authorized expansion in a rather leisurely manner.

## Planning for War

The Commandant of the Corps, Major General George Barnett, planned to extend the expansion over a period of one year from the date of the passage of the Act, and formulated a more or less indefinite program for a further expansion, in the event of national emergency, to 800 officers and 20,000 marines. He stated that the organization "was practically on a wartime basis at all times, that its war procurement had been perfected for purchase, delivery, and inspection of stores." Recruiting for the newly authorized strength proceeded very slowly and by the end of 1916 it had been augmented by less than a thousand men, and no new officers were commissioned until February, 1917, when only ten were appointed. When we entered the war (April 6, 1917) the Corps had an actual strength of 419 officers and a few over 13,000 enlisted men.

The duties of the Marine Corps as laid down in Navy Regulations in effect December 31, 1916, were: to provide detachments for certain vessels of the Navy; to garrison regular navy yards and naval stations both within and without the continental limits of the United States; to defend when necessary naval stations beyond the continental limits of the United States; to provide a force of marines for seizing and defending advanced naval bases in time of war; to help garrison the Canal Zone; and to furnish such garrisons and expeditionary forces for duty beyond the seas as might be necessary in time of peace. The principal service rendered by the Corps during the World War—with the Army on the Western Front—had not apparently been anticipated at the passage of the National Defense Act.

Such emergency plans as the Marine Corps had, or were formulated prior to our actual entry into the World War, were vague and indefinite. No staff or office for emergency planning had ever been maintained by the Corps and most of its officers had only a vague realization, as our entry into the war approached, that the Marine Corps should by all means get into action wherever and whenever there was an opportunity. In the event we should become involved in the World War, it was commonly thought that there would be considerable expansion in the duties of marines guarding the Navy's shore establishments, particularly in the eastern part of the United States, by increasing the strength of posts already in existence and establishing a number of new ones. Aside from the necessary expansion for such routine peacetime duties, the Marine Corps expected only to supply a mobile force of a few thousand men to seize and hold advanced bases for the Navy.

The principal concern of the Marine Corps as war became more and more imminent was, to make ready its advanced base force, a part of which was serving in Haiti and Santo Domingo, for service with the fleet. Several companies of marines returned to their advanced base units in Philadelphia a short time before the declaration of war or soon thereafter. And it was found necessary to replace part of these units immediately by new and comparatively untrained ones, hastily organized for the purpose.

## The Virgin Islands

A few days prior to our actual declaration of war, the transfer of the Virgin Islands from the possession of Denmark to the United States was completed, and a battalion of marines, acting as an occupying force, helped to take them over. One company established a garrison at Christiansted on St. Croix (March 29) and two companies went to St. Thomas (April 21). The islands had been purchased largely to prevent their falling into the hands of the Germans, who it was feared might use them as submarine bases for operations in the western Atlantic. The Navy Department was constantly in fear of such a possibility even after the United States had taken possession of the islands. About one year later a small base-defense force (a battalion of marines), equipped with searchlights and fixed naval guns, was organized and sent to the islands, where they established defenses which they maintained throughout the remainder of the war.

## Interned German Vessels

A number of German vessels, including vessels of war, had been interned in various American ports prior to the time that the United States entered the war. These vessels were taken possession of immediately after our declaration of war; the marines in some cases participated in taking them over. An interesting instance of such action occurred on the island of Guam.

The German cruiser *Cormoran* had been chased into the harbor of that island by the Japanese more than two years previously and the vessel had been interned, but only partially disarmed, and its crew allowed to live on board. The failure fully to disarm the vessel caused considerable anxiety for many months preceding our entry into the World War, as the crew of the German vessel was of about equal strength to the entire American garrison on the island. This condition was rectified a few weeks prior to the war and the vessel, supposedly, was completely disarmed. On the early morning of April 7, after the news of the declaration of war had reached the American authorities on the island, preparations were made for the sinking of the vessel by gunfire of batteries on shore, manned by marines, in case it refused to surrender. The Governor's aide was sent out to demand the surrender of the *Cormoran*. The Germans pretended to acquiesce, momentarily, by hauling down their colors, but refused actual surrender to the boarding officer, and as soon as he had left the ship again raised the colors and blew up their own vessel which sank within a few minutes. The Germans jumped into the bay, were rescued by the Americans, made prisoners of war, brought to the United States by an escort of marines (commanded by the writer), and taken to an army prison camp at Fort Douglas, Utah.

## Duty With the Army

In every major war and in a number of less important belligerent affairs, the Marine Corps had served with the Army, and the President was authorized by law to order marines to duty with that branch of the service when he saw fit. Nevertheless, there was considerable difficulty at first in getting marines made available for duty with the Army on the Western Front, where American forces were so seriously needed. As noted above, in the preparations which took place prior to our actual entry into the war, little thought had been given to having the marines serve with the Army. There was considerable opinion in the Navy Department that their services should be exclusively with the Navy. The Chief of Naval Operations, Admiral Benson, initially recommended against marines being ordered to such duty. The Commandant of the Marine Corps, with a proper vision of the Corps's larger usefulness, felt, however, that the most urgent need for armed forces was on the Western Front and that the marines should participate in any expeditionary force sent to France. He held fast to that belief throughout the war and made it a basic part of his policy.

Just prior to our entry into the war a still greater expansion of the naval services was planned. Recommendations had been made for the Navy's enlisted personnel to be increased to 150,000, and that the Marine Corps be authorized to have 20 per cent of that number—its normal proportionate strength. This became the basis for the first increase (May 22, 1917), made in the naval establishment during the war. It was then planned to use this increase in the Marine Corps: to meet the ever-growing demands for protection of naval establishments in the United States; to augment slightly the expeditionary forces in Haiti, Santo Domingo, and Cuba; to make more men available for the increasing number of ships' detachments; to bring the advanced base force up to its authorized strength of approximately 5,000 men; and to provide about 7,000 marines for expeditionary duty with the Army.

In the meantime the Army had been organizing the initial contingent of an expeditionary force to join the Allies in France. On May 16 the Secretary of War requested a regiment of marines, organized as infantry, to accompany the expedition and a base detachment of about 1,000 marines to be sent later as replacements for the regiment. The Fifth Marines at Philadelphia was reorganized for the purpose, and on May 27 President Wilson directed that the necessary orders be issued for it to be sent to France for duty with the Army.

### Guarding Shore Establishments

Despite the fact that the United States was far removed from the war zone, and there was not the slightest danger of invasion or the wholesale entry of spies into the country, a great deal of fear prevailed that enemy sympathizers would interfere in some way with our preparations for war and with the operation of our naval shore establishments. Throughout the entire war calls for new guards for naval shore activities and increases in such guards already in existence poured into Marine Corps Headquarters. As the war neared its end, the number of detachments, guarding such establishments in the United States alone, had grown to seventy-five which required approximately 250 officers and 7,788 marines—nearly equaling the entire prewar strength of the Marine Corps. The greatest single increase in the number of such detachments was for new radio stations and commercial cable and telegraph offices, to protect our war communications system. There was doubtless much unnecessary extension of guarding shore establishments by marines which resulted in the absorption of all too many of them in non-combat activities.

## Training Centers

The rapid expansion of the naval shore establishments, incident to preparation for war, and their taking over nearly all near-by space kept the marines from expanding their training facilities at most of the navy yards. The expansion of the Corps, first to 17,400 and not long afterwards to 30,000, necessitated far larger camp facilities for sheltering the men than had ever been anticipated. The housing problem was solved by the Marine Corps in the same manner as it was by the Army—by the development of large temporary cantonments. Barracks space at Mare Island, California, was considerably expanded but the Corps's main developments were made in the eastern part of the country—at Parris Island, South Carolina, and Quantico, Virginia.

The Marine Corps had maintained a small post at an inactive naval station near Port Royal, South Carolina, for a number of years. There it had trained the recruits from the eastern part of the country since November, 1915. The station was located on Parris Island, having an area of about ten square miles, exclusive of marsh and tide lands. The entire island was gradually acquired, and the difficult task of developing a cantonment suitable for training several thousand men, in a comparatively isolated locality which had neither railway nor highway transportation, was initiated. Practically all the facilities for the necessary water transportation, including wharves, barges, tugs, boats, etc. from the nearest railway terminal, had to be provided. Before temporary buildings could be erected in sufficient number, it was necessary to place several thousand recruits under canvas. The development of the plant at Parris Island, in the course of the war, cost nearly four million dollars. More than 46,000 marines were accommodated—after a fashion—and given their initial training. The maximum capacity of the cantonment, approximately 16,600, was reached after the Marine Corps had been more than doubled in strength for the second time during 1918.

The effort to expand the advanced base force to a war strength organization, with a brigade of infantry in addition to the necessary technical units and artillery, necessitated larger camp facilities than were available in the Philadelphia Navy Yard, where the organization had theretofore maintained itself when not on expeditionary duty. A tract having suitable terrain for the training of both artillery and infantry was essential, and it was desirable that it could be readily reached by transport vessels. Such a supposedly suitable area was found at Quantico, Virginia, about forty miles below Washington on the Potomac River. Most of the desired land was at the time in the hands of a land-speculating company, which was making little progress in disposing of it. Six thousand acres of land were leased initially, and on May 14 the first marine detachment was transferred to Quantico from Annapolis. A temporary housing development on a large scale was immediately undertaken. The initial plans provided for temporary barracks buildings (accommodating fifty men each), kitchens, mess halls, bath houses, etc., for approximately 3,500 men, and a hospital, a headquarters building, storehouses, and necessary utilities.

## Recruiting

The efforts to augment the Marine Corps to its newly authorized strength proceeded rapidly after the declaration of war. Its recruiting stations were stormed with many times more applicants than could be accepted. An unusually high type of men presented themselves for enlistment; three hundred students, for example, from the University of Minnesota, enlisted en bloc. Successful business and professional men accepted the humble status of a private without reservation. A number of these were later made temporary officers and some became regular officers in the Marine Corps after the war. The Corps was filled to its allowed strength within a few weeks and was asking for an additional substantial increase. Temporary recruit depots were operated at Philadelphia and Norfolk, and the regular recruit training establishments at Parris Island, South Carolina, and Mare Island, California, were expanded to take care of the remaining recruits who rushed to the colors.

The process of procuring officers proceeded rather slowly, but within a little over four months the number of Marine officers was more than doubled. The new officers were given a few days training, while obtaining the necessary uniforms and equipment and immediately sent to duty with troops. A considerable number were commissioned from the ranks, while others were selected from colleges and universities throughout the country, that maintained military departments.

The initial temporary increase in the strength of the Corps was followed by a still greater one in 1918. Each increase was followed by a wave of recruiting and the filling of the recruit camps to more than their capacity with men outfitting and undergoing the preliminary instruction prior to being turned over for advanced training or other duties. The recruiting service, at its maximum expansion, had 374 stations and required 26 officers and 428 enlisted men. Enlistments were voluntary until near the close of the war, when a quota of 5,000 drafted men monthly was assigned the Marine Corps and volunteering was no longer allowed. All men who served in the Marine Corps during the World War were volunteers with the exception of 7,088 drafted men, inducted into the Corps during the last few weeks of the war; but none of the drafted men reached the war zone before the armistice.

The vast army of recruits trained at Parris Island were assigned to recruit companies as they arrived; as soon as a company was filled to its desired strength and the men issued their military clothing and equipment, it started on a schedule of intensive training. The period of training varied, according to the need for the men elsewhere, from eight to twelve weeks, including as a rule two weeks of firing on the rifle range. Training of recruits was carried on in a similar manner, but on a far less extensive scale, at Mare Island, California. In addition to giving the prescribed recruit training, Parris Island also operated establishments for the special training of noncommissioned officers, field musicians, radio and signal communications men, bandsmen, cooks, and bakers. It gave such specialized training to approximately 3,700 marines during the war.

## Advanced Base Force

The Navy Department, from the beginning of the war, seriously considered the possibility of the German fleet reaching the high seas, in spite of the efforts of the British Fleet to keep it in German ports or at least in the North Sea. The possibility of having to establish an advanced naval base somewhere in the Caribbean area, to defend the Panama Canal, or possibly to develop a naval base in Europe, caused the Navy Department to order the early development of an effective Marine Corps advanced base force, and in June, 1917, directed that as soon as possible it be maintained at full war strength of 360 officers and 7,598 marines. The force, when fully organized, was to consist of: a headquarters organization, containing an aerial company; an armored car squadron and signal and engineer companies; a fixed defense force, consisting of four batteries of 5-inch naval guns (later changed to heavy howitzers), two submarine mine companies and two searchlight companies; a mobile artillery force, consisting of a battalion of light artillery, a battery of medium artillery, and two antiaircraft batteries; and a brigade of infantry, organized into two regiments of approximately one thousand men each. Some of the more experienced companies of marines were withdrawn from Haiti and Santo Domingo and resumed their regularly assigned positions in the Advanced Base Force.

The decision to maintain a force for the protection of advanced naval bases during the World War proved to be unnecessary; the German fleet never attempted to make its way out to sea, and the Advanced Base Force proved to be an organization which served only to keep men from more actively participating in the war. Some of the batteries of the Advanced Base Force were equipped and trained with 5-inch naval guns, but these were taken away from them early in the war and mounted on merchant ships. Eight-inch howitzers were requisitioned for the Marines to use instead. The heavy howitzers were intended for the long range defense of advanced naval bases and were eventually supplied to the Marine Corps as tractor-drawn heavy mobile artillery.

A light artillery battalion, equipped with 3-inch guns, went into training at Quantico in May, 1917. The Eighth Marines was organized at Quantico (October 9, 1917) under Lieut. Colonel George C. Reid to make up part of the infantry brigade. The Allies at that time were depending largely upon the Mexican oil fields for fuel. A few of our naval vessels were on duty protecting oil tankers, coming and going from the Mexican fields. It was feared that the Germans would take advantage of the generally chaotic conditions in Mexico and interrupt oil production in the principal area—the Tampico fields. The Eighth Marines was transferred to Fort Crockett, near Galveston, Texas, soon after it was organized, to be in readiness to guard the Mexican oil fields and to pursue its war training.

The Ninth Marines, the other infantry regiment for the Brigade of the Advanced Base Force, was organized at Quantico in November, 1917. It was transferred soon afterwards to Guantanamo Bay, Cuba, to assist in the intervention then in progress in that country (see Chapter XII). Each of the regiments had a strength of approximately 1,000 marines; part of the men for these units had been transferred from California for special assignment to them.

Headquarters of the Advanced Base Force and the First Marines, to which was allotted most of the technical equipment for the fixed defense of a naval base, were retained at Philadelphia, where they continued training and equipping. A signal battalion was formed in July, 1917, at Philadelphia as part of the headquarters troops, but it functioned more as a training school for communication units and replacements for such units in expeditionary forces.

## Artillery Units

As the war progressed with no call for the Advanced Base Force to assume its wartime functions, other possible uses for Marine Corps artillery units were considered. The battalion of 3-inch artillery and later a battery of 4.7-inch guns continued to train at Quantico, in the hope that the detachment might be expanded into a regiment and sent to the war zone. This hope was crushed in April, 1918, when the War Department advised the Marine Corps that no 3-inch field artillery was being used in France and that none would be used. The War Department then also advised that an additional brigade of marines would be acceptable in the American Expeditionary Force but "no artillery regiment could be accepted." In anticipation that only 75 mm. guns would be used in the war, the Navy Department, in the meantime, had requisitioned twenty-four guns of that caliber to equip a regiment of marines. The guns were not received, however, due to not being available, until after the close of the war. Still another effort to equip a regiment of marine artillery for the war zone proved futile.

Early in 1918 the War Department approved a naval project to send some heavy artillery units to join the American Expeditionary Force; 14-inch railway guns and 7-inch converted naval guns on caterpillar mounts were selected for the purpose. The Marine Corps was assigned the task of organizing a 7-inch gun regiment, while the railway guns were manned by Navy personnel. The Tenth Marines was organized January 14, 1918, to man the 7-inch guns and absorbed the other artillery units then in training at Quantico. The regiment continued to train with the 3-inch artillery until the following July when, in anticipation of receiving its heavy guns, it moved to the Naval Proving Grounds at Indian Head, Maryland, where it gained considerable experience by helping in the test firing of naval guns of all calibers. The regiment received only two of its 7-inch guns prior to the armistice. At that time it was scheduled for duty in France during the more extensive operations planned for 1919.

The War Department apparently meant something different, in the reference made above about accepting *no* regiments of Marine Corps artillery, from what the Navy Department thought was meant. The Tenth Marines as a 7-inch gun regiment proceeded with its training under naval direction, in anticipation of going to France as a part of the naval artillery. On August 23, 1918, however, the War Department requested that the twenty 7-inch naval guns, then being made ready for the Marine Corps, as well as sixteen 8-inch howitzers be turned over to the Army and stated that soldiers had been trained for those weapons, which were urgently needed in the war zone. The protest of the Commandant of the Marine Corps saved the guns, but the signing of the armistice ended all hope for the marines to see active service as heavy artillery units.

The efforts to procure the 8-inch howitzers for the artillery units of the Advanced Base Force also proved disappointing. In anticipation of the early receipt of those weapons, after having lost their 5-inch naval guns, four companies of the First Marines were transferred to Quantico and organized (November 16, 1917) into a heavy artillery force under Colonel Charles S. Hill. Hill waited until early June, 1918, before receiving the first of his howitzers and the full allowance of those arms was not received until August. A balloon company was organized and attached to the force in June, 1918. Hill's artillery unit continued in existence at Quantico throughout the remainder of the war, narrowly avoided losing its weapons to the Army as noted above, but, like the remainder of the Advanced Base Force, was never assigned to active service.

In addition to its other artillery efforts, the Marine Corps, in accordance with Navy Department orders, organized the Eleventh Marines as artillery early in January, 1918. It had a strength of 32 officers and 637 enlisted men organized into six batteries. Two of its batteries were detached in April, 1918, to form an antiaircraft battalion, the guns for which had been requisitioned from the Army but not yet received. The antiaircraft battalion was built up to a strength of nearly 500 men by June, 1918. It received only enough guns for one battery, and in September the other battery was transferred to other duty. In the meantime one of the batteries of the Eleventh Marines was sent to the Virgin Islands as a coast defense unit. That regiment was finally discontinued as an artillery unit early in September by the transfer of its three remaining batteries to form a separate artillery battalion equipped with 3-inch field pieces. This new artillery unit remained at Quantico until after the close of the war.

The Marine Corps was planning to make still greater artillery effort, if the war had continued another year. On August 30, 1918, it requisitioned twenty-eight 3-inch antiaircraft guns and sixteen 155 mm. guns in addition to the 75 mm. guns for a regiment, then on requisition. Both the 75 mm. and the 155 mm. guns were delivered after the armistice and formed an artillery reserve for a number of years thereafter.

## THIRD BRIGADE

The Eighth Marines with its approximate initial strength was maintained at Fort Crockett and not used for field duty at any time during the war. The situation in Cuba improved considerably by the summer of 1918; the Ninth Marines was withdrawn from that country and joined the Eighth Marines at Fort Crockett during August. The two were formed into the Third Brigade, commanded by Brigadier General J. E. Mahoney. The brigade, like the regiment before it, was considered a part of the Advanced Base Force and was retained in Texas for possible use in the Mexican oil fields until it was demobilized early in 1919.

The Advanced Base Force was maintained until the end of the war as part of the Navy Department's readiness for any emergency. None of its organizations, except the Ninth Marines, which performed guard duty for a few months in Cuba, left the United States. It now appears most doubtful, due to the lack of prewar planning and procurement of material, whether the organization could have performed the duties, outlined for it, earlier than the winter of 1918-1919. It was obviously a military organization which needed to be arranged for in time of peace and could not be hastily improvised during the first few months of war. It may be charged off, however, as one of the many undertakings during the World War resulting from erroneous estimates as to what course the war would take, and how long it would continue.

## SEA DUTY

At the time of our entry into the World War, the Marine Corps was maintaining detachments on thirty-five ships of the Navy, with a total strength of 35 officers and 1,805 marines. Soon after the declaration of war the size of some of the detachments was increased, and marines were placed on several older vessels which had been recommissioned. It was not necessary for our Navy to send all of its capital ships into the war zone; therefore, marines were not so extensively used at sea. A vital problem for the Allies was to replace the ships sunk by German submarines. The United States placed every possible ship into war purposes and entered upon a vast shipbuilding program. A great need for trained crews resulted, and many of our naval vessels, not needed in the war zone, were used primarily for training seamen. At times some of the ships had doubled their normal personnel on board. To make room for more seamen under training, the marines—nine detachments in all—were removed (in the spring of 1918) from the vessels of Battleship

Major General Harry Lee  Brigadier General Albertus W. Catlin

Leaders of the Sixth Marines

Major General Ben H. Fuller
1930-1934

Major General John H. Russell
1934-1936

Major General Thomas Holcomb
1936-

Commandants of the Marine Corps

Force Number One and sent to Quantico where they were absorbed into various units.

Several new ships were completed during the war and they, as well as a few others taken over by the Navy, were given marine guards. As a result of the many changes the total number of detachments and the number of marines at sea remained almost constant throughout the war. After the armistice a number of larger naval vessels, having marine detachments, were used for returning troops from France, and, in order to make more room for troops, the marines were also removed from these vessels and replaced when the ships were no longer needed as transports.

## With the Grand Fleet

A division of United States battleships under Rear Admiral Rodman joined the British Grand Fleet in the North Sea during November, 1917. The *New York, Wyoming, Florida, Delaware, Arkansas,* and *Texas* served with that division; each had the usual marine detachments, performing the normal functions of marines on such vessels. The division functioned as an integral part of the Grand Fleet, taking part in many maneuvers against the enemy and performing a number of auxiliary missions in the North Sea, such as escorting vessels engaged in laying the North Sea mine barrage. The American battleships were engaged only with German submarines—the one general naval engagement during the war having taken place before our vessels joined the Grand Fleet. It was feared for a time that German cruisers would escape to the Atlantic and raid United States convoys. The *Utah, Nevada,* and *Oklahoma,* all having marine detachments, were based at Bantry, Ireland, and guarded convoys far out to sea against the danger of raiders.

An American naval headquarters, which controlled all of our naval activities in European waters, was established under Admiral Sims in London. A detachment of marines was assigned to it for guard duty and to supply sentries for the American Embassy. As the American Expeditionary Force grew to great strength, its need for coal and other fuels, as well as the similiar need of our allies, reached enormous proportions. A fleet of vessels, taken principally from the Great Lakes, was sent to Europe for the purpose of transporting coal from Cardiff, Wales, to different French ports. In compliance with the request of General Pershing, to furnish a marine detachment at Cardiff to protect the base of operation of those vessels, the 136th Company of marines was sent there during September, 1918, and guarded that base until June, 1919. An American naval headquarters was established in Paris soon after the armistice, and a small marine detachment was attached to it for a number of months.

Incident to the Russian Revolution of 1918 and to the movement of Czechoslovakian troops across Siberia to the Pacific, the United States Asiatic Fleet became engaged in a wartime mission. Early that year the flagship *Brooklyn* of the fleet went to Vladivostok, where the Czechs and the Bolsheviki were fighting, to protect Allied interests. The Czechs finally got control of the city during June. In order to protect the American consulate and to assist an international force in maintaining order, the marine detachment of the *Brooklyn* was placed on duty ashore for a period of about six weeks during the summer of 1918. A marine patrol was maintained over the Russian navy yard during August, and on two occasions, even after the war was over, marine detachments went ashore on similar missions.

## Activities at Quantico

The country surrounding Quantico, which it was necessary to use for military training, was mostly quite hilly, covered with shrub timber and located in the semi-wilderness part of Virginia. The reservation contained only a few cleared areas. United States Highway No. 1 passed along the western edge of the initially procured tract of land. Aside from the fact that the locality had excellent railway transportation and most transports could be docked at Quantico, it was almost completely lacking in suitable terrain for the training of troops. It was difficult to lay out rifle ranges without endangering the inhabitants of the country, and it was well-nigh impossible in such a place to fire even light artillery. Since one of the main functions of the Marine Corps was to provide an advanced base force for service with the fleet and another to train units to serve with the Army, the Marine Corps determined to make Quantico its permanent base of military operations on the East Coast, notwithstanding its many disadvantages.

In January, 1918, the Marine Corps asked Congress for an appropriation to purchase not only the tract of land then under lease but also an additional 1,200 acres lying to the west of Highway No. 1, which was desired as additional space for machine-gun and artillery ranges, despite the fact that the highway then would run directly across the proposed reservation. An appropriation of $575,000 was allowed by Congress, the land company agreed to reduce its original price by $100,000, and the combined tract of 4,900 acres was purchased.

As early as May, 1917, a battalion of the Fifth Marines had been hurriedly mobilized at Quantico and after a few days' training joined its regiment at Philadelphia. The President soon afterwards directed the sending of an additional regiment of marines to France, to be brigaded with the Fifth. It then became the task of Quantico, in addition to forming advanced base units, to form as rapidly as possible the Sixth Marines, organized as a greatly augmented army infantry regiment, and a brigade machine-gun battalion to complete the Fourth Brigade. While every effort was being made to form and train the units for duty in France, at the direction of the Navy Department, the Seventh, Eighth, and Ninth Marines were also being formed for the duties noted above. The completion of the Fourth Brigade was delayed until February, 1918.

The last contingent of troops for the Fourth Brigade of Marines had not yet left Quantico for overseas, before Pershing requested three replacement battalions for the brigade, in early anticipation of battle casualties. Quantico's principal task for a time thereafter was to organize and train these three battalions, which were sent overseas during the first three months of 1918. Scarcely had the first of the replacement units been sent, however, when Pershing changed his estimate to five battalions, to provide for an advanced training unit in addition to replacements. As soon as the Fourth Brigade became actively engaged in June, 1918 (See Chapter XVII), and began to suffer more than normal battle casualties, the Marine Corps received repeated calls for replacements. It was necessary to dispatch two replacement battalions to that brigade nearly every month during the remainder of the war.

The necessity for providing large numbers of trained marines and officers for replacements and the task of furnishing an additional brigade of marines to serve in the American Expeditionary Force, which had been assigned to the Marine Corps early in 1918, led to the establishment of an intensive training organization at Quantico, called the Overseas Depot. It was started in May, 1918, and, with a specialized corps of instructors, gave short and intensive periods of training and instruction in all of the specialties of troops in an infantry brigade. When thoroughly organized and in full operation, it took over the task not only of training all personnel due for duty in France but of organizing new tactical units, replacement battalions, and the units of the additional brigade. From the time of the organization of the Overseas Depot until the close of the war, it gave specialized training to approximately 16,000 officers and enlisted men.

## Fifth Brigade

The increase of the Marine Corps to 30,000 men was practically complete by the end of August, 1917. For a number of months thereafter comparatively few men were enlisted. It became quite apparent towards the end of the year that a still larger increase in the Corps would soon be authorized by Congress. While the actual authorization was not enacted for the Corps's expansion to approximately 3,000 officers and 75,500 enlisted men until July, 1918, recruiting in anticipation thereof was begun in April with a resultant further expansion of nearly 50 per cent by the time the increase was authorized, followed by a further rapid expansion to nearly 65,000 by the end of the war. The increase was made to permit the Corps to maintain two brigades, or possibly a complete infantry division, with a 50 per cent allotment for replacements in France and for naval needs anticipated for the fiscal year. During its second expansion phase the Corps's facilities for recruiting, equipping, sheltering, and training were taxed to the utmost and forced to expand further in order to care for the great number of men absorbed into its ranks. The Marine Corps reached its all-time maximum on December 11, 1918—75,101 officers and enlisted men, including 269 female reservists.

The sending of replacements to France, the forming of advanced base units, and the furnishing of various other detachments absorbed most of the available trained personnel in the Corps until August, 1918. By that time men who had been recruited during the second increase began finishing their recruit training and were increasingly available to form new units. It was only then possible to begin organizing the Fifth Brigade of Marines at Quantico for duty in France. The Eleventh and Thirteenth Marines and the Fifth Machine Gun Battalion were organized to form the brigade. The Thirteenth, commanded by Colonel Smedley D. Butler, began organizing in July, but the necessary trained personnel for its battalions was not available until the following month. After a brief period of unit training, the regiment was transferred in contingents to Brest, France, where the last of it arrived by the end of September. The Eleventh Marines, under Colonel George Van Orden, was formed during September and transferred almost immediately to France; the last of its units arrived at Brest near the end of October. The brigade machine-gun battalion was formed, under Major E. A. Perkins, during late September and October, and reached France just before the armistice.

The Fifth Brigade of Marines was sent to France without previously being assigned as part of an infantry division by the War Department. Practically all combat troops sent overseas were organized and received some training as units of divisions before leaving the United States. When Pershing was notified of the departure of the Fifth Brigade for France, it was not quite clear to him just how it should be used. He cabled the War Department, who advised him that the Brigade was not assigned to any regular division or other organization and was to be used as he saw fit. At the time of its arrival in France the commanding general of the S.O.S. (Service of Supply) was much in need of dependable troops for guard duty and upon his request the Fifth Brigade was assigned to the S.O.S. (September 23, 1918) with the restriction that it should not be used for replacements nor for labor purposes. When the Brigade Commander, Brigadier General Eli K. Cole, arrived in France he was transferred to St. Aignon with his headquarters and assigned to the 41st Division—a depot division for the advanced training of replacements. Cole was given command of the division late in October which position he held until January, 1919.

The Thirteenth Marines soon found itself scattered and doing miscellaneous guard duty along the western coast of France; the regimental companies and most of the Second and Third Battalions guarded various supply facilities in the St. Nazaire area, while the First Battalion was stationed in and around Bordeaux, guarding docks, camps, and supply facilities. Most of the Eleventh Marines moved to the general area of Tours, the headquarters of the S.O.S. It performed duties similar to those of the Thirteenth, guarded the aviation training center at Issouden, and furnished some companies for military police duty. The regimental machine-gun company was sent to Le Havre and a rifle company to Marseilles for guard duty. The brigade machine-gun battalion was assigned to duty at Camp Pontanezan (Brest), where it remained until it returned to the United States.

The Fifth Brigade of Marines considered itself the equal of the Fourth Brigade and was very anxious to be assigned to combat duty. As a result of its being sidetracked to the duties noted above, it suffered considerable humiliation. Had it been assigned as part of a division prior to leaving the United States its fate would no doubt have been entirely different; and the responsibility for it not being so assigned was probably that of the War Department. The type of officers and men assigned to the Fifth Brigade, its training and *esprit*, made it a potential equal to the Fourth and the failure to use it for combat purposes, had the war not ended suddenly, would no doubt have meant considerable loss to the nation.

The units of the Fifth Brigade continued to perform the general duties noted above until July, 1919, when the Brigade assembled at Brest and returned to Hampton Roads, where it arrived early in August and demobilized soon afterwards. Butler, who was promoted to brigadier general after his arrival in France, added considerably to his reputation by his energetic efforts in the development and operation of Camp Pontenezan—the largest embarkation camp for the return of the American Army to the United States. He received the Distinguished Service Medal for those services to add to his already much envied collection of decorations.

The use of the entire Fifth Brigade of Marines by the S.O.S. did not satisfy the wants of that tremendous organization for dependable guard units. Only part of the marines who were evacuated for illness or wounds from the Fourth Brigade recovered sufficiently to return to their organizations. Upon being discharged from hospitals other men, who were able to perform guard duty, were organized into guard companies—some permanently assigned, others temporarily pending further classification. The first of these companies was organized on July 23, 1918, and became a prisoner of war escort company. Twelve guard companies of two officers and approximately one hundred marines were formed from Marine Corps personnel discharged from hospitals at various times during October and November, 1918, and were sent to guard S.O.S. establishments in various parts of France. Eleven other companies, designated Guard Companies Nos. 62 to 72 inclusive, were formed during the first three months of 1919 and performed various guard duties until July, 1919, when they were disbanded and their personnel returned to the United States with the Fifth Brigade.

Prior to the departure of the Fourth and Fifth Brigades of Marines from France, arrangements were made for a battalion of marines to assist in conducting a plebiscite in Schleswig-Holstein. The battalion, consisting of 18 officers and 737 marines under Major Charles F. B. Price, was organized at Brest (July 21, 1919) from personnel selected from the two Marine Brigades and the Twelfth Separate Battalion of Marines, which had recently arrived in France. The plans for the use of this battalion were changed, however; it was transferred to Bordeaux in September and to the United States on board the *Henderson* in December, 1919.

Despite the fact that at the beginning of the war, it had not been contemplated that the Marines would serve with the Army, by the time the armistice was signed 781 officers and 30,208 marines had reported for duty with the Army, in France. In addition, more than two thousand marines were undergoing advanced training at Quantico for that duty and over six thousand recruits were in training at Parris Island, as potential reinforcements for units in France. Approximately half of the entire Marine Corps was either on duty with the Army or being prepared for that duty.

## AVIATION

At the time the United States entered the World War, aviation in the Navy and the Marine Corps had scarcely developed beyond its experimental stage. The Navy had begun to experiment with planes during 1911; on May 22, 1912, the first marine officer (First Lieut. A. A. Cunningham) was assigned to naval aviation duty. By April 6, 1917, four additional marine officers and thirty marines were being trained at the Naval Air Station, Pensacola, Florida. This little group (all that the Marine Corps had at the time), expanded into a number of squadrons before the close of the war. It was transferred to Philadelphia soon after the outbreak of the war and organized into the Marine Aeronautic Company. During the next six months it grew to 34 officers and 330 enlisted men and trained with land planes on its own flying field near Philadelphia. Advantage was also taken of other training establishments, both Army and Navy, for the instruction of its personnel. On October 12, 1917, it was divided into the First Marine Aviation Squadron and the First Marine Aeronautic Company.

The Aviation Squadron was transferred to Roosevelt Field, Mineola, Long Island, and trained with army land planes until the end of the year. It then went to an army aviation field at Lake Charles, Louisiana, and continued training with the same type of planes until March 31, when it moved to a newly established Marine Corps flying field at Miami, Florida. During this period of training the squadron continued to expand and, by the end of June, 1918, had 91 officers and 825 marines. It was again subdivided to form a group headquarters and four squadrons, preparatory to being sent to the war zone.

## THE NORTHERN BOMBING GROUP

Major Cunningham went to the war zone to study conditions and saw an opportunity for extensive land-based bombing aviation, to operate against the troublesome German submarine bases along the English Channel. When he returned to the United States in January, 1918, he recommended that four Marine Corps squadrons operate as a day wing of a proposed naval bombing group to be stationed in the general vicinity of Calais. The project was eventually approved and preparations were started during May for the

Navy to send as many night bombing squadrons as possible and the Marine Corps to send the day bombing units. Captain D. C. Hanrahan, U.S.N., was given command of the combined organization (the Northern Bombing Group), and it began moving overseas during June. Headquarters and three squadrons of the Day Wing, with a total strength of 109 officers and 657 marines, sailed from Miami and arrived at Brest on July 31, 1918.

The Marine Corps and the Navy personnel for the group then moved into the Calais-Dunkirk area and began developing airdromes. Squadron D of the Marine Corps wing and the 88th Company (from the First Regiment), equipped with searchlights, arrived in that area during September. The first planes for the marine squadrons were not delivered until late in September; but in the meantime the pilots received advanced training with some near-by pursuit and bombing squadrons of the Royal Flying Corps and with a French squadron. Several marine officers took part in raids over the German lines as pilots of British planes.

Sufficient planes had been received early in October for the Day Wing to begin operations with their own equipment. Squadron No. 9 made its first raid (October 13) over the enemy lines with a British aviation group. The marine squadrons made only one raid on the submarine bases before the Germans began the general withdrawal of their line and abandoned their submarine bases at Ostend, Zebrugge, and Bruges, which had been the special objectives for the Northern Bombing Group. This complete change in the situation left no assigned mission, and the group was attached to the American Expeditionary Force. Pershing assigned it to duty with the British Army with which it operated until the armistice. Its mission thereafter was to attack any rear area targets, the bombing of which would hinder the retreat of the German Army. The Day Wing carried out several bombing raids behind the German lines.

It was necessary to advance the airdromes to some abandoned German landing fields, after the Germans had retreated a considerable distance. This interrupted flights for several days, near the close of the war. The Marine aviators managed to carry on several more operations, however, before the end came. They shot down four German planes and one of their own planes was forced, due to damage by antiaircraft fire, to land in Holland. They rendered considerable service to a French battalion, cut off by the Germans for several days, by dropping it large quantities of food. After the armistice the squadrons moved back to their old airdromes. One of them returned to the United States late in November; the others were withdrawn early in the following month. The marine wing lost four of its officer pilots killed during the several operations. The name of one of these officers, Ralph Talbot, was fittingly commemorated by the naming of a destroyer of the Navy after him in 1936.

## The Azores

The Germans had occasionally been able to send submarines far out into, and even across, the Atlantic during the latter part of 1917, and the Allies feared that they might establish a submarine base in the Azores. The British had been guarding the islands but during September, 1917, turned part of the job over to our Navy and arranged for the United States forces to assume full control. United States cruisers and a few submarines based at Ponta Delgado during October but had no shore facilities. The harbor of that city was very weakly defended. With permission of the Portuguese Government, our Navy decided (in December) to establish an advanced shore base, with the necessary supply facilities for ships operating in that vicinity. The Marine Corps was assigned the task of defending the base with aviation and with some medium caliber guns mounted on shore.

The First Marine Aeronautic Company had been transferred to Cape May, New Jersey, on October 14, 1917. It took over the flying field at that place, began training with seaplanes, and further expanded its personnel. Early in December it was equipped with seaplanes and flying boats and, under the command of Major F. T. Evans, prepared for duty in the Azores. A detachment of marines was formed in Philadelphia under Captain Maurice G. Holmes to mount and operate two 7-inch naval guns, to protect Ponta Delgado. The two marine organizations, together with certain naval contingents and naval supplies, were transferred to the naval base, Azores, in January, 1918. The 7-inch gun detachment mounted its guns—one on each side of Ponta Delgado Harbor—constructed the necessary magazines and other facilities, and manned the guns until after the close of the war. The guns were by special agreement later turned over to the Portuguese.

The Aeronautic Company developed an air station and, in about a month after its arrival, began making antisubmarine patrols at varying distances out to sea. It operated eighteen planes in all and continued patrolling until the close of the war, making as many as thirty-one scouting flights a week. Aside from the hazards of flying the crude equipment of the time, its experiences were rather uneventful; the Germans by that time were no longer attempting distant operations with their submarines. Neither the aeronautic company nor the 7-inch battery engaged the enemy in combat. One officer lost his life in a wrecked plane at sea soon after the armistice. The aviation unit returned to the United States in January, 1919, and was demobilized. The gun detachment remained at Ponta Delgado until the naval station was withdrawn during the following August.

## BALLOONS

Marine Corps aviators, not content with operating heavier-than-air machines, trained with different types of balloons and formed a balloon company. Their training with balloons began at Philadelphia, shortly after the Marine Aeronautic Company arrived there in the spring of 1917, and several marines received instruction at Army balloon schools. They organized a balloon company at Quantico in June, 1918. The company operated and trained with the heavy artillery units during the remainder of the war but, like the artillery, never went to field duty. It also operated two or three seaplanes—the beginning of a permanent aviation establishment at Quantico.

During the period between our entry into the World War and the armistice, Marine Corps aviation grew from thirty-five officers and marines to a force of approximately 280 officers and 2,200 enlisted men. By November 11, 1918, its flight equipment had grown to approximately 340 machines. In addition to training most of its officers and some of the enlisted men as pilots, Marine Corps aviation trained 175 aviation cadets. The flying personnel gained invaluable experience, which made possible the further successful development of Marine Corps aviation during the years following the World War.

## SLOWING DOWN

A German general, after reading the terms of the armistice, declared that it was nothing short of unconditional surrender. It was designed to cripple the German armies by taking from them a large proportion of their fighting equipment, practically to demobilize Germany's armed forces, and to place Allied armies in the heart of Germany. Despite the terms of the armistice, which made further resistance by Germany all but impossible, there was a hesitancy, within the American services, to admit that the war was over. The Marine Corps did not instantly stop its war activities from further expansion; the strength of the Corps continued to increase for another month and reached an aggregate of 75,101. Approximately two thousand more men were enlisted and nearly one hundred additional officers were commissioned. No further tactical units were sent overseas. The marines, who were in training for that duty at Quantico, were formed into the Fourteenth and Fifteenth Marines, each having the approximate peace strength of a Marine Corps regiment. Training of troops and the courses of instruction at officers' training camps were continued for several months.

The first step towards demobilization was made on November 20, when Headquarters of the Corps issued an order providing for the release of members of the Marine Corps Reserve and those marines enlisted for the duration of the war, who for urgent reasons wished to be discharged. More than half of the Corps, however, was serving in foreign countries and could not immediately be made available for demobilization. Appropriation was made for an enlisted strength of 27,400 for the fiscal year 1920, and it became necessary to effect a rapid demobilization. The strength of the Corps was reduced to approximately 43,000 by July 10, 1919. The Fourth and Fifth Brigades of Marines returned from France soon afterwards and were demobilized. Several thousand other men were discharged from various organizations. By early September the Corps had less than its authorized peace strength. It continued to drop, due to the discharge of duration-of-war men, to slightly over 15,000 by March, 1920. Recruiting to replace the temporary marines proved very difficult.

## Résumé

As a result of the vast expansion of the Marine Corps during the World War, practically all of its prewar officers were advanced into the grades of major and above. The field forces did not require a great many officers of the higher grades and as a result the talent of many trained officers was not made use of for real war purposes; an all too large a proportion were required to serve throughout the war in administrative positions where they gained little or no war experience. Only about one-sixth of the Corps's officers, with two or more years of commissioned service, had actual combat experience. The leadership of companies having a strength of upward of 250 men fell upon young men who had been commissioned from civil life after the outbreak of the war or upon officers who had been recently promoted from the ranks. Many of both classes, however, despite their lack of experience as officers, made brilliant records on the battlefields.

While much of this chapter may appear to be the story of misdirected efforts which resulted from wrong estimates, the Marine

Corps's record in the World War is believed to be comparable with the other branches of our military and naval service.

### Distribution of the Marine Corps—November 11, 1918

| *In the United States* | *Officers* | *Enl. Men* |
|---|---|---|
| Headquarters | 103 | 547 |
| On duty at Naval Establishments | 114 | 11,069 |
| Recruit Depots, Training Establishments | 273 | 13,924 |
| Advance Base Force | 278 | 6,019 |
| Total | 768 | 31,559 |
| *Foreign Shore Duties* | | |
| Guarding Naval Stations | 53 | 1,772 |
| Intervening Forces | 243 | 5,014 |
| Legation Guards | 16 | 389 |
| Total | 312 | 7,175 |
| *In War Zone* | | |
| Serving with A.E.F. | 857 | 23,700 |
| Northern Bombing Group | 160 | 935 |
| Azores | 11 | 188 |
| On Ships of the Grand Fleet | 12 | 476 |
| Naval Headquarters, London, England | 2 | 78 |
| Cardiff, Wales | 2 | 93 |
| Total | 1,044 | 25,470 |
| *On Ships* (not with the Grand Fleet) | 52 | 1,533 |
| Miscellaneous, in U. S., Overseas, en route, etc. | 298 | 4,752 |
| Grand Total | 2,474 | 70,489 |

## Chapter XVII
## ON THE WESTERN FRONT

THE Fifth Regiment of Marines, commanded by Colonel Charles A. Doyen, sailed from New York on board the *Henderson, DeKalb,* and *Hancock* on June 14, 1917, and by July 2 the entire regiment had arrived at St. Nazaire, France. Until then it had been under naval control but upon his arrival in France on June 27 Doyen reported the regiment for duty with the Army. It was attached to the First Division, American Expeditionary Force, which arrived at about the same time, but was not made an integral part of that tactical unit as the division was filled to its authorized allowance of four infantry regiments. The marines went into camp at St. Nazaire, as they disembarked, and on July 9 began performing provost and guard duty.

After considerable discussion of the matter with the Allied Powers, it had been decided that the American Army would be assigned a sector of operations near the middle of the stabilized Western Front, then extending through northeastern France from Switzerland to the North Sea. The First American Division went into a training and billeting area around Gondrecourt, Department of Meuse, in the rear of the proposed American sector. On July 16 the Fifth Marines, less the Third Battalion which remained at St. Nazaire, proceeded to the Gondrecourt training area and was billeted in Naix-aux-Forges and Menaucourt.

The first method of individual training of American troops in France was to place them under experienced French soldiers. The marines began their training under the instruction of the 30th, 70th, and 151st battalions of Alpine Chasseurs—the blue devils of France. The French taught them many things about the technique of trench warfare, while the tactical training was carried on under their own regimental officers.

## The Base Detachment

The problem of supplying replacements for the Fifth Marines had been anticipated, and the Base Detachment commanded by Lieutenant Colonel H. I. Bearss, consisting of one machine-gun company and four rifle companies, was organized at Quantico, in June, 1917, and sent to France on the *Henderson* during August. By this time the Service of Supply of the American Army in France had begun to take form and in addition to the Third Battalion which was performing guard and provost duty in the vicinity of St. Nazaire, the Base Detachment was called upon to furnish part of its personnel for that duty. Bordeaux was selected as one of the base ports for the A.E.F., and plans were formulated for its extensive development for receiving troops and supplies and for training artillery units in the general vicinity. Engineering supplies already had begun to arrive at Bordeaux, and on September 8 Bearss took command at the newly designated Base Section No. 2. The headquarters and three companies of the Base Detachment were transferred there early in October and took over a number of duties, principally guard and police. A part of the 30th Company of Marines had, in the meantime, been sent to Paris, which was then the headquarters of the Service of Supply, and the Seventh Company was transferred to Chaumont, the new headquarters of the A.E.F., for guard duty. The marines at Bordeaux remained there until early in January, 1918, when they were withdrawn from duty in the S.O.S. and consolidated with the Fifth Marines.

## The Second Division

The Marine regiment soon found itself to be only a fifth wheel attached to the First Division. One of its companies was doing guard duty at Nevers and the Third Battalion was still at St. Nazaire. The 67th Company had been transferred late in September to Southampton, England, which later became an important port for handling American troops en route to France, to establish a rest camp. In the meantime plans were made for the organization of the Second American Division in France. The Marine Corps was given the mission of supplying one of its two infantry brigades. Army units for the new division began to arrive in France during September, 1917, and were assigned to a divisional billeting area around Bourmont in eastern Haute-Marne. The machine-gun companies of the Fifth Marines remained in the First Division area for advanced training; the remainder of the regiment, less detachments, moved to the new Second Division area on September 24. Doyen, who by that time had been promoted to brigadier general, took command of the division. The Fifth Marines was billeted with its headquarters and Second Battalion in the village of Damblain and the First Battalion in Breuvannes.

During the remainder of 1917 the troops carried on such training as the weather and other conditions would permit. General Headquarters decided that training under the instruction of the French had failed. A new system was established which provided for a month or more of training of smaller units after arrival in France, while their headquarters and staff made intensive studies of their functions in the type of warfare then in progress. The battalions were then to go to the front and, under the supervision of the French, have a period of actual experience in quiet sectors. Each division would then reassemble for another training period before being pronounced ready for all combat duties.

The composition of some of our military units was considerably changed during December, 1917. The infantry regiments particularly were greatly enlarged; a machine-gun battalion of four companies was provided for each infantry brigade; one rifle company was added to each battalion and the rifle companies were enlarged. In order to provide the necessary units and personnel, two additional companies of marines were sent from the United States, and they, with the three rifle companies and the headquarters and supply companies of the Base Detachment, were absorbed into the Fifth Marines. By the end of January, 1918, the Third Battalion rejoined from St. Nazaire; the reorganized regiment was complete with the exception of the 67th Company at Southampton.

## The Sixth Marines

The providing of an additional regiment for the brigade of marines to form part of the Second Division was rather a difficult problem for the Marine Corps, which was at the time also being called upon to raise certain other regiments as well as replacements for units in France. The Sixth Marines was organized in August, 1917, at Quantico and transported to France piecemeal. The First Battalion arrived at St. Nazaire on October 5 and performed various guard and police duties in that vicinity, at Brest and at Le Havre during the remainder of the year. Headquarters of the regiment, Colonel A. W. Catlin commanding, and the supply and machine-gun companies were the next to arrive at St. Nazaire on November 1. Together with the Third Battalion, which arrived in France on November 12, they were sent to Bordeaux for duty. The Second Battalion arrived in France on February 5, 1918, and was sent directly to the

Second Division area. In the meantime the remainder of the units performed guard and provost duties at various places in the S.O.S. and assisted in the construction of docks at Bordeaux. They were relieved of all such duties early in January, 1918, assembled in the Second Division area, billeted in the villages of Blevaincourt, Chaumont-la-ville, Robecourt, and Germainvilliers, in an area to the northeast of that occupied by the Fifth Marines, and began preliminary training.

### Sixth Machine Gun Battalion

To provide a machine-gun battalion for the Marine Brigade, battalion headquarters and two companies, Major E. B. Cole commanding, arrived at St. Nazaire late in December, 1917, and proceeded directly to the training area of the marines. It was joined by the two machine-gun companies from the Fifth Marines which had been left in Gondrecourt, and its organization completed. This battalion, the Fifth and Sixth Marines, and a brigade headquarters made up the Brigade of Marines. The 67th Company returned from Southampton on March 10, just prior to the Brigade's first duty at the front. In the meantime the Second Division had completed its organization and was under the command of Major General Omar Bundy.

The Fourth Brigade, which had, after so many months of delay, finally been assembled and given some of the preliminaries of war training, was about to take its place as a regular infantry brigade with the Allied armies on the Western Front. It had an aggregate strength of 280 officers and 9,164 enlisted men and was by far the largest tactical unit of marines that had ever been assembled. While it had a sprinkling of older men who had seen some service in the Caribbean countries, it was composed mostly of men who came in for the duration of the war. The field officers and part of the company commanders had been regular officers in the Marine Corps, and some of them had had experiences in minor warfare. The junior officers had either been promoted from the ranks or had been appointed since the outbreak of the war. All were yet to be tried on the field of battle, some to fail and some to be brilliantly successful, while others proved physically incapable of enduring the hardships of war.

### The Defense of the Toulon Sector

The Fourth Brigade went about the middle of March, 1918, with the Second Division for its preliminary tour of duty in a quiet defensive sector. The Division was assigned to the X Corps of the

MAJOR GENERAL JOHN A. LEJEUNE (RETIRED)
AS HE APPEARED WHILE COMMANDING THE SECOND DIVISION, A.E.F.

TYPICAL UNIFORMS AND EQUIPMENT OF MARINES ON THE
WESTERN FRONT

BELLEAU WOOD, 1918

Second French Army which held a sector a few miles southeast of Verdun. The front line there had been stabilized for about two years; its defenses were highly developed, and its back areas provided with rest camps. With the exception of the motor elements the Division moved up on standard French military trains, detrained about fifteen miles south of Verdun, and the various units marched to their assigned positions. At the beginning only one battalion of each infantry regiment was placed in front line battalion areas, called centers of resistance. The French whom they were to relieve did not leave until every man was instructed in his particular duties.

The Second Battalion of the Fifth, during the night of March 17-18, was the first to occupy a front line position, C.R. (center of resistance) Montgirmont, located at the point of a large salient, near the center of the corps sector. The First Battalion was placed in support on the second battle position while the Third went into a camp still farther to the rear and continued training. The Sixth Marines was similarly disposed and performed like duties. Its Third Battalion relieved the French on the night of March 18-19 in C.R. Mont-sous-les-Cotes, with a French battalion in line between it and the front line battalion of the Fifth. The Ninth and 23d Infantry of the Third Brigade, Second Division, were similarly disposed several miles farther to the south.

It was initially planned that the battalions of each regiment would have about ten days in each position, rotating in such manner as to give each a tour of duty in the front lines. In accordance with this plan the First Battalion of the Fifth and the Second Battalion of the Sixth were next to go into the front line. The first of the great German drives against the Western Front in 1918 was launched towards Amiens on March 21 and advanced in a startling manner, almost separating the British from the French. In order to make more divisions available, the French withdrew, in addition to others, one from their X Corps and one from the corps on its left, leaving the troops in the line the task of spreading out to hold the gaps. This necessitated the complete rearrangement of the infantry units of the Second Division. The Fifth Marines was withdrawn from the line and together with a French regiment took over an entire divisional sector, east of Verdun, relieving a French division. The marines took the left half of the front line of the divisional sector with the First Battalion occupying C.R. Eix on the extreme left, the Third Battalion taking over C.R. Chatillon on its right, while the Second Battalion went into reserve. The Sixth Marines continued to hold its original center of resistance and with the First

Battalion took over C.R. Montgirmont and an intervening battalion sector.

The marines of the Fourth Brigade had a great many valuable experiences during their occupation of that highly developed defensive position. They learned among other things the difficult art of relieving troops in front line positions, always at night, and learned to co-ordinate the fire of their battalion weapons and attached machine guns with that of the supporting artillery. It fell to their lot to carry on many patrols in "no man's land," to repair barbed-wire entanglements at night, to take part in raiding German positions, and to repel German raids. They were subjected to several concentrations of artillery fire.

### Raided and Gassed

The 74th Company, in the ruined village of Tresavaux, was raided by the enemy on the night of April 6 but successfully repulsed the Germans. The same company a week later, while in reserve at camp Fontaine St. Robert, billeted in hutment barracks, was heavily bombarded with gas shells, one of which exploded inside a building where some men were sleeping. Due partly to the severity and suddenness of the gassing and partly to the inexperience of the organization, the results were most disastrous. Practically the entire company and some other men had to be evacuated, an immediate loss of nearly three hundred, including all officers of the company.

The bad effects of the disaster were offset on the night of April 20-21 by the determined defense put up by a platoon of the 45th Company, commanded by Second Lieutenant Edward B. Hope. Hope with his platoon together with the rest of the battalion had just finished relieving in C.R. Eix. The platoon was holding the extreme left of the divisional and corps sector on a commanding ridge; the Germans, after a severe bombardment, raided the position with one of their specially trained raiding parties. The Germans, who were repulsed by the front line marines, left behind two of their officers and a soldier dead and one wounded. Hope's platoon lost three killed and eleven wounded by the enemy artillery barrage and raiding party. The French commander immediately recognized the heroic conduct of the marines and awarded French *Croix de Guerres* to a number of officers and men who had participated in the operations. This was the first award of that decoration to marines, although later the same decoration was given to Second Lieutenant Gilfillan and Sergeant Cukela for the part they took in a raid made by marines and French soldiers a few days before. The 84th Company, Sixth Marines, successfully repelled a raid of the Germans, made with flame throwers and grenades, the night that the 45th Company was raided.

## A Brigade Sector

The front held by the two marine regiments was separated by two French battalions, holding C.R. Watronville and C.R. Haudiomont. The Sixth Marines was relieved late in March by the French and it in turn relieved the intervening French Battalions, thus making the line held by the Fourth Brigade continuous and forming a brigade sector with four battalions in the line and two in reserve, all supported by their own Twelfth Field Artillery. By the beginning of May the Second Division had had considerable experience, and the time was approaching for it to be withdrawn from the line to receive a hurried period of training of its larger units preparatory to being used wherever desired. Repeated German attacks on the Western Front had at last induced the Allies to accept a unified command under Marshal Ferdinand Foch, and General Pershing placed all American forces unreservedly at its disposal.

## The Relief

The French relieved the Second Division between May 9 and 16, and it moved by marching, trucks, and trains to a new training area, a few miles west of Bar-le-Duc and just northeast of Vitry-le-François. Doyen was sent home, physically disqualified, and Brigadier General J. G. Harbord, U.S.A., took command of the Fourth Brigade. Scarcely had its organizations reached their new billets, than they were called upon to help stop a determined German drive. The enemy after having almost cut the Allies in two, south of Amiens, next attacked the British on the Lys and drove them back a considerable distance. The French shifted a number of their reserve divisions to the support of the British, and Foch ordered the Second American Division to move to a reserve position between Paris and Beauvais. The Division moved by trains between May 18 and 22 to Pontoise and then marched to the vicinity of Chaumont en Vixen, where it went into vigorous training in anticipation of taking its place at the front as a first line division.

## Helping to Save Paris

The Second Division had scarcely established itself in the new area and began to make plans to relieve the First American Division at Cantigny, when the Germans launched a still more threatening drive, begun by a surprise attack May 27 on the Chemin des Dames, northwest of Reims. The weakened French and British divisions, which had been sent into the theretofore quiet sector for rest and reorganization, were completely routed and in a remarkably short time the Germans reached the Marne at Château-Thierry and created a situation so perilous that it threw the French capital into panic. The French were unable to stop the Germans by sending additional troops into the line, as they too were driven back in the general retreat. Several reserve divisions, including our Second Division, were rushed into the breach. The Second Division on May 30 was ordered to proceed by trucks, rail, and marching to Meaux on the Paris-Metz Road, about half way between Paris and Château-Thierry, to assist the French in forming a defensive line in rear of the retiring front in the hope of stopping the rapid advance of the enemy towards Paris.

The retreating French Army and the fleeing refugees had so congested Meaux, before the Second Division arrived, that it could not be used as an assembly point and the leading units were routed to the village of May-en-Multien, several miles farther to the northeast. As the units arrived in that area they were ordered by the XXI French Corps to concentrate in the region of Montreuil-aux-Lions. The infantry units, equipped only with what they carried, were the first to arrive by trucks. They hurriedly debussed and took up the march towards the front. The Ninth Infantry, the leading regiment, formed a defensive line with its left resting at the village of Thiolet on the Paris-Metz Road and its right extending nearly to the Marne. The Sixth Marines, the next to arrive, took up a line nearly 7,000 yards long, extending generally northwest from Le Thiolet with two battalions in the line and one in reserve. The French 43d Division was gradually being driven back through the marines. The two American regiments covered the entire front of the XXI Corps. The Fifth Marines moved up in support of the Sixth on the following morning. The Division's supporting units, supply and ammunition trains did not begin to arrive until June 2. The Second Battalion of the Fifth was next placed in line, to the left of the Sixth, and the 23d Infantry extended the line, held by the Division, to Gandelu making a total divisional front of nearly eleven miles, from which, according to its orders, "no retirement will be thought of on any pretext whatsoever"—a precariously, thinly held front with practically no reserves, but desperate measures were necessary if the German advance was to be stopped. The deployment of our troops had been made in the midst of the greatest confusion of fleeing refugees and retreating French soldiers.

So far, scattering remnants of French units were between the line occupied by the Second Division and the enemy. During the night of June 3-4 most of the advanced detachments withdrew leaving the Americans holding the front line. The divisional front was shortened to approximately 9,000 yards by the French relieving battalions on both flanks. On June 4, which proved to be a quiet day, the front was reorganized into two brigade sectors with the Marine Brigade on the left, with each of its regiments having two battalions in the line and one in reserve. The Twelfth Field Artillery (75-mm.) supported the marines. A general line to hold back the German advance had been reformed, though greatly extended and only slightly organized.

The demoralization of the retreating French soldiers was anything but encouraging to the Americans. Numerous suggestions were made by the French for our troops to join the general retreat. One Marine officer when ordered by a French officer to retire with his unit gave the famous reply, "Retreat hell, we just got here." Captain Lloyd W. Williams, who shortly afterwards lost his life in the battle, countermanded the order of another French officer for the marines to retire.

The German success on that front had been far greater than they anticipated. They had massed all available reserves in preparation for another attack against the British in the north of France and were not prepared to exploit their unexpected break-through towards Paris. They halted their advance when they encountered the line held by the Second Division and began redisposing their troops for defense.

### The Marines Assume the Offensive

The commander of the French corps, to which the Second Division was assigned, not content with a mere passive defense, ordered a general advance to begin on June 6 to rectify the line and secure stronger ground. It was on this general mission that the Marine Brigade, during the next twenty days, was engaged in some of the most desperate fighting ever performed by any troops.

The first advance was ordered on the extreme left of the Brigade in conjunction with the adjoining French division. Part of the First Battalion, Fifth Marines (Major Turrill), on a front of about eight hundred yards lying between two decided ravines, advanced to the north, in conjunction with the French, a distance of about 1,000 yards. The attack, the first undertaken by the Marines in France, was successfully carried out with the support of the divisional artillery and a company of the Sixth Machine Gun Battalion. The Third Battalion, Fifth Marines (Major Berry), on the right of Turrill's battalion had also been ordered to advance its left, keeping in contact with the First Battalion. It advanced only very slightly, however, leaving the First Battalion in a badly exposed position. The French on the left also failed to keep up but fortunately the Germans, who could have easily enfiladed Turrill's battalion, were satisfied to leave it alone. The Fifth Marines had 10 officers and about 400 men killed and wounded and took 20 prisoners during the operation. The attack was made at the dividing line between two German divisions and came as a complete surprise to the enemy and caused him to shift several reserve units to stop any further advance by the marines.

## THE FIRST ATTACK ON BELLEAU WOOD

After Turrill's successful attack the Germans were holding a decided salient at Lucy-le Bocage. The French corps, at noon of June 6, directed that measures be taken to reduce the salient. Harbord immediately began making plans to carry out an attack to capture the Bois de Belleau, followed by taking Bouresches and then effect a general straightening of his front line. He ordered the Third Battalion, Fifth Marines, to attack east on approximately a mile of front, from where it was then holding with its right about 500 yards north of Lucy-le Bocage, and capture all except the southern end of Belleau Wood. Harbord ordered the Third Battalion, Sixth Marines (Major Sibley), on the right of Berry's Battalion, to attack east at the same time on a narrow front and capture the southern edge of Belleau Wood and the town of Bouresches. The two battalions were then expected to occupy a new front line running from in front of Bouresches around the northeast edge of Belleau Wood and along the ridge south of Torcy. The First Battalion, Fifth Marines, on the extreme left of the brigade sector was directed to conform to the movements of the attacking battalions, while the Second Battalion, Sixth Marines, on the extreme right of the sector, was ordered to advance its left to conform to the progress of Sibley's battalion.

The positions against which the attack was directed were held by two German divisions. Belleau Wood had been occupied by the 461st Infantry Regiment, having a strength of 28 officers and 1,141 enlisted men and a few auxiliary troops. It had two battalions in line organized for defense and a protective artillery barrage had been provided. Belleau Wood was approximately a mile in length and of irregular shape as shown on the accompanying sketch. It was mostly heavily wooded, cut by a deep ravine near the southern end, and at places filled with huge boulders. The Marine Brigade had prac-

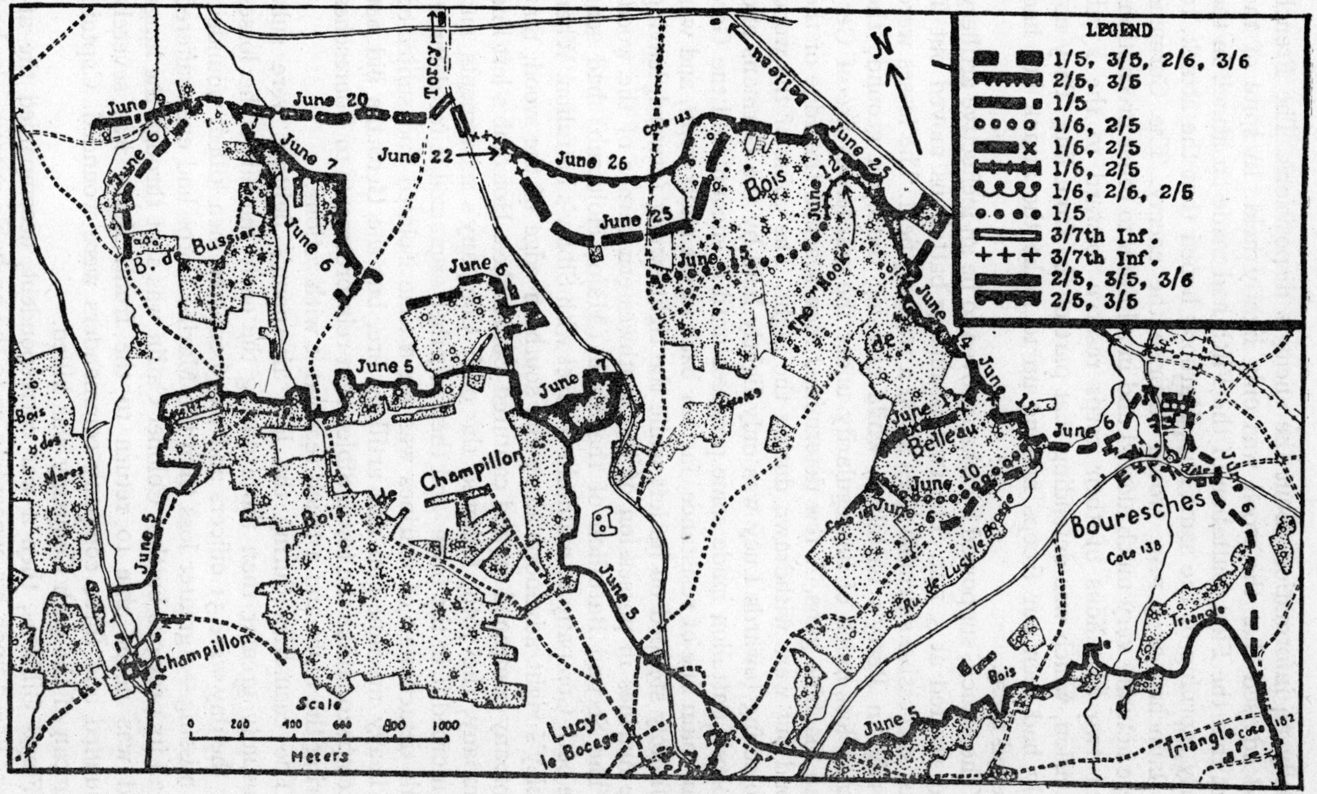

BELLEAU WOOD

tically no information about the enemy's dispositions. The French had advised that the wood was only lightly held. In spite of the fact that the First Battalion of the Fifth had made an attack in the early morning of the same day, Harbord hoped that the attack, to be launched at 5 P.M., would surprise the enemy. The Germans were actually very much alerted and in addition to other precautions sent two battalions of their corps reserve forward to the 237th Division, which was defending that part of the front line. They not only had seen our troops moving up to make the attack but had shelled them.

The attack, supported by what proved to be an ineffective artillery fire, started at 5 P.M. The two assaulting battalions moved out in four successive skirmish lines as on a training field. The losses were terrific in Berry's battalion, while crossing the open ground; the attack lost much of its regularity under the murderous fire of German machine guns. A few determined men reached the edge of the wood but were withdrawn during the night. The point of the wood projecting towards Lucy was only lightly held by the Germans and Sibley's battalion made some progress until it encountered the German main line of resistance, farther back in the main wood, and was definitely stopped on its left while the right swung forward, leaving the marines in possession of the southwestern corner of the wood.

The Second Battalion of the Sixth (Major Holcomb) had sent the 96th Company to maintain contact with Sibley's battalion. When Sibley's right advanced along the southern edge of the wood, that company continued on and captured Bouresches. Holcomb's left line company, the 79th, followed the 96th Company's movements and reinforced it in the town, and they together organized it for defense. This detachment of marines was for a time isolated and subjected to heavy machine-gun and artillery fire, but the Germans did not attempt to retake the town. Sibley sent reinforcements to Bouresches during the night and a truck reached it with rations.

The casualties during the late afternoon's fighting were substantially greater than those during the early morning: the losses for the day were 31 officers and 1,056 enlisted men killed, wounded, or missing—a greater loss than the Marine Corps had ever suffered in all its previous battles. Colonel Catlin was shot through the lungs and was never able to return to the front. Berry was severely wounded and three company commanders were wounded. Captain Duncan of the 96th Company was killed.

Floyd Gibbons, then a war correspondent, accompanied the attack. Based upon his conception as to the probable outcome, he had sent back a story to the censor in Paris written in his usual colorful style, intending to fill in a few words after the fight. His left eye was shot out. His being wounded was reported, but since he had not appeared at the dressing station, the rumor started that he had been killed. Upon hearing this the censor, thinking that he would do a last favor for Gibbons, released the dispatch as it was and on the following day the United States was electrified by glaring headlines and blood-curdling accounts of the exploits of the Marine Brigade. Since no other units had been so mentioned in dispatches, considerable jealousy was aroused by the incident. The fault was not due to anyone in the Marine Corps but to an inadvertent slip in the instructions relative to mentioning the kind of troops, issued by the chief censor of the A.E.F.

June 7 was devoted to preparations for the resumption of the attack on the wood. The Germans relieved the divisions on each flank of the 237th Division, a regiment of which was holding the wood, and narrowed its sector by placing some troops of the 28th Division in the southwestern corner of the wood, facing Sibley's battalion. Our artillery shelled the wood during the night; at 4 A.M., June 8, Sibley attempted to advance his line to the north but each position that he reached was flanked by German machine guns, and he finally withdrew to the southern edge of Belleau Wood and later moved into a ravine south of the wood to permit free use of the artillery fire on the enemy front line.

## Attack of June 9

A limited attack by the First Battalion, Sixth Marines, preceded by a heavy artillery bombardment on the southern half of the wood, was made in the early morning of June 9. It was the first attack made with adequate artillery support and had the promise of yielding substantial results. The battalion commander made several optimistic reports of his progress and finally reported that he had gained his objective across the narrow neck which separates the northern from the southern part of the wood. Actually he had only reached the German main line of resistance in its southern edge, where Sibley's battalion had been stopped three days before.

## Wise's Attack

Plans were then made for another determined attack to clear the entire wood, but based on the assumption that its lower half was in the possession of the marines. Arrangement was made for considerably less artillery fire than had supported the previous attack. The main infantry attack was made by the Second Battalion of the Fifth on the early morning of June 11. It advanced with its left following the road which passes just west of Belleau Wood; the expectation was that its right would make contact with the battalion of the Sixth at the narrow neck near the center of the wood. The battalion shifted to the right as it advanced, seeking its supporting troops which were to advance with it and, not finding them, moved over until its left was where its right was intended to be and finally advanced with the First Battalion of the Sixth to a line across the narrow part of the wood which was already supposed to be held. The advance was stopped after heavy losses and with no foothold yet in the larger northern part of the wood. The troops of the German 28th Division were driven from the southern part of the wood with a loss of nearly 800. They attempted to retake their old position by a counterattack early the following morning but failed.

The indomitable Wise was not satisfied with the results and wanted immediately to make another effort. He was reinforced by two companies of engineers and given 150 replacements. After an artillery preparation, he started north at 5 P.M. the next day, in an attempt to cover the entire wood. The artillery had very little effect in the dense wood and never seriously molested the German main line of resistance, which was farther south than supposed. Wise's front line hit the German position, broke up into small groups, and lost all organization. Groups of marines under determined officers and sergeants then began to work their way forward independently, eliminating German machine-gun groups as they found them. They went through the German main line, completely disorganized it, and pushed on to the northeastern edge of the wood, where they finally stopped at about 8:40 P.M. and reorganized. A battalion of the German 110th Grenadiers was driven out and only part of the German 461st Infantry remained in the northwest part of the wood, holding out among the boulders.

A detachment of Germans under a white flag surrendered to Wise's battalion, and a wounded German officer reported that the enemy planned to counterattack early the following morning. During the night they reinforced their few remaining troops in the portion of the wood which they still held and reorganized their positions. Wise's left flank was badly exposed; he bent it back through the wood and formed "the hook." His losses during the day's fighting were about 150, not excessive considering what he had accomplished, as within two days the two marine battalions had captured over 400 prisoners and 60 machine guns. The expected German counter blow, preceded by an intense bombardment, struck at 4 A.M., June 13, against the entire eastern edge of the wood and extended as far south as Bouresches. Their infantry attack was ineffective except that against the town, which they vigorously assaulted, and it was thought for a time that they had retaken it. There was little infantry activity during the remainder of the day, but the Germans continued their harassing artillery fire with high explosive and mustard gas shells. The gassing was particularly severe along the front of the First Battalion of the Sixth in the southeastern edge of the wood and in Bouresches, where it caused about 450 marine casualties.

### Exhaustion and Relief

Wise's battalion was reduced to about one-third of its normal strength; there was danger of still more determined attacks from the east. The First Battalion, Fifth Marines, then in Bois de Champillon, west of Belleau Wood, joined up with it by forming a thin line with one company across the remainder of the wood to the west. The situation by this time was rather precarious for the Marine Brigade, as its losses had been very heavy, its personnel was exhausted by the long period of continuous fighting, and its units were hopelessly mixed. The Germans continued to reinforce that part of the wood still held by them; the marines made no further advances at that time. The real danger to the marines was not as great as they thought, as the German Fourth Reserve Corps was also badly used up and had few reserves. Since a corps counterattack had failed to retake any ground, the enemy was probably not very optimistic about driving the marines from Belleau Wood and allowed them to remain in their weakly held positions without making further counterattacks. The Germans contented themselves by keeping up a harassing artillery fire and occasional gassing of the positions of the Brigade.

The Second Battalion, Sixth Marines, was on its way to relieve Wise's battalion during the gas attack mentioned above and lost so heavily that it did not have enough men to effect the relief. Both battalions remained in the wood. Holcomb placed the scattered remnants of his battalion along the eastern edge of the wood between Wise's battalion on the left and Hughes's on the right. Wise refused to leave with his depleted companies. Lieutenant Colonel Logan Feland took direct command of the remnants of the three battalions, reorganized the whole position, and made it more tenable. The 23rd Infantry relieved the marine battalion in Bouresches and it went to Lucy in reserve. By one of the many shifts of battalions the Third of the Sixth (Sibley's) had been placed in the line on the extreme left of the brigade sector. It was relieved by an adjoining French division; a few more reserves were thereby made available.

The Seventh Infantry of the American Third Division was being held in army reserve and, upon the urgent request of General Bundy, was made available for his use for the period between June 15 and June 22. Its battalions moved into the marine sector, one each night, and relieved for a few days the four front line battalions. Its three battalions held the entire Fourth Brigade front which remained under the control of Colonel W. C. Neville, commanding the Fifth Marines, with Feland in command in the wood. The 237th German Division, with whom the marines had been mostly engaged, was relieved at about the same time. The 28th Division on its left was relieved a few days later. Thereafter the Fourth Brigade was faced with the 87th Infantry Division.

During a brief period, when out of the front line, the battalions of the Fourth Brigade were partly refilled with approximately 2,800 replacements. The units were reorganized, given all available equipment, and were soon in a condition to resume their places in the line.

### Belleau Wood Cleared

During the time that the Seventh Infantry held the sector the front line remained practically unchanged. On the night of June 21-22 the Third Battalion, Fifth Marines, then commanded by Major M. E. Shearer, took over the center battalion area in the northern part of Belleau Wood; on the following night the Third Battalion of the Sixth took over the line along the eastern edge of the wood. The Second Battalion, Fifth Marines, then commanded by Major Ralph E. Keyser, took over the front line on the extreme left of the division sector on the night of June 23-24.

Plans were next formulated to drive the Germans from the northern end of the wood. In spite of the experience thus far a tactical error was again made and another failure resulted. Shearer, according to orders, attempted to capture the remainder of the wood which was held by a battalion of the German 347th Infantry fully organized for a determined defense. The attack started at 7 P.M., June 23, after an ineffective preparation with trench mortars and rifle grenades, and depended mainly on the tactics employed by Wise's battalion in its spectacular advance through the wood on June 12. This time such tactics did not succeed, as the enemy had skillfully placed his machine guns so as closely to support each other: when a machine-gun position was captured the crew usually escaped with part of the mechanism and the position was immediately brought under fire by other guns. Shearer's attack con-

*Courtesy of Radio Corporation of America*

MAJOR GENERAL JAMES G. HARBORD, U.S.A. (RETIRED)
COMMANDED THE MARINE BRIGADE IN FRANCE

Belleau Wood

tinued well into the night; the battalion suffered heavy casualties and gained no ground.

The higher command then conceded that strong artillery support was necessary to help drive the enemy from his last stronghold. An artillery preparation lasting fourteen hours was fired by the Second Field Artillery Brigade reinforced by heavy and light batteries of the French. The bursting of shells upon hitting trees was especially demoralizing to the enemy. Shearer withdrew his front lines clear of the artillery preparation and at 5 P.M., June 25, a rolling barrage crept through the remainder of the wood, followed by Shearer's marines. The German resistance was still energetic despite heavy losses and the demoralizing effect of the artillery preparation and barrage. They attempted to reinforce the position but were prevented by artillery interdiction fire. By 9:30 P.M. Shearer's battalion had possession of the wood with the exception of a narrow fringe, held by a few scattered enemy machine-gun groups which were captured without great difficulty the following day. The marines then began to organize the northern edge for defense. They fully expected another counterattack, but the Germans had no such intention and contented themselves by reorganizing a new line in the rear. In this final phase of the fighting at Belleau Wood the Germans lost 7 officers and 423 men including 260 captured—a loss which prompted the comment of the German high command, who reprimanded the division and corps commanders for allowing so many men to be trapped in an exposed position.

## The *Pas Fini* Sector

The clearing of Belleau Wood ended the offensive operations of the marines in that sector. The Third Brigade, after remaining comparatively inactive up to that time, captured Vaux on the evening of July 1, in a determined and well co-ordinated attack supported by tremendous artillery fire. The division then redisposed itself and organized its sector in the usual manner for defense. When it was making its way to the front past the fleeing refugees and French soldiers on June 1, the panic-stricken French shouted despairingly, *"La guerre est fini."* The Americans promptly replied, *"Pas fini,"* and the words of the reply became the nickname for the sector and was finally recognized as its official designation. The division was organized in considerable depth with several successive battle positions, to provide an elastic defense which at that time had come to be recognized as the only way to stop the drives designed by Ludendorff.

## The Relief

The Second Division was long overdue for a period of rest, reorganization, and training. The Marine Brigade had approximately 4,000, or 55 per cent casualties—the heaviest losses suffered by any American brigade during a single offensive operation in the World War. It had inflicted a total loss, including prisoners, of about 3,000 to the German front line units.

The 26th American Division, which had been in army reserve near the Second Division sector, was ordered to make the relief. The 52d Brigade relieved the marines on the night of July 4-5. The relief of the remainder of the Division was delayed for a short time on account of persistent rumors of a planned German attack. During that brief interval the Marine Brigade was attached to the 26th Division. The relief was completed shortly afterwards, and the Second Division was assigned a line nine miles long across the entire Corps sector and approximately six miles in rear of the front to organize as a reserve battle position. It remained there until it went to take part in the attack which initiated the general Allied offensive.

## Results

The fighting qualities demonstrated by the marines of the Fourth Brigade contributed substantially to the respect which the German Army was rapidly learning to have for the more experienced American divisions. Their intelligence reports at the beginning of the operations showed more or less contempt for the supposedly inexperienced American troops, but that estimate gradually changed and by the time the Second Division was withdrawn from the line the German reports were giving it their highest classification of battle efficiency—"a shock unit." As Colonel Ernst Otto of the German Army in writing about the matter some years afterwards said, "The Second Division had answered the question, How would the Americans act in a real battle?" The discouraging effect that such a discovery had upon the German Army had, of course, a corresponding awakening of hope in the French and other Allies: Clemenceau then frankly admitted that the timely arrival and determined stand made by the Second and other American divisions had saved Paris. The Sixth French Army, in recognition of the services performed by the marines, issued an order on June 30, 1918, which changed the name of the Bois de Belleau to the Bois de la Brigade de Marine, and the Brigade received a citation of the French Army signed by General Pétain for its gallant conduct. The ground lying between Belleau Wood and the village of Belleau was made one of the five American National Cemeteries in France. The entire wood was purchased by Mrs. James Carroll Fraser and it has since passed to the jurisdiction of the American Battle Monuments Commission and is perhaps the battlefield most visited by Americans traveling in Europe.

## THE MOVEMENT TO SOISSONS

The Germans had not yet given up hope of winning a decision on the Western Front and continued their attacks, but the Allied Powers were making preparations to take the offensive from them at the earliest opportunity. The Germans started new drives both to the east and west of Reims. Foch began concentrating troops to the north of Paris to attack the flank of the German salient extending to the Marne. The enemy was aware of that danger but anticipated that his successes farther east would draw all reserve forces and prevent any aggressive action by the Allied armies.

The Second Division remained in its reserve position until the middle of July, when it began to be shifted by various means to the Villers-Cotterets (or Retz) Forest for use in the planned offensive. Harbord had been made commander of the Division and Colonel Harry Lee was, for the time being, commander of the Fourth Brigade. The movement to the north was carried on under the greatest secrecy, without even the general officers knowing definitely where the troops were going or what they were expected to do, and under conditions of the greatest confusion. In order to effect the surprise of the Germans, the Second Division as well as other troops being assembled for the attack were kept hidden in the forest.

The plan for the use of the Second Division for the attack about to be made on a wide front extending south from the vicinity of Soissons was finally made known to Harbord after it was almost too late to get his troops into position. The Second Division was put in the line as the right division of the XX French Corps which, with the American First Division on the left and the First Moroccan in the center, was expected to make a deep penetration at the most critical point on the western flank of the Marne salient. The country over which the attack was to be made was comparatively open terrain, covered with fields of wheat with occasional wooded ravines. It was particularly well adapted for a rapid advance, supported by tanks which were provided in considerable numbers. The marines as well as the other infantry units were brought as near as possible to their positions in trucks and were then required to find their way forward, as best they could, through the great forest on a dark, rainy night. The confusion was increased by the Second Division Headquarters not knowing the order of arrival of its troops. In the initial disposition for the attack, the Third Brigade covered most of the division sector, while the Fifth Marines covered the remainder and joined up with the Moroccans on the left. The Sixth was held out as the corps reserve. In order to surprise the enemy only a few minutes' artillery preparation was made.

## THE ATTACK OF JULY 18

The marines, as well as the remainder of the infantry, had practically no sleep during the movement by trucks; they spent the entire night of July 17-18 making their way to the front over the hopelessly congested road through the forest, most of the time by holding on to each other in the darkness. The Fifth was, unfortunately, the last infantry unit to arrive, and Feland, its commander, who had received orders for the attack in the late afternoon, did not find his battalions until 10 P.M.; the machine-gun units were even then not available. Machine-gun companies were attached from the division machine-gun battalion and from the Sixth Marines. Even then some battalions went into the attack without proper machine-gun support. When told that the traffic conditions made it impossible to make more machine guns available, an officer retorted, "Very well we will take the Boche machine guns." The rear units of the assault battalions had to double time and did not get into position before their artillery barrage started forward. The Fifth Marines, which had a broad front initially, placed the First Battalion (Turrill) as left assault battalion, with the added duty of keeping contact with the Moroccans, and the Second Battalion (Keyser) as right assault battalion, while the Third (Shearer) occupied the old front line as the support.

The advance of the troops of the XX Corps was along sectors running a little south of east. The German sectors extended back to the northeast; this caused a drift of the retiring German troops across the corps front as the attack progressed. At the beginning of the attack the right front of the Second Division was faced by the 14th Reserve Division, and the left front by the 42d Division of the XIII (Royal Wurtemburg) Corps. The German front line in the eastern edge of the forest was weakly held by a battalion of the 138th Infantry and one of the 17th Infantry. They had a thinly held outpost line, with the main line of resistance a few hundred yards to the rear, and an artillery protective line about one mile in rear of the front. A second defensive position was arranged on what they called the Chaudun position, running along the ridge east of Chau-

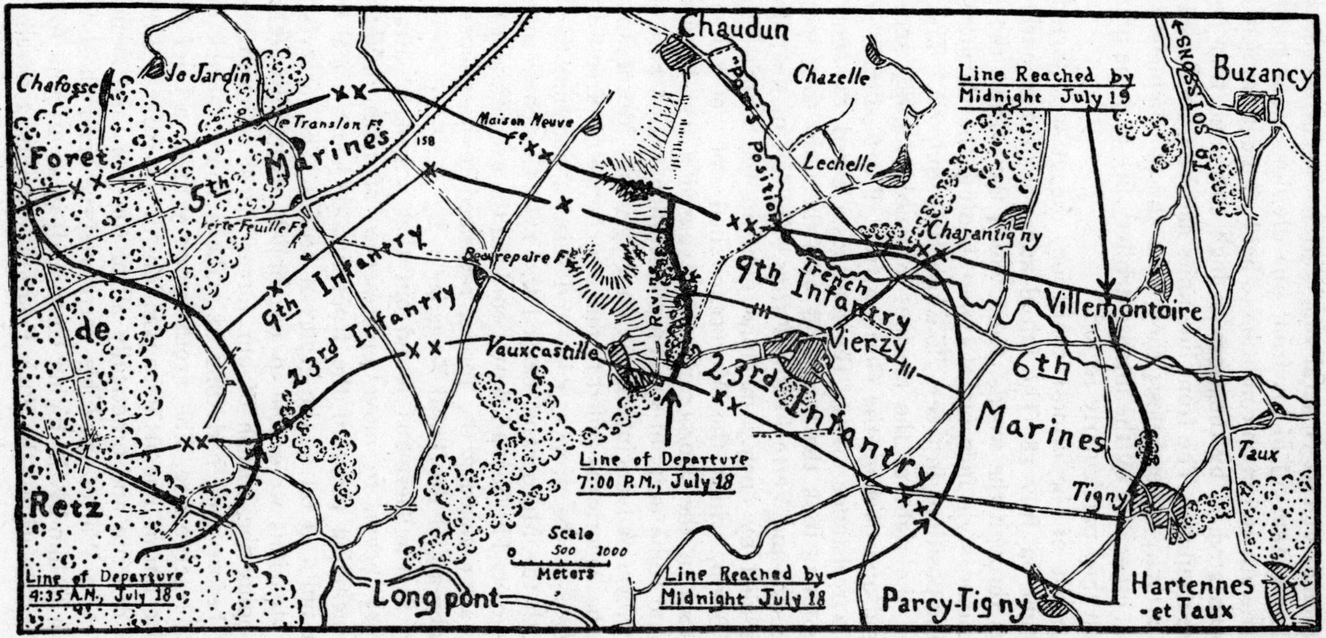

THE SOISSONS ATTACK

dun and through Vierzy. General von Watter, the corps commander, had complained that all of his front line divisions were greatly depleted in strength and in no condition to hold off a determined attack, but had been advised by the German high command that no more troops were available. The front line units had been cautioned about a possible attack; nevertheless, they were almost completely taken by surprise, especially by the intense artillery fire and the numerous tanks which they particularly feared.

In the midst of the utmost confusion, the attack started soon after daylight on July 18. The initial advance of the marine battalions was through the woods, from which they drove the enemy by close Indian style fighting, at times shooting the Germans from their sniping positions in trees, "like shooting squirrels." The Third Brigade on the right of the marines advanced rapidly across the open ground and overran the German front line positions, encountering little resistance. When the marines cleared the woods the supporting tanks took the lead, and with their aid they soon captured Translon and Verte Feuille Farms. The left of their line was badly enfiladed by enemy machine guns in the woods north of Translon Farm, which the Moroccans had not yet taken. The slowing down of the Moroccans' right caused a gap between the divisions and some units of the First Battalion, which bore too far to their left, were advancing almost entirely in the Moroccan sector. A part of the Americans failed to make a change of direction to the south of east at the proper point and this, in addition to seeking contact with the Moroccans, caused the 17th Company to get far out of its sector. The Second Battalion, with the exception of its 55th Company, after clearing the forest, remained in its proper sector and kept abreast of the Third Brigade.

As soon as the Germans found out that a general attack had started, they began to move up reserves of both infantry and artillery, including those of the front line divisions back through the higher units as far as the group of armies. The reserves of the front line divisions were able to accomplish practically nothing towards stopping the onrush of our forces. Most of them were encountered before they had time to make a counterattack or even establish a reserve line. The 219th Infantry made a brief stand at Beaurepaire Farm. The artillery positions of the front line divisions were soon overrun and practically all of the guns and ammunition captured. Von Watter used his corps reserves and those initially turned over to him by the higher commands in an attempt to occupy an old trench position—the Paris Position—running generally southeast of Chaudun for a distance of about one mile, and attempted to build up a line running south through Vierzy. His reserves began to occupy that line soon after the attack started, and reserve artillery pushed forward to support it. That position finally stopped the onward rush of the Second Division during the afternoon of June 18 and held it up until artillery could be shifted forward and coordinated plans for a further advance made.

### The Taking of Vierzy

So far only two complete battalions of marines had been in the front of the attack. Practically all of the Third Battalion of the Fifth, however, had been absorbed into the other two. None of the smaller unit commanders had maps and only a few had notes on the battle orders, including such data as compass bearings for the advance. Before the advance had progressed very far several units drifted far out of their sectors. The 17th Company of the First Battalion veered off to the north and with the help of a few Moroccans captured Chaudun about 9 A.M. The commander of the 55th Company of the Second Battalion seeing a town at some distance which he mistook for Vierzy, and knowing that his objective was to the left of that town, took his company to a position just west of Chaudun. He reported that Vierzy had been captured and caused considerable confusion to the staffs of the Brigade and of the Second Division. The commanders of the front line battalions, in their attempts to maintain contact to the rear, lost contact with some of their front line troops. The Third Brigade, on the right, after having overcome resistance at several points during its advance, pushed on towards Vierzy where the Germans were forming a new line. Scattering and more or less mixed companies of marines held a line from the left of the Third Brigade north for a considerable distance into the Moroccan sector.

The attack succeeded even better than was hoped for and during the afternoon the French Corps ordered another advance to the Soissons—Château-Thierry road. The units of the Second Division were still badly mixed. A hasty reorganization was made to enable the Third Brigade to continue the advance during the remainder of the day. Its initial task was to capture Vierzy and drive the Germans from their hastily organized line through that village. The Ninth Infantry, on the left, was ordered to pass to the north of the town and the 23d Infantry to capture Vierzy.

A battalion of the Fifth Marines was attached to each of these regiments. Turrill managed to collect part of the scattered First Battalion, and with some of the Third and a portion of the Eighth Marine Machine Gun Company, joined the 23d Infantry. He went through Vierzy and assisted that regiment in partially clearing the town of numerous snipers, all of whom were not eliminated for several days. The Second Battalion of the Fifth, with the exception of the 55th Company, still near Chaudun, was in the ravine north of Vauxcastille in the late afternoon and was attached to the Ninth Infantry. It was ordered to be the left assault battalion in the attack, with a battalion of infantry on its right and another in its rear in support.

The reinforced regiment started forward again at about 7 P.M. Keyser's battalion had neither tank nor artillery support. After it had advanced about one kilometer, it came under the fire of the Chaudun position; its left was held up while its right continued to advance with the front line troops of the Ninth Infantry. While Keyser's marines were attempting to dislodge some German machine gunners, several French tanks retreated through his line, drawing considerable artillery fire, which not only destroyed several of the tanks but also inflicted severe casualties upon the marines. The 55th Company finally rejoined the battalion, and with its help the left flank advanced a short distance only to be again stopped by enemy machine guns which suddenly began firing from a wheat field just at dark. The right flank elements of the battalion by that time had reached a position just south of the woods at Lechelle. Unable to advance further without support and on account of darkness, the battalion halted for the night in an old trench system, from which they had driven the enemy. They remained there until withdrawn two days later.

The Third Brigade was able to advance nearly a mile east of Vierzy before it stopped for the night. By this time the Fifth Marines as well as the Third Brigade were so completely exhausted and used up that they could make no further effort.

## The Attack of the Sixth Marines

The Sixth Marines, from its initial position in corps reserve, had advanced to Beaurepaire Farm but had not taken part in the operations. The French Army ordered a continuation of the attack on the 19th, with the objective of the Second Division still the Soissons—Château-Thierry road. The order was late in reaching the Second Division, and it was not until 6:30 A.M. that the leading battalion of the Sixth Marines, which was ordered to lead the attack during that day, left its bivouac to move forward to an attack, supported by the Second Field Artillery Brigade and a group of French tanks. The First Battalion, Second Engineers, and a machine-gun battalion made up the reserve. The Germans had been making every effort to build up a line to stop the Allies' advance before it reached the Soissons—Château-Thierry road. Entire divisions from the general reserve were hurried to that position. The situation for the Marne salient was so grave that all the higher commands were ordering that line held at all costs. Particular effort was made to reorganize the artillery defense since the German infantry would not stand against tank attacks.

The Sixth Marines, commanded by Lieutenant Colonel Harry Lee, advancing to the attack on a front of about 2,500 yards with the First Battalion (Hughes) leading on the right, the Second (Holcomb) on the left, and the Third (Sibley) in support, passed through the line held by the Third Brigade at 8:25 A.M. The ground over which the advance was made was practically level and contained no cover with the exception of an occasional field of wheat. The attack started with insufficient artillery support; it was in perfect view of the enemy and had none of the chances of success of the attack on the previous day. The accompanying tanks were slow, and the advance had to conform to their pace. The German artillery, with ample air observation, promptly put down a destructive fire upon the advancing troops; this, together with the fire from occasional machine-gun groups, caused a veritable slaughter in the ranks of the leading battalions. Within one-half hour so many men had been cut down that it was necessary to send forward two companies from the support battalion to fill the ever-widening gaps. The right of the line was soon definitely stopped by the enemy's strongly organized position in Tigny.

The 84th Company, sent forward from the support, was able to rush and seize a small wood north of Tigny, which afforded some cover. The remainder of the support battalion had merged with the front line by noon. The Second Battalion managed to reach the shelter of the wood about five hundred yards west of Villemontoire. The losses to the original front line battalions had averaged more than 50 per cent. It had been almost impossible to evacuate the wounded. The enemy had built up a strong line, well supported with artillery, just west of the Soissons—Château-Thierry highway; it was hopeless for the decimated regiment to attempt further advance without substantial reinforcements, which were not available. Lee accordingly ordered his troops to dig in during the early afternoon. The regiment was harassed by artillery during the remainder of the day. It was relieved by French units during the following night and went to the rear. In the course of these operations the Fifth Marines had experienced the thrill of pursuing a demoralized enemy, who had been taken completely by surprise, while the Sixth had the hopeless and bitter experience of trying to overcome machines with their bare bodies.

## Relief

The Fourth Brigade withdrew during the night of July 19-20 to its original starting position, in the eastern edge of the forest. Together with the remainder of the Second Division it was moved farther to the rear, and by July 26 the entire Division was reassembled thirty miles northeast of Paris. The Fourth Brigade lost approximately 2,000 killed and wounded during its two days' participation in the attack. The Sixth Marines suffered about two-thirds of the losses. The Division together with the First American and French Moroccan Divisions was given credit for constituting the spearhead of the initial attack which started the general retreat of the German Army, which continued until the war was over.

After a few days' rest the Division, except its motor elements, was moved to the vicinity of Nancy where a concentration of American divisions had already begun for the purpose of forming an American army and taking over a part of the front. Approximately 2,000 replacements were absorbed into the Marine Brigade shortly after its arrival in its new area. Brigadier General John A. Lejeune took command of the Fourth Brigade on July 26 and of the Second Division three days later. He was promoted to major general shortly afterwards. Neville, who had been promoted to brigadier general, continued in command of the Fourth Brigade for the remainder of the war. Lieutenant Colonel Earl H. Ellis, one of the most brilliant officers in the Marine Corps, took over the position of brigade adjutant, and from that time until the end of the war directed the brigade staff work and was responsible more than any other individual for the thoroughgoing manner in which the Brigade functioned in the succeeding operations.

## The Marbache Sector

After a few days' rest the Second Division was ordered to take over a defensive sector at Pont-a-Mousson, which took its name from the town of Marbache where the divisional headquarters was located. The sector was an unusually quiet one and extended over an extremely wide front of about ten miles. The movements for the relief began on August 4. The Fourth Brigade was assigned the left half of the sector lying generally in the valley of the Moselle River with one regiment on each side of the river—the Fifth on the east bank and the Sixth on the west. The Second Battalion of each regiment was placed in the front line, which extended generally east and west for a distance of about two miles from a point just north of Pont-a-Mousson.

This time the marines allowed the quiet sector to remain quiet, carried on some improvements in the trench system, and trained the new men in the technique of trench warfare. The only incident that caused any excitement occurred in the sector of the Second Battalion of the Fifth. A party of Germans, apparently engaged in a stealth raid to destroy wire, were wandering about in "no man's land" about 2 A.M., August 8, and ran into the marines' front line. They were promptly driven off, but both sides put down barrages of machine-gun and artillery fire, which they kept up for nearly an hour.

The war was progressing too rapidly to permit a division with the reputation that the Second had gained to continue long at such child's play. On August 12 it was ordered out of the line, relieved by the 82nd American Division, and assembled in the area of Colombey-les-Belles, south of Toul, on August 20 to prepare itself for more important duties.

## The St. Mihiel Offensive

In the meantime the war on the Western Front had been making favorable progress for the Allies. The Germans had evacuated the entire Marne salient and the British as well as French armies had made successful attacks and driven back the Germans. The American Army was about to have its long-sought-for opportunity to crush the St. Mihiel salient, which had existed since the early phases of the war. The Germans were aware that extensive preparations were being made for a drive against the salient; there had been considerable discussion in their high command as to the advisability of withdrawing from it and straightening out their line across its base along what they called the Michel position—a part of the Hindenburg Line. Some historians have claimed that such an evacuation had already been initiated before the salient was attacked, but a careful search of the German records fails to disclose that any troops had been withdrawn from it, although a redistribution of front line units to make the defense more elastic was in progress when the attack started.

As the attack was finally arranged, the I and IV Corps of the American First Army made the principal efforts by attacking north from a line running west from Pont-a-Mousson while the American V Corps, led by our 26th Division, attacked southeast from the western side of the salient. The double attack was expected to pinch off the salient. The Second Division was placed in the center of the main attack, as the left division of the I (right) Corps. The attack was planned in great detail and no cost or effort was spared to assure the rapid advance of the assaulting troops. A four-hour artillery bombardment, with the normal artillery support more than doubled, and machine-gun barrages preceded the attack. The Second Division faced the German 77th Reserve Division, which had held the position for a number of weeks. It covered the approximate front of the Second Division with a thinly held line occupied by two battalions of the 419th German Infantry. In an effort to maintain the secrecy of the intended attack, the entire front of the Second Division was taken over by the Second Battalion, Fifth Marines (Major Messersmith), on the night of September 11-12.

The attack started in the early morning of September 12. The Second Division was in column of brigades, Third Brigade leading, regiments abreast in column of battalions. The Ninth Infantry on the right was followed by the Fifth Marines in support; the 23d Infantry on the left was followed by the Sixth Marines. The German front line battalions were in the act of deepening their outpost zones and withdrawing their main line of resistance farther to the rear when the artillery preparation began. This added greatly to their confusion. The heavy bombardment and the rolling barrages which preceded the infantry advance enabled the Second Division together with the units on its flank to sweep rapidly to the first objective, encountering little resistance. After a halt for reorganization, the advance was again resumed, and the objective for the first day was reached by 1 P.M. without the necessity of the Marine Brigade being put into the front line.

## The Fourth Brigade

The Sixth Machine Gun Battalion took part in the initial barrage and together with the marine regiments followed the advance of the Third Infantry Brigade. The First Battalion, Fifth Regiment (Barker) maintained contact with the 89th Division on the left during the advance. The German corps attempted a counterattack which was entirely ineffective, on the front of the Second Division. As soon as the German higher command saw the extent of the break in their lines, they ordered their troops to evacuate the salient and move back to the Michel position, with strong outposts only to be maintained in front of that line. The withdrawal was successfully accomplished by a considerable proportion of the all but trapped Germans, during the late afternoon and early evening. The American forces made contact across the salient at 9 A.M. the following day.

The Second Division's front line halted on a generally east and west line about 1,000 yards north of Thiacourt. Both regiments of the Third Brigade pushed patrols farther to the front and occupied Xammes and Jaulny. Little change took place in the sector during the 13th, and on the evening of that day the Marine Brigade took over the front line with the Fifth Marines on the right and the Sixth on the left. The Third Battalion of the Sixth took over the front line and the remainder of that regiment occupied successive support positions. The task of the Fourth Brigade during the rest of the operation was to drive back the German outposts in front of the Michel position.

### Attacks on the German Outposts

Each regiment of marines sent forward strong patrols on the evening of September 14 to reconnoiter and take possession of a series of woods which screened the brigade front. The Third Battalion, Fifth Marines, sent the 45th Company into the Bois de Hailbat, in the right part of its sector, and the 47th Company into the eastern edge of the Bois de la Montagne located farther west. The two companies acting as outposts held the northern edges of those woods until the following day when the remainder of the battalion moved up, reinforced them, and established a new front line. The enemy counterattacked the new position in the afternoon of September 15 but was successfully repulsed. The Fifth Marines was relieved during the following night.

The operations in the woods to the front of the Sixth were more complex. The First Battalion sent two companies to the northern edge of the Bois de la Montagne during the evening of September 14. The rest of the battalion came up the following day, reinforced the position, and made it the new front line. The Second Battalion of the Sixth (Major E. C. Williams) moved forward to reconnoiter the woods farther west and to extend the line of the First Battalion. It advanced, expecting to find the woods unoccupied by the enemy, but, soon after entering it, discovered a detachment of forty Germans retiring to the north, who ran when fired upon. The battalion sergeant major (now major, U. S. M. C., retired), William Ulrich, himself a born German, ran after the fleeing enemy and persuaded all of them to surrender to him. The battalion went towards its assigned position but found that the enemy still held most of the woods. Williams attacked and, after considerable fighting, cleared the woods to its northern edge, where he established a new front line. The enemy then made three or four counterattacks attempting to recapture the position. A composite regiment, formed from the remnants of the Tenth German Division, supported by short artillery bombardments, made the attack but each time was driven back by Williams' battalion. The Sixth Marines was relieved during the night of September 15-16 by units of the 78th American Division which was taking over from the Second Division.

The smashing victory which reduced the St. Mihiel salient was accomplished with relatively few losses. This was due largely to the smothering artillery fire and to the fact that the enemy evacuated the salient shortly after the battle began. The Marine Brigade suffered only 132 killed and died of wounds and 574 wounded in action. The losses which the marines caused the enemy cannot even be approximated. The Second Division captured approximately 3,300 prisoners during the operation, most of whom were captured by the Third Brigade during the first day of the battle. The operation greatly added to the prestige of the American Army and gave the Marine Brigade considerable battle experience, which proved valuable in the more difficult operations that followed.

## BLANC MONT

Even before the operations which resulted in the reduction of the St. Mihiel salient had been completed, feverish efforts were being made to begin an attack by the American Army between the Meuse and the Argonne forest, in co-operation with the French Fourth Army west of that forest, in the hopes of driving the enemy back far enough to intercept his principal railway communications, which converged in the vicinity of Mezières. Should the Germans permit the operation to succeed it would imperil all their armies between the Argonne and the North Sea; they therefore resisted to the utmost.

At the urgent request of Marshal Foch, Pershing allotted the Second Division and the incomplete 36th Division to the French Fourth Army. After a brief period of reorganization, absorbing replacements, and training near Toul, the Second Division moved by rail and marching to Chalons where it began to arrive on September 26. The French desired to use the Americans as shock troops to lead their attack and were not at all anxious for them to operate as larger American units. Lejeune soon learned that they wanted to break up his division temporarily and put its brigades in line to reinforce French divisions. He vigorously opposed such a plan, and the division was allowed to attack as a unit.

The high hills east of Reims were strongly held and could not be readily taken from the front. The French Fourth Army attacked farther to the east to outflank them. The general attack of that army and the American Army started on September 26 and considerable ground was gained by both. The key to the situation in the French sector became Blanc Mont Ridge; the taking of this important position was delegated to the American Second Division. The Division was assigned to the French XXI Corps, and the Fourth Brigade took over a front line position about two miles long, in an old German trench system just north of Somme-Py on the night of October 1-2. Both regiments went into the line, the Fifth on the right and the Sixth on the left. During the following night they made a short advance to Essen trench, which was being evacuated by the Germans at the time.

The German high command had by this time decided that a general retirement along most of the western front was necessary, but, while this was going on, every effort was to be made to inflict the greatest possible casualties on the Allies. It had ordered a series of step by step withdrawals along the immediate front which had been taken over by the Second Division. Ground lost, however, essential to the holding of any successive defensive line, they ordered retaken by counterattack. All their troops were expected to make a determined stand and avoid giving ground except as ordered.

The Second Division was given a front of more than three miles on which to attack in the early morning of October 3, 1918. It put both brigades in line, Fourth Brigade on the left, with sectors converging on Blanc Mont Ridge, leaving a triangular area between the two of more than one mile at its base, in which no troops advanced. The triangle was to be outflanked and cleared out after it had been passed. The Fourth Brigade attacked from the line held by the Sixth Marines. That regiment led the advance in column of battalions on a front of approximately one mile. The Fifth, after it had withdrawn from the Essen trench area, followed in support and had the tasks of clearing out the triangle and protecting the flanks of the leading regiment. The Marine Brigade had a battalion of French tanks attached; each of its battalions was, as usual, closely supported by a machine-gun company. In addition to that of its own, the infantry was supported by the artillery of two French divisions and several other artillery units—forty-eight batteries in all. This vast aggregation of guns fired an intense five-minute artillery preparation. Thereafter part of the light artillery furnished a rolling barrage for the leading units to follow. The Second Battalion, Sixth Marines (Williams), led the assault with the First and Third following in the order named. The marines could count on the Third Brigade on their right, but it appeared doubtful whether the French division on their left would be able to advance at all.

The zone of attack assigned to the Marine Brigade was at the beginning in the defensive sector of the 51st Reserve German Division but soon led into that of the 200th Division. The front line, organized as outposts, was held by a battalion of the 235th Reserve German Infantry, having at the time a strength of slightly over 200 officers and men, most of whom were exhausted by long service in the front line. The main line of resistance was located along a system of trenches on the Blanc Mont Ridge, nearly three kilometers in the rear of the covering troops.

## The Initial Advance

The Second Battalion, Sixth Marines, with all four of its companies in line, advanced rapidly in the brigade sector, resisted only by an occasional machine-gun group and flanking fire from the left where the French had not advanced. It reached its objective along the Blanc Mont—Medeah Farm Road by 8:30 A.M. and began consolidating its position. It captured the German main line of resistance in its assigned sector except on the western slope of Blanc Mont.

The attack of the Second Battalion was marked by extraordinary dash and gallantry, some of its members performing the most outstanding acts of heroism in the American Army during the World War. The deeds of two men of the 78th Company particularly are worthy of special mention, as during that attack they performed such conspicuous acts of bravery as to be awarded the Congressional Medal of Honor (two of the five awarded to men of the Fourth Brigade during the war). At about 6:20 A.M. the advance of the battalion was being seriously impeded by a determined enemy machine-gun crew, firing from in front of our artillery barrage. Undaunted by the obvious perils of the situation, Private James J. Kelly dashed forward through the intense barrage, killed the machine-gun operator with a grenade, shot another member of the crew with his pistol, and brought the other eight members of the crew back with him, through the line of bursting shells. The acts of Corporal John H. Pruitt were no less extraordinary. Single-handed and alone he attacked two German machine guns, captured them, and killed two of the enemy. A short time afterwards he captured forty prisoners in a near-by dugout. Before the assault was over he was mortally wounded by shellfire, while sniping at the enemy. Pruitt's name has been commemorated in the naval service by the naming of Destroyer No. 347 in honor of his heroic conduct.

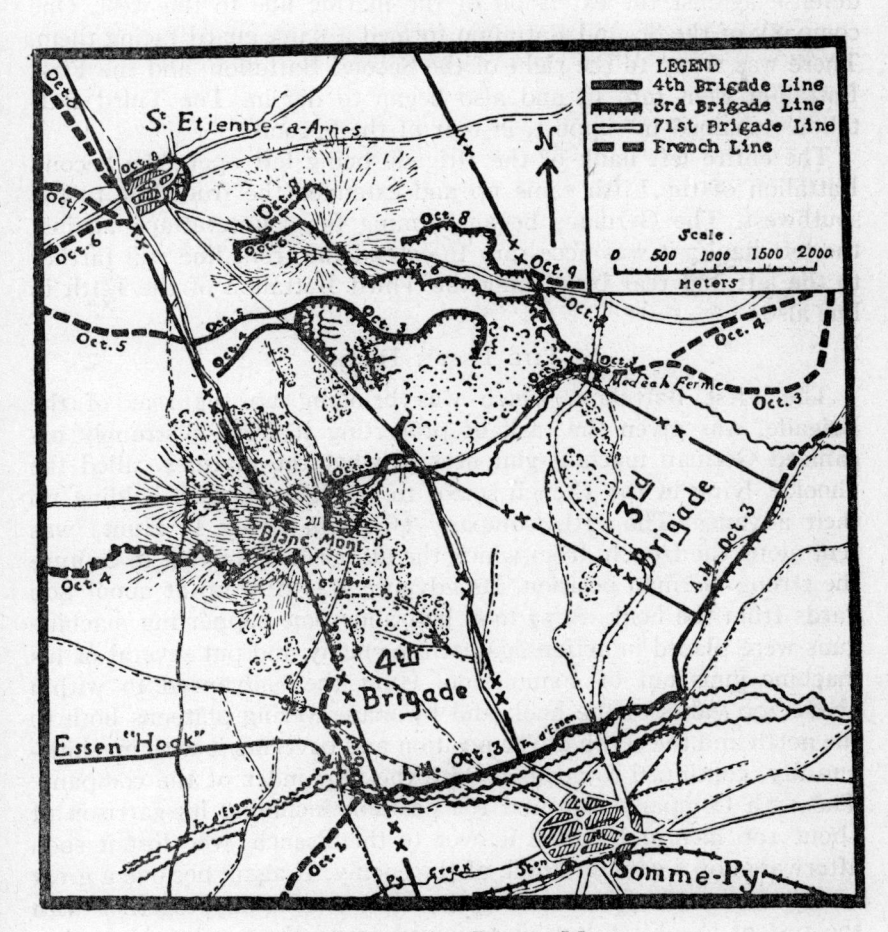

THE ATTACK OF BLANC MONT

The flanking fire and the strongly held hill caused the leading battalion to drift somewhat to the right as it approached its objective. The Germans remaining on Blanc Mont, the headquarters units of both an artillery and an infantry brigade, made a stubborn defense against the extension of the marine line to the west. One company of the Second Battalion formed a flank guard facing them. There was a gap to the right of the Second Battalion, and the First Battalion went into it, and also began to dig in. The Third Battalion remained in support, in rear of the Second.

The entire left flank of the Brigade being left open, the Second Battalion of the Fifth came up and extended the front line to the southwest. The Germans began forming for counterattack against the left flank; it was necessary to extend the front line still farther to the left and rear by placing the Third Battalion of the Fifth in line also.

### The Essen Hook

The First Battalion, which was bringing up the rear of the Brigade, was given the task of protecting it from a strongly organized German machine-gun nest in what the marines called the "hook," lying in the French sector to the left and still holding up their advance. The 17th Company (Captain Leroy P. Hunt) was sent along the trench, from which the attack had started, to capture the strong German position. Its advance was held up at about 800 yards from the hook. A 37 mm. gun and some supporting machine guns were placed in action against the enemy and put several of his machine guns out of commission. Hunt then advanced to within about 300 yards of the hook and by maneuvering platoons both to the north and the south of the position and covering it with machine-gun fire, continued to advance with the remainder of the company. The 17th Company captured the position including its garrison of about 100 men and turned it over to the French, who lost it soon afterwards by a counterattack of the enemy. It again became a great annoyance to the Marine Brigade. Hunt's company together with the rest of the First Battalion moved on to the north and further extended the left flank of the line towards the rear.

### The Advance Renewed

The success of the operation astonished the higher French command, and it ordered another attack in the same general formation by the Second Division for the late afternoon of the same day. The Third Brigade on the right received the order, attacked with its support regiment, the 23d Infantry, and made a further gain of nearly two kilometers in the direction of St. Etienne. The Fifth Marines, which was assigned to make the attack for the Fourth Brigade, did not receive the order until too late to carry it out that day. By mutual agreement of the battalion commanders the operation was postponed, and the attack was made early the following morning without co-ordination by the regimental or brigade commanders. The delay was most unfortunate as during the late afternoon of October 3, the sector in which the marines were to have advanced was practically undefended, but the enemy strongly reinforced and reorganized it during that night. Furthermore the Third Brigade, after its advance, was left in a highly exposed position, as the French on its right had also failed to go forward.

The deep penetration effected by the Second Division caused the German high command to order a gradual withdrawal of their line from the hills east of Reims to the Arnes and the Suippes, as the old line was under observation from Blanc Mont. The withdrawal was made gradually, however, with violent efforts by the Germans to hold back the advance of the Americans, and at times to drive them from commanding positions which they had taken. The American operations during the succeeding days were in the face of determined German resistance. During the night of October 3-4 several Bavarian units and a dismounted cavalry regiment built up a line running south from the eastern edge of St. Etienne, facing the sharp salient which had been made by the Second Division. A number of other German reserve units were ordered to the vicinity, and additional harassing artillery and machine-gun fire was directed for the following day.

OCTOBER 4

The attack of the Fifth Marines in the early morning of October 4 was led by the Third Battalion (Major H. L. Larsen). After passing the front line held by the Sixth Marines, the Fifth in column of battalions, advanced about two kilometers in the direction of St. Etienne without encountering any considerable resistance—the German line, which had been built up during the night, was farther to the west. Larsen reached the front line of the Third Brigade and extended it to the west a distance of nearly one mile. After a brief halt he again resumed the advance and gained several hundred yards more but found his troops enfiladed from both flanks and was forced to retire to a position in a woods in line with the Third Brigade. The other battalions of the Fifth had followed in support. All three battalions were on very exposed terrain and subjected to heavy artillery and machine-gun fire.

The Germans, determined to crush the salient thrust into their lines, ordered a number of reserve units to make a counterattack against it and continued to subject it to artillery and machine-gun fire. The strong and co-ordinated counterattack which they had planned failed to materialize—probably due to difficulties of communication. The enemy made an unsuccessful local counterattack against Larsen's battalion from the west during the afternoon; at 7:30 P.M. several hundred Germans approached his exposed line from the southwest and rear, forcing him to change his front in order to beat off the attack. The Fifth Marines suffered extremely severe casualties from flanking machine-gun and harassing artillery fire. The day proved to be the darkest of the entire war for the marines, who lost over 1,100 killed and wounded—mostly from the Fifth Marines. The divisions on each flank were still unable to keep up. The Third Brigade met heavy resistance during the day, and all its attempts to advance proved practically futile. A portion of Blanc Mont was still in possession of the enemy; this was the next situation to be dealt with.

## BLANC MONT CLEARED

Lee had ordered the First and Third Battalions of the Sixth to attack the enemy position on Blanc Mont, on October 4. The position was strongly held; the marines' supporting artillery fire appeared entirely ineffective, and the two battalion commanders, believing it impossible to carry out the operation successfully, postponed the attack until sufficient artillery fire could be provided. The attack was successfully made by the Third Battalion early the following morning, and an enemy garrison of about 275, whose retreat had been cut off, together with eighty machine guns and numerous other weapons were captured. The way was then open for the advance of the French on the left of the Second Division. They moved forward and extended the front line to the west.

The Sixth Marines, with the Second Battalion leading, passed through the front line held by the Fifth at 3 P.M., October 5, in a further advance towards St. Etienne. The leading battalion with only about 300 men, attempted to advance on nearly one mile of front. It moved forward only a few hundred yards, when its right was stopped by a strong German machine-gun nest on a hill; being unable to gain further ground, the troops dug in. The Germans had withdrawn to a generally east and west main line of resistance, passing just north of St. Etienne, with a salient around the hill located about one mile southeast of St. Etienne, held by machine guns which had stopped Williams' advance.

An attack with adequate artillery support against that German position was arranged for the early morning of October 6. The entire Second Field Artillery Brigade participated in an hour's bombardment of the hill and its immediate rear. The assault made by the Third Battalion, Sixth Marines, and a battalion of the 23d Infantry followed a rolling artillery barrage. The marines took the enemy's line in flank and gradually rolled it up, but the infantry, who met more resistance, did not gain much ground. The hill was captured after an advance of about one kilometer by the marine battalion. Aside from this brief but important operation, the front remained relatively quiet and stable during that day.

### Relief and St. Etienne

By this time the Second Division had again about made its utmost effort and was overdue for relief. The incomplete 36th American Division, also attached to the French Fourth Army, made the relief with its 71st Brigade, taking over the entire divisional front, on the night of October 6-7. Only the front line units were relieved, however, and the newly arrived infantry brigade functioned temporarily as a part of the Second Division. It attacked on the early morning of October 8 but, after making a substantial gain, was driven back almost to its former front line.

During that operation the First Battalion, Sixth Marines, was assigned as a connecting group to maintain contacts with the French to the west and to capture St. Etienne. The town was captured by the 76th Company (Captain Macon C. Overton) assisted by a few French soldiers. The 75th Company on its right was left in a desperate position by the retirement of the 71st Brigade, but despite the fact that the strength of the company was reduced to a mere handful of men under Sergeant Aralzaman C. Marsh and all of the officers were killed or wounded, it held on to its advanced position. The Germans made a counterattack to retake the town during the early evening of October 8 but were successfully repulsed. The Third Battalion, like most of the other battalions of the Marine Brigade, was by this time reduced to fewer than 300 men but during the following night was reinforced by two companies of the Second Engineers. The Third Battalion, the last marine unit to hold a front line position in the Champagne sector, was relieved on October 10.

By that time the Germans were retreating to the Aisne, where they formed a new line on October 13. The infantry brigades of the 36th Division supported by the artillery and other auxiliary troops of the Second Division, closely followed the retiring enemy. The infantry brigades of the Second Division, in the meantime, had been sent to the rear for rest and reorganization.

## LEFFINCOURT

During the week of almost continuous combat in the Champagne sector, the Marine Brigade suffered its second largest losses for a single operation. Approximately 494 were killed or died of wounds, and approximately 1,864 were wounded. The percentage of casualties among the officers was particularly high. By way of slight compensation the Fifth and Sixth Marines were again cited by the French Army for the gallant part they had played during the many days of the trying battle. This made the third citation for each of those regiments, and they as well as the Sixth Machine Gun Battalion, which had been cited on two previous occasions, met the requirements of the French Army of two such citations for making the *fourragère* in the colors of the French *Croix de Guerre* a part of the uniform of the organizations. The authorization was later confirmed by the United States Government, and the *fourragère* has become a part of the uniform of the Fifth and Sixth Marines (the Sixth Machine Gun Battalion was discontinued immediately after the war). Any individual, who belonged to a unit of the Fourth Brigade and participated in two of the battles for which the French Army citation was given, was thereafter authorized to wear the *fourragère* as a part of his uniform.

The depleted ranks of the organizations were refilled by replacements, sent from the First Marine Training Regiment to the brigade camp north of Chalons. This had scarcely been accomplished when a movement was set on foot, which again threatened the disintegration of the Division. Its artillery brigade as well as a portion of the auxiliary troops were already separated from it, but on October 19 the French Fourth Army ordered one brigade to return to the line and relieve a French division. The Fourth Brigade was designated for this task. It marched north again on October 21, and during the following night its advanced units stayed in Leffincourt, while the Brigade Staff carried out preliminary arrangements for the relief of the French division. A prompt report to American General Headquarters resulted in the cancellation of the plan; the Fourth Brigade on the following day marched back to the area north of Chalons. Arrangements had been completed for the entire Division to join the American First Army in the Argonne. On October 25 the Fourth Brigade moved by trucks and marching to Les Islettes. From there, together with the infantry of the rest of the Division, it marched

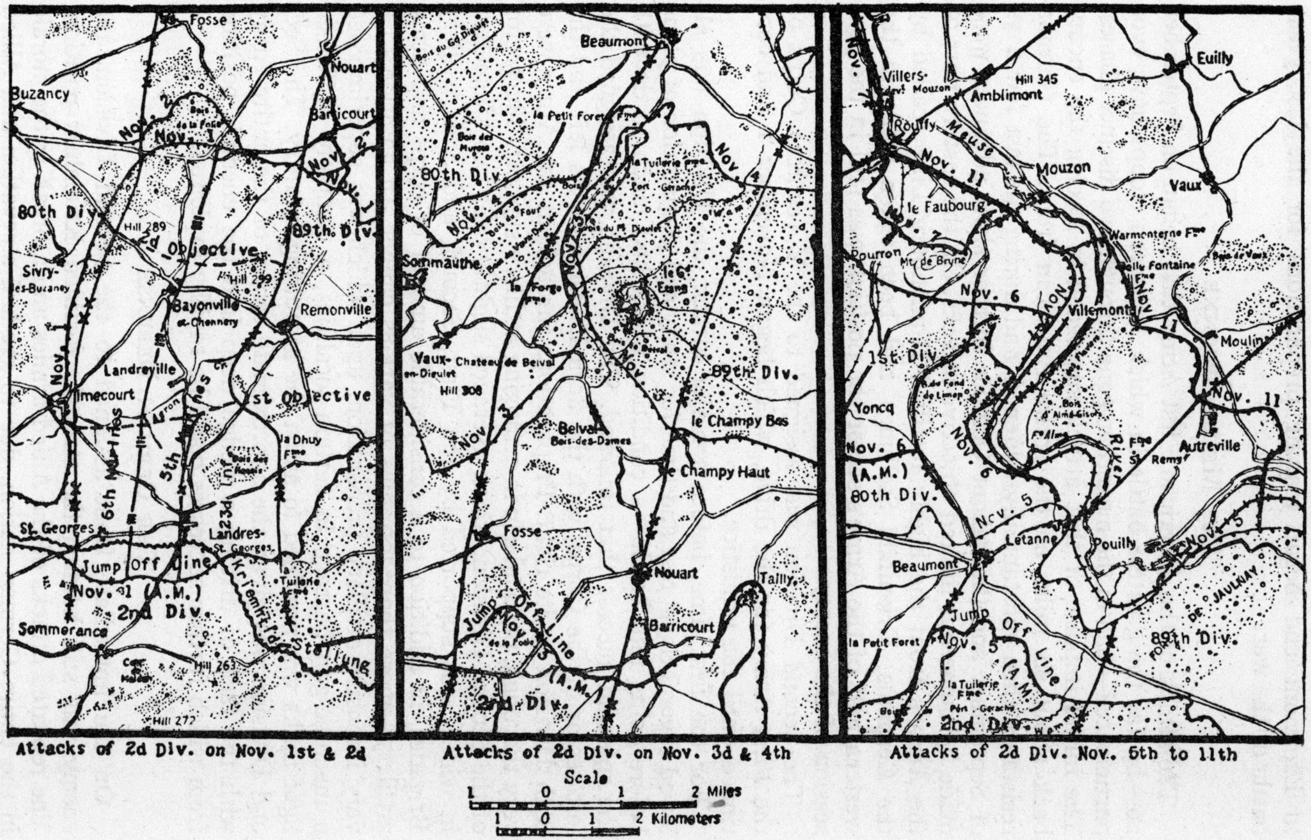

THE MEUSE-ARGONNE SECTOR

to Exermont and began making preparations for the last great battle of the war.

## The Meuse-Argonne

The attack of the American First Army that began on September 26—by far the greatest battle in which American troops have ever participated—had in the meantime gone through two distinct phases. The initial impulse of that attack succeeded in forcing the enemy back about six miles on the entire American front. The German resistance then substantially stiffened, and during the last few days of September and throughout October further short advances were made by numerous limited objective attacks. On the eastern part of the Army's front the highly fortified Hindenburg Line (called by the Germans, Kriemhild Stellung) had been taken while in the western half of the Army's sector the position was still in the possession of the enemy.

The Second Division was assigned to the V (center) Corps of the First Army for the drive, which began November 1 and continued until the armistice.

For the first time, before a major attack, the Division was allowed several days' rest and time for study and preparation of plans before going into battle—a condition which had much to do with the splendid success that followed. The Division was assigned the left sector of the Corps, with the 80th Division on its left and the 89th Division on its right. Preparations throughout the Army were very thorough, particularly in arranging artillery support. The sector of the Second Division, which averaged slightly over two kilometers in width, was supported by the First, Second, and 42d Artillery Brigades, in addition to a considerable amount of corps and army artillery—more than 300 guns of various caliber. In addition to a very intensive artillery preparation, upon which was superimposed a machine-gun barrage in certain localities, a company of fifteen light tanks was provided to assist the assaulting infantry. The Second Division was given the approximate center of the entire Army with the task of driving a wedge deep into the enemy's position from which further successes could be rapidly exploited.

## The German Defense

On the immediate front assigned to the Second Division, the enemy was still holding the strongly fortified Kriemhild position. The repeated attacks of the Allied armies and a break in the morale in the entire German nation, due to gradual starvation and Allied propaganda, had continued to undermine the fighting power of the

German Army. It was attempting by this time to withdraw from France, delaying the Allied forces as much as possible by rear guard actions. Preliminary plans were ready for withdrawing to the Antwerp-Meuse Line, which, on the American front, would mean a retreat of nearly twenty-five miles, to the east bank of the Meuse. The front facing the Second Division was held by the German 41st Division and just west of it was the Fifteenth Bavarian, against which the marines had fought at Blanc Mont. The 52d Division was in the process of relieving the 41st, when the American attack started on the morning of November 1, and the units of both divisions were still in the sector. The actual front line was held by one battalion on the hill south of Landres-St. Georges while in the vicinity of St. Georges were mixed units of the two divisions. The sector was held in considerable depth with support and reserve troops farther to the rear, and the supporting artillery was disposed in depth.

## The Break Through

The attack of the Second Division, with the exception of capturing the Bois de Hazois in the right of the division sector by the 23d Infantry, was made in column of brigades. The Marine Brigade led the attack with the Fifth Marines on the right and the Sixth on the left, each deployed in column of battalions. The artillery preparation and the rolling barrage, which preceded the attack throughout the entire first day's battle, almost completely broke up the enemy defense. The fire was so intense, particularly in its initial stages, that scarcely a square foot of ground in the enemy's front line area was left unturned by bursting shells. The attack proceeded through three phases with the artillery barrage standing for a short period just beyond each of the objectives, giving the next battalion in column an opportunity to leap-frog the front line battalion. The First Battalion of the Fifth (Hamilton) and the First Battalion of the Sixth (Barker) led the assault followed by the Second (Captain Dunbeck) and the Third (Larsen) in the Fifth's sector and the Third (Shuler) and Second (Williams) in the sector of the Sixth. The companies of the Brigade Machine Gun Battalion, after taking part in a preliminary barrage, and the regimental machine-gun companies were assigned one in support of each battalion. The infantry attack started at 5:30 A.M., with the leading troops following closely the artillery barrage. The task of maintaining contact with the 89th Division on the right was carried out by the Eighteenth Company of the Fifth Marines. An improvised battalion, under Major George A. Stowell, U.S.M.C., consisting of the 95th Company of the Sixth

Marines, Company G of the 319th Infantry, and two machine-gun platoons, taken from the two divisions, performed the difficult task on the left of maintaining contact between the I and V Corps.

The German main line of resistance was overrun after a few local skirmishes. The two villages on the division front were almost completely demolished by the artillery preparation. The German protective artillery barrage, which they as usual laid down in front of their advanced lines, was more or less effectively maintained until their artillery positions were overrun. It inflicted more casualties on the first day of the battle than all of the other German efforts combined. The heavy belts of wire caused considerable delay initially but they, like all other obstacles, were surmounted in time for the troops to catch up with the creeping artillery barrage.

Hamilton's battalion, leading the assault on the right, soon outflanked the German positions in Landres and on the ridge south of that village and thereafter, without difficulty, kept up with the barrage as far as its objective, a few hundred yards south of Landreville. Barker's battalion encountered considerable resistance from enemy machine guns in a small wood south of St. Georges, which the artillery for some reason had not effectively covered. While leading the 76th Company in an attack against that position, Captain Macon C. Overton, one of the most gallant young officers of the Marine Corps, was killed. The Battalion reached its objective along the stream line running east from Imecourt without further difficulty.

The center division of the V Corps had failed to advance, and the 80th Division had made very little progress. Stowell with his liaison battalion came into action to protect the left of the marines. He attacked Imecourt and, after a brief skirmish, captured its entire garrison of about 150 and, thereafter for a time, advanced in the sector of the 80th Division, keeping abreast of the leading assault units of the Second Division.

The first objective having been reached along the entire division front at about 8 A.M., the Second Battalion of the Fifth and the Third Battalion of the Sixth passed through the front line and assumed the lead, covering the entire division front, as by this time the 23d Infantry had completed its limited task. The Second Battalion of the Fifth encountered considerable resistance of enemy machine guns firing from the windows of the houses in Landreville. The village was soon taken, however, and approximately 100 Germans surrendered. The second German defensive line, known as the Freya Stellung, ran generally east and west through Bayonville. Hill 299, which was covered by woods, contained a considerable number of enemy machine guns as well as some heavy artillery; all of which were captured together with their personnel by Dunbeck's battalion which reached its objective—an east and west line about 500 yards north of Bayonville—about noon.

The Third Battalion of the Sixth passed through the First Battalion and, during the second phase, led the attack. It encountered little resistance until reaching the villages of Chennery and Bayonville which were taken with the aid of tanks. About 100 Germans, a number of machine guns, and several artillery pieces in the villages were captured. Stowell was still protecting the flank of the Division; the 80th was several kilometers behind.

The original rear battalions of the Brigade, the Third Battalion of the Fifth on the right and the Second Battalion of the Sixth on the left, passed through the front line about noon and continued the advance to the final objective. By this time all of the enemy's organized positions had been overrun, and he was resisting the advance only with small rear guards. Larsen's battalion of the Fifth reached its objective along a generally east and west line about one kilometer southwest of Barricourt soon after 2 P.M. while Williams' battalion, advancing through a more wooded region, reached its objective, in the Bois de la Folie, about one hour later. Stowell's connecting battalion reached the woods on the Second Division's left boundary, southwest of the leading battalion of the Sixth, and organized it for defense. A few troops of the 80th Division finally reached their objective, in line with the front held by the marines, late during the day. The enemy having retreated out of his sector during the night, the 80th Division advanced early on the 2nd and relieved Stowell of his theretofore difficult task.

## The Exploitation

A line of exploitation about two miles to the front of the third objective had been assigned. The front line battalions sent forward a number of patrols during the night. The brigade sector was organized into a series of defensive lines to guard against the possibility of a German counterattack, particularly against the western flank of the pronounced salient. Thanks to complete plans, thorough artillery support and their own dash, the marines had made an advance against organized resistance at least equal to that ever made during the war by an American division in a single day.

The enemy as usual attempted to bring forward reserves to stop the vigorous advance of the American forces as soon as a salient was developed by the Second Division. The German higher command ordered a counterattack by several regiments, to be delivered southeast of Buzancy. The American advance was so rapid that the attack could not be prepared before the Americans had gained still more ground. Instead of counterattacking, the Germans formed an outpost line just north of Buzancy and across the front of the Fourth Brigade with remnants of a number of divisions, to cover their withdrawal during the night. They withdrew that outpost line on the following day. The Germans decided on November 2 to begin withdrawing behind the Meuse as rapidly as possible, delaying the Allies only enough to avoid serious engagements and to permit the development of a new line.

The Second Division spent the night of November 1-2 making and unmaking plans for exploiting the success gained. The Third Brigade was ordered to pass through the Fourth and resume the advance the second day. The plans were changed, and the Brigade did not advance until the next night. In the meantime Williams' battalion advanced its front line by pushing forward patrols into the Bois de la Folie until stopped by the enemy's outpost line. The remainder of the Marine Brigade took a day of respite, after the mad dash of November 1. During the night of November 2-3 the enemy continued his retreat across the entire Army front. The Third Brigade, which was now in the lead, made an advance of approximately seven miles, during that night and on the following day and night. The Fourth Brigade followed the Third in close reserve. The neighboring divisions across the entire I and V Corps fronts were then advancing parallel to the Second Division.

The night advance of the Third Brigade was along a single road with no effort to cover the remainder of the division front. November 4 was spent in cleaning out the entire division sector and advancing the front a short distance to near the road running southeast from Beaumont. The Second Battalion, Fifth Marines, and later the entire regiment, went into the front line on the right of the Third Brigade, to connect up with the 89th Division and helped to clean out its sector. The Sixth Marines remained in reserve, south of the Bois de Belval. On the following day the front line was advanced about a mile farther. The Marine Brigade assisted the 89th Division in clearing the enemy from the Jaulny Forest—mostly in the 89th Division sector—and in gaining a position on the bank of the Meuse, preparatory to forcing a crossing.

## The Pursuit

During the night of November 5-6 the Germans withdrew their outpost line from the ridge north of Beaumont and continued their retirement across the Meuse. On the following day American reconnaisance groups pushed up the river along the entire corps front. The First Division relieved the 80th, on the left of the Second. During the night of 6-7 its commander, desiring his troops to be the first to enter Sedan, marched his division to the northwest across the front of the entire I Corps, leaving his proper sector practically unoccupied. The Fourth Brigade was at the time on the right of the Third with its front line along the Meuse. Flank marching across the front having apparently become the order of the day, the Marine Brigade then moved across the rear of the Third and assembled, preparatory to forcing a crossing of the river.

The troops had almost completely outrun all of their supply facilities. The congestion in the back areas, due to very few and poor roads and the necessity for bringing up bridge materials, delayed the crossing. Traffic jams had been so frequent, that it had been impossible even to evacuate the sick and wounded, who had to be cared for at improvised hospitals on the battlefield. The crossing continued to be postponed from day to day. The two marine regiments were gradually moved towards the front and concentrated in the wooded area between Yoncq and the Meuse on November 10, by which time detailed plans had been worked out and the necessary materials provided for the crossing.

By this time all the German armies to the northwest were in full retreat and making little effort to hold back their pursuing enemies. Along the Meuse, however, to the immediate front of the American I and V Corps, they were making considerable efforts to hold back the Allies, in order to protect a route of retreat for their armies. On the immediate front of the Second Division the remnants of several German divisions were attempting to hold the Meuse River line. They had an outpost line along the river held by a half dozen depleted battalions and a main line of resistance on the ridge farther to the northeast. They had practically no reserves but still had considerable artillery, well supplied with ammunition. Although badly demoralized they were determined if possible to hold off the Americans for a time.

### The Crossing of the Meuse

The crossing of the Meuse on the front of the V Corps was planned as a joint operation of the Second and 89th Divisions for the purpose of taking the important ridge lying from two to four miles back from the river. The Fourth Brigade was assigned to help carry out the infantry part of the operation. Artillery support, by the Second Field Artillery Brigade and some corps artillery, was arranged by the Corps. The main crossing of the marines was planned at a point about one mile northwest of Mouzon; an auxiliary crossing, jointly by a battalion from each of the two divisions, was arranged at a point about one mile southwest of Villemontry, near the bend of the river. The three battalions of the Sixth, the writer in command of the Second Battalion, and the Third Battalion of the Fifth were assigned to make the main crossing and seize the ridge north of Mouzon. The Second Battalion of the Fifth was assigned to take part in the auxiliary crossing with the First Battalion in close support, but remaining in the woods on the west bank of the river.

Although the operation had been in mind for several days, orders were not received by the battalion commanders at Yoncq until about 5 P.M., and all of the troops were still in the Bois de Fond de Limon. There was some confusion as to the time the operation should start, and the artillery preparation, which was planned to begin one hour before the troops reached the river, actually began before the troops left the woods where they were bivouacked, and most of the supporting fire, which was to cover their advance after they had crossed the river, was delivered before they reached the river. Two pontoon footbridges were ready to be thrown across the river for the main crossing, but the enemy soon located them and prevented their being put in place, by keeping them under machine-gun and artillery fire. The enemy's artillery also fired upon the roads leading to the front, but fortunately the four battalions of marines were disposed along a railroad leading towards the point of crossing and were never hit by the searching artillery fire. As dawn approached with the bridges still unconstructed, the battalion commanders mutually agreed that there was nothing to do but retire from the exposed position, back into the woods before daylight arrived. On their return they learned that the armistice had been signed, to become effective at 11 A.M. They considered themselves triply lucky—the enemy's artillery never found them, their engineers were prevented from constructing the bridges, and the war was over anyway.

The battalion of the 89th Division failed to arrive in time to take part in the secondary crossing southwest of Villemontry. The support battalion of marines went in its stead; Major Hamilton took command of the two battalions. The fortunes of these battalions, during what proved to be an entirely unnecessary operation, were quite the reverse of those of the remainder of the Marine Brigade. The enemy's artillery bombardment came down upon them, during their approach to the river, and inflicted many casualties. The engineers successfully installed the footbridges, but the enemy located them almost immediately, subjected them to both machine-gun and artillery fire, and made it impossible to use one of them. The First Battalion managed to cross the other bridge by 10:30 P.M., followed by the Second Battalion about one hour later. They drove the enemy from the immediate vicinity and remained in the woods, just east of where they had crossed, until morning.

By this time the battalion of the 89th Division had effected its crossing, and all three battalions took up the advance to the northeast. The Second Battalion, on the left, advanced along the east bank of the river to the national highway between Mouzon and Moulins. Its companies encountered very little resistance, but as they advanced their communications lengthened; some of them did not receive news of the armistice until 11:30 A.M. By that time the 18th Company was more than a mile beyond the river. The First Battalion advanced initially in support of the battalion of the 89th Division and later moved rapidly forward parallel to the Second Battalion. It was approaching Moulins with its leading company and did not receive news of the armistice until about 11:45 A.M.

## THE ARMISTICE

The news of the armistice was disseminated rather slowly to the front line units, both German and American. In some cases German units were informed of the armistice before the marines. Of the coming of that all-important historical event, a German front line battalion commander facing the Second Division reported: "At 11:15 hostilities cease. Not a shot is fired. Among our own men quiet, depressed mood, and quiet joy, while among the enemy there is loud manifestation of joy over the armistice." To the writer, as well as to the other officers of the first line battalions, who at the time were none too well informed of the general collapse of the German Army and knew nothing of the terms of the armistice, its conclusion was received with considerable skepticism as being too good to be true. Most of the men were so exhausted from recent experiences and from living outdoors in a cold damp climate, that they were incapable of responses. The realization that the war was over only slowly permeated their benumbed minds. After a time it was observed that marines began to build bonfires and form in groups, to talk and sing songs. On the following night they fired off most of the pyrotechnics as a manifestation of their joy. There was little of the tremendous outburst of enthusiasm among these men that occurred among the Allied civil populations throughout the world.

Along the entire Western Front the war had actually ceased several hours before. The armistice had been expected for several days by the higher commanders, and it was only the American forces, who prosecuted the war to its bitter last moments. As noted above some of the marines actually were engaged for some little time after the armistice went into effect. The two battalions of marines which forced the crossing on the night before suffered losses of 31 killed and 148 wounded. Since the beginning of the battle on November 1 the Marine Brigade had suffered the following casualties: 323 killed and 1,109 wounded.

## The March to the Rhine

The Germans were given a few days to turn over material, required by the terms of the armistice and to withdraw their troops away from the Allied armies, before the latter started the march into Germany to establish the armies of occupation and three bridgeheads beyond the Rhine. The Second Division, being a regular division, was assigned to the Army of Occupation and on November 17 started its long march into the heart of Germany. It was divided into two columns with the Fourth Brigade and its supporting artillery in the northern column. The first day's march was still in the more or less devastated war zone. On the following day the columns crossed the Belgian frontier and spent that night amidst the ruins of Belgian villages, which had been burned by the Germans in 1914. The next day practically completed the march across the narrow corner of Belgium. The outburst of gratitude of the liberated French and Belgian people, who had been under enemy domination for more than four years, was a considerable source of satisfaction to the exhausted veterans of the trying campaigns. The simple villagers made their coming a festive affair and received them with pathetic gratitude, shouting, *"Vive nos liberateurs!"*

The wreckage of war was soon passed, and the march led on through the beautiful rolling country across the Grand Duchy of Luxembourg. Day by day the columns advanced, keeping close behind the retiring German Army, but always having a deadline, which would prevent them from overtaking the Germans. The Luxembourgers everywhere greeted the Americans most cordially, and at times prepared for their reception before the German troops had left their towns. The German frontier was reached at Diekirch on November 23; in accordance with the terms of the armistice a halt was made until December 1.

The marines, like the rest of the men of the badly used-up divisions, were in worn and tattered uniforms and much of their equipment was in a run-down condition. During the week's halt on the frontier they were partially resupplied with clothing—army uniforms, such as had been used after casting aside their marine uniforms, which were worn out since arriving in France. Precaution against hostile action by the Germans was still maintained—outposts while at a halt and advanced guards on the march.

On the early morning of December 1, with the Marine Brigade still on the left, the Second Division, together with the French on its left and other American troops on its right, made its first long march into Germany. As the march continued during the first week, the wooded and hilly country became more and more rugged. Finally the divide was crossed, and one column started down the winding picturesque valley of the Ahr. During each halt the troops were scattered for billeting in the towns and farmhouses. The Germans were reserved but showed no hostility; many of the Americans felt more at home with them than they had with the French.

### The Watch on the Rhine

The scarcity of roads made it necessary for the entire Second Division to march in one column down the Ahr, the Marine Brigade leading. The front units reached the Rhine at Zinzig on December 9; the Marine Brigade marched up the river for a short distance and billeted in towns along the western bank until December 13, when they again resumed the advance to their sector of the Coblenz bridgehead. It had been arranged for the American Third Army to occupy with a corps the northern two-thirds of the semi-circular bridgehead area on the east bank of the Rhine with the French holding the remainder of it. The Marine Brigade held the front of the entire Division with the Third Brigade in second line. A complete defensive organization and occupation of the sector was planned but was never resorted to.

The experiences of the marines during their seven months stay with the Army of German Occupation were uneventful and monotonous. They were of course anxious to return home, and a spirit of unrest permeated the organizations. Every possible means was used to keep them occupied and interested. Extensive athletic activities, amateur theatrical productions, professional entertainers and speakers, and educational schemes were employed to keep up their spirit during the indefinite wait for final conclusion of peace and for the Division's turn to be withdrawn.

In June, 1919, serious friction in the peace conference initiated a further advance of the Allied armies into Germany. The marines together with some other units of the Second Division advanced a two days' march to the east, but upon final agreement of the German delegates soon afterwards withdrew to their former positions along the Rhine. The long-hoped-for return to the United States finally came in the middle of July, when several trains daily began taking the units of the Division to Brest. The Fourth Brigade arrived back in the United States early in August. It participated with the remainder of the Division in a parade in New York and was reviewed by President Woodrow Wilson in Washington. It then returned to Quantico, where its demobilization began almost immediately.

### American and French Decorations of Marine Corps Personnel for World War Service

| | |
|---|---|
| Medals of Honor (Navy) | 7 |
| Medals of Honor (Army) | 5 |
| Distinguished Service Medals (Navy) | 22 |
| Distinguished Service Medals (Army) | 12 |
| Navy Crosses | 393 |
| Distinguished Service Crosses (Army) | 351 |
| Croix de Guerre (French) | 1633 |
| Legion of Honor (French) | 22 |
| Medaille Militaire (French) | 23 |

### Battle Casualties of Fourth Brigade of Marines

| | | Killed in Action and Died of Wounds | Wounded and Gassed |
|---|---|---|---|
| Toulon Sector, Verdun | Officers | 0 | 11 |
| | Enl. Men | 51 | 412 |
| | Total | 51 | 423 |
| Aisne Defensive | Officers | 2 | 13 |
| | Enl. Men | 75 | 308 |
| | Total | 77 | 321 |
| Chateau-Thierry Sector | Officers | 25 | 87 |
| | Enl. Men | 931 | 2950 |
| | Total | 956 | 3037 |
| Aisne-Marne (Soissons) | Officers | 13 | 70 |
| | Enl. Men | 407 | 1482 |
| | Total | 420 | 1552 |

| | | | |
|---|---|---:|---:|
| *St. Mihiel Offensive* | Officers | 5 | 18 |
| (Including Marbache Sector) | Enl. Men | 129 | 567 |
| | Total .. | 134 | 585 |
| *Champagne Offensive* | Officers | 22 | 97 |
| (Oct. 1-10, 1918) | Enl. Men | 472 | 1770 |
| | Total .. | 494 | 1867 |
| *Meuse Argonne* | Officers | 10 | 48 |
| (Nov. 1-11, 1918) | Enl. Men | 313 | 1061 |
| | Total .. | 323 | 1109 |

## Chapter XVIII
## TWENTY YEARS AFTER

During the twenty years since the close of the World War (to November, 1938), the Marine Corps has again experienced many far-reaching changes. A decided letdown, which came just after the war, was followed by six or seven years of more or less routine existence, during which the organization was attempting to readjust itself to meet the conditions of the postwar period. It sent out no expeditions of importance and, during a part of those years, had only a small brigade to maintain in Haiti and was therefore able to maintain a substantial expeditionary force in the United States. This brief period was characterized by considerable playing to the spectacular, in an attempt to counteract the waning interest in the military forces which had swept the country. Early in 1927, however, the Corps was again swept into a period of intense activity, maintaining a large expeditionary force in Nicaragua and later an additional one in China. This period, which ended in the withdrawal of the Marine Brigade from Nicaragua early in 1933, was one of many valuable field experiences, but with little opportunity to advance the educational, training, and other facilities of the Corps, looking to the preparation of the organization for a major war. Following the withdrawal from Nicaragua and Haiti, the Corps entered upon a new phase of its existence; Latin American interventions, which had long been its principal preoccupation, were definitely relegated to the past. Its principal efforts since then have been directed towards raising the efficiency of its personnel by various methods, reorganizing and training itself as an auxiliary of the fleet, and in developing both its peace and wartime facilities.

### Disillusionment

The enthusiasm, characteristic of wartime, continued for a number of months after the close of the World War. Men returning from the war were for a time enthusiastically received. As time went on, however, a period of postwar disillusionment set in, which was dramatically presented on the stage and in the motion pictures by "What Price Glory." Captain Lawrence T. Stallings, U.S.M.C., was the co-author and largely responsible for the extremely disillusioning tone of the great drama, the influence of which swept the entire country. Stallings had joined the Third Battalion of the Fifth Marines as a second lieutenant near the beginning of the fighting at Belleau Wood; he commanded a platoon for a time in Bouresches and on June 25, while leading his men in a charge against a German machine-gun nest, received multiple machine-gun wounds which caused him to be hospitalized until his final retirement as a captain in the Marine Corps on July 2, 1920. His brief but harrowing experiences, succeeded by two years of hospitalization, followed further by a long period of convalescence, when he had great difficulty in re-establishing himself as a writer, and during which time he brooded a great deal over the futility of the war, amply prepared his sensitive nature for leadership in the reaction against war.

The period of reaction made it very difficult to re-establish the Marine Corps on its new and greatly enlarged peacetime basis. The glory of war having been largely debunked, the youth of the land was not interested in the military service. The Corps had lost the greater part of its prewar noncommissioned officers, on whom it had previously depended for much of its cohesion. Other advantages than that of the attraction of wearing a uniform and serving the flag had to be found in order to interest new men sufficiently to join the organization. Sports, educational advantages, and demonstrations to arouse public interest were hit upon as the necessary inducements.

In addition to the usual sports carried on for the recreation of its personnel, the Marine Corps organized football and baseball teams and went into competition with some of the leading colleges and universities. Under the dynamic leadership of Smedley D. Butler, the football enthusiasm rose to unexpected heights and reached its climax when several special train loads of marines accompanied the Marine Corps football team to play the University of Michigan at Ann Arbor, on November 10, 1923. Many of the marines pledged their pay for a considerable period in order to meet the expenses of the trip. The enthusiasm over its football team caused a considerable loss of the sense of proportion in the Marine Corps; it set about building at Quantico what was planned to be the nation's largest stadium. No appropriation, of course, was available for such a project, but it was enthusiastically embarked upon, using marines as labor, salvaged scrap iron from navy war activities, and sand and gravel procured locally by the marines. Only cement was to be purchased, and the entire gigantic structure was planned to be erected for only $5,000. Little thought was apparently given as to where the great number of people to fill such a huge arena would come from or how they could arrive and depart over the limited means of communication that the locality afforded. There were other ambitious construction projects entered upon in the same spirit and without funds. The futility of these exploits was well expressed by a Secretary of the Navy, who, upon looking at the incompleted stadium remarked that, "It was all damned foolishness to have ever started such a thing under such circumstances." The enthusiasm over maintaining athletic teams of national reputation outlived its initial usefulness; the Marine Corps football team was discontinued in 1930, and the baseball team ceased to exist the following year.

## The Marine Corps Institute

It was commonly felt by those in authority in the Marine Corps that the average young man of the country, who gave four of the best years of his life to the service of his country, usually did so at a sacrifice, and, if possible, the Government should give him something more than a record of honorable service to take back to his usual walk of life. Post schools for enlisted men were experimented with as a means of continuing the education of the men while they were in the Marine Corps, but this idea was superseded by an educational project designed to cover the entire Marine Corps. An arrangement was made with the International Correspondence Schools for the supply of necessary textbooks and lesson papers for practically all correspondence courses put out by that institution. The Marine Corps established what was called the "Marine Corps Institute" in November, 1920. It organized its own staff of instructors and, by using the material of the I.C.S., started its own correspondence school, following the same general system. A large proportion of marines enrolled for courses and within the brief period of three years nearly one-third of the Corps was studying different subjects under the Institute's guidance. The experiment has so far proved to be permanent, and many thousands of men who have served in the Corps have taken its courses for the purpose of advancing themselves in the Marine Corps and for bettering their chances for success after returning to civil life.

## Maneuvers

The Marine Corps was able to reorganize itself on a peacetime basis by the autumn of 1921 and began a series of land maneuvers with its expeditionary force stationed at Quantico, Virginia. The first of these maneuvers took place near the scenes of the Battle of the Wilderness. A reinforced brigade with a considerable amount of heavy equipment, including 155 millimeter guns pulled by 10-ton tractors, marched to that area from Quantico. As part of its effort to obtain favorable publicity, President Harding was induced to attend the maneuvers. During the following summer similar field exercises, but on a larger scale, were staged at Gettysburg with a small army of about 4,000 marines, armed with all manner of equipment left over from the World War. They even had a platoon of tanks. The Commandant of the Corps commented that the organization was "a miniature army small but highly trained and powerfully armed." President Harding again attended the maneuvers. A bid for publicity was made by the re-enactment of Pickett's famous charge in the Battle of Gettysburg. During the following year the marines from Quantico went into the Shenandoah Valley for maneuvers. Together with the corps of cadets from the Virginia Military Institute, they re-enacted the Civil War battle of New Market, in which battle the cadets of that institution had formed part of the Confederate forces. The summer maneuvers of 1924 were held in the vicinity of Sharpsburg, Maryland, with more than three thousand marines from Quantico and ended with the spectacular re-enactment of the Civil War battle of Antietam, carried out as a modern attack. This time the reinforced brigade returned through Washington where it was reviewed by President Coolidge.

In the meantime maneuvers with the fleet had been resumed by the expeditionary force of marines, normally stationed at Quantico. Early in 1924 the Fifth Marines went to Panama on maneuvers, and the East Coast Expeditionary Force from Quantico went through extensive maneuvers on the Island of Culebra, just off the eastern coast of Porto Rico. During the spring of 1925, 1,500 officers and marines from Quantico, representing a large constructive expeditionary force, participated in joint Army and Navy maneuvers on the Island of Oahu, Hawaii. The affair, as far as the marines were concerned, was highly theoretical and, judging from present day standards, rather impractical. The maneuvers served to draw the attention of the naval service to one of the basic missions of the Marines—supporting the fleet in overseas operations.

Maneuvers, with the President in attendance, were discontinued but the marines still continued to have their annual contacts with the Chief Executives at their favorite places of recreation. President Coolidge's "Summer White House" was located in an old mansion at Swampscott, Massachusetts, which the marines assisted in putting into a state of repair. They also furnished detachments for guarding the President during his several visits to that place. Coolidge's successor, Herbert Hoover, preferred a mountain retreat as his place of recreation. The marines developed a Summer White House, called Camp Rapidan, near Criglersville, Virginia, in the Blue Ridge Mountains. They not only guarded the President during his visits to his favorite retreat but helped to maintain and develop it. President Franklin D. Roosevelt has as one of his recreation places, Warm Springs, Georgia, where a foundation for victims of infantile paralysis is maintained under his sponsorship. Detachments of marines usually go to Warm Springs to guard President Roosevelt during his stay at that place.

## Guarding the Mails

Among the postwar reactions in the United States was a more or less pronounced crime wave, which manifested itself extensively in mail, bank, and other spectacular robberies. The Post Office Department found itself unable to cope with the increasing number of mail robberies; the Postmaster General called upon President Harding for protection. On November 7, 1921, Harding directed the Secretary of the Navy, "to detail as guards for the United States mails a sufficient number of officers and men of the United States Marine Corps to protect the mails from depredations by robbers and bandits." Approximately 53 officers and 2,200 marines were sent to the principal mail distributing centers of the country; they not only guarded the mails in those cities but protected many mail trains and formed virtually a nation-wide system of mail protection. They were given strict orders as to how they should carry out their duties. When necessary they were ordered to use their weapons, for "shooting or otherwise killing or disabling any person engaged in the theft or robbery, or the attempted theft or robbery of the mails entrusted to" their protection. They operated usually in small groups of only two or three men and maintained a remarkable record in carrying out their duties. Mail robberies ceased almost immediately after the protective system by marines had been completely established. By the following March conditions had so improved that it was no longer necessary for the marines to continue guarding the mails.

There was a recurrence of spectacular mail robberies during the

The Transport of the Marines—U.S.S. *Henderson*

GENERAL OFFICERS OF THE MARINE CORPS

autumn of 1926. At the request of the Postmaster General a force of about 2,500 marines went out on October 20 and again formed a nation-wide system of mail protection, organized in a manner almost identical with that of 1921. This time the country was divided into two zones: an eastern zone under Brigadier General Logan Feland, with headquarters in New York City; and a smaller western zone, under Brigadier General S. D. Butler, with headquarters at San Francisco. Again mail robberies ceased upon the marines taking over the protection of the mails. Neither on this occasion nor during the previous guarding of the mails did any marines have direct contact with mail robbers. The second outbreak of mail robberies prompted the Post Office Department to provide effective means of its own, for the guarding of the mails. While the marines were engaged in this second mission of enforcing the law, but after mail robberies had been definitely stopped, they were relieved to help provide the necessary troops for the expeditionary force to Nicaragua early in 1927.

## In China Since the World War

The activities of the Marines in the several countries of the Caribbean area during the postwar period are described in the preceding chapters, devoted especially to the interventions in that area. Most of the Corps's energy was absorbed in those extensive operations. This delayed for some time the development of the Marine Corps's educational and training system and prevented the Corps from building up an organized and trained expeditionary force, such as it now has in the Fleet Marine Force. Such a large proportion of the Marines were engaged in various foreign tasks, that at times men were returned for a second or third tour of foreign duty almost as soon as they had got back to the United States. But in addition to their operations in the several Latin American countries—their more usual theater of operations—the Marines have been called upon to keep a force of varying size in China ever since the World War.

The prestige of the white man in China suffered greatly during the World War. Civil wars, the domination of war lords, and the general chaotic state of economic and social affairs in that country entered upon a new phase with the beginning of the Chinese Nationalist movement in 1923. At first the movement was considerably under the influence of the Russian Bolsheviki, but, as it progressed, it became more conservative and represented a strong nationalistic, democratic tendency, attempting the unification of China and the freeing of the country from all outside domination. China's desire to get rid of the foreign control—gradually extended by European powers and Japan during the previous hundred years—manifested its attitude by outbreaks against foreign residents and their property. These outbreaks were similar to the Boxer movement of 1900, but were less violent. Resentment was especially strong against the British during the early stages of the Nationalist movement, but, as time passed, Great Britain succeeded in pacifying the Chinese to some extent, and their strongest resentment against foreigners gradually shifted to the Japanese.

During several outbreaks a number of the powers sent additional naval vessels as well as expeditionary forces to important centers of foreign property and population, for the protection of their nationals. During a contest between factions led by General Wu Pei-Fu and Marshal Chang Tso-lin for the control of northern China, the Americans in Peking were endangered. In order to provide additional protection for our Legation, the marines of the Asiatic Fleet were formed into a battalion and sent to Tientsin, where they arrived on May 5, 1922, and remained at the barracks of the 15th U. S. Infantry for a brief period, in readiness to rush to Peking. However, the crisis passed within a few days after the arrival of the marines, and they returned to their ships. The Nationalist forces threatened to seize the maritime customs house at Canton in November, 1923; the commander in chief of our Asiatic Fleet sent four destroyers and two gunboats, carrying a detachment of marines, to that place. The British and French sent landing forces ashore, to protect their interests, but our naval forces, by their mere presence, were able to accomplish their mission.

Conflict between the contending factions, for the control of northern China, was resumed during the autumn of 1924; conditions around Peking were again somewhat menacing to the foreign legations. Upon request of the American Minister, 225 additional marines were provided from the U.S.S. *Huron* and from the Philippines, to reinforce the Legation Guard. A detachment of fifty marines was again stationed at the U. S. Army barracks at Tientsin, as a potential reinforcement for the Legation Guard. A new government was set up at Peking, however, and conditions improved. The marine detachment at Tientsin was withdrawn and the Legation Guard at Peking was reduced during June of the following year.

Conditions throughout China continued very uncertain, and several vessels of the Asiatic Fleet, some of which carried small additional contingents of marines, moved from one threatened port to another, as the scene of possible trouble shifted. When the war lord controlling the general vicinity of Shanghai at the end of 1924 was faced with an invasion of his territory by an opposing faction, his troops mutinied; he fled to Shanghai for safety. The foreign settlements were endangered by the disorderly elements, and additional protection was provided. The marine detachment of the U.S.S. *Sacramento* was landed on January 15 and, together with other naval forces, helped to protect the foreign quarter until the danger had passed early in February. The marines then returned to their ships. However, in view of impending trouble, which soon took place, an additional force of 140 marines was sent there from the Philippines.

Civil war again broke out around Shanghai during the summer of 1925; the International Settlement was again protected by marine detachments from ships of the Asiatic Fleet and by a small expeditionary force—2 officers and 125 marines—from the Philippines and Guam. The immediate need for such protection passed by the end of August; the marines ashore in Shanghai were placed on board various naval vessels and remained in Chinese waters, awaiting the development of the situation. Throughout the remainder of 1925 and the following year, disorders occurred at various Chinese ports as well as in the interior. The Asiatic Fleet kept a greater portion of its vessels, several of which had extra complements of marines, in readiness to protect our nationals and their property. The vessels together with small expeditionary forces of marines shifted to different parts of the China coast but made no landing operations during this period.

The Nationalist forces gradually extended their control over more of the country. They discovered in 1927 that the Soviet representatives, who had been "assisting" in organizing the government as well as the army, were plotting its overthrow. This led to a split in the Kuomintang (Nationalist Party), and the Bolshevik sympathizers, driven from it, became a radical faction and stood in the way of national unity. The more conservative Nationalists, nevertheless, were able gradually to strengthen their control to include practically all of the country. Their insistence on recovering rights from foreigners resulted in strong anti-foreign feelings, which at times led to massacres of foreigners. An outbreak occurred at Hankow in March, 1927, when several foreign consulates were violated by Nationalist soldiers. Some of the powers demanded the punishment of the offending commanders, reparations, and apologies.

The situation at Shanghai became very critical for the foreign settlements during February, 1927. A Nationalist army was approaching the city, and a sympathetic political strike broke out in

Shanghai. The local Nationalist commander retaliated against the strikers by beheading a number of them. The various interested foreign powers inaugurated extensive schemes for the defense of their settlements.

The danger to Americans had been anticipated by the commander in chief of the Asiatic Fleet, who mobilized all available marines in the Far East, including a small battalion from Guam, caused them to be transferred to Shanghai, and on February 9 placed a force of 15 officers and 326 marines ashore to assist in protecting the International Settlement. Ill-feeling against foreigners ran high; the danger appeared so threatening that more extensive measures for protection were in order. A battalion of marines was obviously inadequate for the American portion of an allied force which, it was contemplated, would be increased to a strength of approximately forty thousand. The Fourth Marines, consisting of 66 officers and 1,162 enlisted men under Colonel Charles S. Hill, was sent from San Diego and arrived at Shanghai on February 24. The regiment landed about ten days later and, together with the expeditionary battalion already ashore, took over an area of the International Settlement for the "protection of American and foreign life and property." Hill's efforts were co-ordinated with the other foreign forces by the senior commander, Major General John Duncan of the British Army. The marines, in close support of the British troops, concerned themselves initially with preventing mobs and other undesirable elements from entering the International Settlement and with maintaining order. They were not at this time assigned to the defense of the boundary line.

The Nationalists took possession of Shanghai on March 21 with little actual fighting, as the defending leader went over to their side. There was some disorder in the Chinese quarter of the city, but the foreign troops had by this time developed the defenses of the foreign settlement, and it was little affected. The situation at Shanghai soon settled down, but almost immediately a crisis occurred at Nanking.

The Nationalist forces captured Nanking on March 23. On the following day, in the midst of considerable disorder and looting, the Nationalist soldiers and also a mob made some attacks upon foreigners. Some Americans as well as other foreigners were killed. A group of foreign refugees sought shelter on Socony Hill, near the river, and were there protected by a barrage fired by American and British naval vessels and later evacuated to safety. Those attacks on foreigners by Chinese soldiers and the hazardous position of the foreign settlements in several other Chinese cities prompted additional protective measures to be taken for Americans residing in China.

The Navy Department dispatched three additional cruisers from Hawaii to Chinese waters and ordered the sending of additional marine units to China. The Sixth Marines was hurriedly reorganized at Philadelphia, with personnel drawn from various Marine Corps posts in the eastern part of the United States, and rushed by rail to San Diego for transfer to China. Brigadier General Smedley D. Butler was designated to command all the marines in China, and Headquarters ordered the marines for duty in that country organized into a reinforced brigade. Butler proceeded to organize his headquarters and several units of brigade special troops, including artillery, tanks, engineers, and service troops, at San Diego. With his headquarters, one battery of artillery, and the Sixth Marines, Butler sailed on the *Henderson* April 7 and arrived at Shanghai on May 2. The remainder of the troops to form the brigade, including two extra battalions—one for each of the regiments—were mobilized at San Diego and sailed on the S.S. *President Grant* April 17. The *Henderson* was kept at Shanghai during the month following its arrival, with most of the marines who came out on it remaining on board. The marines on the *President Grant* were taken to Olongapo, Philippine Islands, and from there sent on to Shanghai on the *Chaumont*. After the arrival of all of Butler's troops at Shanghai, the then designated Third Brigade of Marines had a total strength of 238 officers, 18 warrant officers, and 4,170 enlisted men.

The Nationalist forces continued to extend their control northward, and the commander in chief of the Asiatic Fleet as well as the representatives of the other powers, prepared to send forces to protect their nationals in northern China. An aggregate force of 16,000 allied troops was ordered to the Tientsin-Peking area. Butler with his brigade, less the Fourth Marines, moved up to Tientsin early in June and established themselves in camp. Butler announced that their object was "solely for the defense of life and property." The 15th Infantry and other U. S. Army units, aggregating approximately 1,800, were stationed at Tientsin or along the Peking-Tientsin railway. The Legation Guard at Peking then had a total of 17 officers and 499 marines, making our armed forces in the general vicinity about 5,200. The foreign powers had the right, under the Boxer protocol of 1901, to keep the railroad to Peking open; they appeared well prepared to do so.

In spite of the considerable concentration of troops which had been hurried off to China, the "war" proved to be a very uneventful affair when compared to the experiences of the marines in China during 1900. Marines at all of the principal stations made extensive plans for all manner of emergencies—most of which never occurred. Initially the marines at Shanghai were given only missions of the internal security of the International Settlement. Later, however, they were given a regular sector to defend against invasion by mobs or organized armed forces. The mission of the Third Brigade was announced as being primarily for the protection of American lives and property. The general principle adhered to was that conflict with the Chinese, when not absolutely necessary to carry out the primary mission, was to be carefully avoided. Co-ordination with other foreign forces was sanctioned only for protecting the lives of Americans and other foreigners. The positions held by the marines provided a refuge for Americans residing in their general vicinity. The Brigade was under the command of the commander in chief of the Asiatic Fleet and was not subject to the orders of any foreign officer. It carefully avoided being placed in the position of a "cat's paw" to further the interests of any of the associated powers. Its adherence to such a policy had much to do with furthering the traditional friendly feeling of the Chinese towards the United States.

After a few weeks the marines settled down to more or less of a garrison routine and concerned themselves largely with drills, parades, and carrying on such field training as the limited training areas available would permit. They, together with some of the other foreign military units, made extensive use of athletics to maintain their morale. Butler made every effort to promote the good will of the Chinese, and on a number of occasions rendered assistance in various ways to the Chinese Government. In order to impress Chinese and other officials of the importance of the American forces and their military efficiency, Butler put forth every effort to make all marine units "snappy" in appearance and precise in all their drills. They put on numerous military parades, sometimes for moral effect, but often as a compliment to Chinese and other officials, for the purpose of fostering good will.

The general situation in China continued throughout 1927 and early 1928 about the same, with the Nationalists in control of the southern part of the country and certain war lords, with few affiliations, in control of the remaining parts of the country. Anti-foreign demonstrations subsided; some of the foreign powers, particularly the British, reduced their forces in China during the fall of 1927. The Third Brigade was maintained at approximately its original strength throughout 1928. On March 1 of that year duty with the organization was made "permanent," indicating little anticipation of an early withdrawal. During the spring and summer of 1928 the Nationalist forces, again under the leadership of Chiang Kai-shek, advanced farther north and occupied Peking. They discontinued that city as the national capital and renamed it Peiping. Soon afterwards they occupied Tientsin and had some control over practically all of China. Chiang Kai-shek was chosen president of the country on October 10. General political conditions had greatly improved during the year; plans were again formulated for a partial withdrawal of the marines from the country. All units of the Third Brigade in Tientsin were withdrawn in January, 1929; those not used for replacements in China, the Philippines, Guam, or the Asiatic Fleet were returned to the United States. The Legation Guard at Peiping was increased to five hundred enlisted men. The Fourth Marines, which remained in Shanghai, was increased to 1,150.

The apparent unification of China suffered a serious set-back during 1929 by a rift in the Nationalist Party. Soviet influence had reached much farther than was desired by many party leaders. The Nationalist Government broke off its connections with its Russian advisers and attempted to purge itself of "Red" influence. The party broke into two factions who fought each other at various times until the war with Japan in 1937 induced the communists to join with the Nanking Government. The Nationalist Government continued for a time to strengthen its hold over the entire country and, except for the communist-bandit activities, there was better prospect for unity and peace by the beginning of 1931 than at any time during the previous ten years. Banditry made it necessary, however, for the United States to maintain a number of small naval vessels in Chinese waters—some around the seaport towns and others on the larger rivers. Several of these vessels had clashes with bandit or communist groups. The Fourth Marines, with an average strength of about 1,200 men, remained at Shanghai.

Japan's sponsoring the movement for the separation of Manchuria from China in September, 1931, in a manner which suggested eventual Japanese domination, aroused strong anti-Japanese feeling throughout China. Boycotts against Japanese goods and Japanese-owned cotton mills broke out. In January, 1932, mobs clashed with Japanese; Japan made a formal demand on China for the cessation of the boycotts and other anti-Japanese activities. The Japanese garrison in the International Settlement at Shanghai attacked the Chinese district at Chapei on January 28. The Chinese strongly resisted, and the Japanese bombed and set fire to the densely populated area. Both Great Britain and the United States protested the act; they, together with several other foreign governments, rushed additional troops to Shanghai. The Fourth Marines was reinforced by a detachment of 8 officers and 326 marines and by the marine detachment of the U.S.S. *Houston*. The 31st Infantry from the Philippines arrived at Shanghai on February 5, 1932. Upon the outbreak of hostilities the Fourth Marines had occupied defensive positions to prevent the belligerents from entering the International Settlement. The 31st Infantry, soon after it arrived, took over part of the American sector.

The Chinese gradually built up a substantial force around Shanghai, including among other troops the Nineteenth Route Army, while the Japanese continued to bring in reinforcements until nearly fifty thousand faced the Chinese positions. During the period from the initial outbreak until the Chinese troops evacuated the area, the marines in Shanghai were kept constantly on the alert. A number of stray shells as well as some misdirected bombs fell in their sector. Hostilities were more or less continuous for more than a month and on several occasions fighting occurred within a few hundred yards of the American positions. A number of marines had narrow escapes, but they suffered no casualties. From their various vantage points they watched the fighting between the two armies and came to have great admiration for the splendid defense that the hastily improvised Chinese Army made against the well equipped and trained Japanese forces. When the Chinese finally retired on March 3, they did so in perfect order and without being observed by the Japanese. Their retirement put an end to hostilities. Order was gradually restored, and the defense of the marines' sector gradually became less trying and was maintained with fewer and fewer men. The state of emergency was declared ended on June 13, 1932; the holding of the defense sector was discontinued. The 31st Infantry returned to its regular station in the Philippines. The Fourth Marines again resumed its peaceful routine of carrying on training and maintaining itself in readiness for any emergency.

The Fourth Marines during the entire period of its occupation of Shanghai had consisted of only two battalions, regimental headquarters, and service troops. After the withdrawal of the 31st Infantry the commander in chief of the Asiatic Fleet recommended that the strength of the marine regiment in Shanghai be increased sufficiently for it to properly hold the American sector and obviate the future necessity of having to call upon the Army for additional troops. Sufficient personnel was sent from the United States to form an additional battalion. The regiment then had an aggregate strength of 64 officers and 1,745 enlisted men. It remained at approximately that strength until December, 1934, when one of the battalions was disbanded, and the strength of the regiment was reduced to 58 officers and 1,005 enlisted men.

During the period between the withdrawal of the Japanese forces from Shanghai and the beginning of their invasion in 1937, internal conditions in China continued to show many cross currents. Civil wars between the Nationalist Government, the communists, and certain war lords recurred throughout the period with the Nationalists becoming stronger, particularly in the west of China. Despite the more or less continued pressure by Japan, internal strife prevented the country from presenting a united front against the common enemy. However, material progress was made in many parts of the country, despite the unsettled conditions. The Asiatic Fleet and the Fourth Marines at Shanghai continued to have frequent periods of concern over the safety of Americans and their property. In January, 1934, the Nationalist forces advanced against a revolutionary force at Foochow. The American consul at that place, fearing for the safety of our nationals, called upon the commanding officer of the U.S.S. *Tulsa*, which was lying in a near-by anchorage, to provide protection until the danger had passed. While the rebel forces were retiring from the city, the *Tulsa*'s marine detachment went ashore and guarded the consulate, until the Nationalists took possession and restored order. During the following year small detachments of marines were used in conjunction with the vessels of the Yangtze Patrol for the protection of commerce on the Yangtze River. Some twenty-six small detachments in all, sent out for periods of about one month each, performed various protective missions on vessels plying that river—usually during their trips into the interior.

With a total frontage of about 6,000 yards, the defensive sector assigned to the Fourth Marines at Shanghai faced generally the boundary of the International Settlement along Soochow Creek. The strength of the regiment remained on an average of about eleven hundred until it was augmented during the later emergency. The regiment continued to concern itself largely with promoting good will with the Chinese and the various foreign powers represented in Shanghai, and in maintaining itself at the highest possible state of training and readiness for future emergencies.

After Japan succeeded in cutting off Manchuria from China in 1931-32, Japan kept up an almost continuous pressure in northern China with the object of bringing more and more of that area under her control. The province of Jehol was separated in 1933 and, two years later, by having friendly officials installed in some of the other northern provinces, Japan still further extended her control. Chahar Province was made a demilitarized zone in June, 1936, and, in the meantime, four other important northern provinces were set off for future domination by Japan. When the government of China was reorganized in December, 1935, Chiang Kai-shek was made a virtual dictator. For some time he made every effort to build up the defenses of the country, and, under the tutelage of German officers, he built up a sizable army, which gave a splendid account of itself during the undeclared war that began in 1937.

During the early summer of that year the Japanese began to press more vigorously their efforts to gain control of northern China. This resulted in friction with Chinese forces, and on July 12 fighting broke out in Peiping and soon afterwards in Tientsin. The Chinese sent no reinforcements from their main army in the South. The Japanese, who were continually being reinforced, encountered little resistance in the northern part of the country. Japan demanded a large autonomous area in northern China. Chiang Kai-shek's government determined to resist to the utmost any further aggression on the part of Japan. With a comparatively small force the Japanese took possession of the Tientsin-Peiping Railway. They set up military rule in that part of China and began to extend their conquests to the west and south. Our embassy guard of about five hundred marines and the several other contingents of foreign troops found themselves in the midst of the fighting around Peiping but successfully avoided being drawn into it.

Trouble started in Shanghai on August 9, when a few Japanese were killed. Japan concentrated some thirty-two warships in the vicinity and started offensive operations on August 12 by invading the Chinese city. The fighting increased in severity; the Japanese attack was supported by heavy bombing operations, which played havoc with important parts of Shanghai and killed many hundreds of noncombatants. At first the Japanese used only naval landing forces but later rushed their army into the area to relieve the pressure by the Chinese, who had rapidly augmented their army in an effort to drive out the Japanese. After Japan had landed about forty thousand troops to the north of Shanghai, the Chinese retreated on August 28 to a stronger defensive position, which they held for several weeks before being driven farther back.

Soon after the outbreak in Shanghai, the commander in chief of the Asiatic Fleet requested that a thousand extra marines be sent to Shanghai to augment our forces there to a sufficient strength for the proper defense of their sector. While waiting for this additional force, which could be supplied only from the United States, landing forces including marine detachments went ashore from vessels of the Asiatic Fleet to assist the Fourth Marines. Two additional companies of marines were formed at Cavite and proceeded to Shanghai. With the approval of the Navy Department, the Major General Commandant of the Marine Corps decided to increase the strength of the marines in Shanghai to a reinforced brigade. Brigadier General J. C. Beaumont was selected as brigade commander. Brigade headquarters troops, the Sixth Marines, and a battery of antiaircraft artillery were made ready in a very short time at San Diego, but their transfer to China was delayed for several days until the U.S.S. *Chaumont* could be made available. Brigade Headquarters and the Sixth sailed on the *Chaumont* on August 28, and the U.S.S. *Marblehead*, escorting that transport, carried the battery of antiaircraft artillery. These additional troops arrived in Shanghai on September 19, 1937. The reorganized Second Brigade of Marines then had an aggregate strength of 2,536. Together with the other foreign forces, which have been substantially augmented, it was able to defend the International Settlement and maintain its neutrality.

The Second Brigade in Shanghai carried on its duties during the fighting of the Chinese and Japanese around that city pretty much the same as during the previous taking of Shanghai by the Japanese. The situation for the marines was at times somewhat strained; there was occasionally some danger from bombs, shells, and small arms bullets. By February, 1938, the war zone had moved considerably to the west of the city, and it was no longer considered necessary to maintain an entire American brigade in Shanghai. The headquarters of the brigade and the Sixth Marines left Shanghai on February 18, 1938, proceeded via Manila and Guam to Honolulu, and, after participating in fleet maneuvers, returned to their regular station at San Diego some time afterwards.

The marine detachment at Peiping continued to be maintained at about its last-mentioned strength. At about the time it was decided to withdraw part of the marines from Shanghai, our government also decided to withdraw the part of the 15th Infantry stationed at Tientsin and turn that foreign post over to marines, taken from Peiping. A detachment of approximately 200 men under Lieut. Colonel W. C. James was organized at Peiping, proceeded to Tientsin on February 28, 1938, and established a Marine Corps post at the barracks which had been maintained for a number of years by the U. S. Army. The last of the Army troops left the post on March 2. With the Japanese in almost complete control in the Peiping-Tientsin area nothing unusual happened to the marines in northern China during the following months.

## Personnel Problems

An act of Congress, July 11, 1919, provided for an authorized peace strength of the Marine Corps of 1,093 officers and 27,400 enlisted men. Appropriation was made for approximately the full number of officers, but the allowed enlisted strength has never even been approximated. The problem of selecting suitable men for the permanent officers of the Corps and arranging them in grades, in accordance with the above-mentioned act, proved very difficult and was never satisfactorily solved. A great many temporary officers were anxious to obtain permanent commissions. They varied in age and experience from young men, who had barely reached their majority at the time they entered the Marine Corps during the war, to older men who had served thirty or more years in the ranks of the organization. The permanent officers remaining after the war were only sufficient to fill the upper part of the captains' grade and the higher ranks. The positions to be filled in the remainder of the captains' grade and in the two lieutenants' grades greatly exceeded these. The problem of arranging a large group, having, with few exceptions, practically the same military experience, was impossible to solve from a long period point of view. Nearly all of the group naturally grew older together and created a serious "hump," preventing a normal flow of promotions, which haunted the Marine Corps for many years. The commissions were distributed, however, though with great dissatisfaction to the men placed far down on the list. The problem of overcoming the all but impossible hump was only solved by the drastic elimination of officers from the active list of the Corps which began in 1935.

The desire of Congress to restrict the appropriations for military purposes during the postwar period made it impossible for the Marine Corps ever to approach its authorized enlisted strength. Its strength has more often been at least ten thousand less than full strength. Only the dominating personality and persistence of Lejeune, during the years that he was Commandant of the Corps, kept the organization as large as it was. At times since the war the strength of the Corps has been so low, when a greater portion of its personnel were on foreign duty, that it was very difficult to carry on all of the duties which were expected of it. When the marines withdrew first from Santo Domingo in 1924 and later from China, Nicaragua, and Haiti, instead of relieving the shortage of personnel and leaving a reserve for training purposes, the Corps was usually promptly reduced by the curtailment of appropriations for enlisted men. The economy act of 1933 reduced the enlisted personnel to slightly over 15,000, but during the last few years, when military preparedness has been embarked upon by almost the entire world, appropriations for both officers and enlisted men have been gradually increased, and the organization is once more (December, 1938) undergoing an expansion.

Throughout the history of the Marine Corps its officers had been promoted through the different grades almost exclusively by seniority. At times, some individuals who were not really qualified for the positions reached relatively high rank. Some manner of selection, particularly to the higher grades, had been advocated for a number of years. The Navy resorted at first to a system of eliminating officers who were not believed to be up to the desired standard, and in 1916 it adopted a system of selection prior to promotion to the higher grades. During the time he was Commandant, Lejeune tried repeatedly to have a selective system similar to that used in the Navy made applicable to the Marine Corps. All efforts to effect the necessary legislation, with the exception of selection to general officers and the retirement of unselected colonels at the age of fifty-six, failed until 1934, when an act of Congress was passed that not only established promotion by selection but also provided for a proportionate increase in the higher grades to facilitate the flow of promotions—particularly in the lower grades.

The effects of the new order of things have been far-reaching: a number of officers have been pushed into retirement. The system has been modified by practically every Congress since 1934; selection and forced retirements now apply to all grades except second lieutenant, and the proportionate number in the higher grades has been further increased to meet the growing complexity of the duties of the Corps and because of a prospective general increase in the Corps over a period of years. A number of officers have been rapidly promoted—often more than offsetting their slow promotions during the leaner years—but the increasing number of officers in the higher grades has not at the same time permitted their assignment to duties really commensurate with their new ranks; in many cases they find themselves performing the same duties to which they were assigned before being promoted.

## COMMANDANTS

During these twenty years the Marine Corps has had six major general commandants, who served for various periods from slightly more than one year to about nine years and had varied influence on the affairs of the Corps during the postwar years.

George Barnett, the first commandant to serve under a four-year appointment, completed his regular detail during the World War, and he, together with several chiefs of bureaus of the Navy Department, were again detailed in order to prevent a disruption of the Department in the midst of the war; but, according to Secretary of the Navy Daniels, each and all of those officers were expected to resign their bureau positions at the expiration of the war. During early 1920 the Secretary reminded Barnett of the circumstances of his reappointment, but Barnett, who was apparently under the impression that his reappointment for four additional years as Commandant of the Marine Corps was in no way subject to qualification, maintained that he was entitled, by virtue of the appointment, to continue in office for the entire period. The Secretary disagreed, however, and relieved him from duty as Commandant on July 1, 1920, and appointed John A. Lejeune as his successor.

Major General Lejeune, a man of exceptionally strong character who always commands the respect of all who come in contact with him, had acquired one of the best reputations for integrity and ability of any officer who had ever served in the Marine Corps. He served as commandant during the remainder of the Wilson administration. He was given a reappointment at the beginning of the Harding administration and again reappointed at the beginning of the Coolidge administration. As the expiration of his last term approached in 1929, he still had more than two years to serve before reaching the statutory age for retirement (64 years) and was given to understand that he could retain the office until his retirement, but declined the reappointment, retired from the Marine Corps, and accepted the office of Superintendent of the Virginia Military Institute from which position he also retired in 1937.

For a number of years after the World War, under the leadership of Lejeune, whose opinions always carried a great deal of weight with Congress because of the extreme friendliness of Congressman Thomas Butler—father of Major General Smedley D. Butler and for many years prior to his death in May, 1928, the senior member of the House Naval Affairs Committee—and because of the enhanced reputation of the Corps for services rendered during the World War and at other times, the Marine Corps was more liberally appropriated for than some other branches of the service. It was during Lejeune's tenure as commandant that the regular Marine Corps re-established itself on a permanent peacetime basis following the World War. Lejeune stood for a number of constructive policies such as the development of a thorough educational system for officers and for enlisted men serving in key positions and the continuance of training in the Marine Corps, which would keep it prepared for experiences similar to that which it had in the World War, as well as for any national emergency that might arrive.

His influence for the general betterment of his organization undoubtedly marks him as one of the more outstanding commandants of the Marine Corps. It must be conceded, however, that he was entirely human and therefore made mistakes. It has been noted that while he was commandant, several selections of officers to important positions were made that did not work out to the best advantage, and it was necessary to relieve them with more suitable officers before the desired results were accomplished.

Upon Lejeune's retirement from the Marine Corps, he recommended Wendell C. Neville to succeed him as commandant; Neville was appointed to the position March 5, 1929. Throughout his career he was one of the more colorful characters of the Corps and one of its most decorated officers. He had won a substantial reputation, particularly during the World War, first as Colonel of the Fifth Marines and later as Commanding General of the Fourth Brigade. During his brief tenure of office, ending with his untimely death on July 8, 1930, he could only carry on the multitude of tasks in which the Marine Corps was involved at the time.

The problem of selecting a successor for Neville proved somewhat embarrassing. Smedley D. Butler was the ranking general officer of the Corps and, of course, strongly felt that his brilliant record in the organization entitled him to the honor. The office remained vacant for nearly one month while a successor was being considered, and intense feeling arose over the affair. Brigadier General Ben H. Fuller had been assistant commandant under Neville and had been running the job during Neville's long illness and after his death. Fuller was, by length of commissioned service, the senior officer of the Marine Corps, and on August 6, 1930, he was restored to his old relative position by being made its commandant. Butler, obviously greatly disappointed, remained on active duty slightly more than one year and then went into retirement. He made known his opinions of the entire affair in an article published in *Liberty*, entitled "To Hell with the Admirals." Fuller, affectionately called "Uncle Ben" by many of his contemporaries, served as commandant until he retired for age March 1, 1934. The course of events of the organization was pretty well laid out by circumstances; Fuller largely concerned himself with carrying on the policy of his predecessors and with attempting to prevent drastic reduction of the organization upon the coming of the great depression in 1929.

Fuller was succeeded in office by John H. Russell, who, it will be recalled, served for many years in Haiti first with troops in various capacities and for more than eight years as American High Commissioner. Russell had only slightly more than two years to serve before being retired for age on December 1, 1936. During his brief tenure of office the Marine Corps saw the end of Spanish-American interventions and with it apparently the beginning of a new era in its history in which expeditionary activities would probably be much less than during the eventful years since the turn of the century. Under Russell's leadership a system of drastic selection for promotion of officers was established, and the Fleet Marine Force came forward as one of the principal functions of the Marine Corps.

The selection of a successor to Russell closely paralleled the drastic action taken by Gideon Welles in 1864. The President reached downward and picked a relatively junior and younger general officer to fill the position of Commandant of the Corps. Brigadier General Thomas Holcomb, previously mentioned in connection with experiences of the Marine Corps on the Western Front during the World War, was selected for the position. Holcomb, a direct descendant of Commodore Joshua Barney, entered upon the duties of his new responsibility with the same vigorous thoroughgoing spirit demonstrated by his distinguished ancestor. This time the other general officers of the Corps who had ambition to be promoted to the highest position in the organization accepted the situation. No dramatic retirements occurred.

Throughout the history of the Marine Corps its commandants have been selected by the President, who, on numerous occasions, made the selection upon recommendation from the Secretary of the Navy. The position is largely administrative and somewhat political. As the titular head of the Marine Corps it is largely the responsibility of the commandant to obtain the necessary support of the organization by Congress. Whether or not an officer made an outstanding record as commandant often depended upon the opportunities which arose during his tenure of office. With few exceptions, the officers appointed as commandants have been able to rise to the occasion in a commendable manner, and under their leadership the Corps has rendered valuable services to the nation. So long as they followed the policy of using the Marine Corps in such a way that it could properly serve the nation, they have been generally successful.

## Towards a Higher Intellectual Plane

The rapid drift to a more and more complicated existence during recent years has found its counterpart in the activities of the Marine Corps. Throughout the entire history of the Corps, marines were concerned almost exclusively with the use of the rifle and pistol and, occasionally at sea, in the manning of a few naval guns. Proficiency with the trusty musket and, in more recent years, the rifle, was about all the technical ability required of a marine. The profession of arms, as far as any military organization was concerned, was a comparatively simple and practical one, which could be readily learned by a few years of experience. The officers boasted of being practical soldiers, and any tendency towards theorizing or making their profession a scholarly affair was looked upon as entirely unnecessary. With the tremendous intellectual advancement in the country during the last few decades, in which the proportion of people receiving higher education has greatly increased and the professions have all become scholarly, there has been a parallel increase in the mental equipment of the personnel of the Marine Corps. Prior to the World War, and even in the reorganization of the Corps following the war, it was not considered necessary for an officer to have a college or university education; it was the exception rather than the rule that officers were men of such training. A great many officers did not even have the equivalent of a high school education and many, as in other walks of life, were largely self-educated. A corresponding lack of education prevailed in the ranks as well.

The Marine Corps today has a high percentage of men who are high school graduates and a sprinkling of men of college education in its ranks. Most of the officers, commissioned during the last few years, are graduates with high standing from our leading colleges and universities maintaining cadet corps or from the U. S. Naval Academy. In addition to the greater advancement prior to entry into the Corps, both officers and enlisted men are given further schooling in order to fit them for the more and more complicated duties that have developed during the last few years. Each officer attends the Basic School, immediately upon his entrance into the Corps; a few years later he attends the Company Officers School, or its equivalent, one of the Army schools of the different branches; and before or shortly after being made a field officer is given a year's course in the advanced Marine Corps schools or in one of the advanced schools for Army or Navy officers. In addition to this general training for the average officer, a number of them attend special schools in communications, gas warfare, the handling of motor transport, and aeronautical engineering. Schools are also maintained for the specialized training of enlisted men, and a considerable number of marines attend courses at specialized schools operated by the Army and the Navy.

The growing complexity of modern warfare has necessitated that the Marine Corps become more and more a highly complicated military organization with the multiplicity of its duties promising to become even more intricate in the near future.

But, with the better educated Corps of both officers and enlisted men who have been pressed into the same mold by the standardizing processes of our educational system, colorful characters have practically ceased to exist in the organization. As in any other military organization the favorite topic of conversation in barracks, in the mess hall, and with groups of officers, wherever assembled, had, from the very beginning, been the actions and remarks of the Corps's highly colorful and sometimes more or less eccentric characters. The remarks of such persons as "Fritz" Wise, "Hiking Hiram" Bearss, "Jim" Boots, "Pop" Hardee, and many other colorful characters, which have so often been repeated, will soon pass from the memory of the Marine Corps.

In the older Marine Corps with its relatively simple organization and administration, practically no staff organization was considered necessary. Because of the experiences during the World War and the growing complexity of modern military organizations and warfare, it has been found necessary to assign more and more personnel to staff duties. The Headquarters of the Corps, for example, had, practically throughout the entire history of the organization, been administered by the commandant, assisted by a quartermaster, an adjutant and inspector, a paymaster, one or two aides, a few other officers, and some marines and civilians acting in a clerical capacity. Since the outbreak of the World War the organization of Headquarters has grown far more complex, and the personnel required to operate it is now several times as many as before the war. A most notable change has been the development of the Operations and Training Section, which now performs practically all of the functions of, and has an organization similar to, a general staff. The problem of supply in the Corps has grown far more complex and even within the Quartermaster Department a high degree of specialization has become necessary. The larger units of the Corps, which were formerly administered by the commanding officer and his adjutant, are now provided with completely organized staffs.

## Improved Conditions for Marines

The standing of the Marines in the naval service and in the country in general has greatly improved since the World War. Their splendid fighting record on the Western Front served greatly to raise the general estimate of their real worth, not only within the naval service but in the minds of the people. The lot of a marine is filled with far fewer hardships except, of course, while on field duty. More of the ordinary comforts of life have been provided for him both on board ship and in barracks. The means for maintaining discipline are far less severe now than they were even two decades ago—prison sentences, for example, are less frequently resorted to. The routine duties which the average marine is called upon to do are far less trying than in former years. Facilities for his recreation and amusement in barracks, on board ship, and in near-by cities have been greatly extended. In the prewar years a marine was more or less a social outcast when away from his ship or barracks; he was usually welcome only in the ordinary saloon or in the house of ill-fame. Payday in the older Marine Corps was nearly always a time for overindulgence in drink, and all too frequently the average marine returned from liberty more or less under the influence of liquor. Such conditions of course no longer exist, because of the higher type of men now enlisted in the Corps, which is in turn caused by fewer opportunities for young men, the increased facilities within the service for amusement and recreation, the general extension of our system of education, and other reasons. The average marine is now everywhere well received. Payday no longer presents a problem of discipline, nor is considered a time for general "hell-raising."

The number of detachments of marines serving on board vessels of the Navy has been gradually increased since the World War, and at this writing (December, 1938) there were fifty-two such detachments, having approximately 125 officers and 2,800 marines. Duties of marines on board vessels of the Navy have undergone some further changes. They still man parts of the secondary battery on the larger vessels, and, since the more recent extensive development and use of antiaircraft guns on several vessels, they have been assigned the additional task of helping to man the antiaircraft batteries, which are now composed of both guns and machine guns. With the rapid expansion of the Navy, taking place at the writing, several additional marine detachments are scheduled to be added to the complements afloat each year until the expansion program is completed.

For a number of years after the war, when appropriations for military expenditures were drastically reduced, the Marine Corps as well as the other branches of the military and naval service had to get along with prewar establishments and the temporary developments, made during the war, and, to a large extent, used supplies left over from the war. This condition continued to some extent until after the coming of the great depression in 1929, when building projects were initiated for unemployment relief; then the Marine Corps as well as the other branches of the service began to receive funds for the permanent development of barracks. The process has continued up to the writing and by the time the present building program is carried out practically every marine will be housed in the most modern barracks, which have comforts far beyond the wildest imagination of the old-time marines. Utilities, recreation facilities, and ample numbers of officers' and noncommissioned officers' quarters are also being rapidly developed at all the larger posts of the Marine Corps. The development of the Marine Corps Base, San Diego, was begun in 1920 for the purpose of housing the West Coast Expeditionary Force, which later became a brigade of the Fleet Marine Force. That base is now the second largest post of the Marine Corps and is undergoing further development.

## Rifle Marksmanship

Even before the World War, the Marine Corps took a pardonable pride in the excellence of its rifle marksmanship. Colonel W. C. Harllee's score book, which, in addition to the purpose suggested by the name, served as a basis of instruction in rifle shooting for many years prior to and following the World War, aided materially in raising the marksmanship of marines. The Corps has continued to place great importance on the shooting ability of its personnel and considers straight shooting the most important qualification of a marine. It has maintained a particularly keen interest in national and international shooting competitions. The National Rifle Matches, in which teams from various branches of the military and naval service as well as civilian teams compete, were started in 1903 for the purpose of promoting excellence in marksmanship. The Marine Corps has made a special effort to develop rifle and pistol shooters of the highest possible skill to compete in such shooting competitions. Competition in all such matches has become more and more keen; the shooting quality of the ammunition and the arms have been constantly improved; but the Marine Corps's team has been able to carry off more honors in these matches perhaps than all other teams combined. During the last twenty years the Marine Corps's team has won first place twelve times out of sixteen competitions and during the remainder won either second or third place, and prior to 1938 won first place in five consecutive national matches.

The development of highly specialized shots in these competitions has helped to raise the general shooting ability throughout the Corps, by the interest the competitions have stimulated and by using the highly trained marksmen as instructors for the Corps in general. The high standard of rifle shooting by marines has been carried over to some extent into their shooting of naval guns, to which they are regularly assigned as gun crews.

## Artillery

As noted in Chapter XVI, the Marine Corps did not receive its artillery equipment designed for use in the World War until a short time before the armistice, when a limited quantity was received, and some time after the armistice, when a considerable quantity of 75 mm. and 155 mm. guns with accessory equipment, tractors, etc., were turned over to the organization. For several years thereafter the marines, particularly at Quantico, continued to take their artillery quite seriously. A battery of antiaircraft guns of World War make together with all accessories such as listening devices and searchlights was later added to the artillery equipment. The Tenth Marines was maintained as artillery for a number of years, using both heavy and light guns. For some time officers continued to be assigned to duty with the organization more in accordance with their interests than their ability as artillerists. As the years have passed, however, a considerable number of Marine officers have attended both the Field and Coast Artillery Schools of our Army or otherwise qualified themselves in the technique of artillery. Unquestionably, the efficiency of the present Marine Corps artillery units, which are all assigned to the Fleet Marine Force, are on a par with most any regular artillery.

Since the tendency to still greater mechanization of armed forces has set in, the Marine Corps artillery has begun to acquire more modern and additional weapons. With the increased prominence given to aviation, antiaircraft defenses have been developed, and the Marine Corps in keeping with the more modern practices has added 50-caliber machine guns and up to date 3-inch antiaircraft artillery to its regular equipment. In order to provide trained officers for these new and highly specialized weapons and to provide officers for artillery with advanced naval base troops, the Marine Corps established a base defense weapons school at Quantico, which has turned out several classes to add to the growing number of its trained artillerists.

## The Fleet Marine Force

Perhaps the most significant development within the Marine Corps during the last few years has been the prominence assigned to and the growth of the Fleet Marine Force. Since the experience of our Navy in Cuban waters and in the Philippines during the war with Spain, the Navy has felt the need of a well-organized military force to accompany its fleet for the purpose of taking and holding advanced bases of operations. It will be recalled that during the war with Spain, marines were used to hold Guantanamo Bay, Cuba, and Cavite, Philippine Island. Not long after the close of the war, the Marine Corps and the Navy began to consider organizing and equipping a contingent of marines, to be kept available and trained, for advanced base purposes. Such organizations were formed from time to time prior to the World War, but the exigencies of the service usually soon forced their disbandment and necessitated the use of the marines who were in the organizations for emergency duties.

The expeditionary forces, formed soon after the World War, were partly intended for advanced base purposes. The postwar maneuvers with the fleet served to attract attention and show the possibilities of a well-trained and equipped organization of marines as a fleet auxiliary. The pressing need of marines in the Caribbean Area and in China prevented the organization of such a force until a considerable portion of the marines had been withdrawn from such emergency duties abroad. Finally in the fall of 1933 following the withdrawal of marines from Haiti and Nicaragua, a sufficient number of men was at last available to begin the organization of an expeditionary force designed especially to operate with the United States Fleet.

The Fleet Marine Force, as now organized, is an integral part of the United States Fleet and serves under the orders of the commander in chief of that organization. The troops regularly assigned to the force are normally stationed at the two larger Marine Corps posts—the Marine Corps Base, San Diego, California, and the Marine Barracks, Quantico, Virginia. Major General Louis McCarty Little, in command of the organization, maintains his headquarters at San Diego. The Second Marine Brigade of that force, commanded by Brigadier General John C. Beaumont, is also stationed at San Diego, while the First Marine Brigade, commanded by Brigadier General R. P. Williams, is stationed at the Marine Barracks, Quantico. Each of these brigades consists of an infantry regiment, a battalion of light artillery (pack howitzers), a battalion of antiaircraft artillery, an aviation group, a light tank company, and suitable con-

MISCELLANEOUS VIEWS, FLEET MARINE FORCE

MISCELLANEOUS VIEWS, MARINE CORPS AVIATION

*Official U. S. Navy Photograph*

No. 1. A. A. Cunningham at the Controls of "Noisy Nan"
No. 2. Colonel Ross E. Rowell
No. 3. Colonel Roy S. Geiger at Pensacola in 1916
No. 4. DeHaviland Type of Plane Used by Northern Bombing Group, France, 1918
No. 5. Marine Aviation at Dress Parade, Quantico, Va.
No. 6. Assembling Training Planes ("Jennies") Miami, 1918
No. 7. Marine Amphibian on the Hai Ho River, China, 1927
No. 8. Bizoton, Haiti, 1920
No. 9. Transporting Wounded Marines in Nicaragua
No. 10. Amphibian Transport
No. 11. Fighting Plane
No. 12. Transport

tingents of engineers and chemical troops. The aggregate strength of the Fleet Marine Force is now approximately 4,585 officers and enlisted men. Its units are kept constantly trained for their specialized duties with the fleet and are ready to embark for such duty within a few hours' notice.

It should not be understood, however, that the entire efforts of the Marine Corps's organized field forces are directed solely towards their preparation as a fleet auxiliary. The troops in the Fleet Marine Force as well as all other marines are kept trained for any necessary duties to which they might in the future be called upon to perform.

## Marine Corps Reserve

As early as 1914 the necessary laws had been enacted for the beginning of a reserve organization of marines to reinforce the regular establishment in the event of a national emergency. Very little was accomplished, however, before the war and on April 6, 1917, the Corps's Reserve numbered only thirty-six men. During the war, part of the new officers were commissioned as reserve officers; by November 11, 1918, 463 reserve officers were on the rolls of the Corps. The Reserve was also authorized to make enlistments. The enlisted reservists gradually increased until a few days after the armistice, when they reached a total of 6,773, including approximately 250 women enlisted as "marinettes." During the demobilization period the reservists were transferred to an inactive status as fast as they could be spared from active duty. By the time demobilization had been completed all reservists, with the exception of a few reserve officers, had been transferred to inactive status.

The interest in a Marine Corps reserve suffered a similar setback to that of the other military and naval services during the postwar period of disillusionment. There was "lack of a definite policy and appropriation for the purpose of equipment and training" the reserves. Marine Corps recruiting officers were presumed to keep in contact with reservists throughout the country but actually they could accomplish very little. Some World War officers and enlisted men continued to belong to the organization—mostly for sentimental reasons. In July, 1925, an Act of Congress went into effect which made a general reorganization of the Reserve. It provided for a fleet Marine Corps and a volunteer reserve. There were several classes of the former, the more important of which were: those who were transferred to it after 16 to 20 years of active service; marines who had completed a regular enlistment in the Marine Corps and enlisted for another period of four years in the Reserve; and former marines who had served at least one year on active duty. A limited amount of funds was thereafter available; the Reserve then took on new life and gradually increased in strength and efficiency. Two years after its re-establishment, it had a paper strength of approximately 5,800 which rose to nearly 10,000 a few years afterwards. The success of the organization was rather remarkable when it is considered that its personnel received very little pay and were expected to give a great deal of their time; at times they had expenses contingent with their reserve duties in excess of their reserve pay. Most of its men remained faithful to it largely on account of patriotic motives and through devotion to the Marine Corps.

The Marine Corps Reserve has gone through several reorganizations and changes of policy during the last few years. As now constituted, it is organized into the Fleet Marine Corps Reserve, the Organized Marine Corps Reserve, and the Volunteer Marine Corps Reserve. The Organized Marine Corps Reserve comprises eighteen infantry battalions, an artillery battalion, and twelve aviation squadrons. These reserve units are organized and active, and are required to engage in weekly drills and undergo an intensive period of field training annually. The Fleet Marine Corps Reserve comprises officers and enlisted men, now in an inactive status, who have previously served with the regular naval and military forces. The Volunteer Marine Corps Reserve comprises officers and enlisted men, also in an inactive status, who have had previous military experience. The strength of the combined Marine Corps Reserve is approximately one thousand officers and fourteen thousand enlisted men. All Marine Corps reservists are available for active duty in time of war or national emergency.

## Aviation

The Marine Corps came out of its experiences in the World War with a few "flying crates"—DH4-B's, "H"-boats, single-engine sea planes, and "Jennys," Curtiss trainers—and a few officers and enlisted men, principally young men who had come into the Corps during the World War, some of whom had had considerable experience in a training capacity or in the war zone. Aviation continued as a more or less separate specialization for marines. The few flying facilities at Quantico were developed into an aviation field that became the Corps's principal aviation center. A smaller aviation field was maintained for a few years at Parris Island, South Carolina, and a contingent of Marine Corps aviation was assigned to the Naval Aviation Station at San Diego, California, in August, 1924. Student aviators were commonly trained as pilots in Marine

Corps aviation at the Naval Air Station at Pensacola, Florida. More modern planes were gradually acquired, and in 1921 more than a thousand officers and enlisted men were assigned exclusively to aviation duty. As mentioned in the chapters devoted to each of several countries of the Caribbean area, units of Marine Corps aviation participated with the intervening forces in those countries. At times the maintenance of aviation units abroad absorbed most of the available personnel and equipment. A small aviation squadron, operating principally with scouting planes, was stationed on the Island of Guam from 1921 to 1927, and then transferred to duty with the Third Brigade in China.

By 1922 the aviation strength at Quantico was large enough to form a small aviation group of one observation and one fighting squadron in addition to a balloon section. Available personnel and equipment continued to be added; by 1927 the Marine Corps was maintaining five aviation squadrons, as part of the Expeditionary Force at Quantico, and three squadrons at San Diego, in addition to four squadrons serving outside the United States. Late in that year one of the squadrons at San Diego was transferred to China. From 1932 until 1934 a marine observation squadron was assigned to each of the two larger airplane carriers, the *Lexington* and *Saratoga*. Ever since Lieutenant Cunningham began flying in 1912, Marine Corps aviation had been going through the developing or pioneering stages with the attendant risk and danger. A considerable proportion of both its officers and enlisted men who engaged in actual flying lost their lives during this developing stage. The hazards of flying, particularly over the jungles of tropical countries, were far greater than those in commercial aviation at that time. More recent developments in airplane construction plus the advantages of years of experience have of course made Marine Corps aviation considerably less hazardous. With the coming of the Fleet Marine Force in 1933, practically all of Marine Corps aviation was assigned to that part of the Marine Corps. Each brigade of the F.M.F. now has an aviation group assigned to it.

The present authorized strength of Marine Corps aviation is 112 airplanes of modern standard navy types, exclusive of spare, experimental, training, and obsolete machines. It has in all nine squadrons, seven of which are maintained for tactical purposes and two for general utility. The tactical organizations consist of two fighting, two bombing, and three observation squadrons. The utility squadrons are equipped with transports, amphibians, and odd types of planes. The operating personnel of Marine Corps aviation consists of approximately 175 officers, 40 flying cadets, and 1,100 enlisted men. Marine aviators are trained to operate planes from airplane carriers as well as from landing fields and from the water. One of the observation squadrons is at this writing maintaining a regular aviation station at Charlotte Amalie, St. Thomas, Virgin Islands, and serves as the military garrison for those islands.

## Present and Probable Future Duties

In conformity with the approved naval policy the fundamental tasks of the Marine Corps are:

(a) To provide trained marine detachments for vessels of the Navy.
(b) To maintain the Fleet Marine Force in immediate readiness as a unit of the United States Fleet.
(c) To guard naval property and naval shore establishments within the continental limits of the United States and outlying possessions.
(d) To educate and train officers and enlisted men to perform their duties in peace and war.
(e) To protect American lives and interests in disturbed areas where operations on shore are involved.
(f) To maintain a trained reserve of officers and enlisted men.
(g) To maintain an emergency reserve of munitions and equipment.

It is contemplated of course that each of these duties will be continued at least in the immediate future. Throughout the entire history of the United States Marines, they have served on board vessels of the Navy and guarded naval establishments ashore; so long as there is a Marine Corps these will probably be among their fundamental duties. As previously stated the Fleet Marine Force is a comparatively recent development and as such has never been used in a national emergency. Whether or not it would actually be used for its primary purpose in war would obviously depend upon the mission assigned to the fleet and the conditions under which it would operate. If no advanced bases were required by the fleet, and none within the theater of operations needed to be denied to the enemy, the F.M.F. would no doubt then be available for diversion to other duties.

When it is considered how complex warfare is today and conceded—as it is entirely logical to concede—that warfare will become still more complicated, the mission of educating and training officers and enlisted men will continue indefinitely, and probably become more important. With regard to the mission of maintaining a reserve, such an organization would undoubtedly prove useful in times of emergency, but the Reserve might be discontinued, of course, as a change in our plans for national defense. The maintenance of emergency reserves of munitions and equipment will probably become more important in the future but will be governed almost entirely by appropriations by Congress.

The preceding chapters of this work show that in addition to their prescribed duties, marines have participated in: raiding and punitive operations undertaken for various reasons; conquests; various interventions in foreign countries; operations in support of the civil power; and service directly with the Army in time of war. The armed forces of the United States have not participated in raiding and punitive expeditions, except as incident to war, for a great many years and will probably not do so again. Our country has undertaken no conquests for many years and it does not at present appear likely that it will again—at least until world-wide conditions are considerably altered. Military interventions, at least in the Latin-American countries, appear to have ceased, as the result of changes in our foreign policy and because of certain treaties referred to heretofore. The Marines have in the past rendered many valuable services to the civil powers, both local and national. There appears to be no logical reason to suppose that they will not continue to do so in the future.

This work points out, that, with the single exception of the Spanish-American War, marines have been called to serve with the Army in all our major wars and during some of our lesser belligerent experiences. Had sufficient marines been available, it is highly probable that they would have been used by the Army during the war with Spain. During each of our wars the Army has found itself in great need of additional troops, well-trained and equipped and immediately available. Our national policy has always been to maintain a small standing army, which cannot be as rapidly expanded at the outbreak of war as can the armies of most other first class powers. Neither the National Guard nor the Army Reserve could come to the assistance of the Regular Army as rapidly as could the Marines. So long as this condition prevails, it appears as taking too much for granted to assume that in the event of a major national emergency, when all of the Marines are not needed with the Navy, a part of them would not as usual be ordered to duty with the Army. If one adheres to the theory of continuity in history, he must conclude that the future mission of the Marine Corps, both in peace and in war, will continue to be not very much unlike what it has been during the past few decades.

# INDEX

## A

Abaco, Hopkins' Squadron to, 14
Acapulco, Mexico, 300
Act establishing Marine Corps, 31
Act of March 2, 1807, 47
Act of June 30, 1834, Corps increased, 82
Act, National Defense, August 29, 1916, 449-50
Adams, John, 42, 110; appoints first commandant, 31
Administration of the Corps, 546
Advanced training of officers, 545-6
Advanced Base Force, 310-11
Advancement of learning, 305-6, 545-6
Aeronautic Company in World War, 469-70
Aeroplanes, types used, 552-3
*Aetna,* bomb ketch, 49
African slave trade, 181-3
African tribes, war with, 182-3
Aguinaldo, Emilio, 256, 268
Ahr River, Germany, march down, 521
Aiding the Civil Power, 246-7
"Aircraft One" and "Two," 553-4
Aisne-Marne Operation, *see* Soissons
Aizpuru-McCalla difficulties, 233-4
Aizpuru of Panama, 232 *et seq.*
*Alabama,* Confederate raider, captures marines, 217
Alaska, 226
*Alaska* at Korea, 1871, 240
*Albany,* 122, 308-9
*Alert,* fight of, with *Lexington,* 17; in Nicaragua, 1894, 236
Alexandria, Egypt, 224
*Alfred,* 13; marines placed on, 1775, 12
Algerine cruisers attack American Commerce, 28; vessels, capture of, 87
Algiers, treaty with, 29; war with, 1815, 87
*Al-Ki,* in Alaskan waters, 226-7
Allen, Ethan, 6
Allen, William H., officer, U.S.M.C., 89
*Alliance,* 22-3, 225; in Holland, 24; last ship of the Continental Navy, 27; in 1885, 232

Allowances, early Corps, 84
Alpine Chasseurs, French, 473
Alvarado, Mexico, 112-14; capture of, 120-21; marines at, 136
Amador, rebel, Panama, 291, 296-7
Amelia Island, Florida, 76, 201; capture of, 1810, 50; pirates on, 1816, 88
American flag, raised over Guam, 264; at Manila, 256; over Porto Rico, 262
"American Fort," Derne, Tripoli, 46
American Government in Guam, 264
American Legation: Chile, guarding, 230; at Seoul, Korea, guarded, 244
American Minister: to Japan, guarded by marines, 1868, 237; to Korea, 1894, 244
American property owners in Cuba, 325
Amiens, France, 477
Ammunition expended at Canton, China, 1856, 176
Amory, lieutenant, U.S.M.C., 35
*Amphitrite,* landing force, 262
Ancon, Panama, 297
*Andrea Doria,* 13, 14
*Annapolis,* 410; Nicaragua, 414
Antiaircraft artillery, 549-50
Anti-foreign riots, Canton, China, 92
Anthony, William, private, U.S.M.C., 254, 263
Anton Lizardo, Mexico, 113, 116
Apalachicola, Florida, 99
Apalachicola River, Florida, pirates on, 88
Appropriations, reductions in, 547-8
Arab mutiny before Derne, Tripoli, 45
Arabian cavalry with Eaton in Tripoli, 44
Arctic expeditions, 225-6
Argentine: difficulties with in Falkland Islands, 90; landing in, 1890, 230
*Argus,* 44-5
Argonne attack, 503 *et seq.*
Argonne Forest, France, 502, 510
Arias Rebellion, Dominican Republic, 343 *et seq.*
*Ariel,* mail steamer, 217
*Arkansas,* 461

557

## INDEX

Armistice: Mexican War, 165; World War, 282, 519-20
Arms Commission, Cuba, 321
Armstrong, commodore, U.S.N., 173
Army: balloon schools, World War, 470; takes over California, 155; campaign against Seminoles, 100-2; relieved at Cavite by marines, 1900, 270; marines on duty with, 1861, 195; marines on duty with in World War, 452-3, 466-7; in East Florida, 50-51; expedition to Vera Cruz, 1914, 303-04; expeditionary force to Cuba, 321; at Fort Fisher, 215-6; joint maneuvers with Navy, 527; marines assist, in California, 249; joint operations with Navy in Florida, 1817, 88; at La Paz, Mexico, 159-60; 271, 279, 285, 303
Army of Cuba Pacifications, 320-24
Army, German, 468, 470
Army of Occupation, Germany, 521-2
Arnold, Benedict, expedition to Ticonderoga, 5
Arnold's Fleet, 8
Arriete, Cuba, 318
Artillery: antiaircraft, 549-50; Army, to Mediterranean, 1815, 87; with Barney at Bladensburg, 73; battalion in Dominican Republic, 347; light pack howitzers, 550; in Guam, 265; in Nicaragua, 414; of the present, 549-50; schools, 549; in World War, 458-9; 349, 456-7
Ashepoo River, South Carolina, 201
*Ashuelot* Formosa, 1867, 238
Asia, eastern, operations in, 236-45
Asiatic Fleet: legation guard from, Korea, 244; at Shanghai, 266, 270, 308-9, 462, 530, 532, 534, 537, 539
Asiatic Squadron, after Civil War, 225; 255
Asiatic station, 270
Assinpink, Battle of, 17
*Atlantic*, captured by Porter, 64. Renamed *Essex Jr.*
Atlantic Blockading Squadron, 212-3
Atlantic Squadron, 220
Attacks: on Alvarado, Mexico, 113; in the Argonne, 502; marines' first, in Belleau Wood, 482-4; on Charleston, S. C., 207-10; on Chapultepec, Mexico, 130-33; on Cochori, Mexico, 158-9; on Derne, Tripoli, 45-6; on Fortaleza, San Francisco de Marcoris, Dominican Republic, 353; on Fort Fisher, S. C., 214-7; second, on Fort Fisher, S. C., 215-6; on Fort George, 1813, 56; on Fort Sumter, 208-10; on Las Trencheras, Dominican Republic, 348-9; on Mobile, 211-12; of New Orleans, preparation for, 202; on New Orleans, 1862, 202-04; on Norfolk, Va., 1813, 70; of Peking, China, 285-6; of Sixth Marines on July 19, 1918, 496-8; of Tampico, 117-8; of Tripoli, 43

Atwood, first sergeant, U.S.M.C., killed in Dominican Republic, 352
Aulick, John H., officer, U.S.N., in Rio Grande Expedition, 111
Authorized marines for ships of new navy, 1797-1799, 32
Aviation: squadron, in Dominican Republic, 364; Squadron One, 369; squadron, in Nicaragua, 424; detachment, Eastern Area, 435; in World War, 467-70; in Azores, 469; stations, 552-3; since World War, 552-4; today, strength, number of planes, 427, 429, 442, 552, 553-4
Aviators, lost, 429; locate bandits, 436; as pilots for British planes, 468
Azores, World War, 469-70

### B

Bacoor, P. I., 267
Badger, admiral, U.S.N., 302
Bahamas, expedition to, 1776, 13
Bahon, Haiti, 383
Bainbridge, William, officer, U.S.N., 64
Balangiga, Samar, P. I., massacre of soldiers, 271; marines at, 272
Baldwin, Samuel, officer, U.S.M.C., 49
Balloons, 470
*Baltimore*, 244, 255, 266-7, 280; Tientsin, 1894, 239
*Baltimore* affair, Chile, 230
Baltimore, Md., defense of, 1813, 74-5; bombarded, 75; strikes, 1877, 248-9
Bamboo guns, in P. I., 273
Bancroft, George, Secretary of the Navy, 106
Bandit contacts, Dominican Republic, 358-9, 363-4
Banditry: in Dominican Republic, 1918, 357 *et seq.;* increase of, 1919, 363; recurrence of, 365-6; end of, 367-8; in Haiti, 368, 398-9
Bandits, Nicaraguan, 437; leaders of, 440
Bank of Haiti, 372
Bannon, Philip M., officer, U.S.M.C., 308-9, 319
Bantry, Ireland, 461
Baracoa, Cuba, 319
Barataria, attack on pirates at, 76-7
Barbary corsairs, 41-7; 1815, 87-8
Barker, F. A., officer, U.S.M.C., in Haiti, 381; in France, 500, 513
Barnett, George, officer, U.S.M.C., 317-19, 450, 542
Barney, Joshua, officer, U.S.N., his flotilla, 71-3; in Battle of Bladensburg, 73
Barricourt, France, 55
Barton, Thomas B., officer, U.S.M.C., 89
Baseball, 526
Base Defense Weapons School, 549
Base Detachment, Fifth Regiment, 474
Base Section No. 2, France, 474
Bas Obispo, Panama, 294-5, 297

## INDEX

Basey, P. I., 272, 274-5, 277
Basilon Island, P. I., 271
Bates, George D., officer, U.S.M.C., 226
Batista, Roman, Dominican Republic, 352
Baton Rouge, La., 49
Battalion to Panama, 290; in Dominican Republic, 345
Battalion, Second, guards Washington Arsenal, 249
Battle, between *Bon Homme Richard* and *Serapis*, 23-4
Battle casualties in France, 522-3
Battles: Bladensburg, 73; Bull Run, 198; Coyotepe Hill, Nicaragua, 413-14; Cherabusco, 129; Cuzco Well, Cuba, 258; Guartanamo Bay, 257-8; Hatchee-Lustee, 100-1; El Molino del Rey, 129-30; Lake Borgne, 77-8; Lake Champlain, 8; Lake Erie, 57-8; La Mesa, 154; Los Angeles, 154; Manila Bay, 255-6; Mobile Bay, 211-12; New Orleans, 77-80; Novaleta, P. I., 267-8; Palo Alto, 109; San Gabriel, 152-3; San Pasqual, 149-50; Santiago, 261-2; Tientsin, 283; of the World War, 522-3
Battleship Force Number One, 460-61
Bay Point, S. C., 201-213
Bayonville, France, 515
Beadle, Elias R., officer, U.S.M.C., 425, 433, 438
*Beagle*, 89
Bear Republic, 140
Bearss, Hiram I., officer, U.S.M.C., 273-5; 277; in Dominican Republic, 350; *vs.* Chacha, 356; in France, 474
Beaumont, John C., officer, U.S.M.C., 539, 550
Beaumont, France, 516
Bejucal, Cuba, 319
Belgium, march across, 520
Bell, admiral, U.S.N., Japan, 1867, 237-8
Belleau Wood, first attack, 482-4; attack of June 9, 485; Wise's attack, 485; the "hook," 486; relief by Seventh Infantry, 488; German defense of, 482, 484-5, 486-8; losses in, 489-90; relief from, 487-8; results of and appreciation expressed, 489; renamed, 490-91
Bellevue, Francis B. de, officer, U.S.M.C., 78
*Benicia*, in Korea, 1871, 240
*Bennington*, at Guam, 265
Benoit Batraville, Haitian bandit leader, 398; attacks on, 400-1
Bering Sea, expedition into, 226-7
Berkeley, Randolph C., officer, U.S.M.C., 301, 424, 448
Berribee Tribe, Africa, 182-3
Berry, B. S., officer, U.S.M.C., 481-2, 484
Biddle, James, commodore, U.S.N., 155
Biddle, William P., officer, U.S.M.C., 270
Biebush, F. H., officer, U.S.M.C., 364
Big Cypress Swamp, Fla., 102
Bigelow, commander, U.S.N., 125

Birthday of Marines, 11
Bizaton, Haiti, 376
*Black Hawk*, 218
Bladensburg, Battle of, 1813, 73
Blake, H. C., officer, U.S.N., in expedition to Korea, 241
Blanc Mont operation, 502-510; first attack, 503-4; second advance, 506-7; Essen Hook, 506; heroism of, 504; German defense of, 504; 506-8; attack of Oct. 4, severest test, 507-8; cleared, 508; further advance, 509; attack of 36th Division, 509; capture of St. Etienne, 509; losses in, 509-10
Blandon, Pedro, bandit in Nicaragua, 444
Blevaincourt, France, 476
Blockade, method of, west coast, Mexico, 156-7; of Mexico, 106, 115
"Blue devils" of France, 473; *see also* Alpine Chasseurs
Bluefields, Nicaragua, 236; landings at, 409, 411, 415, 419
Boarding parties, 84
Boat expeditions, in Florida, 100-4, 208
Bobo, Rosalvo, of Haiti, 375 *et seq.;* his rebellion, 377-8
Boca de Cupe, Panama, 295
Bocay, Nicaragua, 435-6
Bogac, P. I., 269
Bois de la Bridge de Marine, 490
Bois de Belleau, France, 482
Bois de Champillon, France, 487
Bolshevik influence in China, 529, 531
Bombardment of Fort Fisher, 215-16
*Bon Homme Richard*, engagement with *Serapis*, 23-4; marines on, 22-4
*Bonita*, schooner, 117, 123
Bordeaux, France, 465-6, 474-6
Borno, Louis, of Haiti, 403
Boston, 39, 317; fire at, 247; prison riot, 1833, 86-7
*Boston*, in Haiti, 36
*Boston*, 280, 293-5
Bouresches, France, 484, 487
Bourmont, France, 474
*Boxer*, fight with *Enterprise*, 62
Boxer rebellion, 270, 279-85, 307
Boyd's Neck, S. C., 213
Blunderbusses, 26
Bradman, F. L., officer, U.S.M.C., 337, 445
*Brandywine*, frigate to China, 91-2
Brazil, 184
Brazil Squadron, 181; in 1858, 185; operations of, 183-5
Brazil Station, 1833, 105
Breckinridge, Henry B., officer, U.S.M.C., 70
Breese, James B., officer, U.S.M.C., 247
Brest, France, 464, 466, 468, 475
Breuvannes, France, 474
Brigade of Marines, to Panama 1885, 233-5; prepared for Mexico, 1913, 298;

Brigade of Marines—*cont'd*
  in Cuba, 1912, 326; in Haiti, 379; in China, 1937, 539
Brigade sector, marines' first, 479
British African Squadron, 182
British Army at Shanghai, 532
British Fleet, World War, 456
British Isles, Jones's cruise around, 1779, 22
British Navy, 13; on the Penobscot, 22; at New Orleans, 76; *vs* pirates in the West Indies, 89-90
British on Lake Ontario, 54-8
British planes, marines used, 468
British raid of Sackett's Harbor, 56-7
British repulsed at Baltimore, 75
British troops, 283-4
Broad River Expedition, 212-14
Broke, captain, British Navy, captured the *Chesapeake*, 61
*Brooklyn*, 261, 462
Brooks, John, officer, U.S.M.C., 55; on *Wasp*, 60
Broom, James, officer, U.S.M.C., 62
Broome, John L., officer, U.S.M.C., 177, 204
Broome's battalion at New Orleans, 1862, 204
Brown, Charles, corporal, U.S.M.C., in Korea, 243
Brown, John, captured at Harpers Ferry, 188-9
Bruges, Belgium, 468
Bryan, William J., policy toward Dominican Republic, 343; Haiti, 374-5
Buchanan, R. B., officer, U.S.M.C., killed, 423
Buchanan, Secretary of State, 139; his administration, 197
Buenos Aires, 1833, 183; 1852, 183; 1890, 230
Building a navy, 1794, 28
Bull Run, Battle of, 198
Bunau-Varilla, in Panama, 291
Bundy, Omar, general, U.S.A., 476
Burning of the *Philadelphia*, 42
Burning of Sackett's Harbor, 56-7
Burning of Washington, 74
Burr Conspiracy, 48
Burrita, Mexico, 111
Burrows, William W., first commandant of Marine Corps, 31; resigned, 38
Bush, William, officer, U.S.M.C., on *Constitution*, 59
Butler, Benj. F., general, U.S.A., 199, 202
Butler, Smedley D., officer, U.S.M.C., 294, 391, 525, 529; in Haiti, 380-5; in Nicaragua, 409-14, 416; World War, 464, 466; in China 533-4; influence, 542; retires, 543-4
Butler's Battalion, Nicaragua, 410-14, 416
Butler, Thomas, congressman, 542-3
Button, William R., corporal, U.S.M.C., 397, 398

Buzancy, France, 516
Byrd, William C., officer, U.S.M.C.C, 359, 364

C

*Cabot*, detachment for, 1775, 12-14
Cacos, 378-80, 397; first war with, 380-6; campaign against at Cap Haitien, 381-86; attack Port au Prince, 386; chiefs agree to give up, 382; end of the first war with, 385-6; caco resistance, 401
Cadwalader, George, officer, Amer. Army, Rev. War, 16-17
Cahuenga, Cal., peace at, 154
Cairo, Ill., 217-8
Calais, France, 467-8
Caldwell, C. H. B., officer, U.S.N., 178
California: in 1848, 93; operations in, 138 *et seq.;* California Battalion, 132; volunteers, 141, 155; railroad strikes, 1894, 249; revolt of, 133 *et seq.*
*California*, in Nicaragua, 414; battalion in Nicaragua, 414
Calixte, Demosthenes P., Haitian, 407
Callao, Peru, 92
*Callao*, gunboat, 268
Camaguey, Cuba, 318-20, 336-7
Camp, marines, first in D. C., 38
Camp Rapidan, Va., 528
Campaigns: *vs* cacos at Cap Haitien, 381-2; *vs* Creek Indians, 98-9; *vs* Seminoles, 100-1; in Samar, 271 *et seq.;* in the South, Revolutionary War, 25
Campbell, Chandler, officer, U.S.M.C., 381
Canal, surveying expeditions, 236
Canal Zone, 296-7, 409, 450
Canton, China, 1835, 44; 1844, 92; protecting Americans, 1856, 172 *et seq.*, 530
Cap Haitien, 91, 374-5; fight with cacos near, 381-2; 402, 404
Cape Disappointment, Ore., landing at, 91
Cape Florida, 99
Cape Gracias, 436
Cape Henlopen, 14
Cape May, N. J., 469
Cape of Good Hope, 169
Cape Verde Islands, *Constitution* at, 63; base of African Squadron, 181
Caperton, William B., officer, U.S.N., 343-5; in Haiti, 375, 377; his report, Haiti, 386
Capois, Haiti, 396
Cardiff, Wales, 461
Caribbean area: naval war in 1798, 33; piracy in, 88; 186, 286-97, 408, 410, 456
Caribbean countries, 476
Caribbean Sea, 76; Squadron, 293
Carlosahatchee River, 103
Carmick, Daniel, officer, U.S.M.C., 31, 35, 48-9; with marines in Battle of New Orleans, 78

# INDEX  561

*Carolina,* at New Orleans, 78
Carranza, Mexican general, 305
Carson, Kit, 149
Cartegena, 292
Cash, John C., officer, U.S.M.C., 196
*Castine,* in Dominican waters, 1816, 344
Castle of Chapultepec, 130-2
Castro, Mexican officer, 144
Casualties: in Cuba, 258; in Nicaragua, 415-436, 446-7; of Fourth Brigade, France, 522-3
Catlin, Albertus W., officer, U.S.M.C., 302, 315-6, 475, 484
Cat-o'-nine-tails, 85
Caunao, Cuba, 318
Cavite, P. I., 255, 268-79; naval station, 266
Cavite Province, 267, 271
Cavite Viejo, P. I., 267
Cayes District, Haiti, 405
Cecil Furnace, 74
Censorship, World War, 485
Central American countries, 408
Central Area, Haiti, 442
Cerro Gordo, Battle of, 126
Cervera, Pascual, Spanish admiral, 256, 261
Chacha, Dominican bandit leader, 356
Chacha's group, contact with, 356
Chaffee, general, U.S.A., 284
Chagres River, 180
Chahar, Province, China, 538
Chalons, France, 502
Chamorro, Emiliano, Nicaraguan, 410, 417, 433
Champagne Offensive, *see* Mont Blanc
Champlain Lake, 7; Battle of Arnold's Fleet on, 8; struggle for control of, 1775, 8
Chapultepec, storming of, 130-2
Characters, colorful, passing of, 546
Charlemagne Peralte, Haitian leader, 394-6
*Charleston,* 263-4, 266
Charleston, S. C., capture of by British, 1780, 25; marines from, to Lakes, 55; attacks on, 207-10.
Charlotte River, expedition up, 96
Château-Thierry, 480
Chattahoochie River, guards on, 99
Chaudun, France, taken by 17th Co., 495
*Chaumont,* 474, 533, 539
Chaumont-en-Vexin, France, 479
Chaumont-la-Ville, France, 476
Chauncey, Isaac, officer, U.S.N., on Lake Ontario, 54-8
Chauncey's Squadron, providing marines for, 54-5; attack on Fort George, 56; captures York, Ontario, 56
Cheering ship, 110
Chefoo, China, 239, 309
Chemical troops, 551
Chemulpo, Korea, 244

Chennery, France, 515
Cherokee country, marines in, 104
*Cherub,* British vessel, captures Gamble, 68
Cherubusco, Battle of, 129
*Chesapeake,* 42; captured by *Shannon,* 61
Chesapeake, raids in, War of 1812, 69-75
*Chester,* 302
Chicharones, D. R., 368-9
Chichigalpa, Nicaragua, 415
Chief of Gendarmerie, Haiti, 393-4
Chile, difficulties in, 1890
China: opening up to trade, 91-2; supporting trade with, 171-2; disorders in 1840's, 172; post-civil war period, 238; protection of Americans in, 1866, 238; disorders in, 238-9; 280; 280-5; 307-9; battalion sent to, 308; duty in since 1918, 529 *et seq.;* postwar conditions in, 529 *et seq.;* Sixth Marines sent to, 533; Third Brigade in China, 1927, 533-4; anti-Japanese activities, 535; Third Brigade withdrawn from, 535; situation in, 1928, 534-5; political conditions, 1927, 535; war with Japan, 538 *et seq.*
Chinandega, Nicaragua, 419, 444
Chinese Army, at Shanghai, 1932, 536
Cholera epidemic, marines combat, 1892, 248
Christophe of Haiti, relations with U. S., 91
Church, Jonathan, officer, U.S.M.C., 36
Cienfuegos, Cuba, 315-6, 318
*Cincinnati,* naval detachment, 262, 290
"Citadel," Korean fort, 242; renamed Fort McKee, 243
Citations by French Army, 490-1
Civil powers: *see* Domestic Disturbances; aid to, 86, 309-10
Civil War, 192-221; Civil War officers, 184; losses, 220; résumé of service in, 220-1; battles re-enacted, 527; disintegration at beginning of, 192-3; distribution, marines, 253
Civil War, in Haiti, 372
Civil War, in Nicaragua, 417
Clark, George Rogers, marines in Northwest with, 20
Clemenceau, comments on marines, 490
*Cleveland,* 417-9
Cliff defenses, Samar, 272-3
Clinch, Bartholomew, officer, U.S.M.C., 32, 34
Clinch, general, U.S.A., 95
Clothing, allowance, 85
Cochori, Mexico, attack on, 158
Cochrane, Henry C., officer, U.S.M.C., 225-7, 250
Cockburn, George, British admiral, 69
Coco River, 434, 436, 440
Coco Solo, Canal Zone, 298
Cole, E. B., officer, U.S.M.C., 476

Cole, Eli K., officer, U.S.M.C., to Haiti, 376; to Cap Haitien, 379; negotiations with caco chiefs, 381; 465
Colombey-les-Belles, France, 499
Colombia, 290-6, 288-93, 295; relations with, 230-1
Colon, Panama, 217; in 1885, 232; 287-88, 290-5, 298
Colonial Background, 3-4
Colonial Wars, 3-4
*Colorado*, flagship of Asiatic Fleet, Korea, 1871, 240; in Nicaragua, 412
Colored Party in Cuba, 324-5
Colorful characters, passing of, 546
Colt automatic gun, 274
*Columbia*, in Nicaragua, 236
Columbia, Camp, Cuba, 318-9
Columbia River, 91
Columbian Exposition, Chicago, 1893, 250
Columbus, Ga., army at, 97
*Columbus*: marines on, November, 1775, 12; 13, 155
Commandant, early duties of, 31, 33, 305, 310
Commandants, 82-3, 251-2, 544; since the World War, 544
Commanding officers in Cuba, 1906-9, 322
Commission, oldest existing of marine officer, 12
Concentration of marines in Haiti, 387
*Concord*, 266
Conditions in the Marine Corps, 547
Confederacy, officers join, 193
Confederate flotilla, at New Orleans, 202; on the Mississippi, 210
Confederate Marine Corps, 194-5
Conference, Tipitapa, 422
*Congress*, frigate, in Haiti, 1821, 91; 139, 142, 145-6, 152, 155, 160, 163-4, 184, 204-5
Congress, U. S., 255, 299, 310, 462, 464
Congressional Medal of Honor, 243, 398, 430
Conner, David, officer, U.S.N., 113; attack on Tampico, 117
*Connecticut*, in Cuba, 334, 376
Connecticut Marines, 9
Conquest of California, 151 *et seq.*; résumé of naval, 165
*Constellation*: marines authorized for, 29; 30; vs *Insurgente*, 34; vs the *Vengeance*, 34; at Derne, 46; at Norfolk, 69-70
*Constitution*: marines authorized for, 29; 30; at Puerto Plata, 34; 47; vs *Guerrière*, 58; marines in battle with *Guerrière*, 59; fight with *Java*, 1812, 60; cruise of, 62; last cruise in War of 1812, 63; fight with *Cyane* and *Levant*, 63; 250
Consuelo, D. R., 356
Contacts with Dominican bandits, 358 *et seq.*; in D. R., 1920, 364

Continental Congress: acts of, to create Navy, 10-11; acts of, creating Marines, 11; act of June 25, 1776, making marine officers, 12
Continental Marines: authorization of, 11; beginning of, 11-12; in Europe, 18; uniforms of, 25-6; end of, 27
Continental Navy: earliest ships in, 7; origin of, 10-11; end of, 27
Coolidge, Calvin, President, 421-22, 528
Cordon System, in D. R., 366-7
Corinto, Nicaragua, 409-11, 416-17
*Cormoran*, German cruiser, 452
Corporal punishment, 85, 246
*Corvée*, the, 392-4
Couden, A. R., officer, U.S.N., 317
Countersign, the, 397
Courts-martial in the Philippines, 279
Coyotepe Hill, Nicaragua, 413-14
Crabb, Horatio N., officer, U.S.M.C., 89
Craddock, officer, British Navy, 282
Craney Island, near Norfolk, 69-70; marines help hold, 70
Craven, T. A. M., officer, U.S.N., 158
Creek Indians: take warpath, 96; the fighting Creeks, 98-9; moved to Oklahoma, 99
Creek volunteers, in Seminole War, 99-100
Crossing of the Meuse, 517-19
*Croyable*, captured by *Delaware*, 33
Cruces, Cuba, 318
Cruising stations of ships in war with France, 33
Cuba: pirate base, 88, 255, 257, 287, 312, 319, 453, 460; in 1851, 186; in 1875, 228; rebels vs Spain, 1869, 247; occupation of, 262-3; a dependency of U. S., 312; intervention in, 1901-06, 312-24; taken over by U. S., 312-14, 316-18; distribution of marines in, 320, 322-3, 329-30; in 1906 relieved by Army, 321-2; towns held, 322-3; withdrawal from, 1908-9, 323-4; Negro Rebellion, 324-7; protecting property in, 326-7; towns occupied, 1912, 328; withdrawal from, 1912, 331; Sugar Intervention in, 332 *et seq.*; destruction of American property, 1917, 332-3; operations at Guaycanayabo Bay, 1917, 333; sugar plantations guarded, 333; battalion from Haiti in, 333; naval station water problem, 1917, 333; guarding sugar estates, 334; guarding American property, 335; protection of towns, 1917, 335; duties during Sugar Intervention, 336; withdrawal of part of the marines, 1917, 336; Army plans to occupy, 1917, 336; in World War, 336; German agents in World War, 336; Camp San Juan, 337; 1934 battalion of marines in waters only, 338; Army of Pacification, 320-24
Cuban Pacification, the Army of, 316
Cuban towns held, 1917-18, 336-7

## INDEX

Cukela, Louis, officer, U.S.M.C., 478
Culebra, V. I., 300, 310
*Cumberland,* 109-11, 113, 115, 196-7, 204-5
Cumberland Island, Fla., 1811, 50
Cunningham, Alfred A., officer, U.S.M.C., 467
Curaçao, French expedition against, 34
Cushing, Caleb, diplomat, U. S., arrival in China, 91-2
Customs, 190-1
Customs, control by U. S. in Haiti, 374
Customs of the Early Corps, 38-9; of the Navy, 11, 110
Cutts, Richard M., Sr., officer, U.S.M.C., 368
Cuvali, Nicaragua, 436-7
Cuzco Well, Cuba, attack on, 258
*Cyane,* 139-40, 143-4, 152, 156, 160-1, 163; fight with *Constitution,* 63

### D

Dade, major, U.S.A., massacre of his force, 95
Dahlgren, John A., officer, U.S.N., 207
Dahlgren's Squadron, marines ashore from, 213
Daiquiri, Cuba, 261
*Dale,* 142, 150, 201; at Guaymas, Mexico, 158; at La Paz, Mexico, 159
Dale's Squadron in the Mediterranean, 41-2
Dallas, A. J., officer, U.S.N., 95, 99
Damblain, France, 474
Daniels, Josephus, and the Caco War, 385, 542
Darien route for canal, 236
Darnall, G. C., officer, U.S.M.C., 426
Dartiguenave, President of Haiti, 377-8; government, 386
Dartt, V. H., officer, U.S.M.C., killed, 441
Dawson, L. L., officer, U.S.M.C., 216
Dawson's Battalion at Fort Fisher, 216
Day Wing, Northern Bombing Group in World War, 468
Decatur, Stephen, officer, U.S.N., 43; in the Mediterranean, 1815, 87; 1856, 186
Declaration of war against Mexico, 111
Decorations, World War, 478, 522
Defeat of the Californians, 154
*Defense,* South Carolina Navy, marines on, 1775, 10
Defense: of Baltimore, 74-5; of the Marbache Sector, France, 498-9; of Norfolk, 1813, 69-70; program of, 1798, 29-30; of Washington, 72
*DeKalb,* 473
*Delaware,* packet, purchased and marines sent to, 31; captures *Croyable,* 33; 461
Delaware, crossing of with Washington, 16-17
Denig, Robert L., officer, U.S.M.C., 318

Denby, Charles, American minister to Peking, 1894, 239
Denny, Frank L., officer, U.S.M.C., 225
*Denver,* 314; landing force in Nicaragua, 411; 418
Derne, Tripoli, expedition against, 43-7
Desertions, punishments for, 85; in Civil War, 220
*Des Moines,* 314
d'Estaing, French naval officer, 25
Destroyer named for Corporal Pruitt, 504
Destruction of property, Cuba, 1912, 326-7
Detachments at sea, 83-4; 1864, 222
Devil's Bend in Tabasco River, sketch of, 124
Dewey, George, officer, U.S.N., 255, 266
Diabol, Camp in Panama, 297
Diaz, Adolpho, President of Nicaragua, 409, 417-18, 421, 433
Diekirch, Luxembourg, 520
Dios Olivorio, bandit leader, Dominican Republic, 358
Diplomatic representative to Korea, supporting of, 240-2
Diplomatic Mission, supporting, 340
Disarming: Cubans, 321; in Dominican Republic, 354-5; Haitians, 382-3; Nicaragua, 422-3
Discipline: Navy and marines, 1775, 11; marines help enforce, 84; 38, 85, 190-91, 245-6
Disillusionment after the World War, 525-6
Disintegration at beginning of Civil War, 192-3
Disorders, Dominican Republic, 339-40
Distribution: Marine Corps, 1809, 48; 1833, 105; 1847, 166; 1855, 168; at beginning of Civil War, 253; marines in Cuba, 1906, 320; in Army of Cuban Occupation, 322; marine brigade in Cuba, 1912, 329-30; in Dominican Republic, 352; in Haiti, 385; Marine Corps at end of World War, 472
*Dixie,* 293, 397, 314, 317
Dollar Diplomacy, 342
*Dolphin,* 258-9, 299; cutter, 17
Domestic disturbances, 86, 187
Dominica, Island of, Gamble's trip to, 67
Dominican Republic: 339 *et seq.;* disorders in, 339-40; attempts to set up orderly government in, 340; map of, 341; Congress, 351; towns occupied by marines, 351; rebels scattered, 351; distribution of marines in, 352; establishing military government in, 352-3; campaign against bandits in, 357 *et seq.;* natives of, as soldiers, 362; dissatisfaction in, 365; change in attitude of people of, 1920, 367; co-operation of, 367-8; government of returned to local control, 368; stations of marines in, 1924, 369; improvements of during occupation, 369-70

"Don't Give Up the Ship," 61
Dooley, sergeant, U.S.M.C., 278
Dorward, general, British Army, Boxer Rebellion, 1900, 283
Doughty, Isaac T., officer, U.S.M.C., 202
Doyen, Charles A., officer, U.S.M.C., 232; in Dominican Republic, 342; in World War, 473-4
Draft Riots, 218
*Drake,* Jones's battle with, 18
Draper, Henry L., officer, U.S.M.C., 269-70
Drumming out of garrison, 38
Drummond's Island, relief expedition to, 1841, 93
Dulany, William, officer, U.S.M.C., 1837, 102; in Mexico, 127
Dulany's marines at Fort Brooke, 104
Dulany's Regiment, 136
Dunbeck, Charley, officer, U.S.M.C., 513, 515
Duncan, Donald F., officer, U.S.M.C., killed in World War, 484
Dunlap, Robert H., officer, U.S.M.C., 275-77, 431-2
Dunlap's Battalion in Dominican Republic, 347
Dunkirk, 468
DuPont, S. F., officer, U.S.N., 201-2
DuPont's Squadron, 201
Dutch at Curaçao aided by marines, 34
Duties of marines: Revolutionary War, 26-7; early 1800's, 82; on shore and at sea, 83-4; general, 1815 to 1846, 86; with Army against the Cherokees, 104; 1847, 166; in the African Squadron, 181-3; general routine, 191; at sea, 209-10; in battles at sea, 215; routine, peacetime, 1890, 244; in the Gilded Age, 244-5; in the Philippines, 270-2; in Cuba in Sugar Intervention, 336; in Dominican Republic, 358; in Haitian Gendarmerie, 390; 1916, 450; U. S. and foreign shore, World War, 472; with Army, World War, Chap. XVII; since World War, 524; at sea, 547; prescribed by Naval Policy, 554; 1939, 554; past and present, 554-5; probable future, 555; in China since World War, 529 *et seq.*
Dutton, Robert McN., officer, U.S.M.C., 280

E

Earliest marines, 3; in Revolution, 6-7
Earliest marine officers, 12
Early, Jubal, Confederate general, 211; Early's Corps on raid, 211
Early officers, U.S.M.C., 32
Early years of the Marine Corps, 33 *et seq.;* résumé of, 51-2
Earthquake, at San Francisco, 309; Managua, Nicaragua, 445
East Coast Expeditionary Force, 527

East Florida, marines operating in, 49-51
East India Squadron, formed, 91; at Canton, 92; 169, 171-2; operations taking forts of Canton, 172 *et seq.*
East India Station, 1853-4, 170
Eastern Area, of Nicaragua, 434-5, 437, 440, 442
Eastern Branch of Potomac River, naval vessels in, 37; 72
Eastern District of Dominican Republic, 363
Eaton, William, commander of expedition against Derne, 44; attack on Derne, 46
Eberle, E. W., officer, U.S.N., 342-3
Economic conditions in Dominican Republic, 1919, 365
Edelin, James, officer, U.S.M.C., at Norfolk, 197
Edson, Alvin, officer, U.S.M.C., 115; at Panuco, Mexico, 117; Edson's Battalion at Vera Cruz, 119-20; on Tabasco River, 123-4
Edson, M. A., officer, U.S.M.C., 435-6; Edson's patrol up the Coco River, 435 *et seq.;* 436
Education, 305-6; for marines, 526; in the Marine Corps, 545-6; of officers, 245
Edwards, Philip, early marine officer, 30
Egypt, 44; in 1882, 224-5
Eight-inch howitzers, 459
Eightieth Division, 515
Eighth Marines, 398, 457, 460, 463
Eighty-eighth Company, 468
Eighty-ninth Division, 517
Eix, center of resistance, France, 477-8
El Caney, Cuba, 261
El Chipote, Nicaragua, attack on, 430; Sandino's Camp, 431
El Molino del Rey, Mexico, 129
El Tejar, Mexico, 303-4; march to relieve, 304
Election riots in Washington, 187
Elections, Nicaragua, supervision of, 421-2, 437-8
Eleventh Regiment, 422, 424, 459, 464 *et seq.;* in Nicaragua, 431, 433, 435, 440, 442
Elizabeth River, Va., 69-70, 204
Elliott, George F., officer, U.S.M.C., 258, 266, 267, 295-6, 310; to Peking, 238; in Korea, 1871, 244
Ellis, Earl H., officer, U.S.M.C., 498
Empire, Panama, 294-6
Engineers of the Marine Corps, 551
English Channel, 467
English troops, 281-2
*Enterprise,* captures *Flambeau,* 35; on Guadeloupe station, 35; 42, 47, 50; fight with *Boxer,* 62; with *L'Aigle,* 35
*Enterprize,* sloop on Lake Champlain, 6; record of earliest marines on, 6
Equipment, for marines, 1775, 12; furnished by Pennsylvania, 13; in Revolu-

## INDEX

Equipment—*cont'd*
  tion, 25-6; in Indian wars, 97-8; *see also* Uniforms
Erie, Lake, 54; Perry's squadron on, 55
Erie, Pa., marines at, 83
Escondida River, Nicaragua, 419
Esperanza, Cuba, 318
Essen "Hook," Blanc Mont operation, 506
*Essex*, cruise of, 1813, 63-6; defeated at Valparaiso, 66
*Essex Junior*, 64-6
Estenoy, Evaristo, Cuban rebel, 324-5
Estili, Nicaragua, 424
Estrada, Juan, Nicaraguan general, 409
European Squadron, 224-5
European waters, 1776-77, marines and Navy in, 17-18
Evans, F. T., officer, U.S.M.C., 469
Everglades, hunting Seminoles in, 102-3
Expeditions: against Derne, 43-7; down the St. Lawrence, 58; into Florida, 1836-42, 100-4; to Arctic, 225-6; Alvarado, Mexico, 120-21; *vs* Barataria pirates, 76-7; Cuba, 1906, 314-15; 317; Cuba, 1912, 326; against Derne, 43-7; into Florida, 1836-42, 100-4; Korea, 239, 242-3; Japan, 169 *et seq.*; Matagalpa, 426; New Providence, 13-15, 18-19; Panama, 1885, 232-5; Paraguay, 1855, 185; Philippines, 272; Poteca, 436; up the Rio Grande, 111-13; Samar, P. I., 271-9; Sumatra, 90; Tabasco, 114-16; 123-4; Tunis, 47; Vera Cruz, 1914, 298 *et seq.*
Exposition Guards, 250

### F

Fagan, Louis E., officer, U.S.M.C., at Fort Fisher, 216
Falkland Islands, 1831, marines in, 90
*Falmouth*, 185
Farragut, David G., U.S.N., 202; his attack on Mobile, 211-2
Fauntleroy, D., officer, U.S.N., 147
Feland, Logan, officer, U.S.M.C., 319, 336, 420, 431, 435, 438, 487, 529
Fernandina, East Florida, capture of, 50; 201
Fifth Battalion, 270
Fifth Corps, A.E.F., 517
Fifth Marines, in Haiti, 374; in Nicaragua, 420, 423-4, 440; World War, 453; in Belleau Wood, 481-2; 585; 587-8; at Soissons, 492, 494-5; taking Vierzy, 495-6, 497, 501, 503, 507
Fifth Brigade, authorized, 464; sent to France, 465; assigned to S.O.S., 465-6; 467, 471
Fifth Machine Gun Battalion, 464
Fifty-fifth Company, Cuba, 334
Fifteenth Regiment of Marines in Dominican Republic, 363, 471
Fifteenth Infantry, 309, 530, 533

Fifty-first Company, 419
Fighting Spirit of Navy, 35-6; marines, 130
Fiji Islands, Wilkes' ship at, 92; second expedition to, 93; in 1855, 177
Filibusters: Walker in Nicaragua, 236; on Long Island, 1869, 247, 408
Filibustering Vessel, 410
Financial Supervision over Dominican Government, 339
Firearms Collected in Dominican Republic, 355, 366
Fire, at Boston, 1872, 247; Portland, Maine, 247
First Advanced Base Brigade, 300-302
First Army, Americans, 499, 510
First Corps, at St. Mihiel, 499-500
First Division, U.S.A., 473-4, 491
First landing operation by marines, 15
First marines, 3
First marine officer, 12
First Marine Aeronautic Company (World War), 467, 469
First Marine Aviation Squadron (World War), 467
First Marine Brigade, P. I., 271-9; 308; in Haiti, 376, 386, 407; Fleet Marine Force, 500
First Marine Training Regiment, 510
First Moroccan Division, 491, 494
First Provisional Regiment, Cuba, 324, 326
First real brigade, 270
First Regiment, 270; in China, 283; battalions of, 295-6; 300, 302, 307, 317-18; 368; in Haiti, 379 *et seq.*; 457, 459, 468
Fisherman's Point, Cuba, 257
"Fita-Fita" of Samao, 306
Fleet Marine Force, 529, 544; organization and stations, 550
Fletcher, F. F., rear admiral, U.S.N., 300, 302-4
Flintlock muskets, 26
Flogging, 38, 85
Flores, Jose M., of California, 145
Florida Indian War, 81
*Florida*, 461
Florida Expedition, 103
Florida Keyes, operations along, 99
Florida pirates, 88
Floyd, Oliver, officer, U.S.M.C., 426, 428
*Fly*, schooner, 13, 14
Flying in the Marine Corps, 553
Foch, Marshal of France, 479, 502
Fokker transport planes, 432
Folly Island, S. C., 209
Football, 525
Foote, commander, U.S.N., at Canton, 174
Foochow, China, 537
Forest of Retz, France, 491, *see* Villers-Cotterets Forest
Foreign Policy, marines' support of, 286; in Caribbean Sea, 286; changes in, 338, 447

## INDEX

Formosa, punitive operations in, 237
Forney, James, officer, U.S.M.C., 211, 261; in Formosa, 1867, 238; strike duty, 247
Forrest, French, officer, U.S.N., 114, 185
Fort Accachappa, Mexico, 115
Fort Adams, near New Orleans, 49
Fort Brooke, Fla., 95-6, 99
Fort Clark, N. C., 199
Fort Crockett, Texas, Eighth Marines at, 457, 460
Fort Dallas, Fla., 103
Fort Dipitie, Haiti, capture of, 383-4
Fort Donelson, 210
Fort Douglas, Utah, 452
Fort Drane, Fla., 95
Fort Fisher, N. C., attack on, 214-17
Fort Gaines, Ala., 211
Fort George, attack on, 56
Fort Hamilton, N. Y., 127
Fort Hatteras, N. C., 199
Fort Henry, 210
Fort Jackson, La., 202
Fort King, Fla., 95
Fort Lauderdale, Fla., 103
Fort Liberte, Haiti, 382
Fort McHenry, Baltimore, Md., 195
Fort Madison, 65
Fort Mervine, San Francisco, Cal., 141
Fort Montague, New Providence, 14
Fort Morgan, Ala., 211
Fort Nassau, New Providence, 15, 18
Fort National, Haiti, 377
Fort Ozama, D. R., 369
Fort Pickens, Fla., 196
Fort Pillow, 210
Fort Pitt, marines with Willing at, 20
Fort Polk, Texas, 1847, 111; sketch of, 112
Fort Riviere, Haiti, capture of, 384-5; destruction of, 385
Fort St. John, La., marines at, 1808, 49
Fort St. Philip, La., 202
Fort San Geronimo, D. R., landing at, 344-5
Fort Santa Cruz, Guam, 263
Fort Sumter, S. C., 1861, 195, 208
Fort Wagner, S. C., 207
Fort Washington, 74; 1861, 195
Fortress Monroe, 97, 196
Forts of Canton, bombardment of, 173; destruction of, 176
Forts of Santiago, occupied, 381
Forbes, W. Cameron, 406
Forbes Commission in Haiti, 406
Foreign stations, 306
Forty-fifth Company, 478
Forty-first Division, A.E.F., 465
Forty-fourth Infantry, 76
Forty-third Company in Cuba, 335
*Forward*, pirate ship, 229
Fourragere, French, 510
Fourteenth Marines, 471
Fourteenth Infantry in China, 284
Fourth Army, French, 502, 509

Fourth Brigade, 463, 465-6, 471, 476-7, 479-80; return to U. S. and casualties of, 522; *see* Belleau Wood, Soissons attack, St. Mihiel, Mont Blanc, Meuse-Argonne, and Army of German Occupation
Fourth Company at Santo Domingo City, D. R., 344
Fourth Division, U.S.A., in Mexican War, 128
Fourth Regiment Marines, 300, 304; in Dominican Republic, 348 *et seq.;* march to Santiago, 348-9; 368; to Shanghai, 532, 535; reinforced, 536; 1937 to date, 538-9
*Fox*, schooner, 89
Foxado, Porto Rico, landing at, 89
France, difficulties with, 1798, 29-30; Paris Exposition, 250; first marines, 1917, 373; marine aviation in, 367-8; duty in S.O.S., 473-6
Fraser, Mrs. James C., purchased Belleau Wood, 491
Frederic, Md., marines at, 37
French and Indian War, 4
French Army, aid of Washington, 25
French Canal Company, Panama, 232, 290-94
French decoration for World War, 522
French land at Port au Prince, Haiti, 376-7
French privateer capturing U. S. vessels, 1798, 29
French retire from Curaçao, 34
French Revolution in Haiti, 372
Fremont, John C., officer, U.S.M.C., activities in California, 139-150, 154-6
Fremont Battalion, 143, 155, 156
Frigates, six, authorized by Congress, 28
*Frolic vs Wasp*, War of 1812, 59
Frontera, Mexico, capture of, 115-16, 123
Fuller, Ben H., officer, U.S.M.C., 267, 402; as commandant, 543
Fuller, Paul, diplomatic representative to Haiti, 374-5
Funston, Frederick, brigadier general, U.S.A., 303-4, 321

### G

Gaines, general, U.S.A., 95
Gainesville, Florida, 95
Galapagos Islands, Porter at, 1813, 64
Gale, Anthony, made commandant, 82; dismissed, 83
*Galena*, 229, 232
Galveston, 298, 303, 337, 457
*Galvez, Bernardo de,* Spanish governor, New Orleans, 9
Gamble, John M., officer, U.S.M.C., 63-9; at Nukuhiva, 65; war with Marquesans, 66-7; mutineers, 68; sails for Hawaii, 68; captured, 68-9; later life, 69
Gandelu, France, 480

## INDEX

*Ganges,* 30; marines for, 31
Garde D'Haiti, 403-6
Garland, Addison, officer, U.S.M.C., 180, 217
Garrisons, standard strength of, 39
Garrisoning the Dominican Republic, 355
Garrobo, Nicaragua, 436-7
Gassed in World War, 478; gas attacks, 487
Gates, colonel, U.S.A., 118
Gatling guns, 251
Gendarmerie of Haiti, 386, 388-94, 396, 402-5
*General Arnold,* privateer, captured the *Nanny,* 24-5
*General Greene,* supporting Toussaint, 36
General Headquarters, A.E.F., 510
*General Sherman,* in Korea, 239
"Gentleman Sailors," Marines on privateers, 24
Georgia State Navy, 10
Georgia Volunteers, 49
Germainvilliers, France, 476
Germany, 470
German advance on Paris, 479-81
German Army retreats into Germany, 520
German fleet, World War, 456-7
German submarines, 460-61
*Germantown,* in Uruguay, 184
German vessels, interned, 452
Gettysburg, maneuvers, 527
Gibbons, Floyd, at Belleau Wood, 484
Gilded Age, 252 *et seq.*
Gilfillon, officer, U.S.M.C., 478
Gillespie, Archibald H., officer, U.S.M.C., agent to Cal., 139; activities in Cal., 140, 143, 144; besieged at Los Angeles, 145-6; retreat, 146; with Kearny, 149-50
Gillespie's riflemen, 147
Gillespie's volunteers, 150
Gillmore, general, U.S.A., 207
Glass, Henry, commander, U.S.N., 263
Glenn, Harry, private, U.S.M.C., 273-4
Goave, Grant and Petit, 36
Goldsborough, officer, U.S.N., 206
Good, Henry, sergeant major, U.S.M.C., 258
Good Neighbor Policy, 407, 447
Gomez, José, of Cuba, 313
Gomez Rebellion, Cuba, 1917, 332
Gonaives, Haiti, 380; operations *vs* cacos at, 380-81
Gonave, Island of, 390
Gondrecourt, France, 473, 476
Gosport, Va., 69
Government, in Dominican Republic by U. S. forces, 354; regular re-established, 369
Government, Imperial of China, 280-81, 285
*Governor,* transport, 200
Grahamville, S. C., 213
Granada, Nicaragua, relief of, 412-13

Grand Fleet, duty with, in World War, 461-2
Grande Riviere, Haiti, 378, 381, 383, 397-8
Grant, U. S., officer, U.S.A., 133
Grayson, J. C., officer, U.S.M.C., Civil War, 218
Grenades, hand, in the Revolution, 26
Great Britain and seal protection, 226
Great Lakes, 1812, 54
Great Lakes, Training Station, Ill., 461
Greeks with Eaton at Derne, 44
Greeley Polar Expedition, 226
Green Mountain Boys, 6
Green, Israel, officer, U.S.M.C., 188-9
*Greenwich,* 67; commanded by Gamble, 64; captured *Seringapatam,* 64; burned, 68
Gregory, F. H., officer, U.S.N., 110
Greytown, Nicaragua, 1852, 178; raided, 179
Grog, 85
Gross, Samuel, private, U.S.M.C., 385

**H**

Haines, Henry C., officer, U.S.M.C., 262
Haiti, early operations in, 36; relations with, 1817-21, 91; 1888, 229, 287; marines from Dominican Republic to, 344; financial troubles, 371; conditions in, 371 *et seq.;* gold reserve removed, 372; colonial history, 372; policy of United States to, 372-5; map of, 372; marines in, 385; the *corvée,* 392-3; supervision over, 403; normal conditions in, 402; unity of command, 402-403; strikes of 1929, 404-5; disturbances of 1929, 404-6; withdrawal from, 407
Haiti, caco revolt, 393 *et seq.,* 401-2; curfew order, 404; campaign of 1920, 399-400; peace restored in 1921, 402
Haitian Government, Bryan plan to control, 374
Haitian, Laws about Gendarmerie, 386; psychology, 391
Haitian Revolution of 1915, 375-6
Haitian troops disarmed, 382
Haitian towns, occupied, 379
Haitians as soldiers, 388-9
Haitianization of Garde, 406
Halford, Frank, officer, U.S.M.C., 275; in Cuba, 336
Hall, Newt, officer, U.S.M.C., 281, 345
Halls of Montezuma, 133
Hamet, deposed Pasha of Tripoli, U. S. effort to restore, 44
Hamilton, George W., officer, U.S.M.C., 513, 518
Hampton Roads, British Squadron in, 70, 200, 204, 215; 466
*Hancock,* marines of, 16
*Hancock,* 300, 302, 374, 473

## INDEX

Hankow, China, 308; outbreak of 1927, 531
Hanneken, Herman H., officer, U.S.M.C., 396; kills Charlemagne, 396-8
Hanrahan, D. C., captain, U.S.N., of North Bombing Group, 468
Harboard, J. G., U.S.A., takes command of Fourth Brigade, 479, 482; at Soissons, 491
Harding, Warren G., 527
Harding, Arthur E., officer, U.S.M.C., 342
Hardships of duty in Dominican Republic, 358
Harllee, W. C., officer, U.S.M.C., 318; in Dominican Republic, 366; 544
Harpers Ferry, John Brown at, 188-9
*Harriet Lane*, 199
Harrington, Francis H., officer, U.S.M.C., 245
Harris, John, officer, U.S.M.C., 136; made commandant, 190, 198; death, 219
Harris, J. C., lieutenant, U.S.M.C., at New Orleans, 1862, 203
Harrison, General William H., 57
*Hartford*, at New Orleans, 203; at Mobile, 212; at Formosa, 1867, 238
Hatch, Charles B., officer, U.S.M.C., 346, 372
Hatch's Battalion at Monte Cristi, 347
Hatchee-Lustee, battle of, 100-1
Hatfield, G. D., officer, U.S.M.C., 426
Hato Mayo, D. R., 359
Hatteras Inlet, 1861, 199
Havana, 254; marines at, 263, 313-19
Havana Province, Cuba, 319
Hawaiian Islands, 307
Hawaiian Maneuvers, 527
Headquarters, at Philadelphia, 31; moved to Washington, 38; organization of, 546
Heavy artillery, 459-60, 469
*Helena*, 308
Helmet, 250, *see* Uniform
Henderson, Archibald, officer, U.S.M.C., early record, 83; made commandant, 83; in Indian Wars, 96-101, 187; death, 189; résumé of life, 189-90
*Henderson*, 466, 473-74, 533
Heywood, Charles, officer, U.S.M.C., 205; at Mobile, 212, 228, 233, 248; made commandant, 251
Heywood's Battalion, 248
High Commissioner to Haiti, John H. Russell, 402, 403, 406
Higsbee, John H., officer, U.S.M.C., 233
Higsbee's Battalion in Panama, 233-4
Hill, Charles S., officer, U.S.M.C., 459, 532
Hilton Head, island, S. C., 201
Hinche, Haiti, 394-5
Hirshinger, J. H., officer, U.S.M.C., killed, 346
Holcomb, T., officer, U.S.M.C., 484, 487; 497; made commandant, 544
Holland, in World War, 468

Hollins, John, officer, U.S.N., 178-9
Holmes, Maurice G., officer, U.S.M.C., 469
Home Squadron, 106, 111, 118, 127, 167, 186
Honduras, 440-41; bandits retreat to, 433
Honey Hill, S. C., attack on, 213
Hong Kong, 1842, 91; 169, 254
Honolulu, 306
Hoover, Herbert, President, 528
Hope, Edward B., officer, U.S.M.C., 478
Hopkins, Esek, commodore, 11, 12, 15
Hopkins' Squadron, marines for, 12; fitting out, 12, 13; plans for use, 13; on New Providence Expedition, 15
Hormiguero, Cuba, 315
*Hornet*, sloop, 13, 14; at Derne, 45, 47; fight with *Peacock*, 61; in Haiti, 1821, 91
Hotchkiss revolving cannon, 251
*Houston*, 536
Howitzers, 459
Huerta, Mexican general, 298, 299, 305
Huertas, Panamanian general, 296
Hughes, J. R., officer, U.S.M.C., 497
Hull, Jos. B., officer, U.S.M.C., 142
Humphrey, M. B., officer, U.S.M.C., 422
Hunt, Leroy P., officer, U.S.M.C., 507
Hunter, lieutenant, U.S.N., at Alvarado, Mexico, 120-21
Hunter, Robert, officer, U.S.M.C., mortally wounded, 437
Huntington, Robert W., officer, U.S.M.C., 255; Huntington's Battalion at Guantanamo Bay, 256-60; reviewed by President, 263
*Huron*, in China, 530

I

Iams, Ross L., U.S.M.C., in Haiti, 385
Idea of marines, 2, 4
Ill-fated march across Samar, 275 *et seq.*
Imperial Government of China, 176-7
Improved conditions today, 547
Imus, P. I., 267
Increases in Corps, 1799, 1856, and 1858, 168; 1809, 47; 1834, 81; during Mexican War, 126; during Civil War, 194; World War, 450, 464
*Independence*, 160, 163; marines on, 464; at Panama, 180
*Indiana*, marines operate guns, 261; 317
Indian Head, Md., marines at, 1813, 75; 458
Indian attacks, 156; boat crews in Nicaragua, 436; fighting, 186; fighting in East Florida, 51
Indians, movement to the West, 94-105; reservation, 94; wars, 1836-42, 94-105
Insignia, Marine Corps, adopted, 250
Institute, Marine Corps, 526
Instruction of marines, 1897, 245
*Insurgente*, captured by *Constellation*, 34
Insurrection in Philippines, 271 *et seq.*

## INDEX

Intervention, *see* Occupation.
Intervention: in Cuba in 1906-9, 312 *et seq.*; in 1912, 324-7; in 1917-22, 332 *et seq.*; in the Dominican Republic, Chapter XIII; cause of, 339-40; in Haiti, Chapter XIV; in Mexico in 1914, 298 *et seq.*; in Nicaragua in 1850's, 178-9; in 1912, 410-11; in 1927, 420 et seq.; résumé of, 446-7; in Panama, 179 *et seq.*, 287-98; in Uruguay, 228-9
Interventions in Cuba under the Platt Amendment, Chapter XII.
Investigations of affairs in Haiti, 1930, 406
*Iowa*, 287
Irish Sea, Jones's cruise in, 18
"Irishtown," Brooklyn, 1867, 247
*Iroquois*, at Japan, 1868, 237
Islands, *see* name of
Issoudun, France, 465
Isthmus of Panama, protecting transit, 230-1; 236
Izard, general, U.S.A., 76

### J

Jackson, Andrew, general, 77-80
Jackson's Army at New Orleans, 78-80
Jackson, private, U.S.M.C., killed in Nicaragua, 423
Jacmel, Haiti, 36; occupied, 380; 404
James, W. C., officer, U.S.M.C., 539
Japan: with Perry in, 168-71; opening of, 169; in revolution, 171; protecting Americans in, 236; forts bombarded in, 236; activities in 1867, 237; treaty ports opened, 1868, 237; foreign residents guarded by marines, 1868, 237; troops of in Boxer Rebellion, 1900, 283, 285; 307; domination of China by, 535 *et seq.*
*Java*, fight with *Constitution*, 60; 74
Jaulny, France, 501
Jefe Director, Nicaragua, 425, 446
Jefferson reduces the Marine Corps, 37
Jesup, T. H., general, U.S.A., 98
Jesup's Army against Seminoles, 1837, 101
Jiminez, President of Dominican Republic, 343
Jicaro, Nicaragua, 441
Jinotega, Nicaragua, 434, 442
Joint expedition: to Hatteras Inlet, 199; to Port Royal, S. C., 199-200; to Fort Fisher, 214-17
Jones, Secretary of Navy, 75
Jones, James H., officer, U.S.M.C., 172
Jones, John Paul, marines with, 1777, 18
Jones's Second cruise, 22-4
Jones, Thomas ap C., defends New Orleans, 77-8; in California, 93; landing at Monterey, 1842, 94
*Junon*, British ship, attempts to capture, 70
*Jupiter*, 300

### K

Kalakan River, 266
Kane, Theodore P., officer, U.S.M.C., 319; in Dominican Republic, 346; 402
Karmany, Lincoln, officer, U.S.M.C., 298; in Cuba, 1912, 326; in Cuba, 331-2
Kearny, general, U.S.A., march to California, 149; met by Gillespie, 149; Gillespie with, 150; 152
Kellogg, Secretary of State, 418
Kelly, James J., private, U.S.M.C., 504
Kelton, Allen C., officer, U.S.M.C., 265
Kelton's Battalion in Guam, 264-5
*Kentucky*, 317
Keyser, Ralph S., officer, U.S.M.C., 488, 492, 496
Key West, Fla., 99, 254-5, 317; as base, 1822, 89; fleet at, 1873, 227-8
Kimberly, A. L., officer, U.S.N., commanded landing force, Korea, 1871, 241
Kincade, G. M., officer, U.S.M.C., 318
Kingsbury, R. S., officer, U.S.M.C., 356
Kirkman, W. W., officer, U.S.M.C., at Canton, China, 173; 175
Kirkpatrick, Edgar G., officer, U.S.M.C., 400
Klemann, J. V., officer, U.S.N., 315-16
Knapp, Harry S., officer, U.S.N., Military Governor of Dominican Republic, 352; in Haiti, 377
Know-Nothing Party, 187
Knox, Secretary of State, 325, 408
Korea; *General Sherman* burned by natives, 1866, 239; punitive expedition to, 239-44; attacks on forts, 240-44; landing of sailors and marines at, 1871, 241; "Citadel," storming of, 242; expedition to, 1871, 242-3; landing of sailors and marines at, 1894, 244; guarding legation in, 244

### L

*L'Aigle*, captured by *Enterprise*, 35
"La Fuerza," Havana, 314
Lafitte brothers, 76-7
La Luz Mine, Nicaragua, raided by Sandino, 434-6
La Paz, Mexico, 156
La Vega, D. R., occupied, 351; 353-4
Labor Riots, 248-9
*Lachawanna* at Mobile, 212
Ladrone Islands, 263
Laguna, Mexico, marines at, 135-6
Lake Borgne, British advance *via*, 76; battle on, 77-8
Lake Champlain, 5; in 1812, 75
Lake Charles, La., 467
Lake Erie, Perry's squadron, 55
Lake Erie, Battle of, 57-8
Lake Okeechobee, Fla., battle on, 102
Lake Thompson, 103
La Mesa, Battle of, 154

Lanang River, Samar, P. I., 275-6
Lanang, Samar, P. I., 76-8
Lancaster, Pa., prison camp at, 37
Landing Force of marines, first, 13-14
Landings at: Alexandria, Egypt, 225; Alvarado, Mexico, 113; in Argentina, 1890, 230; in Brazil, 184; in California, 1842, 93-4; at Canton, 1856, 174; Cap Haitien, 1915, 375; Colon, Panama, 1903, 292; Cuba, June 1898, 257; Fiji Islands, 1855, 177; Formosa, 1867, 238; Fort Fisher, 215-16; Fort Sumter, 209; Guacanaybo Bay, 1917, 333-4; Guaymas, Mexico, 157; Havana, 1906, 314; Japan, 1853, 170; Korea, 1871, 241; Korea, 1894, 244; Mazatlan, 163-4; Monte Cristi, D. R., 346-7; at Monterey, 1842, 94; Monterey, 1846, 140-1; Navassa Island, 226; Nicholas' battalion of marines at New Providence, 14-15; Nicaragua, 1894, 236; at Bluefields, 415, 417; Nicaragua, from *Tacoma*, 411; from *California* and *Denver* in Nicaragua, 411; Point Isabel, Texas, 109; Port Olongapo, P. I., 266; in Panama, 1800, 180-1; Panama, 1856, 180, 231; Panama, 1901, 287, 292-3; Port au Prince, 376; Port Olongapo, P. I., 1899, 266; Port Royal, S. C., 201; Puerto Plata, D. R., 1916, 346; Santa Barbara, 142-3; San Francisco, 141; San Juan Bautista, 116, 122; San Pedro, 143, 148; Santo Domingo City, 344; Shanghai, 1854, 172; Shanghai, 1924, 531; Sumatra, 1832, 90; Tampico, Mexico, 117-8; Tuxpan, 122; Vera Cruz, 119-20; 1914, 300-3; Yokohama, 1868, 237
Landings, *see also* Operations and attacks on coast localities
Landres-St. George, France, 513
Landsmen, marines for, 168, 194
Lane, Rufus H., officer, U.S.M.C., 354
Lang, William, officer, U.S.M.C., 111
Lang's Battalion at Fort Polk, 111
La Paz Centro, Nicaragua, 423
Larkin, Thomas O., 94, 139
Larsen, Henry L., officer, U.S.M.C., 507, 513, 515
Las Cahobas, Haiti, 395, 400
Las Canitas, D. R., 357
Last marine of the Revolution, 27
Las Trencheras, D. R., 348-9; attack on by Fourth Regiment, tactics used, 349
Latin-American countries, 407; Republics, 408
Laurens, John, colonel of S. C. Marines, 25
Lavallette, E. A. F., officer, U.S.N., his squadron, 157; 163-4
La Vega, D. R., 353-4
*Lawrence,* on Lake Erie, 55
Laws, U. S. and Haitian, about Gendarmerie, 389
Leathernecks, 40

Lee, Robert E., 189
Lee, Harry, officer, U.S.M.C., 308; in Dominican Republic, 369; Military Governor, 369; report on D. R., 370; 491; at Soissons, 497
Leffincourt, France, march of the Fourth Brigade to, 510
Legations at Peking, defense of, 281-2
Legation Guard, China, 530; Peking, 285, 308
Legation Guard in Korea, 307
Legation Guard, Nicaragua, 411, 416-17; withdrawal of, 425
Legation, landing to protect, 344
Le Havre, France, 465, 475
Lejeune, John A., officer, U.S.M.C., 262, 293-7, 302-4; in Cuba, 327; 431; 502; as commandant, 542
Leogane, Haiti, occupied, 379, 404
Leon, Nicaragua, 410-12; occupation of, 415; 444
Le Trou, Haiti, 384
*Levant*, fight with *Constitution*, 63; 140; at Canton, 1856, 173, 176
Levonski, Charles J., sergeant, U.S.M.C., 441
*Lexington,* 17
*Lexington,* sloop, 90
Liberals, in Nicaragua, 409-10, 416-17, 438
Liberia, 182
*Liberty*, schooner, on Lake Champlain, marines on, 6
Life in the Marine Corps in 1850's, 190
Li Hung Chang, Chinese viceroy, 244
Lincoln, Abraham, 193, 207
Lincoln, Benjamin, general, Amer. Army, 25
Lincoln's Army, captured by British at Charleston, 25
Line of communications, in D. R., 349
Linscott, H. D., officer, U.S.M.C., 435
Little, L. McCarty, officer, U.S.M.C., 398, 550
Livingston, Richard, officer, U.S.M.C., 430
Lobos Island, 119
Loma Fortress, Nicaragua, 409, 416-17; occupied, 420
London, 461
Long, Charles G., officer, U.S.M.C., 297, 302, 415
Long's Battalion, in Nicaragua, 416
Long Island, filibusters on, 1869, 247
Longstreet, Daniel, Continental Marine officer, at New Orleans, 20
Los Angeles, 138; Gillespie besieged, 144 *et seq.;* first taking of, 143
Los Huertas, near Mexico City, 133
Losses, in Civil War, 220; in Dominican Rep., 349; in Nicaragua, 446-7; the first day at Belleau Wood, 484
*Louisiana,* 317
Louisiana, first marines in, 48
Louisiana Purchase Exposition, 310
Lovell, Solomon, Massachusetts general, 21

INDEX 571

Low, A. A., American minister to China, 240
Low, W. W., officer, U.S.M.C., killed in D. R., 352
Lower California, 144, 161
Lowndes, Edward R., officer, U.S.M.C., 317, 319
Lucas, Lewis C., officer, U.S.M.C., 258, 294-5
Luchu Islands, 170; Perry at, 169
Lucy-le-Bocage, France, 482, 484
Ludendorff, 489
Luxembourg, Grand Duchy of, 520
Luzon, Island of, 268
Lybian Desert, march over, 44
Lyman, Charles H., officer, U.S.M.C., 334

## M

Maas, Mexican general, 301
Macacca River, campaign, 96
Macao, 1844, legation at, 91
MacCarthy, Eugene, Marine officer on *Bonhomme Richard*, 22
Macdonough, Thos., officer, U.S.N., 75
*Macedonian*, fight with *United States*, 60; in war with pirates, 88-9
Machado, President of Cuba, 338
*Machias*, 287-8
Machine-gun units, 476; 50-caliber, 549
MacNulty, William K., officer, U.S.M.C., 432
Macoris, Dominican Republic, naval forces at, 344; Macoric Province, 353, 363
MacSwiney, sergeant, U.S.M.C., killed in Samar, 279
Maddox, Wm. A. T., officer, U.S.M.C., 142, 144, 146; *vs* Sanchez group, 151
Maddox's Volunteers, 155
Madero, Francisco, President of Mexico, 298-9
Madison, President, desired to control Lakes, 54
Madison Island, 64
Magill, Louis J., officer, U.S.M.C., 259
Magoon, Chas., provisional governor of Cuba, 323
Mahoney, J. E., officer, U.S.M.C., 259, 295, 297; in Cuba, 1912, 326; in 1917, 337; 409, 460
*Mahoning*, 1869, 247
Mail, U. S., robberies of, 528-9; guarding, 1921, 528; 1926, 529
*Maine*, blown up, 254-5
Maissade, Haiti, 394
Malta, 42
Mamelukes, 44
Mameluke Sword, 46-7, 251
Managua earthquake, marines in, 445
Managua, Nicaragua, 409, 411-12, 416
*Manassas*, Confederate ram, 203
Manchu dynasty, 279-80, 308
Manchuria, 537

Maneuvers, postwar, 527-8
Manicaragua, Cuba, 318
Manifest Destiny, supporting, 135-8
Manila, P. I., 266, 310; occupied, 256
Manila Bay, Battle of, 255-6
Manzanilla, Cuba, 260
Marbache Sector, France, defense of, 498-9
*Marblehead*, 236, 257, 539
March: from Egypt to Derne, 44-6; to Pueblo, Mexico, 127-8; of Mervine's force to Los Angeles, 147; to Los Angeles by Stockton's force, 151-2; to Peking, 284-5; to El Tejar, Mexico, 304; of Fourth Regiment to Santiago, D. R., 348-50; to the Rhine, 520-21
Mare Island, Cal., 217, 249, 266, 268, 300, 309, 454-6
*Marietta*, 315-16
Marina, Juan, Spanish governor, Guam, 264
Marinette, 464, 551
Marine Aviation in Nicaragua, 442
Marine Aeronautic Company, 467
Marine Band, 39, 250
Marine Battalions to Philippines, 266
Marine Brigade in Dominican Republic, 355
Marine Corps: establishment of, 31; early years of, 33 *et seq.*; artillery in Nicaragua, 414; Base, San Diego, 548; Institute, 526; Reserve, 471, 551-2; Schools, 545
Marine detachments at Sea, 244
Marine officer, first to be commissioned by Congress, 12
Marine officers, list of 1833, 105
Marines: from Continental Army, 12; in Philadelphia, 16; on Penobscot Expedition, 21; on privateers in Revolution, 24-5; before a Marine Corps, 28; first authorized under the constitution, 29; for the New Navy, 1798, 30; in Battle of Lake Erie, 57-8; on *Wasp*, 62; shortage in Civil War, 194 *et seq.*; in Haitian service, 387-8
Marksmanship, 309, 548
Marquesans, Porter's war with, 64; trouble with, 65-8
Marquesas Island, Porter's squadron at, 64-5
Marseilles, France, 465
Marsh, Aralzaman C., sergeant, U.S.M.C., 509
Marston, Ward, officer, U.S.M.C., 140, 142, 147, 151
Martinsburg, W. Va., 249
Maryland Navy and Marines, 10
Masaya, Nicaragua, 410-14
Maskoff, sergeant, U.S.M.C., 395
Massachusets Navy and Marines, 8-9
Massachusetts Navy on Penobscot Expedition, 20-22
Matachin, Panama, 233

Matagalpa, Nicaragua, 416, 420, 421, 436; Expedition, 426
Matanzas, province, Cuba, 313
Matthews, Calvin B., officer, U.S.M.C., 446
May-en-Multien, France, 480
Mayer, John L., officer, U.S.M.C., killed, 395
Mayo, Isaac, officer, U.S.N., 121
Maximum strength of Corps, 1918, 464
Mazatlan, Mexico, 139, 140, 156; operations at, 163 et seq.; Marine garrisons, 164-5, 300
McCalla, B. H., officer, U.S.N., 1885; his expeditionary force, 233-5; in Cuba, 257; in China, 280-82.
McCawley, Chas. G., officer, U.S.M.C., 207-10, 251
McClellan, general, U.S.A., 206
McCoy, Frank R., officer, U.S.A., 437
McCrea, officer, U.S.N., 288
McCreary, Wirt, officer, U.S.M.C., 318
McDougal, corporal, U.S.M.C., at Canton, 175
McDougal, Douglas C., officer, U.S.M.C., 438 et seq.
McKee, lieutenant, U.S.N., killed in Korea, 243
McKelvy, Wm. N., officer, U.S.M.C., 319, 413, 416
McKelvy's Battalion in Nicaragua, 414
McKenzie, lieutenant commander, U.S.N., in Formosa, 238
McKinley, President, reviews marines, 263
McLaughlin, John T., officer, U.S.N., Mosquito Fleet, 102-4
*McLane*, revenue cutter, 113
*Meade*, army transport, 298
Meade, James J., officer, U.S.M.C., 419
Meade, R. L., officer, U.S.M.C., 283
Meade's Battalion in Nicaragua, 419
Meaux, France, 480
Medals of Honor, 243, 359, 384, 504, 522
Mediterranean Squadron, 41, 43; operations of, 41-7; reduced, 1806, 47; in 1815, 86-7; 186
Mediterranean station, 1833, 105
Memphis, Tenn., 210
Mena, Nicaraguan general, 410-13
Menaucourt, France, 473
Mendieta, Cuban general, 329
Merkel, C. F., officer, U.S.M.C., 359
Mervine, Wm., officer, U.S.N., 140; defeated near San Pedro, 146-7
Mercine's March to Los Angeles, 147
*Merrimac*, attacks of, 204-6; *vs Monitor*, 206; Collier, 256
*Merrimack*, 34
Messersmith, major, U.S.M.C., 500
Meuse-Argonne, operations, 512-18; German defense, 512-14; plans for, 512-13; first day, 513-15; the break-through, 514-15; pursuit, 515-17; crossing of the Meuse, 516-18; losses, 520

Mexican Army, 119, 127
Mexican oil fields, 400
Mexican War, 106; theaters of operation, 107; naval preparedness, 113; plans for, 120; west coast operations, 156 et seq.; end of, 165
Mexican War to Civil War, 167-191
Mexico, readiness for duty in, 1913, 298; intervention in, 299-305
Mexico City, Scott's advance to, 120; attacks of, 128 et seq.; entered, 135
Miami, Florida, 99, 467-8
*Michigan*, 1917, in Cuba, 334
Middleton, James, officer, U.S.M.C., 34
Midway Island, 307
Miles, Nelson A., general, U.S.A., 262
Military government at Mazatlan, Mexico, 164; established in Dominican Republic, 352-3; officers in, 354; marines supporting, 355; in Haiti, 377, 385
Military governor of Dominican Republic, Harry Lee as, 369
Military Interventions, 407
Mill Prison, Plymouth, England, 17
Miller, Samuel, officer, U.S.M.C., 69; with Barney, 71; captured at Bladensburg, 73; 98; at Fort Brooks, Florida, 101
Mindanao Island, P. I., 271
Mindi, Panama, 297
Miniature army, 527
Minister: to Nicaragua, 1853, 179; to Cuba, 325
*Minneapolis*, 314
Minnesota, 199
Minnesota University students enlist, 455
Mirebalais, Haiti, 395
Missions of marines: in Mexican War, 107; in Cuba, 1912, 328-9; in Haiti, 379
Mississippi, operations on in Revolutionary War, 20; Union vessels in Civil War, 210
Mississippi Flotilla, 210
*Mississippi*, steamer, U.S.N., 113-15, 117, 122, 125, 135, 168, 177
*Mississippi*, U.S.S., 300, 303
Mitchell, governor of Georgia in East Florida affair, 50-51
Mobile, Ala., 76
Mobile Bay, Battle of, 211-12
Mobs in Haiti, 375
Moca, Dominican Republic, occupied, 351
Modern attacks, first by marines, 349
*Mohican*, 1870, 229
*Monata*, schooner, 117
Moncada, José, Nicaraguan, 417, 419, 422, 438-9, 446
*Monocacy*, in Japan, 1868, 237; Korea, 1871, 240-42; Taku, China, 1894, 239
Monroe Doctrine, 286, 299, 369, 408; Roosevelt's corollary to, 339
Mont Blanc, *see* Blanc Mont
*Montana*, in Cuba, 1917, 333

## INDEX

573

Monterey, Cal., landing in 1842, 93-4; during Mexican War, 138-41, 143, 155
Montevideo, 228-9
Montezuma, Halls of, 133
Montgirmont, France, 477-8
Montgomery, John B., officer, U.S.N., 141, 158
Monti Cristi, D. R., landing at 346-7
Mont-sous-les-Cotes, France, 477
Morale of Marines: in Civil War, 220; 245-6; in Dominican Republic, 365; in Germany, 521
Morong, P. I., 269
Moros, Samar Campaign, 271, 273-5, 279
Morristown, N. J., with Washington at, 17
*Morris,* at New Orleans, 1778, 19
Morris, R. V., officer, U.S.N., 42
Morris Island, S. C., 207, 209
*Morro Castle,* S. S., 303
Moselle River, France, 498
Moses, Franklin J., officer, U.S.M.C., 236, 317, 319, 340
Mosquito Fleet in Florida, 102-4
Mosquito Confederation, 178
Mosquito Indians, 437
Mound City, Ill., 218
Mount Hope, Panama, 297
Mouzon, France, 518
Mt. Vernon, marines at, 1813, 74
Mulejé, Mexico, landing at, 162
Mullan, Robt., Continental Marine officer, 12
Munro, Dana G., 406
Muse, Wm. S., officer, U.S.M.C., 230
Muskets in Revolution, 26; rifled, of 1870, 250
Musketry of Marines, 59, 60
Muth, Lawrence, sergeant, U.S.M.C., 400
Mutiny, prevented on *Bon Homme Richard,* 22
Mutinies, on ships in Revolution, 26; at Nukuhiva, 66-8; in Nicaragua of Guardias, 431, 440-42
Muy Muy, Nicaragua, 420
Myers, John T., officer, U.S.M.C., 264, 266, 280-81

### N

Naix-aux-Forges, France, 473
Nanking, protecting foreigners, 532-33
*Nashville,* 269, 291-3
Natchez, Miss., 49
*Natchez,* 183
National Bridge, Mexico, 128
National City Bank, 372
National Rifle Matches, 548
National Railroad of Haiti, 371
Native troops, officers over, 100
Nautilus Island, 21
*Nautilus,* in attack on Derne, 45
Navarette, D. R., marines join at, 350-51
Naval air station, Pensacola, 553

Naval aviation station, San Diego, 552
Naval base, Guam as, 265
Naval brigade, in South Carolina, 1864, 213; 302
Naval duels in war with France, 33-4
Naval expedition to Paraguay, 1855, 185
Naval forces, assist Army in Florida, 199; in Dominican waters; 342-3; to Nicaragua, 416, 20
Naval gun support of landing, 114
Naval preparedness for Mexican War, 106-113
Naval station, Cairo, Ill., 218
Naval vessels in American waters, 1777-79, 19
Naval vessels at Corinto, Nicaragua, 419
Naval war with France, marines in, 33-7
Navassa Island, landing on, 226
Navy: in War of 1812, 62; preparation for Civil War, 197; post-Civil War period, 224 *et seq.;* in War of 1812, use of, 58, 62; new, 1883, 251
Navy Department, 290, 292-4, 300, 314-15
Navy, Secretary of, 270, 298, 315
Navy Yard, Norfolk, 11; loss of, 196-7; marines reoccupy, 207
Negro Rebellion, Cuba, 324-7
*Nevada,* 461
Neptune Mine, Nicaragua, 435
Neutral rights, 1798, 29
Neutral zones, Nicaragua, 416-17
Neuvitas, Cuba, 318
Neville, Wendell C., officer, U.S.M.C., 258, 301-2, 319, 488; as commandant, 543
Nevers, France, 474
New Granada, treaty with, 287
*New Jersey,* marines in Dominican Republic, 346
New Orleans, vessels at, 1806, 49; battle of, 77-80; capture of, 1862, 202-4; marines occupy, 204; 300, 314
New Providence, Navassa Island, 13; expeditions to, 13-15, 18
New York, 39, 290, 461, 473; British in, 25; Civil War draft riots, 218
*New York,* 42, 271
New York volunteers, in Mexican war, 161; in Civil War, 213
*Newark,* 280
Newcastle, Del., marines at, 74
Newport News, Va., 317
Nicaragua: early interventions in, 178-9; 287, 297; intervention of 1912, 408 *et seq.;* marines supporting government, 409-16; growing unrest in, 416-17; Liberal revolt, 417-20; intervention of 1927, 419-46; Moncada revolt, 419 *et seq.;* force of marines establish neutral zone, 418-20; settlement by agreement, 421; disarming the country, 422-3; policing it, 423-40; police force, *see* Guardia National; results, 447

## 574  INDEX

Nicholas, Samuel, commissioned, 12; his landing at New Providence, 14-16
Nicholas' Battalion in battle of Trenton, 17
Nicholson, Augustus S., officer, U.S.M.C., 184-5
Nicoll, Wm., officer, U.S.M.C., 91
Nineteenth Company at Port de Paix, Haiti, 379
Ninety-sixth Company at Bouresches, 484
Ninth Infantry, 271-2, 283, 307, 477
Ninth Company at Puerto Plata, D. R., 350
Ninth Marines, 457, 460, 463; to Cuba, 1917, 337
Norfolk, 290, 314, 317, 455; defense of, 1813, 69-70
Norfolk Navy Yard, 70; loss and burning of, 196; retaken, 207
North Atlantic Blockading Squadron, 215
North Island, Cal., 305
North Sea, 456, 461, 473
Northern Area, Nicaragua, 433-4, 437, 439-40
Northern Bombing Group, 467-9
Nouel, Archbishop, 340
Novaleta, P. I., battle at, 267-8
Nueva Segovia Expedition, 426
Nueva Segovia, Nicaragua, 428, 430; reinforced, 432; neutralized, 433-4
Nukuhiva, marines at, 63-9; taken possession of, 64

### O

Oahu, Gamble at, 68, 527
O'Bannon, P. N., officer, U.S.M.C., 44-7; at Derne, 45-6; resignation, 47
Occupation: of Cap Haitien, 379; of Dominican Republic, cost and results of, 369-70; of Haiti, Chap. XIV, 379; of Leon, Nicaragua, 415; see also Interventions
Occupied towns, in Haiti, 1915, 385
Ocotal, Nicaragua, 424, 430; attack by Sandino, 426-7
Officers, appointment of, 81-2; Civil War, 194; Spanish War, 244
Officers: early Marine, 32; Continental Navy and Marines, commissioning of, 11; new Marine Corps, 545; in Service Schools, 545; on duty in Gendarmerie D'Haiti, 389-90
O'Day, E. F., officer, U.S.M.C., 432
Oglesby, D. G., officer, U.S.M.C., 364
O'Kelly, James J., marine officer on *Bon Homme Richard*, 22
*Oklahoma*, 461
Oldest branch of the Service, 4, 11
Old Fields, Md., Barney at, 72
Olongapo, P. I., 269-79, 308
Old Marine Corps, 546
One Hundred Thirty-Sixth Company, 461
*Oneida*, 1812, 54

*Oneida*, in Japan, 1868, 237
*Ontario*, 91
Operations: advanced base, 310-11; vs Alvarado, 113; in East Florida, 49-51; at Guaymas, 157; in Gulf of California, 162; at Hatteras Inlet, 1861, 199; at Mazatlan, 163; in the Mediterranean, 41-7; in Panama, 287-98; in Porto Rico, 262; at Puerta Plata, 346-7; at Subig Bay, 269; against Tuxpan, 122-3; (second) up Tabasco River, 123-6; on west coast of Mexico, 156 *et seq.*; at Vigan, 268; see also Landings
Operations and Training Section, 546
Oregon Territory, 1818, 91; 1842, 93
*Oregon*, 257; at Santiago, 268, 280
Oriente, Cuba, 334
Oriente Province, Cuba, 325, 328
Osaka, Japan, 237
Oscar, Haitian general, 375
Osceola, Seminole Chief, 94 *et seq.*
Ostermann, E. A., officer, U.S.M.C., 383
Ostend, Belgium, 468
Overseas Depot, 463
Overton Macon C., officer, U.S.M.C., 509; killed, 514
Ouanaminthe, Haiti, 395
Outbreaks against foreigners, China, 1866, 238
Owen, Clarence S., officer, U.S.M.C., 307

### P

Pacific Cable Company, 307
Pacific Coast, first marines to, 217
Pacific Squadron, 106, 139, 294-6; in Mexican War, 165; ships and marines, 1847, 166; 1850's, 186; 1855, 233
Pacific Station, 1833, 105, 138
*Paducah*, 409
Pakenham, Sir Edward, at New Orleans, 79
*Pallas*, 23; engagement with *Countess of Scarborough*, 23-4
Palma, Lomas Estrada, of Cuba, 313-14, 316-17
Palmira, Cuba, 316
Palo Alto, battle of, 111
*Palos*, Korea, 1871, 240-41
Panama, 301, 409; 1903, independence of, 291-8
Panama Canal, 287-91; defense of, 295-8, 456
Panama City, 288-92, 295; marines hold, 1885, 234
Panama, Isthmus of, 287-98
Panama maneuvers, 527
Panama, map of, 289
Panama, operations in, 287-98
Panama Railroad, 234-5
Panama Republic recognized by State Dept., 293
Panama, rioting, 1856, 180; 1873, 231; disorders, 1835, 232

## INDEX

Pan-American Exposition, Buffalo, 310
Panuco River, Mexico, 117; expedition up, 117-18
*Panther,* 257
Parades, memorable, 250
Paraguay Expedition, 185
Paris, France, Universal Exposition, 1878, 250; 461, 474; naval headquarters in, 461; helping to save, 479 *et seq.*
Paris-Metz Road, marines on, 480
Parker, W. E., officer, U.S.M.C., 315
Parris Island, S. C., 454-6, 467
*Pas Fini* Sector, 489-90
Pass Christian, Jones's squadron at, 77
Passmore, sergeant, U.S.M.C., 400
*Patapsco,* 34
Patillon, Haitian bandit leader, 400
"Patriots" in East Florida, 50
Patrolling, in Nicaragua, 429, 442; in Haiti, 402; in Dominican Republic, 357 *et seq.*
Patterson, Daniel T., officer, U.S.N., at New Orleans, 76, 79; attack on Barataria, 77
Patuxent, Barney's flotilla in, 71
Paulding, Hiram, officer, U.S.N., 196
*Pawnee,* 1861, 196, 200
Pay (early 1800's), 84; pay and allowance, 1870's, 246
Peace Establishment Act, 37
Peace, in northern California, 151; in Dominican Republic, 364
Peacetime duties, 1890, 244
*Peacock,* 89; vs *Hornet,* 61
Pearl Harbor, T. H., 306
Pearl Lagoon, Nicaragua, 418
Pearl, R. W., officer, U.S.M.C., 430
Peck, midshipman, U.S.N., 44
"Pedregal," Mexico, 129
Peffley, Harlan, captain, U.S.M.C., killed, 444
Pei-ho River, China, 284
Peiping, 538
Peking, advance on, 1900, 284-5; legation guard established, 1898, 280-85; capture of, 285; 307-9; 530
Peking, legation guard, 533; increase of, 535; part sent to Tientsin, 539
Pendleton, Joseph H., officer, U.S.M.C., 354, 411-14, 416; in Dominican Republic, 348; occupies Santiago, 350-1
Pendleton's "Flying Column," 349; marines in Nicaragua, 413
Pennsylvania Committee of Public Safety provides arms, etc., for marines, 1775, 12
Pennsylvania Navy and Marines, 16; on Delaware, 9
Penobscot Bay, battle in, 20-1
Penobscot Expedition, 9; marines with, 20-22
Pensacola, Florida, 113; 1861, 195, 231, 300-03; British Base at, 77; marines at, 83; naval base, 1822, 89

Peralte, Charlemagne, 394
Perez' rebel group in Dominican Republic, 353-5
Perkins, E. A., officer, U.S.M.C., 464
Perkins, Jesse L., officer, U.S.M.C., 400
Perry, M. C, officer, U.S.N., 114-15, 127, 135, 287; attack of Tuxpan, 122; to Japan, 168-71; negotiations with Japan, 169; second trip to Japan, 170; in China, 172; in Africa, 182-3
Perry, O. H., officer, U.S.N., on Lake Erie, 55-6
Perry's Squadron, soldiers used for marines, 55
Pershing, John J., general, U.S.A., 461, 463, 465, 468, 479
Personnel, laws and legislation, 540-1; problems of the postwar period, 540
Personnel problems, 1861, 192
Petain, French general, 490
Petion, of Haiti, 91
Petit Goave, Haiti, 404; occupied by 12th Co., 379
Petit Riviere, Haiti, 382
*Petrel,* 136, 267
*Philadelphia,* 39; captured, 42; burned, 42-43
Philadelphia, Pa., 32; rioting at, 1887, 248; marines maintain order, 248-9; 293-6, 303, 314, 317, 411, 451, 454, 455, 357, 463, 467, 469-70
Philadelphia Navy Yard, 454
Philippine Brigade, 270 *et seq.*
Philippine Insurrection, 266
Philippines, 70, 283-5, 307-8
Picaroons in Haiti, 36
Pierce, H. C., officer, U.S.M.C., 424
Pierce, President, 127
Pile, John, second lieutenant, U.S.M.C., 215
Pillon, general, U.S.A., 132
Pilot Town, La., 204
Pinar del Rio, Cuba, 313, 319
Pines, Isle of, Cuba, 1898, 260, 319
Pirates of Barataria, 76-7; in West Indies, 76, 88-90; in Florida, 88; in Sumatra, 90
Pistols, 26
Piti, Guam, 264
*Pittsburg,* 300
Planes, British, marines as pilots, 468
Platt Amendment, 286, 312; repealed, 338
Platt, John, sergeant, U.S.M.C., 382
Plattsburg Bay, battle of, 76
"Plug-Uglies," 187
*Plymouth* in China, 172
*Poictiers* captures the *Wasp,* 60
Point Isabel, Texas, landing at, 109; 111
Pointe Coupee, La., 49
Polar Expeditions, 225-6
*Policia Nacional,* Dominican Republic, 367-9
Policy of marines in China, 1927, 533-4
Policy of Navy for using marines, 452-3

# 576  INDEX

Policy of United States: toward Dominican Republic, 342; toward Haiti, 372; toward Nicaragua, 408 et seq.; during interventions, 439; changes in, 447
Policies of Cuba, 324; of Dominican Republic, 351
Polloc, P. I., 271-79
Pollock, Oliver, 19
Pollock's fleet and marines, 19-20
Ponce, Porto Rico, 262
Pont-a-Mousson, France, 499
Ponta Delgada, Azores, 469-70
Pontanezan, Camp, Brest, France, 465-6
Pontoise, France, 479
Pope, general, U.S.A., 210
Pope, Percival C., officer, U.S.M.C., 266
Port au Prince, Haiti, 391; attack on, 395-6, 399; 402, 404, 407
Port de Paix, Haiti, 379
Port Isabela, P. I., 270-1
Port Olongapo, P. I., landing at, 1899, 266
Port Royal, S. C., expedition to, 199-200; 454
Porter, David, officer, U.S.N., 42; cruise in Pacific, 63-6; to Nukuhiva, 65; defeated at Valparaiso, 66; in Porto Rico, 89; court-martial, 89
Porter, D. D., officer, U.S.N., 215
Porter, David D., officer, U.S.M.C., 271-8
Portland, Maine, fire 1866, 247
Porto Rico, 89; operations in, 262
Portsmouth, N. H., 39, 260, 261
Portsmouth, Va., 152
*Portsmouth*, 140, 142, 156-8, 160; marines of, 164; at Canton, 173, 176
Portuguese Government, 469; Portuguese West Africa, 183
Post-Civil War Navy, 224
Post-Civil War period, 223 et seq.
Postwar disillusionment, 524-5; efforts to offset, 525-7; postwar psychology, 525-6; postwar reduction, 540; post-World War period, Chapter XVIII
Postwar reaction, War of 1812, 81
Postwar reduction after Mexican war, 167
Posts, development of, 547-8
Poteca, Nicaragua, 436-7
*Potomac*, 110-11
Powell, L. M., officer, U.S.N., 96
*Powhatan*, steam frigate, at Shanghai, 172
*Prairie*, 296, 298-302, 317, 319; to Cuba 1912, 326; 340; to Dominican Republic, 344
Preble, commander, U.S.N., 42
Pre-Civil War period, characteristics of, 167
Pre-Marine Corps marines, 29-30
Pre-Revolutinary marines, 3
Preparation for War of 1812, 53-4
Preparing for War with Spain, 254-5
*President Grant*, 533
President of Dominican Republic, struggle over election, 345-6

Presidential Commission, 405-6
Presidents, contracts with, 527-8
Preston, Pedro, Panama, 232
Price, Charles F. B., officer, U.S.M.C., 466
*Princeton*, steamer, 113, 119
Prinzapolka, Nicaragua, 419
Prisoners of war, marines as in the Revolution, 25; French guarded, 36-7; 452
Prisons, British during Revolution, 25
Privateers in the Revolution, 24-5; War of 1812, 80
Prize crews, marines in, 84
Promotion of officers, 1890's, 245; 254; systems of, 540-41
Propaganda, 399, 405
Protecting: Americans at Canton, 92; in Japan, 236; in China, 238; Minister in Peking, 1894, 239; in Cuba, 325-7; in Nicaragua, 411; foreign property in Cuba, 1912, 329
Protectorate over Cuba ended, 338
*Providence*, sloop, 13, 14, 18
Provisional Government in Dominican Republic, 342, 368
Pruitt, John H., corporal, U.S.M.C., 504
Public Work, Haiti, 403
Publicity, 1898, 263
Puebla, Mexico, 126; marines march to, 127-8
Pueblo Nuevo, Nicaragua, 428
Puerto Cabezas, Nicaragua, 418, 435-6; bandits at, 444
Puerto Plata, D. R., cutting out expedition, 34-5; marines attack, 35; in 1914, 342; naval force at, 344; landing at, 346; advance to Santiago, 350; 368
Puget Sound, 1850's, 186
Punishments, 85; mode of 1872-82, 246
Purvis, Hugh, private, U.S.M.C., in Korea, 243

## Q

Quallah, Battoo, Sumatra, 90
Quantico, Va., 454-5, 457-9, 461; World War activities in, 462-4; purchased as reservation, 462-3; 466-7, 470-1, 474-5
Quarters, 39
Quartermaster Department, 5-46
Quartier Morin, Haiti, 382
Queenstown, Canada, 56
Quick, John H., sergeant, U.S.M.C., 259, 274-8
Quilali, Nicaragua, 428 et seq., 437
Quinapandon, Samar, P. I., 272, 279
Quitman, John A., officer, U.S.A., 121, 128, 134

## R

Racial wars in Haiti, 372
Raids of: York, Ontario, 55-6; Washington, 72-4

# INDEX 577

Raids (British) in the Chesapeake, 69-75
*Rainbow,* 308-9
"Railroad battalion" in R. D., 350
Railroad strikes, 1877, 248-9
Raleigh, 280
Ranchuelo, Cuba, 318
*Randolph,* battle with *Yarmouth,* 19
Rama, Nicaragua, 419
*Ranger,* marines on, in Europe, 1777, 18
*Ranger,* 290
Rank, devices, 40
*Raritan,* frigate, 110, 113, 115
Rations, 39, 85
*Rattletrap,* boat on Ohio and Mississippi, 20
Reading, Pa., 249
Rebel groups in Dominican Republic, pursuit of, 355
Rebellion, in Cuba, 1912, 324-7; 1912, 332; 1917, 335; Santo Domingo City, 343-4
Receiving ships, 1833, 105
Recruit Depots, 456
Recruit training in the World War, 454-5
Recruiting, first marines, 12; inducement for in 1775, 12; for early Marine Corps, 31; War of 1812, 53; World War, 455-6
Reduction after: War of 1812, 81; Mexican War, 167; Civil War, 223; in Haiti, 387
Reduction of Navy and Marine Corps, 37
*Reefer,* 122
Regiment of marines for Mexico, 1847, 127; with Cuban Army of Occupation, 322
Regulations of the U. S. Navy, 11
Reid, George, officer, U.S.M.C., 301-3
Reid, George C., officer, U.S.M.C., 457
Reilly's battery in China, 284
*Reindeer vs Wasp,* 62
Reisinger, H. C., officer, U.S.M.C., 319
Relief: of Kearny, 150; of Granada, Nicaragua, 412-13
Remey, George C., officer, U.S.N., 270, 282
Reorganization of Corps, 1861, 194
Replacements, training of: at Quantico, 463; for France, 474, 488
*Reprisal,* to Europe, 1776, 17
Reputation of the Corps, 53
Reserve, Marine Corps, 551
Reserve vessels, marines on, 37
Reservists, female, 464
Resignations to join Confederacy, 193
*Resolute,* marine transport, 260
Results of occupation of Dominican Republic, 369-70
Retaliation: in Sumatra, 1838, 90; at Canton, 1856, 172 *et seq.*
Retirement laws, 193; of older men, 219
"Retreat hell," etc., 481
Retreat of Mervine's force at San Pedro, 147

Revenue Cutter Service, marines in, 28
Revolt and mutiny at Nukuhiva, 66-8
Revolt at Puerto Plata, D. R., 1914, 342
Revolt of the Californians, 144-6, 150-1
Revolution: in Cuba, 1906, 313; 1934, 388; in Haiti, 375-6; in Panama, 287-98
Reynolds, John G., officer, U.S.M.C., 185, 198, 200, 208
Reynolds' Battalion, at Bull Run, 198; 200; at Port Royal, S. C., 201
Rhea, Robert Y., officer, U.S.M.C., 425
Rhine River, march to, 520-21; watch on, 521-2
Richal, M. A., officer, U.S.M.C., wounded, 430
*Richmond's* marines, 204
Rifles, 200, 250-51; Colt rifles, 98
Rifle marksmanship, 548-9
Rigaud, operations against, in Haiti, 36
Rio Grande River, 107; expedition up, 111-13
Rio Grande, Nicaragua, 418
Rio de Janeiro, 69
Riots: Charlestown, Mass., 86; in New York, 247-8; in Washington, 1857, 187; on Staten Island, 188
Riots, draft, Civil War, 218; in Nicaragua, 409
Rivas, Nicaragua, 424
Roads in Haiti, 391, 393, 399, 403
Robecourt, France, 476
*Rochester,* 417-18
Rodgers, commodore, U.S.N., in Mediterranean, 46; at Tunis, 47
Rogers, John, officer, U.S.N., 73, 104, 240
Roosevelt, Theodore, 286-92, 310, 313-14, 316, 339
Roosevelt, Franklin D., 528
Ross, Andrew, officer, U.S.M.C., killed, 100
Ross, Robert, British general, 71-3; burns Washington, 73; killed, 75
Rowell, Ross E., officer, U.S.M.C., 429
Roy, Eugene, Haiti, 406
Royal Flying Corps, 468
Royal Marines, 3, 59; *vs* pirates in West Indies, 89-90
Royal Navy on Lake Champlain, 7-8
Royal Welsh Fusiliers, 283
Royal Wurtemburg Corps, 492
Rum ration, 39
Rural police in Haiti, 390, 407
Rushforth, private, U.S.M.C., gallant stand of, 359
Russell, Benjamin R., officer, U.S.M.C., 250, 290
Russell, John H., officer, U.S.M.C., 303-4, 398, 402-3, 405-6; as commandant, 544
Russell, W. W., officer, U.S.M.C., 164
Russell, W. W., minister to Dominican Republic, 343, 348
Russia, 226, 307; Russian troops, 281-5
Russian Revolution, 462

## S

*Sabine,* frigate, 188, 200
Sacasa, Juan, Nicaragua, 417
Sackett's Harbor, N. Y., 55-7, 83
*Sacramento*: bombards Puerto Plata, D. R., 346; marines at Shanghai, 531
Sagua la Grande, Cuba, 316
St. Aignan, France, 465
St. Augustine, Fla., with Army at, 51
St. Croix, V. I., 451
St. Etienne, France, 507-8
St. Georges, France, 513
St. Helena Sound, S. C., 201
St. John, Porto Rico, 89
St. Johns, expedition to, 6
St. Lawrence, Wilkinson's expedition to, 58
*St. Lawrence,* 185
St. Leonard's Creek, 71
*St. Louis,* sloop, in China, 91, 92
*St. Louis,* 210, 261, 257
St. Louis, Mo., 310
St. Marc, Haiti, 378, 379
St. Mark, landing at, 99
*St. Mary's,* at Panama, 180
St. Michel, Haiti, 395, 402
St. Mihiel offensive, 499-502; German defenses, 499-500; attack on German outposts, 501-502; losses in, 502
St. Mihiel salient, France, 499
St. Nazaire, France, 465, 473-6
St. Thomas, fire at, 86; 451
Salladay, J. M., officer, U.S.M.C., 294
*Sally,* sloop, at Puerto Plata, 35
Sam, Guillaume, of Haiti, 375
Samar, P. I., 271; campaign in, 272-9; march across, 275-8
*Samar,* gunboat, 268
Samoa, 306
Samoan Island, 1839-42, 93
Samana Bay, D. R., 361, 366
Sampson, Wm. P., rear admiral, U.S.N., 256
San Agustin, Mexico, 129
San Albino Mines, Nicaragua, 428, 430-31
San Bernardo Ranch, Cal., 150
San Bernardino Straits, P. I., 279
Sanchez, D. R., 353
Sanchez, Francisco, 150; Sanchez group, operations against, 151
San Cosme gate, of Mexico City, 133
Sancti Spiritus, Cuba, 318
San Diego, Cal., 138, 148, 155, 300, 305; captured, 143-4; base at, 548
Sandino, Augusto, Nicaraguan bandit, 423-7; supported by radicals, 428; demagogue, 428; fortified camp, 429; raids gold mines, 434-5; 436-7, 442-3; last attack, 443
*Sandoval,* Spanish gunboat, 257
*Sandwich,* cutting out of, at Puerto Plata, 34-5

Sandwich Islands, Gamble at, 68
San Fernando, Nicaragua, 428
San Francisco, capture of, 141, 142; earthquake, 309
*San Francisco,* 302, marines in Cuba, 334
San Francisco Bay, 140, 150
San Francisco de Macoris, D. R., occupied, 351; battle at, 353
San Gabriel, Battle of, 152-3
Sangley Point, 255
Sanitation, Guam, marines improve, 265
*San Jacinto,* at Canton, 1856, 173
San José, Cal., 162
San Juan Bautista, Mexico, captured, 115-6, 123-4
San Juan Mission, Cal., 141
San Juan, Porto Rico, 262, 317
San Juan de Ulloa, Mexico, 120, 301
San Juan del Sur, Nicaragua, 178, 411
San Juan Hill, Cuba, 336
San Lucas, Mexico, 156
San Luis Rey, Cal., 144
San Marcus, Cuba, 318
San Pasqual, Cal., battle at, 149-50
San Pedro, Cal., 143, 147, 148, 155
San Pedro de Macoris, D. R., 342, 368
San Rafael, Nicaragua, 424
Santa Anna's Army, defense of Mexico City, 128 *et seq.*
Santa Cruz, Nicaragua, 437-8
Santa Barbara, Cal., landing, 142, 143; 150
Santa Clara, Cal., fight near, 151
Santa Clara Province, Cuba, 313, 315, 318, 320
Santo Domingo City, 340, 368
Santo Domingo, 287, 396, 407, 451, 453, 457; *see also* Dominican Republic
Santo Domingo, Cuba, 318
Santiago, Cuba, operation at, 260, 319, 327
Santiago, D. R., occupied, 350-1, 368
Santiago, naval battle, 261
Sash, wearing of, 40
*Savannah,* 138, 140, 146, 201; marines from, 164
Savannah, S. C., 10, 13; captured by British, 25
Second Battalion, Fifth Marines, in Nicaragua, 419; in France, 477
Schilt, Christian, officer, U.S.M.C., 430
Schleswig-Holstein, plebiscite, 466
Schley, Winfield S., U.S.N., in Korea, 243, 256, 261
Schmidt, Harry, officer, U.S.M.C., 309
Schmierer, Edward H., U.S.M.C., killed, 445
School of Application, 245
Schools of the Dominican Republic, 364, 370
Schooner gunboats, 114
Scott, Winfield, general, U.S.A., 97; at Vera Cruz, 118-20; Scott's Army in

# INDEX

Scott—*cont'd*
  Mexico, at Pueblo, 126; marines with, 126 *et seq.*
*Scourge*, gunboat, 121
Sea duels, War of 1812, 58-63
Sea duty, 83-4, 224-6, 254; in 1845, 106; in 1847, 166; in 1855, 168; in Civil War, 209-10; World War, 460-61; today, 547
Seals, protecting, 226-7
Seattle, 1856, defending, 186
Second Army, French, 477
Second Battalion, Fifth Marines, 480
Second Battalion, Sixth Marines, 477, 484; *see* Sixth Marines
Second Brigade, commanders of, 448
Second Brigade, Dominican Republic, 365 *et seq.*; Nicaragua, 423, 438, 448; Shanghai, 1937, 539 *et seq.*; F.M.F., 554
Second Division, A.E.F., assigned to, 474-5; training area, 476; operations with, Chapter XVII
Second Engineers, U.S.A., 486, 509
Second Machine Gun Battalion, 337
Second Regiment in Panama, 271, 295-6, 300-3, 319, 328; in Haiti, 376
Second Seminole War, 104
Secretaries of State: Knox, 408; Kellogg, 418
Seibo Province, D. R., 356, 363
Selby, Edward, officer, U.S.M.C., 441
Selection in the Marine Corps, 540-1
Selfridge, T. O., officer, U.S.N., 158
Selkirk, Earl of, 18
Sellers, David F., rear admiral, U.S.N., 427, 433, 438
Seminole Indian War, 94-105
Sentences of courts-martial, 246; *see also* Punishments and Discipline
Sentries, marines as, 26
Seoul, Korea, naval force at, 244, 307
*Serapis*, British frigate, engaged by *Bon Homme Richard*, 23-4
*Seringapatam*, 64-8
Services of marines in gilded age, 252
Seven-inch gun regiment, 458; company, Azores, 469
Seventh Company: at Gonaives, Haiti, 379; in France, 474; at Soissons, 494-5
Seventh Infantry, U.S.A.: in Samar campaign, 275-6; in France, 488
Seventeenth Infantry, U.S.A., Samar campaign, 271
Seventh Marines in Cuba, 1917-19, 336-7, 395, 463
Seventy-fourth Company in France, 478
Seventy-seventh Company in Nicaragua, 420
Seymour, Sir Edward, British Navy, 280-2
Shafter, general, U.S.A., 261
Shanghai, landing at, 1854, 172, 177; in 1866, 239; 308-9
Shanghai: conditions in 1924, 531-2; marines from Guam and Philippine Islands to, 531; Fourth Marines to, 532; Sector, 537; conditions, 1932-37, 537; reinforced by 31st Infantry, 536; fighting, 1937, 538-9; brigade to, 1937, 539
*Shannon* captures the *Chesapeake*, 61
Sharpsburg maneuvers, 527
Shaw, Melvelle J., U.S.M.C., 336
*Shenandoah*, 233-4
Shepard, R. L., officer, U.S.M.C., 315
Shearer, M. E., officer, U.S.M.C., 488-9; at Soissons, 492
Sherman, general, U.S.A., march to the sea, 212-3
Ships, marines on, 1864, 222
Ships of New Navy, date procured, marines allowed, etc., 32
Shooting in the Marine Corps, 548-9
Shore establishments in the World War, 453-4
Shubrick, W. B., officer, U.S.N., 155-6
Shuttleworth, Wm. L., officer, U.S.M.C., 123
Siberia, 462
Sibley, officer, U.S.M.C., 482; at Soissons, 497-8
Siege of Vera Cruz, 120
Sigsbee, Charles D., captain, U.S.N., 254
Sims, admiral, U.S.N., 461
Sims, John D., officer, U.S.M.C., 133, 173-4, 193
Sinking of the *Maine*, 254-5
Sino-Japanese War, 234; 1937, 538-9
*Sir Andrew Hammond*, 66-8
Siribao River, Samar, P. I., 276
Sixth Battalion, 270
Sixth Cavalry, 284
Sixth Machine Gun Battalion, 476, 481, 513
Sixth Marine Brigade, Cuba, 337
Sixth Marines, 463, 475-6; Château-Thierry, 480; Belleau Wood, 482 *et seq.*; at Soissons, 492, 496-8; 500, 501; Blanc Mont, 503-4, 508-9; in China, 533-5; 1937, 539
Sixty-seventh Company, France, 474-6
Sixth Marines, Third Battalion, in Dominican Republic, 369
Skenesborough, N. Y., 6
Slave trade, African, 181-3
Sleeper, Chargé d'Affaires, Cuba, 314
Sloan, officer, U.S.M.C., 103
Sloat, John D., commodore, U.S.N., instructions of, 138-9
Smith, H. C., sergeant, U.S.M.C., 258
Smith, Julian C., officer, U.S.M.C., 337
Smith, Jacob M., general, U.S.A., in Samar, 272
Smith, Richard, officer, U.S.M.C., 55
Smyrna, burning of, 86
Snowden, Thomas S., military governor, Dominican Republic, 360; difficulties in, 366

Sohotan Cliffs, Samar, P. I., 273; attack on, 274-7
Sohotan River, 272-5
Soissons attack: 491-8; movement to, 491; first day, 492-6; German defense, 492, 494, 496-7; Chaudun position, 492; map, 493; machine guns in, 495; attached to 9th and 23rd Infantry, 495; Vierzy, 495-6; Sixth Marines, 496-8; 84th Company, 497; relief, 498; losses, 498
Soldiers used for marines, 76
Soledad, Cuba, 315-6, 318
Somme-Py, France, 503
Somotillo, Nicaragua, 424; mutiny at, 431
Somoto, Nicaragua, 428; mutiny, 442
Somoza, Anastacio, of Nicaragua, 446
Sonoma, Cal., 140, 156
S.O.S. (Services of Supply) France, 465-6, 474-6
Sousa, John Philip, leader of Marine Band, 250
South Atlantic Squadron, 201; blockading, 202-207; duties, 1866, 225; at Montevideo, 228
South Atlantic Squadron marines, 208
*South Carolina*, in Cuba, 1917, 334; marines from, 374
South Carolina Marines on the *Randolph*, 19
South Carolina Navy, Third New Providence Expedition, 14; siege of Charleston, 1780, 10
*South Dakota*, 300
South Edisto River, S. C., 201
Southerland, W. H. H., rear admiral, 411, 414-15
Southern navy yards, loss of, 195-6
Southampton, England, 474-6
South Pacific Squadron, 225
South Seas, 90; Wilkes' expedition, to, 92-3
South Sea Islands, 67
Southwest Pass, La., 76
Spain, 247-56, 305; disputes with in Louisiana, 48-9; war with, 253 *et seq.;* 312
Spanish-American War, 252
Spanish colonies, 88; revolt of, 90-91
Spanish prisoners, 261, 268
Spanish Squadron, 255; in Cuban waters, 256; sunk, 261; survivors, 261
Spanish troops, 258
Spicer, William F., officer, U.S.M.C., 258
*Spitfire*, steamer, 117, 122
Sports, 525
Springfield Rifle: model 1884, 250; model 1903, 251
Squadron marines, Mexican war, 110; battalion of, 115, 120
Squadrons of the Navy: 1847, 166; 1855, 168; 1864, 222
Stock, Edward, marine officer, on *Bon Homme Richard*, 22-3

Stadium, 526
Staff authorized for early Marine Corps, 31
Standard Fruit Company, Nicaragua, 444
Standard Oil Co., 308
*Star of the West*, 195
Stars and Stripes over Derne, 46
Starving out the Seminoles, 101
Stalemate in Nicaragua, 439
Stallings, Lawrence T., officer, U.S.M.C., 525
State Department, 41, 314, 410, 413, 417, 419
State Marines, 8; *see* names of States
State Navies, 1775, 8
Stations of early Marine Corps, 39
Stations of Marines: 1846, 166; 1855, 168; 1864, 222; in Cuba, 1906, 320; same 1907, 323; same 1912, 329-30; in Dominican Republic, 1922, 368; on ships, 84
Steedman, admiral, U.S.N., 231
*Sterling*, 146
Stillman, C. A., officer, U.S.M.C., 201
Stimson, Henry L., 420
Stimson Agreement, 423, 437, 447
Stocks, leather, 40
Stockton, commodore, U.S.N., 139, 146; command of Pacific Squadron, 142; at San Pedro, 148; at San Diego, 148; march on Los Angeles, 151
Stoddard, George G., officer, U.S.M.C., 213
Stoddard's Battalion, 214
Storming, Chapultepec, 131-3; forts of Canton, 1856, 172 *et seq.*
Stowell, George A., major, U.S.M.C., 513 *et seq.*
Strength and distribution, Guardia, Nicaragua, 439
Strength of Brigades, Cuba, 1906, 319; Haiti, 399; Nicaragua, 440, 442
Strength of Corps: 1803, 37; 1809, 48; 1812, 53; 1817, 81; 1855, 168, 194; 1897, 245, 253; World War, 450, 472
Strength of marines: in Dominican Republic, 352; China 1927, 533
Strength, on sea duty, 254
Strength, pre-Civil War, 253
Strike, in Haiti, 404
Strikes, 248-9
Stuart, J. E. B., officer, U.S.A., 189
"Sub-chasers" in Haiti, 399
Subig Bay, P. I., 269-71
Submarines, German, 460-61, 468, 470; bases for, 467, 469
Sugar Intervention, Cuba, 332 *et seq.*
Sumatra, pirates in, punished, 90
Summer White House, 527-8
*Supply*, 309
Supply of Army in Creek campaign, 98
Supply, problem of, in California, 1846, 147, 152
Support, diplomatic mission, 340

INDEX 581

Suppressing pirates in Caribbean, 88-90
Suppressing riots, Washington, 178-9; labor, 1877, 248
Surveying expeditions for Isthmian Canal, 1870, 236
*Susquehanna*, 188
Susquehanna River, 211
Swampscott, Mass., 528
Sword, Mameluke, 46-7, 251
Sword Rack Hoo, of China, 238
*Swatara*, 233
*Sydney*, troop ship, 264

T

Tabasco River, 115, 124; first expedition up, 114-6; second, 123-5
*Tacoma*, 314, 318; landing, Nicaragua, 411
Tactics: in Caco War, 384-5; of Californians, 150; at Canton, China, 1856, 174-5; used in Dominican Republic, 348-9, 364; of landing operations, 208-9; at Mazatlan, 164; in the Philippines, 267; at St. Mihiel, 500; at Soissons, 492, 494; Upton's and Wagner's, 245; woods fighting, 486, 488; in World War, 482, 484; 147, 152-3, 158-9, 215, 506, 513-15
Taft, William H., President, 298, 316-17, 319, 410
Taipi, war with, 64-5
Tapa, Formosa, 1867, 238
Taking of Guaymas, Mexico, 15-17
Taking of Puerto Plata, 1916, 346
Taku, China, 280, 282
Talbot, Ralph, officer, U.S.M.C., killed, 469
Tallahassee, Florida, 99
Tampa Bay, Florida, 95, 96, 100; Seminoles assembled at, 101
Tampico, expedition, 116-8; surrender of, 117; Army takes over, 118
Tampico affair, 299-300
Tank Company, 550
Tansill, Robert, officer, U.S.M.C., 156, 158-9
Tarbell, captain, U.S.N., 70
Taussig, Edward D., officer, U.S.N., 265
Taylor, Algernon S., officer, U.S.M.C., 184
Taylor, Zachary, officer, U.S.A., 101, 107
Taylor's Army in Mexico, 118
Tehauntepec, Isthmus of, 136
Telles, Rafael, Mexican colonel, 163-4
Telpaneca, Nicaragua, 424; mutiny of garrison, 440-41
Temulty, Mexico, skirmish at, 125
*Tennessee*, Confederate ram, 211-12, 233
Tennessee River, 210
Tenth Corps, French, 476-7
Tenth Infantry, U.S.A., relieves marines in Canal Zone, 298
Tenth Marines, 458

Terhune, Warren J., commodore, U.S.N., 411
Terrett, George H., officer, U.S.M.C., 132-4, 193
Terry, general, U.S.A., at Fort Fisher, 215
*Texas*, 317, 461
Texas, 49; annexed, 107; 460
Theaters of operation, Mexican War, 107
Theodore of Haiti, 375
Thiacourt, France, 501
Thiolet, France, 480
Third Artillery, 119, 248
Third Battalion in Philippines, 268
Third Battalion, Fifth Marines in World War, 477
Third Battalion, Sixth Marines in World War, 477
Third Brigade, U.S.A., 477; attack on Vaux, France, 489; 494-5; at Soissons, France, 496; at Blanc Mont, France, 506-7
Third Brigade, U.S.M.C., in Cuba, 1917-18, 337; in Texas, World War, 460; in China, 1927, 533-4; withdrawn, 535
Third Field Artillery, 103
Third Regiment, U.S.M.C., 302
Thirteenth Company in Haiti, 383-4
Thirteenth Marines in World War, 464-5
Thirtieth Company, World War, 474
Thirty-first Infantry, U.S.A., to Shanghai, 536
Thirty-sixth Division, A.E.F., 509
Thomonde, Haiti, 395
Thrasher, Thomas E., officer, U.S.M.C., 383
Ticonderoga, Fort, 5, 6
Tientsin, China, marines of *Baltimore* at, 1894, 239; 280-84, 309, 530; Third Brigade at, 533; taken over from Army, 539
Tilton, McLane, officer, U.S.M.C., 204, 241-2
Tipitapa Conference, 422
Todos Santos, Mexico, 160
Tokyo Bay, Perry in, 169
Tomas, colonel, Cuban Army, 258
Torcy, France, 482
Torres, colonel, Colombian Army, 292
Toulon Sector, France, defense of, 476-9
Tours, France, 465
Toussaint L'Ouverture, 36
Towns occupied in Dominican Republic, 352
Townsend, Robert, commander, U.S.N., 238
Training centers, World War, 454-5
Training in Dominican Republic, 369
Training Haitians, 390
Transit of Isthmus of Panama, 179 *et seq.*
Translon Farm, near Vierzy, France, 494
Treadwell, Thomas C., officer, U.S.M.C., 337

Treasury of U. S., fire in, 86
Treaty: with Algiers, 87; of Cahuenga, 154; of Guadelupe Hidalgo, 136; Hay-Herran, with Colombia, 291; with Japan, 1854, 171; Japan, ports opened, 1868, 237; Jay, 29; with Korea, 244; with Mexico, 129; with New Granada, 1846, 179; for Panama Canal rights, 1901, 293; of 1847, with Panama, 294; of Paris, ending War with Spain, 312; with Tripoli, 41; Webster-Ashburton, 181
Trenton, Battle of, 16-17
Tresavaux, France, 478
Trevett, John, continental marine officer, 12, 18
Tribute-paying, 87
Tripoli, 41; attacks of, 43; squadron to, 1815, 87
Tripolitan ships, fight with, 42
Trist, N. P., representative of State Department, 129
Trogler, Lewis S., sergeant, U.S.M.C., 440
Troop training, 551
Truck movements, France, 491, 510
Trujillo, Raphael, Dominican, 370
*Truxton*, guns of, recovered, 122
Tuira River, Panama, 294
*Tulsa*, in Nicaragua, 429; 537
Tullifinney Creek, S. C., 213
Tullifinney Cross Roads, S. C., 214
Tumas, Cuba, 318
Tun Tavern, 12
Tunis, Bay of, expedition to, 47; squadron to, 1815, 87
Tung Chow, China, 1900, 285
Tung Chow Foo, China, 1866, 239
Turrill, Julius S., officer, U.S.M.C., 481-2, 492, 495
*Tuscarora*, 231
Tuxpan, Mexico, capture of, 122-3
Twelfth Company, 379
Twelfth Field Artillery, U.S.A., supports marines, 479; 481
Twelfth Separate Battalion, France, 466
Twentieth French Corps, Soissons, 491
Twenty-first French Corps, duty with, 480 *et seq.*; 503
Twenty-fourth Company, U.S.M.C., at Puerto Plata, D. R., 350; to Haiti, 376
Twenty-third Infantry, U.S.A., 477
Twiggs, Levi, officer, U.S.M.C., 98, 127; 131-2
Tybee Island, Ga., landing on, 201
Tyler, Henry B., officer, U.S.M.C., 187; adjutant and inspector, 193

U

Ulrich, William, major, U.S.M.C., 501
Underwood, Robert W., officer, U.S.M.C., 416
Uniform Regulations, 40

Uniform and equipment, Revolutionary War, 25-6
Uniforms: 85; of the Continental Marines, 25-6; of the Royal Marines, worn by Jones's marines, 26; of early Marine Corps, 39-40 (*see* illustrations); Civil War, 250
Union Army at Port Royal, S. C., 212-3
United Fruit Co., 288
United States, 405, 409, 417; policy of, 408; Senate, 291
United States Government, 409
*United States*, frigate, 29; fight with *Macedonian*, 60, at Monterey, Cal., 1842, 92
Upper Marlboro, Md., 72
Upshur, W. P., officer, U.S.M.C., 383-4
Upton Mills, Ga., 98
Uruguay, landings in, 184-5, 228-9
*Utah*, 303, 461
Utley, Harold H., officer, U.S.M.C., 436

V

Vallejo, Cal., 217
Valparaiso, Porter at, 1813, 65; Gamble at, 69; riots, 230
*Vandalia* marines: in Florida, 96, 99; 146; in the Fijis, 178
Van Orden, George, officer, U.S.M.C., 376, 464
Van Valkenburg, minister to Japan, 1867, 237
Vaux, France, 489
Vauxcastille, France, 496
*Vengeance*, 22-3
*Venus*, Nicaraguan gunboat, 409
Verdun, France, 477
Verdun Sector, France, 476-9
Vergara, Mexico, 120, 303
Vernon, admiral, British Navy, 4
Verte Feuille Farm, near Vierzy, France, 494
*Vesuvius*, bomb ketch, 49
Veterans movement in Cuba, 324
*Vicksburg*, 272
Vicksburg, Miss., 216
Vierzy, France, 494-6
Vigan, P. I., capture of, 268
Villa, Pancho, Mexican rebel leader, 305
Villers-Cotterets Forest, France, 491
Vincent, Stenio, Haiti, 406
Vincentico Evangelista, Dominican bandit leader, 357
Virgin Islands, taken over, 451-2; marines occupy, 459; aviation squadron in, 554
Virginia Marines, 9-10
*Virginius* affair, 227-8
Viti Levu, South Seas, 177
*Vixen*, steamer, U. S., 113-4, 116, 135

W

*Wabash*, 202
*Wachusett*, 238

## INDEX

Wahoo Swamp, Seminoles in, 100
Wainwright, Robert D., officer, U.S.M.C., 55, 86-7
Waldron, N. S., officer, U.S.M.C., 95, 99
Walker, William, filibuster, 236
Walker, William W., officer, U.S.M.C., 435
Walla Walla Indians, 146
Waller, Littleton W. T., officer, U.S.M.C.: in Egypt, 1882, 225; 268; in Samar, 271-9; in China, 282-4; 304; 318; to Haiti, 376; Waller's Brigade in Haiti, 380; in Caco Campaign, 382-6
Wallingford, Samuel, Continental Marine officer, 18
War of 1812, résumé of, 80
War planning, 1917, 450-1
War training, France, 473-6
*Warren*, at Mazatlan, 142; 156
Warm Springs, Ga., 528
Wars with: African tribes, 182-3; Algiers, 87; Barbary Corsairs, 41-7; of 1812, 53-80; France, 30 *et seq.*; Seminoles, 95-105; Spain, 253 *et seq.*
Wartime duties, early 1800's, 84
War Zone, World War, marines in, 472
Washington Arsenal, 249
Washington Conference, 266
Washington, D. C., 270, 296
Washington, defense of, 1813, 72, 74-5
*Washington* in Haiti, 375-6
Washington marines with Barry, 71-3
Washington Navy Yard, 38
Washington's Army, marines with, 15-17
Washington's Fleet: at Boston, 4; at New York, 5
*Wasp*, schooner, 13, 14
*Wasp*, sloop: fight with *Frolic*, 59; captured by *Poictien*, 60; fight with *Reindeer*, 62; sinks the sloop *Avon*, 63
Waspuc, Nicaragua, 434
Watch on the Rhine, 521-2
Waterman, W. M., last Continental Marine officer, 27
Watson, Henry B., officer, U.S.M.C., 141, 153, 161
Watson, James, earliest marine officer, 6
Watson, Samuel E., officer, U.S.M.C., 127 *et seq.*
Watson's Battalion: 127; at Vera Cruz, 127; march to Puebla, 127; at Chapultepec, 130-2; in Mexico City, 133
Watson's Brigade, 129
Waya, Fiji Islands, war with, 1858, 178
Weapons: carried by marines in Revolution, 26; used by marines at sea, 84; 250-1
Weaver, James, officer, U.S.M.C., 36
Webster-Ashburton Treaty, 181
Welles, Gideon, Secretary of Navy, 199, 207, 544
Western Front, marines on, Chapter XVII
Western frontier, marines on, 20
West Florida, 48

West Indies, 33; piracy in, 88-90
West India Squadron *vs* Pirates, 89; in Indian Wars, 95-105
West India Station, 1833, 105
Western Gulf Blockading Squadron, 202
Whaling fleet, British, Porter's raiding, 64
Whampoo, Canton, 92, 176
Wharton, Franklin, officer, U.S.M.C.: early experiences, 38; 54, 73; death, 82
What Next?, 555
"What Price Glory," 525
Whipple, Abraham, commodore, at Charleston, S. C., 25
White House, summer, 527-8
"White King of Gonave," 390
Wilkinson's expedition down the St. Lawrence, 58
Wilkes, John, officer, U.S.N., 92; exploring expedition, 92-3
Williams, Alexander S., officer, U.S.M.C., 275-78, 393
Williams, Dion, officer, U.S.M.C., 256, 268, 319
Williams, E. C., officer, U.S.M.C., 353, 501, 503, 513, 515
Williams, G. A., officer, U.S.M.C., 442
Williams, John, officer, U.S.M.C., 49-50; killed by Indians, 51
Williams, Lloyd W., officer, U.S.M.C., 481
Williams, Richard P., officer, U.S.M.C., 550
Willings, James, captain, marines with, 20
Wilson, Woodrow, President, 286, 298-9, 305, 365, 453; plan in Dominican Republic, supporting, 342-3; orders military government in Dominican Republic, 352
Winder, brigadier general, U.S.A., attempts to defend Washington, 72-5
Wirkus, Faustin, sergeant, U.S.M.C., 390
Wise, F. M., officer, U.S.M.C., 344, 347, 485; Wise's attack of Belleau Wood, 485-6
Withdrawal from Derne, 46-7; from Mexico, 136-7
Wood, Thomas N., officer, U.S.M.C., 297
Woosung, China, 1859, 177
World War, activities other than France, Chapter XVI
World War, 449-523; home duty, 453-4; planning for, 450-51; aviation in, 467-8; distribution of men at end, 472; demobilization, 470-71; résumé of experience, 471-2; peace conference, 521-2
Worth, general, U.S.A., 119, 120-132
*Wyoming*: bombarded Japanese forts, 236; at Formosa, 238; 294; 461

X

X. Y. Z. despatches, 29
Xammes, France, 501

# INDEX

## Y

Yang Tsun, China, 284
Yangste Patrol, marines on, 537
*Yankee,* 257
*Yantic,* 229
Yaqui Indians, 160-61
*Yarmouth,* engagement with *Randolph,* 19
Yaviza, Panama, 294-5
Yedo, Japan, 1868, 237; *see also* Tokyo
Yeh, Chinese Commission, 45, 176
Yellow fever: in Mexico, 125; epidemics, 188
Yeo, Sir James, British Navy, 56
Yerba Bueno, Cal., 138; *see also* San Francisco
Yerba Buena Island, 309
Yokohama, Japan, 237
Yorktown, Va., marines at, 9-10; Maryland marines at, 10

*Yosemite* at Guam, 265
Young, Archibald, officer, U.S.M.C., 430
Young, general, U.S.A., 268
*Yperanga,* German steamer, 299, 303
Yucatan, Mexico, 135
Yusuf Karamali, Pasha of Tripoli, 43, 45

## Z

Zebrugge, Belgium, 468
Zeilin, Jacob, officer, U.S.M.C., 142, 143, 150, 152, 164; to Japan, 169-170; made commandant, 219; résumé of life, 219, 251
Zeilin's regiment at Charleston, S. C., 208
Zelaya, José, of Nicaragua, 408
Zeledon, Nicaraguan rebel, 412, 414
Zinzig, Germany, 521

YA Sp Quezad
Quezadas, Juan Carlos, 1970-
Barras bravas /
$26.95      ocn966850433